FREEDOM OF EXPRESSION IN THE SUPREME COURT

FREEDOM OF EXPRESSION IN THE SUPREME COURT

THE DEFINING CASES

EDITED BY TERRY EASTLAND

ROWMAN & LITTLEFIELD PUBLISHERS, INC.
LANHAM • BOULDER • NEW YORK • OXFORD

ETHICS AND PUBLIC POLICY CENTER

ROWMAN & LITTLEFIELD PUBLISHERS, INC.

Published in the United States of America
by Rowman & Littlefield Publishers, Inc.
4720 Boston Way, Lanham, Maryland 20706
http://www.rowmanlittlefield.com

12 Hid's Copse Road
Cumnor Hill, Oxford OX2 9JJ, England

This book was produced in conjunction with the Ethics and Public Policy Center.

British Library Cataloguing in Publication Information Available

Library of Congress Cataloging-in-Publication Data

Freedom of expression in the Supreme Court : the defining cases / edited by Terry Eastland.
    p. cm.
    Includes bibliographical references and index.
    ISBN 0-8476-9710-X (alk. paper) ISBN 0-8476-9711-8 (pbk. : alk. paper)
    1. Freedom of speech—United States—Cases.   2. Freedom of the press—United States—Cases.
I. Eastland, Terry.
KF4770.A7F74   2000
342.73'0853—dc21   00-029083

Printed in the United States of America

CONTENTS

PREFACE

The First Amendment freedoms of speech, the press, assembly, and petition as the Supreme Court has construed them in sixty important cases are the subject of this book. These freedoms together make up what the Court calls "freedom of expression." Traditionally understood, the activities of publishing, assembling, and petitioning—not to mention speaking—all involve speech, but in the Court's cases "expression" encompasses not only speech but wordless acts that are said to communicate messages—so-called symbolic speech, a recent example of which is flag-burning. The title of this book uses "Freedom of Expression" to represent the gamut of what the Court has seen fit to bring within the protection of the First Amendment.

The First Amendment actually says this: "Congress shall make no law . . . abridging the freedom of speech, or of the press, or the right of the people peaceably to assemble, and to petition the Government for a redress of grievances." Note that it is *Congress* that the First Amendment restrains, forbidding it to pass laws of a certain kind. The Court has read the amendment also to bar the executive branch and—significantly—the states from abridging the several freedoms. Note also that the First Amendment does not say that "Congress shall make no law abridging *speech*"; it does not guarantee us the right to say whatever we want to say whenever, wherever, and however we choose. It is the *freedom* of speech, and the other freedoms, that government may not abridge.

The nature of the freedom claimed and the measure of protection it may enjoy are the issues at the heart of every First Amendment case. And in deciding such cases—which number in the hundreds and concern a wide range of free expression claims—the Supreme Court has substantially broadened First Amendment freedoms.

This is a modern development. The First Amendment was added to the Constitution in 1791. But most of the Court's cases, and certainly all its important ones, date from the first years after World War I. There is now a substantial body of First Amendment law, and it grows every year as the Court reviews new First Amendment claims.

The introduction to this book provides the background for understanding this body of law. It discusses the origins of the First Amendment, the history of the several First Amendment freedoms from 1791 through the Civil War, and the judicial understanding of those freedoms in the several decades before World War I.

The first case in the book is *Schenck* v. *United States* (1919), a subversive-speech case, and the last is *National Endowment for the Arts* v. *Finley* (1998), which concerned the congressional effort to encourage "decency and respect" among NEA-funded artistic expressions. The sixty cases are presented chronologically, in the order the Court decided them.

I briefly introduce each case by describing its origins and reporting the decisions by the lower courts and then indicating why it is significant. A case may be important as a statement of legal doctrine. It may extend First Amendment protection to some new activity (such as commercial speech). It may show the Court reversing a decision made by Congress or the states, or even reversing one of its own rulings. Also, a case may be notable as a reflection of, or a statement about, its times. Each case in this book is significant for at least one and perhaps more than one of these reasons.

After the introduction to the case I present, in abridged form, the Court's opinion and any concurring or dissenting opinion that especially sheds light on disputed issues. As in other areas of constitutional law, certain concurrences and dissents in First Amendment cases have suggested doctrinal roads—even U-turns—later taken.

Finally, to convey some sense of how the country responded to the Court's decisions at the time they were handed down, twenty-three of the cases are followed by commentaries from leading newspapers and magazines of the day. These commentaries underscore the fact that free expression claims have been parts of significant chapters in many, probably most, of the big stories of our century, including World War I, the Cold War, the Vietnam War, the civil rights movement, and the ongoing battle over abortion.

Four other items appear at the end of the book. First is a table of the justices who have served on the Court since 1900, including for each the appointing president, the departing justice, and the years of service on the Court. Second is a short bibliography of useful books and articles on the First Amendment. Last are two indexes. The general index of names and legal concepts is followed by an index of cases.

ACKNOWLEDGMENTS AND CREDITS

This book could not have been produced without the contributions of many persons, in particular several staff members and interns of the Ethics and Public Policy Center. As with two other books of mine published with the Center, Senior Editor Carol Griffith superbly handled the manuscript, offering excellent editorial suggestions and readying the text for publication. Former or current staffers Marianne Geers, Diane Bryhn, Ethan Reedy, Jason Boffetti, and Josh Good helped in various ways, most of them computer-related. Several interns assisted in retrieving and reviewing cases and other materials, among them Jon Rothchild, Heidi Metcalfe, and Jennifer Swift; Jennifer in particular did exceptional work in helping me finish the book, efficiently performing a variety of research and word-processing tasks. I am also grateful to George Weigel and Elliott Abrams for their interest and support; George was president of the Center when I began the book and Elliott when I finished.

Finally, I want to thank John Raisian and Tom Henriksen of the Hoover Institution for their hospitality. The time I spent at Hoover in early 1999 enabled me to make enough progress on this book to believe it could be completed on something approximating its original schedule.

I am grateful to the publishers listed below for permitting me to reprint editorials and op-ed pieces in the sampling of editorial responses that follows various cases in this book. Most of the pieces appear in excerpted form, with ellipses to show omissions within (but not before or after) the sections reprinted.

America: On *Rust* v. *Sullivan*, "Rust v. Sullivan: A Better Debate," June 8, 1991 (© 1991 America Press; all rights reserved).

Atlanta Journal-Constitution: On *Texas* v. *Johnson*, "Conservative Court, Libertarian Streak," June 25, 1989 (used by permission of *The Atlanta Journal* and *The Atlanta Constitution*).

Boston Herald American: On *Miller* v. *California*, editorial, June 26, 1973.

The Christian Century: On *Thornhill* v. *Alabama*, "Peaceful Picketing Gets Supreme Court Sanction," May 8, 1940 (© 1940 Christian Century Foundation). / On *West Virginia Board of Education* v. *Barnette*, "Court Upholds Freedom of Conscience," June 23, 1943 (© 1943 Christian Century Foundation).

The Commonweal: On *Roth* v. *United States*, "Obscenity and Freedom," July 12, 1957.

Dallas Morning News: On *R.A.V.* v. *St. Paul*, "Hate Crimes," June 24, 1992.

Harvard Law Review: On *Schenck* v. *United States*, "Freedom of Speech in War Time," by Zechariah Chafee, Jr., June 1919 (© 1919 Harvard Law Review Association).

Indianapolis Star-News: On *Texas* v. *Johnson*, editorial, June 23, 1989.

INTRODUCTION

The four freedoms involving expression are part of a quintet of freedoms named in the First Amendment, the fifth being religious liberty. In full, the amendment provides: "Congress shall make no law respecting an establishment of religion, or prohibiting the free exercise thereof; or abridging the freedom of speech, or of the press, or the right of the people peaceably to assemble, and to petition the Government for a redress of grievances." This amendment and nine others were known, when they were added to the Constitution, as the Bill of Rights, and they were understood to protect the rights of the people and the states against overreaching by the newly established federal government.

Why did the makers of the Constitution think it necessary to amend the newly minted document so substantially by adding a bill of rights? And why did this bill of rights include an amendment instructing Congress that it could not abridge certain freedoms?

For the answers to these questions, recall the famous passage from the Declaration of Independence:

> We hold these truths to be self-evident, that all men are created equal, that they are endowed by their Creator with certain unalienable rights, that among these are life, liberty, and the pursuit of happiness—that to secure these rights, governments are instituted among men, deriving their just powers from the consent of the governed, that whenever any form of government becomes destructive of these ends, it is the right of the people to alter or to abolish it, and to institute new government, laying its foundation on such principles and organizing its powers in such forms, as to them shall seem most likely to effect their safety and happiness.

In the understanding of the Founders, it was a "self-evident truth" that every human being, simply by virtue of having been created by God, had the same rights as any other. These rights were regarded as "unalienable," which meant that they could not rightfully be taken away. They could not "be taken from us by any human power," John Dickinson declared in 1766, "without taking our lives." The Declaration did not specify all of the unalienable or "natural rights," as they were also called, noting only that the rights of "life, liberty, and the pursuit of happiness" were "among [them]." The Declaration made clear the relationship between these fundamental rights and government by stating that it is "to secure these rights" that "governments are instituted," and that these governments must have "the consent of the governed." This passage assumed an unalienable right to self-government, and "the right of the people to alter or to abolish" a government destructive of its proper ends was a means of vindicating that right.

The Declaration was adopted by the Second Continental Congress on July 4, 1776. By it the signatories declared that the United Colonies were "free and independent states," with no further allegiance or political connection to the British Crown. The people of these infant states then fell to the task of instituting state governments and, eventually, the national government. And they understood that it was "to secure these rights," the unalienable rights that include life, liberty, and the pursuit of happiness, that they went about establishing their governments. They accomplished this purpose in written constitutions, which defined and limited the powers of the new governments.

RIGHTS IN THE STATE AND FEDERAL CONSTITUTIONS

There was a striking difference between the state constitutions, which were adopted between 1776 and 1780, and the federal Constitution submitted to the states for ratification in 1787. This difference concerned the extent to which they explicitly protected rights—both the natural rights of the Declaration and the rights that were considered means of vindicating those natural rights. All of the constitutions, state and federal alike, sought to secure rights in the very design of the governments they created; in this sense they all were constitutions of liberty. But more than the federal Constitution did, the state constitutions specified the rights meriting protection. Some of them did so in a "bill of rights."

The idea of explicitly protecting rights, and doing so in a bill of rights, had English roots. In 1215 the rights of the criminally accused won protection in the "great charter" (Magna Carta) extracted from King John at Runnymede. Over the centuries the English common law provided more and more protection for individual rights, and in the seventeenth century Parliament passed a series of "rights" measures that limited the authority of the Crown—the Habeas Corpus Act of 1679, the Bill of Rights of 1689, and the Toleration Act of 1689. The American colonies, heirs to this rights tradition, advanced it by defining rights more precisely and expansively and then, once they had become "free and independent states" in 1776, writing them into their organic law.[1]

This itself was a significant move, for in the understanding that had developed in the colonies over a century and a half, a constitution was law superior to the government it created and the actions that government might take. "In all free States," the Massachusetts General Court said in 1768, the legislative branch "derives its power and authority from the Constitution" and "cannot overleap the bounds of it, without destroying its own foundation." England had no written constitution and therefore no paramount law that constrained the actions of government.

In thinking about rights, of course, the people of the free states began with those "certain unalienable rights." These were known, in the works of English political philosophers well known to Americans, as "natural rights"—rights that everyone has equally in the prepolitical (and mythical) state of nature. These included the rights to life and liberty, the right to work to acquire property, the right to believe and to speak one's beliefs, and the right to join with others in order to leave the state of nature and fashion a civil society—i.e., the right to self-government.

The bulk of the rights that the states explicitly protected in their constitutions were those of individuals who already had formed a civil society. The merits of many of these rights—such as those for the criminally accused—had been concretely demonstrated by the English struggles against the Crown dating back to the Magna Carta. While these rights were not natural, they came to be considered as fundamental as natural rights because they served ultimately to protect natural rights. Freedom of the press, for example, was not a natural right, because printing presses were a feature of civil society. But it was considered instrumental to securing freedom of speech, and it was central to the conduct of politics and thus to the exercise of the natural right to self-government.

The state constitutions did not all protect the same rights. For example, while ten state constitutions protected freedom of the press, only two secured freedom of speech. It is also true that the federal Constitution was in at least one respect more protective of rights than the state constitutions. For though it contained no provision securing religious liberty, the Constitution, unlike the state constitutions, explicitly prohibited religious tests for office.[2] The framers of the Constitution also were clearly mindful of the natural right to liberty when they included in Article I prohibitions against bills of attainder (legislative judgments of individual guilt and impositions of criminal penalties without judicial proceedings) and ex post facto laws (which criminalized an activity after its occurrence). Still the state constitutions went further than the federal Constitution in protecting both natural rights and the prudential ones that experience taught would help secure the natural ones.

The framers of the Constitution could have done more to protect these rights. Indeed, they had opportunities to do so. Toward the end of their deliberations, a motion was offered to prepare a bill of rights. But by unanimous vote the motion was defeated. A motion then was made to include in the Constitution a declaration that "the liberty of the press should be inviolably observed." It lost as well. Without a declaration of rights, the Constitution was submitted to the states for ratification.

The framers were not opposed in theory to a bill of rights; they just thought it was unnecessary. They said that the states had bills of rights and the Constitution did not repeal them; that the purpose of the Constitution was to establish a federal government of only limited and enumerated powers, none of which invaded natural rights; and that the Constitution was by its very design a bill of rights, as Alexander Hamilton argued in *The Federalist.*

Nine states had to ratify the Constitution for it to take effect, and New Hampshire was the ninth. But in voting its approval, New Hampshire also urged adoption of a bill of rights as soon as the new government was established. New York and Virginia voted next. Though their blessing was not needed in a legal sense for the Constitution to become law, it was important politically, for it was unimaginable that the new nation could prosper unless those two states were part of it. And in ratifying the Constitution both New York and Virginia called for a bill of rights. North Carolina, the twelfth state to ratify, made the same demand. The state ratifying conventions wound up making more than seventy recommendations for provisions in a federal bill of rights. Four conventions recommended freedom of the press; three, freedom of speech; and three, freedom of assembly and petition.

Some of those "for" a bill of rights during the ratification debates were in fact against the Constitution. Anti-Federalists seized upon the absence of a bill of rights in order to galvanize opposition to the Constitution they would have rejected anyway. Realizing that the Constitution might not be approved unless there was a promise to add a bill of rights, key Federalists who were formerly opposed to the idea—the most important being James Madison—relented and said they would work to add a bill of rights. The Federalists nonetheless were not enthusiastic about this project.

In this peculiar political setting, Madison, as a member of the First Congress, became the central figure. By the time he had decided to run for the House, Madison had endorsed a bill of rights that would include "the freedom of the press, trials by jury, and security against general warrants." Though he still was not impressed with the substantive arguments for a bill of rights, he grasped as few others did its immediate practical necessity, for only a bill of rights could calm public fears and expose the true nature of the Anti-Federalists seeking to subvert the Union. In the long term, Madison thought a bill of rights might help educate the people and restrain their majoritarian impulses. He did not foresee, as Thomas Jefferson did, the role of the courts in enforcing rights.

MAKING THE FIRST AMENDMENT

On June 8, 1789, Madison gave a speech introducing proposals taken from the states' bills of rights and the recommendations made by the state ratifying conventions. Madison suggested placing some proposals in a prefix to the Constitution and inserting others in Articles I, III, and VI. In Article I, Section 9, between clauses 3 and 4, Madison recommended for insertion a series of clauses, including:

> The people shall not be deprived or abridged of their right to speak, to write, or to publish their sentiments; and the freedom of the press, as one of the great bulwarks of liberty, shall be inviolable.

> The people shall not be restrained from peaceably assembling and consulting for their common good; nor from applying to the legislature by petitions, or remonstrances for redress of their grievances.

Madison also recommended for insertion in Article I, Section 10, between clauses 1 and 2, this clause:

> No state shall violate the equal rights of conscience, of the freedom of the press, or the trial by jury in criminal cases.

The place he proposed for insertion of this clause was appropriate, for all three clauses of Article I, Section 10, bind the states, not Congress. Notably, Madison thought this particular amendment "the most valuable of the whole list." Not all of the state constitutions safeguarded these rights. And he believed, as he put it in his speech on the House floor, that "there is more danger of those powers being abused by the state governments than by the government of the United States." Indeed, as a general matter, he thought that "every government should be disarmed of powers which trench upon those particular rights."[3]

The House did not show much interest in moving Madison's proposals; the members believed they had more pressing business. Eventually, Madison's list was given to a special committee. Among the few substantive changes the committee made was to add freedom of speech to the rights that "no state shall violate." The committee also combined the two clauses addressed to Congress and rewrote them to read: "The freedom of speech and of the press, and the right of the people peaceably to assemble and consult for their common good, and to apply to the Government for redress of grievances, shall not be infringed." During the subsequent debate on the committee's recommendations, the House—for reasons unknown—rejected the idea of interspersing amendments within the text of the Constitution and decided to append them to the Constitution as a separate bill of rights.

The House approved seventeen amendments and sent them to the Senate, which by combination and deletion reduced the number to twelve. Curiously—and here again we do not know why—Madison's "most valuable" amendment was struck, which meant that none of the amendments eventually added to the Constitution as the Bill of Rights limited the states. Even so, the question arose early in the nineteenth century as to whether the Bill of Rights also restrained the states, and in the 1833 case *Barron* v. *Baltimore* the Supreme Court held that it applied only to the federal government. In the twentieth century, the Court decided that certain provisions in the Bill of Rights, including those concerning freedom of expression, do apply to the states. It is likely that litigation over alleged state infringements of freedom of speech and of the press would have arisen well before it did in the twentieth century had Madison's "most valuable" protection made its way into the Constitution.

The Senate did not strike the other amendment that eventually became our First Amendment but rewrote it to read: "That Congress shall make no law abridging the freedom of speech, or of the press, or the right of the people peaceably to assemble and consult for their common good, and to petition the government for a redress of grievances." The Senate then combined these provisions with the ones concerning religious liberty into a single amendment. A conference committee resolved some differences concerning the ban on an established religion, and then both houses approved this amendment (along with the Senate versions of the others).

On September 25, 1789, the twelve amendments were submitted to the states for ratification. What became the First Amendment was originally the third of the twelve. It became the first when the first two amendments—dealing with the number of representatives and with the compensation of senators and representatives—met with defeat. The remaining ten amendments won the approval of the necessary number of states and became part of the Constitution on December 15, 1791.[4]

THE MEANING OF THE FIRST AMENDMENT

Not much can be learned about the original meaning of the First Amendment from the history of its framing and ratification. The movement arising from the states for a bill of rights did not define the rights for which it sought protection. During the actual framing and proposing of the amendment, the Senate kept no records of its deliberations, and the House debates are not illuminating. There are no records of the relevant debates in the state legislatures.

We do know, however, something about the origins of these freedoms and how they were generally regarded by Americans during the period of state and federal constitution-making. To take the last named liberty first, the right to petition, which was formally declared in England in the bill of rights of 1689, enabled subjects to petition the king. The American colonists tried to exercise this right, but to no avail, and the Declaration of Independence put forth the flouting of "our repeated petitions" for redress as one of the main grievances against King George III. The obvious contribution the states made to the right to petition was to republicanize it. In its recommendations for a bill of rights, for example, Virginia said that "every freeman should have the right to petition or apply to the legislature for redress of grievances."

The related right to assemble peaceably also had English roots. In the seventeenth century the House of Commons resolved that every commoner had "the inherent right to prepare and present petitions" to it "in case of grievance," and it was understood that commoners would join together in preparing to present petitions. In the colonies and then the states this notion of meeting to prepare petitions came to be understood as assembling for a political purpose. Not surprisingly, given their common origins, the rights of assembly and petition were brought together in the First Amendment: "Congress shall make no law . . . abridging . . . the right of the people peaceably to assemble, and to petition the Government for a redress of grievances."

Also yoked together in the First Amendment were the freedoms of speech and of the press. Freedom of speech drew its meaning from freedom of the press, and that freedom was commonly understood in the colonies in terms of the liberty achieved in England with the abolition of "prior restraint," under which the Crown had licensed printing presses and printers and nothing could be published without previous approval.[5]

As significant as this measure of press liberty was at the time, from our perspective today it was quite limited. No prior restraint meant that a publisher could publish freely, but what he published might still be punishable. This distinction between liberty and license (defined as the abuse of liberty) was made plain by William Blackstone, the famous compiler of English law, who was a major influence in eighteenth-century America. Blackstone wrote that freedom of the press

> consists in laying no previous restraints upon publications, and not in freedom from censure for criminal matter when published. Every freeman has an undoubted right to lay what sentiments he pleases before the public; to forbid this, is to destroy the freedom of the press: but if he publishes what is improper, mischievous, or illegal, he must take the consequences of his own temerity. Thus, the will of individuals is still left free: the abuse only of that free will is the object of legal punishment.

In the states, obscenity was an object of legal punishment. So was—and this is a major chapter in First Amendment history—seditious libel.

In the English common law, "seditious libel" was criticism that threatened to diminish respect for the government, its laws, or public officials. Most states adopted the English common law, and most also passed seditious-libel statutes. The states included in their constitutions free-press provisions, but there is no evidence that these provisions were intended to prohibit what the common and statutory law allowed. While seditious-libel charges were infrequently brought against a press increasingly given to vituperative criticism of government and public officials, the lack of enforcement did not lead to demise of the law. Thus the America that ratified the Bill of Rights was simultaneously for a free press and for seditious-libel law.

Nor did the America of that era qualify this law by the teachings of the Zenger trial, held half a century earlier. John Peter Zenger, the publisher of the *New York Weekly Journal,* was tried for seditious libel after he published criticism of the New York governor. Zenger admitted publishing the material in question, but in defense he contended for the right to print the truth about public officials. The colonial jury found Zenger innocent of the charges. His case stood for the principles that jurors, not judges, should decide whether something was libelous, and that defendants should be able to plead truth as a defense. But no state embraced these principles in its law in the years before the Bill of Rights was submitted for ratification; in fact, New York actually repudiated them in its constitution of 1777, which formally embraced the English common law. In 1790, Pennsylvania became the first state to adopt the Zengerian principles, followed by Delaware and Kentucky in 1792. But that was the extent of this libertarian trend, and of course in all three of these states seditious libel—criticism that threatened to diminish respect for the government or its officials—remained formally a crime.

At the end of the eighteenth century a more libertarian understanding of freedom of the press would emerge. But when the First Amendment was added to the Constitution, the prevailing view of press liberty was that it did not preclude punishment for seditious libel. "The security of the state against libelous advocacy or attack," observes Leonard Levy,

> outweighed any social interest in open expression, at least through the period of the adoption of the First Amendment. The thought and experience of a lifetime, indeed the taught traditions of law and politics extending back many generations, supplied an a priori belief that freedom of political discourse, however broadly conceived, stopped short of seditious libel.[6]

THE SEDITION ACT OF 1798

During the Adams administration, the Federalists believed that the opposition Republicans would undermine the young nation by promoting the radical ideas of the French Revolution. War with France seemed likely to many Americans, and the Federalist majority in Congress passed legislation aimed at curbing the Republicans' criticisms. Embracing the English common law of seditious libel, the Sedition Act of 1798 criminalized speech that disparaged government and public officials.[7] Punishment included fines of as much as $2,000 and prison terms of up to two years. Because the Sedition Act incorporated the Zengerian principles of allowing the jury to judge criminality and the defendant to plead truth as a defense, it was more libertarian than the understanding of seditious libel that had prevailed in the states through at least 1791. Even so, every case the government brought resulted in conviction, and three newspapers had to quit publishing. The act expired in 1801 without having come under Supreme Court review,[8] and the Republican attack against it, led by Thomas Jefferson and James Madison, helped drive the Federalists from power and into oblivion as a political party. President Jefferson pardoned those convicted under the act, and Congress repaid their fines.

The Sedition Act forced a reconsideration of the substantive meaning of speech and press freedom. Yet this did not happen immediately. When the bill was debated in Congress, Republicans attacked it as a violation of states' rights—the right in particular to punish libel. After the Sedition Act was passed, Republicans carried on this same attack by means of the Virginia and Kentucky Resolutions, which were written by Madison and Jefferson, respectively. Only after other states failed to pass similar resolutions did some Republicans offer a principled argument against the doctrine of seditious libel. They began to question, wrote Walter Berns, "whether the Blackstone view of free press as merely an uncensored press was compatible with republican government, state or national."[9] What emerged from this questioning was not an absolute repudiation of seditious libel: even the most libertarian of the Republicans still thought the states could punish libels of public officials. What many of them did reject was the idea that any government could punish speech critical of that government.[10]

Here again Madison played a key intellectual role. There were differences between England and the United States, he said, that rendered Blackstone's definition of press liberty inappropriate to the latter. In England the legislature is seen as omnipotent, he explained, but in America the people, "not the Government, possess the absolute sovereignty," and it is therefore necessary to secure "the great and essential rights of the people . . . against legislative as well as against executive ambition." This is done in written constitutions that are paramount to ordinary laws, he continued, and freedom of speech and press enjoy constitutional protection because they are crucial to the exercise of the right of self-government. Madison saw freedom of speech and press as nothing less than a necessary condition of republican government; it followed that criticism of government could never be a crime.[11]

Elected to power in 1800, the Republicans did not live up to their states' rights rhetoric. The Jefferson administration brought seditious-libel cases on the basis not of the Sedition Act, which had expired, but of the common law. One case charged that the *Connecticut Current* had libeled the President and the Congress by publishing an allegation that they had secretly voted to approve a $2 million present to Napoleon Bonaparte. An issue from this case was later reviewed by the Supreme Court in *United States* v. *Hudson*, which asked whether the federal courts have a common-law jurisdiction in criminal cases. The Court flatly said no. "The legislative authority of the Union must first make an act a crime, affix a punishment to it, and declare the Court that shall have jurisdiction of the offence."[12] *Hudson* denied the ability of the federal government to prosecute crimes unless Congress had declared them in the first place—and Congress was not about to pass another sedition act. Dealing with the crime of seditious libel fell to the states.

Over time, state prosecutions for seditious libel ground to a halt. Libel became a concern of not the criminal but the civil law, and individuals, including public officials, who thought they had been defamed went to court to invoke the law's protection. The states typically incorporated Zengerian principles into their libel laws, with some requiring that defendants pleading truth as a defense also show that they published from "good motives." Libel law remained a matter for the states alone to decide until 1964, when the Court lifted it into the First Amendment in *New York Times Co.* v. *Sullivan.*

THE CIVIL WAR AND FREE SPEECH

In the first decades of the nineteenth century, Southern states saw anti-slavery speech as a direct threat to an institution on which their economies were heavily dependent. They moved to suppress such speech locally and then asked Northern states to pass criminal laws "prohibiting the printing . . . of all such publications as may have a tendency to make our slaves discontented," as a resolution by the North Carolina legislature put it. They even asked for laws suppressing abolitionist societies.

When these requests were rebuffed, some communities in the South took matters into their own hands by persuading local postmasters to refuse to deliver abolitionist mail and anti-slavery newspapers.[13] The Southern states also turned to Washington and asked Congress to use its postal authority to exclude abolitionist literature from the mails. President Andrew Jackson took up their cause, arguing that the "painful excitement produced in the South" by such "incendiary" literature was sufficient reason to ban it. Senator John C. Calhoun of South Carolina, chair of the committee to which Jackson's recommendation was assigned, objected to it on states' rights grounds. Contending that the federal government should not be able to determine which material was "incendiary" and therefore subject to restraint, Calhoun instead offered a substitute measure giving the Southern states in effect veto power over the post office's distribution of "any paper . . . touching the subject of slavery." Calhoun's measure failed.[14]

So, too, though it took a while, did the effort to "gag" the House of Representatives. In 1836 the House passed the first of a series of resolutions denying itself the ability to consider any petition relating to the subject of slavery or even to permit any discussion of such petitions. The last of these gag rules was rescinded in 1845, thanks mainly to the efforts of John Quincy Adams, who contended that they were "a direct violation of the Constitution of the United States."

The Southern states were not alone in believing that some speech was so dangerous that it should be suppressed. During the Civil War, a grand jury sitting in New York was disturbed by opposition in the city's press to the Northern war effort. Although the *Tribune*, the *Herald*, and the *Times* generally supported the effort, other papers in the city did not. One non-supporter was the *New York Journal of Commerce*, which declared in print that more than a hundred Northern newspapers opposed "the present unholy war." The jurors asked the presiding judge whether this criticism was indictable. Because the grand jury was soon to be discharged, the judge declined to answer. The jurors then asked that the *Journal of Commerce* and four other New York papers opposing the war effort be brought to the attention of the succeeding grand jury.

The next step was taken by the Lincoln administration. Concerned about the disproportionate influence upon the nation exerted by the New York newspapers, the administration moved against the five papers by excluding them from the mails. Newspapers of that era were distributed almost entirely by mail, and the action effectively shut down the five. The *New York News* tried using private express to send papers out of town and newsboys to deliver them locally. But U.S. marshals seized all copies of the paper, and the *News* gave up.

In recounting this story in a speech, Chief Justice William Rehnquist has observed that "other New York newspapers did not rally round the sheets that the government was suppressing. Instead of crying out that the First Amendment rights of these papers had been abridged—as they surely would do today—their rivals simply gloated." The press did not see its interest in terms of the First Amendment.

The Civil War also produced the famous case of Clement L. Vallandigham, a former Ohio congressman who was the leader of the Peace Democrats. This group opposed the war effort and had considerable support in the Democratic Party. Lincoln told a friend that he feared "the fire in the rear"—meaning the anti-war rhetoric from the Peace Democrats and others of like mind—more than the fire on the battlefield; he thought this "fire" could so weaken military morale that substantial numbers of soldiers might desert, and there is evidence that he was right. Democratic newspapers circulating among the Northern troops published editorials proclaiming the illegality of the war and also letters allegedly written by relatives of soldiers decrying the "unholy" and "unconstitutional" war and urging them to desert. "Such propaganda had its intended effect," writes James M. McPherson in *Battle Cry of Freedom*. "So many members of two southern Illinois regiments deserted rather than help free the slaves that General Grant had to disband the regiments. Soldiers from several other regiments allowed themselves to be captured so they could be paroled and sent home."[15]

Vallandigham was a constant source of "the fire in the rear"—indeed, Lincoln regarded him as more responsible than any other anti-war activist for "hindrance" of the military. After Vallandigham gave a speech denouncing the war as "wicked, cruel, and unnecessary," with a goal of "crushing out liberty and erecting a despotism," General Ambrose Burnside arrested him at his Ohio home. The charge was "implied treason." Tried by a military court and found guilty, he was sentenced to prison for the war's duration. Lincoln commuted the sentence to banishment, but Vallandigham's case remained controversial, not least because it raised the question whether speech could be treason. His supporters vigorously protested to Lincoln that he had been prosecuted "for no other reason than words addressed to a public meeting." Lincoln replied that had there been no other reason for the arrest, it would have been wrong, but that there had been "a very different reason"—that Vallandigham "was laboring, with some effect, to prevent the raising of troops, to encourage desertions from the army, and to leave the rebellion without an adequate military force to suppress it." The life of the nation depended upon the army, Lincoln said, and "armies can not be maintained unless desertion shall be punished by the severe penalty of death." Then he asked: "Must I shoot a simple-minded soldier boy who deserts, while I must not touch a hair of a wiley agitator who induces him to desert? . . . I think that in such a case, to silence the agitator, and save the boy, is not only constitutional, but, withal a great mercy."[16]

THE FIRST CASES

Post–Civil War legislation quickly produced the Supreme Court's first opportunity to interpret the First Amendment. The Enforcement Act of 1870 prohibited interference with the free exercise and enjoyment of any constitutional right or privilege. Louisiana whites were indicted under the law for having deprived blacks of their rights to assemble with other citizens "for a peaceful and lawful purpose." The defendants appealed, and in *United States* v. *Cruikshank* (1876) the Court found their case inadequate because they did not allege a denial of *federal* rights. The First Amendment, said the Court, protected persons only from congressional interference, not from actions taken by the states or by private individuals.

The 1870s marked the start of a period of societal change and social unrest that included radical activity. Cases involving free speech and press were brought more frequently than before, in both state and federal courts, not only by workers, anarchists, socialists, and religious minorities but also by editors and publishers, businessmen, movie distributors, candidates for office, and government employees.[17] Seldom were these cases successful, and not until 1931, in *Stromberg* v. *California* and *Near* v. *Minnesota*, did the Supreme Court actually vindicate First Amendment claims.

During these decades the Court declined opportunities to accept the argument that the Constitution bars the states from abridging free expression.[18] It did not object to the understanding of freedom of speech and press that was commonly shared in the states when the Bill of Rights was added to the Constitution. In fact, it suggested that the common-law crime of libel, possibly including seditious libel, was not forbidden by the First Amendment.[19] It stated flatly that the amendment did not "permit the publication of libels, blasphemous or indecent articles, or other publications injurious to public morals or private reputation."[20] And it denied that the amendment compelled Congress to use "its facilities for the distribution of matter deemed injurious to the public morals."[21] The Court also refused to accept the claim that public property is open to the public by right as a place where free-speech rights may be exercised.[22] It did not see free speech implicated when it upheld a statute forbidding federal employees to solicit or receive money for political purposes from other employees.[23] Nor did it see a commercial speech claim in a case in which it sustained a state law prohibiting the use of the American flag in advertisements.[24] The Court also rejected the notion that films deserve First Amendment protection; showing films is a profit-making business that should not be regarded "as part of the press of the country or as organs of public opinion."[25] On most of the key issues in these cases, the Court eventually changed its mind.

Of most relevance to the story of the First Amendment as it takes shape in the initial cases found in this volume is the Court's treatment of when speech may constitutionally be punished. In *Patterson* v. *Colorado* (1907) the Court sustained a contempt conviction of an editor who had criticized judicial behavior and had not had the opportunity to assert truth as a defense. The Court did not rest its judgment on the First Amendment, which it had yet to apply to the states. But it nonetheless observed, with Justice Oliver Wendell Holmes writing, that the First Amendment prevents all "previous restraints" upon publications but permits "the subsequent punishment of such as may be deemed contrary to the public welfare. . . . The preliminary freedom extends as well to the false as to the true; the subsequent punishment may extend as well to the true as to the false." Holmes said that a publication criticizing judicial behavior "would tend to obstruct the administration of justice." The truth or falsity of such criticism did not matter; the issue was the way such criticism "tends."

Here the Court was simply acknowledging the continuing vitality of the "bad tendency test," as it was called. Part of the English common law of libel, which had been adopted in eighteenth-century America, the test measured the legality of speech by its tendency to produce an illegal action. Eight years after *Patterson*, in *Fox* v. *Washington* (1915), the Court was asked to review a state law making it a misdemeanor to publish articles "having a tendency to encourage or incite the commission of any crime, breach of the peace or act of violence, or to encourage or advocate disrespect for a law or for any court or courts of justice." Writing for the Court, Holmes found that the article in question, "The Nude and the Prudes," which encouraged boycotts of those who interfered with nude bathing, had indeed a bad tendency. "By indirection but unmistakably," he said, the article encouraged violations of laws against indecent exposure.

Four years later, in *Schenck* v. *United States* (1919)—the first case in this volume—Holmes again applied the bad-tendency test in sustaining convictions under the Espionage Act of 1917 for speech that obstructed military recruitment. "If the act (speaking, or circulating a paper), its tendency, and the intent with which it is done are the same," Holmes wrote, "we perceive no ground for saying that success alone warrants making the act a crime." Holmes also employed the bad-tendency test in writing the Court's opinions in two subsequent cases sustaining convictions for speech of a similar kind, *Frohwerk* v. *United States* (1919) and *Debs* v. *United States* (1919). "A little breath would be enough to kindle a flame," he wrote in *Frohwerk*. And in *Debs*, Holmes said that the defendant's anti-war speeches "had as their natural tendency and reasonably probable effect to obstruct the recruitment service." It did not matter whether the relation between the words and the crime had been indirect and incidental; for Holmes, the tendency of the language was evidence of the speaker's intent.[26]

In *Schenck*, Holmes also wrote: "The question in every case is whether the words used are used in such circumstances and are of such a nature as to create a clear and present danger that they will bring about the substantive evils that Congress has a right to prevent." In the June 1919 issue of the *Harvard Law Review*, Zechariah Chafee, a professor at the Harvard Law School, wrote that Holmes had used the term "clear and present danger" to make "the punishment of words for their bad tendency impossible."[27] This was almost certainly a wrong interpretation of Holmes's use of this term. Holmes had employed the bad-tendency test in previous cases, as we have seen, and he relied on it to decide not only *Schenck* but also the subsequent cases of *Frohwerk* and *Debs*. In neither of those cases did he mention "clear and present danger."

Chafee's article appeared before the Court decided *Abrams* v. *United States* (the second case in this book) in the fall of 1919. Citing *Schenck* and *Frohwerk* against the First Amendment claims of the defendants, the Court again sustained convictions for subversive speech.

Chafee's arguments had found an audience, however, for Holmes, in a dissent joined by Justice Louis Brandeis, defended "the sweeping command of the First Amendment" and held that the government had failed to make a showing of "clear and present danger." First Amendment scholar David Rabban observes that Holmes and Brandeis "accepted as their own the libertarian meaning Chafee erroneously read into those words, and thus were able, beginning with *Abrams*, to reject the bad-tendency theory."[28]

The *Oxford Companion to the Supreme Court* calls Chafee "the father of modern free speech law."[29] Yet as Rabban points out, Chafee was influenced by intellectuals of the late nineteenth and early twentieth century who argued for a more libertarian understanding of the First Amendment.[30] Not all the scholarship of these intellectuals survives scrutiny, however, and Chafee himself shared with some of them a view of First Amendment history that has rightly been described as "more polemical than scholarly."[31] Contrary to what Chafee contended, for example, the First Amendment was not designed to abolish the law of seditious libel.[32] In his *Abrams* dissent, Holmes repeated this mistaken view of history when he wrote: "I wholly disagree with the argument of the government that the First Amendment left the common law as to seditious libel in force."

The more serious flaw in Holmes's opinion lay in its "theory of the First Amendment," which the justice refined six years later in his *Gitlow* dissent. Under this theory, there is no intrinsically superior political idea, no political truth. The only true ideas are those that majorities accept— i.e., those which are true "for them." The role of the First Amendment is to protect the expression of all ideas—none should be suppressed. The amendment thus permits a "free trade in ideas," and the ones that "the dominant forces of the community" accept are that society's truths.

Holmes's theory in its philosophical underpinnings was diametrically opposed to the understanding of the American founders, who held in the Declaration of Independence that there are ideas that are true for all people at all times and in all places, one of them being that everyone has the same unalienable rights, including that of self-government. And his theory had startling implications, which Holmes did not hesitate to point out. *Gitlow* was a case in which the defendant advocated violent action by a minority in order to impose a dictatorship, and in *Gitlow* Holmes wrote: "If, in the long run, the beliefs expressed in proletarian dictatorship are destined to be accepted by the dominant forces of the community, the only meaning of free speech is that they should be given their chance and have their way." In other words, those who would advocate a violent end to republican government must be allowed to speak their mind in "the free trade in ideas"—but if their doctrine prevailed, there would be no free trade in ideas because there would be no First Amendment; nonetheless, those who might suppress speech of this kind for the sake of republican government and the self-evident truths that provide its foundation must not be allowed to do that since, after all, the First Amendment guarantees a "free trade in ideas." Free speech, constitutional scholar Walter Berns has observed of Holmes's theory, "turns out to mean that it is worse to suppress the advocacy of Stalinism or Hitlerism than to be ruled by Stalin or Hitler. The reasons for this are not, one might say, readily apparent."[33]

THE FIRST AMENDMENT TODAY

Abrams marks the beginning of modern First Amendment law, for it is in their *Abrams* dissent that Holmes and Brandeis insisted that the Court should take free-speech claims more seriously. A decade later the Court began to do that. During the 1930s the Court held in behalf of every one of the four freedoms now referred to as freedom of expression. Informing the Court's work during these years was the view, perhaps best expressed in *Palko* v. *Connecticut* (1937), that "freedom of thought and speech" is "the matrix, the indispensable condition, of every other form of freedom."

Although the First Amendment mentions only Congress and its law-making function, these early cases arose from the states. The Court had made this possible by a series of decisions beginning in 1925, in *Gitlow* v. *New York*, in which it said that the states, and not just Congress, are restrained by the First Amendment.

In 1942, in *Chaplinsky* v. *New Hampshire*, the Court undertook to say which speech is not free speech—i.e., is unprotected by the First Amendment. Sustaining a conviction under New Hampshire law prohibiting offensive speech and name-calling in public, the Court said that "fighting" words as well as lewd, obscene, profane, and libelous words are unprotected because "such utterances are no essential part of any exposition of ideas, and are of such slight social value as a step to truth that any benefit that may be derived from them is clearly outweighed by the social interest in order and morality." Under *Chaplinsky*, expression falling within its five categories was unprotected, period; but expression falling outside those categories was covered by the First Amendment.

Over the decades the Court has in effect rewritten *Chaplinsky*, broadening the First Amendment freedoms that governments at all levels must respect. "Fighting words" appear to have been moved into the "protected" category, though the Court has never explicitly repudiated its view of such speech in *Chaplinsky*. The Court has also brought libel firmly within the shelter of the First Amendment. And it has so narrowed the definition of obscenity as to make secure all but hard-core pornography. Diverging from this generally libertarian trend is the Court's 1982 decision to categorize child pornography as unprotected speech (*New York* v. *Ferber*).

The same year the Court decided *Chaplinsky* (1942), it also ruled in *Valentine* v. *Chrestenson* that commercial speech lacks First Amendment protection. But on this issue, too, the Court has changed its mind. Commercial speech now enjoys substantial protection, though less than non-commercial speech, and seems likely to gain more security as the Court continues to review commercial-speech claims.

The year after *Chaplinsky*, the Court ruled in one of its most famous cases ever— *West Virginia Board of Education* v. *Barnette*—that a state may not force students to say the Pledge of Allegiance and salute the American flag. Here the Court recognized a First Amendment right not to speak and a right not to salute. The First Amendment remains today a sturdy defense against governments that would compel a citizen's speech.

In the 1950s, in yet another expansion of First Amendment freedoms, the Court declared the existence of a right of association. In the Court's cases, this right is seen either as part and parcel of the right to assemble peaceably or as derived from that right.

Finally, the Court has extended shelter to a substantial amount of non-verbal expression. In one of its early cases it held that the First Amendment encompasses a right to picket, a decision that was not based on the words actually appearing on the signs. In similar fashion, the Court later decided that the First Amendment includes a right to march or demonstrate, and to conduct a sit-in or stand-in. The Court observed, however, that expressive-conduct claims are not to be equated with "pure speech" claims, since the former involve non-speech elements that may be lawfully proscribed. In *United States* v. *O'Brien* (1968) the Court sustained a federal law outlawing draft-card destruction in a case in which a draft card had been burned in protest of the Vietnam War. But a year later, in *Tinker* v. *Des Moines School District,* the Court said that a public school student's wearing of a black armband to protest the Vietnam War was protected speech. And in 1989 and 1990, the Court held that burning the American flag was also protected speech. In sum, with non-verbal as with verbal expression, the trend in the Court's cases has been a generally libertarian one.

It bears emphasis that the Court has extended the reach of the First Amendment beyond politics to many other areas. "It is no doubt true that a central purpose of the First Amendment 'was to protect the free discussion of governmental affairs,'" the Court said in *Abood* v. *Detroit Board of Education* (1977). "But our cases have never suggested that expression about philosophical, social, artistic, economic, literary, or ethical matters—to take a nonexclusive list of labels—is not entitled to full First Amendment protection."

In deciding First Amendment claims, the Court has not employed a single mode of analysis. Instead it has used a variety of legal concepts and tests, revising or discarding them as new cases arise. The introductions to the cases in this book alert readers to the Court's use of such doctrines as "prior restraint" and the "time, place, and manner" rule, and to such tests as "bad tendency," "clear and present danger" (in its several forms), and "First Amendment balancing."

A case is by definition a controversy, and some of the Court's decisions remain controversial. Campaign financing is an example of an issue about which some think the Court has been too libertarian and others think it has been too strict. For the most part, however, the First Amendment decisions that are still criticized today are deemed too libertarian, the obscenity and flag-burning decisions being the most conspicuous examples.

Generally speaking, the libertarian thrust of First Amendment law enjoys broad public support. Even many of those who object to a particular decision or line of decisions salute this overall tendency. Today, in part because of the First Amendment, no nation conducts its politics more freely, and no nation has more freedom of expression.

NOTES

1. Leonard Levy, *Origins of the Bill of Rights* (New Haven: Yale University Press, 1999), 1–5. Levy's book is an excellent, concise account of the origins of the Bill of Rights and the First Amendment in particular.

2. Ibid., 19. One natural right enjoys explicit protection in the original Constitution: the right of contract—i.e., the right of individuals to make promises in the state of nature that are binding upon them. It is protected by Article I's prohibition of laws (though only those enacted by the states, not those of the federal government) "impairing the obligation of contracts." Ibid., 26.

3. *James Madison: Writings* (New York: Library of America, 1999), 451.

4. Georgia, Massachusetts, and Connecticut voted against. One hundred and fifty years later, on the sesquicentennial anniversary of the Bill of Rights, these states formally ratified the Bill of Rights.

5. Freedom of the press in terms of freedom from prior restraint was John Milton's cause in *Areopagitica: A Speech for the Liberty of Unlicensed Printing* (1644).

6. Levy, *Origins*, 120.

7. For a worthy account of the Sedition Act and the controversies surrounding it, see Walter Berns, *The First Amendment and the Future of American Democracy* (Washington: Regnery Gateway, 1985), 86–119.

8. The man who soon (in 1801) would become chief justice of the Supreme Court, John Marshall, apparently did express a view of the Sedition Act. When Virginia passed its resolution, the legislators in the minority published their dissent, which is thought to have been written by Marshall. Marshall said of the Act that to "contend that there does not exist a power to punish writings coming within the description

of this law, would be to assert the inability of our nation to preserve its own peace, and to protect themselves from the attempt of wicked citizens, who incapable of quiet themselves are incessantly employed in devising means to disturb the public repose." Marshall wrote that the First Amendment did not prohibit such laws, observing that a "punishment of the licentiousness is not . . . a restriction of the freedom of the press." Berns, *The First Amendment*, 109–10.

9. Ibid., 111.

10. Ibid., 113.

11. Ibid., 117–18. In *New York Times* v. *Sullivan* (1964), the landmark case that constitutionalized the law of libel, the Court declared the Sedition Act of 1798 "inconsistent with the First Amendment."

12. 11 U.S. 32 (1812).

13. Berns, *The First Amendment*, 120–22.

14. Ibid., 126.

15. James M. McPherson, *Battle Cry of Freedom: The Civil War* (New York: Oxford University Press, 1988), 595.

16. Roy Basler, ed., *The Collected Works of Abraham Lincoln* (New Brunswick: Rutgers University Press, 1953), 6:266–67.

17. David M. Rabban, "The First Amendment in Its Forgotten Years," *Yale Law Journal* 90 (January 1981): 523. I have drawn on Rabban's account for information on some of these early cases.

18. *Spies* v. *Illinois* (1887) was an appeal by anarchists convicted of aiding and abetting murder after a fatal bomb exploded in a town square where they were pushing their doctrines and passing out literature. The anarchists claimed that the Fourteenth Amendment incorporated the Bill of Rights and that the cases brought against them abridged their free-speech rights. Discerning no federal question requiring decision, the Court did not address incorporation. Twenty years later, in *Patterson* v. *Colorado*, the Court, with Justice Oliver Wendell Holmes writing, sustained the contempt conviction of a Colorado newspaper editor by denying his argument that Colorado had abridged press liberty. The Court noted that it left "undecided the question whether there is to be found in the Fourteenth Amendment a prohibition [the ban on abridging the freedom of the press] similar to that in the First." In 1922 the Court stated in *Prudential Insurance Co.* v. *Cheek* that the Fourteenth Amendment did not impose upon the states the obligation to protect "the right of free speech." Three years later, in *Gitlow* v. *New York*, the third case presented in this book, the Court held the opposite without offering any reasoning for its new position, describing its statement in *Cheek* as mere "dicta."

19. *United States* v. *Press Publishing Co.* (1911).

20. *Robertson* v. *Baldwin* (1897).

21. The quotation is from *Ex parte Jackson* (1878), in which the Court upheld the constitutionality of a federal law prohibiting the mailing of lottery advertisements. In passing, it also sanctioned the Comstock Act, which barred from the mails all publications of an "obscene" or otherwise "indecent character." The Court later upheld such restrictions, most recently in *United States* v. *Reidel* (1971). The exception occurred in 1965, when restrictions on foreign mailings of "communist propaganda" were struck down in *Lamont* v. *Postmaster General*, a case included in this book and the very first in which the Court invalidated an act of Congress on First Amendment grounds.

22. *Davis* v. *Massachusetts* (1897). The Court stated: "For the legislature absolutely or conditionally to forbid public speaking in a highway or public park is no more an infringement of rights of a member of the public than for the owner of a private house to forbid it in the house." Four decades later the Court changed its mind and embraced the idea of a public forum in *Hague* v. *CIO* (1939).

23. *Ex parte Curtis* (1882).

24. *Halter* v. *Nebraska* 205 U.S. 34 (1907). The Court extended the First Amendment to commercial speech in *Virginia Pharmacy Board* v. *Virginia Consumers Council* (1976).

25. *Mutual Film Corp.* v. *Industrial Commission of Ohio* (1915). At issue was a state law requiring approval of all films by a board of censors before they could be shown. In 1952 the Court extended First Amendment protection to films in *Burstyn* v. *Wilson*.

26. Rabban, "The First Amendment," 582–86.

27. Ibid., 590. (An excerpt from the Chafee essay is printed in the *Schenck* chapter of the present volume.)

28. Ibid., 534.

29. Kermit L. Hall, ed., *The Oxford Companion to the Supreme Court* (New York: Oxford University Press, 1992), 133.

30. Ibid., 579.

31. Samuel Walker, *In Defense of American Liberties: A History of the ACLU* (Carbondale: Southern Illinois University Press, 1990), 28. See also Rabban, "The First Amendment," 587.

32. In *Legacy of Suppression: Freedom of Speech and Press in Early American History* (Cambridge: Belknap Press, 1960) Leonard Levy first advanced the result of his historical investigations into the First Amendment—that it was not written to abolish seditious libel. Levy commented that Chafee "'anticipated the past' by succumbing to an impulse to recreate it so that its image may be seen in a manner consistent with our rhetorical tradition of freedom, thereby yielding a message which will instruct the present" (2–3).

33. Berns, *The First Amendment*, 160–61.

Note to the Reader

The Opinions. Opinions have been abridged with the intention of preserving the fundamentals of the justices' reasoning in an abbreviated form. An ellipsis after the boldface introductory line (e.g., Justice Holmes delivered the opinion of the Court . . .) indicates the omission of one or more paragraphs at the beginning of the opinion. An ellipsis within an opinion shows that one or more words, sentences, or paragraphs have been omitted. An ellipsis sometimes replaces numerous pages of an opinion.

Most bracketed words etc. Omissions within the reprinted text are denoted with ellipses, but omissions before the reprinted section are not so indicated. An ellipsis at the beginning or end of a paragraph or within a paragraph indicates that one or more words, sentences, or paragraphs have been omitted. An ellipsis sometimes replaces numerous pages of an opinion.

Most bracketed words and ellipses have been added by the editor of this volume. In the very few places in which brackets or ellipses are present in an opinion (i.e., in quoted material), these have not been distinguished from those added by the editor.

Footnotes, most references to books and articles, and some references to other cases have been omitted from the opinions, without ellipses. Most references to other cases are included, usually in a shortened form.

Case Names and Citations. For each of the sixty cases presented in this book, the full citation to the *United States Reports*, the official edition of the Supreme Court's decisions, appears on the chapter title page. For cases referred to within an opinion, a bracketed year has been added in lieu of the citation, e.g., *Schenck* v. *United States* [1919]; subsequent references in the same opinion use a shortened form of the case name, e.g., *Schenck*.

Accuracy. Care has been taken to present the Court's opinions accurately. However, minor typographical or other insignificant errors are possible. The complete, official texts of Supreme Court opinions may be found in the *United States Reports*.

SCHENCK V. UNITED STATES
249 U.S. 47 (1919)

Charles Schenck, the general secretary of the Socialist Party, mailed circulars to 15,000 potential draftees urging them to "assert their rights" in opposition to the Great War and to sign an anti-draft petition. Schenck was prosecuted under the Espionage Act of 1917, which prohibited attempts to obstruct military recruitment. Appealing his conviction, Schenck argued that the statute was at odds with the First Amendment's free speech clause because the clause guarantees "absolutely unlimited discussion" of public affairs, even that which condemns the government of the United States. A unanimous Supreme Court declined this invitation to strike down an act of Congress.

In *Schenck* the Court for the first time reviewed a free speech challenge to a federal statute, and it used the occasion to articulate its first significant interpretation of the free speech clause. Before *Schenck,* both federal and state courts had employed the "bad tendency test" in analyzing free speech and free press claims. Derived from the common law, this test assumed that the purpose of the First Amendment (like that of all other constitutional provisions) was to promote the public good, and it measured the legality of speech by the tendency of its effects. Speech tending to cause good effects enjoyed constitutional protection; but speech tending to cause bad effects—those that threatened the order or morality of a community, or the security of society—did not, and thus was subject to legislative regulation. In the typical case before *Schenck,* a law affecting speech was presumed constitutional and did not require more exacting scrutiny than other legislation. The bad-tendency test did not, one might say, tend to support free speech claims.

Nor did the Court in *Schenck* support the free speech claim before it. But the opinion, written by Justice Holmes, seemed to suggest a new and more stringent test for measuring the legality of speech. Called the "clear and present danger test," it came from this passage: "The question in every case is whether the words used are used in such circumstances and are of such a nature as to create a clear and present danger that they will bring about the substantive evils that Congress has a right to prevent. It is a question of proximity and degree."

Holmes, who had used the bad-tendency test in previous cases, concluded that the circulars mailed to the potential draftees had created the kind of clear and present danger that Congress constitutionally could punish. Left for another day was development of the clear-and-present-danger test and its employment to invalidate legislation affecting speech.

In two 1919 cases decided soon after *Schenck*—*Frohwerk* v. *United States* and *Debs* v. *United States*—the Court, with Holmes writing the opinions in both, unanimously upheld convictions under the Espionage Act that had been challenged on free speech grounds. The Court did not refer in these cases to "clear and present danger" but regarded the speech of the defendants as having a bad tendency.

Opinion of the Court: **Holmes**, White, McKenna, Day, Van Devanter, Pitney, McReynolds, Brandeis, Clarke.

Schenck v. *United States* was decided on March 3, 1919.

OPINION

JUSTICE HOLMES DELIVERED THE OPINION OF THE COURT . . .

The document in question upon its first printed side . . . said that the idea embodied in [the Thirteenth Amendment, i.e., that slavery and involuntary servitude are forbidden except as a punishment for crime] was violated by the conscription act and that a conscript is little better than a convict. In impassioned language it intimated that conscription was despotism in its worst form and a monstrous wrong against humanity in the interest of Wall Street's chosen few. It said, "Do not submit to intimidation," but in form at least confined itself to peaceful measures such as a petition for the repeal of the act. The other and later printed side of the sheet was headed "Assert Your Rights." It stated reasons for alleging that anyone violated the Constitution when he refused to recognize "your right to assert your opposition to the draft," and went on, "If you do not assert and support your rights, you are helping to deny or disparage rights which it is the solemn duty of all citizens and residents of the United States to retain." It described the arguments on the other side as coming from cunning politicians and a mercenary capitalist press, and even silent consent to the conscription law as helping to support an infamous conspiracy. It denied the power to send our citizens away to foreign shores to shoot up the people of other lands, and added that words could not express the condemnation such cold-blooded ruthlessness deserves, . . . winding up, "You must do your share to maintain, support, and uphold the rights of the people of this country." Of course the document would not have been sent unless it had been intended to have some effect, and we do not see what effect it could be expected to have upon persons subject to the draft except to influence them to obstruct the carrying of it out. The defendants do not deny that the jury might find against them on this point.

But it is said, suppose that was the tendency of this circular, it is protected by the First Amendment to the Constitution. . . . It may well be that the prohibition of laws abridging the freedom of speech is not confined to previous restraints, although to prevent them may have been the main purpose. . . . We admit that in many places and in ordinary times the defendants in saying all that was said in the circular would have been within their constitutional rights. But the character of every act depends upon the circumstances in which it is done. . . . The most stringent protection of free speech would not protect a man in falsely shouting fire in a theater and causing a panic. It does not even protect a man from an injunction against uttering words that may have all the effect of force. . . . The question in every case is whether the words used are used in such circumstances and are of such a nature as to create a clear and present danger that they will bring about the substantive evils that Congress has a right to prevent. It is a question of proximity and degree. When a nation is at war, many things that might be said in times of peace are such a hindrance to its effort that their utterance will not be endured so long as men fight and that no Court could regard them as protected by any constitutional right. It seems to be admitted that if an actual obstruction of the recruiting services were proved, liability for words that produced that effect might be enforced. The statute of 1917 . . . punishes conspiracies to obstruct as well as actual obstruction. If the act (speaking, or circulating a paper), its tendency, and the intent with which it is done are the same, we perceive no ground for saying that success alone warrants making the act a crime. . . .

[JUDGMENT] AFFIRMED.

RESPONSE

FROM THE *HARVARD LAW REVIEW*, JUNE 1919, ZECHARIAH CHAFEE, JR. "FREEDOM OF SPEECH IN WAR TIME" (GREATLY ABRIDGED, NOTES OMITTED)

. . . The real issue in every free-speech controversy is this—whether the state can punish all words which have some tendency, however remote, to bring about acts in violation of law, or only words which directly incite to acts in violation of law.

If words do not become criminal until they have an immediate tendency to produce a breach of the peace, there is no need for a law of sedition, since the ordinary standards of criminal solicitation and attempt apply. Under those standards the words must bring the speaker's unlawful intention reasonably near to success. Such a limited power to punish utterances rarely satisfies the zealous in times of excitement like a war. They realize that all condemnation of the war or of conscription may conceivably lead to active resistance or insubordination. Is it not better to kill the serpent in the egg? All writings that have a tendency to hinder the war must be suppressed.

Such has always been the argument of the opponents of free speech. And the most powerful weapon in their hand, since the abolition of the censorship, is this doctrine of indirect causation, under which words can be punished for a supposed bad tendency long before there is any probability that they will break out into unlawful acts. Closely related to it is the doctrine of constructive intent, which regards the intent of the defendant to cause violence as immaterial so long as he intended to write the words, or else presumes the violent intent from the bad tendency of the words on the ground that a man is presumed to intend the consequences of his acts. When rulers are allowed to possess these weapons, they can by the imposition of severe sentences create an *ex post facto* censorship of the press. The transference of that censorship from the judge to the jury is indeed important when the attack on the government which is prosecuted expresses a widespread popular sentiment, but the right to jury trial is of much less value in times of war or threatened disorder when the herd instinct runs strong, if the opinion of the defendant is highly objectionable to the majority of the population, or even to the particular class of men from whom or by whom the jury are drawn. . . .

Although the free-speech clauses were directed primarily against the sedition prosecutions of the immediate past, it must not be thought that they would permit unlimited previous restraint. They must also be interpreted in light of more remote history. The framers of those clauses did not invent the conception of freedom of speech as a result of their own experience of the last few years. The idea had been gradually molded in men's minds by centuries of conflict. It was the product of a people of whom the framers were merely the mouthpiece. Its significance was not fixed by their personality, but was the endless expression of a civilization. It was formed out of past resentment against the royal control of the press under the Tudors, against the Star Chamber and the pillory, against the Parliamentary censorship which Milton condemned in his *Areopagitica,* by recollections of heavy newspaper taxation, by hatred of the suppression of thought which went on vigorously on the Continent during the eighteenth century. Blackstone's views also had undoubted influence to bar out previous restraint. The censor is the most dangerous of all the enemies of liberty of the press, and cannot exist in this country unless made necessary by extraordinary perils.

Moreover, the meaning of the First Amendment did not crystallize in 1791. The framers would probably have been horrified at the thought of protecting books by Darwin or Bernard Shaw, but "liberty of speech" is no more confined to the speech they thought permissible than "commerce" in another clause is limited to the sailing vessels and horse-drawn vehicles of 1787. Into the making of the constitutional conception of free speech have gone, not only men's bitter experience of the censorship and sedition prosecutions before 1791, but also the subsequent development of the law of fair comment in civil defamation, and the philosophical speculations of John Stuart Mill. Justice Holmes phrases the thought with even more than his habitual felicity. "The provisions of the Constitution are not mathematical formulas having their essence in their form; they are organic living institutions transplanted from English soil."

It is now clear that the First Amendment fixes limits upon the power of Congress to restrict speech either by a censorship or by a criminal statute, and if the Espionage Act exceeds those limits it is unconstitutional. It is sometimes argued that the Constitution gives Congress the power to declare war, raise armies, and support a navy, that one provision of the Constitution cannot be used to break down another provision, and consequently freedom of speech cannot be invoked to break down the war power. I would reply that the First Amendment is just as much a part of the Constitution as the war clauses, and that it is equally accurate to say that the war clauses cannot be invoked to break down freedom of speech. The truth is that all provisions of the Constitution must be construed together so as to limit each other. In war as in peace, this process of mutual adjustment must include the Bill of Rights. . . .

. . . If the First Amendment is to mean anything, it must restrict the powers which are expressly granted by the Constitution to Congress, since Congress has no other powers. It must apply to those activities of government which are most liable to interfere with free discussion, namely, the postal service and the conduct of war.

The true meaning of freedom of speech seems to be this. One of the most important purposes of society and government is the discovery and spread of truth on subjects of general concern. This is possible only through absolutely unlimited discussion, for . . . once force is thrown into the argument, it becomes a matter of chance whether it is thrown in on the false side or the true, and truth loses all its natural advantage in the contest. Nevertheless, there are other purposes of government, such as order, the training of the young, protection against external aggression. Unlimited discussion sometimes interferes with these purposes, which must then be balanced against freedom of speech, but freedom of speech ought to weigh very heavily in the scale. The First Amendment gives binding force to this principle of political wisdom. . . .

. . . To find the boundary line of any right, we must get behind rules of law to human facts. In our problem, we must regard the desires and needs of the individual human being who wants to speak and those of the great group of human beings among whom he speaks. That is, in technical language, there are individual interests and social interests, which must be balanced against each other, if they conflict, in order to determine which interest shall be sacrificed under the circumstances and which shall be protected and become the foundation of a legal right. . . .

The First Amendment protects two kinds of interests in free speech. There is an individual interest, the need of many men to express their opinion on matters vital to them if life is to be worth living, and a social interest in the attainment of truth, so that the country may not only adopt the wisest course of action but carry it out in the wisest way. This social interest is especially important in war time. Even after war has been declared there is bound to be a confused mixture of good and bad arguments in its support, and a wide difference of opinion as to its objects. Truth can be sifted out from falsehood only if the government is vigorously and constantly cross-examined, so that the fundamental issues of the struggle may be clearly defined, and the war may not be diverted to improper ends, or prolonged after its just purposes are accomplished. . . .

The great trouble with most judicial constructions of the Espionage Act is that this social interest has been ignored and free speech has been regarded as merely an individual interest, which must readily give way like other personal desires the moment it interferes with the social interest in national safety. The judge [Justice Holmes] who has done most to bring social interests into legal interests said years ago, "I think that the judges themselves have failed adequately to recognize their duty of weighing considerations of social advantage. The duty is inevitable, and the result of the often proclaimed judicial aversion to deal with such considerations is simply to leave the very ground and foundation of judgments inarticulate and often unconscious." The failure of the courts in the past to formulate any principle for drawing a boundary line around the right of free speech has not only thrown the judges into the difficult questions of the Espionage Act without any well-considered standard of criminality, but has allowed some of them to impose standards of their own and fix the line at a point which makes all opposition to this or any future war impossible. . . .

The true boundary line of the First Amendment can be fixed only when Congress and the courts realize that the principle on which speech is classified as lawful or unlawful involves the balancing against each other of two very important social interests, in public safety and in the search for truth. Every reasonable attempt should be made to maintain both interests unimpaired, and the great interest in free speech should be sacrificed only when the interest in public safety is really imperiled, and not, as most men believe, when it is barely conceivable that it may be slightly affected. In war time, therefore, speech should be unrestricted by the censorship or by punishment, unless it is clearly liable to cause direct and dangerous interference with the conduct of the war. . . .

The United States Supreme Court did not have the opportunity to consider the Espionage Act until 1919, after the armistice was signed and almost all the District Court cases had been tried. Several appeals from conviction had resulted in a confession of error by the government, but at last four cases were heard and decided against the accused. Of these three were clear cases of incitement to resist the draft, so that no real question of free speech arose. Nevertheless the defense of constitutionality was raised, and denied by Justice Holmes. His fullest discussion is in *Schenck* v. *United States*:

> We admit that in many places and in ordinary times the defendants in saying all that was said in the circular would have been within their constitutional rights. But the character of every act depends upon the circumstances in which it is done. . . . *The question in every case is whether the words used are used in such circumstances and are of such a nature as to create a clear and present danger that they will bring about the substantive evils that Congress has a right to prevent.* It is a question of proximity and degree. When a nation is at war many things that might be said in time of peace are such a hindrance to its effort that their utterance will not be endured so long as men fight and that no Court could regard them as protected by any constitutional right [italics added].

This portion of the opinion, especially the italicized sentence, substantially agrees with the conclusion reached by . . . investigation of the history and political purpose of the First Amendment. It is unfortunate that "the substantive evils" are not more specifically defined, but if they mean overt acts of interference with the war, then Justice Holmes draws the boundary line very close to the test of incitement at common law and clearly makes the punishment of words for their bad tendency impossible. . . .

If the Supreme Court had applied this same standard of "clear and present danger" to the utterances of Eugene V. Debs, . . . it is hard to see how he could have been held guilty. . . .

Justice Holmes seems to discuss the constitutionality of the Espionage Act of 1917 rather than its construction. There can be little doubt that it is constitutional under any test if construed naturally, but it has been interpreted in such a way as to violate the free-speech clause and the plain words of the statute, to say nothing of the principle that criminal statutes should be construed strictly. If the Supreme Court test had been laid down in the summer of 1917 and followed in charges by the District Courts, the most casual perusal of the utterances prosecuted makes it sure that there would have been many more acquittals. Instead, bad tendency has been the test of criminality, a test which this article has endeavored to prove wholly inconsistent with freedom of speech, or any genuine discussion of public affairs.

Furthermore, it is regrettable that Justice Holmes did nothing to emphasize the social interest behind free speech, and show the need of balancing even in war time. The last sentence of the passage quoted from the *Schenck* case seems to mean that the Supreme Court will sanction any restriction of speech that has military force behind it, and reminds us that the Justice used to say when he was young "that truth was the majority vote of that nation that could lick all others." His liberalism seems held in abeyance by his belief in the relativity of values. It is not by giving way to force and the majority that truth has been won. Hard it may be for a court to protect those who oppose the cause for which men are dying in France, but others have died in the past for freedom of speech.

2

ABRAMS V. UNITED STATES
250 U.S. 616 (1919)

Jacob Abrams and four other Russian immigrants distributed in New York City two leaflets, one in English and the other in Yiddish, condemning the United States for sending troops to Russia. The Yiddish leaflet also urged a strike by munitions workers to protest the government's intervention in Russia. Abrams and his comrades were prosecuted under the Sedition Act of 1918, which punished speech critical of the government and subversive of the war effort. Sentenced to prison terms of fifteen to twenty years, the defendants appealed on grounds that their free speech rights had been violated. The Supreme Court sustained their convictions. For the first time in a seditious speech case, however, the Court split, with Justice Holmes, joined by Justice Brandeis, in dissent.

Writing for the majority, Justice Clarke held that the leaflets indeed created a clear and present danger. Holmes, who had set forth the clear-and-present-danger test eight months earlier in *Schenck* v. *United States*, replied in his dissent that they did not. Holmes (and Brandeis) obviously understood the test to mean more than the majority did. "It is only the present danger of immediate evil or an intent to bring it about," Holmes wrote, adding to what he had said in *Schenck*, "that warrants Congress in setting a limit to the expression of opinion." Holmes observed that "the surreptitious publishing of a silly leaflet by an unknown man [Abrams]" hardly presented any such immediate danger, and that Abrams lacked the necessary intent, since his leaflet sought only to stop U.S. intervention in Russia.

Holmes sought to ground his clear-and-present-danger doctrine in the Constitution. Its "theory," he wrote in a famous passage, is that the public interest is best served by "free trade in ideas—that the best test of truth is the power of the thought to get itself accepted in the competition of the market." Because this marketplace is the best means for discovering truth, government should not suppress speech unless it imminently or intentionally threatens harm.

In subsequent free speech cases, Holmes and Brandeis continued to argue for a more rigorous clear-and-present-danger test. Not until 1937, in *Herndon* v. *Lowry*, did the Court actually use the test in sustaining a free speech claim.

Opinion of the Court: **Clarke**, White, Van Devanter, Pitney, McReynolds, Day, McKenna. Dissenting opinion: **Holmes**, Brandeis.

Abrams v. *United States* was decided on November 10, 1919.

OPINIONS

JUSTICE CLARKE DELIVERED THE OPINION OF THE COURT . . .

It will not do to say . . . that the only intent of these defendants was to prevent injury to the Russian cause. Men must be held to have intended, and to be accountable for, the effects which their acts were likely to produce. Even if their primary purpose and intent was to aid the cause of the Russian Revolution, the plan of action which they adopted necessarily involved, before it could be realized, defeat of the war program of the United States, for the obvious effect of this appeal, if it should become effective, as they hoped it might, would be to persuade persons of character such as those whom they regarded themselves as addressing, not to aid government loans and not to work in ammunition factories, where their work would produce "bullets, bayonets, cannon" and other munitions of war, the use of which would cause the "murder" of Germans and Russians. . . .

This is not an attempt to bring about a change of administration by candid discussion, for no matter what may have incited the outbreak on the part of the defendant anarchists, the manifest purpose of such a publication was to create an attempt to defeat the war plans of the government of the United States, by bringing upon the country the paralysis of a general strike, thereby arresting the production of all munitions and other things essential to the conduct of the war. . . .

That the interpretation we have put upon these articles, circulated in the greatest port of our land, from which great numbers of soldiers were at the time taking ship daily, and in which great quantities of war supplies of every kind were at the time being manufactured for transportation overseas, is not only the fair interpretation of them, but that it is the meaning which their authors consciously intended should be conveyed by them to others is further shown by the additional writings found in the meeting place of the defendant group and on the person of one of them. . . .

. . . [W]hile the immediate occasion for this particular outbreak of lawlessness, on the part of the defendant alien anarchists, may have been resentment caused by our government sending troops into Russia as a strategic operation against the Germans on the eastern battle front, yet the plain purpose of their propaganda was to excite, at the supreme crisis of war, disaffection, sedition, riots, and, as they hoped, revolution, in this country for the purpose of embarrassing and if possible defeating the military plans of the government in Europe. . . . [T]he language of these circulars was obviously intended to provoke and to encourage resistance to the United States in the war, . . . and the defendants . . . plainly urged and advocated a resort to a general strike of workers in ammunition factories for the purpose of curtailing the production of ordnance and munitions necessary and essential to the prosecution of the war. . . . Thus it is clear not only that some evidence but that much persuasive evidence was before the jury tending to prove that the defendants were guilty as charged . . . and . . . the judgment of the District Court must be

AFFIRMED.

JUSTICE HOLMES, DISSENTING . . .

I never have seen any reason to doubt that the questions of law that alone were before this Court in the cases of *Schenck* [1919], *Frohwerk* [1919], and *Debs* [1919] were rightly decided.

I do not doubt for a moment that by the same reasoning that would justify punishing persuasion to murder, the United States constitutionally may punish speech that produces or is intended to produce a clear and imminent danger that it will bring about forthwith certain substantive evils that the United States constitutionally may seek to prevent. The power undoubtedly is greater in time of war than in time of peace because war opens dangers that do not exist at other times.

But as against dangers peculiar to war, as against others, the principle of the right to free speech is always the same. It is only the present danger of immediate evil or an intent to bring it about that warrants Congress in setting a limit to the expression of opinion where private rights are not concerned. Congress certainly cannot forbid all effort to change the mind of the country. Now nobody can suppose that the surreptitious publishing of a silly leaflet by an unknown man, without more, would present any immediate danger that its opinions would hinder the success of the government arms or have any appreciable tendency to do so. Publishing those opinions for the very purpose of obstructing, however, might indicate a greater danger and at any rate would have the quality of an attempt. So I assume that the second leaflet if published for the purposes alleged . . . might be punishable. But it seems pretty clear to me that nothing less than that would bring these papers within the scope of this law. An actual intent in the sense that I have explained is necessary to constitute an attempt, where a further act of the same individual is required to complete the substantive crime. . . . It is necessary where the success of the attempt depends upon others because if that intent is not present the actor's aim may be accomplished without bringing about the evils sought to be checked. An intent to prevent interference with the revolution in Russia might have been satisfied without any hindrance to carrying on the war in which we were engaged.

I do not see how anyone can find the intent required by the statute in any of the defendant's words. The second leaflet is the only one that affords even a foundation for the charge, and there, without invoking the hatred of German militarism expressed in the former one, it is evident from the beginning to the end that the only object of the paper is to help Russia and stop American intervention there against the popular government—not to impede the United States in the war that it was carrying on. . . .

In this case sentences of twenty years imprisonment have been imposed for the publishing of two leaflets that I believe the defendants had as much right to publish as the Government has to publish the Constitution of the United States now vainly invoked by them. . . .

Persecution for the expression of opinions seems to me perfectly logical. If you have no doubt of your premises or your power and want a certain result with all your heart you naturally express your wishes in law and sweep away all opposition. To allow opposition by speech seems to indicate that you think the speech impotent, as when a man says that he has squared a circle, or that you do not care wholeheartedly for the result, or that you doubt either your power or your premises. But when men have realized that time has upset many fighting faiths, they may come to believe even more than they believe the very foundations of their own conduct that the ultimate good desired is better reached by free trade in ideas—that the best test of truth is the power of the thought to get itself accepted in the competition of the market, and that truth is the only ground upon which their wishes safely can be carried out. That at any rate is the theory of our Constitution. It is an experiment, as all life is an experiment. Every year if not every day we have to wager our salvation upon some prophecy based upon imperfect knowledge. While that experiment is part of our system I think that we should be eternally vigilant against attempts to check the expression of opinions that we loathe and believe to be fraught with death, unless they so imminently threaten immediate interference with the lawful and pressing purposes of the law that an immediate check is required to save the country. I wholly disagree with the argument of the Government that the First Amendment left the common law as to seditious libel in force. History seems to me against the notion. I had conceived that the United States through many years had shown its repentance for the Sedition Act of 1798 . . . by repaying fines that it imposed. Only the emergency that makes it immediately dangerous to leave the correction of evil counsels to time warrants making any exception to the sweeping command, "Congress shall make no law abridging the freedom of speech." Of course I am speaking only of expressions of opinion and exhortations, which were all that were uttered here, but I regret that I cannot put into more impressive words my belief that in their conviction upon this indictment the defendants were deprived of their rights under the Constitution of the United States.

RESPONSE

FROM *THE NEW REPUBLIC*, NOVEMBER 26, 1919, "THE CALL TO TOLERATION"

At the present time American public opinion in relation to freedom of speech, as expressed by the Supreme Court itself, is in danger of sacrificing the benefits of liberty to a headstrong impulse to cure its abuses. We are seeking a remedy not in a temper of mind which is too self-possessed to be stampeded and which is willing to stand or fall by the facts, but in repression and in impatient denunciation. Administrative officers and the courts, instead of patiently estimating whether or not the expression of an opinion which as patriotic Americans they may loathe is or is not an imminent and actual source of danger to social order, prefer to repress all suspicious utterances and to inflict savage punishments on their perpetrators. We are acting on the supposition that every utterance which expresses hostility to the social establishment and which may possess a tendency or be prompted by a purpose to undermine it, is actually accomplishing all that it may tend or purpose to accomplish. The patriotic American seems to have lost all his former imperturbability, all his confidence in the stability of the American political and social fabric. He is panic-stricken lest a few hundred agitators can rend it to pieces by repeating the phrases of the Communist manifesto—phrases which the less tolerant and less stable governments of Europe have rarely considered it necessary to suppress, even when accompanied by direct provocation to acts of violence. . . .

   If we in America ever suffer the awful affliction of a class revolution, it will come about not because of the indirect appeals to violence on the part of an insignificant minority of revolutionists, but as a consequence of the intolerance, the inflammation of spirit, the stupidity, and the faith in force rather than in the justice of the existing majority of educated and well-to-do Americans. They are adopting a course which, if pursued to the end, will do far more to provoke revolutionary violence than vague and empty appeals to the proletarians for union and rebellion. Educated and responsible Americans are allowing irresponsible agitators to mold their psychology and their ethics. The suicidal error of the Bolshevists consists in their attempt to force on society by means of a class military dictatorship what they believe to be a program of economic and social liberation for the workers. The suicidal error of American counter-Bolshevism consists in its attempts to protect the safety of a free democracy by a feverish outbreak of moral and physical violence which will in the long run destroy the moral self-control and the intellectual candor and integrity which the operation of democratic institutions requires. Democracy is capable of curing the ills it generates by means of peaceful discussion and unhesitating acquiescence in the verdict of honestly conducted elections, but its self-curative properties are not unconditional. They are the creation of a body of public opinion which has access to the facts, which can estimate their credibility and significance, and which is in effective measure open to conviction. The most articulate public opinion in America is temporarily indifferent to the facts and impervious to conviction. Its fear of revolutionary agitation betrays it into an impotent and feverish devotion to symbols and phrases which do not permit the candid consideration of social evils and abuses and the adoption of thoroughgoing remedies. American educators and lawyers no longer act as if the government and Constitution of the United States is, as Justice Holmes says, an experiment which needs for its own safety an agency of self-adjustment and which seeks it in the utmost possible freedom of opinion. They act as good Catholics formerly acted in relation to the government and creed of the Catholic church—as if the government and Constitution were the embodiment of ultimate political and social truth, which is to be perpetuated by persecuting and exterminating its enemies rather than by vindicating its own qualifications to carry on under new conditions the difficult job of supplying political salvation to mankind. If they begin by sacrificing freedom of speech to what is supposed to be the safety of constitutional government they will end by sacrificing constitutional government to the dictatorship of one class.

3

GITLOW V. NEW YORK
268 U.S. 652 (1925)

New York's Criminal Anarchy Act, enacted in 1902, made it a crime to advocate the forcible overthrow of organized government. In 1921 Benjamin Gitlow, a radical socialist, was convicted under the law; his crime was that he had published and distributed 16,000 copies of a tract entitled "The Left Wing Manifesto" that condemned moderate socialism and urged the establishment of a Communist regime though strikes and mass revolutionary action. On appeal, Gitlow argued that the law violated his free speech rights. The Supreme Court disagreed and thus declined to overturn his conviction. But it did embrace his contention that not only Congress but also the states may not abridge the First Amendment.

The Court split on by now familiar terms, with Justice Sanford writing for the Court and Justice Holmes joined by Justice Brandeis filing a dissent. Sanford said that the clear-and-present-danger test announced in *Schenck* v. *United States* did not apply; he instead employed the bad-tendency test. Sanford conceded that there was no evidence of any effects produced by the publication of Gitlow's tract or of what those effects were likely to be; it was enough for him and his colleagues in the majority to know that the manifesto advocated forcible overthrow of the government. Such utterances, he wrote, are by their very nature "so inimical to the general welfare and involve such danger of substantive evil" that a state may punish the responsible persons. Sanford discounted the need to define the danger in imminent or immediate terms, as Holmes had done in dissent in *Abrams* v. *United States* (1919). "The State cannot reasonably be required," wrote Sanford, "to measure the danger from every such utterance in the nice balance of a jeweler's scale. A single revolutionary spark may kindle a fire that, smoldering for a time, may burst into a sweeping and destructive conflagration."

Holmes said that the clear-and-present-danger test did apply, and he found that Gitlow's tract did not create the necessary danger. "[W]hatever may be thought of the redundant discourse before us," he wrote, "it had no chance of starting a present conflagration."

All the justices agreed that the states—and not just the federal government—are governed by the First Amendment. "[F]or present purposes," wrote Sanford, "we may and do assume that freedom of speech and of the press . . . are among the fundamental personal rights and liberties protected by the due process clause of the Fourteenth Amendment from impairment by the States." In a case decided only three years earlier (*Prudential Ins. Co. v. Cheek*), the Court had stated the opposite: "[T]he Constitution of the United States imposes upon the states no obligation to confer upon those within their jurisdiction . . . the right of free speech." Justice Sanford did not explain why the Court had changed its mind, nor did he attempt to justify the new position, noting only that the Court did not regard its earlier statement as "determinative of this question."

The great significance of *Gitlow* lies in its announcement that the states, too, are bound by the First Amendment speech and press clauses. Since *Gitlow*, the majority of the Court's speech and press cases have concerned challenges not to federal but to state enactments. As a result of the development of doctrine more friendly to First Amendment claims, many of the parties raising speech and press claims against the states have prevailed—as Benjamin Gitlow did not.

Six years after *Gitlow*, in *Stromberg* v. *California* (1931), the Court for the first time struck down a state law on free speech grounds. Not until 1965, in *Lamont* v. *Postmaster General*, did the Court invoke the free speech clause to nullify a federal law.

Opinion of the Court: **Sanford**, Taft, Van Devanter, McReynolds, Sutherland, Butler, Stone. Dissenting opinion: **Holmes**, Brandeis.

Gitlow v. *New York* was decided on June 8, 1925.

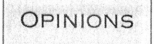

OPINIONS

JUSTICE SANFORD DELIVERED THE OPINION OF THE COURT . . .

. . . The sole contention here is, essentially, that as there was no evidence of any concrete result flowing from the publication of the Manifesto or of circumstances showing the likelihood of such result, the statute as construed and applied by the trial court penalizes the mere utterance, as such, of "doctrine" having no quality of incitement, without regard either to the circumstances of its utterance or to the likelihood of unlawful sequences; and that, as the exercise of the right of free expression with relation to government is only punishable "in circumstances involving likelihood of substantive evil," the statute contravenes the due process clause of the Fourteenth Amendment. The argument in support of this contention rests primarily upon the following propositions: 1st, that the "liberty" protected by the Fourteenth Amendment includes the liberty of speech and of the press; and 2d, that while liberty of expression "is not absolute," it may be restrained "only in circumstances where its exercise bears a causal relation with some substantive evil, consummated, attempted or likely," and as the statute "takes no account of circumstances," it unduly restrains this liberty and is therefore unconstitutional.

The precise question presented . . . is, whether the statute, as construed and applied in this case, by the State courts, deprived the defendant of his liberty of expression in violation of the due process clause of the Fourteenth Amendment.

The statute does not penalize the utterance or publication of abstract "doctrine" or academic discussion having no quality of incitement to any concrete action. It is not aimed against mere historical or philosophical essays. It does not restrain the advocacy of changes in the form of government by constitutional and lawful means. What it prohibits is language advocating, advising, or teaching the overthrow of organized government by unlawful means.

These words imply urging to action. Advocacy is defined in the *Century Dictionary* as: "1. The act of pleading for, supporting, or recommending; active espousal." It is not the abstract "doctrine" of overthrowing organized government by unlawful means which is denounced by the statute, but the advocacy of action for the accomplishment of that purpose. . . .

The Manifesto, plainly, is neither the statement of abstract doctrine nor, as suggested by counsel, mere prediction that industrial disturbances and revolutionary mass strikes will result spontaneously in an inevitable process of evolution in the economic system. It advocates and urges in fervent language mass action which shall progressively foment industrial disturbances and through political mass strikes and revolutionary mass action overthrow and destroy organized parliamentary government. It concludes with a call to action in these words:

> The proletariat revolution and the Communist reconstruction of society—the struggle for these—is now indispensable. . . . The Communist International calls the proletariat of the world to the final struggle!

This is not the expression of philosophical abstraction, the mere prediction of future events; it is the language of direct incitement.

The means advocated for bringing about the destruction of organized parliamentary government, namely, mass industrial revolts usurping the functions of municipal government, political mass strikes directed against the parliamentary state, and revolutionary mass action for its final destruction, necessarily imply the use of force and violence, and in their essential nature are inherently unlawful in a constitutional government of law and order. That the jury were warranted in finding that the Manifesto advocated not merely the abstract doctrine of overthrowing organized government by force, violence, and unlawful means, but action to that end, is clear.

For present purposes we may and do assume that freedom of speech and of the press—which are protected by the First Amendment from abridgment by Congress—are among the fundamental personal rights and "liberties" protected by the due process clause of the Fourteenth Amendment from impairment by the States. We do not regard the incidental statement in *Prudential Ins. Co.* v. *Cheek* [1922], that the Fourteenth Amendment imposes no restrictions on the States concerning freedom of speech, as determinative of this question.

It is a fundamental principle, long established, that the freedom of speech and of the press which is secured by the Constitution does not confer an absolute right to speak or publish, without responsibility, whatever one may choose, or an unrestricted and unbridled license that gives immunity for every possible use of language and prevents the punishment of those who abuse this freedom. . . .

That a State in the exercise of its police power may punish those who abuse this freedom by utterances inimical to the public welfare, tending to corrupt public morals, incite to crime, or disturb the public peace, is not open to question. . . .

And, for yet more imperative reasons, a State may punish utterances endangering the foundations of organized government and threatening its overthrow by unlawful means. These imperil its own existence as a constitutional State. Freedom of speech and press . . . does not protect disturbances to the public peace or the attempt to subvert the government. . . . It does not protect publications or teachings which tend to subvert or imperil the government or to impede or hinder it in the performance of its governmental duties. It does not protect publications prompting the overthrow of government by force; the punishment of those who publish articles which tend to destroy organized society being essential to the security of freedom and the stability of the State. . . . And a State may penalize utterances which openly advocate the overthrow of the representative and constitutional form of government of the United States and the several States, by violence or other unlawful means. . . . In short this freedom does not deprive a State of the primary and essential right of self preservation; which, so long as human governments endure, they cannot be denied. . . .

By enacting the present statute the State has determined, through its legislative body, that utterances advocating the overthrow of organized government by force, violence, and unlawful means, are so inimical to the general welfare and involve such danger of substantive evil that they may be penalized in the exercise of its police power. That determination must be given great weight. Every presumption is to be indulged in favor of the validity of the statute. . . . That utterances inciting to the overthrow of organized government by unlawful means, present a sufficient danger of substantive evil to bring their punishment within the range of legislative discretion, is clear. Such utterances, by their very nature, involve danger to the public peace and to the security of the State. They threaten breaches of the peace and ultimate revolution. And the immediate danger is none the less real and substantial, because the effect of a given utterance cannot be accurately foreseen. The State cannot reasonably be required to measure the danger from every such utterance in the nice balance of a jeweler's scale. A single revolutionary spark may kindle a fire that, smoldering for a time, may burst into a sweeping and destructive conflagration. It cannot be said that the State is acting arbitrarily or unreasonably when in the exercise of its judgment as to the measures necessary to protect the public peace and safety, it seeks to extinguish the spark without waiting until it has enkindled the flame or blazed into the conflagration. It cannot reasonably be required to defer the adoption of measures for its own peace and safety until the revolutionary utterances lead to actual disturbances of the public peace or imminent and immediate danger of its own destruction; but it may, in the exercise of its judgment, suppress the threatened danger in its incipiency. . . .

We cannot hold that the present statute is an arbitrary or unreasonable exercise of the police power of the State unwarrantably infringing the freedom of speech or press; and we must and do sustain its constitutionality.

This being so it may be applied to every utterance . . . which is of such a character and used with such intent and purpose as to bring it within the prohibition of the statute. . . . In other words, when the legislative body has determined generally, in the constitutional exercise of its discretion, that utterances of a certain kind involve such danger of substantive evil that they may be punished, the question whether any specific utterance coming within the prohibited class is likely, in and of itself, to bring about the substantive evil, is not open to consideration. It is sufficient that the statute itself be constitutional and that the use of the language comes within its prohibition.

It is clear that the question in such cases is entirely different from that involved in those cases where the statute merely prohibits certain acts involving the danger of substantive evil, without any reference to language itself, and it is sought to apply its provisions to language used by the defendant for the purpose of bringing about the prohibited results. There, if it be contended that the statute cannot be applied to the language used by the defendant because of its protection by the freedom of speech or press, it must necessarily be found, as an original question, without any previous determination by the legislative body, whether the specific language used involved such likelihood of bringing about the substantive evil as to deprive it of the constitutional protection. In such case it has been held that the general provisions of the statute may be constitutionally applied to the specific utterance of the defendant if its natural tendency and probable effect was to bring about the substantive evil which the legislative body might prevent. *Schenck* v. *United States* [1919]. . . . And the general statement in the *Schenck* case, that the "question in every case is whether the words used are used in such circumstances and are of such a nature as to create a clear and present danger that they will bring about the substantive evils"—upon which great reliance is placed in the defendant's argument . . . has no application to [cases] like the present, where the legislative body itself has previously determined the danger of substantive evil arising from utterances of a specified character.

. . . It was not necessary, within the meaning of the statute, that the defendant should have advocated "some definite or immediate act or acts" of force, violence, or unlawfulness. It was sufficient if such acts were advocated in general terms; and it was not essential that their immediate execution should have been advocated. Nor was it necessary that the language should have been "reasonably and ordinarily calculated to incite certain persons" to acts of force, violence, or unlawfulness. The advocacy need not be addressed to specific persons. Thus, the publication and circulation of a newspaper article may be an encouragement or endeavor to persuade to murder, although not addressed to any person in particular. . . .

. . . [F]inding, for the reasons stated, that the statute is not in itself unconstitutional, and that it has not been applied in the present case in derogation of any constitutional right, the judgment of the Court of Appeals is AFFIRMED.

JUSTICE HOLMES, DISSENTING . . .

Justice Brandeis and I are of opinion that this judgment should be reversed. . . . I think that the criterion sanctioned by the full Court in *Schenck* v. *United States* [1919] applies:

> The question in every case is whether the words used are used in such circumstances and are of such a nature as to create a clear and present danger that they will bring about the substantive evils that [the State] has a right to prevent.

It is true that in my opinion this criterion was departed from in *Abrams* v. *United States* [1919], but the convictions that I expressed in that case are too deep for it to be possible for me as yet to believe that it and *Schaefer* v. *United States* [1920] have settled the law. If what I think the correct test is applied, it is manifest that there was no present danger of an attempt to overthrow the government by force on the part of the admittedly small minority who shared the defendant's views. It is said that this manifesto was more than a theory, that it was an incitement. Every idea is an incitement. It offers itself for belief, and if believed it is acted on unless some other belief outweighs it or some failure of energy stifles the movement at its birth. The only difference between the expression of an opinion and an incitement in the narrower sense is the speaker's enthusiasm for the result. Eloquence may set fire to reason. But whatever may be thought of the redundant discourse before us it had no chance of starting a present conflagration. If in the long run the beliefs expressed in proletarian dictatorship are destined to be accepted by the dominant forces of the community, the only meaning of free speech is that they should be given their chance and have their way.

If the publication of this document had been laid as an attempt to induce an uprising against government at once and not at some indefinite time in the future, it would have presented a different question. The object would have been one with which the law might deal, subject to the doubt whether there was any danger that the publication could produce any result, or in other words, whether it was not futile and too remote from possible consequences. But the indictment alleges the publication and nothing more.

RESPONSES

FROM THE *NEW YORK TIMES*, JUNE 9, 1925, "WHEN ANARCHY IS CRIMINAL"

Yesterday's decision of the Supreme Court in the *Gitlow* case is, in its essence, simply a reaffirmation of an old principle of law and government. Any constituted Government is entitled to protect itself against overthrow by violence. It can make the use of force against itself a crime. It is not, as the Supreme Court said, a question of an abstract or doctrinaire discussion of what may be the best form of government. What the State of New York made criminal, and what our highest tribunal has now upheld its right to make criminal, is advocacy of the destruction of the Government by arms. Two dissenting Justices argue that the utterances of Benjamin Gitlow did not involve an "immediate danger" to the Government of New York. Doubtless this is true. The vaporings of one anarchist, or of 10,000 anarchists, could not make the authorities tremble. But there is such a thing as moral peril in addition to one merely physical. And the Supreme Court is of the opinion that an open incitement to violence against the State is a moral peril against which the State may lawfully protect itself by a stringent statute.

This is no denial of free speech. But the free speakers must be ready to face their responsibility to the law for what they say. The Supreme Court does not rule against a political revolution. But the revolutionists must be prepared to undergo the penalty of failure. Were not Washington and Adams justified in rebelling against the British Government and attempting to overthrow its rule in this country? Certainly they were, but they knew what would happen to them if they were caught in arms as rebels. . . . That is one trouble with our theoretic revolutionists of today. They want to eat their cake and have it too. They wish to bear themselves as rebels, yet be treated as good and worthy citizens. The Supreme Court has decided that this can't be done. Revolutionists retain their old privilege of perishing gloriously in arms, but they can't incite others to perish and hope to get off themselves scot free.

FROM THE *EVENING STAR*, WASHINGTON, D.C., JUNE 9, 1925, "THE GITLOW DECISION"

Denial of the freedom of speech is not involved in the enactment and enforcement of laws which are designed to protect the state from subversive radicalism. Advocacy of a different form of government is not denied. But in this case, as in many others that have not come to the point of prosecution and punishment, in large degree in consequence of a policy of tolerance, there was actually a call for action, a summoning of the forces of disruption, a mandate for revolt.

"I was only theorizing, only pointing out the way to ideal government," says the anarchist who is held for seditious utterances. "I was only exercising the right of free speech in expressing my opinion of what government should be, not raising the standard of rebellion." Such in effect was the defense in the *Gitlow* case. The Supreme Court says now that that is no defense, that incitation to revolution for the overturning of government is a crime against the United States or against any State that has a specific statute such as that of New York, which is now sustained. This decision will strengthen the defenses of this country against radical subversion. Even though the defendant in this case, who has already served a considerable length of time in prison, should now be pardoned by Gov. Smith of New York, the decision stands as a safeguard for sound government.

FROM *THE NEW REPUBLIC*, JULY 1, 1925, "THE GITLOW CASE"

In the United States Supreme Court the only question was the constitutionality of the Criminal Anarchy Act. Unlike the other famous free speech decisions, the case did not come up under the First Amendment, which restricts only Congress, but under the Fourteenth, ". . . Nor shall any State deprive any person of . . . liberty . . . without due process of law," that is, by arbitrary and unreasonable legislation. In several cases the Court had carefully refrained from deciding whether "liberty" protects liberty of speech as well as liberty of the person and of contracts, but the recent holding that liberty to teach a foreign language in private schools was within the Fourteenth Amendment naturally led the way to the unanimous statement of the Court that "we may and do assume that freedom of speech and of the press . . . are among the fundamental personal rights and 'liberties' protected . . . from impairment by the States."

The majority of the Court, however, held, through Justice Sanford, that this statute did not wrongfully impair Gitlow's liberty of speech. The state courts had expressly repudiated the test laid down by the Supreme Court in a leading Espionage Act case that words were punishable only when their nature and the surrounding circumstances created a "clear and present danger" of wrongful acts, and there was no evidence of such danger in this case. Consequently Gitlow's counsel contended that he had been punished merely for doctrines and words because of their supposed bad tendency to result at a remote time in acts. This bad-tendency test is an English eighteenth-century doctrine, wholly at variance with any true freedom of discussion because it permits the government to go outside the proper field of acts, present or probable, into the field of ideas, and to condemn them by the judgment of a judge or jury, who, human nature being what it is, consider a doctrine they dislike as so liable to cause harm someday that it had better be nipped in the bud. The danger test, on the other hand, leaves the doctrine to be proved or disproved by argument and the course of events. It avoids the risk of suppressing disagreeable truths, so long as there is no immediate risk of unlawful acts.

Justice Sanford virtually adopts the bad-tendency test. The words "tend" and "tending" are as frequent in his opinion as in an English charge during the prosecution of a reformer in the French Revolutionary Wars. As for the "clear and present danger" test, he declares that it merely served to decide how far the Espionage Act, which dealt primarily with acts, should be interpreted to extend to words. He rejects it altogether as a test of the constitutionality of a statute expressly directed against words of incitement which the legislature considers dangerous. Thus words may be punished for their bad nature regardless of the Court's opinion that there is no danger of bad acts. The injudicious choice of language becomes a crime.

> A single revolutionary spark may kindle a fire that, smoldering for a time, may burst into sweeping and destructive conflagration. It cannot be said that the State is acting arbitrarily . . .

when . . . it seeks to extinguish the spark without waiting until it has enkindled the flame or blazed into the conflagration.

The trouble is that in extinguishing the spark we cause much damage that might be avoided if the spark were left to go out by itself. There is no better way to increase discontent than to impose severe sentences for acts which the accused and his friends do not consider criminal at all.

Justice Holmes's brief dissent stands by the danger test, which cannot apply to suppress this Manifesto concerned with an uprising in some vague future. . . .

A profit and loss account of the *Gitlow* case shows one new gain, the possibility of federal protection against state suppression. A more liberal Court may prevent a checker-board nation, with ultra-conservative states into which moderately radical Americans come at peril of imprisonment for sedition. Not much can be hoped today. Such extreme laws as the Tennessee evolution statute may be invalidated, but the intolerance of the California Syndicalism Act will not be checked by Justice Sanford. State freedom must be secured through state legislatures and state governors like Alfred E. Smith, who pardoned Gitlow's associates and stopped further Anarchy Act prosecutions.

The losses are much clearer. Without the danger test, freedom of speech means little more than the right to say what a considerable number of citizens regard as sound, which consequently is not likely to be prosecuted. For novel and unpopular ideas, where alone it is really needed, it seems no longer to exist as a legal right. . . .

The victories of liberty of speech must be won in the mind before they are won in the courts. In that battle-field of reason we possess new and powerful weapons, the dissenting opinions of Justices Holmes and Brandeis. Out of this long series of legal defeats has come a group of arguments for toleration that may fitly stand beside the *Areopagitica* and Mill's *Liberty*. The majority opinions determined the cases, but these dissenting opinions will determine the minds of the future.

WHITNEY V. CALIFORNIA
274 U.S. 357 (1927)

Between 1917 and 1920 some twenty states, including California, passed "criminal syndicalism" laws that made it a crime to defend, advocate, or establish an organization committed to violent means of effecting change in government or in industrial ownership or control. These statutes took aim at a radical labor organization called the Industrial Workers of the World.

California passed its syndicalism act in 1919. Late that year, Charlotte Anita Whitney attended a convention of the Communist Labor Party of California. The CLP endorsed many IWW objectives, and though by the time of her arrest after the convention she had resigned from the party, Whitney had, at least for a short while, been a member of the CLP. That, essentially, was the case against her, and the jury returned a guilty verdict. Whitney ultimately appealed to the Supreme Court, but no justice voted to overturn her conviction.

Whitney's significance lies in the concurring opinion filed by Justice Brandeis, joined by Justice Holmes. Following *Gitlow* v. *New York* (1925) in presuming the constitutionality of the challenged law, the majority opinion by Justice Sanford concluded that California's decision to criminalize "the combining of others in an association for the accomplishment of the desired ends through the advocacy and use of criminal and unlawful methods" did not "unwarrantably" infringe "any right of free speech, assembly, or association." Brandeis said he was "unable to assent to the suggestion in the opinion of the Court that assembling with a political party, formed to advocate the desirability of a proletarian revolution by mass action at some date necessarily far in the future, is not a right within the protection of the Fourteenth Amendment." But he felt he could not dissent from the result in the case because there were other grounds on which Whitney's conviction could have been based. He wrote separately to endorse the relevance of the clear-and-present-danger test, which had not been raised by Whitney in her challenge to the law. Brandeis restated and added to the test: Not only must the danger be imminent and substantive, but there must also be "the probability of serious danger to the state."

The governor of California later pardoned Whitney, for reasons similar to those advanced by Brandeis in his dissent. And in 1969, the Court explicitly overruled *Whitney* in *Brandenburg* v. *Ohio*.

Opinion of the Court: **Sanford**, Taft, Butler, Sutherland, Stone, McReynolds, Van Devanter. Concurring opinion: **Brandeis**, Holmes.

Whitney v. *California* was decided on May 26, 1927.

OPINIONS

JUSTICE SANFORD DELIVERED THE OPINION OF THE COURT . . .

. . . [T]he Syndicalism Act . . . [is not] repugnant to the due process clause as a restraint of the rights of free speech, assembly, and association.

That the freedom of speech which is secured by the Constitution does not confer an absolute right to speak, without responsibility, whatever one may choose, or an unrestricted and unbridled license giving immunity for every possible use of language and preventing the punishment of those who abuse this freedom; and that a State in the exercise of its police power may punish those who abuse this freedom by utterances inimical to the public welfare, tending to incite to crime, disturb the peace, or endanger the foundations of organized government and threaten its overthrow by unlawful means, is not open to question. . . .

By enacting the provisions of the Syndicalism Act the State has declared, through its legislative body, that to knowingly be or become a member of or assist in organizing an association to advocate, teach, or aid and abet the commission of crimes or unlawful acts of force, violence, or terrorism as a means of accomplishing industrial or political changes, involves such danger to the public peace and the security of the State, that these acts should be penalized in the exercise of its police power. That determination must be given great weight. Every presumption is to be indulged in favor of the validity of the statute . . . ; and it may not be declared unconstitutional unless it is an arbitrary or unreasonable attempt to exercise the authority vested in the State in the public interest. . . .

The essence of the offense denounced by the Act is the combining with others in an association for the accomplishment of the desired ends through the advocacy and use of criminal and unlawful methods. It partakes of the nature of a criminal conspiracy. . . . That such united and joint action involves even greater danger to the public peace and security than the isolated utterances and acts of individuals is clear. We cannot hold that, as here applied, the Act is an unreasonable or arbitrary exercise of the police power of the State, unwarrantably infringing any right of free speech, assembly, or association, or that those persons are protected from punishment by the due process clause who abuse such rights by joining and furthering an organization thus menacing the peace and welfare of the State. . . .

. . . [T]he . . . judgment of the Court of Appeal [is]

AFFIRMED.

JUSTICE BRANDEIS, CONCURRING . . .

. . . The right of free speech, the right to teach, and the right of assembly are, of course, fundamental rights. . . . These may not be denied or abridged. But, although the rights of free speech and assembly are fundamental, they are not in their nature absolute. Their exercise is subject to restriction, if the particular restriction proposed is required in order to protect the state from destruction or from serious injury, political, economic, or moral. That the necessity which is essential to a valid restriction does not exist unless the speech would produce, or is intended to produce, a clear and imminent danger of some substantive evil which the state constitutionally may seek to prevent has been settled. See *Schenck* v. *United States* [1919]. It is said to be the function of the Legislature to determine whether at a particular time and under the particular circumstances the formation of, or assembly with, a society organized to advocate criminal syndicalism constitutes a clear and present danger of substantive evil; and that by enacting the law here in question the Legislature of California determined that question in the affirmative. . . . The Legislature must obviously decide, in the first instance, whether a danger exists which calls for a particular protective measure. But where a statute is valid only in case certain conditions exist, the enactment of the statute cannot alone establish the facts which are essential to its validity. Prohibitory legislation has repeatedly been held invalid, because unnecessary, where the denial of liberty involved was that of engaging in a particular business. The powers of the courts to strike down an offending law are no less when the interests involved are not property rights, but the fundamental personal rights of free speech and assembly.

This court has not yet fixed the standard by which to determine when a danger shall be deemed clear; how remote the danger may be and yet be deemed present; and what degree of evil shall be deemed sufficiently substantial to justify resort to abridgment of free speech and assembly as the means of protection. To reach sound conclusions on these matters, we must bear in mind why a state is, ordinarily, denied the power to prohibit dissemination of social, economic, and political doctrine which a vast majority of its citizens believes to be false and fraught with evil consequence. Those who won our independence believed that the final end of the state was to make men free to develop their faculties, and that in its government the deliberative forces should prevail over the arbitrary. They valued liberty both as an end and as a means. They believed liberty to [be] the secret of happiness and courage to be the secret of liberty. They believed that freedom to think as you will and to speak as you think are means indispensable to the discovery and spread of political truth; that without free speech and assembly discussion would be futile; that with them, discussion affords ordinarily adequate protection against the dissemination of noxious doctrine; that the greatest menace to freedom is an inert people; that public discussion is a political duty; and that this should be a fundamental principle of the American government. . . .

Fear of serious injury cannot alone justify suppression of free speech and assembly. Men feared witches and burnt women. It is the function of speech to free men from the bondage of irrational fears. To justify suppression of free speech there must be reasonable ground to fear that serious evil will result if free speech is practiced. There must be reasonable ground to believe that the danger apprehended is imminent. There must be reasonable ground that the evil to be prevented is a serious one. Every denunciation of existing law tends to in some measure increase the probability that there will be violation of it. Condonation of a breach enhances the probability. Expressions of approval add to the probability. Propagation of the criminal state of mind by teaching syndicalism increases it. Advocacy of lawbreaking heightens it still further. But even advocacy of violation, however reprehensible morally, is not a justification for denying free speech where the advocacy falls short of incitement and there is nothing to indicate that the advocacy would be immediately acted on. The wide difference between advocacy and incitement, between preparation and attempt, between assembling and conspiracy, must be borne in mind. In order to support a finding of clear and present danger it must be shown either that immediate serious violence was to be expected or was advocated, or that the past conduct furnished reason to believe that such advocacy was then contemplated. Those who won our independence by revolution were not cowards. They did not fear political change. They did not exalt order at the cost of liberty. To courageous, self-reliant men, with confidence in the power of free and fearless reasoning applied through the processes of popular government, no danger flowing from speech can be deemed clear and present, unless the incidence of the evil apprehended is so imminent that it may befall before there is opportunity for full discussion. If there be time to expose through discussion the falsehood and fallacies, to avert the evil by the processes of education, the remedy to be applied is more speech, not enforced silence. Only an emergency can justify repression. Such must be the rule if authority is to be reconciled with freedom. Such, in my opinion, is the command of the Constitution. It is therefore always open to Americans to challenge a law abridging free speech and assembly by showing that there was no emergency justifying it.

Moreover, even imminent danger cannot justify resort to prohibitions of these functions essential to effective democracy, unless the evil apprehended is relatively serious. Prohibition of free speech and assembly is a measure so stringent that it would be inappropriate as the means of averting a relatively trivial harm to society. A police measure may be unconstitutional merely because the remedy, although effective as means of protection, is unduly harsh or oppressive. Thus, a state might, in the exercise of its police power, make any trespass upon the land of another a crime, regardless of the results or of the intent or purpose of the trespasser. It might, also, punish an attempt, a conspiracy, or an incitement to commit the trespass. But it is hardly conceivable that this court would hold constitutional a statute which punished as a felony the mere voluntary assembly with a society formed to teach that pedestrians had the moral right to cross unenclosed, unposted, waste lands and to advocate their doing so, even if there was imminent danger that advocacy would lead to a trespass. The fact that speech is likely to result in some violence or in destruction of property is not enough to justify its suppression. There must be the probability of serious injury to the State. Among free men, the deterrents ordinarily to be applied to prevent crime are education and punishment for violations of the law, not abridgment of the rights of free speech and assembly. . . .

Whether in 1919, when Miss Whitney did the things complained of, there was in California such clear and present danger of serious evil, might have been made the important issue in the case. She might have required that the issue be determined either by the court or the jury. She claimed . . . that the statute as applied to her violated the federal Constitution; but she did not claim that it was void because there was no clear and present danger of serious evil, nor did she request that the existence of these conditions of a valid measure thus restricting the rights of free speech and assembly be passed upon by the court or a jury. On the other hand, there was evidence on which the court or jury might have found that such danger existed. I am unable to assent to the suggestion in the opinion of the court that assembling with a political party, formed to advocate the desirability of a proletarian revolution by mass action at some date necessarily far in the future, is not a right within the protection of the Fourteenth Amendment. In the present case, however, there was other testimony which tended to establish the existence of a conspiracy, on the part of members of the [Industrial] Workers of the World, to commit present serious crimes, and likewise to show that such a conspiracy would be furthered by the activity of the society of which Miss Whitney was a member. Under these circumstances the judgement of the State court cannot be disturbed. . . .

STROMBERG V. CALIFORNIA
283 U.S. 359 (1931)

During the summer of 1929, 19-year-old Yetta Stromberg taught in a summer camp for children in San Bernardino County, California, that was supported by Communist groups. The Russian Soviet flag was flown in the camp, and each morning Stromberg led the children in saluting that flag and pledging allegiance to it as "the workers' red flag and the cause for which it stands, one aim throughout our lives, freedom for the working class." Stromberg was convicted under California's "red flag" law, which provided that "any person who displays a red flag . . . as a sign, symbol or emblem of opposition to government, or as an invitation or stimulus to anarchistic action or as an aid to propaganda that is of a seditious character, is guilty of a felony."

Rejecting Stromberg's claim that the law was "an unwarranted limitation" on free speech rights, the California appeals court sustained her conviction. But Stromberg prevailed in the Supreme Court. Writing for the majority, Chief Justice Hughes said that "the maintenance of the opportunity for free political discussion to the end that government may be responsive to the will of the people and that changes may be obtained by lawful means" is a "fundamental principle of the constitutional system." The red flag law, he concluded, violated the free speech clause.

In *Stromberg* the Court for the first time voided a state law on First Amendment grounds. The Court did so in a case involving not spoken or written words but non-verbal or symbolic expression, also known as "expressive conduct."

Opinion of the Court: **Hughes**, Holmes, Van Devanter, Brandeis, Sutherland, Stone, Roberts. Separate opinion: **McReynolds**. Dissenting opinion: **Butler**.

Stromberg v. *California* was decided on May 18, 1931.

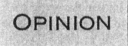

OPINION

CHIEF JUSTICE HUGHES DELIVERED THE OPINION OF THE COURT . . .

. . . The principles to be applied have been clearly set forth in our former decisions. It has been determined that the conception of liberty under the due process clause of the Fourteenth Amendment embraces the right of free speech. *Gitlow* v. *New York* [1925]. . . . The right is not an absolute one, and the State in the exercise of its police power may punish the abuse of this freedom. There is no question but that the State may thus provide for the punishment of those who indulge in utterances which incite to violence and crime and threaten the overthrow of organized government by unlawful means. There is no constitutional immunity for such conduct abhorrent to our institutions. . . . We have no reason to doubt the validity of the second and third clauses of the statute. . . .

The question is . . . narrowed to that of the validity of the first clause, that is, with respect to the display of the flag "as a sign, symbol or emblem of opposition to organized government," and the construction which the state court has placed upon this clause removes every element of doubt. The state court recognized the indefiniteness and ambiguity of the clause. The court considered that it might be construed as embracing conduct which the State could not constitutionally prohibit. Thus it was said that the clause "might be construed to include the peaceful and orderly opposition to a government as organized and controlled by one political party by those of another political party equally high minded and patriotic, which did not agree with the one in power. It might also be construed to include peaceful and orderly opposition to government by legal means and within constitutional limitations." The maintenance of the opportunity for free political discussion to the end that government may be responsive to the will of the people and that changes may be obtained by lawful means, an opportunity essential to the security of the Republic, is a fundamental principle of our constitutional system. A statute which upon its face, and as authoritatively construed, is so vague and indefinite as to permit the punishment of the fair use of this opportunity is repugnant to the guaranty of liberty contained in the Fourteenth Amendment. The first clause of the statute being invalid upon its face, the conviction of the appellant, which so far as the record discloses may have rested upon that clause exclusively, must be set aside. . . .

JUDGMENT REVERSED.

RESPONSE

FROM *THE NATION*, JUNE 3, 1931

Despite the decision of the United States Supreme Court in the Yetta Stromberg case, it is still illegal to display a red flag in California for propaganda or similar purposes. In setting aside the conviction in this case the court merely held that the conviction was invalid because it had been obtained under a State law, one of the essential clauses of which is unconstitutional. This clause, making it a felony to display the traditional revolutionary banner as a symbol of opposition to organized government, was considered by the court to be "repugnant to the guaranty of liberty contained in the Fourteenth Amendment." By inference, however, the court ruled that the other two major clauses of the statute are still valid, so that convictions can still be had under the notorious "red-flag" law if in bringing charges against accused radicals the authorities disregard the first clause. The still valid clauses make it a felonious offense to display a red flag as a means of inviting or stimulating anarchistic action, or for the purpose of promoting propaganda of seditious character.

6

NEAR V. MINNESOTA
283 U.S. 697 (1931)

The *Saturday Press*, a weekly newspaper in Minneapolis, published a series of articles charging that city officials were incompetent and corrupt, and were associated with boot-legging and racketeering. The paper called for a special grand jury investigation. Under a 1925 Minnesota law authorizing abatement of a "malicious, scandalous, and defamatory" newspaper, the state obtained a temporary court order forbidding publication of the *Press.* At trial, the *Press* was found in violation of the statute and enjoined from publication. On appeal, the state supreme court affirmed the trial court, rejecting the argument of the paper's manager, J. M. Near, that the injunction abridged his First Amendment free press rights. The Supreme Court, by a vote of 5 to 4, reversed.

In *Near* the Court for the first time held a law in violation of the free press clause. The law at issue was a *state* law, and because it was, the Court reiterated what it had announced in *Gitlow* v. *New York* (1925): that the states, like the federal government, are bound by the free press clause.

Near also established important First Amendment doctrine. The case presented the Court with its first opportunity to address the question of prior or previous restraint—i.e., censorship. The Court observed that in England the common law prohibited systems of prior restraint under which publications were illegal unless they received previous governmental approval, and that the First Amendment codified this prohibition. In holding that Minnesota's Public Nuisance Abatement Law, as it was called, was a prior restraint in violation of the First Amendment, the Court did not declare that prior restraints were inherently unconstitutional. But clearly it believed they were presumptively so. The Court noted "exceptional cases" in which prior restraint may be constitutional—such as those involving wartime obstruction of recruitment and publication of military secrets, obscenity, and incitements to riot or to forcible overthrow of the government.

The Minnesota Public Nuisance Abatement Act, an effort to deal with the "yellow journalism" of that day, was drafted with the help of the mainstream press in the state but mostly opposed by newspapers around the country.

Opinion of the Court: **Hughes**, Holmes, Brandeis, Stone, Roberts. Dissenting opinion: **Butler**, Van Devanter, McReynolds, Sutherland.

Near v. *Minnesota* was decided on June 1, 1931.

OPINIONS

CHIEF JUSTICE HUGHES DELIVERED THE OPINION OF THE COURT . . .

This statute, for the suppression as public nuisance of a newspaper or periodical, is unusual if not unique and raises questions of grave importance transcending the local interests involved in the particular action. It is no longer open to doubt that the liberty of the press and of speech is within the liberty safeguarded by the due process clause of the Fourteenth Amendment from invasion by state action. . . . In maintaining this guaranty, the authority of the state to enact laws to promote the health, safety, morals, and general welfare of its people is necessarily admitted. . . .

. . . If we cut through mere details of procedure, the operation and effect of the statute in substance is that public authorities may bring the owner or publisher of a newspaper or periodical before a judge upon charge of conducting a business of publishing scandalous and defamatory matter—in particular that the matter consists of charges against public officers of official dereliction—and, unless the owner or publisher is able and disposed to bring competent evidence to satisfy the judge that the charges are true and are published with good motives and for justifiable ends, his newspaper or periodical is suppressed and further publication is made punishable as a contempt. This is of the essence of censorship.

. . . The question is whether a statute authorizing such proceedings in restraint of publication is consistent with the conception of the liberty of the press as historically conceived and guaranteed. In determining the extent of the constitutional protection, it has been generally, if not universally, considered that it is the chief purpose of the guaranty to prevent previous restraints upon publication. The struggle in England . . . resulted in renunciation of the censorship of the press. The liberty deemed to be established was thus described by Blackstone:

> The liberty of the press is indeed essential to the nature of the free state; but this consists in laying no previous restraints upon publications, and not in freedom from censure for criminal matter when published. Every freeman has an undoubted right to lay what sentiments he pleases before the public; to forbid this, is to destroy the freedom of the press; but if he publishes what is improper, mischievous, illegal, he must take the consequence of his own temerity. . . .

The criticism upon Blackstone's statement has not been because immunity from previous restraint upon publication has not been regarded as deserving of special emphasis, but chiefly because that immunity cannot be deemed to exhaust the conception of the liberty guaranteed by State and Federal Constitutions. . . . But it is recognized that punishment for the abuse of the liberty accorded to the press is essential to the protection of the public, and that the common-law rules that subject the libeler to responsibility for the public offenses, as well as for the private injury, are not abolished by the protection extended in our Constitutions. The law of criminal libel rests upon that secure foundation. . . .

The objection has also been made that the principle as to immunity from previous restraint is stated too broadly, if every such restraint is deemed to be prohibited. That is undoubtedly true; the protection even as to previous restraint is not absolutely limited. But the limitation has been recognized only in exceptional cases. "When a nation is at war many things that might be said in time of peace are such a hindrance to its effort that their utterance will not be endured so long as men fight and that no Court could regard them as protected by any constitutional right." *Schenck* v. *United States* [1919]. . . . On similar grounds, the primary requirements of decency may be enforced against obscene publications. The security of the community life may be protected against incitements to acts of violence and the overthrow by force of orderly government. . . . These limitations are not applicable here. Nor are we now concerned with questions as to the extent of authority to prevent publications in order to protect private rights according to the principles governing the exercise of the jurisdiction of courts of equity.

The exceptional nature of its limitations places in a strong light the general conception that liberty of the press, historically considered and taken up by the Federal Constitution, has meant, principally although not exclusively, immunity from previous restraints or censorship. The conception of the liberty of the press in this country has broadened with the exigencies of the colonial period and with the efforts to secure freedom from oppressive administration. That liberty was especially cherished for the immunity it afforded from previous restraint of the publication of censure of public officers and charges of official misconduct. . . .

The fact that for approximately one hundred and fifty years there has been almost an entire absence of attempts to impose previous restraints upon publications relating to the malfeasance of public officers is significant of the deep-seated conviction that such restraints would violate constitutional right. Public officers, whose character and conduct remain open to debate and free discussion in the press, find their remedies for false accusations in actions under libel laws providing for redress and punishment, and not in proceedings to restrain the publication of newspapers and periodicals. The general principle that the constitutional guaranty of the liberty of the press gives immunity from previous restraints has been approved in many decisions under the provisions of state constitutions.

The importance of this immunity has not lessened. While reckless assaults upon public men, and efforts to bring obloquy upon those who are endeavoring faithfully to discharge official duties, exert a baleful influence and deserve the severest condemnation in public opinion, it cannot be said that this abuse is greater, and it is believed to be less, than that which characterized the period in which our institutions took shape. Meanwhile, the administration of government has become more complex, the opportunities for malfeasance and corruption have multiplied, crime has grown to most serious proportions, and the danger of its protection by unfaithful officials and of the impairment of the fundamental security of life and property by criminal alliances and official neglect, emphasizes the primary need of a vigilant and courageous press, especially in great cities. The fact that the liberty of the press may be abused by miscreant purveyors of scandal does not make any the less necessary the immunity of the press from previous restraint in dealing with official misconduct. Subsequent punishment for such abuses as may exist is the appropriate remedy, consistent with constitutional privilege. . . .

For these reasons, we hold the statute . . . to be an infringement of the liberty of the press guaranteed by the Fourteenth Amendment. . . .

JUDGMENT REVERSED.

JUSTICE BUTLER, DISSENTING . . .

The decision of the Court in this case declares Minnesota and every other state powerless to restrain by injunction the business of publishing and circulating among the people malicious, scandalous, and defamatory periodicals that in due course of judicial procedure has been adjudged to be a public nuisance. It gives to freedom of the press a meaning and a scope not heretofore recognized, and construes "liberty" in the due process clause of the Fourteenth Amendment to put upon the states a federal restriction that is without precedent. . . .

The act was passed in the exertion of the state's power of police, and this court is by well-established rule required to assume, until the contrary is clearly made to appear, that there exists in Minnesota a state of affairs that justifies this measure for the preservation of the peace and good order of the state. . . .

It is of the greatest importance that the states shall be untrammeled and free to employ all just and appropriate measures to prevent abuses of the liberty of the press. . . .

The Court quotes Blackstone in support of its condemnation of the statute as imposing a previous restraint upon publication. But the *previous restraints* referred to by him subjected the press to the arbitrary will of an administrative officer. . . .

It is plain that Blackstone taught that under the common law liberty of the press means simply the absence of restraint upon publication in advance as distinguished from liability, civil or criminal, for libelous or improper matter so published. . . .

The Minnesota statute does not operate as a *previous* restraint on publication within the proper meaning of that phrase. It does not authorize administrative control in advance such as was formerly exercised by the licensors and censors, but prescribes a remedy to be enforced by a suit in equity. In this case there was previous publication made in the course of the business of regularly producing malicious, scandalous, and defamatory periodicals. The business and publications unquestionably constitute an abuse of the right of free press. The statute denounces the thing done as a nuisance on the ground, as stated by the state Supreme Court, that they threaten morals, peace, and good order. There is no question of the power of the state to denounce such transgressions. The restraint authorized is only in respect of continuing to do what has been duly adjudged to constitute a nuisance. . . .

The judgment should be affirmed.

RESPONSES

FROM THE *MINNEAPOLIS TRIBUNE*, JUNE 2, 1931, "PRESS SUPPRESSION LAW INVALID"

The decision of the Supreme Court invalidating the Minnesota law which permitted the suppression of "scandal sheets" will no doubt be hailed with joy by the great majority of newspapers throughout the land. Newspapers for the most part are so sensitively jealous of their freedom of speech that they oppose to the utmost the slightest curtailment. The Minnesota law, enacted to meet a particular situation, attained nation-wide notoriety and disapproval.

The jubilation over the decision of the Supreme Court will be much more enthusiastic outside of Minnesota. For some unexplained reason this state seems to have been particularly fertile in the production of blackmailing and scandal sheets. The suppression law put an end to them, but no doubt they will be back with us, now that the law has been declared unconstitutional.

Chief Justice Hughes, in the majority opinion, says that the present libel laws are a sufficient protection against the abuses of the press. This is unquestionably true as far as the legitimate newspaper is concerned. But it is hardly true for the blackmailing and scandal sheets, which have no responsibility whatever. They possess no physical property and the editors are judgment proof. A person who has been libeled by one of these sheets may, if he desires, go to the cost and trouble of suing, and in due course of time get a verdict which is not worth the paper on which the judgment is written. To say that a citizen has an adequate recourse in the courts against these sheets is to say something that most emphatically is not so, unless an uncollectable judgment is considered a recompense for the injury sustained.

The blackmailing activities of these sheets are particularly vicious. An individual who is so unfortunate as to be an object of their attention is as defenseless as the victim of a highwayman who is looking into a loaded revolver. There is no defense against blackmail and certainly there is no redress at law. Blackmailing is the safest of rackets. The blackmail victim is the most helpless of all victims. Legal redress is about as available as the moon.

It may well be that the dangers inherent in any suppression law are such that the public must pay for their avoidance by risking libel and blackmail by sheets that are morally and financially irresponsible.

Certainly the *Tribune*, as a newspaper, is not at all anxious to see even the beginnings of a press censorship. At the same time it recognizes the existence of these scandal mongering blackmailing sheets which thrive and prosper under the guarantee of a free press. Thus it is that our satisfaction over the vindication by the Supreme Court of [the] right of the press to a free existence is diluted by the knowledge that the scandal sheets will quickly revive in Minnesota.

FROM THE *WASHINGTON POST,* JUNE 3, 1931, "LIBERTY OF PRESS"

In making void the Minnesota law attempting to abridge the liberty of the press the United States Supreme Court has swept aside a subtle and dangerous innovation which, if not thus stopped, might have worked great mischief to that State. . . .

The suppression of a periodical on the ground that it is a public nuisance is illogical, as well as a denial of liberty. If the publisher has been guilty of libel there is a remedy; and it is absurd to punish him in anticipation of what he might publish. If the libel law of Minnesota is inadequate it can be amended, but it is truly "the essence of censorship" to suppress a periodical instead of holding the publisher to account for abuse of liberty of the press.

The power to suppress a periodical, if lodged in public officers would lead to irremediable wrong, whereas abuse of liberty of the press is a wrong that can be remedied. The Supreme Court has decided this case on the solid ground of public interest. The press is and ought to be responsible for abuse of its liberty. This liberty should not be snuffed out because it is sometimes abused.

FROM THE *LOS ANGELES TIMES,* JUNE 5, 1931, "AN IMPORTANT DECISION"

The decision of the United States Supreme Court voiding the Minnesota press gag law is the most important victory the right of free publication has won since the First Amendment was adopted to the Constitution. The Minnesota case was not so important in itself, but as the entering wedge for censorship it represented real peril to all press channels of public information and consequently to the public itself. The high court's decision establishes the broad principle that no publication can be suppressed because some of its notions are objectionable to persons in official authority. . . .

. . . The Minnesota press gag law permitted the suppression by a court (without jury trial) of any publication which the judge considers to be "malicious, scandalous, or defamatory."

. . . Now no reputable newspaper, of course, holds any brief for "malicious, scandalous, or defamatory" matter, nor do newspapers of any standing publish such matter. Nevertheless, such a law obviously goes much too far. There are already ample safeguards against abuses of the privileges of a free press in provisions already existing for punishing a publisher who oversteps the bounds—a very different thing from suppressing a publication outright and permanently.

If any public official should be able to prevent criticism of his acts by merely going before a court and asking for an injunction, it is plain that official corruption and misfeasance could never be brought to public attention. Corrupt officialdom, linked to corrupt judiciary, could entrench itself in power and never be dislodged if it had the power of silencing any newspaper which attacked it. Nor is it fanciful to suppose that the law would be so used. Officials who are the subject of unfavorable newspaper comment nearly always feel that such comment is "malicious, scandalous, and defamatory" and if they had the opportunity would be rushing into court, sometimes in the utmost good faith, to demand suppression orders against the press.

Officers and citizens unfairly and improperly criticized have their remedy, if they can prove their case to the satisfaction of a jury, in a suit at law. There is no necessity for giving them suppression power as an additional remedy—and it would be highly dangerous to do so.

No abuse on the part of a free press can be so dangerous to the public welfare as its suppression.

GROSJEAN V. AMERICAN PRESS CO.
297 U.S. 233 (1936)

In 1934 the Louisiana legislature imposed a license tax of 2 percent on the gross advertising revenues of all newspapers, magazines, and other publications with a weekly circulation of more than 20,000 copies. Of the 165 newspapers in the state, only thirteen met this circulation requirement. Twelve of these were opponents of the Huey Long administration—which had pushed for the tax. The publishers of the thirteen papers joined in a lawsuit declaring the tax an abridgment of the First Amendment. A unanimous Supreme Court agreed, finding that the tax was "a deliberate and calculated device . . . to limit the circulation of [public] information."

In *Grosjean* the Court elaborated on its holding in *Near* v. *Minnesota* (1931). "The conclusion there stated," said the Court, in an opinion written by Justice Sutherland, "is that the object of the constitutional provisions was to prevent previous restraints on publication; and the court was careful not to limit the protection of the right to any particular way of abridging it." The Court concluded that a tax hostile to the press was a form of prior restraint as unconstitutional as the gag law struck down in *Near*.

The justices noted that nothing they said was intended "to suggest that the owners of newspapers are immune from any of the ordinary forms of taxation." In a case decided a year after *Grosjean,* the Court dismissed a claim for such an exemption. Subsequent cases made it plain that the First Amendment press liberty does not encompass exemption from non-discriminatory general taxation (or regulation).

Opinion of the Court: **Sutherland**, Van Devanter, McReynolds, Brandeis, Butler, Stone, Hughes, Roberts, Cardozo.

Grosjean v. *American Press Co.* was decided on February 10, 1936.

OPINION

JUSTICE SUTHERLAND DELIVERED THE OPINION OF THE COURT . . .

That freedom of speech and of the press are rights . . . safeguarded by the due process of law clause of the Fourteenth Amendment against abridgment by state legislation has . . . been settled by a series of decisions of this court beginning with *Gitlow* v. *New York* [1925] and ending with *Near* v. *Minnesota* [1931]. . . .

The tax imposed is designated a "license tax for the privilege of engaging in such business," that is to say, the business of selling, or making any charge for, advertising. As applied to appellees, it is a tax of 2 per cent on the gross receipts derived from advertisements carried in their newspapers when, and only when, the newspapers of each enjoy a circulation of more than 20,000 copies per week. It thus operates as a restraint in a double sense. First, its effect is to curtail the amount of revenue realized from advertising; and, second, its direct tendency is to restrict circulation. This is plain enough when we consider that, if it were increased to a high degree, . . . it well might result in destroying both advertising and circulation.

A determination of the question whether the tax is valid in respect of the point now under review requires an examination of the history and circumstances which antedated and attended the adoption of the abridgment clause of the First Amendment. . . . The history is a long one; but for present purposes it may be greatly abbreviated.

For more than a century prior to the adoption of the amendment—and, indeed, for many years thereafter—history discloses a persistent effort on the part of the British government to prevent or abridge the free expression of any opinion which seemed to criticize or exhibit in an unfavorable light, however truly, the agencies and operations of the government. The struggle between the proponents of measures to that end and those who asserted the right of free expression was continuous and unceasing. As early as 1644, John Milton, in an "Appeal for the Liberty of Unlicensed Printing," assailed an act of Parliament which had just been passed providing for censorship of the press previous to publication. He vigorously defended the right of every man to make public his honest views "without previous censure," and declared the impossibility of finding any man base enough to accept the office of censor and at the same time good enough to be allowed to perform its duties. . . . The act expired by its own terms in 1695. It was never renewed; and the liberty of the press thus became, as pointed out by Wickwar (*The Struggle for the Freedom of the Press*, p. 15), merely "a right or liberty to publish *without* a license what formerly could be published only with one." But mere exemption from previous censorship was soon recognized as too narrow a view of the liberty of the press.

In 1712, in response to a message from Queen Anne . . . Parliament imposed a tax upon all newspapers and upon advertisements. That the main purpose of these taxes was to suppress the publication of comments and criticisms objectionable to the Crown does not admit of doubt. . . . There followed more than a century of resistance to, and evasion of, the taxes, and of agitation for their repeal. . . . [T]hese taxes constituted one of the factors that aroused the American colonists to protest against taxation for the purposes of the home government; . . . the revolution really began when, in 1765, that government sent stamps for newspaper duties to the American colonies.

These duties were quite commonly characterized as "taxes on knowledge," a phrase used for the purpose of describing the effect of the exactions and at the same time condemning them. That the taxes had, and were intended to have, the effect of curtailing the circulation of newspapers, and particularly the cheaper ones whose readers were generally found among the masses of the people, went almost without question, even on the part of those who defended the act. . . .

. . . [I]n the adoption of the English newspaper stamp tax and the tax on advertisements, revenue was of subordinate concern; . . . the dominant and controlling aim was to prevent, or curtail the opportunity for, the acquisition of knowledge by the people in respect of their governmental affairs. It is idle to suppose that so many of the best men of England would for a century of time have waged, as they did, stubborn and often precarious warfare against these taxes if a mere matter of taxation had been involved. The aim of the struggle was not to relieve taxpayers from a burden, but to establish and preserve the right of the English people to full information in respect of the doings or misdoings of their government. . . .

In 1785, only four years before Congress had proposed the First Amendment, the Massachusetts Legislature, following the English example, imposed a stamp tax on all newspapers and magazines. The following year an advertisement tax was imposed. Both taxes met with such violent opposition that the former was repealed in 1786, and the latter in 1788. . . .

The framers of the First Amendment were familiar with the English struggle, which then had continued for nearly eighty years and was destined to go on for another sixty-five years, at the end of which time it culminated in a lasting abandonment of the obnoxious taxes. The framers were likewise familiar with the then recent Massachusetts episode; and while that occurrence did much to bring about the adoption of the amendment . . . the predominant influence must have come from the English experience. It is impossible to concede that by the words "freedom of the press" the framers of the amendment intended to adopt merely the narrow view then reflected by the law of England that such freedom consisted only in immunity from previous censorship; for this abuse had then permanently disappeared from English practice. It is equally impossible to believe that it was not intended to bring within the reach of these words such modes of restraint as were embodied in the two forms of taxation already described. Such belief must be rejected in the face of the then well-known purpose of the exactions and the general adverse sentiment of the colonies in respect of them. Undoubtedly, the range of a constitutional provision phrased in terms of the common law sometimes may be fixed by recourse to the applicable rules of that law. But the doctrine which justifies such recourse, like other canons of construction, must yield to more compelling reasons whenever they exist. . . .

In the light of all that has now been said, it is evident that the restricted rules of the English law in respect of the freedom of the press in force when the Constitution was adopted were never accepted by the American colonists, and that by the First Amendment it was meant to preclude the national government, and by the Fourteenth Amendment to preclude the states, from adopting any form of previous restraint upon printed publications, or their circulation, including that which had theretofore been effected by these two well-known and odious methods.

This court had occasion in *Near* to discuss at some length the subject in its general aspect. The conclusion there stated is that the object of the constitutional provisions was to prevent previous restraints on publication; and the court was careful not to limit the protection of the right to any particular way of abridging it. Liberty of the press within the meaning of the constitutional provision, it was broadly said, meant "principally although not exclusively, immunity from previous restraints or (from) censorship." . . .

It is not intended by anything we have said to suggest that the owners of newspapers are immune from any of the ordinary forms of taxation for support of the government. But this is not an ordinary form of tax, but one single in kind, with a long history of hostile misuse against the freedom of the press.

The predominant purpose of the grant of immunity here invoked was to preserve an untrammeled press as a vital source of public information. The newspapers, magazines, and other journals of the country, it is safe to say, have shed and continue to shed, more light on the public and business affairs of the nation than any other instrumentality of publicity; and since informed public opinion is the most potent of all restraints upon misgovernment, the suppression or abridgment of the publicity afforded by a free press cannot be regarded otherwise than with grave concern. The tax here involved is bad not because it takes money from the pockets of the appellees. If that were all, a wholly different question would be presented. It is bad because, in the light of its history and of its present setting, it is seen to be a deliberate and calculated device in the guise of a tax to limit the circulation of information to which the public is entitled in virtue of the constitutional guaranties. A free press stands as one of the great interpreters between the government and the people. To allow it to be fettered is to fetter ourselves.

In view of the persistent search for new subjects of taxation, it is not without significance that, with the single exception of the Louisiana statute, so far as we can discover, no state during the one hundred fifty years of our national existence has undertaken to impose a tax like that now in question.

The form in which the tax is imposed is in itself suspicious. It is not measured or limited by the volume of advertisements. It is measured alone by the extent of the circulation of the publication in which the advertisements are carried, with the plain purpose of penalizing the publishers and curtailing the circulation of a selected group of newspapers. . . .

DECREE AFFIRMED.

8

DEJONGE V. OREGON
299 U.S. 353 (1937)

Dirk DeJonge helped conduct a meeting in Portland held by the Communist Party, of which he was a member. The purpose of the meeting was to protest police shootings of striking longshoremen and raids on workers' homes and halls. Police arrived during the event and arrested DeJonge, who subsequently was convicted under a state law making it a crime to assist in conducting a meeting convened by a group that advocated criminal syndicalism— "the doctrine," in the words of the statute, "which advocates crime, physical violence, sabotage, or any unlawful acts or methods as a means of accomplishing or effecting industrial or political change or revolution." On appeal, the Oregon Supreme Court upheld DeJonge's conviction. But a unanimous Supreme Court reversed.

There was no dispute in the case that the Communist Party advocated criminal syndicalism, but the record contained no evidence that DeJonge himself had actually done so during the meeting. "His sole offense as charged," wrote Chief Justice Hughes for the Court, "was that he had assisted in the conduct of a public meeting, albeit otherwise lawful, which was held under auspices of the Communist Party." This activity, the Court concluded, cannot be made a crime, and therefore DeJonge's conviction was a violation of his "rights of free speech and peaceable assembly."

The Court did not employ the clear-and-present-danger test in upholding DeJonge's free speech rights. But it left the impression that this test—or any other that might be used—should ask whether the speech under review was used "to incite to violence or crime." As for the right of peaceable assembly, the Court emphasized the importance of this liberty in *DeJonge* and declared, for the first time, that the right is one that, under the Fourteenth Amendment, the states may not abridge.

Whitney v. *California* (1927) permitted what might be called "guilt by association." *DeJonge*, together with the earlier case *Stromberg* v. *California* (1931) and with *Herndon* v. *Lowry* (1937), decided four months later, denied that guilt may be inferred from the company a person keeps.

Opinion of the Court: **Hughes**, Van Devanter, McReynolds, Brandeis, Sutherland, Butler, Roberts, Cardozo. Not participating: Stone.

DeJonge v. *Oregon* was decided on January 4, 1937.

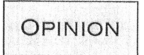

CHIEF JUSTICE HUGHES DELIVERED THE OPINION OF THE COURT . . .

. . . Having limited the charge to defendant's participation in a meeting called by the Communist Party, the state court sustained the conviction upon that basis regardless of what was said or done at the meeting.

We must take the indictment as thus construed. Conviction upon a charge not made would be sheer denial of due process. It thus appears that, while defendant was a member of the Communist Party, he was not indicted for participating in its organization, or for joining it, or for soliciting members, or for distributing its literature. He was not charged with teaching or advocating criminal syndicalism or sabotage or any unlawful acts, either at the meeting or elsewhere. He was accordingly deprived of the benefit of evidence as to the orderly and lawful conduct of the meeting and that it was not called or used for the advocacy of criminal syndicalism or sabotage or any unlawful action. His sole offense as charged, and for which he was convicted and sentenced to imprisonment for seven years, was that he had assisted in the conduct of a public meeting, albeit otherwise lawful, which was held under the auspices of the Communist Party.

The broad reach of the statute as thus applied is plain. While defendant was a member of the Communist Party, that membership was not necessary to conviction on such a charge. A like fate might have attended any speaker, although not a member, who "assisted in the conduct" of the meeting. However innocuous the object of the meeting, however lawful the subjects and tenor of the addresses, however reasonable and timely the discussion, all those assisting in the conduct of the meeting would be subject to imprisonment as felons if the meeting were held by the Communist Party. . . .

While the States are entitled to protect themselves from the abuse of the privileges of our institutions through an attempted substitution of force and violence in the place of peaceful political action in order to effect revolutionary changes in government, none of our decisions go to the length of sustaining such a curtailment of the right of free speech and assembly as the Oregon statute demands in its present application. . . .

Freedom of speech and of the press are fundamental rights which are safeguarded by the due process clause of the Fourteenth Amendment of the Federal Constitution. *Gitlow* v. *New York* [1925]; *Stromberg* v. *California* [1927]; *Near* v. *Minnesota* [1931]; *Grosjean* v. *American Press Co.* [1936]. The right of peaceable assembly is a right cognate to those of free speech and free press and is equally fundamental. As this Court said in *United States* v. *Cruikshank* [1875], "The very idea of a government, republican in form, implies a right on the part of its citizens to meet peaceably for consultation in respect to public affairs and to petition for a redress of grievances."

The First Amendment of the Federal Constitution expressly guarantees that right against abridgment by Congress. But explicit mention there does not argue exclusion elsewhere. For the right is one that cannot be denied without violating those fundamental principles of liberty and justice which lie at the base of all civil and political institutions—principles which the Fourteenth Amendment embodies in the general terms of its due process clause.

These rights may be abused by using speech or press or assembly in order to incite to violence and crime. The people through their Legislatures may protect themselves against that abuse. But the legislative intervention can find constitutional justification only by dealing with the abuse. The rights themselves must not be curtailed. The greater the importance of safeguarding the community from incitements to the overthrow of our institutions by force and violence, the more imperative is the need to preserve inviolate the constitutional rights of free speech, free press, and free assembly in order to maintain the opportunity for free political discussion, to the end that government may be responsive to the will of the people and that changes, if desired, may be obtained by peaceful means. Therein lies the security of the Republic, the very foundation of constitutional government.

It follows from these considerations that, consistently with the Federal Constitution, peaceable assembly for lawful discussion cannot be made a crime. The holding of meetings for peaceable political action cannot be proscribed. Those who assist in the conduct of such meetings cannot be branded as criminals on that score. The question, if the rights of free speech and peaceable assembly are to be preserved, is not as to the auspices under which the meeting is held but as to its purpose; not as to the relations of the speakers, but whether their utterances transcend the bounds of the freedom of speech which the Constitution protects. If the persons assembling have committed crimes elsewhere, if they have formed or are engaged in a conspiracy against the public peace and order, they may be prosecuted for their conspiracy or other violation of valid laws. But it is a different matter when the State, instead of prosecuting them for such offenses, seizes upon mere participation in a peaceable assembly and a lawful public discussion as the basis for a criminal charge. . . .

REVERSED.

9

HERNDON V. LOWRY
301 U.S. 242 (1937)

Angelo Herndon joined the Communist Party while living in Kentucky and moved to Atlanta to work in its behalf. There he was arrested by local authorities and charged under state law with attempting to incite insurrection. At trial, Herndon was convicted and sentenced to imprisonment for eighteen to twenty years. The Georgia Supreme Court sustained the judgment, but the U.S. Supreme Court, by a vote of 5 to 4, reversed.

The record in the case showed that Herndon had held meetings designed to recruit members for the party and had solicited contributions for its support, and that literature in his possession at the time of his arrest yielded proof of what the party believed. Skeptical of Georgia's case against Herndon, the Court, with Justice Roberts writing, employed the clear-and-present-danger test in reviewing the defendant's First Amendment appeal.

"[P]enalizing even . . . utterances of a defined character must find its justification," said the Court, "in a reasonable apprehension of danger to organized government"—specifically, in "a clear and present danger of forcible obstruction of a particular state function." But there was no evidence in the case that Herndon had actually distributed any documents advocating forcible subversion of government, nor that he had urged by speech or written word any doctrine or action implying as much. The Court concluded that Herndon's rights had been abridged by the enforcement of a law that "unreasonably limits freedom of speech and assembly."

Herndon was the first case since *Schenck* v. *United States* (1919) in which a majority endorsed the clear-and-present-danger test. It was also the first case in which use of the test resulted in a defeat for government.

For the next decade and a half—until *Dennis* v. *United States* (1951)—the Court employed the clear-and-present-danger test to protect First Amendment rights in a variety of contexts. It did not use the test in a case in which it rejected First Amendment claims.

Opinion of the Court: **Roberts**, Brandeis, Stone, Hughes, Cardozo. Dissenting opinion: **Van Devanter**, McReynolds, Sutherland, Butler.

Herndon v. *Lowry* was decided on April 26, 1937.

39

OPINIONS

JUSTICE ROBERTS DELIVERED THE OPINION OF THE COURT . . .

The affirmance of conviction upon the trial record necessarily gives section 56 [of the Georgia Penal Code] the construction that one who seeks members for or attempts to organize a local unit of a party which has the purposes and objects disclosed by the documents in evidence may be found guilty of an attempt to incite.

The questions are whether this construction and application of the statute deprives the accused of the right of freedom of speech and of assembly guaranteed by the Fourteenth Amendment, and whether the statute so construed and applied furnishes a reasonably definite and ascertainable standard of guilt.

The appellant, while admitting that the people may protect themselves against abuses of the freedom of speech safeguarded by the Fourteenth Amendment by prohibiting incitement to violence and crime, insists that legislative regulation may not go beyond measures forefending against "clear and present danger" of the use of force against the state. For this position he relies upon our decisions under the Federal Espionage Acts and cognate state legislation. These made it criminal willfully to cause or to attempt to cause, or incite or attempt to incite, insubordination, disloyalty, mutiny, or refusal of duty in the military or naval forces of the United States or willfully to obstruct or attempt to obstruct the recruiting or enlistment service of the United States or to conspire for these purposes. We sustained the power of the government or a state to protect the war operations of the United States by punishing intentional interference with them. We recognized, however, that words may be spoken or written for various purposes and that willful and intentional interference with the described operations of the government might be inferred from the time, place, and circumstances of the act. "The question in every case is whether the words used are used in such circumstances and are of such a nature as to create a clear and present danger that they will bring about the substantive evils that Congress has a right to prevent. It is a question of proximity and degree." [*Schenck* v. *U.S.* (1919).]

The legislation under review differs radically from the Espionage Acts in that it does not deal with a willful attempt to obstruct a described and defined activity of the government.

The state, on the other hand, insists that our decisions uphold state statutes making criminal utterances which have a "dangerous tendency" towards the subversion of government. It relies particularly upon *Gitlow* v. *New York* [1925]. There, however, we dealt with a statute which, quite unlike section 56 of the Georgia Criminal Code, denounced as criminal certain acts carefully and adequately described. . . .

The power of a state to abridge freedom of speech and of assembly is the exception rather than the rule, and the penalizing even of utterances of a defined character must find its justification in a reasonable apprehension of danger to organized government. The judgment of the Legislature is not unfettered. The limitation upon individual liberty must have appropriate relation to the safety of the state. Legislation which goes beyond this need violates the principle of the Constitution. If, therefore, a state statute penalize innocent participation in a meeting held with an innocent purpose merely because the meeting was held under the auspices of an organization membership in which, or the advocacy of whose principles, is also denounced as criminal, the law, so construed and applied, goes beyond the power to restrict abuses of freedom of speech and arbitrarily denies that freedom. [*DeJonge* v. *Oregon* (1937).] And, where a statute is so vague and uncertain as to make criminal an utterance or an act which may be innocently said or done with no intent to induce resort to violence or on the other hand may be said or done with a purpose violently to subvert government, a conviction under such a law cannot be sustained. Upon this view we held bad a statute of California . . . providing that "any person who displays a red flag, . . . in any public place or in any meeting place or public assembly, or from or on any house, building, or window as a sign, symbol, or emblem of opposition to organized government . . . is guilty of a felony." [*Stromberg* v. *California* (1931).] . . .

1. The appellant had a constitutional right to address meetings and organize parties unless in so doing he violated some prohibition of a valid statute. The only prohibition he is said to have violated is that of section 56 forbidding incitement or attempted incitement to insurrection by violence. If the evidence fails to show that he did so incite, then, as applied to him, the statute unreasonably limits freedom of speech and freedom of assembly and violates the Fourteenth Amendment. We are of opinion that the requisite proof is lacking.

. . . The only objectives appellant is proved to have urged are those having to do with unemployment and emergency relief which are void of criminality. His membership in the Communist Party and his solicitation of a few members wholly fails to establish an attempt to incite others to insurrection. Indeed, so far as appears, he had but a single copy of the booklet the state claims to be objectionable; that copy he retained. The same may be said with respect to the other books and pamphlets, some of them of more innocent purport. In these circumstances, to make membership in the party and solicitation of members for that party a criminal offense, punishable by death, in the discretion of a jury, is an unwarranted invasion of the right of freedom of speech.

2. The statute, as construed and applied in the appellant's trial, does not furnish a sufficiently ascertainable standard of guilt. . . . If the jury conclude that the defendant should have contemplated that any act or utterance of his in opposition to the established order or advocating a change in that order, might, in the distant future, eventuate in a combination to offer forcible resistance to the state, or, as the state says, if the jury believe he should have known that his words would have "a dangerous tendency" then he may be convicted. To be guilty under the law, as construed, a defendant need not advocate resort to force. He need not teach any particular doctrine to come within its purview. Indeed, he need not be active in the formation of a combination or group if he agitate for a change in the frame of government, however peaceful his own intent. If, by the exercise of prophecy, he can forecast that, as a result of a chain of causation, following his proposed action a group may arise at some future date which will resort to force, he is bound to make the prophecy and abstain, under pain of punishment, possibly of execution. Every person who attacks existing conditions, who agitates for a change in the form of government, must take the risk that if a jury should be of opinion he ought to have foreseen that his utterances might contribute in any measure to some future forcible resistance to the existing government he may be convicted of the offense of inciting insurrection. Proof that

the accused in fact believed that his effort would cause a violent assault upon the state would not be necessary to conviction. It would be sufficient if the jury thought he reasonably might foretell that those he persuaded to join the party might, at some time in the indefinite future, resort to forcible resistance of government. The question thus proposed to a jury involves pure speculation as to future trends of thought and action. Within what time might one reasonably expect that an attempted organization of the Communist Party in the United States would result in violent action by that party? If a jury returned a special verdict saying twenty years or even fifty years, the verdict could not be shown to be wrong. The law, as thus construed, licenses the jury to create its own standard in each case. . . .

The statute, as construed and applied, amounts merely to a dragnet which may enmesh anyone who agitates for a change of government if a jury can be persuaded that he ought to have foreseen his words would have some effect in the future conduct of others. No reasonably ascertainable standard of guilt is prescribed. So vague and indeterminate are the boundaries thus set to the freedom of speech and assembly that the law necessarily violates the guarantees of liberty embodied in the Fourteenth Amendment. . . .

REVERSED and remanded.

JUSTICE VAN DEVANTER, DISSENTING.

I am of opinion that the Georgia statute, as construed and applied by the Supreme Court of the state of Herndon's case, prescribes a reasonably definite and ascertainable standard by which to determine the guilt or innocence of the accused, and does not encroach on his right of freedom of speech or of assembly.

It plainly appears, I think, that the offense defined in the statute, and of which Herndon was convicted, was not that of advocating a change in the state government by lawful means, such as an orderly exertion of the elective franchise or of the power to amend the State Constitution, but was that of attempting to induce and incite others to join in combined forcible resistance to the lawful authority of the state. . . .

There was no direct testimony that Herndon distributed . . . literature. . . . No member of the Communist Party came forward to tell what he did in their meetings or in inducing them to become members. Nor does this seem strange when regard is had to the obligation taken by members and to the discipline imposed. Nevertheless there was evidence from which distribution by him reasonably could be inferred. It was shown that he was an active member, was sent to Atlanta as a paid organizer, and was subject to party discipline; also that he received the literature for distribution in the course of his work and had copies of it, together with current membership and collection books, under his arm when he was arrested; and further that he had been soliciting and securing members, which was part of the work in which the literature was to be used. He had declared his "adherence to the program and statutes" of the party and had taken like declarations from those whom he secured as members; and this tended strongly to show not only that he understood the party program and statutes as outlined in the literature, but also that he brought them to the attention of others whom he secured as members. Besides, at the trial he made an extended statement to the court and jury in his defense, but did not refer in any wise to the literature or deny that he had been using or distributing it. Thus there was in the evidence not merely some but adequate and undisputed basis for inferring that he had been using the literature for the purposes for which he received it. Evidently, and with reason, the jury drew this inference.

It should not be overlooked that Herndon was a negro member and organizer in the Communist Party and was engaged actively in inducing others, chiefly southern negroes, to become members of the party and participate in effecting its purposes and program. The literature placed in his lands by the party for that purpose was particularly adapted to appeal to negroes in that section, for it pictured their condition as an unhappy one resulting from asserted wrongs on the part of white landlords and employers, and sought by alluring statements of resulting advantages to induce them to join in an effort to carry into effect the measures which the literature proposed. These measures included a revolutionary uprooting of the existing capitalist state, as it was termed; confiscation of the landed property of white landowners and capitalists for the benefit of negroes; establishment in the black belt of an independent state, possibly followed by secession . . . [;] demonstrations, strikes, and tax boycotts in aid of this measure; adoption of a fighting [sic] the United States; organization of mass alliance with the revolutionary white proletariat; revolutionary overthrow of capitalism and establishment of Communism through effective physical struggles against the class enemy. Proposing these measures was nothing short of advising a resort to force and violence, for all know that such measures could not be effected otherwise. Not only so, but the literature makes such repelling use of the terms "revolution," "national rebellion," "revolutionary struggle," "revolutionary overthrow," "effective physical struggle," "smash the National Guard," "mass strikes," and "violence," as to leave no doubt that the use of force in an unlawful sense is intended.

The purpose and probable effect of such literature, when under consideration in a prosecution like that against Herndon, are to be tested and determined with appropriate regard to the capacity and circumstances of those who are sought to be influenced. In this instance the literature is largely directed to a people whose past and present circumstances would lead them to give unusual credence to its inflaming and inciting features.

And so it is that examination and consideration of the evidence convince me that the Supreme Court of the state applied the statute, conformably to its opinion, as making criminal an attempt to induce and incite others to join in combined forcible resistance to the lawful authority of the state.

That the constitutional guaranty of freedom of speech and assembly does not shield or afford protection for acts of intentional incitement to forcible resistance to the lawful authority of a state is settled by repeated decisions of this Court [*Gitlow* v. *New York* (1925); *Whitney* v. *California* (1927); *Fiske* v. *Kansas* (1927); *Stromberg* v. *California* (1931); *Near* v. *Minnesota* (1931)]; and the Georgia decisions are to the same effect.

Under the statute as construed and applied, it is essential that the accused intended to induce combined forcible resistance. The presence of the intent aggravates the inducement and brings it more certainly within the power of the state to denounce it as a crime than otherwise it would be. The Supreme Court of the state in both of its opinions [in this case] was dealing with a statute and a charge in which the intent of the accused was an element of the offense. In the original opinion the court incautiously said "it would be sufficient that he intended it (the combined and forcible resistance) to happen at any time." In its opinion on rehearing it said the phrase "at any time" had not been intended to mean any time in the indefinite future; and by way of avoiding such a meaning the court changed that part of the original opinion by making it read "at any time within which he might reasonably expect his influence to continue to be directly operative in causing such action by those whom he sought to induce." I do not perceive that this puts the standard of guilt at large or renders it inadmissibly vague. The accused must intend that combined forcible resistance shall proximately result from his act of inducement. There is no uncertainty in that. The intended point of time must be within the period during which he "might reasonably expect" his inducement to remain directly operative in causing the combined forcible resistance. The words "might reasonably expect" have as much precision as is admissible in such a matter, are not difficult to understand, and conform to decisions heretofore given by this Court in respect of related questions. I therefore am of opinion that there is no objectionable uncertainty about the standard of guilt and that the statute does not in that regard infringe the constitutional guaranty of due process of law. . . .

10

LOVELL V. CITY OF GRIFFIN
303 U.S. 444 (1938)

An ordinance of Griffin, Georgia, prohibited the distribution of pamphlets without written permission from the city manager. Alma Lovell, a Jehovah's Witness, passed out Witness literature on city streets without applying for the necessary permit, and she was arrested. Lovell said she had not sought a permit because she regarded herself as sent "by Jehovah to do His work": to apply for a permit, she said, would be "an act of disobedience to His commandment." When she was found in violation of the ordinance she appealed on First Amendment grounds, contending that the city law ran afoul of the free exercise of religion and free press clauses. Voting unanimously to reverse, the Supreme Court held that the ordinance was an unconstitutional abridgment of freedom of the press.

Understanding *Lovell* as a prior-restraint case, the Court expanded the definition of the press that enjoys constitutional liberty to include not only newspapers but also pamphlets and leaflets. The Court found "censorship" in the "broad sweep" of the ordinance. It was not limited to categories of expression that the Court had previously identified as without First Amendment protection—literature "that is obscene or offensive to public morals or that advocates unlawful conduct." Nor was it limited to ways of distributing literature that might be regarded as "inconsistent with the maintenance of public order, or as involving disorderly conduct, the molestation of the inhabitants, or the misuse or littering of the streets." The ordinance, said the Court, summing up its objection, "prohibits the distribution of literature of any kind at any time, at any place, and in any manner without a permit."

In subsequent cases the Court developed doctrine allowing prior licensing so long as the discretion of the public authorities was not complete, as it had been in *Lovell*, but was limited to issues of "time, place, and manner."

Lovell was the first in a series of cases in which Jehovah's Witnesses asserted First Amendment speech, press, and free exercise rights, and often the Court treated their claims, as it did in *Lovell*, without reaching the free exercise issues.

Opinion of the Court: **Hughes**, McReynolds, Stone, Brandeis, Butler, Roberts, Black, Reed. Not participating: Cardozo.

Lovell v. *City of Griffin* was decided on March 28, 1938.

OPINION

CHIEF JUSTICE HUGHES DELIVERED THE OPINION OF THE COURT . . .

Freedom of speech and freedom of the press, which are protected by the First Amendment from infringement by Congress, are among the fundamental personal rights and liberties which are protected by the Fourteenth Amendment from invasion by state action. . . . It is also well settled that municipal ordinances adopted under state authority constitute state action and are within the prohibition of the amendment. . . .

The ordinance in its broad sweep prohibits the distribution of "circulars, handbooks, advertising, or literature of any kind." It manifestly applies to pamphlets, magazines, and periodicals. The evidence against appellant was that she distributed a certain pamphlet and a magazine called the "Golden Age." Whether in actual administration the ordinance is applied, as apparently it could be, to newspapers does not appear. . . . The ordinance is not limited to "literature" that is obscene or offensive to public morals or that advocates unlawful conduct. . . . The ordinance embraces "literature" in the widest sense.

The ordinance is comprehensive with respect to the method of distribution. It covers every sort of circulation "either by hand or otherwise." There is thus no restriction in its application with respect to time or place. It is not limited to ways which might be regarded as inconsistent with the maintenance of public order, or as involving disorderly conduct, the molestation of the inhabitants, or the misuse or littering of the streets. . . .

We think that the ordinance is invalid on its face. Whatever the motive which induced its adoption, its character is such that it strikes at the very foundation of the freedom of the press by subjecting it to license and censorship. The struggle for the freedom of the press was primarily directed against the power of the licensor. It was against that power that John Milton directed his assault by his "Appeal for the Liberty of Unlicensed Printing." And the liberty of the press became initially a right to publish "without a license what formerly could be published only with one." [Wickwar, "The Struggle for the Freedom of the Press," p. 15.] While this freedom from previous restraint upon publication cannot be regarded as exhausting the guaranty of liberty, the prevention of that restraint was a leading purpose in the adoption of the constitutional provision. . . . Legislation of the type of the ordinance in question would restore the system of license and censorship in its baldest form.

The liberty of the press is not confined to newspapers and periodicals. It necessarily embraces pamphlets and leaflets. These indeed have been historic weapons in the defense of liberty, as the pamphlets of Thomas Paine and others in our own history abundantly attest. The press in its connotation comprehends every sort of publication which affords a vehicle of information and opinion. . . . What we have had recent occasion to say with respect to the vital importance of protecting this essential liberty from every sort of infringement need not be repeated. . . .

The ordinance cannot be saved because it relates to distribution and not to publication. . . . The license tax in *Grosjean* v. *American Press Co.* [1936] was held invalid because of its direct tendency to restrict circulation. . . .

REVERSED and remanded.

THORNHILL V. ALABAMA
310 U.S. 88 (1940)

The American Federation of Labor ordered a strike of the Brown Wood Preserving Company in Tuscaloosa, Alabama. Employee Byron Thornhill, a union member, joined others on the picket line, and was arrested. Found in violation of an Alabama law that made picketing illegal, Thornhill appealed on First Amendment grounds to the Alabama Supreme Court and was unsuccessful. But the U.S. Supreme Court, with only one justice in dissent, reversed.

The Court first suggested that picketing was a form of expression in sustaining a Wisconsin statute authorizing peaceful picketing (*Senn* v. *Tile Layers Union*, 1937). In *Thornhill* the Court developed the logic of this suggestion by holding that picketing in fact merits First Amendment protection. The Court took care, however, to define the kind of picketing worthy of protection as educational—e.g., that which serves to inform the public of the facts of a labor dispute. In later cases the Court balanced the general police power of the state against First Amendment rights in sustaining efforts to curtail picketing marked by violence and destruction of property.

As in other cases before and after World War II, the Court in *Thornhill* applied the clear-and-present-danger test in sustaining a First Amendment claim. In his opinion for the majority, Justice Murphy concluded that there was no clear and present danger "of destruction of life or property, or invasion of the right of privacy, or breach of the peace" inherent in the activities of a person "who approaches the premises of an employer and publicizes the facts of a labor dispute involving the latter."

Opinion of the Court: **Murphy**, Stone, Hughes, Roberts, Black, Reed, Frankfurter, Douglas. Dissenting opinion: **McReynolds**.

Thornhill v. *Alabama* was decided on April 22, 1940.

JUSTICE MURPHY DELIVERED THE OPINION OF THE COURT . . .

The numerous forms of conduct proscribed by Section 3448 [of the Alabama penal code] are subsumed under two offenses: the first embraces the activities of all who "without a just cause or legal excuse" "go near to or loiter about the premises" of any person engaged in a lawful business for the purpose of influencing or inducing others to adopt any of certain enumerated courses of action; the second, all who "picket" the place of business of any such person "for the purpose of hindering, delaying, or interfering with or injuring any lawful business or enterprise of another." It is apparent that one or the other of the offenses comprehends every practicable method whereby the facts of a labor dispute may be publicized in the vicinity of the place of business of an employer. The phrase "without a just cause or legal excuse" does not in any effective manner restrict the breadth of the regulation; the words themselves have no ascertainable meaning either inherent or historical. . . . The courses of action, listed under the first offense, which an accused—including an employee—may not urge others to take, comprehends those which in many instances would normally result from merely publicizing, without annoyance or threat of any kind, the facts of a labor dispute. An intention to hinder, delay, or interfere with a lawful business, which is an element of the second offense, likewise can be proved merely by showing that others reacted in a way normally expectable of some upon learning the facts of a dispute. The vague contours of the term "picket" are nowhere delineated. Employees or others, accordingly, may be found to be within the purview of the term and convicted for engaging in activities identical with those proscribed by the first offense. In sum, whatever the means used to publicize the facts of a labor dispute, whether by printed sign, by pamphlet, by word of mouth or otherwise, all such activity without exception is within the inclusive prohibition of the statute so long as it occurs in the vicinity of the scene of the dispute. . . . We think that Section 3448 is invalid on its face.

The freedom of speech and of the press guaranteed by the Constitution embraces at the least the liberty to discuss publicly and truthfully all matters of public concern without previous restraint or fear of subsequent punishment. The exigencies of the colonial period and the efforts to secure freedom from oppressive administration developed a broadened conception of these liberties as adequate to supply the public need for information and education with respect to the significant issues of the times. . . . Freedom of discussion, if it would fulfill its historic function in this nation, must embrace all issues about which information is needed or appropriate to enable the members of society to cope with the exigencies of their period.

In the circumstances of our times the dissemination of information concerning the facts of a labor dispute must be regarded as within that area of free discussion that is guaranteed by the Constitution. . . . It is recognized now that satisfactory hours and wages and working conditions in industry and a bargaining position which makes these possible have an importance which is not less than the interests of those in the business or industry directly concerned. The health of the present generation and of those as yet unborn may depend on these matters, and the practices in a single factory may have economic repercussions upon a whole region and affect widespread systems of marketing. The merest glance at State and Federal legislation on the subject demonstrates the force of the argument that labor relations are not matters of mere local or private concern. Free discussion concerning the conditions in industry and the causes of labor disputes appears to us indispensable to the effective and intelligent use of the processes of popular government to shape the destiny of modern industrial society. The issues raised by regulations, such as are challenged here, infringing upon the right of employees effectively to inform the public of the facts of a labor dispute are part of this larger problem. . . .

It is true that the rights of employers and employees to conduct their economic affairs and to compete with others for a share in the products of industry are subject to modification or qualification in the interests of the society in which they exist. This is but an instance of the

power of the State to set the limits of permissible contest open to industrial combatants. . . .
It does not follow that the State in dealing with the evils arising from industrial disputes may
impair the effective exercise of the right to discuss freely industrial relations which are matters of public concern. A contrary conclusion could be used to support abridgment of freedom of speech and of the press concerning almost every matter of importance to society.

The range of activities proscribed by Section 3448, whether characterized as picketing or
loitering or otherwise, embraces nearly every practicable, effective means whereby those interested—including the employees directly affected—may enlighten the public on the nature
and causes of a labor dispute. The safeguarding of these means is essential to the securing of
an informed and educated public opinion with respect to a matter which is of public concern.
It may be that effective exercise of the means of advancing public knowledge may persuade
some of those reached to refrain from entering into advantageous relations with the business
establishment which is the scene of the dispute. Every expression of opinion on matters that
are important has the potentiality of inducing action in the interests of one rather than another
group in society. But the group in power at any moment may not impose penal sanctions on
peaceful and truthful discussion of matters of public interest merely on a showing that others
may thereby be persuaded to take action inconsistent with its interests. Abridgment of the liberty of such discussion can be justified only where the clear danger of substantive evils arises
under circumstances affording no opportunity to test the merits of ideas by competition for
acceptance in the market of public opinion. We hold that the danger of injury to an industrial
concern is neither so serious nor so imminent as to justify the sweeping proscription of freedom of discussion embodied in Section 3448.

The State urges that the purpose of the challenged statute is the protection of the community from the violence and breaches of the peace, which, it asserts, are the concomitants
of picketing. The power and the duty of the State to take adequate steps to preserve the peace
and to protect the privacy, the lives, and the property of its residents cannot be doubted. But
no clear and present danger of destruction of life or property, or invasion of the right of privacy, or breach of the peace can be thought to be inherent in the activities of every person
who approaches the premises of an employer and publicizes the facts of a labor dispute involving the latter. . . .

REVERSED.

RESPONSES

FROM THE *NEW YORK TIMES*, APRIL 24, 1940, "PICKETING AS FREE SPEECH"

. . . Picketing, under this decision, is a form of "free discussion." A very little observation in
our own city may suggest that it is often a futile and annoying form of discussion. But the crux
of free speech is that the right to engage in discussions which seem to many persons both futile and annoying should be protected.

Of course these decisions do not dispose of all picketing problems. Local authorities must
still decide when "free discussion" becomes coercion, to what extent the obstruction of busy

city streets should be permitted, to what lengths pickets may go in language or gestures, and what tests can be or ought to be applied to determine whether a given picket is engaged in a genuine labor dispute. Picketing can and has been a racket, which no community is obligated to tolerate. It can be and has been as harmful to labor as to the employer and the public.

The decisions do seem to mean that the burden of proof in a particular case must lie on those who want picketing stopped. At times this may seem to be a hard doctrine, but it is safer in the long run than the doctrine that a local or State Government can decide for itself on what subjects free speech shall be permitted and on what subjects it shall not be permitted. The further deduction may be made that if labor union pickets are protected, the right of an employer to state his own case, in any orderly fashion he likes, is guaranteed by the same line of reasoning.

FROM *THE CHRISTIAN CENTURY*, MAY 8, 1940, "PEACEFUL PICKETING GETS SUPREME COURT SANCTION"

. . . The ground of the decision may seem a little surprising, for it has not been customary to think of picketing as primarily a form of speech. Yet the argument seems sound and the conclusion is praiseworthy. It carried the approval of eight members of the court, only the staunchly conservative Justice McReynolds dissenting. When picketing is not accompanied by violence, as both parties agreed that it was not in the cases under consideration, it is, said Justice Murphy, who wrote the majority opinion, a form of free discussion, a legitimate method by which striking workers can get their side of the case before their fellow workers and the public. It is still a matter for determination in each specific case whether the actions of pickets are confined to free discussion or whether they also include violence and intimidation. The court's decision cannot be cited in defense of discussion carried on by brandishing lengths of lead pipe or by threats of personal assault or by jamming the entrance of plants to the exclusion of employees and customers. But the burden of proof now rests upon those who allege that such violence is used. Picketing is not punishable as such. By the same logic it would seem that the publication of arguments on a labor question by employers should not be considered as *ipso facto* a threat of discrimination against workers who do not accept their views. Here also the question should be treated as one of fact to be determined by the evidence. This matter of free speech and discussion works both ways, and it is of the essence of it that it includes the right to express opinions that are not generally popular among those to whom they are addressed. The picketing decision is important because it assures to labor the right to use a useful instrument, and also because it lays upon labor a serious responsibility to use it lawfully and peaceably.

COX V. NEW HAMPSHIRE
312 U.S. 569 (1941)

A Manchester, New Hampshire, ordinance required that those wishing to conduct a "parade" or "procession" on a public street first obtain a license and pay a fee. Without getting a license, a group of Jehovah's Witnesses marched through city streets carrying placards stating their religious views and handing out leaflets announcing a public meeting. They were arrested and found in violation of the law. The state supreme court and then the U.S. Supreme Court rejected the Witnesses' arguments that the ordinance unconstitutionally deprived them of their First Amendment rights to freedom of worship, speech and press, and assembly.

The Court regarded the licensing requirement as an exercise of a government's traditional authority to control traffic. "The question in a particular case," wrote Chief Justice Hughes in his opinion for the Court, "is whether that control is exerted so as not to deny or unwarrantedly abridge the right of assembly and the opportunities for the communication of thought and the discussion of public questions immemorially associated with resort to public places." In this case, said Hughes, Manchester had not abused its authority.

Cox introduced a long line of cases in which the Court elaborated a narrow exception to the ban on prior restraint by allowing permit systems—what has been called "prior licensing." Accordingly, such systems may concern only considerations of "time, place, and manner," and they must not be manipulated to prevent speech or to favor some groups over others.

Opinion of the Court: **Hughes**, Stone, Roberts, Black, Reed, Frankfurter, Douglas, Murphy. *Cox* v. *New Hampshire* was decided on March 31, 1941.

Opinion

CHIEF JUSTICE HUGHES DELIVERED THE OPINION OF THE COURT . . .

Civil liberties, as guaranteed by the Constitution, imply the existence of an organized society maintaining public order without which liberty itself would be lost in the excesses of unrestrained abuses. The authority of a municipality to impose regulations in order to assure the safety and convenience of the people in the use of public highways has never been regarded as inconsistent with civil liberties but rather as one of the means of safeguarding the good order upon which they ultimately depend. The control of travel on the streets of cities is the most familiar illustration of this recognition of social need. Where a restriction of the use of highways in that relation is designed to promote the public convenience in the interest of all, it cannot be disregarded by the attempted exercise of some civil right which in other circumstances would be entitled to protection. One would not be justified in ignoring the familiar red traffic light because he thought it his religious duty to disobey the municipal command or sought by that means to direct public attention to an announcement of his opinions. As regulation of the use of the streets for parades and processions is a traditional exercise of control by local government, the question in a particular case is whether that control is exerted so as not to deny or unwarrantedly abridge the right of assembly and the opportunities for the communication of thought and the discussion of public questions immemorially associated with resort to public places. . . .

In the instant case, we are aided by the opinion of the Supreme Court of the State which construed the statute and defined the limitations of the authority conferred for the granting of licenses for parades and processions. The court observed that if the clause of the Act requiring a license "for all open-air public meetings upon land contiguous to a highway" was invalid, that invalidity did not nullify the Act in its application to the other situations described. Recognizing the importance of the civil liberties invoked by appellants, the court thought it significant that the statute prescribed "no measures for controlling or suppressing the publication on the highways of facts and opinions, either by speech or by writing"; that communication "by the distribution of literature or by the display of placards and signs" was in no respect regulated by the statute; that the regulation with respect to parades and processions was applicable only "to organized formations of persons using the highways"; and that "the defendants separately or collectively in groups not constituting a parade or procession" were "under no contemplation of the act." In this light, the court thought that interference with liberty of speech and writing seemed slight, that the distribution of pamphlets and folders by the groups "traveling in unorganized fashion" would have had as large a circulation, and that "signs carried by members of the groups not in marching formation would have been as conspicuous, as published by them while in parade or procession."

It was with this view of the limited objective of the statute that the state court considered and defined the duty of the licensing authority and the rights of the appellants to a license for their parade, with regard only to considerations of time, place, and manner so as to conserve the public convenience. The obvious advantage of requiring application for a permit was noted as giving the public authorities notice in advance so as to afford opportunity for proper policing. And the court further observed that, in fixing time and place, the license served "to prevent confusion by overlapping parades or processions, to secure convenient use of the streets by other travelers, and to minimize the risk of disorder." But the court held that the licensing board was not vested with arbitrary power or an unfettered discretion; that its discretion must be exercised with "uniformity of method of treatment upon the facts of each application, free from improper or inappropriate considerations and from unfair discrimination"; that a "systematic, consistent and just order of treatment, with reference to the convenience of public use of the highways, is the statutory mandate." The defendants, said the court, "had a right, under the act, to a license to march when, where, and as they did, if after a required investigation it was found that the convenience of the public in the use of the streets would not thereby be unduly disturbed, upon such conditions or changes in time, place, and manner as would avoid disturbance."

If a municipality has authority to control the use of its public streets for parades or processions, as it undoubtedly has, it cannot be denied authority to give consideration, without unfair discrimination, to time, place, and manner in relation to the other proper uses of the streets. We find it impossible to say that the limited authority conferred by the licensing provisions of the statute in question as thus construed by the state court contravened any constitutional right. . . .

Nor is any question of peaceful picketing here involved, as in *Thornbill* v. *Alabama* [1940] and *Carlson* v. *People of California* [1940]. . . . The statute, as the state court said, is not aimed at any restraint of freedom of speech, and there is no basis for an assumption that it would be applied so as to prevent peaceful picketing as described in the cases cited.

The argument as to freedom of worship is also beside the point. No interference with religious worship or the practice of religion in any proper sense is shown, but only the exercise of local control over the use of streets for parades and processions.

The judgment of the Supreme Court of New Hampshire is AFFIRMED.

13

CHAPLINSKY V. NEW HAMPSHIRE
315 U.S. 568 (1942)

While distributing his sect's literature on the streets of Rochester, New Hampshire, Walter Chaplinsky, a Jehovah's Witness, told those within earshot that organized religions are a "racket." A hostile crowd gathered, and the city marshall was summoned. Chaplinsky called him a "damned racketeer" and "a damned Fascist," adding that "the whole government of Rochester are Fascists or agents of Fascists." Chaplinsky was prosecuted under a state law prohibiting offensive and derisive speech or name calling in public. Appealing his conviction on free speech grounds, Chaplinsky lost in the New Hampshire Supreme Court and then in the U.S. Supreme Court.

In *Chaplinsky* a unanimous Court set forth a "two-tier theory" by which certain "well-defined and narrowly limited" classes of speech receive no constitutional protection—"the lewd and the obscene, the profane, the libelous, and the insulting or 'fighting' words—those which by their very utterance inflict injury or tend to incite an immediate breach of the peace." These classes of speech, the Court said, are "no essential part of any exposition of ideas"; any "slight social value . . . that may be derived from them is clearly outweighed by the social interest in order and morality."

Time has weathered the two-tier theory. Libelous publications and even verbal challenges to police officers have been granted constitutional protection. Not since *Chaplinsky*, in fact, has the Court explicitly sustained a conviction for "fighting words" spoken to public officials.

Opinion of the Court: **Murphy**, Roberts, Black, Reed, Frankfurter, Douglas, Stone, Byrnes, Jackson.

Chaplinsky v. *New Hampshire* was decided on March 9, 1942.

Opinion

JUSTICE MURPHY DELIVERED THE OPINION OF THE COURT . . .

Allowing the broadest scope to the language and purpose of the Fourteenth Amendment, it is well understood that the right of free speech is not absolute at all times and under all circumstances. There are certain well-defined and narrowly limited classes of speech, the prevention and punishment of which has never been thought to raise any Constitutional problem. These include the lewd and obscene, the profane, the libelous, and the insulting or "fighting" words—those which by their very utterance inflict injury or tend to incite an immediate breach of the peace. It has been well observed that such utterances are no essential part of any exposition of ideas, and are of such slight social value as a step to truth that any benefit that may be derived from them is clearly outweighed by the social interest in order and morality. . . .

. . . On the authority of its earlier decisions, the state court declared that the statute's purpose was to preserve the public peace, no words being "forbidden except such as have a direct tendency to cause acts of violence by the person to whom, individually, the remark is addressed." It was further said: "The word 'offensive' is not to be defined in terms of what a particular addressee thinks. . . . The test is what men of common intelligence would understand would be words likely to cause an average addressee to fight. . . . The English language has a number of words and expressions which by general consent are 'fighting words' when said without a disarming smile. . . . Such words, as ordinary men know, are likely to cause a fight. So are threatening, profane or obscene revilings. Derisive and annoying words can be taken as coming within purview of the statute as heretofore interpreted only when they have this characteristic of plainly tending to excite the addressee to a breach of the peace. . . . The statute, as construed, does no more than prohibit the face-to-face words plainly likely to cause a breach of the peace by the addressee, words whose speaking constitute a breach of the peace by the speaker—including 'classical fighting words,' words in current use less 'classical' but equally likely to cause violence, and other disorderly words, including profanity, obscenity and threats."

We are unable to say that the limited scope of the statute as thus construed contravenes the constitutional right of free expression. It is a statute narrowly drawn and limited to define and punish specific conduct lying within the domain of state power, the use in a public place of words likely to cause a breach of the peace. . . . This conclusion necessarily disposes of appellant's contention that the statute is so vague and indefinite as to render a conviction thereunder a violation of due process. A statute punishing verbal acts, carefully drawn so as not unduly to impair liberty of expression, is not too vague for a criminal law. . . .

Nor can we say that the application of the statute to the facts disclosed by the record substantially or unreasonably impinges upon the privilege of free speech. Argument is unnecessary to demonstrate that the appellations "damn racketeer" and "damn Fascist" are epithets likely to provoke the average person to retaliation, and thereby cause a breach of the peace.

. . . Our function is fulfilled by a determination that the challenged statute, on its face and as applied, does not contravene the Fourteenth Amendment.

AFFIRMED.

$$14$$

WEST VIRGINIA STATE BOARD
OF EDUCATION V. BARNETTE
319 U.S. 624 (1943)

In *Minersville School District v. Gobitis* (1940), the Supreme Court by a vote of 8 to 1 sustained the power of Pennsylvania to expel from its schools children who on religious grounds—the children were Jehovah's Witnesses—refused to join in a flag-salute ceremony and recite the pledge of allegiance. Two years later the West Virginia State Board of Education adopted a resolution ordering the same compulsory ceremony for its schools. Walter Barnette sued on behalf of his children to block enforcement. Like the plaintiffs in *Gobitis*, Barnette and the other parents who joined his complaint were Jehovah's Witnesses who regarded the flag as an "image" that they must not "bow down to." They argued that the compulsory ceremony denied both religious freedom and freedom of speech. Though federal lower courts typically adhere to Supreme Court decisions, even those they believe were wrongly decided, the federal district court rejected the decision in *Gobitis* and sided with the parents. The Board of Education appealed to the Supreme Court, which this time was of a different mind. By a vote of 6 to 3, the Court overruled *Gobitis* and held against West Virginia.

Gobitis was a free exercise case. In overruling it, the Court placed the greater weight of its argument on the free speech clause. "Here . . . we are dealing with a compulsion of students to declare a belief," wrote Justice Jackson for the Court. "[The state] requires the individual to communicate by word and sign his acceptance of the political ideas" that the state believes the flag symbolizes. As this passage shows, the Court saw *Barnette* as involving not only literal speech (the saying of the pledge of allegiance) but also symbolic speech (the flag salute). The Court took care to observe that "the flag salute is a form of utterance," and it cited its first symbolic-speech case, *Stromberg* v. *California* (1931), in arguing that West Virginia was in violation of the First Amendment.

Barnette is a free speech case—specifically, a case about compelled speech. More than thirty years later, in *Wooley* v. *Maynard* (1977), the Court reiterated its position against compelled speech when it struck down New Hampshire's requirement that its citizens display the motto "Live Free or Die" on their license plates.

Barnette made clear that the Court was willing to subject to greater scrutiny those exercises of state power said to infringe upon certain "fundamental rights," as Jackson called them,

56

chief among them "freedoms of speech and of press, of assembly, and of worship." They may be restricted, he said, "only to prevent grave and immediate danger to interests which the state may lawfully protect."

In dissent, Justice Felix Frankfurter, who wrote for the Court in *Gobitis*, took issue with the notion that some freedoms guaranteed in the Bill of Rights deserve greater protection than others. "The right not to have property taken without just compensation," he wrote, "has . . . the same constitutional dignity as the right to be protected against unreasonable searches and seizures, and the latter has no less claim than freedom of the press or freedom of speech or religious freedom."

Opinion of the Court: **Jackson**, Stone, Rutledge. Concurring opinions: **Black**, Douglas; **Murphy**. Dissenting opinion: **Frankfurter**. Dissenting: Roberts, Reed.

West Virginia State Board of Education v. *Barnette* was decided on June 14, 1943.

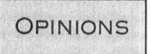

OPINIONS

JUSTICE JACKSON DELIVERED THE OPINION OF THE COURT . . .

Here . . . we are dealing with a compulsion of students to declare a belief. They are not merely made acquainted with the flag salute so that they may be informed as to what it is or even what it means. The issue here is whether this slow and easily neglected route to aroused loyalties constitutionally may be short-cut by substituting a compulsory salute and slogan. . . .

There is no doubt that, in connection with the pledges, the flag salute is a form of utterance. Symbolism is a primitive but effective way of communicating ideas. The use of an emblem or flag to symbolize some system, idea, institution, or personality is a short cut from mind to mind. Causes and nations, political parties, lodges and ecclesiastical groups seek to knit the loyalty of their followings to a flag or banner, a color or design. The State announces rank, function, and authority through crowns and maces, uniforms and black robes; the church speaks through the Cross, the Crucifix, the altar and shrine, and clerical raiment. Symbols of State often convey political ideas just as religious symbols come to convey theological ones. Associated with many of these symbols are appropriate gestures of acceptance or respect: a salute, a bowed or bared head, a bended knee. A person gets from a symbol the meaning he puts into it, and what is one man's comfort and inspiration is another's jest and scorn.

Over a decade ago Chief Justice Hughes led this Court in holding that the display of a red flag as a symbol of opposition by peaceful and legal means to organized government was protected by the free speech guaranties of the Constitution. *Stromberg* v. *California* [1937]. Here it is the State that employs a flag as a symbol of adherence to government as presently organized. It requires the individual to communicate by word and sign his acceptance of the political ideas it thus bespeaks. Objection to this form of communication when coerced is an old one, well known to the framers of the Bill of Rights.

It is also to be noted that the compulsory flag salute and pledge requires affirmation of a belief and an attitude of mind. It is not clear whether the regulation contemplates that pupils forego any contrary convictions of their own and become unwilling converts to the prescribed ceremony or whether it will be acceptable if they simulate assent by words without belief and by a gesture barren of meaning. It is now a commonplace that censorship or suppression of expression of opinion is tolerated by our Constitution only when the expression presents a clear and present danger of action of a kind the State is empowered to prevent and punish. It would seem that involuntary affirmation could be commanded only on even more immediate and urgent grounds than silence. But here the power of compulsion is invoked without any allegation that remaining passive during a flag salute ritual creates a clear and present danger that would justify an effort even to muffle expression. To sustain the compulsory flag salute we are required to say that a Bill of Rights which guards the individual's right to speak his own mind, left it open to public authorities to compel him to utter what is not in his mind.

Whether the First Amendment to the Constitution will permit officials to order observance of ritual of this nature does not depend upon whether as a voluntary exercise we would think it to be good, bad, or merely innocuous. Any credo of nationalism is likely to include what some disapprove or to omit what others think essential, and to give off different overtones as it takes on different accents or interpretations. If official power exists to coerce acceptance of any patriotic creed, what it shall contain cannot be decided by courts, but must be largely discretionary with the ordaining authority, whose power to prescribe would no doubt include power to amend. Hence validity of the asserted power to force an American citizen publicly to profess any statement of belief or to engage in any ceremony of assent to one presents questions of power that must be considered independently of any idea we may have as to the utility of the ceremony in question.

Nor does the issue as we see it turn on one's possession of particular religious views or the sincerity with which they are held. While religion supplies appellees' motive for enduring the discomforts of making the issue in this case, many citizens who do not share these religious views hold such a compulsory rite to infringe constitutional liberty of the individual. It is not necessary to inquire whether non-conformist beliefs will exempt from the duty to salute unless we first find power to make the salute a legal duty.

The *Gobitis* decision, however, assumed, as did the argument in that case and in this, that power exists in the State to impose the flag salute discipline upon school children in general. The Court only examined and rejected a claim based on religious beliefs of immunity from an unquestioned general rule. The question which underlies the flag salute controversy is whether such a ceremony so touching matters of opinion and political attitude may be imposed upon the individual by official authority under powers committed to any political organization under our Constitution. . . .

The *Gobitis* opinion reasoned that this is a field "where courts possess no marked and certainly no controlling competence," that it is committed to the legislatures as well as the courts to guard cherished liberties, and that it is constitutionally appropriate to "fight out the wise use of legislative authority in the forum of public opinion and before legislative assemblies rather than to transfer such a contest to the judicial arena," since all the "effective means of inducing political changes are left free."

The very purpose of a Bill of Rights was to withdraw certain subjects from the vicissitudes of political controversy, to place them beyond the reach of majorities and officials, and to establish them as legal principles to be applied by the courts. One's right to life, liberty, and property, to free speech, a free press, freedom of worship and assembly, and other fundamental rights may not be submitted to vote; they depend on the outcome of no elections. In weighing arguments of the parties it is important to distinguish between the due process clause of the Fourteenth Amendment as an instrument for transmitting the principles of the First Amendment and those cases in which it is applied for its own sake. The test of legislation which collides with the Fourteenth Amendment, because it also collides with the principles of the First, is much more definite than the test when only the Fourteenth is involved. Much of the vagueness of the due process clause disappears when the specific prohibitions of the First become its standard. The right of a State to regulate, for example, a public utility may well include, so far as the due process test is concerned, power to impose all of the restrictions which a legislature may have a "rational basis" for adopting. But freedoms of speech and of press, of assembly, and of worship may not be infringed on such slender grounds. They are susceptible of restriction only to prevent grave and immediate danger to interests which the state may lawfully protect. It is important to note that while it is the Fourteenth Amendment which bears directly upon the State it is the more specific limiting principles of the First Amendment that finally govern this case.

Nor does our duty to apply the Bill of Rights to assertions of official authority depend upon our possession of marked competence in the field where the invasion of rights occurs. True, the task of translating the majestic generalities of the Bill of Rights, conceived as part of the pattern of liberal government in the eighteenth century, into concrete restraints on officials dealing with the problems of the twentieth century, is one to disturb self-confidence. These principles grew in soil which also produced a philosophy that the individual was the center of society, that his liberty was attainable through mere absence of governmental restraints, and that government should be entrusted with few controls and only the mildest supervision over men's affairs. We must transplant these rights to a soil in which the laissez-faire concept or principle of non-interference has withered at least as to economic affairs, and social advancements are increasingly sought through closer integration of society and through expanded and strengthened governmental controls. These changed conditions often deprive precedents of reliability and cast us more than we would choose upon our own judgment. But we act in these matters not by authority of our competence but by force of our commissions. We cannot, because of modest estimates of our competence in such specialties as public education, withhold the judgment that history authenticates as the function of this Court when liberty is infringed.

. . . [T]he *Gobitis* opinion . . . reasons that "National unity is the basis of national security," that the authorities have "the right to select appropriate means for its attainment," and hence reaches the conclusion that such compulsory measures toward "national unity" are constitutional. Upon the verity of this assumption depends our answer in this case.

National unity as an end which officials may foster by persuasion and example is not in question. The problem is whether under our Constitution compulsion as here employed is a permissible means for its achievement.

Struggles to coerce uniformity of sentiment in support of some end thought essential to their time and country have been waged by many good as well as by evil men. Nationalism is a relatively recent phenomenon, but at other times and places the ends have been racial or territorial security, support of a dynasty or regime, and particular plans for saving souls. As first and moderate methods to attain unity have failed, those bent on its accomplishment must resort to an ever-increasing severity. As governmental pressure toward unity becomes greater, so strife becomes more bitter as to whose unity it shall be. Probably no deeper division of our people could proceed from any provocation than from finding it necessary to choose what doctrine and whose program public educational officials shall compel youth to unite in embracing. Ultimate futility of such attempts to compel coherence is the lesson of every such effort from the Roman drive to stamp out Christianity as a disturber of its pagan unity, the Inquisition as a means to religious and dynastic unity, the Siberian exiles as a means to Russian unity, down to the fast failing efforts of our present totalitarian enemies. Those who begin coercive elimination of dissent soon find themselves exterminating dissenters. Compulsory unification of opinion achieves only the unanimity of the graveyard.

It seems trite but necessary to say that the First Amendment to our Constitution was designed to avoid these ends by avoiding these beginnings. There is no mysticism in the American concept of the State or of the nature or origin of its authority. We set up government by consent of the governed, and the Bill of Rights denies those in power any legal opportunity to coerce that consent. Authority here is to be controlled by public opinion, not public opinion by authority.

The case is made difficult not because the principles of its decision are obscure but because the flag involved is our own. Nevertheless, we apply the limitations of the Constitution with no fear that freedom to be intellectually and spiritually diverse or even contrary will disintegrate the social organization. To believe that patriotism will not flourish if patriotic ceremonies are voluntary and spontaneous instead of a compulsory routine is to make an unflattering estimate of the appeal of our institutions to free minds. We can have intellectual individualism and the rich cultural diversities that we owe to exceptional minds only at the price of occasional eccentricity and abnormal attitudes. When they are so harmless to others or to the State as those we deal with here, the price is not too great. But freedom to differ is not limited to things that do not matter much. That would be a mere shadow of freedom. The test of its substance is the right to differ as to things that touch the heart of the existing order.

If there is any fixed star in our constitutional constellation, it is that no official, high or petty, can prescribe what shall be orthodox in politics, nationalism, religion, or other matters of opinion or force citizens to confess by word or act their faith therein. If there are any circumstances which permit an exception, they do not now occur to us.

We think the action of the local authorities in compelling the flag salute and pledge transcends constitutional limitations on their power and invades the sphere of intellect and spirit which it is the purpose of the First Amendment to our Constitution to reserve from all official control.

The decision of this Court in *Minersville School District* v. *Gobitis* . . . [is] overruled, and the judgment enjoining enforcement of the West Virginia Regulation is
AFFIRMED.

JUSTICE FRANKFURTER, DISSENTING.

One who belongs to the most vilified and persecuted minority in history is not likely to be insensible to the freedoms guaranteed by our Constitution. Were my purely personal attitude relevant I should whole-heartedly associate myself with the general libertarian views in the Court's opinion, representing as they do the thought and action of a lifetime. But as judges we are neither Jew nor Gentile, neither Catholic nor agnostic. We owe equal attachment to the Constitution and are equally bound by our judicial obligations whether we derive our citizenship from the earliest or the latest immigrants to these shores. As a member of this Court

I am not justified in writing my private notions of policy into the Constitution, no matter how deeply I may cherish them or how mischievous I may deem their disregard. The duty of a judge who must decide which of two claims before the Court shall prevail, that of a State to enact and enforce laws within its general competence or that of an individual to refuse obedience because of the demands of his conscience, is not that of the ordinary person. It can never be emphasized too much that one's own opinion about the wisdom or evil of a law should be excluded altogether when one is doing one's duty on the bench. The only opinion of our own even looking in that direction that is material is our opinion whether legislators could in reason have enacted such a law. In the light of all the circumstances, including the history of this question in this Court, it would require more daring than I possess to deny that reasonable legislators could have taken the action which is before us for review. Most unwillingly, therefore, I must differ from my brethren with regard to legislation like this. I cannot bring my mind to believe that the "liberty" secured by the Due Process Clause gives this Court authority to deny to the State of West Virginia the attainment of that which we all recognize as a legitimate legislative end, namely, the promotion of good citizenship, by employment of the means here chosen. . . .

The admonition that judicial self-restraint alone limits arbitrary exercise of our authority is relevant every time we are asked to nullify legislation. The Constitution does not give us greater veto power when dealing with one phase of "liberty" than with another, or when dealing with grade school regulations than with college regulations that offend conscience. . . . In neither situation is our function comparable to that of a legislature or are we free to act as though we were a superlegislature. Judicial self-restraint is equally necessary whenever an exercise of political or legislative power is challenged. There is no warrant in the constitutional basis of this Court's authority for attributing different roles to it depending upon the nature of the challenge to the legislation. Our power does not vary according to the particular provision of the Bill of Rights which is invoked. The right not to have property taken without just compensation has, so far as the scope of judicial power is concerned, the same constitutional dignity as the right to be protected against unreasonable searches and seizures, and the latter has no less claim than freedom of the press or freedom of speech or religious freedom. In no instance is this Court the primary protector of the particular liberty that is invoked. This Court has recognized, what hardly could be denied, that all the provisions of the first ten Amendments are "specific" prohibitions. *United States* v. *Carolene Products Co.* [1937]. But each specific Amendment, in so far as embraced within the Fourteenth Amendment, must be equally respected, and the function of this Court does not differ in passing on the constitutionality of legislation challenged under different Amendments. . . .

We are told that a flag salute is a doubtful substitute for adequate understanding of our institutions. The states that require such a school exercise do not have to justify it as the only means for promoting good citizenship in children, but merely as one of diverse means for accomplishing a worthy end. We may deem it a foolish measure, but the point is that this Court is not the organ of government to resolve doubts as to whether it will fulfill its purpose. Only if there be no doubt that any reasonable mind could entertain can we deny to the states the right to resolve doubts their way and not ours.

That which to the majority may seem essential for the welfare of the state may offend the consciences of a minority. But, so long as no inroads are made upon the actual exercise of religion by the minority, to deny the political power of the majority to enact laws concerned with civil matters, simply because they may offend the consciences of a minority, really means that the consciences of a minority are more sacred and more enshrined in the Constitution than the consciences of a majority.

We are told that symbolism is a dramatic but primitive way of communicating ideas. Symbolism is inescapable. Even the most sophisticated live by symbols. But it is not for this Court to make psychological judgments as to the effectiveness of a particular symbol in inculcating concededly indispensable feelings, particularly if the state happens to see fit to utilize the symbol that represents our heritage and our hopes. And surely only flippancy could be responsible for the suggestion that constitutional validity of a requirement to salute our flag implies equal validity of a requirement to salute a dictator. The significance of a symbol lies in what it represents. To reject the swastika does not imply rejection of the Cross. And so it bears repetition to say that it mocks reason and denies our whole history to find in the allowance of a requirement to salute our flag on fitting occasions the seeds of sanction for obeisance to a leader. To deny the power to employ educational symbols is to say that the state's educational system may not stimulate the imagination because this may lead to unwise stimulation.

The right of West Virginia to utilize the flag salute as part of its educational process is denied because, so it is argued, it cannot be justified as a means of meeting a "clear and present danger" to national unity. In passing it deserves to be noted that the four cases which unanimously sustained the power of states to utilize such an educational measure arose and were all decided before the present World War. But to measure the state's power to make such regulations as are here resisted by the imminence of national danger is wholly to misconceive the origin and purpose of the concept of "clear and present danger." To apply such a test is for the Court to assume, however unwittingly, a legislative responsibility that does not belong to it. To talk about "clear and present danger" as the touchstone of allowable educational policy by the states whenever school curricula may impinge upon the boundaries of individual conscience, is to take a felicitous phrase out of the context of the particular situation where it arose and for which it was adapted. Justice Holmes used the phrase "clear and present danger" in a case involving mere speech as a means by which alone to accomplish sedition in time of war. By that phrase he meant merely to indicate that, in view of the protection given to utterance by the First Amendment, in order that mere utterance may not be proscribed, "the words used are used in such circumstances and are of such a nature as to create a clear and present danger that they will bring about the substantive evils that Congress has a right to prevent." *Schenck* v. *United States* [1919]. The "substantive evils" about which he was speaking were inducement of insubordination in the military and naval forces of the United States and obstruction of enlistment while the country was at war. He was not enunciating a formal rule that there can be no restriction upon speech and, still less, no compulsion where conscience balks, unless imminent danger would thereby be wrought "to our institutions or our government."

The flag salute exercise has no kinship whatever to the oath tests so odious in history. For the oath test was one of the instruments for suppressing heretical beliefs. Saluting the flag suppresses no belief nor curbs it. Children and their parents may believe what they please, avow their belief, and practice it. It is not even remotely suggested that the requirement for saluting the flag involves the slightest restriction against the fullest opportunity on the part both of the children and of their parents to disavow as publicly as they choose to do so the meaning that others attach to the gesture of salute. All channels of affirmative free expression are open to both children and parents. Had we before us any act of the state putting the slightest curbs upon such free expression, I should not lag behind any member of this Court in striking down such an invasion of the right to freedom of thought and freedom of speech protected by the Constitution. . . .

. . . [P]atriotism cannot be enforced by the flag salute. But neither can the liberal spirit be enforced by judicial invalidation of illiberal legislation. Our constant preoccupation with the constitutionality of legislation rather than with its wisdom tends to preoccupation of the American mind with a false value. The tendency of focusing attention on constitutionality is to make constitutionality synonymous with wisdom, to regard a law as all right if it is constitutional. Such an attitude is a great enemy of liberalism. Particularly in legislation affecting freedom of thought and freedom of speech, much which should offend a free-spirited society is constitutional. Reliance for the most precious interests of civilization, therefore, must be found outside of their vindication in courts of law. Only a persistent positive translation of the faith of a free society into the convictions and habits and actions of a community is the ultimate reliance against unabated temptations to fetter the human spirit.

RESPONSES

FROM *THE CHRISTIAN CENTURY*, JUNE 23, 1943, "COURT UPHOLDS FREEDOM OF CONSCIENCE"

Appropriately, the Supreme Court chose Flag Day to hand down its decision enjoining the West Virginia board of education from requiring a flag salute of all pupils in the public schools of that state. . . . [T]he court did far more than to set right a legal blunder [*Minersville School District* v. *Gobitis*] which had far reaching consequences for the freedom of conscience of Americans. In the decision, written by Justice Jackson, it incorporated at least one section which should become part of the "American scriptures," to be memorized and taken to heart by every patriot. "If there is any fixed star in our constitutional constellation," said the court, "it is that no official, high or petty, can prescribe what shall be orthodox in politics, nationalism, religion, or other matters of opinion or force citizens to confess by word or act their faith therein. If there are any circumstances which permit an exception, they do not now occur to us."

By this flag salute decision the court has cleared up the whole range of cases involving freedom of conscience and freedom for the propagation of religious beliefs, all of them an outgrowth of the activities of Jehovah's Witnesses. The constitutional guarantees of religious liberty have been reaffirmed; the encroachments of the state in the realm of conscience have received a salutary check. But the sobering experience of the past three years should warn the churches that only their eternal vigilance will insure that the rights thus vindicated will be maintained.

FROM THE *EVENING STAR*, WASHINGTON, D.C., JUNE 16, 1943, "FLAG-SALUTE DECISION"

It is not difficult to agree with the thought of the majority that the tribute to the flag becomes an empty and meaningless gesture when forced on an unwilling participant as the price of public education. The religious scruples of a sect which views the ceremony as a violation of the doctrinal proscription against the worship of "images" also are due consideration. But, granting these things, there will be grave doubts as to the wisdom of the court's action in overriding the judgment of the State Legislature to hold that compliance with a reasonable regulation, applied almost universally to promote good citizenship, depends on nothing more stable than the whim of the individual. By that logic the dissidents become the rule-makers and no regulation is safe.

FROM THE *NEW YORK TIMES*, JUNE 19, 1943, "THE COURT ON THE FLAG SALUTE"

The layman may well be confused by the able reasoning on both sides of this case. If he has seen the [Jehovah's] Witnesses in action he may also be confused by an emotion of dislike. Yet the simple fact stands that a school child compelled to salute the flag, when he has been taught the flag is an "image" which the Bible forbids him to worship, is in effect made to say what he does not believe. It seems to be true, also, that real loyalty "to the flag of the United States of America and to the Republic for which it stands" is expressed by a willing salute, but neither expressed nor created by a reluctant one. The voluntary principle is the essence of civil rights as of common sense.

FROM *THE NEW REPUBLIC*, JUNE 19, 1943, "THE FLAG SALUTE CASE"

The opinion of the Court in the *Barnette* case might have been stronger had it not been so preponderantly devoted to answering the arguments which Justice Frankfurter made earlier for the Court in sustaining the flag-salute requirement in the *Gobitis* case. This destructive polemic was not a difficult task, and it was done with entire adequacy by Justice Jackson. One of the important points in his opinion for the Court is that the liberty here given constitutional sanction is not confined to cases where the objections to compulsion to participate in ceremonials are based on religious grounds. The freedom of silence and the freedom of abstention extend to those who have other than religious objections to compulsion of public avowals.

15

THOMAS V. COLLINS
323 U.S. 516 (1945)

In September 1943 R. J. Thomas, the president of the United Automobile Workers, CIO, was scheduled to address a labor rally near an oil refinery in Bay Town, Texas. Six hours before he was to speak, Thomas was served with a court order restraining him from soliciting workers to become union members until he had obtained an organizer's card, as required by state law. Having consulted with his attorneys and concluded that the order abridged his rights of freedom of speech and assembly, Thomas went ahead with his speech and indeed solicited union memberships. Arrested and charged with violating the court order, he was held in contempt, sentenced to three days in jail, and fined $100. Thomas sought relief in the Texas Supreme Court, which held that the law was a valid exercise of the state's police power because it did not impose a "previous general restraint upon the right of free speech." The U.S. Supreme Court reversed by a vote of 5 to 4.

In *Thomas* the Court offered its clearest articulation of what has been called the "preferred position" doctrine. In development since *Abrams* v. *United States* (1919), the doctrine maintained that First Amendment liberties have a "preferred place," as the Court put it in *Thomas*, meaning they are so fundamental to a free society that they may not be restricted as other liberties may, simply by the demonstration of a "rational connection between the remedy provided and the evil to be curbed." Instead, restrictions of preferred freedoms must be "justified by clear public interest, threatened not doubtfully or remotely, but by clear and present danger"—danger that is "actual or impending."

The preferred-position doctrine was soon absorbed into other concepts that also demanded greater judicial protection for First Amendment (as well as some other) constitutional liberties.

Opinion of the Court: **Rutledge**, Black, Douglas, Murphy, Jackson. Concurring opinions: **Douglas**, Black, Murphy; **Jackson**. Dissenting opinion: **Roberts**, Stone, Reed, Frankfurter.

Thomas v. *Collins* was decided on January 8, 1945.

OPINIONS

JUSTICE RUTLEDGE DELIVERED THE OPINION OF THE COURT . . .

The case confronts us again with the duty our system places on this Court to say where the individual's freedom ends and the State's power begins. Choice on that border, now as always delicate, is perhaps more so where the usual presumption supporting legislation is balanced by the preferred place given in our scheme to the great, the indispensable democratic freedoms secured by the First Amendment. . . . That priority gives these liberties a sanctity and a sanction not permitting dubious intrusions. And it is the character of the right, not of the limitation, which determines what standard governs the choice. Compare *United States* v. *Carolene Products Co.* [1937].

For these reasons any attempt to restrict those liberties must be justified by clear public interest, threatened not doubtfully or remotely, but by clear and present danger. The rational connection between the remedy provided and the evil to be curbed, which in other contexts might support legislation against attack on due process grounds, will not suffice. These rights rest on firmer foundation. Accordingly, whatever occasion would restrain orderly discussion and persuasion, at appropriate time and place, must have clear support in public danger, actual or impending. Only the gravest abuses, endangering paramount interests, give occasion for permissible limitation. It is therefore in our tradition to allow the widest room for discussion, the narrowest range for its restriction, particularly when this right is exercised in conjunction with peaceable assembly. It was not by accident or coincidence that the rights to freedom in speech and press were coupled in a single guaranty with the rights of the people peaceably to assemble and to petition for redress of grievances. All these, though not identical, are inseparable. They are cognate rights, cf. *De Jonge* v. *Oregon* [1937], and therefore are united in the First Article's assurance. . . .

The idea is not sound therefore that the First Amendment's safeguards are wholly inapplicable to business or economic activity. And it does not resolve where the line shall be drawn in a particular case merely to urge, as Texas does, that an organization for which the rights of free speech and free assembly are claimed is one "engaged in business activities" or that the individual who leads it in exercising these rights receives compensation for doing so. Nor, on the other hand, is the answer given, whether what is done is an exercise of those rights and the restriction a forbidden impairment, by ignoring the organization's economic function, because those interests of workingmen are involved or because they have the general liberties of the citizen, as appellant would do.

These comparisons are at once too simple, too general, and too inaccurate to be determinative. Where the line shall be placed in a particular application rests, not on such generalities, but on the concrete clash of particular interests and the community's relative evaluation both of them and of how the one will be affected by the specific restriction, the other by its absence. That judgment in the first instance is for the legislative body. But in our system where the line can constitutionally be placed presents a question this Court cannot escape answering independently, whatever the legislative judgment, in the light of our constitutional tradition. . . . And the answer, under that tradition, can be affirmative, to support an intrusion upon this domain, only if grave and impending public danger requires this.

That the State has power to regulate labor unions with a view to protecting the public interest is, as the Texas court said, hardly to be doubted. They cannot claim special immunity from regulation. Such regulation however, whether aimed at fraud or other abuses, must not trespass upon the domain set apart for free speech and free assembly. . . . The right thus to discuss, and inform people concerning, the advantages and disadvantages of unions and joining them is protected not only as part of free speech, but as part of free assembly. . . . The Texas court . . . did not give sufficient weight to this consideration, more particularly by its failure to take account of the blanketing effect of the prohibition's present application upon public discussion and also of the bearing of the clear and present danger test in these circumstances.

. . . The present application does not involve the solicitation of funds or property. Neither Section 5 [of the Texas law in question] nor the restraining order purports to prohibit or regulate solicitation of funds, receipt of money, its management, distribution, or any other financial matter. Other sections of the Act deal with such things. And on the record Thomas neither asked nor accepted funds or property for the union at the time of his address or while he was in Texas. Neither did he "take applications" for membership, though he offered to do so "if it was necessary"; or ask anyone to join a union at any other time than the occasion of the Pelly mass meeting and in the course of his address.

Thomas went to Texas for one purpose and one only—to make the speech in question. Its whole object was publicly to proclaim the advantages of workers' organization and to persuade workmen to join Local No. 1002 as part of a campaign for members. These also were the sole objects of the meeting. The campaign, and the meeting, were incidents of an impending election for collective bargaining agent, previously ordered by national authority pursuant to the guaranties of national law. Those guaranties include the workers' right to organize freely for collective bargaining. And this comprehends whatever may be appropriate and lawful to accomplish and maintain such organization. It included, in this case, the right to designate Local No. 1002 or any other union or agency as the employees' representative. It included their right fully and freely to discuss and be informed concerning this choice, privately or in public assembly. Necessarily correlative was the right of the union, its members and officials, whether residents or nonresidents of Texas and, if the latter, whether there for a single occasion or sojourning longer, to discuss with and inform the employees concerning matters involved in their choice. These rights of assembly and discussion are protected by the First Amendment. Whatever would restrict them, without sufficient occasion, would infringe its safeguards. The occasion was clearly protected. The speech was an essential part of the occasion, unless all meaning and purpose were to be taken from it. And the invitations, both general and particular, were parts of the speech, inseparable incidents of the occasion and of all that was said or done.

That there was restriction upon Thomas' right to speak and the rights of the workers to hear what he had to say, there can be no doubt. The threat of the restraining order, backed by the power of contempt, and of arrest for crime, hung over every word. A speaker in such circumstances could avoid the words "solicit," "invite," "join." It would be impossible to avoid the idea. The statute requires no specific formula. It is not contended that only the use of the word "solicit" would violate the prohibition. Without such a limitation, the statute forbids any language which conveys, or reasonably could be found to convey, the meaning of invitation. That Thomas chose to meet the issue squarely, not to hide in ambiguous phrasing, does not counteract this fact. General words create different and often particular impressions on different minds. No speaker, however careful, can convey exactly his meaning, or the same meaning, to the different members of an audience. How one might "laud unionism," as the State and the State Supreme Court concede Thomas was free to do, yet in these circumstances not imply an invitation, is hard to conceive. This is the nub of the case, which the State fails to meet because it cannot do so. Workingmen do not lack capacity for making rational connections. They would understand, or some would, that the president of U.A.W. and vice president of C.I.O., addressing an organization meeting, was not urging merely a philosophic attachment to abstract principles of unionism, disconnected from the business immediately at hand. The feat would be incredible for a national leader, addressing such a meeting, lauding unions and their principles, urging adherence to union philosophy, not also and thereby to suggest attachment to the union by becoming a member.

Furthermore, whether words intended and designed to fall short of invitation would miss that mark is a question both of intent and of effect. No speaker, in such circumstances, safely could assume that anything he might say upon the general subject would not be understood by some as an invitation. In short, the supposedly clear-cut distinction between discussion, laudation, general advocacy, and solicitation puts the speaker in these circumstances wholly at the mercy of the varied understanding of his hearers and consequently of whatever inference may be drawn as to his intent and meaning.

Such a distinction offers no security for free discussion. In these conditions it blankets with uncertainty whatever may be said. It compels the speaker to hedge and trim. He must take care in every word to create no impression that he means, in advocating unionism's most central principle, namely, that workingmen should unite for collective bargaining, to urge those present to do so. The vice is not merely that invitation, in the circumstances shown here, is speech. It is also that its prohibition forbids or restrains discussion which is not or may not be invitation. The sharp line cannot be drawn surely or securely. The effort to observe it could not be free speech, free press, or free assembly, in any sense of free advocacy of principle or cause. The restriction's effect, as applied, in a very practical sense was to prohibit Thomas not only to solicit members and memberships, but also to speak in advocacy of the cause of trade unionism in Texas, without having first procured the [organizer's] card. . . .

The assembly was entirely peaceable, and had no other than a wholly lawful purpose. The statements forbidden were not in themselves unlawful, had no tendency to incite to unlawful action, involved no element of clear and present, grave and immediate danger to the public welfare. Moreover, the State has shown no justification for placing restrictions on the use of the word "solicit." We have here nothing comparable to the case where use of the word "fire" in a crowded theater creates a clear and present danger which the State may undertake to avoid or against which it may protect. *Schenck* v. *United States* [1919]. We cannot say that "solicit" in this setting is such a dangerous word. So far as free speech alone is concerned, there can be no ban or restriction or burden placed on the use of such a word except on showing of exceptional circumstances where the public safety, morality, or health is involved or some other substantial interest of the community is at stake.

If therefore use of the word or language equivalent in meaning was illegal here, it was so only because the statute and the order forbade the particular speaker to utter it. When legislation or its application can confine labor leaders on such occasions to innocuous and abstract discussion of the virtues of trade unions and so becloud even this with doubt, uncertainty and the risk of penalty, freedom of speech for them will be at an end. A restriction so destructive of the right of public discussion, without greater or more imminent danger to the public interest than existed in this case, is incompatible with the freedoms secured by the First Amendment. . . .

Apart from its "business practice" theory, the State contends that Section 5 is not inconsistent with freedom of speech and assembly, since this is merely a previous identification requirement which, according to the State court's decision, gives the Secretary of State only "ministerial, not discretionary" authority. . . .

As a matter of principle a requirement of registration in order to make a public speech would seem generally incompatible with an exercise of the rights of free speech and free assembly. Lawful public assemblies, involving no element of grave and immediate danger to an interest the state is entitled to protect, are not instruments of harm which require previous identification of the speakers. And the right either of workmen or of unions under these conditions to assemble and discuss their own affairs is as fully protected by the Constitution as the right of businessmen, farmers, educators, political party members, or others to assemble and discuss their affairs and to enlist the support of others.

We think the controlling principle is stated in *DeJonge* v. *Oregon* [1937]. In that case this Court held that "consistently with the Federal Constitution, peaceable assembly for lawful discussion cannot be made a crime." . . .

If the exercise of the rights of free speech and free assembly cannot be made a crime, we do not think this can be accomplished by the device of requiring previous registration as a condition for exercising them and making such a condition the foundation for restraining in advance their exercise and for imposing a penalty for violating such a restraining order. So long as no more is involved than exercise of the rights of free speech and free assembly, it is immune to such a restriction. If one who solicits support for the cause of labor may be required to register as a condition to the exercise of his right to make a public speech, so may he who seeks to rally support for any social, business, religious, or political cause. We think a requirement that one must register before he undertakes to make a public speech to enlist support for a lawful movement is quite incompatible with the requirements of the First Amendment.

Once the speaker goes further, however, and engages in conduct which amounts to more than the right of free discussion comprehends, as when he undertakes the collection of funds or securing subscriptions, he enters a realm where a reasonable registration or identification requirement may be imposed. In that context such solicitation would be quite different from the solicitation involved here. It would be free speech plus conduct. . . .

The judgment is
REVERSED.

JUSTICE JACKSON, CONCURRING.

As frequently is the case, this controversy is determined as soon as it is decided which of two well-established, but at times overlapping, constitutional principles will be applied to it. The State of Texas stands on its well-settled right reasonably to regulate the pursuit of a vocation, including—we may assume—the occupation of labor organizer. Thomas, on the other hand, stands on the equally clear proposition that Texas may not interfere with the right of any person peaceably and freely to address a lawful assemblage of workmen intent on considering labor grievances. . . .

Though the one may shade into the other, a rough distinction always exists. . . . A state may forbid one without its license to practice law as a vocation, but I think it could not stop an unlicensed person from making a speech about the rights of man or the rights of labor. . . .

This wider range of power over pursuit of a calling than over speech-making is due to the different effects which the two have on interests which the state is empowered to protect. The modern state owes and attempts to perform a duty to protect the public from those who seek for one purpose or another to obtain its money. When one does so through the practice of a calling, the state may have an interest in shielding the public against the untrustworthy, the incompetent, or the irresponsible, or against unauthorized representation of agency. A usual method of performing this function is through a licensing system.

But it cannot be the duty, because it is not the right, of the state to protect the public against false doctrine. The very purpose of the First Amendment is to foreclose public authority from assuming a guardianship of the public mind through regulating the press, speech, and religion. In this field every person must be his own watchman for truth, because the forefathers did not trust any government to separate the true from the false for us. *West Virginia State Board of Education* v. *Barnette* [1943]. Nor would I. Very many are the interests which the state may protect against the practice of an occupation, very few are those it may assume to protect against the practice of propagandizing by speech or press. These are thereby left great range of freedom.

This liberty was not protected because the forefathers expected its use would always be agreeable to those in authority or that its exercise always would be wise, temperate, or useful to society. As I read their intentions, this liberty was protected because they knew of no other way by which free men could conduct representative democracy.

The necessity for choosing collective bargaining representatives brings the same nature of problem to groups of organizing workmen that our representative democratic processes bring to the nation. Their smaller society, too, must choose between rival leaders and competing policies. This should not be an underground process. The union of which Thomas is the head was one of the choices offered to these workers, and to me it was in the best American tradition that they hired a hall and advertised a meeting, and that Thomas went there and publicly faced his labor constituents. How better could these men learn what they might be getting into? By his public appearance and speech he would disclose himself as a temperate man or a violent one, a reasonable leader that well-disposed workmen could follow or an irresponsible one from whom they might expect disappointment, an earnest and understanding leader or a self-seeker. If free speech anywhere serves a useful social purpose, to be jealously guarded, I should think it would be in such a relationship.

But it is said that Thomas urged and invited one and all to join his union, and so he did. This, it is said, makes the speech something else than a speech; it has been found by the Texas courts to be a "solicitation" and therefore its immunity from state regulation is held to be lost. It is not often in this country that we now meet with direct and candid efforts to stop speaking or publication as such. Modern inroads on these rights come from associating the speaking with some other factor which the state may regulate so as to bring the whole within official control. Here, speech admittedly otherwise beyond the reach of the states is attempted to be brought within its licensing system by associating it with "solicitation." Speech of employers otherwise beyond reach of the Federal Government is brought within the Labor Board's power to suppress by associating it with "coercion" or "domination." Speech of political malcontents is sought to be reached by associating it with some variety of "sedition." Whether in a particular case the association or characterization is a proven and valid one often is difficult to resolve. If this Court may not or does not in proper cases inquire whether speech or publication is properly condemned by association, its claim to guardianship of free speech and press is but a hollow one.

Free speech on both sides and for every faction on any side of the labor relation is to me a constitutional and useful right. Labor is free to turn its publicity on any labor oppression, substandard wages, employer unfairness, or objectionable working conditions. The employer, too, should be free to answer, and to turn publicity on the records of the leaders or the unions which seek the confidence of his men. And if the employees or organizers associate violence or other offense against the laws with labor's free speech, or if the employer's speech is associated with discriminatory discharges or intimidation, the constitutional remedy would be to stop the evil, but permit the speech, if the two are separable; and only rarely and when they are inseparable to stop or punish speech or publication. . . .

I concur in the opinion of Justice Rutledge that this case falls in the category of a public speech, rather than that of practicing a vocation as solicitor. Texas did not wait to see what Thomas would say or do. I cannot escape the impression that the injunction sought before he had reached the state was an effort to forestall him from speaking at all and that the contempt is based in part at least on the fact that he did make a public labor speech.

I concur in reversing the judgment.

JUSTICE ROBERTS, DISSENTING . . .

The right to express thoughts freely and to disseminate ideas fully is secured by the Constitution as basic to the conception of our government. A long series of cases has applied these fundamental rights in a great variety of circumstances. Not until today, however, has it been questioned that there was any clash between this right to think one's thoughts and to express them and the right of people to be protected in their dealings with those who hold themselves out in some professional capacity by requiring registration of those who profess to pursue such callings. . . . The question before us is as to the power of Texas to call for such registration within limits precisely defined by the Supreme Court of that State in sustaining the statute now challenged. . . .

Stripped to its bare bones, [the appellant's] argument is that labor organizations are beneficial and lawful; that solicitation of members by and for them is a necessary incident of their progress; that freedom to solicit for them is a liberty of speech protected against state action by the Fourteenth Amendment and the National Labor Relations Act, and hence Texas cannot require a paid solicitor to identify himself. I think this is the issue and the only issue presented to the courts below and decided by them, and the only one raised here. The opinion of the court imports into the case elements on which counsel for appellant did not rely; elements which in fact counsel strove to eliminate in order to come at the fundamental challenge to any requirement of identification of a labor organizer. The position taken in the court's opinion that in some way the statute interferes with the right to address a meeting, to speak in favor of a labor union, to persuade one's fellows to join a union, or that at least its application in this case does, or may, accomplish that end is, in my judgment, without support in the record. . . .

Since its requirements are not obviously burdensome, we cannot void the statute as an unnecessary or excessive exercise of the State's police power on any a priori reasoning. The State Supreme Court has found that conditions exist in Texas which justify and require such identification of paid organizers as the law prescribes. There is not a word of evidence in the record to contradict these conclusions. In the absence of a showing against the need for the statute this court ought not incontinently to reject the State's considered views of policy.

The judgment of the court below that the power exists reasonably to regulate solicitation, and that the exercise of the power by the Act in question is not unnecessarily burdensome, is not to be rejected on abstract grounds. . . .

We are asked then, on this record, to hold, without evidence to support such a conclusion, and as a matter of judicial notice, that Texas, has no bona fide interest to warrant her law makers in requiring that one who engages, for pay, in the business of soliciting persons to join unions shall identify himself as such. That is all the law requires. We should face a very different question if the statute attempted to define the necessary qualifications of an organizer; purported to regulate what organizers might say; limited their movements or activities; essayed to regulate time, place, or purpose of meetings; or restricted speakers in the expression of views. But it does none of these things.

. . . The solicitation at which the Texas Act is aimed . . . involves the assumption of business and financial liability by him who is persuaded to join a union. The transaction is in essence a business one. Labor unions are business associations; their object is generally business dealings and relationships as is manifest from the financial statements of some of the national unions. Men are persuaded to join them for business reasons, as employers are persuaded to join trade associations for like reasons. Other paid organizers, whether for business or for charity, could be required to identify themselves. There is no reason why labor organizers should not do likewise. I think that if anyone pursues solicitation as a business for profit, of members for any organization, religious, secular, or business, his calling does not bar the state from requiring him to identify himself as what he is, a paid solicitor.

We may deem the statutory provision under review unnecessary or unwise, but it is not our function as judges to read our views of policy into a Constitutional guarantee, in order to overthrow a state policy we do not personally approve, by denominating that policy a violation of the liberty of speech. The judgment should be affirmed.

16

UNITED PUBLIC WORKERS V. MITCHELL
330 U.S. 75 (1947)

Section 9 of the Hatch Act, enacted in 1940 and enforced by the Civil Service Commission, made it illegal for executive branch employees to "take any active part in political management or in political campaigns." Challenges to the law asked whether the government, which may not forbid other citizens from engaging in these activities, may do so in the case of its own employees. Declining to consider the claims of executive employees (represented in part by the United Public Workers of America) who had not yet engaged in the prohibited activities, the Supreme Court reviewed the case of the one employee among the plaintiffs, George Poole, a mechanical employee of the Mint, who had done so. By a vote of 4 to 3, the Court denied his First Amendment challenge and sided with the government.

This case revealed a court divided in its First Amendment jurisprudence. The opinion of the Court, by Justice Reed, recognized that the rights at issue were "fundamental" but said they were not "absolutes," and it used a balancing test to weigh these non-absolute rights against a law designed "to protect a democratic society against the supposed evil of political partisanship by classified employees of the government." Justice Douglas, in a partial dissent, did not dispute the need to "balance" but argued for doing so in terms of "clear and present danger"—language the majority did not use. "In other situations where the balance was between constitutional rights of individuals and a community interest which sought to qualify those rights," wrote Douglas, "we have insisted that the statute be 'narrowly drawn to define and punish specific conduct as constituting a clear and present danger to a substantial interest' of government. . . . That seems to me the proper course to follow here." Finally, Justice Black, in a sharp dissent, understood the rights at stake as almost absolutes whose restriction could be justified only in the most demanding terms of a clear and present danger. Laws to this end, he wrote, "must be narrowly drawn to meet the evil aimed at and to affect only the minimum number of people imperatively necessary to prevent a grave and imminent danger to the public."

Opinion of the Court: **Reed**, Vinson, Frankfurter, Burton. Concurring opinion: **Frankfurter**. Dissenting opinion: **Black**. Dissenting opinion, in part: **Douglas**. Dissenting: Rutledge. Not participating: Murphy, Jackson.

United Public Workers v. *Mitchell* was decided on February 10, 1947.

OPINIONS

JUSTICE REED DELIVERED THE OPINION OF THE COURT . . .

Our duty in this case ends if the Hatch Act provision under examination is constitutional.

. . . Again this Court must balance the extent of the guarantees of freedom against a congressional enactment to protect a democratic society against the supposed evil of political partisanship by classified employees of government.

As pointed out hereinbefore in this opinion, the practice of excluding classified employees from party offices and personal political activity at the polls has been in effect for several decades. Some incidents similar to those that are under examination here have been before this Court, and the prohibition against certain types of political activity by office holders has been upheld. . . .

. . . The prohibitions now under discussion are directed at political contributions of energy by Government employees. These contributions . . . have a long background of disapproval. Congress and the President are responsible for an efficient public service. If, in their judgment, efficiency may be best obtained by prohibiting active participation by classified employees in politics as party officers or workers, we see no constitutional objection.

Another Congress may determine that on the whole, limitations on active political management by federal personnel are unwise. The teaching of experience has evidently led Congress to enact the Hatch Act provisions. To declare that the present supposed evils of political activity are beyond the power of Congress to redress would leave the nation impotent to deal with what many sincere men believe is a material threat to the democratic system. Congress is not politically naïve or regardless of public welfare or that of the employees. It leaves untouched full participation by employees in political decisions at the ballot box and forbids only the partisan activity of federal personnel deemed offensive to efficiency. With that limitation only, employees may make their contributions to public affairs or protect their own interests, as before the passage of the act. The argument that political neutrality is not indispensable to a merit system for federal employees may be accepted. But because it is not indispensable does not mean that it is not desirable or permissible. Modern American politics involves organized political parties. Many classifications of Government employees have been accustomed to work in politics—national, state, and local—as a matter of principle or to assure their tenure. Congress may reasonably desire to limit party activity of federal employees so as to avoid a tendency toward a one-party system. It may have considered that parties would be more truly devoted to the public welfare if public servants were not over active politically.

Appellants urge that federal employees are protected by the Bill of Rights and that Congress may not "enact a regulation providing that no Republican, Jew, or Negro shall be appointed to federal office, or that no federal employee shall attend Mass or take any active part in missionary work." None would deny such limitations on Congressional power, but because there are some limitations it does not follow that a prohibition against acting as ward leader or worker at the polls is invalid. A reading of the [Hatch] Act and [Civil Service] Rule 1 together with the [Civil Service] Commission's determination ["Political Activity and Political Assessments," January 1944] shows the wide range of public activities with which there is no interference by the legislation. It is only partisan political activity that is interdicted. It is active participation in political management and political campaigns. Expressions, public or private, on public affairs, personalities, and matters of public interest, not an objective of party action, are unrestricted by law so long as the Government employee does not direct his activities toward party success.

It is urged, however, that Congress has gone further than necessary in prohibiting political activity to all types of classified employees. It is pointed out by appellants "that the impartiality of many of these is a matter of complete indifference to the effective performance" of their duties. Mr. Poole would appear to be a good illustration for appellants' argument. The complaint states that he is a roller in the Mint. We take it this is a job calling for the qualities of a skilled mechanic and that it does not involve contact with the public. Nevertheless, if in free time he is engaged in political activity, Congress may have concluded that the activity may promote or retard his advancement or preferment with his superiors. Congress may have thought that Government employees are handy elements for leaders in political policy to use in building a political machine. For regulation of employees it is not necessary that the act regulated be anything more than an act reasonably deemed by Congress to interfere with the efficiency of the public service. There are hundreds of thousands of United States employees with positions no more influential upon policy determination than that of Mr. Poole. Evidently what Congress feared was the cumulative effect on employee morale of political activity by all employees who could be induced to participate actively. It does not seem to us an unconstitutional basis for legislation. There is a suggestion that administrative workers may be barred, constitutionally, from political management and political campaigns while the industrial workers may not be barred, constitutionally, without an act "narrowly drawn to define and punish specific conduct." A ready answer, it seems to us, lies in the fact that the prohibition of 9(a) of the Hatch Act "applies without discrimination to all employees whether industrial or administrative" and that the Civil Service Rules, by 15 made a part of the Hatch Act, makes clear that industrial workers are covered in the prohibition against political activity. Congress has determined that the presence of government employees, whether industrial or administrative, in the ranks of political party workers is bad. . . . The use of the constitutional power of regulation is for Congress, not for the courts. . . .

AFFIRMED.

JUSTICE BLACK, DISSENTING.

The sentence in 9 of the statute, here upheld, makes it unlawful for any person employed in the executive branch of the Federal Government, with minor numerical exceptions, to "take any active part in political management or in political campaigns." The punishment provided is immediate discharge and a permanent ban against reemployment in the same position. The number of federal employees thus barred from political action is approximately three million. Section 12 of the same Act affects the participation in political campaigns of many thousands of state employees. No one of all these millions of citizens can, without violating this law, "take any active part" in any campaign for a cause or for a candidate if the cause or candidate is "specifically identified with any National or State political party." Since under our common political practices most causes and candidates are espoused by political parties, the result is that, because they are paid out of the public treasury, all these citizens who engage in public work can take no really effective part in campaigns that may bring about changes in their lives, their fortunes, and their happiness. . . .

. . . I think Poole's challenge to the constitutionality of the provision should be sustained. And since I agree with Justice Douglas that all the petitioners' complaints state a case or controversy, and show threats of imminent irreparable damages, I think that the contention that the challenged provision is unconstitutional on its face should be sustained as to all of them.

Had this measure deprived five million farmers or a million businessmen of all right to participate in elections, because Congress thought that federal farm or business subsidies might prompt some of them to exercise, or be susceptible to, a corrupting influence on politics or government, I would not sustain such an Act on the ground that it could be interpreted so as to apply only to some of them. Certainly laws which restrict the liberties guaranteed by the First Amendment should be narrowly drawn to meet the evil aimed at and to affect only the minimum number of people imperatively necessary to prevent a grave and imminent danger to the public. . . .

The right to vote and privately to express an opinion on political matters, important though they be, are but parts of the broad freedoms which our Constitution has provided as the bulwark of our free political institutions. Popular government, to be effective, must permit and encourage much wider political activity by all the people. Real popular government means "that men may speak as they think on matters vital to them and that falsehoods may be exposed through the processes of education and discussion. . . . Those who won our independence had confidence in the power of free and fearless reasoning and communication of ideas to discover and spread political and economic truth." *Thornhill* v. *State of Alabama* [1940]. Legislation which muzzles several million citizens threatens popular government, not only because it injures the individuals muzzled, but also because of its harmful effect on the body politic in depriving it of the political participation and interest of such a large segment of our citizens. Forcing public employees to contribute money and influence can well be proscribed in the interest of "clean politics" and public administration. But I think the Constitution prohibits legislation which prevents millions of citizens from contributing their arguments, complaints, and suggestions to the political debates which are the essence of our democracy; prevents them from engaging in organizational activity to urge others to vote and take an interest in political affairs; bars them from performing the interested citizen's duty of insuring that his and his fellow citizens' votes are counted. Such drastic limitations on the right of all the people to express political opinions and take political action would be inconsistent with the First Amendment's guaranty of freedom of speech, press, assembly, and petition. . . .

There is nothing about federal and state employees as a class which justifies depriving them or society of the benefits of their participation in public affairs. They, like other citizens, pay taxes and serve their country in peace and in war. The taxes they pay and the wars in which they fight are determined by the elected spokesmen of all the people. They come from the same homes, communities, schools, churches, and colleges as do the other citizens. I think the Constitution guarantees to them the same right that other groups of good citizens have to engage in activities which decide who their elected representatives shall be. . . .

It is argued that it is in the interest of clean politics to suppress political activities of federal and state employees. It would hardly seem to be imperative to muzzle millions of citizens because some of them, if left their constitutional freedoms, might corrupt the political process. All political corruption is not traceable to state and federal employees. Therefore, it is possible that other groups may later be compelled to sacrifice their right to participate in political activities for the protection of the purity of the Government of which they are a part.

It may be true, as contended, that some higher employees, unless restrained, might coerce their subordinates or that Government employees might use their official position to coerce other citizens. But is such a possibility of coercion of a subordinate by his employer limited to governmental employer-employee relationships? The same quality of argument would support a law to suppress the political freedom of all employees of private employers, and particularly of employers who borrow money or draw subsidies from the Government. Nor does it seem plausible that all of the millions of public employees whose rights to free expression are here stifled, might, if they participate in elections, coerce other citizens not employed by the Government or the States. Poole . . . is a roller in a government printing office. His job is about on a par in terms of political influence with that of most other state, federal, and private business employees. Such jobs generally do not give such employees who hold them sufficient authority to enable them to wield a dangerous or coercive influence on the political world. If the possibility exists that some other public employees may, by reason of their more influential positions, coerce other public employees or other citizens, laws can be drawn to punish the coercers. It hardly seems consistent with our system of equal justice to all to suppress the political and speaking freedom of millions of good citizens because a few bad citizens might engage in coercion.

It may also be true, as contended, that if public employees are permitted to exercise a full freedom to express their views in political campaigns, some public officials will discharge some employees and grant promotion to others on a political rather than on a merit basis. For the same reason other public officials, occupying positions of influence, may use their influence to have their own political supporters appointed or promoted. But here again, if the practice of making discharges, promotions, or recommendations for promotions on a political basis is so great an evil as to require legislation, the law could punish those public officials who engage in the practice. To punish millions of employees and to deprive the nation of their contribution to public affairs, in order to remove temptation from a proportionately small number of public officials, seems at the least to be a novel method of suppressing what is thought to be an evil practice.

Our political system, different from many others, rests on the foundation of a belief in rule by the people—not some, but all the people. Education has been fostered better to fit people for self-expression and good citizenship. In a country whose people elect their leaders and decide great public issues, the voice of none should be suppressed—at least such is the assumption of the First Amendment. That Amendment, unless I misunderstand its meaning, includes a command that the Government must, in order to promote its own interest, leave the people at liberty to speak their own thoughts about government, advocate their own favored governmental causes, and work for their own political candidates and parties. The section of the Act here held valid reduces the constitutionally protected liberty of several million citizens to less than a shadow of its substance. It relegates millions of federal, state, and municipal employees to the role of mere spectators of events upon which hinge the safety and welfare of all the people, including public employees. It removes a sizable proportion of our electorate from full participation in affairs destined to mold the fortunes of the Nation. It makes honest participation in essential political activities an offense punishable by proscription from public employment. It endows a governmental board with the awesome power to censor the thoughts, expressions, and activities of law-abiding citizens in the field of free expression from which no person should be barred by a government which boasts that it is a government of, for, and by the people— all the people. Laudable as its purpose may be, it seems to me to hack at the roots of a Government by the people themselves; and consequently I cannot agree to sustain its validity.

JUSTICE DOUGLAS, DISSENTING IN PART . . .

. . . The difficulty lies in attempting to preserve our democratic way of life by measures which deprive a large segment of the population of all political rights except the right to vote. Absent coercion, improper use of government position or government funds, or neglect or inefficiency in the performance of duty, federal employees have the same rights as other citizens under the Constitution. They are not second class citizens. If, in exercise of their rights, they find common political interests and join with each other or other groups in what they conceive to be their interests or the interests of the nation, they are simply doing what any other group might do. In other situations where the balance was between constitutional rights of individuals and a community interest which sought to qualify those rights, we have insisted that the statute be "narrowly drawn to define and punish specific conduct as constituting a clear and present danger to a substantial interest" of government. *Cantwell* v. *State of Connecticut* [1940].

That seems to me the proper course to follow here. The prohibition in 9(a) of the Hatch Act against government employees taking an "active part in political management or in political campaigns" applies without discrimination to all employees whether industrial or administrative. The same is true of the Civil Service Rules. . . . But the supposed evils are both different and narrower in the case of industrial workers than they are in the case of the administrative group. The public interest in the political activity of a machinist or elevator operator or charwoman is a distinct and different problem. In those cases the public concern is in the preservation of an unregimented industrial group, in a group free from political pressures of superiors who use their official power for a partisan purpose. Then official power is misused, perverted. The Government is corrupted by making its industrial workers political captives, victims of bureaucratic power, agents for perpetuating one party in power.

Offset against that public concern are the interests of the employees in the exercise of cherished constitutional rights. The nature and importance of those rights have been fully expounded in Justice Black's opinion. If those rights are to be qualified by the larger requirements of modern democratic government, the restrictions should be narrowly and selectively drawn to define and punish the specific conduct which constitutes a clear and present danger to the operations of government. It seems plain to me that that evil has its roots in the coercive activity of those in the hierarchy who have the power to regiment the industrial group or who undertake to do so. To sacrifice the political rights of the industrial workers goes far beyond any demonstrated or demonstrable need. Those rights are too basic and fundamental in our democratic political society to be sacrificed or qualified for anything short of a clear and present danger to the civil service system. No such showing has been made in the case of these industrial workers which justifies their political sterilization as distinguished from selective measures aimed at the coercive practices on which the spoils system feeds.

KOVACS V. COOPER
336 U.S. 77 (1949)

In *Saia* v. *New York* (1948) the Supreme Court struck down as an unconstitutional "previous restraint" on free speech a Lockport, New York, ordinance prohibiting the use of loudspeakers except by permission of the chief of police. A year later the Court was asked to decide whether the city of Trenton, New Jersey, could totally bar from its streets any sound system emitting "loud and raucous" noises. This ordinance the Court, by a vote of 5 to 4, held constitutional.

In *Kovacs* the Court, again dividing on its approach to the First Amendment, was unable to find a rationale agreeable to a majority. Justice Reed announced the judgment of the Court in an opinion joined by only two others. "A state or city may prohibit acts or things reasonably thought to bring evil or harm to its people," he wrote, and Trenton had made such a reasonable conclusion. Reed cautioned that "even the fundamental rights of the Bill of Rights are not absolute," and he observed that "the preferred position of freedom of speech in a society that cherishes liberty for all does not require legislators to be insensible to claims by citizens to comfort and convenience." Reed's reference to "the preferred position of freedom of speech" was too much for Justice Frankfurter, who, in a concurring opinion, said the phrase had "uncritically crept" into recent opinions of the Court. Frankfurter contended that the phrase is "mischievous" and argued that the implicit doctrine behind it—that "any law touching communication is infected with presumptive invalidity"—is wrong.

Judgment of the Court: **Reed**, Vinson, Burton. Concurring opinions: **Frankfurter**; **Jackson**. Dissenting opinions: **Black**, Douglas, Rutledge; **Rutledge**. Dissenting: Murphy.

Kovacs v. *Cooper* was decided on January 31, 1949.

JUSTICE REED ANNOUNCED THE JUDGMENT OF THE COURT AND AN OPINION IN WHICH CHIEF JUSTICE VINSON AND JUSTICE BURTON JOIN . . .

The use of sound trucks and other peripatetic or stationary broadcasting devices for advertising, for religious exercises, and for discussion of issues or controversies has brought forth numerous municipal ordinances. The avowed and obvious purpose of these ordinances is to prohibit or minimize such sounds on or near the streets since some citizens find the noise objectionable and to some degree an interference with the business or social activities in which they are engaged or the quiet that they would like to enjoy. A satisfactory adjustment of the conflicting interests is difficult as those who desire to broadcast can hardly acquiesce in a requirement to modulate their sounds to a pitch that would not rise above other street noises nor would they deem a restriction to sparsely used localities or to hours after work and before sleep—say 6 to 9 p.m.—sufficient for the exercise of their claimed privilege. Municipalities are seeking actively a solution. . . . Unrestrained use throughout a municipality of all sound amplifying devices would be intolerable. Absolute prohibition within municipal limits of all sound amplification, even though reasonably regulated in place, time, and volume, is undesirable and probably unconstitutional as an unreasonable interference with normal activities.

We have had recently before us an ordinance of the City of Lockport, New York, prohibiting sound amplification whereby the sound was cast on public places so as to attract the attention of the passing public to the annoyance of those within the radius of the sounds. The ordinance contained this exception:

> Section 3. Exception. Public dissemination, through radio loudspeakers, of items of news and matters of public concern and athletic activities shall not be deemed a violation of this section provided that the same be done under permission obtained from the Chief of Police.

This Court held the ordinance "unconstitutional on its face," *Saia* v. *New York* [1948], because the quoted section established a "previous restraint" on free speech with "no standards prescribed for the exercise" of discretion by the Chief of Police. When ordinances undertake censorship of speech or religious practices before permitting their exercise, the Constitution forbids their enforcement. . . .

This ordinance is not of that character. It contains nothing comparable to the above quoted [Section] 3 of the ordinance in the *Saia* case. It is an exercise of the authority granted to the city by New Jersey "to prevent disturbing noises," . . . nuisances well within the municipality's power to control. The police power of a state extends beyond health, morals, and safety, and comprehends the duty, within constitutional limitations, to protect the well-being and tranquility of a community. A state or city may prohibit acts or things reasonably thought to bring evil or harm to its people. . . .

Of course, even the fundamental rights of the Bill of Rights are not absolute. The *Saia* case recognized that in this field by stating "The hours and place of public discussion can be controlled." It was said decades ago in an opinion of this Court delivered by Justice Holmes, *Schenck* v. *United States* [1919], that:

> The most stringent protection of free speech would not protect a man in falsely shouting fire in a theatre and causing a panic. It does not even protect a man from an injunction against uttering words that may have all the effect of force.

Hecklers may be expelled from assemblies, and religious worship may not be disturbed by those anxious to preach a doctrine of atheism. The right to speak one's mind would often be an empty privilege in a place and at a time beyond the protecting hand of the guardians of public order. . . .

City streets are recognized as a normal place for the exchange of ideas by speech or paper. But this does not mean the freedom is beyond all control. We think it is a permissible exercise of legislative discretion to bar sound trucks with broadcasts of public interest, amplified to a loud and raucous volume, from the public ways of municipalities. On the business streets of cities like Trenton, with its more than 125,000 people, such distractions would be dangerous to traffic at all hours useful for the dissemination of information, and in the residential thoroughfares the quiet and tranquility so desirable for city dwellers would likewise be at the mercy of advocates of particular religious, social, or political persuasions. We cannot believe that rights of free speech compel a municipality to allow such mechanical voice amplification on any of its streets.

The right of free speech is guaranteed every citizen that he may reach the minds of willing listeners, and to do so there must be opportunity to win their attention. This is the phase of freedom of speech that is involved here. We do not think the Trenton ordinance abridges that freedom. It is an extravagant extension of due process to say that because of it a city cannot forbid talking on the streets through a loud speaker in a loud and raucous tone. Surely such an ordinance does not violate our people's "concept of ordered liberty" so as to require federal intervention to protect a citizen from the action of his own local government. Cf. *Palko* v. *Connecticut* [1937]. Opportunity to gain the public's ears by objectionably amplified sound on the streets is no more assured by the right of free speech than is the unlimited opportunity to address gatherings on the streets. The preferred position of freedom of speech in a society that cherishes liberty for all does not require legislators to be insensible to claims by citizens to comfort and convenience. To enforce freedom of speech in disregard of the rights of others would be harsh and arbitrary in itself. That more people may be more easily and cheaply reached by sound trucks, perhaps borrowed without cost from some zealous supporter, is not enough to call forth constitutional protection for what those charged with public welfare reasonably think is a nuisance when easy means of publicity are open. Section 4 of the ordinance bars sound trucks from broadcasting in a loud and raucous manner on the streets. There is no restriction upon the communication of ideas or·discussion of issues by the human voice, by newspapers, by pamphlets, by dodgers. We think that the need for reasonable protection in the homes or business houses from the distracting noises of vehicles equipped with such sound amplifying devices justifies the ordinance.

AFFIRMED.

JUSTICE FRANKFURTER, CONCURRING . . .

To dispose of this case on the assumption that the *Saia* case . . . was rightly decided would be for me to start with an unreality. While I am not unaware of the circumstances that differentiate this case from what was ruled in *Saia,* further reflection has only served to reinforce the dissenting views I expressed in that case. . . . In the light of them I conclude that there is nothing in the Constitution of the United States to bar New Jersey from authorizing the City of Trenton to deal in the manner chosen by the City with the aural aggressions implicit in the use of sound trucks. The opinions in this case prompt me to make some additional observations. My brother Reed speaks of "The preferred position of freedom of speech," though, to be sure, he finds that the Trenton ordinance does not disregard it. This is a phrase that has uncritically crept into some recent opinions of this Court. I deem it a mischievous phrase, if it carries the thought, which it may subtly imply, that any law touching communication is infected with presumptive invalidity. It is not the first time in the history of constitutional adjudication that such a doctrinaire attitude has disregarded the admonition most to be observed in exercising the Court's reviewing power over legislation, "that it is a constitution we are expounding," *McCulloch* v. *Maryland* [1804]. I say the phrase is mischievous because it radiates a constitutional doctrine without avowing it. Clarity and candor in these matters, so as to avoid gliding unwittingly into error, make it appropriate to trace the history of the phrase "preferred position." The following is a chronological account of the evolution of talk about "preferred position" except where the thread of derivation is plain enough to be indicated.

1. *Herndon* v. *Lowry* [1937]. "The power of a state to abridge freedom of speech and of assembly is the exception rather than the rule and the penalizing even of utterances of a defined character must find its justification in a reasonable apprehension of danger to organized government. The judgment of the Legislature is not unfettered. The limitation upon individual liberty must have appropriate relation to the safety of the state."

2. *United States* v. *Carolene Products Co.* [1937]. A footnote hardly seems to be an appropriate way of announcing a new constitutional doctrine, and . . . [*Carolene* footnote 4] did not purport to announce any new doctrine; incidentally, it did not have the concurrence of a majority of the Court. It merely rephrased and expanded what was said in *Herndon* and elsewhere. It certainly did not assert a presumption of invalidity against all legislation touching matters related to liberties protected by the Bill of Rights and the Fourteenth Amendment. It merely stirred inquiry whether as to such matters there may be "narrower scope for operation of the presumption of constitutionality" and legislation regarding them is therefore "to be subjected to more exacting judicial scrutiny."

The *Carolene* footnote is cited in *Thornhill* v. *Alabama* [1940] in an opinion which thus proceeds: "Mere legislative preference for one rather than another means for combating substantive evils, therefore, may well prove an inadequate foundation on which to rest regulations which are aimed at or in their operation diminish the effective exercise of rights so necessary to the maintenance of democratic institutions. It is imperative that, when the effective exercise of these rights is claimed to be abridged, the courts should 'weigh the circumstances' and 'appraise the substantiality of the reasons advanced' in support of the challenged regulations. *Schneider* v. *State* [1939]." . . .

The *Carolene* footnote was last cited in an opinion of this Court in . . . *Thomas* v. *Collins* [1945].

3. *Schneider* v. *State of New Jersey* [1939]. "In every case, therefore, where legislative abridgment of the rights (freedom of speech and of the press) is asserted, the courts should be astute to examine the effect of the challenged legislation. Mere legislative preferences or beliefs respecting matters of public convenience may well support regulation directed at other personal activities, but be insufficient to justify such as diminishes the exercise of rights so vital to the maintenance of democratic institutions. And so, as cases arise, the delicate and difficult task falls upon the courts to weigh the circumstances and to appraise the substantiality of the reasons advanced in support of the regulation of the free enjoyment of the rights."

4. *Bridges* v. *California* [1941]. "Moreover, the likelihood, however great, that a substantive evil will result cannot alone justify a restriction upon freedom of speech or the press. The evil itself must be substantial," Brandeis, J., concurring in *Whitney* v. *California* [1937]; it must be "serious." And even the expression of "legislative preferences or beliefs" cannot transform

minor matters of public inconvenience or annoyance into substantive evils of sufficient weight to warrant the curtailment of liberty of expression. *Schneider.*

> What finally emerges from the "clear and present danger" cases is a working principle that the substantive evil must be extremely serious and the degree of imminence extremely high before utterances can be punished.

This formulation of the "clear-and-present-danger" test was quoted and endorsed in *Pennekamp* v. *Florida* [1946].

5. A number of Jehovah's Witnesses cases refer to the freedoms specified by the First Amendment, as in a "preferred position." The phrase was apparently first used in the dissent of Chief Justice Stone in *Jones* v. *Opelika* [1942]. . . .

6. *West Virginia State Board of Education* v. *Barnette* [1943]. "The test of legislation which collides with the Fourteenth Amendment, because it also collides with the principles of the First, is much more definite than the test when only the Fourteenth is involved. Much of the vagueness of the due process clause disappears when the specific prohibitions of the First become its standard. The right of a State to regulate, for example, a public utility may well include, so far as the due process test is concerned, power to impose all of the restrictions which a legislature may have a 'rational basis' for adopting. But freedoms of speech and of press, of assembly, and of worship may not be infringed on such slender grounds. They are susceptible of restriction only to prevent grave and immediate danger to interests which the state may lawfully protect."

7. *Thomas* v. *Collins* [1945]. "For these reasons any attempt to restrict those liberties must be justified by clear public interest, threatened not doubtfully or remotely, but by clear and present danger. The rational connection between the remedy provided and the evil to be curbed, which in other contexts might support legislation against attack on due process grounds, will not suffice. These rights rest on firmer foundation. Accordingly, whatever occasion would restrain orderly discussion and persuasion, at appropriate time and place, must have clear support in public danger, actual or impending. Only the gravest abuses, endangering paramount interests, give occasion for permissible limitation." This is perhaps the strongest language dealing with the constitutional aspect of legislation touching utterance. But it was the opinion of only four members of the Court, since Justice Jackson, in a separate concurring opinion, referred to the opinion of Justice Rutledge only to say that he agreed that the case fell into "the category of a public speech, rather than that of practicing a vocation as solicitor."

In short, the claim that any legislation is presumptively unconstitutional which touches the field of the First Amendment and the Fourteenth Amendment, insofar as the latter's concept of "liberty" contains what is specifically protected by the First, has never commended itself to a majority of this Court.

Behind the notion sought to be expressed by the formula as to "the preferred position of freedom of speech" lies a relevant consideration in determining whether an enactment relating to the liberties protected by the Due Process Clause of the Fourteenth Amendment is violative of it. In law also, doctrine is illuminated by history. The ideas now governing the constitutional protection of freedom of speech derive essentially from the opinions of Justice Holmes.

The philosophy of his opinions on that subject arose from a deep awareness of the extent to which sociological conclusions are conditioned by time and circumstance. Because of this awareness Justice Holmes seldom felt justified in opposing his own opinion to economic views which the legislature embodied in law. But since he also realized that the progress of civilization is to a considerable extent the displacement of error which once held sway as official truth by beliefs which in turn have yielded to other beliefs, for him the right to search for truth was of a different order than some transient economic dogma. And without freedom of expression, thought becomes checked and atrophied. Therefore, in considering what interests are so fundamental as to be enshrined in the Due Process Clause, those liberties of the individual which history has attested as the indispensable conditions of an open as against a closed society come to this Court with a momentum for respect lacking when appeal is made to liberties which derive merely from shifting economic arrangements. Accordingly, Justice Holmes was far more ready to find legislative invasion where free inquiry was involved than in the debatable area of economics. . . . The objection to summarizing this line of thought by the phrase "the preferred position of freedom of speech" is that it expresses a complicated process of constitutional adjudication by a deceptive formula. And it was Mr. Justice Holmes who admonished us that "To rest upon a formula is a slumber that, prolonged, means death." *Collected Legal Papers*, 306. Such a formula makes for mechanical jurisprudence.

Some of the arguments made in this case strikingly illustrate how easy it is to fall into the ways of mechanical jurisprudence through the use of oversimplified formulas. It is argued that the Constitution protects freedom of speech: Freedom of speech means the right to communicate, whatever the physical means for so doing; sound trucks are one form of communication; ergo that form is entitled to the same protection as any other means of communication, whether by tongue or pen. Such sterile argumentation treats society as though it consisted of bloodless categories. The various forms of modern so-called "mass communications" raise issues that were not implied in the means of communication known or contemplated by Franklin and Jefferson and Madison. . . . Movies have created problems not presented by the circulation of books, pamphlets, or newspapers, and so the movies have been constitutionally regulated. . . . Broadcasting in turn has produced its brood of complicated problems hardly to be solved by an easy formula about the preferred position of free speech. . . .

Only a disregard of vital differences between natural speech, even of the loudest spellbinders, and the noise of sound trucks would give sound trucks the constitutional rights accorded to the unaided human voice. Nor is it for this Court to devise the terms on which sound trucks should be allowed to operate, if at all. These are matters for the legislative judgment controlled by public opinion. So long as a legislature does not prescribe what ideas may be noisily expressed and what may not be, nor discriminate among those who would make inroads upon the public peace, it is not for us to supervise the limits the legislature may impose in safeguarding the steadily narrowing opportunities for serenity and reflection. Without such opportunities freedom of thought becomes a mocking phrase, and without freedom of thought there can be no free society.

JUSTICE JACKSON, CONCURRING . . .

I agree with Justice Black that this decision is a repudiation of that in *Saia* v. *New York* [1948]. Like him, I am unable to find anything in this record to warrant a distinction because of "loud and raucous" tones of this machine. The *Saia* decision struck down a more moderate exercise of the state's police power than the one now sustained. Trenton, as the ordinance reads to me, unconditionally bans all sound trucks from the city streets. Lockport relaxed its prohibition with a proviso to allow their use, even in areas set aside for public recreation, when and where the chief of police saw no objection. Comparison of this our 1949 decision with our 1948 decision, I think, will pretty hopelessly confuse municipal authorities as to what they may or may not do.

I concur in the present result only for the reasons stated in dissent in *Saia*.

JUSTICE BLACK, JOINED BY JUSTICE DOUGLAS AND JUSTICE RUTLEDGE, DISSENTING . . .

In *Saia* we had before us an ordinance of the City of Lockport, New York, which forbade the use of sound amplification devices except with permission of the chief of police. The ordinance was applied to keep a minister from using an amplifier while preaching in a public park. We held that the ordinance, aimed at the use of an amplifying device, invaded the area of free speech guaranteed the people by the First and Fourteenth Amendments. The ordinance, so we decided, amounted to censorship in its baldest form. And our conclusion rested on the fact that the chief of police was given arbitrary power to prevent the use of speech amplifying devices at all times and places in the city, without regard to the volume of the sound. We then placed use of loud speakers in public streets and parks on the same constitutional level as freedom to speak on streets without such devices, freedom to speak over radio, and freedom to distribute literature.

In this case the Court denies speech amplifiers the constitutional shelter recognized by our decisions and holding in the *Saia* case. This is true because the Trenton, New Jersey, ordinance here sustained goes beyond a mere prior censorship of all loud speakers with authority in the censor to prohibit some of them. This Trenton ordinance wholly bars the use of all loud speakers mounted upon any vehicle in any of the city's public streets.

In my view this repudiation of the prior *Saia* opinion makes a dangerous and unjustifiable breach in the constitutional barriers designed to insure freedom of expression. Ideas and beliefs are today chiefly disseminated to the masses of people through the press, radio, moving pictures, and public address systems. To some extent at least there is competition of ideas between and within these groups. The basic premise of the First Amendment is that all present instruments of communication, as well as others that inventive genius may bring into being, shall be free from governmental censorship or prohibition. Laws which hamper the free use of some instruments of communication thereby favor competing channels. Thus unless constitutionally prohibited, laws like this Trenton ordinance can give an overpowering influence to views of owners of legally favored instruments of communication. This favoritism, it seems to me, is the inevitable result of today's decision. For the result of today's opinion in upholding this statutory prohibition of amplifiers would surely not be reached by this Court if such channels of communication as the press, radio, or moving pictures were similarly attacked.

There are many people who have ideas that they wish to disseminate but who do not have enough money to own or control publishing plants, newspapers, radios, moving picture studios, or chains of show places. Yet everybody knows the vast reaches of these powerful channels of communication which from the very nature of our economic system must be under the control and guidance of comparatively few people. On the other hand, public speaking is done by many men of divergent minds with no centralized control over the ideas they entertain so as to limit the causes they espouse. It is no reflection on the value of preserving freedom for dissemination of the ideas of publishers of newspapers, magazines, and other literature, to believe that transmission of ideas through public speaking is also essential to the sound thinking of a fully informed citizenry. It is of particular importance in a government where people elect their officials that the fullest opportunity be afforded candidates to express and voters to hear their views. It is of equal importance that criticism of governmental action not be limited to criticisms by press, radio, and moving pictures. In no other way except public speaking can the desirable objective of widespread public discussion be assured. For the press, the radio, and the moving picture owners have their favorites, and it assumes the impossible to suppose that these agencies will at all times be equally fair as between the candidates and officials they favor and those whom they vigorously oppose. And it is an obvious fact that public speaking today without sound amplifiers is a wholly inadequate way to reach the people on a large scale. Consequently, to tip the scales against transmission of ideas through public speaking as the Court does today, is to deprive the people of a large part of the basic advantages of the receipt of ideas that the First Amendment was designed to protect.

There is no more reason that I can see for wholly prohibiting one useful instrument of communication than another. If Trenton can completely bar the streets to the advantageous use of loud speakers, all cities can do the same. In that event preference in the dissemination of ideas is given those who can obtain the support of newspapers, etc., or those who have money enough to buy advertising from newspapers, radios, or moving pictures. This Court should no more permit this invidious prohibition against the dissemination of ideas by speaking than it would permit a complete blackout of the press, the radio, or moving pictures. It is wise for all who cherish freedom of expression to reflect upon the plain fact that a holding that the audiences of public speakers can be constitutionally prohibited is not unrelated to a like prohibition in other fields. And the right to freedom of expression should be protected from absolute censorship for persons without, as for persons with, wealth and power. At least, such is the theory of our society.

I am aware that the "blare" of this new method of carrying ideas is susceptible of abuse and may under certain circumstances constitute an intolerable nuisance. But ordinances can be drawn which adequately protect a community from unreasonable use of public speaking devices without absolutely denying to the community's citizens all information that may be disseminated or received through this new avenue for trade in ideas. I would agree without reservation to the sentiment that "unrestrained use throughout a municipality of all sound amplifying devices would be intolerable." And of course cities may restrict or absolutely ban the use of amplifiers on busy streets in the business area. A city ordinance that reasonably restricts the volume of sound, or the hours during which an amplifier may be used, does not, in my mind, infringe the constitutionally protected area of free speech. It is because this ordinance does none of these things, but is instead an absolute prohibition of all uses of an amplifier on any of the streets of Trenton at any time, that I must dissent.

I would reverse the judgment.

JUSTICE RUTLEDGE, DISSENTING . . .

I am in accord with the views expressed by my brother Black. I think it important, however, to point out that a majority here agree with him that the issue presented is whether a state (here a municipality) may forbid all use of sound trucks or amplifying devices in public streets, without reference to whether "loud and raucous noises" are emitted. Only a minority take the view that the Trenton ordinance merely forbids using amplifying instruments emitting loud and raucous noises. Yet a different majority, one including that minority and two other justices, sustain the ordinance and its application. In effect Kovacs stands convicted, but of what it is impossible to tell, because the majority upholding the conviction do not agree upon what constituted the crime. How, on such a hashing of different views of the thing forbidden, Kovacs could have known with what he was charged or could have prepared a defense, I am unable to see. How anyone can do either in the future, under this decision, I am equally at loss to say.

In my view an ordinance drawn so ambiguously and inconsistently as to reflect the differing views of its meaning taken by the two groups who compose the majority sustaining it, would violate Fourteenth Amendment due process even if no question of free speech were involved. No man should be subject to punishment under a statute when even a bare majority of judges upholding the conviction cannot agree upon what acts the statute denounces. What the effect of this decision may be I cannot foretell, except that Kovacs will stand convicted and the division among the majority voting to affirm leaves open for future determination whether absolute and total state prohibition of sound trucks in public places can stand consistently with the First Amendment. For myself, I have no doubt of state power to regulate their abuse in reasonable accommodation, by narrowly drawn statutes, to other interests concerned in use of the streets and in freedom from public nuisance. But that the First Amendment limited its protections of speech to the natural range of the human voice as it existed in 1790 would be, for me, like saying that the commerce power remains limited to navigation by sail and travel by the use of horses and oxen in accordance with the principal modes of carrying on commerce in 1789. The Constitution was not drawn with any such limited vision of time, space, and mechanics. It is one thing to hold that the states may regulate the use of sound trucks by appropriately limited measures. It is entirely another to say their use can be forbidden altogether.

To what has been said above and by Justice Black, I would add only that I think my brother Frankfurter demonstrates the conclusion opposite to that which he draws, namely, that the First Amendment guaranties of the freedoms of speech, press, assembly, and religion occupy preferred position not only in the Bill of Rights but also in the repeated decisions of this Court.

18

TERMINIELLO V. CHICAGO
337 U.S. 1 (1949)

Father Terminiello, a Catholic priest, spoke to 800 people meeting in a Chicago auditorium under the auspices of the Christian Veterans of America. A crowd of 1,000 gathered outside the auditorium to protest the event, and police were unable to prevent disturbances. In his speech Terminiello condemned the conduct of the crowd outside the auditorium and criticized various political and racial groups, including Communists, the New Deal, "Queen Eleanor [Roosevelt], . . . one of the world's communists," and "Zionist Jews." Terminiello was arrested and found guilty of disorderly conduct. When he appealed on free speech grounds, the Illinois courts affirmed his conviction under the "fighting words" doctrine of *Chaplinsky* v. *New Hampshire* (1942). But the Supreme Court reversed.

Justice Douglas, writing for the majority of five, declined to assess Terminiello's appeal in terms of whether he had spoken "fighting words," which *Chaplinsky* held were unprotected by the First Amendment. Instead, Douglas reviewed the case according to the trial court's instruction to the jury that it could convict Terminiello if it found he had uttered speech that stirred people to anger. Douglas concluded that the First Amendment could not permit a conviction on such terms. Only when speech is "shown likely to produce a clear and present danger of a serious substantive evil that rises far above public inconvenience, annoyance, or unrest," he said, invoking the test first suggested in *Schenck* v. *United States* (1919), can it be restricted.

Justice Jackson, in dissent, contended that Terminiello's speech did constitute a clear and present danger, because the danger of rioting, "a substantive evil," was present. Jackson chided the majority for judging Terminiello's speech "as if he had spoken to persons as dispassionate as empty benches." "There is a danger," he concluded, "that, if the Court does not temper its doctrinaire logic with a little practical wisdom, it will convert the constitutional Bill of Rights into a suicide pact."

Opinion of the Court: **Douglas**, Black, Reed, Murphy, Rutledge. Dissenting opinions: **Vinson**; **Frankfurter**, Jackson, Burton; **Jackson**, Burton.

Terminiello v. *Chicago* was decided on May 16, 1949.

OPINIONS

JUSTICE DOUGLAS DELIVERED THE OPINION OF THE COURT . . .

The argument here has been focused on the issue of whether the content of petitioner's speech was composed of derisive, fighting words, which carried it outside the scope of the constitutional guarantees. See *Chaplinsky* v. *New Hampshire* [1942]; *Cantwell* v. *Connecticut* [1940]. We do not reach that question, for there is a preliminary question that is dispositive of the case. As we have noted, the statutory words "breach of the peace" were defined in instructions to the jury to include speech which "stirs the public to anger, invites dispute, brings about a condition of unrest, or creates a disturbance. . . ." That construction of the ordinance is a ruling on a question of state law that is as binding on us as though the precise words had been written into the ordinance. . . .

The vitality of civil and political institutions in our society depends on free discussion. As Chief Justice Hughes wrote in *DeJonge* v. *Oregon* [1937], it is only through free debate and free exchange of ideas that government remains responsive to the will of the people and peaceful change is effected. The right to speak freely and to promote diversity of ideas and programs is therefore one of the chief distinctions that sets us apart from totalitarian regimes.

Accordingly a function of free speech under our system of government is to invite dispute. It may indeed best serve its high purpose when it induces a condition of unrest, creates dissatisfaction with conditions as they are, or even stirs people to anger. Speech is often provocative and challenging. It may strike at prejudices and preconceptions and have profound unsettling effects as it presses for acceptance of an idea. That is why freedom of speech, though not absolute, *Chaplinsky* . . ., is nevertheless protected against censorship or punishment, unless shown likely to produce a clear and present danger of a serious substantive evil that rises far above public inconvenience, annoyance, or unrest. . . . There is no room under our Constitution for a more restrictive view. For the alternative would lead to standardization of ideas either by legislatures, courts, or dominant political or community groups.

The ordinance as construed by the trial court seriously invaded this province. It permitted conviction of petitioner if his speech stirred people to anger, invited public dispute, or brought about a condition of unrest. A conviction resting on any of those grounds may not stand.

The fact that petitioner took no exception to the instruction is immaterial. No exception to the instructions was taken in *Stromberg* v. *California* [1931]. But a judgment of conviction based on a general verdict under a state statute was set aside in that case, because one part of the statute was unconstitutional. The statute had been challenged as unconstitutional, and the instruction was framed in its language. The Court held that the attack on the statute as a whole was equally an attack on each of its individual parts. Since the verdict was a general one and did not specify the ground upon which it rested, it could not be sustained. For one part of the statute was unconstitutional, and it could not be determined that the defendant was not convicted under that part.

The principle of that case controls this one. As we have said, the gloss which Illinois placed on the ordinance gives it a meaning and application which are conclusive on us. We need not consider whether as construed it is defective in its entirety. As construed and applied it at least contains parts that are unconstitutional. The verdict was a general one; and we do not know on this record but what it may rest on the invalid clauses.

The statute as construed in the charge to the jury was passed on by the Illinois courts and sustained by them over the objection that as so read it violated the Fourteenth Amendment. The fact that the parties did not dispute its construction makes the adjudication no less ripe for our review, as the *Stromberg* decision indicates. We can only take the statute as the state courts read it. From our point of view it is immaterial whether the state law question as to its meaning was controverted or accepted. The pinch of the statute is in its application. It is that question which the petitioner has brought here. To say therefore that the question on this phase of the case is whether the trial judge gave a wrong charge is wholly to misconceive the issue.

But it is said that throughout the appellate proceedings the Illinois courts assumed that the only conduct punishable and punished under the ordinance was conduct constituting "fighting words." That emphasizes, however, the importance of the rule of the *Stromberg* case. Petitioner was not convicted under a statute so narrowly construed. For all anyone knows he was convicted under the parts of the ordinance (as construed) which, for example, make it an offense merely to invite dispute or to bring about a condition of unrest. We cannot avoid that issue by saying that all Illinois did was to measure petitioner's conduct, not the ordinance, against the Constitution. Petitioner raised both points—that his speech was protected by the Constitution; that the inclusion of his speech within the ordinance was a violation of the Constitution. We would, therefore, strain at technicalities to conclude that the constitutionality of the ordinance as construed and applied to petitioner was not before the Illinois courts. The record makes clear that petitioner at all times challenged the constitutionality of the ordinance as construed and applied to him.

REVERSED.

JUSTICE JACKSON, DISSENTING . . .

The Court reverses this conviction by reiterating generalized approbations of freedom of speech with which, in the abstract, no one will disagree. Doubts as to their applicability are lulled by avoidance of more than passing reference to the circumstances of Terminiello's speech and judging it as if he had spoken to persons as dispassionate as empty benches, or like a modern Demosthenes practicing his Philippics on a lonely seashore.

But the local court that tried Terminiello was not indulging in theory. It was dealing with a riot and with a speech that provoked a hostile mob and incited a friendly one, and threatened violence between the two. When the trial judge instructed the jury that it might find Terminiello guilty of inducing a breach of the peace if his behavior stirred the public to anger, invited dispute, brought about unrest, created a disturbance, or molested peace and quiet by arousing alarm, he was not speaking of these as harmless or abstract conditions. He was addressing his words to the concrete behavior and specific consequences disclosed by the evidence. He was saying to the jury, in effect, that if this particular speech added fuel to the situation already so inflamed as to threaten to get beyond police control, it could be punished as inducing a breach of peace. When the light of the evidence not recited by the Court is thrown upon the Court's opinion, it discloses that underneath a little issue of Terminiello and his hundred-dollar fine lurk some of the most far-reaching constitutional questions that can confront a people who value both liberty and order. This Court seems to regard these as enemies of each other and to be of the view that we must forego order to achieve liberty. So it fixes its eyes on a conception of freedom of speech so rigid as to tolerate no concession to society's need for public order.

An old proverb warns us to take heed lest we "walk into a well from looking at the stars." To show why I think the Court is in some danger of doing just that, I must bring these deliberations down to earth by a long recital of facts. . . . [Justice Jackson goes on to quote at length from Terminiello's testimony and speech.]

Such was the speech. Evidence showed that it stirred the audience not only to cheer and applaud but to expressions of immediate anger, unrest, and alarm. One called the speaker a "God damned liar" and was taken out by the police. Another said that "Jews, niggers, and Catholics would have to be gotten rid of." One response was, "Yes, the Jews are all killers, murderers. If we don't kill them first, they will kill us." The anti-Jewish stories elicited exclamations of "Oh!" and "Isn't that terrible!" and shouts of "Yes, send the Jews back to Russia," "Kill the Jews," "Dirty kikes," and much more of ugly tenor. This is the specific and concrete kind of anger, unrest, and alarm, coupled with that of the mob outside, that the trial court charged the jury might find to be a breach of peace induced by Terminiello. It is difficult to believe that this Court is speaking of the same occasion, but it is the only one involved in this litigation.

Terminiello, of course, disclaims being a fascist. Doubtless many of the indoor audience were not consciously such. His speech, however, followed, with fidelity that is more than coincidental, the pattern of European fascist leaders. The street mob, on the other hand, included some who deny being communists, but Terminiello testified and offered to prove that the demonstration was communist-organized and communist-led. He offered literature of left wing organizations calling members to meet and "mobilize" for instruction as pickets and exhorting followers: "All out to fight Fascist Smith." [Gerald L. K. Smith, who organized the meeting in the auditorium.]

As this case declares a nation-wide rule that disables local and state authorities from punishing conduct which produces conflicts of this kind, it is unrealistic not to take account of the nature, methods, and objectives of the forces involved. This was not an isolated, spontaneous, and unintended collision of political, racial, or ideological adversaries. It was a local manifestation of a world-wide and standing conflict between two organized groups of revolutionary fanatics, each of which has imported to this country the strong-arm technique developed in the struggle by which their kind has devastated Europe. Increasingly, American cities have to cope with it. One faction organizes a mass meeting, the other organizes pickets to harass it; each organizes squads to counteract the other's pickets; parade is met with counterparade. Each of these mass demonstrations has the potentiality, and more than a few the purpose, of disorder and violence. This technique appeals not to reason but to fears and mob spirit; each is a show of force designed to bully adversaries and to overawe the indifferent. We need not resort to speculation as to the purposes for which these tactics are calculated nor as to their consequences. Recent European history demonstrates both. . . .

The present obstacle to mastery of the streets by either radical or reactionary mob movements is not the opposing minority. It is the authority of local governments which represent the free choice of democratic and law-abiding elements, of all shades of opinion but who, whatever their differences, submit them to free elections which register the results of their free discussion. The fascist and communist groups, on the contrary, resort to these terror tactics to confuse, bully, and discredit those freely chosen governments. Violent and noisy shows of strength discourage participation of moderates in discussions so fraught with violence, and real discussion dries up and disappears. And people lose faith in the democratic process when they see public authority flouted and impotent and begin to think the time has come when they must choose sides in a false and terrible dilemma such as was posed as being at hand by the call for the Terminiello meeting: "Christian Nationalism or World Communism—Which?"

This drive by totalitarian groups to undermine the prestige and effectiveness of local democratic governments is advanced whenever either of them can win from this Court a ruling which paralyzes the power of these officials. This is such a case. The group of which Terminiello is a part claims that his behavior, because it involved a speech, is above the reach of local authorities. If the mild action those authorities have taken is forbidden, it is plain that hereafter there is nothing effective left that they can do. If they can do nothing as to him, they are equally powerless as to rival totalitarian groups. Terminiello's victory today certainly fulfills the most extravagant hopes of both right and left totalitarian groups, who want nothing so much as to paralyze and discredit the only democratic authority that can curb them in their battle for the streets.

I am unable to see that the local authorities have transgressed the Federal Constitution. Illinois imposed no prior censorship or suppression upon Terminiello. . . .

A trial court and jury has found only that in the context of violence and disorder in which it was made, this speech was a provocation to immediate breach of the peace and therefore cannot claim constitutional immunity from punishment. Under the Constitution as it has been understood and applied, at least until most recently, the State was within its powers in taking this action.

Rioting is a substantive evil. . . . In this case the evidence proves beyond dispute that danger of rioting and violence in response to the speech was clear, present, and immediate. If this Court has not silently abandoned this long standing test and substituted for the purposes of this case an unexpressed but more stringent test, the action of the State would have to be sustained.

Only recently this Court held that a state could punish as a breach of the peace use of epithets such as "damned racketeer" and "damned fascists," addressed to only one person, an official, because likely to provoke the average person to retaliation. But these are mild in comparison to the epithets "slimy scum," "snakes," "bedbugs," and the like, which Terminiello hurled at an already inflamed mob of his adversaries. . . .

The Fourteenth Amendment forbade states to deny the citizen "due process of law." But its terms gave no notice to the people that its adoption would strip their local governments of power to deal with such problems of local peace and order as we have here. Nor was it hinted by this Court for over half a century that the Amendment might have any such effect. In 1922, with concurrence of the most liberty-alert Justices of all times—Holmes and Brandeis—this Court declared flatly that the Constitution does not limit the power of the state over free speech. *Prudential Insurance Co.* v. *Cheek.* In later years the Court shifted this dogma and decreed that the Constitution does this very thing and that state power is bound by the same limitation as Congress. *Gitlow* v. *New York* [1925]. I have no quarrel with this history. . . . I recite the method by which the right to limit the state has been derived only from this Court's own assumption of the power, with never a submission of legislation or amendment into which the people could write any qualification to prevent abuse of this liberty, as bearing upon the restraint I consider as becoming in exercise of self-given and unappealable power.

It is significant that provisions adopted by the people with awareness that they applied to their own states have universally contained qualifying terms. The Constitution of Illinois is representative of the provisions put in nearly all state constitutions and reads (Art. II, 4): "Every person may freely speak, write and publish on all subjects, being responsible for the abuse of that liberty." . . . That is what I think is meant by the cryptic phrase "freedom of speech," as used in the Federal Compact, and that is the rule I think we should apply to the states.

This absence from the Constitution of any expressed power to deal with abuse of freedom of speech has enabled the Court to soar aloof from any consideration of the abuses which create problems for the states and to indulge in denials of local authority, some of which seem to me improvident in the light of functions which local governments must be relied on to perform for our free society. Quite apart from any other merits or defects, recent decisions have almost completely immunized this battle for the streets from any form of control.

I do not think we should carry this handicap further, as we do today, but should adhere to the principles heretofore announced to safeguard our liberties against abuse as well as against invasion. It should not be necessary to recall these elementary principles, but it has been a long time since some of them were even mentioned in this Court's writing on the subject, and results indicate they may have been overlooked.

I begin with the oft-forgotten principle which this case demonstrates, that freedom of speech exists only under law and not independently of it. What would Terminiello's theoretical freedom of speech have amounted to had he not been given active aid by the officers of the law? He could reach the hall only with this help, could talk only because they restrained the mob, and could make his getaway only under their protection. . . .

This case demonstrates also that this Court's service to free speech is essentially negative and can consist only of reviewing actions by local magistrates. But if free speech is to be a practical reality, affirmative and immediate protection is required; and it can come only from nonjudicial sources. It depends on local police, maintained by law-abiding taxpayers, and who, regardless of their own feelings, risk themselves to maintain supremacy of law. Terminiello's theoretical right to speak free from interference would have no reality if Chicago should withdraw its officers to some other section of the city, or if the men assigned to the task should look the other way when the crowd threatens Terminiello. Can society be expected to keep these men at Terminiello's service if it has nothing to say of his behavior which may force them into dangerous action? . . .

In considering abuse of freedom by provocative utterances it is necessary to observe that the law is more tolerant of discussion than are most individuals or communities. Law is so indifferent to subjects of talk that I think of none that it should close to discussion. Religious, social, and political topics that in other times or countries have not been open to lawful debate may be freely discussed here.

Because a subject is legally arguable, however, does not mean that public sentiment will be patient of its advocacy at all times and in all manners. So it happens that, while peaceful advocacy of communism or fascism is tolerated by the law, both of these doctrines arouse passionate reactions. A great number of people do not agree that introduction to America of communism or fascism is even debatable. Hence many speeches, such as that of Terminiello, may be legally permissible but may nevertheless in some surrounding, be a menace to peace and order. When conditions show the speaker that this is the case, as it did here, there certainly comes a point beyond which he cannot indulge in provocations to violence without being answerable to society.

Determination of such an issue involves a heavy responsibility. Courts must beware lest they become mere organs of popular intolerance. Not every show of opposition can justify treating a speech as a breach of peace. Neither speakers nor courts are obliged always and in all circumstances to yield to prevailing opinion and feeling. As a people grow in capacity for civilization and liberty their tolerance will grow, and they will endure, if not welcome, discussion even on topics as to which they are committed. They regard convictions as tentative and know that time and events will make their own terms with theories, by whomever and by whatever majorities they are held, and many will be proved wrong. But on our way to this idealistic state of tolerance the police have to deal with men as they are. The crowd mind is never tolerant of any idea which does not conform to its herd opinion. It does not want a tolerant effort at meeting of minds. It does not know the futility of trying to mob an idea. Released from the sense of personal responsibility that would restrain even the worst individuals in it if alone, and brave with the courage of numbers, both radical and reactionary mobs endanger liberty as well as order. The authorities must control them, and they are entitled to place some checks upon those whose behavior or speech calls such mobs into being. When the right of society to freedom from probable violence should prevail over the right of an individual to defy opposing opinion, presents a problem that always tests wisdom and often calls for immediate and vigorous action to preserve public order and safety.

I do not think that the Constitution of the United States denies to the states and the municipalities power to solve that problem in the light of local conditions, at least so long as danger to public order is not invoked in bad faith, as a cover for censorship or suppression. The preamble declares domestic tranquility as well as liberty to be an object in founding a Federal Government, and I do not think the Forefathers were naïve in believing both can be fostered by the law.

Certain practical reasons reinforce the legal view that cities and states should be sustained in the power to keep their streets from becoming the battleground for these hostile ideologies to the destruction and detriment of public order. There is no other power that can do it. Theirs are the only police that are on the spot. . . . Every failure of local authority to deal with riot problems results in a demand for the establishment of a federal police or intervention by federal authority. In my opinion, locally established and controlled police can never develop into the menace to general civil liberties that is inherent in a federal police.

The ways in which mob violence may be worked up are subtle and various. Rarely will a speaker directly urge a crowd to lay hands on a victim or class of victims. An effective and safer way is to incite mob action while pretending to deplore it, after the classic example of Antony, and this was not lost on Terminiello. And whether one may be the cause of mob violence by his own personification or advocacy of ideas which a crowd already fears and hates, is not solved merely by going through a transcript of the speech to pick out "fighting words." The most insulting words can be neutralized if the speaker will smile when he says them, but a belligerent personality and an aggressive manner may kindle a fight without use of words that in cold type shock us. True judgment will be aided by observation of the individual defendant, as was possible for this jury and trial court but impossible for us. . . .

In the long run, maintenance of free speech will be more endangered if the population can have no protection from the abuses which lead to violence. No liberty is made more secure by holding that its abuses are inseparable from its enjoyment. We must not forget that it is the free democratic communities that ask us to trust them to maintain peace with liberty and that the factions engaged in this battle are not interested permanently in either. What would it matter to Terminiello if the police batter up some communists or, on the other hand, if the communists batter up some policemen? Either result makes grist for his mill; either would help promote hysteria and the demand for strong-arm methods in dealing with his adversaries. And what, on the other hand, have the communist agitators to lose from a battle with the police?

This Court has gone far toward accepting the doctrine that civil liberty means the removal of all restraints from these crowds and that all local attempts to maintain order are impairments of the liberty of the citizen. The choice is not between order and liberty. It is between liberty with order and anarchy without either. There is danger that, if the Court does not temper its doctrinaire logic with a little practical wisdom, it will convert the constitutional Bill of Rights into a suicide pact.

I would affirm the conviction.

AMERICAN COMMUNICATIONS ASSN. V. DOUDS
339 U.S. 382 (1950)

Section 9(h) of the Taft Hartley Act of 1947 made its protections contingent on whether officers of labor unions signed affidavits stating that they were not Communist Party members or supporters and did not believe in the forcible or illegal overthrow of the United States government. Soon enough a challenge to 9(h) materialized, as unions whose officers declined to sign the affidavits found themselves handicapped when seeking relief for unfair labor practices before the National Labor Relations Board. Challenging 9(h) on First Amendment grounds, the unions lost in the lower courts and, finally, in the Supreme Court.

In *Douds*, decided by a vote of 5 to 1, the Court did not apply the clear-and-present-danger test but instead used a "balancing" test. Addressing the unions' contention that 9(h) failed the older test, Chief Justice Vinson, writing for the Court, said "the considerations that gave birth to the phrase, 'clear and present danger,' not the phrase itself, . . . are vital in our decision of [First Amendment] questions." Those considerations, he explained, include "the right of the public to be protected from evils of conduct." Weighing "the probable effects" of the law upon First Amendment rights against the judgment of Congress that "political strikes are evils of conduct" and that Communists "pose continuing threats" to the public interest when they are union leaders, Vinson easily found for the latter.

Douds revealed a court plainly uncomfortable with the clear-and-present-danger test. "In suggesting that the substantive evil must be serious and substantial, it was never the intention of this Court to lay down an absolutist test measured in terms of danger to the nation," wrote Vinson. "When the effect of a statute or ordinance upon the exercise of First Amendment freedoms is relatively small and the public interest to be protected is substantial, it is obvious that a rigid test requiring a showing of imminent danger to the security of the nation is an absurdity." Though employed a year later in *Dennis* v. *United States*, the clear-and-present-danger test largely vanished from the Court's First Amendment cases over the next two decades.

Opinion of the Court: **Vinson**, Reed, Burton. Concurring in part: **Frankfurter**. Concurring and dissenting, each in part: **Jackson**. Dissenting: **Black**. Not participating: Douglas, Clark, Minton.

American Communications Assn. v. *Douds* was decided on May 8, 1950.

OPINION

CHIEF JUSTICE VINSON DELIVERED THE OPINION OF THE COURT . . .

The unions contend that once it is determined that this is a free speech case, the "clear and present danger" test must apply. See *Schenck* v. *United States* [1919]. But . . . the attempt to apply the term, "clear and present danger," as a mechanical test in every case touching First Amendment freedoms, without regard to the context of its application, mistakes the form in which an idea was cast for the substance of the idea. The provisions of the Constitution, said Justice Holmes, "are not mathematical formulas having their essence in their form; they are organic living institutions transplanted from English soil. Their significance is vital not formal; it is to be gathered not simply by taking the words and a dictionary, but by considering their origin and the line of their growth." *Gompers* v. *United States* [1914]. Still less should this Court's interpretations of the Constitution be reduced to the status of mathematical formulas. It is the considerations that gave birth to the phrase, "clear and present danger," not the phrase itself, that are vital in our decision of questions involving liberties protected by the First Amendment.

Although the First Amendment provides that Congress shall make no law abridging the freedom of speech, press, or assembly, it has long been established that those freedoms themselves are dependent upon the power of constitutional government to survive. If it is to survive it must have power to protect itself against unlawful conduct and, under some circumstances, against incitements to commit unlawful acts. Freedom of speech thus does not comprehend the right to speak on any subject at any time. The important question that came to this Court immediately after the First World War was not whether, but how far, the First Amendment permits the suppression of speech which advocates conduct inimical to the public welfare.

Some thought speech having a reasonable tendency to lead to such conduct might be punished. Justices Holmes and Brandeis took a different view. They thought that the greater danger to a democracy lies in the suppression of public discussion; that ideas and doctrines thought harmful or dangerous are best fought with words. Only, therefore, when force is very likely to follow an utterance before there is a chance for counter-argument to have effect may that utterance be punished or prevented. . . .

But the question with which we are here faced is not the same one that Justices Holmes and Brandeis found convenient to consider in terms of clear and present danger. Government's interest here is not in preventing the dissemination of Communist doctrine or the holding of particular beliefs because it is feared that unlawful action will result therefrom if free speech is practiced. Its interest is in protecting the free flow of commerce from what Congress considers to be substantial evils of conduct that are not the products of speech at all. Section 9(h), in other words, does not interfere with speech because Congress fears the consequences of speech; it regulates harmful conduct which Congress has determined is carried on by persons who may be identified by their political affiliations and beliefs. The Board does not contend that political strikes, the substantive evil at which 9(h) is aimed, are the present or impending products of advocacy of the doctrines of Communism or the expression of belief in overthrow of the Government by force. On the contrary, it points out that such strikes are called by persons who, so Congress has found, have the will and power to do so without advocacy or persuasion that seeks acceptance in the competition of the market. Speech may be fought with speech. Falsehoods and fallacies must be exposed, not suppressed, unless there is not sufficient time to avert the evil consequences of noxious doctrine by argument and education. That is the command of the First Amendment. But force may and must be met with force. Section 9(h) is designed to protect the public not against what Communists and others identified therein advocate or believe, but against what Congress has concluded they have done and are likely to do again. . . .

The contention . . . that this Court must find that political strikes create a clear and present danger to the security of the Nation or of widespread industrial strife in order to sustain 9(h) similarly misconceives the purpose that phrase was intended to serve. In that view, not the relative certainty that evil conduct will result from speech in the immediate future, but the extent and gravity of the substantive evil must be measured by the "test" laid down in the *Schenck* case. But there the Court said that: "The question in every case is whether the words used are used in such circumstances and are of such a nature as to create a clear and present danger that they will bring about the substantive evils that Congress has a right to prevent." *Schenck.* . . .

So far as the *Schenck* case itself is concerned, imminent danger of any substantive evil that Congress may prevent justifies the restriction of speech. Since that time this Court has decided that however great the likelihood that a substantive evil will result, restrictions on speech and press cannot be sustained unless the evil itself is "substantial" and "relatively serious," Brandeis, J., concurring in *Whitney* v. *California* [1927], or sometimes "extremely serious," *Bridges* v. *California* [1941]. And it follows therefrom that even harmful conduct cannot justify restrictions upon speech unless substantial interests of society are at stake. But in suggesting that the substantive evil must be serious and substantial, it was never the intention of this Court to lay down an absolutist test measured in terms of danger to the Nation. When the effect of a statute or ordinance upon the exercise of First Amendment freedoms is relatively small and the public interest to be protected is substantial, it is obvious that a rigid test requiring a showing of imminent danger to the security of the Nation is an absurdity. . . .

On the contrary, however, the right of the public to be protected from evils of conduct, even though First Amendment rights of persons or groups are thereby in some manner infringed, has received frequent and consistent recognition by this Court. . . .

When particular conduct is regulated in the interest of public order, and the regulation results in an indirect, conditional, partial abridgment of speech, the duty of the courts is to determine which of these two conflicting interests demands the greater protection under the particular circumstances presented. The high place in which the right to speak, think, and assemble as you will was held by the Framers of the Bill of Rights and is held today by those who value liberty both as a means and as an end indicates the solicitude with which we must view any assertion of personal freedoms. We must recognize, moreover, that regulation of "conduct" has all too frequently been employed by public authority as a cloak to hide censorship of unpopular ideas. We have been reminded that "It is not often in this country that we now meet with direct and candid efforts to stop speaking or publication as such. Modern inroads on these rights come from associating the speaking with some other factor which the state may regulate so as to bring the whole within official control." [Jackson, J., concurring in *Thomas* v. *Collins*, 1945.]

On the other hand, legitimate attempts to protect the public, not from the remote possible effects of noxious ideologies, but from present excesses of direct, active conduct, are not presumptively bad because they interfere with and, in some of its manifestations, restrain the exercise of First Amendment rights. . . . In essence, the problem is one of weighing the probable effects of the statute upon the free exercise of the right of speech and assembly against the congressional determination that political strikes are evils of conduct which cause substantial harm to interstate commerce and that Communists and others identified by 9(h) pose continuing threats to that public interest when in positions of union leadership. We must, therefore, undertake the "delicate and difficult task . . . to weigh the circumstances and to appraise the substantiality of the reasons advanced in support of the regulation of the free enjoyment of the rights." *Schneider* v. *State* [1939].

The "reasons advanced in support of the regulation" are of considerable weight, as even the opponents of 9(h) agreed. . . . It should be emphasized that Congress, not the courts, is primarily charged with determination of the need for regulation of activities affecting interstate commerce. This Court must, if such regulation unduly infringes personal freedoms, declare the statute invalid under the First Amendment's command that the opportunities for free public discussion be maintained. But insofar as the problem is one of drawing inferences concerning the need for regulation of particular forms of conduct from conflicting evidence, this Court is in no position to substitute its judgment as to the necessity or desirability of the statute for that of Congress. Cf. *United Public Workers* v. *Mitchell* [1947]. . . .

When compared with ordinances and regulations dealing with littering of the streets or disturbance of house-holders by itinerant preachers, the relative significance and complexity of the problem of political strikes and how to deal with their leaders becomes at once apparent. It must be remembered that 9(h) is not an isolated statute dealing with a subject divorced from the problems of labor peace generally. It is a part of some very complex machinery set up by the Federal Government for the purpose of encouraging the peaceful settlement of labor disputes. Under the statutory scheme, unions which become collective bargaining representatives for groups of employees often represent not only members of the union but nonunion workers or members of other unions as well. Because of the necessity to have strong unions to bargain on equal terms with strong employers, individual employees are required by law to sacrifice rights which, in some cases, are valuable to them. . . . The loss of individual rights for the greater benefit of the group results in a tremendous increase in the power of the representative of the group—the union. But power is never without responsibility. And when authority derives in part from Government's thumb on the scales, the exercise of that power by private persons becomes closely akin, in some respects, to its exercise by Government itself. . . .

What of the effects of 9(h) upon the rights of speech and assembly of those proscribed by its terms? The statute does not prevent or punish by criminal sanctions the making of a speech, the affiliation with any organization, or the holding of any belief. But as we have noted, the fact that no direct restraint or punishment is imposed upon speech or assembly does not determine the free speech question. Under some circumstances, indirect "discouragements" undoubtedly have the same coercive effect upon the exercise of First Amendment rights as imprisonment, fines, injunctions, or taxes. A requirement that adherents of particular religious faiths or political parties wear identifying arm-bands, for example, is obviously of this nature.

But we have here no statute which is either frankly aimed at the suppression of dangerous ideas nor one which, although ostensibly aimed at the regulation of conduct, may actually "be made the instrument of arbitrary suppression of free expression of views." *Hague* v. *Com-*

mittee for Industrial Organization [1939]. There are here involved none of the elements of censorship or prohibition of the dissemination of information that were present in the cases mainly relied upon by those attacking the statute. The "discouragements" of 9(h) proceed, not against the groups or beliefs identified therein, but only against the combination of those affiliations or beliefs with occupancy of a position of great power over the economy of the country. Congress has concluded that substantial harm, in the form of direct, positive action, may be expected from that combination. In this legislation, Congress did not restrain the activities of the Communist Party as a political organization; nor did it attempt to stifle beliefs. Compare *West Virginia State Board of Education* v. *Barnette* [1943]. Section 9(h) touches only a relative handful of persons, leaving the great majority of persons of the identified affiliations and beliefs completely free from restraint. And it leaves those few who are affected free to maintain their affiliations and beliefs subject only to possible loss of positions which Congress has concluded are being abused to the injury of the public by members of the described groups. . . .

It is contended that the principle that statutes touching First Amendment freedoms must be narrowly drawn dictates that a statute aimed at political strikes should make the calling of such strikes unlawful but should not attempt to bring about the removal of union officers, with its attendant effect upon First Amendment rights. We think, however, that the legislative judgment that interstate commerce must be protected from a continuing threat of such strikes is a permissible one in this case. The fact that the injury to interstate commerce would be an accomplished fact before any sanctions could be applied, the possibility that a large number of such strikes might be called at a time of external or internal crisis, and the practical difficulties which would be encountered in detecting illegal activities of this kind are factors which are persuasive that Congress should not be powerless to remove the threat, not limited to punishing the act. . . .

Previous discussion has considered the constitutional questions raised by 9(h) as they apply alike to members of the Communist Party and affiliated organizations and to persons who believe in overthrow of the Government by force. The breadth of the provision concerning belief in overthrow of the Government by force would raise additional questions, however, if it were read very literally to include all persons who might, under any conceivable circumstances, subscribe to that belief.

But we see no reason to construe the statute so broadly. It is within the power and is the duty of this Court to construe a statute so as to avoid the danger of unconstitutionality if it may be done in consonance with the legislative purpose. . . . The congressional purpose is . . . served if we construe the clause, "that he does not believe in, and is not a member of or supports any organization that believes in or teaches, the overthrow of the United States Government by force or by any illegal or unconstitutional methods," to apply to persons and organizations who believe in violent overthrow of the Government as it presently exists under the Constitution as an objective, not merely a prophecy. Congress might well find that such persons—those who believe that the present form of the Government of the United States should be changed by force or other illegal methods—would carry that objective into their conduct of union affairs by calling political strikes designed to weaken and divide the American people, whether they consider actual overthrow of the Government to be near or distant. It is to those persons that 9(h) is intended to apply, and only to them. We hold, therefore, that the belief identified in 9(h) is a belief in the objective of overthrow by force or by any illegal or unconstitutional methods of the Government of the United States as it now exists under the Constitution and laws thereof.

As thus construed, we think that the "belief" provision of the oath presents no different problem from that present in that part of the section having to do with membership in the Communist Party. Of course we agree that one may not be imprisoned or executed because he holds particular beliefs. But to attack the straw man of "thought control" is to ignore the fact that the sole effect of the statute upon one who believes in overthrow of the Government by force and violence—and does not deny his belief—is that he may be forced to relinquish his position as a union leader. . . .

To hold that such an oath is permissible . . . is to admit that the circumstances under which one is asked to state his belief and the consequences which flow from his refusal to do so or his disclosure of a particular belief make a difference. The reason for the difference has been pointed out at some length. . . . First, the loss of a particular position is not the loss of life or liberty. We have noted that the distinction is one of degree, and it is for this reason that the effect of the statute in proscribing beliefs—like its effect in restraining speech or freedom of association—must be carefully weighed by the courts in determining whether the balance struck by Congress comports with the dictates of the Constitution. But it is inaccurate to speak of 9(h) as "punishing" or "forbidding" the holding of beliefs, any more than it punishes or forbids membership in the Communist Party.

Second, the public interest at stake in ascertaining one's beliefs cannot automatically be assigned at zero without consideration of the circumstances of the inquiry. If it is admitted that beliefs are springs to action, it becomes highly relevant whether the person who is asked whether he believes in overthrow of the Government by force is a general with five hundred thousand men at his command or a village constable. To argue that because the latter may not be asked his beliefs the former must necessarily be exempt is to make a fetish of beliefs. The answer to the implication that if this statute is upheld "then the power of government over beliefs is as unlimited as its power over conduct and the way is open to force disclosure of attitudes on all manner of social, economic, moral, and political issues," is that that result does not follow "while this Court sits." The circumstances giving rise to the inquiry, then, are likewise factors to be weighed by the courts, giving due weight, of course, to the congressional judgment concerning the need. In short, the problem of balancing the conflicting individual and national interests involved is no different from the problem presented by proscriptions based upon political affiliations. . . .

Considering the circumstances surrounding the problem—the deference due the congressional judgment concerning the need for regulation of conduct affecting interstate commerce and the effect of the statute upon rights of speech, assembly, and belief—we conclude that 9(h) of the National Labor Relations Act, as amended by the Labor Management Relations Act, 1947, does not unduly infringe freedoms protected by the First Amendment. Those who, so Congress has found, would subvert the public interest cannot escape all regulation because, at the same time, they carry on legitimate political activities. . . . To encourage unions to displace them from positions of great power over the national economy, while at the same time leaving free the outlets by which they may pursue legitimate political activities of persuasion and advocacy, does not seem to us to contravene the purposes of the First Amendment. That Amendment requires that one be permitted to believe what he will. It requires that one be permitted to advocate what he will unless there is a clear and present danger that a substantial public evil will result therefrom. It does not require that he be permitted to be the keeper of the arsenal. . . .

AFFIRMED.

FEINER V. NEW YORK
340 U.S. 315 (1951)

On a street corner in Syracuse, New York, a college student named Irving Feiner addressed a gathering of whites and blacks, about eighty people in all. Feiner made derogatory remarks about President Truman, the American Legion, and local public officials, and he urged blacks to rise up in arms and fight for equal rights. Police headquarters received a telephone complaint about the meeting and sent two officers to the scene. Concerned about the apparent effect of Feiner's words upon public order—the crowd was restless, and one person threatened violence if the police did not intervene—the officers asked him to stop speaking. When he refused to do so, they arrested him. Feiner was convicted of disorderly conduct and sentenced to thirty days in jail. He challenged his conviction on free speech grounds but lost in the New York courts and ultimately in the Supreme Court, there by a vote of 6 to 3.

With Chief Justice Vinson writing, the Court deferred to the findings and judgments of the New York courts and saw the case as one in which it was compelled to respect "the interest of the community in maintaining peace and order in the streets." In refusing to "reverse this conviction in the name of free speech," the Court seemed to adopt (without so indicating) the position of Justice Jackson in dissent in *Terminiello* v. *Chicago* (1949): that government has "the right and the duty to prevent and punish" any "clear, present, and immediate" danger of rioting and violence in response to a public speech. Justice Black filed a biting dissent, arguing that as a result of the Court's decision "minority speakers can be silenced in any city" and "criticism of public officials will be too dangerous for all but the most courageous."

Opinion of the Court: **Vinson**, Reed, Jackson, Burton, Clark. Concurring in the result: **Frankfurter**. Dissenting opinions: **Black**; **Douglas**, Minton.

Feiner v. *New York* was decided on January 15, 1951.

OPINIONS

CHIEF JUSTICE VINSON DELIVERED THE OPINION OF THE COURT . . .

In the review of state decisions where First Amendment rights are drawn in question, we of course make an examination of the evidence to ascertain independently whether the right has been violated. Here, the trial judge, who heard the case without a jury, rendered an oral decision at the end of the trial, setting forth his determination of the facts upon which he found the petitioner guilty. His decision indicated generally that he believed the state's witnesses, and his summation of the testimony was used by the two New York courts on review in stating the facts. Our appraisal of the facts is, therefore, based upon the uncontroverted facts and, where controversy exists, upon that testimony which the trial judge did reasonably conclude to be true.

On the evening of March 8, 1949, petitioner Irving Feiner was addressing an open-air meeting at the corner of South McBride and Harrison Streets in the City of Syracuse. At approximately 6:30 p.m., the police received a telephone complaint concerning the meeting, and two officers were detailed to investigate. One of these officers went to the scene immediately, the other arriving some twelve minutes later. They found a crowd of about seventy-five or eighty people, both Negro and white, filling the sidewalk and spreading out into the street. Petitioner, standing on a large wooden box on the sidewalk, was addressing the crowd through a loud-speaker system attached to an automobile. Although the purpose of his speech was to urge his listeners to attend a meeting to be held that night in the Syracuse Hotel, in its course he was making derogatory remarks concerning President Truman, the American Legion, the Mayor of Syracuse, and other local political officials.

The police officers made no effort to interfere with petitioner's speech, but were first concerned with the effect of the crowd on both pedestrian and vehicular traffic. They observed the situation from the opposite side of the street, noting that some pedestrians were forced to walk in the street to avoid the crowd. Since traffic was passing at the time, the officers attempted to get the people listening to petitioner back on the sidewalk. The crowd was restless, and there was some pushing, shoving, and milling around. One of the officers telephoned the police station from a nearby store, and then both policemen crossed the street and mingled with the crowd without any intention of arresting the speaker.

At this time, petitioner was speaking in a "loud, high-pitched voice." He gave the impression that he was endeavoring to arouse the Negro people against the whites, urging that they rise up in arms and fight for equal rights. The statements before such a mixed audience "stirred up a little excitement." Some of the onlookers made remarks to the police about their inability to handle the crowd, and at least one threatened violence if the police did not act. There were others who appeared to be favoring petitioner's arguments. Because of the feeling that existed in the crowd both for and against the speaker, the officers finally "stepped in to prevent it from resulting in a fight." One of the officers approached the petitioner, not for the purpose of arresting him, but to get him to break up the crowd. He asked petitioner to get down off the box, but the latter refused to accede to his request and continued talking. The officer waited for a minute and then demanded that he cease talking. Although the officer had thus twice requested petitioner to stop over the course of several minutes, petitioner not only ignored him but continued talking. During all this time, the crowd was pressing closer around petitioner and the officer. Finally, the officer told petitioner he was under arrest and ordered him to get down from the box, reaching up to grab him. Petitioner stepped down, announcing over the microphone that "the law has arrived, and I suppose they will take over now." In all, the officer had asked petitioner to get down off the box three times over a space of four or five minutes. Petitioner had been speaking for over a half hour.

On these facts, petitioner was specifically charged with violation of 722 of the Penal Law of New York. . . . The bill of particulars, demanded by petitioner and furnished by the State, gave in detail the facts upon which the prosecution relied to support the charge of disorderly conduct. Paragraph C is particularly pertinent here: "By ignoring and refusing to heed and obey reasonable police orders issued at the time and place mentioned in the Information to regulate and control said crowd and to prevent a breach or breaches of the peace and to prevent injury to pedestrians attempting to use said walk, and being forced into the highway adjacent to the place in question, and prevent injury to the public generally."

We are not faced here with blind condonation by a state court of arbitrary police action. Petitioner was accorded a full, fair trial. The trial judge heard testimony supporting and contradicting the judgment of the police officers that a clear danger of disorder was threatened. After weighing this contradictory evidence, the trial judge reached the conclusion that the police officers were justified in taking action to prevent a breach of the peace. The exercise of the police officers' proper discretionary power to prevent a breach of the peace was thus approved by the trial court and later by two courts on review. The courts below recognized petitioner's right to hold a street meeting at this locality, to make use of loud-speaking equipment in giving his speech, and to make derogatory remarks concerning public officials and the American Legion. They found that the officers in making the arrest were motivated solely by a proper concern for the preservation of order and protection of the general welfare, and that there was no evidence which could lend color to a claim that the acts of the police were a cover for suppression of petitioner's views and opinions. Petitioner was thus neither arrested nor convicted for the making or the content of his speech. Rather, it was the reaction which it actually engendered.

The language of *Cantwell* v. *Connecticut* [1940], is appropriate here. "The offense known as breach of the peace embraces a great variety of conduct destroying or menacing public order and tranquility. It includes not only violent acts but acts and words likely to produce violence in others. No one would have the hardihood to suggest that the principle of freedom of speech sanctions incitement to riot or that religious liberty connotes the privilege to exhort others to physical attack upon those belonging to another sect. When clear and present danger of riot, disorder, interference with traffic upon the public streets, or other immediate threat to public safety, peace, or order, appears, the power of the State to prevent or punish is obvious." The findings of the New York courts as to the condition of the crowd and the refusal of petitioner to obey the police requests, supported as they are by the record of this case, are persuasive that the conviction of petitioner for violation of public peace, order, and authority does not exceed the bounds of proper state police action. This Court respects, as it must, the interest of the community in maintaining peace and order on its streets. *Schneider* v. *State* [1939]; *Kovacs* v. *Cooper* [1949]. We cannot say that the preservation of that interest here encroaches on the constitutional rights of this petitioner.

We are well aware that the ordinary murmurings and objections of a hostile audience cannot be allowed to silence a speaker, and are also mindful of the possible danger of giving overzealous police officials complete discretion to break up otherwise lawful public meetings. "A State may not unduly suppress free communication of views, religious or other, under the guise of conserving desirable conditions." *Cantwell*. But we are not faced here with such a situation. It is one thing to say that the police cannot be used as an instrument for the suppression of unpopular views, and another to say that, when as here the speaker passes the bounds of argument or persuasion and undertakes incitement to riot, they are powerless to prevent a breach of the peace. Nor in this case can we condemn the considered judgment of three New York courts approving the means which the police, faced with a crisis, used in the exercise of their power and duty to preserve peace and order. The findings of the state courts as to the existing situation and the imminence of greater disorder coupled with petitioner's deliberate defiance of the police officers convince us that we should not reverse this conviction in the name of free speech.

AFFIRMED.

JUSTICE BLACK, DISSENTING . . .

The record before us convinces me that petitioner, a young college student, has been sentenced to the penitentiary for the unpopular views he expressed on matters of public interest while lawfully making a street-corner speech in Syracuse, New York. Today's decision, however, indicates that we must blind ourselves to this fact because the trial judge fully accepted the testimony of the prosecution witnesses on all important points. . . .

But . . . [e]ven accepting every "finding of fact" below, I think this conviction makes a mockery of the free speech guarantees of the First and Fourteenth Amendments. The end result of the affirmance here is to approve a simple and readily available technique by which cities and states can with impunity subject all speeches, political or otherwise, on streets or elsewhere, to the supervision and censorship of the local police. I will have no part or parcel in this holding which I view as a long step toward totalitarian authority. . . .

The Court's opinion apparently rests on this reasoning: The policeman, under the circumstances detailed, could reasonably conclude that serious fighting or even riot was imminent; therefore he could stop petitioner's speech to prevent a breach of peace; accordingly, it was "disorderly conduct" for petitioner to continue speaking in disobedience of the officer's request. As to the existence of a dangerous situation on the street corner, it seems far-fetched to suggest that the "facts" show any imminent threat of riot or uncontrollable disorder. It is neither unusual nor unexpected that some people at public street meetings mutter, mill about, push, shove, or disagree, even violently, with the speaker. Indeed, it is rare where controversial topics are discussed that an outdoor crowd does not do some or all of these things. Nor does one isolated threat to assault the speaker forebode disorder. Especially should the danger be discounted where, as here, the person threatening was a man whose wife and two small children accompanied him and who, so far as the record shows, was never close enough to petitioner to carry out the threat.

Moreover, assuming that the "facts" did indicate a critical situation, I reject the implication of the Court's opinion that the police had no obligation to protect petitioner's constitutional right to talk. The police of course have power to prevent breaches of the peace. But if, in the name of preserving order, they ever can interfere with a lawful public speaker, they first must make all reasonable efforts to protect him. Here the policemen did not even pretend to try to protect petitioner. According to the officers' testimony, the crowd was restless but there is no showing of any attempt to quiet it; pedestrians were forced to walk into the street, but there was no effort to clear a path on the sidewalk; one person threatened to assault petitioner, but the officers did nothing to discourage this when even a word might have sufficed. Their duty was to protect petitioner's right to talk, even to the extent of arresting the man who threatened to interfere. Instead, they shirked that duty and acted only to suppress the right to speak.

Finally, I cannot agree with the Court's statement that petitioner's disregard of the policeman's unexplained request amounted to such "deliberate defiance" as would justify an arrest or conviction for disorderly conduct. On the contrary, I think that the policeman's action was a "deliberate defiance" of ordinary official duty as well as of the constitutional right of free speech. For at least where time allows, courtesy and explanation of commands are basic elements of good official conduct in a democratic society. Here petitioner was "asked" then "told" then "commanded" to stop speaking, but a man making a lawful address is certainly not required to be silent merely because an officer directs it. Petitioner was entitled to know why he should cease doing a lawful act. . . .

In my judgment, today's holding means that as a practical matter, minority speakers can be silenced in any city. Hereafter, despite the First and Fourteenth Amendments, the policeman's club can take heavy toll of a current administration's public critics. Criticism of public officials will be too dangerous for all but the most courageous. This is true regardless of the fact that in two other cases decided this day, *Kunz* v. *New York, Niemotko* v. *Maryland*, a majority, in obedience to past decisions of this Court, provides a theoretical safeguard for freedom of speech. For whatever is thought to be guaranteed in *Kunz* and *Niemotko* is taken away by what is done here. The three cases read together mean that while previous restraints probably cannot be imposed on an unpopular speaker, the police have discretion to silence him as soon as the customary hostility to his views develops. . . .

JUSTICE DOUGLAS, DISSENTING . . .

Public assemblies and public speech occupy an important role in American life. One high function of the police is to protect these lawful gatherings so that the speakers may exercise their constitutional rights. When unpopular causes are sponsored from the public platform, there will commonly be mutterings and unrest and heckling from the crowd. When a speaker mounts a platform it is not unusual to find him resorting to exaggeration, to vilification of ideas and men, to the making of false charges. But those extravagances, as we emphasized in *Cantwell* v. *Connecticut* [1940], do not justify penalizing the speaker by depriving him of the platform or by punishing him for his conduct.

A speaker may not, of course, incite a riot any more than he may incite a breach of the peace by the use of "fighting words." See *Chaplinsky* v. *New Hampshire* [1942]. But this record shows no such extremes. It shows an unsympathetic audience and the threat of one man to haul the speaker from the stage. It is against that kind of threat that speakers need police protection. If they do not receive it and instead the police throw their weight on the side of those who would break up the meetings, the police become the new censors of speech. Police censorship has all the vices of the censorship from city halls which we have repeatedly struck down. . . .

KUNZ V. NEW YORK
340 U.S. 290 (1951)

A New York City ordinance said that street preachers could not hold public meetings without first obtaining a permit from the city police commissioner. In 1946, Carl J. Kunz, an ordained Baptist minister, applied for and received the necessary permit, but later it was revoked by the police commissioner on grounds that during his meetings Kunz had ridiculed and denounced the religious beliefs of Catholics and Jews. Kunz applied for permits in 1947 and 1948 without success but continued to conduct his "Outdoor Gospel Work." During one of his public meetings in the fall of 1948, he was arrested for speaking without a permit. Convicted and fined $10, Kunz brought a First Amendment challenge. He lost in the New York courts but prevailed in the Supreme Court by a vote of 8 to 1.

Writing for the majority, Chief Justice Vinson found the New York City ordinance an unconstitutional "prior restraint" because it gave "an administrative official"—here the police commissioner—"discretionary power to control in advance the right of citizens to speak on religious matters." Alone in dissent, Justice Jackson contended that prior restraint—a doctrine first elaborated in *Near* v. *Minnesota* (1931)—was most applicable in press cases and could not "reasonably be transposed to the street-meeting field." Jackson found other precedents relevant. Kunz, he said, had uttered the very kind of insulting or "fighting" words that a unanimous Court only nine years earlier in *Chaplinsky* v. *New Hampshire* (1942) had declared unequivocally beyond constitutional protection. Kunz's words, he added, citing Justice Holmes's opinion for the Court in *Schenck* v. *United States* (1919), were "of such a nature as to create a clear and present danger that they will bring about the substantive evils" that New York City has a right to prevent—those evils being "street fighting or riots."

Opinion of the Court: **Vinson**, Reed, Douglas, Burton, Clark, Minton. Concurring in the result: **Black**, Frankfurter. Dissenting opinion: **Jackson**.

Kunz v. *New York* was decided on January 15, 1951.

OPINIONS

CHIEF JUSTICE VINSON DELIVERED THE OPINION OF THE COURT . . .

Although the penalties of the ordinance apply to anyone who "ridicules and denounces other religious beliefs," the ordinance does not specify this as a ground for permit revocation. Indeed, there is no mention in the ordinance of any power of revocation. However, appellant did not seek judicial or administrative review of the revocation proceedings, and any question as to the propriety of the revocation is not before us in this case. In any event, the revocation affected appellant's rights to speak in 1946 only. Appellant applied for another permit in 1947, and again in 1948, but was notified each time that his application was "disapproved," with no reason for the disapproval being given. On September 11, 1948, appellant was arrested for speaking at Columbus Circle in New York City without a permit. It is from the conviction which resulted that this appeal has been taken.

Appellant's conviction was thus based upon his failure to possess a permit for 1948. We are here concerned only with the propriety of the action of the police commissioner in refusing to issue that permit. Disapproval of the 1948 permit application by the police commissioner was justified by the New York courts on the ground that a permit had previously been revoked "for good reasons." It is noteworthy that there is no mention in the ordinance of reasons for which such a permit application can be refused. This interpretation allows the police commissioner, an administrative official, to exercise discretion in denying subsequent permit applications on the basis of his interpretation, at that time, of what is deemed to be conduct condemned by the ordinance. We have here, then, an ordinance which gives an administrative official discretionary power to control in advance the right of citizens to speak on religious matters on the streets of New York. As such, the ordinance is clearly invalid as a prior restraint on the exercise of First Amendment rights.

In considering the right of a municipality to control the use of public streets for the expression of religious views, we start with the words of Justice Roberts that "Wherever the title of streets and parks may rest, they have immemorially been held in trust for the use of the public and, time out of mind, have been used for purposes of assembly, communicating thoughts between citizens, and discussing public questions." *Hague* v. *C.I.O.* [1939]. Although this Court has recognized that a statute may be enacted which prevents serious interference with normal usage of streets and parks, *Cox* v. *New Hampshire* [1941], we have consistently condemned licensing systems which vest in an administrative official discretion to grant or withhold a permit upon broad criteria unrelated to proper regulation of public places. . . .

The court below has mistakenly derived support for its conclusion from the evidence produced at the trial that appellant's religious meetings had, in the past, caused some disorder. There are appropriate public remedies to protect the peace and order of the community if appellant's speeches should result in disorder or violence. "In the present case, we have no occasion to inquire as to the permissible scope of subsequent punishment." *Near* v. *Minnesota* [1931]. We do not express any opinion on the propriety of punitive remedies which the New York authorities may utilize. We are here concerned with suppression—not punishment. It is sufficient to say that New York cannot vest restraining control over the right to speak on religious subjects in an administrative official where there are no appropriate standards to guide his action.

REVERSED.

JUSTICE JACKSON, DISSENTING . . .

Essential freedoms are today threatened from without and within. It may become difficult to preserve here what a large part of the world has lost—the right to speak, even temperately, on matters vital to spirit and body. In such a setting, to blanket hateful and hate-stirring attacks on races and faiths under the protections for freedom of speech may be a noble innovation. On the other hand, it may be a quixotic tilt at windmills which belittles great principles of liberty. Only time can tell. But I incline to the latter view and cannot assent to the decision.

To know what we are doing, we must first locate the point at which rights asserted by Kunz conflict with powers asserted by the organized community. New York City has placed no limitation upon any speech Kunz may choose to make on private property, but it does require a permit to hold religious meetings in its streets. The ordinance, neither by its terms nor as it has been applied, prohibited Kunz, even in street meetings, from preaching his own religion or making any temperate criticism or refutation of other religions; indeed, for the year 1946, he was given a general permit to do so. His meetings, however, brought "a flood of complaints" to city authorities that he was engaging in scurrilous attacks on Catholics and Jews. . . .

At these meetings, Kunz preached, among many other things of like tenor, that "The Catholic Church makes merchandise out of souls," that Catholicism is "a religion of the devil," and that the Pope is "the anti-Christ." The Jews he denounced as "Christ-killers," and he said of them, "All the garbage that didn't believe in Christ should have been burnt in the incinerators. It's a shame they all weren't."

These utterances, as one might expect, stirred strife and threatened violence. . . .

The speeches which Kunz has made and which he asserts he has a right to make in the future were properly held by the courts below to be out of bounds for a street meeting and not constitutionally protected. This Court, without discussion, makes a contrary assumption which is basic to its whole opinion. It says New York has given "an administrative official discretionary power to control in advance the right of citizens to speak on religious matters on the streets." Again, it says that "prior restraint on the exercise of First Amendment rights" invalidates the ordinance. . . . This seems to take the last step first, assuming as a premise what is in question. . . .

This Court today initiates the doctrine that language such as this, in the environment of the street meeting, is immune from prior municipal control. We would have a very different question if New York had presumed to say that Kunz could not speak his piece in his own pulpit or hall. But it has undertaken to restrain him only if he chooses to speak at street meetings. There is a world of difference. The street preacher takes advantage of people's presence on the streets to impose his message upon what, in a sense, is a captive audience. A meeting on private property is made up of an audience that has volunteered to listen. The question, therefore, is not whether New York could, if it tried, silence Kunz, but whether it must place its streets at his service to hurl insults at the passer-by.

What Justice Holmes said for a unanimous Court in *Schenck* v. *United States* [1919] has become an axiom: "The most stringent protection of free speech would not protect a man in falsely shouting fire in a theatre and causing a panic." This concept was applied in one of its few unanimous decisions in recent years, when, through Justice Murphy, the Court said: "There are certain well-defined and narrowly limited classes of speech, the prevention and punishment of which have never been thought to raise any Constitutional problem. These include the lewd and obscene, the profane, the libelous, and the insulting or 'fighting' words—those which by their very utterance inflict injury or tend to incite an immediate breach of the peace. . . ." *Chaplinsky* v. *New Hampshire* [1942].

There held to be "insulting or 'fighting' words" were calling one a "God damned racketeer" and a "damned Fascist." Equally inciting and more clearly "fighting words," when thrown at Catholics and Jews who are rightfully on the streets of New York, are statements that "The Pope is the anti-Christ" and the Jews are "Christ-killers." These terse epithets come down to our generation weighted with hatreds accumulated through centuries of bloodshed. They are recognized words of art in the profession of defamation. They are not the kind of insult that men bandy and laugh off when the spirits are high and the flagons are low. They are not in that class of epithets whose literal sting will be drawn if the speaker smiles when he uses them. They are always, and in every context, insults which do not spring from reason and can be answered by none. Their historical associations with violence are well understood, both by those who hurl and those who are struck by these missiles. . . .

This Court's prior decisions, as well as its decisions today, will be searched in vain for clear standards by which it does, or lower courts should, distinguish legitimate speaking from that acknowledged to be outside of constitutional protection. . . .

What evidences that a street speech is so provocative, insulting, or inciting as to be outside of constitutional immunity from community interference? Is it determined by the actual reaction of the hearers? Or is it a judicial appraisal of the inherent quality of the language used? Or both?

I understand, though disagree with, the minority in the *Feiner* case [decided the same day; see case 20], who, so far as I can see, would require no standards since they recognize no limits at all, considering that some rioting is the price of free speech and that the city must allow all speech and pay the price. But every juristic or philosophic authority recognized in this field admits that there are some speeches one is not free to make. The problem, on which they disagree, is how and where to draw the line.

It is peculiar that today's opinion makes no reference to the "clear and present danger" test which for years has played some part in free-speech cases. . . . If New York has benefit of the rule as Justice Holmes announced it, *Schenck* v. *United States* [1919], it would mean that it could punish or prevent speech if "the words used are used in such circumstances and are of such a nature as to create a clear and present danger that they will bring about the substantive evils" that the City has a right to prevent, among which I should suppose we would list street fighting or riots. As I have pointed out, the proof in this case leaves no doubt that Kunz's words, in the environment of the streets, have and will result in that, unless a police escort attends to awe the hearers into submission.

A hostile reception of his subject certainly does not alone destroy one's right to speak. A temperate and reasoned criticism of Roman Catholicism or Judaism might, and probably would, cause some resentment and protest. But in a free society all sects and factions, as the price of their own freedom to preach their views, must suffer that freedom in others. Tolerance of unwelcome, unorthodox ideas or information is a constitutionally protected policy not to be defeated by persons who would break up meetings they do not relish.

But emergencies may arise on streets which would become catastrophes if there was not immediate police action. The crowd which should be tolerant may be prejudiced and angry or malicious. If the situation threatens to get out of hand for the force present, I think the police may require the speaker, even if within his rights, to yield his right temporarily to the greater interest of peace. Of course, the threat must be judged in good faith to be real, immediate, and serious. But silencing a speaker by authorities as a measure of mob control is like dynamiting a house to stop the spread of a conflagration. It may be justified by the overwhelming community interest that flames not be fed as compared with the little interest to be served by continuing to feed them. But this kind of disorder does not abridge the right to speak except for the emergency and, since the speaker was within his constitutional right to speak, it could not be grounds for revoking or refusing him a permit or convicting him of any offense because of his utterance. If he resisted an officer's reasonable demand to cease, he might incur penalties.

And so the matter eventually comes down to the question whether the "words used are used in such circumstances and are of such a nature" that we can say a reasonable man would anticipate the evil result. In this case the Court does not justify, excuse, or deny the inciting and provocative character of the language, and it does not, and on this record could not, deny that when Kunz speaks he poses a "clear and present" danger to peace and order. Why, then, does New York have to put up with it? . . .

The purpose of constitutional protection of speech is to foster peaceful interchange of all manner of thoughts, information, and ideas. Its policy is rooted in faith in the force of reason. This Court wisely has said, "Resort to epithets or personal abuse is not in any proper sense communication of information or opinion safeguarded by the Constitution." *Cantwell* v. *Connecticut* [1941]. "It has been well observed that such utterances are no essential part of any exposition of ideas, and are of such slight social value as a step to truth that any benefit that may be derived from them is clearly outweighed by the social interest in order and morality." So said we all in *Chaplinsky*. It would be interesting if the Court would expose its reasons for thinking that Kunz's words are of more social value than those of Chaplinsky. . . .

Of course, as to the press, there are the best of reasons against any licensing or prior restraint. Decisions such as *Near* v. *Minnesota* [1931] hold any licensing or prior restraint of the press unconstitutional, and I heartily agree. But precedents from that field cannot reasonably be transposed to the street-meeting field. The impact of publishing on public order has no similarity with that of a street meeting. Publishing does not make private use of public property. It reaches only those who choose to read, and, in that way, is analogous to a meeting held in a hall where those who come do so by choice. Written words are less apt to incite or provoke to mass action than spoken words, speech being the primitive and direct communication with the emotions. Few are the riots caused by publication alone, few are the mobs that have not had their immediate origin in harangue. The vulnerability of various forms of communication to community control must be proportioned to their impact upon other community interests. . . .

DENNIS V. UNITED STATES
341 U.S. 494 (1951)

The Smith Act of 1940 made it a crime to teach or advocate the overthrow of the government by force or violence, or to conspire to do these things. First used in 1941 against eighteen members of the Socialist Workers Party in Minnesota, the law was seldom invoked during World War II. After the war and with the onset of the Cold War, the Justice Department began to enforce the Smith Act against domestic Communists. In 1949, a jury found Eugene Dennis and ten other board members of the American Communist Party guilty of violating the statute. The eleven Communists appealed on multiple grounds, including the First Amendment, to the U.S. Court of Appeals for the Second Circuit. In an opinion by Judge Learned Hand, the court unanimously sustained the convictions and rejected in particular the defendants' First Amendment claims. The Supreme Court, in a plurality opinion by Chief Justice Vinson, affirmed.

Dennis marked the demise of the clear-and-present-danger test. The two dissenting justices—Black and Douglas—contended that faithful application of the test could lead only to a reversal of the convictions. The plurality evidently agreed with this analysis, for otherwise it would not have felt compelled to weaken the test so as to allow the convictions.

This task had already been performed by Judge Hand for the Second Circuit. "In each case," Hand wrote, "[courts] must ask whether the gravity of the 'evil,' discounted by its improbability, justifies such invasion of free speech as is necessary to avoid the danger." Thus diluting the immediacy requirement of the clear-and-present-danger test, Hand effectively made the test into something more akin to the old bad-tendency test. Following Hand's analysis, the Vinson plurality found that "the requisite danger" for government action existed. That there was no attempt by the defendants to overthrow the government by force or violence was beside the point, said Vinson. "It is the existence of the conspiracy which creates the danger. . . . If the ingredients of the reaction are present, we cannot bind the Government to wait until the catalyst is added."

Justices Frankfurter and Jackson voted with the plurality. Significantly, however, neither did so on the basis of a clear-and-present-danger analysis. After *Dennis* the Court mostly ignored the clear-and-present-danger test and developed new doctrines to decide First Amendment claims of an increasing number and variety.

On the authority of *Dennis*, the Justice Department intensified its efforts to prosecute domestic Communists under the Smith Act. By 1957, the department had obtained 145 indictments and 89 convictions under the law. That year, however, the Supreme Court in *Yates* v. *United States* (1957) reviewed Smith Act convictions of fourteen Communists and reversed each one of them. Though the Court did not overrule *Dennis* (and indeed never has), it interpreted *Dennis* to require a distinction between advocacy of forcible overthrow as an abstract doctrine and advocacy of action to that end. As a result of *Yates*, federal prosecutors, in order to obtain a conviction under the Smith Act, had to show specific illegal acts by party members; membership in the party was not enough. *Dennis* thus was weakened, and prosecutions under the Smith Act ground to a halt.

Opinion of the Court: **Vinson**, Reed, Burton, Minton. Concurring opinions: **Frankfurter**; **Jackson**. Dissenting opinions: **Black**; **Douglas**. Not participating: Clark.

Dennis v. *United States* was decided on June 4, 1951.

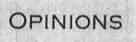

CHIEF JUSTICE VINSON ANNOUNCED THE JUDGMENT OF THE COURT AND AN OPINION IN WHICH JUSTICE REED, JUSTICE BURTON, AND JUSTICE MINTON JOIN . . .

The obvious purpose of the statute is to protect existing Government, not from change by peaceable, lawful, and constitutional means, but from change by violence, revolution, and terrorism. That it is within the *power* of the Congress to protect the Government of the United States from armed rebellion is a proposition which requires little discussion. Whatever theoretical merit there may be to the argument that there is a "right" to rebellion against dictatorial governments is without force where the existing structure of the government provides for peaceful and orderly change. We reject any principle of governmental helplessness in the face of preparation for revolution, which principle, carried to its logical conclusion, must lead to anarchy. No one could conceive that it is not within the power of Congress to prohibit acts intended to overthrow the Government by force and violence. The question with which we are concerned here is not whether Congress has such *power*, but whether the *means* which it has employed conflict with the . . . Constitution.

One of the bases for the contention that the means which Congress has employed are invalid takes the form of an attack on the face of the statute on the grounds that by its terms it prohibits academic discussion of the merits of Marxism-Leninism, that it stifles ideas and is contrary to all concepts of a free speech and a free press. . . .

The very language of the Smith Act negates the interpretation which petitioners would have us impose on that Act. It is directed at advocacy, not discussion. Thus, the trial judge properly charged the jury that they could not convict if they found that petitioners did "no more than pursue peaceful studies and discussions or teaching and advocacy in the realm of ideas." He further charged that it was not unlawful "to conduct in an American college or university a course explaining the philosophical theories set forth in the books which have been placed in evidence." Such a charge is in strict accord with the statutory language, and illustrates the meaning to be placed on those words. Congress did not intend to eradicate the free discussion of political theories, to destroy the traditional rights of Americans to discuss and evaluate ideas without fear of governmental sanction. Rather Congress was concerned with the very kind of activity in which the evidence showed these petitioners engaged. . . .

We pointed out in *American Communications Assn.* v. *Douds* [1950] that the basis of the First Amendment is the hypothesis that speech can rebut speech, propaganda will answer propaganda, free debate of ideas will result in the wisest governmental policies. It is for this reason that this Court has recognized the inherent value of free discourse. An analysis of the leading cases in this Court which have involved direct limitations on speech, however, will demonstrate that both the majority of the Court and the dissenters in particular cases have recognized that this is not an unlimited, unqualified right, but that the societal value of speech must, on occasion, be subordinated to other values and considerations. . . .

. . . [I]n *Douds,* we were called upon to decide the validity of 9(h) of the Labor Management Relations Act of 1947. That section required officials of unions which desired to avail themselves of the facilities of the National Labor Relations Board to take oaths that they did not belong to the Communist Party and that they did not believe in the overthrow of the Government by force and violence. We pointed out that Congress did not intend to punish belief, but rather intended to regulate the conduct of union affairs. We therefore held that any indirect sanction on speech which might arise from the oath requirement did not present a proper case for the "clear and present danger" test, for the regulation was aimed at conduct rather than speech. In discussing the proper measure of evaluation of this kind of legislation, we suggested that the Holmes-Brandeis philosophy insisted that where there was a direct restriction upon speech, a "clear and present danger" that the substantive evil would be caused was necessary before the statute in question could be constitutionally applied. And we stated, "[The First] Amendment requires that one be permitted to believe what he will. It requires that one be permitted to advocate what he will unless there is a clear and present danger that a substantial public evil will result therefrom." But we further suggested that neither Justice Holmes nor Justice Brandeis ever envisioned that a shorthand phrase should be crystallized into a rigid rule to be applied inflexibly without regard to the circumstances of each case. Speech is not an absolute, above and beyond control by the legislature when its judgment, subject to review here, is that certain kinds of speech are so undesirable as to warrant criminal sanction. Nothing is more certain in modern society than the principle that there are no absolutes, that a name, a phrase, a standard has meaning only when associated with the considerations which gave birth to the nomenclature. . . . To those who would paralyze our Government in the face of impending threat by encasing it in a semantic straitjacket we must reply that all concepts are relative.

In this case we are squarely presented with the application of the "clear and present danger" test, and must decide what that phrase imports. . . . Overthrow of the Government by force and violence is certainly a substantial enough interest for the Government to limit speech. Indeed, this is the ultimate value of any society, for if a society cannot protect its very structure from armed internal attack, it must follow that no subordinate value can be protected. If, then, this interest may be protected, the literal problem which is presented is what has been meant by the use of the phrase "clear and present danger" of the utterances bringing about the evil within the power of Congress to punish.

Obviously, the words cannot mean that before the Government may act, it must wait until the *putsch* is about to be executed, the plans have been laid and the signal is awaited. If Government is aware that a group aiming at its overthrow is attempting to indoctrinate its members and to commit them to a course whereby they will strike when the leaders feel the circumstances permit, action by the Government is required. The argument that there is no need for Government to concern itself, for Government is strong, it possesses ample powers to put down a rebellion, it may defeat the revolution with ease, needs no answer. For that is not the question. Certainly an attempt to overthrow the Government by force, even though doomed from the outset because of inadequate numbers of power of the revolutionists, is a sufficient evil for Congress to prevent. The damage which such attempts create both physically and politically to a nation makes it impossible to measure the validity in terms of the probability of success, or the immediacy of a successful attempt. In the instant case the trial judge charged the jury that they could not convict unless they found that petitioners intended to overthrow the Government "as speedily as circumstances would permit." This does not mean, and could not properly mean, that they would not strike until there was certainty of success. What was meant was that the revolutionists would strike when they thought the time was ripe. We must therefore reject the contention that success or probability of success is the criterion. . . .

Chief Judge Learned Hand, writing for the majority below, interpreted the phrase as follows: "In each case [courts] must ask whether the gravity of the 'evil,' discounted by its improbability, justifies such invasion of free speech as is necessary to avoid the danger." . . . We adopt this statement of the rule. As articulated by Chief Judge Hand, it is as succinct and inclusive as any other we might devise at this time. It takes into consideration those factors which we deem relevant, and relates their significances. More we cannot expect from words.

Likewise, we are in accord with the court below, which affirmed the trial court's finding that the requisite danger existed. The mere fact that from the period 1945 to 1948 petitioners' activities did not result in an attempt to overthrow the Government by force and violence is of course no answer to the fact that there was a group that was ready to make the attempt. The formation by petitioners of such a highly organized conspiracy, with rigidly disciplined members subject to call when the leaders, these petitioners, felt that the time had come for action, coupled with the inflammable nature of world conditions, similar uprisings in other countries, and the touch-and-go nature of our relations with countries with whom petitioners were in the very least ideologically attuned, convince us that their convictions were justified on this score. And this analysis disposes of the contention that a conspiracy to advocate, as distinguished from the advocacy itself, cannot be constitutionally restrained, because it comprises only the preparation. It is the existence of the conspiracy which creates the danger. . . . If the ingredients of the reaction are present, we cannot bind the Government to wait until the catalyst is added. . . .

We hold that [the challenged provisions] of the Smith Act do not inherently, or as construed or applied in the instant case, violate the First Amendment. . . . Petitioners intended to overthrow the Government of the United States as speedily as the circumstances would permit. Their conspiracy to organize the Communist Party and to teach and advocate the overthrow of the Government of the United States by force and violence created a "clear and present danger" of an attempt to overthrow the Government by force and violence. They were properly and constitutionally convicted for violation of the Smith Act. The judgments of conviction are
AFFIRMED.

JUSTICE FRANKFURTER, CONCURRING IN THE JUDGMENT . . .

Few questions of comparable import have come before this Court in recent years. The appellants maintain that they have a right to advocate a political theory, so long, at least, as their advocacy does not create an immediate danger of obvious magnitude to the very existence of our present scheme of society. On the other hand, the Government asserts the right to safeguard the security of the Nation by such a measure as the Smith Act. Our judgment is thus solicited on a conflict of interests of the utmost concern to the well-being of the country. This conflict of interests cannot be resolved by a dogmatic preference for one or the other, nor by a sonorous formula which is in fact only a euphemistic disguise for an unresolved conflict. If adjudication is to be a rational process, we cannot escape a candid examination of the conflicting claims with full recognition that both are supported by weighty title-deeds. . . .

But how are competing interests to be assessed? Since they are not subject to quantitative ascertainment, the issue necessarily resolves itself into asking, who is to make the adjustment?—who is to balance the relevant factors and ascertain which interest is in the circumstances to prevail? Full responsibility for the choice cannot be given to the courts. Courts are not representative bodies. They are not designed to be a good reflex of a democratic society. Their judgment is best informed, and therefore most dependable, within narrow limits. Their essential quality is detachment, founded on independence. History teaches that the independence of the judiciary is jeopardized when courts become embroiled in the passions of the day and assume primary responsibility in choosing between competing political, economic, and social pressures.

Primary responsibility for adjusting the interests which compete in the situation before us of necessity belongs to the Congress. . . . We are to set aside the judgment of those whose duty it is to legislate only if there is no reasonable basis for it. . . .

A generation ago this distribution of responsibility would not have been questioned. . . . But in recent decisions we have made explicit what has long been implicitly recognized. In reviewing statutes which restrict freedoms protected by the First Amendment, we have emphasized the close relation which those freedoms bear to maintenance of a free society. . . . Some members of the Court—and at times a majority—have done more. They have suggested that our function in reviewing statutes restricting freedom of expression differs sharply from our normal duty in sitting in judgment on legislation. It has been said that such statutes "must be justified by clear public interest, threatened not doubtfully or remotely, but by clear and present danger. The rational connection between the remedy provided and the evil to be curbed, which in other contexts might support legislation against attack on due process grounds, will not suffice." *Thomas* v. *Collins* [1945]. It has been suggested, with the casualness of a footnote, that such legislation is not presumptively valid, see *United States* v. *Carolene Products Co.* [1937], and it has been weightily reiterated that freedom of speech has a "preferred position" among constitutional safeguards. *Kovacs* v. *Cooper* [1949].

The precise meaning intended to be conveyed by these phrases need not now be pursued. It is enough to note that they have recurred in the Court's opinions, and their cumulative force has, not without justification, engendered belief that there is a constitutional principle, expressed by those attractive but imprecise words, prohibiting restriction upon utterance unless it creates a situation of "imminent" peril against which legislation may guard. It is on this body of the Court's pronouncements that the defendants' argument here is based.

In all fairness, the argument cannot be met by reinterpreting the Court's frequent use of "clear" and "present" to mean an entertainable "probability." In giving this meaning to the phrase "clear and present danger," the Court of Appeals was fastidiously confining the rhetoric of opinions to the exact scope of what was decided by them. We have greater responsibility for having given constitutional support, over repeated protests, to uncritical libertarian generalities. . . .

It is not for us to decide how we would adjust the clash of interests which this case presents were the primary responsibility for reconciling it ours. Congress has determined that the danger created by advocacy of overthrow justifies the ensuing restriction on freedom of speech. The determination was made after due deliberation, and the seriousness of the congressional purpose is attested by the volume of legislation passed to effectuate the same ends.

Can we then say that the judgment Congress exercised was denied it by the Constitution? Can we establish a constitutional doctrine which forbids the elected representatives of the people to make this choice? Can we hold that the First Amendment deprives Congress of what it deemed necessary for the Government's protection?

To make validity of legislation depend on judicial reading of events still in the womb of time—a forecast, that is, of the outcome of forces at best appreciated only with knowledge of the topmost secrets of nations—is to charge the judiciary with duties beyond its equipment. . . .

The wisdom of the assumptions underlying the legislation and prosecution is another matter. In finding that Congress has acted within its power, a judge does not remotely imply that he favors the implications that lie beneath the legal issues. . . .

Civil liberties draw at best only limited strength from legal guaranties. Preoccupation by our people with the constitutionality, instead of with the wisdom, of legislation or of executive action is preoccupation with a false value. Even those who would most freely use the judicial brake on the democratic process by invalidating legislation that goes deeply against their grain, acknowledge, at least by paying lip service, that constitutionality does not exact a sense of proportion or the sanity of humor or an absence of fear. Focusing attention on constitutionality tends to make constitutionality synonymous with wisdom. When legislation touches freedom of thought and freedom of speech, such a tendency is a formidable enemy of the free spirit. Much that should be rejected as illiberal, because repressive and envenoming, may well be not unconstitutional. The ultimate reliance for the deepest needs of civilization must be found outside their vindication in courts of law; apart from all else, judges, howsoever they may conscientiously seek to discipline themselves against it, unconsciously are too apt to be moved by the deep undercurrents of public feeling. A persistent, positive translation of the liberating faith into the feelings and thoughts and actions of men and women is the real protection against attempts to strait-jacket the human mind. Such temptations will have their way, if fear and hatred are not exorcised. The mark of a truly civilized man is confidence in the strength and security derived from the inquiring mind. We may be grateful for such honest comforts as it supports, but we must be unafraid of its incertitudes. Without open minds there can be no open society. And if society be not open the spirit of man is mutilated and becomes enslaved. . . .

JUSTICE JACKSON, CONCURRING . . .

The "clear and present danger" test was an innovation by Justice Holmes in the *Schenck* [v. *United States*, 1919] case, reiterated and refined by him and Justice Brandeis in later cases, all arising before the era of World War II revealed the subtlety and efficacy of modernized revolutionary techniques used by totalitarian parties. In those cases, they were faced with convictions under so-called criminal syndicalism statutes aimed at anarchists but which, loosely construed, had been applied to punish socialism, pacifism, and left-wing ideologies, the charges often resting on farfetched inferences which, if true, would establish only technical or trivial violations. They proposed "clear and present danger" as a test for the sufficiency of evidence in particular cases.

I would save it, unmodified, for application as a "rule of reason" in the kind of case for which it was devised. When the issue is criminality of a hot-headed speech on a street corner, or circulation of a few incendiary pamphlets, or parading by some zealots behind a red flag, or refusal of a handful of school children to salute our flag, it is not beyond the capacity of the judicial process to gather, comprehend, and weigh the necessary materials for decision whether it is a clear and present danger of substantive evil or a harmless letting off of steam. It is not a prophecy, for the danger in such cases has matured by the time of trial or it was never present. The test applies and has meaning where a conviction is sought to be based on a speech or writing which does not directly or explicitly advocate a crime but to which such tendency is sought to be attributed by construction or by implication from external circumstances. The formula in such cases favors freedoms that are vital to our society, and, even if sometimes applied too generously, the consequences cannot be grave. But its recent expansion has extended, in particular to Communists, unprecedented immunities. Unless we are to hold our Government captive in a judge-made verbal trap, we must approach the problem of a well-organized, nation-wide conspiracy . . . as realistically as our predecessors faced the trivialities that were being prosecuted until they were checked with a rule of reason.

I think reason is lacking for applying that test to this case. . . .

JUSTICE BLACK, DISSENTING . . .

At the outset I want to emphasize what the crime involved in this case is, and what it is not. These petitioners were not charged with an attempt to overthrow the Government. They were not charged with overt acts of any kind designed to overthrow the Government. They were not even charged with saying anything or writing anything designed to overthrow the Government. The charge was that they agreed to assemble and to talk and publish certain ideas at a later date: The indictment is that they conspired to organize the Communist Party and to use speech or newspapers and other publications in the future to teach and advocate the forcible overthrow of the Government. No matter how it is worded, this is a virulent form of prior censorship of speech and press, which I believe the First Amendment forbids. I would hold [Section] 3 of the Smith Act . . . unconstitutional on its face and as applied. . . .

. . . [T]he other opinions in this case show that the only way to affirm these convictions is to repudiate directly or indirectly the established "clear and present danger" rule. This the Court does in a way which greatly restricts the protections afforded by the First Amendment. The opinions for affirmance indicate that the chief reason for jettisoning the rule is the expressed fear that advocacy of Communist doctrine endangers the safety of the Republic. Undoubtedly, a governmental policy of unfettered communication of ideas does entail dangers. To the Founders of this Nation, however, the benefits derived from free expression were worth the risk. They embodied this philosophy in the First Amendment's command that "Congress shall make no law . . . abridging the freedom of speech, or of the press. . . ." I have always believed that the First Amendment is the keystone of our Government, that the freedoms it guarantees provide the best insurance against destruction of all freedom. At least as to speech in the realm of public matters, I believe that the "clear and present danger" test does not "mark the furthermost constitutional boundaries of protected expression" but does "no more than recognize a minimum compulsion of the Bill of Rights." *Bridges* v. *California* [1941].

So long as this Court exercises the power of judicial review of legislation, I cannot agree that the First Amendment permits us to sustain laws suppressing freedom of speech and press on the basis of Congress' or our own notions of mere "reasonableness." Such a doctrine waters down the First Amendment so that it amounts to little more than an admonition to Congress. The Amendment as so construed is not likely to protect any but those "safe" or orthodox views which rarely need its protection. . . .

Public opinion being what it now is, few will protest the conviction of these Communist petitioners. There is hope, however, that in calmer times, when present pressures, passions, and fears subside, this or some later Court will restore the First Amendment liberties to the high preferred place where they belong in a free society.

JUSTICE DOUGLAS, DISSENTING.

If this were a case where those who claimed protection under the First Amendment were teaching the techniques of sabotage, the assassination of the President, the filching of documents from public files, the planting of bombs, the art of street warfare, and the like, I would have no doubts. The freedom to speak is not absolute; the teaching of methods of terror and other seditious conduct should be beyond the pale along with obscenity and immorality. This case was argued as if those were the facts. The argument imported much seditious conduct into the record. That is easy and it has popular appeal, for the activities of Communists in plotting and scheming against the free world are common knowledge. But the fact is that no such evidence was introduced at the trial. There is a statute which makes a seditious conspiracy unlawful. Petitioners, however, were not charged with a "conspiracy to overthrow" the Government. They were charged with a conspiracy to form a party and groups and assemblies of people who teach and advocate the overthrow of our Government by force or violence and with a conspiracy to advocate and teach its overthrow by force and violence. It may well be that indoctrination in the techniques of terror to destroy the Government would be indictable under either statute. But the teaching which is condemned here is of a different character. . . .

There comes a time when even speech loses its constitutional immunity. . . . Yet free speech is the rule, not the exception. The restraint to be constitutional must be based on more than fear, on more than passionate opposition against the speech, on more than a revolted dislike for its contents. There must be some immediate injury to society that is likely if speech is allowed.

The nature of Communism as a force on the world scene would, of course, be relevant to the issue of clear and present danger of petitioners' advocacy within the United States. But the primary consideration is the strength and tactical position of petitioners and their converts in this country. On that there is no evidence in the record. If we are to take judicial notice of the threat of Communists within the nation, it should not be difficult to conclude that as a political party they are of little consequence. . . . Communism has been so thoroughly exposed in this country that it has been crippled as a political force. Free speech has destroyed it as an effective political party. It is inconceivable that those who went up and down this country preaching the doctrine of revolution which petitioners espouse would have any success. . . .

How it can be said that there is a clear and present danger that this advocacy will succeed is, therefore, a mystery. Some nations less resilient than the United States, where illiteracy is high and where democratic traditions are only budding, might have to take drastic steps and jail these men for merely speaking their creed. But in America they are miserable merchants of unwanted ideas; their wares remain unsold. The fact that their ideas are abhorrent does not make them powerful.

. . . If we are to proceed on the basis of judicial notice, it is impossible for me to say that the Communists in this country are so potent or so strategically deployed that they must be suppressed for their speech. . . . To believe that petitioners and their followers are placed in such critical positions as to endanger the Nation is to believe the incredible. It is safe to say that the followers of the creed of Soviet Communism are known to the F.B.I.; that in case of war with Russia they will be picked up overnight as were all prospective saboteurs at the commencement of World War II; that the invisible army of petitioners is the best known, the most beset, and the least thriving of any fifth column in history. Only those held by fear or panic could think otherwise.

. . . Free speech—the glory of our system of government—should not be sacrificed on anything less than plain and objective proof of danger that the evil advocated is imminent. On this record no one can say that petitioners and their converts are in such a strategic position as to have even the slightest chance of achieving their aims. . . .

RESPONSES

FROM THE *NEW YORK TIMES*, JUNE 5, 1951, "THE SMITH ACT UPHELD"

Chief Justice Vinson, in writing the majority opinion, fell back, just as Judge Learned Hand of the United States Court of Appeal had done before him, on the doctrine of "clear and present danger." It is obvious that no Government is required to stretch the guarantee of individual liberty to a point where both the Government and the liberty will be imperiled. In any borderline case, such as this admittedly was, the imminence of the danger is the deciding factor. As Judge Hand had argued, an old-style soap-boxer might be permitted extravagances of speech that would be denied to such persons as the titular heads of the American Communist Party. The distinction is clear. The soap-boxers were not an actual menace. The Communist Party is a menace because it is aimed at the security of the existing Government and because it is allied with the nation's enemies.

It was not charged that the convicted Communists had committed any overt act. So far as the indictment went, they were not conspiring to overthrow the Government. What they were charged with doing was an attempt to produce an atmosphere in which the overthrow of the Government would appear right and necessary. They were dealing with words, not acts. It was the intent and efficacy of the words that had to be examined. The question was at what point the words became so dangerous that the defendants had overstepped the freedom guaranteed in the First Amendment. Chief Justice Vinson held that the phrase "clear and present danger cannot mean that before the Government may act it must wait until the putsch is about to be executed, the plans have been laid, and the signal is awaited."

Within the past year we have seen what a "clear and present danger" can be. We have seen American young men thrown into battle in Korea against Communist aggression, and we have seen this aggression applauded and encouraged by Communists here as in other countries. We have felt compelled to divert fabulous sums from peaceful uses to build up our defenses against foreign Communists. Who can say that under these circumstances the enemies within our gates should not be restrained?

Justices Black and Douglas, dissenting from the majority opinion, used language that would have been more cogent in quieter days. Indeed, Justice Black said there was hope "that in calmer times, when present pressures, passions, and fears subside, this or some later court will restore the First Amendment liberties to the high preferred place where they belong in a free society." He neglected to add that the first essential is that the society should remain free. It is the enemies of freedom, not the friends, who stood at the bar in this case. . . .

What is important . . . is . . . the establishment of a principle. The principle is that liberty shall not be abused to its own destruction. We need have little fear of a Communist uprising in this country. We do have reason to fear, however, the harmful activities of Communist spies and traitors operating under the protection of our own laws. The First Amendment was designed to preserve our freedom and not to serve the purposes of a furtive conspiracy allied with foreign Governments to overthrow all freedom.

FROM *THE NATION*, JUNE 14, 1951, "STRAIT-JACKETING FREE SPEECH"

There is grim irony in the fact that the Truman law firm of Vinson, Minton, and Burton has fallen back on the clear-and-present-danger doctrine to uphold the Smith Act. The doctrine was intended, of course, to establish the principle that only the existence of such a danger could justify any interference with the right of free speech guaranteed by the First Amendment. Yet in the decision upholding the conviction of the eleven Communist leaders Chief Justice Vinson has interpreted the doctrine as though its purpose were to sanction an abridgment of freedom of speech.

The convicted Communist leaders were not charged with committing overt acts of any kind designed to overthrow the government or with conspiring to do so. They were not even charged with saying or writing anything that might have this effect. "The charge," as Justice Black points out in his dissenting opinion, "was that they agreed to assemble and to talk and publish certain ideas at a later date: the indictment is that they conspired to organize the Communist Party and to use speech or newspapers or other publications in the future to teach and to advocate the forcible overthrow of government."

In view of the admitted facts, Chief Justice Vinson was compelled to adopt Judge Learned Hand's distinction between discussion and advocacy, to hold, that is, that a distinction exists between reading a book in a college library and reading the same book in the headquarters of the Communist Party; that an old-style soap-boxer can be permitted certain extravagances of speech which must be denied Eugene Dennis. The distinction makes freedom of speech turn not on what is said but on the intent with which the words are spoken. In the world of facts and men the application of this test usually means: Who is speaking? In short, what the court has done is to formulate a rule of political expediency under which an obnoxious opposition can be suppressed by charging that it uses certain words and ideas with intent to violate the Smith Act. "Once we start down that road," to quote from Justice Douglas's dissent, "we enter territory dangerous to the liberties of every citizen." "Once we start" is here polite parlance for "we have started."

FROM THE *WASHINGTON POST*, JUNE 6, 1951, "FREEDOM WITH SECURITY"

The Supreme Court's decision upholding the conviction of the eleven Communist leaders is the most important reconciliation of liberty and security in our time. The five opinions handed down in this case contain ample evidence of long and deep soul-searching. That process brought six of the eight justices who took part in the deliberations to a firm conviction that the Smith Act is constitutional and that the Communist leaders were properly convicted under it. The court has demonstrated once more that our system, with all its respect for individual freedom, is not (to borrow words from Chief Justice Hughes) "an imposing spectacle of impotency."

We do not think the decision belittles the great principle of freedom of speech. The court has said only that individuals engaged in a conspiracy to teach and advocate the overthrow of the Government by force and violence cannot use freedom of speech as a shield for their plot. . . . Freedom of speech for all legitimate purposes remains. Freedom of speech in aid of a conspiracy aimed at the destruction of all freedom is found to have no standing in the context of these times.

BEAUHARNAIS V. ILLINOIS
343 U.S. 250 (1952)

Joseph Beauharnais, president of the White Circle League in Chicago, distributed leaflets that spoke of "the aggressions . . . rapes, robberies, knives, guns, and marijuana of the negro" and called on the mayor and city council to exclude blacks from white neighborhoods. Beauharnais was arrested under a group libel law, state statute 224a, which prohibited the defamation of a race or class of people. At trial, the presiding judge refused to charge the jury—as Beauharnais had requested—that it should convict if it found his leaflets were "likely to produce a clear and present danger of a serious substantive evil that rises far above public inconvenience, annoyance, or unrest." Instead, the judge told the jury it was to convict if it found that Beauharnais had presented his literature "in any public place"—a fact not in dispute. The jury then convicted Beauharnais, and he was fined $200. The defendant challenged the group libel law as a violation of his First Amendment rights but lost in the Illinois courts and, ultimately, by the narrow vote of 5 to 4, in the U.S. Supreme Court.

Writing for the Court, Justice Frankfurter could find no good reason why the states, already able to punish libels of individuals, should not have the power to outlaw the same utterances when directed at defined groups. *Beauharnais* relied on *Chaplinsky* v. *New Hampshire* (1942), in which the Court said that libel was a category of speech that the First Amendment does not protect. In 1964, the Court in *New York Times Co.* v. *Sullivan* decisively rejected this doctrine in a case in which it constitutionalized the law of libel.

Opinion of the Court: **Frankfurter**, Burton, Vinson, Clark, Minton. Dissenting opinions: **Black**, Douglas; **Reed**; **Douglas**; **Jackson**.

Beauharnais v. *Illinois* was decided on April 28, 1952.

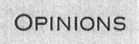

JUSTICE FRANKFURTER DELIVERED THE OPINION OF THE COURT . . .

The Illinois Supreme Court tells us that 224a "is a form of criminal libel law." . . . The defendant, the trial court, and the [Illinois] Supreme Court consistently treated it as such. The defendant offered evidence tending to prove the truth of parts of the utterance, and the courts below considered and disposed of this offer in terms of ordinary criminal libel precedents. Section 224a does not deal with the defense of truth, but by the Illinois Constitution, Art. II, 4, "in all trials for libel, both civil and criminal, the truth, when published with good motives and for justifiable ends, shall be a sufficient defense." . . . Similarly, the action of the trial court in deciding as a matter of law the libelous character of the utterance, leaving to the jury only the question of publication, follows the settled rule in prosecutions for libel in Illinois and other States. Moreover, the Supreme Court's characterization of the words prohibited by the statute as those "liable to cause violence and disorder" paraphrases the traditional justification for punishing libels criminally, namely their "tendency to cause breach of the peace."

Libel of an individual was a common-law crime, and thus criminal in the colonies. Indeed, at common law, truth or good motives was no defense. In the first decades after the adoption of the Constitution, this was changed by judicial decision, statute, or constitution in most States, but nowhere was there any suggestion that the crime of libel be abolished. Today, every American jurisdiction—the forty-eight States, the District of Columbia, Alaska, Hawaii, and Puerto Rico—punish libels directed at individuals. "There are certain well-defined and narrowly limited classes of speech, the prevention and punishment of which have never been thought to raise any Constitutional problem. These include the lewd and obscene, the profane, the libelous, and the insulting or 'fighting' words—those which by their very utterance inflict injury or tend to incite an immediate breach of the peace. It has been well observed that such utterances are no essential part of any exposition of ideas, and are of such slight social value as a step to truth that any benefit that may be derived from them is clearly outweighed by the social interest in order and morality. 'Resort to epithets or personal abuse is not in any proper sense communication of information or opinion safeguarded by the Constitution, and its punishment as a criminal act would raise no question under that instrument.' *Cantwell* v. *Connecticut* [1940]." Such were the views of a unanimous Court in *Chaplinsky* v. *New Hampshire* [1942].

No one will gainsay that it is libelous falsely to charge another with being a rapist, robber, carrier of knives and guns, and user of marijuana. The precise question before us, then, is whether the protection of "liberty" in the Due Process Clause of the Fourteenth Amendment prevents a State from punishing such libels—as criminal libel has been defined, limited, and constitutionally recognized time out of mind—directed at designated collectivities and flagrantly disseminated. There is even authority, however dubious, that such utterances were also crimes at common law. It is certainly clear that some American jurisdictions have sanctioned their punishment under ordinary criminal libel statutes. We cannot say, however, that the question is concluded by history and practice. But if an utterance directed at an individual may be the object of criminal sanctions, we cannot deny to a State power to punish the same utterance directed at a defined group, unless we can say that this is a wilful and purposeless restriction unrelated to the peace and well-being of the State.

Illinois did not have to look beyond her own borders or await the tragic experience of the last three decades to conclude that wilful purveyors of falsehood concerning racial and religious groups promote strife and tend powerfully to obstruct the manifold adjustments required for free, ordered life in a metropolitan, polyglot community. From the murder of the abolitionist Lovejoy in 1837 to the Cicero riots of 1951, Illinois has been the scene of exacerbated tension between races, often flaring into violence and destruction. In many of these outbreaks, utterances of the character here in question, so the Illinois legislature could conclude, played a significant part. The law was passed on June 29, 1917, at a time when the State was struggling to assimilate vast numbers of new inhabitants, as yet concentrated in discrete racial or national or religious groups—foreign-born brought to it by the crest of the great wave of immigration, and Negroes attracted by jobs in war plants and the allurements of northern claims. Nine years earlier, in the very city where the legislature sat, what is said to be the first northern race riot had cost the lives of six people, left hundreds of Negroes homeless, and shocked citizens into action far beyond the borders of the State. Less than a month before the bill was enacted, East St. Louis had seen a day's rioting, prelude to an outbreak, only four days after the bill became law, so bloody that it led to Congressional investigation. A series of bombings had begun which was to culminate two years later in the awful race riot which held Chicago in its grip for seven days in the summer of 1919. Nor has tension and violence between the groups defined in the statute been limited in Illinois to clashes between whites and Negroes.

In the face of this history and its frequent obligato of extreme racial and religious propaganda, we would deny experience to say that the Illinois legislature was without reason in seeking ways to curb false or malicious defamation of racial and religious groups, made in public places and by means calculated to have a powerful emotional impact on those to whom it was presented. . . .

It may be argued, and weightily, that this legislation will not help matters; that tension and on occasion violence between racial and religious groups must be traced to causes more deeply embedded in our society than the rantings of modern Know-Nothings. Only those lacking responsible humility will have a confident solution for problems as intractable as the frictions attributable to differences of race, color, or religion. This being so, it would be out of bounds for the judiciary to deny the legislature a choice of policy, provided it is not unrelated to the problem and not forbidden by some explicit limitation on the State's power. That the legislative remedy might not in practice mitigate the evil, or might itself raise new problems, would only manifest once more the paradox of reform. It is the price to be paid for the trial-and-error inherent in legislative efforts to deal with obstinate social issues. . . .

Long ago this Court recognized that the economic rights of an individual may depend for the effectiveness of their enforcement on rights in the group, even though not formally corporate, to which he belongs. *American Foundries* v. *Tri-City Trade Council* [1921]. Such group-protection on behalf of the individual may, for all we know, be a need not confined to the part that a trade union plays in effectuating rights abstractly recognized as belonging to its members. It is not within our competence to confirm or deny claims of social scientists as to the dependence of the individual on the position of his racial or religious group in the community. It would, however, be arrant dogmatism, quite outside the scope of our authority in passing on the powers of a State, for us to deny that the Illinois legislature may warrantably believe that a man's job and his educational opportunities and the dignity accorded him may depend as much on the reputation of the racial and religious group to which he willy-nilly belongs, as on his own merits. This being so, we are precluded from saying that speech concededly punishable when immediately directed at individuals cannot be outlawed if directed at groups with whose position and esteem in society the affiliated individual may be inextricably involved.

We are warned that the choice open to the Illinois legislature here may be abused, that the law may be discriminatorily enforced; prohibiting libel of a creed or of a racial group, we are told, is but a step from prohibiting libel of a political party. Every power may be abused, but the possibility of abuse is a poor reason for denying Illinois the power to adopt measures against criminal libels sanctioned by centuries of Anglo-American law. "While this Court sits" it retains and exercises authority to nullify action which encroaches on freedom of utterance under the guise of punishing libel. Of course discussion cannot be denied and the right, as well as the duty, of criticism must not be stifled. . . .

Libelous utterances not being within the area of constitutionally protected speech, it is unnecessary, either for us or for the State courts, to consider the issues behind the phrase "clear and present danger." Certainly no one would contend that obscene speech, for example, may be punished only upon a showing of such circumstances. Libel, as we have seen, is in the same class.

We find no warrant in the Constitution for denying to Illinois the power to pass the law here under attack. But it bears repeating—although it should not—that our finding that the law is not constitutionally objectionable carries no implication of approval of the wisdom of the legislation or of its efficacy. These questions may raise doubts in our minds as well as in others. It is not for us, however, to make the legislative judgment. We are not at liberty to erect those doubts into fundamental law.

AFFIRMED.

JUSTICE BLACK, DISSENTING.

This case is here because Illinois inflicted criminal punishment on Beauharnais for causing the distribution of leaflets in the city of Chicago. The conviction rests on the leaflet's contents, not on the time, manner, or place of distribution. Beauharnais is head of an organization that opposes amalgamation and favors segregation of white and colored people. After discussion, an assembly of his group decided to petition the mayor and council of Chicago to pass laws for segregation. Volunteer members of the group agreed to stand on street corners, solicit signers to petitions addressed to the city authorities, and distribute leaflets giving information about the group, its beliefs and its plans. In carrying out this program a solicitor handed out a leaflet which was the basis of this prosecution. Since the Court opinion quotes only parts of the leaflet, I am including all of it as an appendix to this dissent. . . .

That Beauharnais and his group were making a genuine effort to petition their elected representatives is not disputed. Even as far back as 1689, the Bill of Rights exacted of William and Mary said: "It is the Right of the Subjects to petition the King, and all Commitments and Prosecutions for such petitioning are illegal." And 178 years ago the Declaration of Rights of the Continental Congress proclaimed to the monarch of that day that his American subjects had "a right peaceably to assemble, consider of their grievances, and petition the King; and that all prosecutions, prohibitory proclamations, and commitments for the same, are illegal." After independence was won, Americans stated as the first unequivocal command of their Bill of Rights: "Congress shall make no law . . . abridging the freedom of speech, or of the press; or the right of the people peaceably to assemble, and to petition the Government for a redress of grievances." Without distortion, this First Amendment could not possibly be read so as to hold that Congress has power to punish Beauharnais and others for petitioning Congress as they have here sought to petition the Chicago authorities. . . . And we have held in a number of prior cases that the Fourteenth Amendment makes the specific prohibitions of the First Amendment equally applicable to the states.

In view of these prior holdings, how does the Court justify its holding today that states can punish people for exercising the vital freedoms intended to be safeguarded from suppression by the First Amendment? The prior holdings are not referred to; the Court simply acts on the bland assumption that the First Amendment is wholly irrelevant. It is not even accorded the respect of a passing mention. This follows logically, I suppose, from recent constitutional doctrine which appears to measure state laws solely by this Court's notions of civilized "canons of decency," reasonableness, etc. . . . Under this "reasonableness" test, state laws abridging First Amendment freedoms are sustained if found to have a "rational basis." . . .

The Court's holding here and the constitutional doctrine behind it leave the rights of assembly, petition, speech, and press almost completely at the mercy of state legislative, executive, and judicial agencies. I say "almost" because state curtailment of these freedoms may still be invalidated if a majority of this Court conclude that a particular infringement is "without reason," or is "a wilful and purposeless restriction unrelated to the peace and well-being of the State." But lest this encouragement should give too much hope as to how and when this Court might protect these basic freedoms from state invasion, we are cautioned that state legislatures must be left free to "experiment" and to make "legislative" judgments. We are told that mistakes may be made during the legislative process of curbing public opinion. In such event the Court fortunately does not leave those mistakenly curbed, or any of us for that matter, unadvised. Consolation can be sought and must be found in the philosophical reflection that state legislative error in stifling speech and press "is the price to be paid for the trial-and-error inherent in legislative efforts to deal with obstinate social issues." My own belief is that no legislature is charged with the duty or vested with the power to decide what public issues Americans can discuss. In a free country that is the individual's choice, not the state's. State experimentation in curbing freedom of expression is startling and frightening doctrine in a country dedicated to self-government by its people. I reject the holding that either state or nation can punish people for having their say in matters of public concern. . . .

As a result of . . . [the Court's] analysis, the Illinois statute emerges labeled a "group libel law." This label may make the Court's holding more palatable [accepting] for those who sustain it, but the sugar-coating does not make the censorship less deadly. However tagged, the Illinois law is not that criminal libel which has been "defined, limited, and constitutionally recognized time out of mind." For as "constitutionally recognized" that crime has provided for punishment of false, malicious, scurrilous charges against individuals, not against huge groups. This limited scope of the law of criminal libel is of no small importance. It has confined state punishment of speech and expression to the narrowest of areas involving nothing more than purely private feuds. Every expansion of the law of criminal libel so as to punish discussions of matters of public concern means a corresponding invasion of the area dedicated to free expression by the First Amendment.

Prior efforts to expand the scope of criminal libel beyond its traditional boundaries have not usually met with widespread popular acclaim. "Seditious libel" was such an expansion, and it did have its day, particularly in the English Court of Star Chamber. But the First Amendment repudiated seditious libel for this country. . . .

The Court's reliance on *Chaplinsky* v. *New Hampshire* [1942] is . . . misplaced. New Hampshire had a state law making it an offense to direct insulting words at an individual on a public street. Chaplinsky had violated that law by calling a man vile names "face-to-face." We pointed out in that context that the use of such "fighting" words was not an essential part of exposition of ideas. Whether the words used in their context here are "fighting" words in the same sense is doubtful, but whether so or not they are not addressed to or about individuals. Moreover, the leaflet used here was also the means adopted by an assembled group to enlist interest in their efforts to have legislation enacted. And the fighting words were but a part of arguments on questions of wide public interest and importance. Freedom of petition, assembly, speech, and press could be greatly abridged by a practice of meticulously scrutinizing every editorial, speech, sermon, or other printed matter to extract two or three naughty words on which to hang charges of "group libel." The *Chaplinsky* case makes no such broad inroads on First Amendment freedoms. Nothing Justice Murphy wrote for the Court in that case or in any other case justifies any such inference.

Unless I misread history the majority is giving libel a more expansive scope and more respectable status than it was ever accorded even in the Star Chamber. For here it is held to be punishable to give publicity to any picture, moving picture, play, drama, or sketch, or any printed matter which a judge may find unduly offensive to any race, color, creed, or religion. In other words, in arguing for or against the enactment of laws that may differently affect huge groups, it is now very dangerous indeed to say something critical of one of the groups. And any "person, firm, or corporation" can be tried for this crime. "Person, firm, or corporation" certainly includes a book publisher, newspaper, radio or television station, candidate, or even a preacher. . . .

This Act sets up a system of state censorship which is at war with the kind of free government envisioned by those who forced adoption of our Bill of Rights. The motives behind the state law may have been to do good. But the same can be said about most laws making opinions punishable as crimes. History indicates that urges to do good have led to the burning of books and even to the burning of "witches."

No rationalization on a purely legal level can conceal the fact that state laws like this one present a constant overhanging threat to freedom of speech, press, and religion. Today Beauharnais is punished for publicly expressing strong views in favor of segregation. Ironically enough, Beauharnais, convicted of crime in Chicago, would probably be given a hero's reception in many other localities, if not in some parts of Chicago itself. Moreover, the same kind of state law that makes Beauharnais a criminal for advocating segregation in Illinois can be utilized to send people to jail in other states for advocating equality and nonsegregation. What Beauharnais said in his leaflet is mild compared with usual arguments on both sides of racial controversies.

We are told that freedom of petition and discussion are in no danger "while this Court sits." This case raises considerable doubt. Since those who peacefully petition for changes in the law are not to be protected "while this Court sits," who is? I do not agree that the Constitution leaves freedom of petition, assembly, speech, press, or worship at the mercy of a case-by-case, day-by-day majority of this Court. I had supposed that our people could rely for their freedom on the Constitution's commands, rather than on the grace of this Court on an individual case basis. To say that a legislative body can, with this Court's approval, make it a crime to petition for and publicly discuss proposed legislation seems as farfetched to me as it would be to say that a valid law could be enacted to punish a candidate for President for telling the people his views. I think the First Amendment, with the Fourteenth, "absolutely" forbids such laws without any "ifs" or "buts" or "whereases." Whatever the danger, if any, in such public discussions, it is a danger the Founders deemed outweighed by the danger incident to the stifling of thought and speech. The Court does not act on this view of the Founders. It calculates what it deems to be the danger of public discussion, holds the scales are tipped on the side of state suppression, and upholds state censorship. This method of decision offers little protection to First Amendment liberties "while this Court sits."

If there be minority groups who hail this holding as their victory, they might consider the possible relevancy of this ancient remark:

"Another such victory and I am undone."

JUSTICE REED, DISSENTING . . .

In carrying out its obligation to conform state legal administration to the "fundamental principles of liberty and justice" imposed on the states by the Fourteenth Amendment, this Court has steadily affirmed that the general principle against abridgment of free speech, protected by the First Amendment, is included in the command of the Fourteenth. So important to a constitutional democracy is the right of discussion that any challenge to legislative abridgment of those privileges of a free people calls for careful judicial appraisal. It is when speech becomes an incitement to crime that the right freely to exhort may be abridged. . . .

The judgment in this present case followed from a determination of judge and jury that petitioner's publication of the lithograph violated the statute. . . . This conviction must stand or fall upon a determination whether all definitions of the acts proscribed by the statute and charged in the information may be banned under the principles of the First Amendment, for . . . it is impossible to tell upon what phrase of the statute petitioner's conviction was based. Our examination can begin and end with the inquiry as to what meaning lies in the act's declaration, as charged in the information, that it is unlawful to portray in a lithograph a "lack of virtue of a class of citizens . . . which . . . exposes [them to] derision, or obloquy."

The majority opinion asserts that Illinois has given sufficiently clear and narrow meaning to the words "virtue," "derision," and "obloquy" by characterizing 224a as "a form of criminal libel law." But the mere description of this statute as a criminal libel law does not clarify the meaning of these vague words in the statute. To say that the mere presence of the word "virtue" in the individual libel statute makes its meaning clear in the group libel statute is a non sequitur. . . .

These words—"virtue," "derision," and "obloquy"—have neither general nor special meanings well enough known to apprise those within their reach as to limitations on speech. . . . Philosophers and poets, thinkers of high and low degree from every age and race have sought to expound the meaning of virtue, but each teaches his own conception of the moral excellence that satisfies standards of good conduct. Are the tests of the Puritan or the Cavalier to be applied, those of the city or the farm, the Christian or non-Christian, the old or the young? Does the Bill of Rights permit Illinois to forbid any reflection on the virtue of racial or religious classes which a jury or a judge may think exposes them to derision or obloquy, words themselves of quite uncertain meaning as used in the statute? I think not. A general and equal enforcement of this law would restrain the mildest expressions of opinion in all those areas where "virtue" may be thought to have a role. Since this judgment may rest upon these vague and undefined words, which permit within their scope the punishment of incidents secured by the guarantee of free speech, the conviction should be reversed.

JUSTICE DOUGLAS, DISSENTING . . .

My view is that if in any case other public interests are to override the plain command of the First Amendment, the peril of speech must be clear and present, leaving no room for argument, raising no doubts as to the necessity of curbing speech in order to prevent disaster.

The First Amendment is couched in absolute terms—freedom of speech shall not be abridged. Speech has therefore a preferred position as contrasted to some other civil rights. For example, privacy, equally sacred to some, is protected by the Fourth Amendment only against unreasonable searches and seizures. There is room for regulation of the ways and means of invading privacy. No such leeway is granted the invasion of the right of free speech guaranteed by the First Amendment. Until recent years that had been the course and direction of constitutional law. Yet recently the Court in this and in other cases has engrafted the right of regulation onto the First Amendment by placing in the hands of the legislative branch the right to regulate "within reasonable limits" the right of free speech. This to me is an ominous and alarming trend. The free trade in ideas which the Framers of the Constitution visualized disappears. In its place there is substituted a new orthodoxy—an orthodoxy that changes with the whims of the age or the day, an orthodoxy which the majority by solemn judgment proclaims to be essential to the safety, welfare, security, morality, or health of society. Free speech in the constitutional sense disappears. Limits are drawn—limits dictated by expediency, political opinion, prejudices, or some other desideratum of legislative action.

An historic aspect of the issue of judicial supremacy was the extent to which legislative judgment would be supreme in the field of social legislation. The vague contours of the Due Process Clause were used to strike down laws deemed by the Court to be unwise and improvident. That trend has been reversed. In matters relating to business, finance, industrial and labor conditions, health, and the public welfare, great leeway is now granted the legislature, for there is no guarantee in the Constitution that the status quo will be preserved against regulation by government. Freedom of speech, however, rests on a different constitutional basis. The First Amendment says that freedom of speech, freedom of press, and the free exercise of religion shall not be abridged. That is a negation of power on the part of each and every department of government. Free speech, free press, free exercise of religion are placed separate and apart; they are above and beyond the police power; they are not subject to regulation in the manner of factories, slums, apartment houses, production of oil, and the like.

The Court in this and in other cases places speech under an expanding legislative control. Today a white man stands convicted for protesting in unseemly language against our decisions invalidating restrictive covenants. Tomorrow a Negro will be haled before a court for denouncing lynch law in heated terms. Farm laborers in the West who compete with field hands drifting up from Mexico; whites who feel the pressure of orientals; a minority which finds employment going to members of the dominant religious group—all of these are caught in the mesh of today's decision. Debate and argument even in the courtroom are not always calm and dispassionate. Emotions sway speakers and audiences alike. Intemperate speech is a distinctive characteristic of man. Hotheads blow off and release destructive energy in the process. They shout and rave, exaggerating weaknesses, magnifying error, viewing with alarm. So it has been from the beginning; and so it will be throughout time. The Framers of the Constitution knew human nature as well as we do. They too had lived in dangerous days; they too knew the suffocating influence of orthodoxy and standardized thought. They weighed the compulsions for restrained speech and thought against the abuses of liberty. They chose liberty. That should be our choice today no matter how distasteful to us the pamphlet of Beauharnais may be. It is true that this is only one decision which may later be distinguished or confined to narrow limits. But it represents a philosophy at war with the First Amendment—a constitutional interpretation which puts free speech under the legislative thumb. It reflects an influence moving ever deeper into our society. It is notice to the legislatures that they have the power to control unpopular blocs. It is a warning to every minority that when the Constitution guarantees free speech it does not mean what it says.

JUSTICE JACKSON, DISSENTING . . .

In this case, neither the court nor jury found or were required to find any injury to any person, or group, or to the public peace, nor to find any probability, let alone any clear and present danger, of injury to any of these. Even though no individuals were named or described as targets of this pamphlet, if it resulted in a riot or caused injury to any individual Negro, such as being refused living quarters in a particular section, house, or apartment, or being refused employment, certainly there would be no constitutional obstacle to imposing civil or criminal liability for actual results. But in this case no actual violence and no specific injury was charged or proved.

The leaflet was simply held punishable as criminal libel per se irrespective of its actual or probable consequences. No charge of conspiracy complicates this case. The words themselves do not advocate the commission of any crime. The conviction rests on judicial attribution of a likelihood of evil results. The trial court, however, refused to charge the jury that it must find some "clear and present danger," and the Supreme Court of Illinois sustained conviction because, in its opinion, the words used had a tendency to cause a breach of the peace.

Referring to the clear and present danger doctrine in *Dennis* v. *United States* [1951], I said:

> I would save it, unmodified, for application as a "rule of reason" in the kind of case for which it was devised. When the issue is criminality of a hot-headed speech on a street corner, or circulation of a few incendiary pamphlets, or parading by some zealots behind a red flag, or refusal of a handful of school children to salute our flag, it is not beyond the capacity of the judicial process to gather, comprehend, and weigh the necessary materials for decision whether it is a clear and present danger of substantive evil or a harmless letting off of steam. It is not a prophecy, for the danger in such cases has matured by the time of trial or it was never present. The test applies and has meaning where a conviction is sought to be based on a speech or writing which does not directly or explicitly advocate a crime but to which such tendency is sought to be attributed by construction or by implication from external circumstances. The formula in such cases favors freedoms that are vital to our society, and, even if sometimes applied too generously, the consequences cannot be grave. . . .

Not the least of the virtues of this formula in such tendency cases is that it compels the prosecution to make up its mind what particular evil it sought or is seeking to prevent. It must relate its interference with speech or press to some identifiable evil to be prevented. Words on their own account are not to be punished in such cases but are reachable only as the root of punishable evils.

Punishment of printed words, based on their tendency either to cause breach of the peace or injury to persons or groups, in my opinion, is justifiable only if the prosecution survives the "clear and present danger" test. It is the most just and workable standard yet evolved for determining criminality of words whose injurious or inciting tendencies are not demonstrated by the event but are ascribed to them on the basis of probabilities.

Its application is important in this case because it takes account of the particular form, time, place, and manner of communication in question. . . . It would consider whether a leaflet is so emotionally exciting to immediate action as the spoken word, especially the incendiary street or public speech. It will inquire whether this publication was obviously so foul and extreme as to defeat its own ends, whether its appeals for money—which has a cooling effect on many persons—would not negative its inflammatory effect, whether it would not impress the passer-by as the work of an irresponsible who needed mental examination.

One of the merits of the clear and present danger test is that the triers of fact would take into account the realities of race relations and any smouldering fires to be fanned into holocausts. Such consideration might well warrant a conviction here when it would not in another and different environment.

Group libel statutes represent a commendable desire to reduce sinister abuses of our freedoms of expression—abuses which I have had occasion to learn can tear apart a society, brutalize its dominant elements, and persecute, even to extermination, its minorities. While laws or prosecutions might not alleviate racial or sectarian hatreds and may even invest scoundrels with a specious martyrdom, I should be loath to foreclose the States from a considerable latitude of experimentation in this field. Such efforts, if properly applied, do not justify frenetic forebodings of crushed liberty. But these acts present most difficult policy and technical problems, as thoughtful writers who have canvassed the problem more comprehensively than is appropriate in a judicial opinion have well pointed out.

No group interest in any particular prosecution should forget that the shoe may be on the other foot in some prosecution tomorrow. In these, as in other matters, our guiding spirit should be that each freedom is balanced with a responsibility, and every power of the State must be checked with safeguards. Such is the spirit of our American law of criminal libel, which concedes the power to the State, but only as a power restrained by recognition of individual rights. I cannot escape the conclusion that as the Act has been applied in this case it lost sight of the rights.

JOSEPH BURSTYN, INC. V. WILSON
343 U.S. 495 (1952)

A New York state law forbade the commercial showing of any motion picture without a license and authorized the education department to deny a license if it concluded that a film was "obscene, indecent, immoral, inhuman, [or] sacrilegious" or "of such a character that its exhibition would tend to corrupt morals or incite to crime." Pursuant to this law, the department in 1950 examined and issued a license to Joseph Burstyn, Inc., a movie distributor, to show an Italian film entitled *The Miracle*, which concerned a poor girl apparently impregnated by a saint. The film had run for eight weeks at a theater in New York City when the department, having received hundreds of messages both for and against the showing, decided to reconsider. Now finding the film "sacrilegious," it rescinded the license. Burstyn challenged the decision on grounds (among others) of free speech and press. He lost in the New York courts, but the U.S. Supreme Court voted 9 to 0 that the law was an unconstitutional abridgment of free speech and press.

The Court said that the statute established a system of "prior restraint," that prior restraint may be justified only in "exceptional cases," and that this was not one of them. "The state has no legitimate interest in protecting any or all religions from views distasteful to them which is sufficient to justify prior restraints upon the expression of those views," wrote Justice Clark for the Court. "It is not the business of government in our nation to suppress real or imagined attacks upon a particular religious doctrine, whether they appear in publications, speeches, or motion pictures." The Court left for another day whether some state censorship of movies might be permissible "under a clearly drawn statute designed and applied to prevent the showing of obscene films."

In *Burstyn* the Court decided that movies enjoy First Amendment protection because they are "a significant medium for the communication of ideas." The Court explicitly rejected a statement it had made in a 1915 case that "the exhibition of moving pictures is a business . . . not to be regarded . . . as part of the press of the country or as organs of public opinion."

Opinion of the Court: **Clark**, Black, Douglas, Vinson, Minton. Concurring in the judgment: **Reed**; **Frankfurter**, Jackson. Concurring in the opinion of the Court and also joining Frankfurter's opinion: **Burton**.

Burstyn v. *Wilson* was decided on May 26, 1952.

OPINION

JUSTICE CLARK DELIVERED THE OPINION OF THE COURT . . .

In *Mutual Film Corp.* v. *Industrial Comm'n* [1915], a distributor of motion pictures sought to enjoin the enforcement of an Ohio statute which required the prior approval of a board of censors before any motion picture could be publicly exhibited in the state, and which directed the board to approve only such films as it adjudged to be "of a moral, educational, or amusing and harmless character." The statute was assailed in part as an unconstitutional abridgment of the freedom of the press guaranteed by the First and Fourteenth Amendments. The District Court rejected this contention, stating that the first eight Amendments were not a restriction on state action. . . . On appeal to this Court, plaintiff in its brief abandoned this claim and contended merely that the statute in question violated the freedom of speech and publication guaranteed by the Constitution of Ohio. In affirming the decree of the District Court denying injunctive relief, this Court stated:

> It cannot be put out of view that the exhibition of moving pictures is a business pure and simple, originated and conducted for profit, like other spectacles, not to be regarded, nor intended to be regarded by the Ohio constitution, we think, as part of the press of the country or as organs of public opinion.

In a series of decisions beginning with *Gitlow* v. *New York* [1925], this Court held that the liberty of speech and of the press which the First Amendment guarantees against abridgment by the federal government is within the liberty safeguarded by the Due Process Clause of the Fourteenth Amendment from invasion by state action. That principle has been followed and reaffirmed to the present day. Since this series of decisions came after the *Mutual* decision, the present case is the first to present squarely to us the question whether motion pictures are within the ambit of protection which the First Amendment, through the Fourteenth, secures to any form of "speech" or "the press."

It cannot be doubted that motion pictures are a significant medium for the communication of ideas. They may affect public attitudes and behavior in a variety of ways, ranging from direct espousal of a political or social doctrine to the subtle shaping of thought which characterizes all artistic expression. The importance of motion pictures as an organ of public opinion is not lessened by the fact that they are designed to entertain as well as to inform. As was said in *Winters* v. *New York* [1948]:

> The line between the informing and the entertaining is too elusive for the protection of that basic right [a free press]. Everyone is familiar with instances of propaganda through fiction. What is one man's amusement, teaches another's doctrine.

It is urged that motion pictures do not fall within the First Amendment's aegis because their production, distribution, and exhibition is a large-scale business conducted for private profit. We cannot agree. That books, newspapers, and magazines are published and sold for profit does not prevent them from being a form of expression whose liberty is safeguarded by the First Amendment. We fail to see why operation for profit should have any different effect in the case of motion pictures.

It is further urged that motion pictures possess a greater capacity for evil, particularly among the youth of a community, than other modes of expression. Even if one were to accept this hypothesis, it does not follow that motion pictures should be disqualified from First Amendment protection. If there be capacity for evil it may be relevant in determining the permissible scope of community control, but it does not authorize substantially unbridled censorship such as we have here.

For the foregoing reasons, we conclude that expression by means of motion pictures is included within the free speech and free press guaranty of the First and Fourteenth Amendments. To the extent that language in the opinion in *Mutual Film Corp.* is out of harmony with the views here set forth, we no longer adhere to it.

To hold that liberty of expression by means of motion pictures is guaranteed by the First and Fourteenth Amendments, however, is not the end of our problem. It does not follow that the Constitution requires absolute freedom to exhibit every motion picture of every kind at all times and all places. That much is evident from the series of decisions of this Court with respect to other media of communication of ideas. Nor does it follow that motion pictures are necessarily subject to the precise rules governing any other particular method of expression. Each method tends to present its own peculiar problems. But the basic principles of freedom of speech and the press, like the First Amendment's command, do not vary. Those principles, as they have frequently been enunciated by this Court, make freedom of expression the rule. There is no justification in this case for making an exception to that rule.

The statute involved here does not seek to punish, as a past offense, speech or writing falling within the permissible scope of subsequent punishment. On the contrary, New York requires that permission to communicate ideas be obtained in advance from state officials who judge the content of the words and pictures sought to be communicated. This Court recognized many years ago that such a previous restraint is a form of infringement upon freedom of expression to be especially condemned. *Near* v. *Minnesota* [1931]. . . . In the light of the First Amendment's history and of the *Near* decision, the State has a heavy burden to demonstrate that the limitation challenged here presents such an exceptional case.

New York's highest court says there is "nothing mysterious" about the statutory provision applied in this case: "It is simply this: that no religion, as that word is understood by the ordinary, reasonable person, shall be treated with contempt, mockery, scorn, and ridicule. . . ." This is far from the kind of narrow exception to freedom of expression which a state may carve out to satisfy the adverse demands of other interests of society. In seeking to apply the broad and all-inclusive definition of "sacrilegious" given by the New York courts, the censor is set adrift upon a boundless sea amid a myriad of conflicting currents of religious views, with no charts but those provided by the most vocal and powerful orthodoxies. New York cannot vest such unlimited restraining control over motion pictures in a censor. Cf. *Kunz* v. *New York* [1951]. Under such a standard the most careful and tolerant censor would find it virtually impossible to avoid favoring one religion over another, and he would be subject to an inevitable tendency to ban the expression of unpopular sentiments sacred to a religious minority. Application of the "sacrilegious" test, in these or other respects, might raise substantial questions under the First Amendment's guaranty of separate church and state with freedom of worship for all. However, from the standpoint of freedom of speech and the press, it is enough to point out that the state has no legitimate interest in protecting any or all religions from views distasteful to them which is sufficient to justify prior restraints upon the expression of those views. It is not the business of government in our nation to suppress real or imagined attacks upon a particular religious doctrine, whether they appear in publications, speeches, or motion pictures.

Since the term "sacrilegious" is the sole standard under attack here, it is not necessary for us to decide, for example, whether a state may censor motion pictures under a clearly drawn statute designed and applied to prevent the showing of obscene films. That is a very different question from the one now before us. We hold only that under the First and Fourteenth Amendments a state may not ban a film on the basis of a censor's conclusion that it is "sacrilegious."

REVERSED.

ROTH V. UNITED STATES
354 U.S. 476 (1957)

Samuel Roth, a New York City businessman who published and sold books and magazines, was found guilty under the federal obscenity statute of mailing obscene materials. Appealing on First Amendment grounds, Roth lost in the U.S. Court of Appeals for the Second Circuit. The Supreme Court then took his case and decided it together with an appeal from California by David Alberts, who had been convicted under a state law of selling obscene and indecent books. The Supreme Court, with Justice Brennan writing, upheld both convictions.

In *Roth* the Court for the first time addressed whether obscenity is speech protected by the First Amendment and held that it was not. Noting that the Court had previously assumed that obscenity lacks First Amendment protection, Brennan adduced constitutional history to show that "the unconditional phrasing of the First Amendment was not intended to protect every utterance"—and that libel and obscenity were outside its scope. Brennan also based the Court's holding on the view that the First Amendment, while it protects all utterances (however unorthodox or controversial) that contribute to the "unfettered interchange of ideas," cannot shelter obscenity because obscenity is "utterly without redeeming social importance." Because obscenity is constitutionally unprotected, Brennan added, obscene materials in a given case do not have to be examined in terms of "clear and present danger."

A difficulty in *Roth* was that the laws under which Roth and Alberts had been convicted did not define obscenity. The Court tried to. It rejected the widely used test from an English case permitting a work's obscenity to be judged by the effect of an isolated excerpt upon particularly susceptible persons. This test, said the Court, "might well encompass material legitimately treating with sex." The Court instead endorsed a test embraced by some American courts: "whether to the average person, applying contemporary community standards, the dominant theme of the material taken as a whole appeals to prurient interest." A footnote defined such material as that which has "a tendency to excite lustful thoughts," and "prurient interest" as "a shameful or morbid interest in nudity, sex, or excretion." In subsequent cases the Court found itself struggling with definitions of obscenity.

Justice Douglas, joined by Justice Black, dissented, contending that obscenity, like every other form of speech, enjoys First Amendment protection.

Opinion of the Court: **Brennan**, Frankfurter, Burton, Clark, Whittaker. Concurring in the result: **Warren**. Concurring in *Roth* and dissenting in *Alberts*: **Harlan**. Dissenting opinion: **Douglas**, Black.

Roth v. *United States* was decided on June 24, 1957.

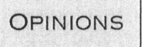

OPINIONS

JUSTICE BRENNAN DELIVERED THE OPINION OF THE COURT . . .

The dispositive question is whether obscenity is utterance within the area of protected speech and press. Although this is the first time the question has been squarely presented to this Court, either under the First Amendment or under the Fourteenth Amendment, expressions found in numerous opinions indicate that this Court has always assumed that obscenity is not protected by the freedoms of speech and press. . . .

The guaranties of freedom of expression in effect in 10 of the 14 States which by 1792 had ratified the Constitution, gave no absolute protection for every utterance. Thirteen of the 14 States provided for the prosecution of libel, and all of those States made either blasphemy or profanity, or both, statutory crimes. As early as 1712, Massachusetts made it criminal to publish "any filthy, obscene, or profane song, pamphlet, libel, or mock sermon" in imitation or mimicking of religious services. . . . Thus, profanity and obscenity were related offenses.

In light of this history, it is apparent that the unconditional phrasing of the First Amendment was not intended to protect every utterance. This phrasing did not prevent this Court from concluding that libelous utterances are not within the area of constitutionally protected speech. *Beauharnais* v. *Illinois* [1952]. At the time of the adoption of the First Amendment, obscenity law was not as fully developed as libel law, but there is sufficiently contemporaneous evidence to show that obscenity, too, was outside the protection intended for speech and press.

The protection given speech and press was fashioned to assure unfettered interchange of ideas for the bringing about of political and social changes desired by the people. . . .

All ideas having even the slightest redeeming social importance—unorthodox ideas, controversial ideas, even ideas hateful to the prevailing climate of opinion—have the full protection of the guaranties, unless excludable because they encroach upon the limited area of more important interests. But implicit in the history of the First Amendment is the rejection of obscenity as utterly without redeeming social importance. This rejection for that reason is mirrored in the universal judgment that obscenity should be restrained, reflected in the international agreement of over 50 nations, in the obscenity laws of all of the 48 States, and in the 20 obscenity laws enacted by the Congress from 1842 to 1956. This is the same judgment expressed by this Court in *Chaplinsky* v. *New Hampshire* [1942]:

> . . . There are certain well-defined and narrowly limited classes of speech, the prevention and punishment of which have never been thought to raise any Constitutional problem. *These include the lewd and obscene. . . . It has been well observed that such utterances are no essen-*

tial part of any exposition of ideas, and are of such slight social value as a step to truth that any benefit that may be derived from them is clearly outweighed by the social interest in order and morality. . . . (Emphasis added.)

We hold that obscenity is not within the area of constitutionally protected speech or press.

It is strenuously urged that these obscenity statutes offend the constitutional guaranties because they punish incitation to impure sexual thoughts, not shown to be related to any overt antisocial conduct which is or may be incited in the persons stimulated to such thoughts. In *Roth*, the trial judge instructed the jury: "The words 'obscene, lewd, and lascivious,' as used in the law, signify that form of immorality which has relation to sexual impurity and has a tendency to excite lustful *thoughts*." (Emphasis added.) In *Alberts*, the trial judge applied the test laid down in *People* v. *Wepplo. . .*, namely, whether the material has "a substantial tendency to deprave or corrupt its readers by inciting lascivious *thoughts* or arousing lustful desires." (Emphasis added.) It is insisted that the constitutional guaranties are violated because convictions may be had without proof either that obscene material will perceptibly create a clear and present danger of antisocial conduct, or will probably induce its recipients to such conduct. But, in light of our holding that obscenity is not protected speech, the complete answer to this argument is in the holding of this Court in *Beauharnais*:

> Libelous utterances not being within the area of constitutionally protected speech, it is unnecessary, either for us or for the State courts, to consider the issues behind the phrase "clear and present danger." Certainly no one would contend that obscene speech, for example, may be punished only upon a showing of such circumstances. Libel, as we have seen, is in the same class.

However, sex and obscenity are not synonymous. Obscene material is material which deals with sex in a manner appealing to prurient interest. The portrayal of sex, e.g., in art, literature, and scientific works, is not itself sufficient reason to deny material the constitutional protection of freedom of speech and press. Sex, a great and mysterious motive force in human life, has indisputably been a subject of absorbing interest to mankind through the ages; it is one of the vital problems of human interest and public concern. As to all such problems, this Court said in *Thornhill* v. *Alabama* [1940]:

> The freedom of speech and of the press guaranteed by the Constitution embraces at the least the liberty to discuss publicly and truthfully *all matters of public concern* without previous restraint or fear of subsequent punishment. The exigencies of the colonial period and the efforts to secure freedom from oppressive administration developed a broadened conception of these liberties as adequate to supply the public need for *information and education with respect to the significant issues of the times*. . . . Freedom of discussion, if it would fulfill its historic function in this nation, must embrace *all issues about which information is needed or appropriate to enable the members of society to cope with the exigencies of their period*. (Emphasis added.)

The fundamental freedoms of speech and press have contributed greatly to the development and well-being of our free society and are indispensable to its continued growth. Ceaseless vigilance is the watchword to prevent their erosion by Congress or by the States. The door barring federal and state intrusion into this area cannot be left ajar; it must be kept tightly closed and opened only the slightest crack necessary to prevent encroachment upon more important interests. It is therefore vital that the standards for judging obscenity safeguard the protection of freedom of speech and press for material which does not treat sex in a manner appealing to prurient interest. *encouraging excessive interest in sexual matters*

The early leading standard of obscenity allowed material to be judged merely by the effect of an isolated excerpt upon particularly susceptible persons. *Regina* v. *Hicklin*, 1868 [an English case]. Some American courts adopted this standard, but later decisions have rejected it and substituted this test: whether to the average person, applying contemporary community standards, the dominant theme of the material taken as a whole appeals to prurient interest. The *Hicklin* test, judging obscenity by the effect of isolated passages upon the most susceptible persons, might well encompass material legitimately treating with sex, and so it must be rejected as unconstitutionally restrictive of the freedoms of speech and press. On the other hand, the substituted standard provides safeguards adequate to withstand the charge of constitutional infirmity.

Both trial courts below sufficiently followed the proper standard. Both courts used the proper definition of obscenity. In addition, in the *Alberts* case, in ruling on a motion to dismiss, the trial judge indicated that, as the trier of facts, he was judging each item as a whole as it would affect the normal person, and in *Roth*, the trial judge instructed the jury as follows:

> . . . The test is not whether it would arouse sexual desires or sexual impure thoughts in those comprising a particular segment of the community, the young, the immature, or the highly prudish or would leave another segment, the scientific or highly educated or the so-called worldly-wise and sophisticated indifferent and unmoved. . . .
>
> The test in each case is the effect of the book, picture or publication considered as a whole, not upon any particular class, but upon all those whom it is likely to reach. In other words, you determine its impact upon the average person in the community. The books, pictures, and circulars must be judged as a whole, in their entire context, and you are not to consider detached or separate portions in reaching a conclusion. You judge the circulars, pictures, and publications which have been put in evidence by present-day standards of the community. You may ask yourselves does it offend the common conscience of the community by present-day standards. . . .
>
> In this case, ladies and gentlemen of the jury, you and you alone are the exclusive judges of what the common conscience of the community is, and in determining that conscience you are to consider the community as a whole, young and old, educated and uneducated, the religious and the irreligious—men, women, and children.

It is argued that the statutes do not provide reasonably ascertainable standards of guilt and therefore violate the constitutional requirements of due process. . . . The federal obscenity statute makes punishable the mailing of material that is "obscene, lewd, lascivious, or filthy . . . or other publication of an indecent character." The California statute makes punishable, inter alia, the keeping for sale or advertising material that is "obscene or indecent." The thrust of the argument is that these words are not sufficiently precise because they do not mean the same thing to all people, all the time, everywhere.

Many decisions have recognized that these terms of obscenity statutes are not precise. This Court, however, has consistently held that lack of precision is not itself offensive to the requirements of due process. . . .

In summary, then, we hold that these statutes, applied according to the proper standard for judging obscenity, do not offend constitutional safeguards against convictions based upon protected material, or fail to give men in acting adequate notice of what is prohibited. . . .

The judgments are

AFFIRMED.

JUSTICE DOUGLAS, DISSENTING.

When we sustain these convictions, we make the legality of a publication turn on the purity of thought which a book or tract instills in the mind of the reader. I do not think we can approve that standard and be faithful to the command of the First Amendment, which by its terms is a restraint on Congress and which by the Fourteenth is a restraint on the States.

In the *Roth* case the trial judge charged the jury that the statutory words "obscene, lewd, and lascivious" describe "that form of immorality which has relation to sexual impurity and has a tendency to excite lustful thoughts." He stated that the term "filthy" in the statute pertains "to that sort of treatment of sexual matters in such a vulgar and indecent way, so that it tends to arouse a feeling of disgust and revulsion." He went on to say that the material "must be calculated to corrupt and debauch the minds and morals" of "the average person in the community," not those of any particular class. "You judge the circulars, pictures, and publications which have been put in evidence by present-day standards of the community. You may ask yourselves does it offend the common conscience of the community by present-day standards."

The trial judge who, sitting without a jury, heard the *Alberts* case and the appellate court that sustained the judgment of conviction, took California's definition of "obscenity" from *People* v. *Wepplo.* That case held that a book is obscene "if it has a substantial tendency to deprave or corrupt its readers by inciting lascivious thoughts or arousing lustful desire."

By these standards punishment is inflicted for thoughts provoked, not for overt acts nor antisocial conduct. This test cannot be squared with our decisions under the First Amendment. Even the ill-starred *Dennis* case conceded that speech to be punishable must have some relation to action which could be penalized by government. *Dennis* v. *United States* [1951]. . . . This issue cannot be avoided by saying that obscenity is not protected by the First Amendment. The question remains, what is the constitutional test of obscenity?

The tests by which these convictions were obtained require only the arousing of sexual thoughts. Yet the arousing of sexual thoughts and desires happens every day in normal life in dozens of ways. . . .

The test of obscenity the Court endorses today gives the censor free range over a vast domain. To allow the State to step in and punish mere speech or publication that the judge or the jury thinks has an undesirable impact on thoughts but that is not shown to be a part of unlawful action is drastically to curtail the First Amendment. . . .

If we were certain that impurity of sexual thoughts impelled to action, we would be on less dangerous ground in punishing the distributors of this sex literature. But it is by no means clear that obscene literature, as so defined, is a significant factor in influencing substantial deviations from the community standards. . . .

The absence of dependable information on the effect of obscene literature on human conduct should make us wary. It should put us on the side of protecting society's interest in literature, except and unless it can be said that the particular publication has an impact on action that the government can control.

As noted, the trial judge in the *Roth* case charged the jury in the alternative that the federal obscenity statute outlaws literature dealing with sex which offends "the common conscience of the community." That standard is, in my view, more inimical still to freedom of expression.

The standard of what offends "the common conscience of the community" conflicts, in my judgment, with the command of the First Amendment that "Congress shall make no law

. . . abridging the freedom of speech, or of the press." Certainly that standard would not be an acceptable one if religion, economics, politics, or philosophy were involved. How does it become a constitutional standard when literature treating with sex is concerned?

Any test that turns on what is offensive to the community's standards is too loose, too capricious, too destructive of freedom of expression to be squared with the First Amendment. Under that test, juries can censor, suppress, and punish what they don't like, provided the matter relates to "sexual impurity" or has a tendency "to excite lustful thoughts." This is community censorship in one of its worst forms. It creates a regime where in the battle between the literati and the Philistines, the Philistines are certain to win. . . .

I assume there is nothing in the Constitution which forbids Congress from using its power over the mails to proscribe conduct on the grounds of good morals. No one would suggest that the First Amendment permits nudity in public places, adultery, and other phases of sexual misconduct.

I can understand (and at times even sympathize) with programs of civic groups and church groups to protect and defend the existing moral standards of the community. I can understand the motives of the Anthony Comstocks who would impose Victorian standards on the community. When speech alone is involved, I do not think that government, consistently with the First Amendment, can become the sponsor of any of these movements. I do not think that government, consistently with the First Amendment, can throw its weight behind one school or another. Government should be concerned with antisocial conduct, not with utterances. Thus, if the First Amendment guarantee of freedom of speech and press is to mean anything in this field, it must allow protests even against the moral code that the standard of the day sets for the community. In other words, literature should not be suppressed merely because it offends the moral code of the censor.

The legality of a publication in this country should never be allowed to turn either on the purity of thought which it instills in the mind of the reader or on the degree to which it offends the community conscience. By either test the role of the censor is exalted, and society's values in literary freedom are sacrificed.

The Court today suggests a third standard. It defines obscene material as that "which deals with sex in a manner appealing to prurient interest." Like the standards applied by the trial judges below, that standard does not require any nexus between the literature which is prohibited and action which the legislature can regulate or prohibit. Under the First Amendment, that standard is no more valid than those which the courts below adopted.

I do not think that the problem can be resolved by the Court's statement that "obscenity is not expression protected by the First Amendment." With the exception of *Beauharnais* none of our cases has resolved problems of free speech and free press by placing any form of expression beyond the pale of the absolute prohibition of the First Amendment. Unlike the law of libel, wrongfully relied on in *Beauharnais*, there is no special historical evidence that literature dealing with sex was intended to be treated in a special manner by those who drafted the First Amendment. . . . I reject too the implication that problems of freedom of speech and of the press are to be resolved by weighing against the values of free expression, the judgment of the Court that a particular form of that expression has "no redeeming social importance." The First Amendment, its prohibition in terms absolute, was designed to preclude courts as well as legislatures from weighing the values of speech against silence. The First Amendment puts free speech in the preferred position.

Freedom of expression can be suppressed if, and to the extent that, it is so closely brigaded with illegal action as to be an inseparable part of it. . . . As a people, we cannot afford to relax that standard. For the test that suppresses a cheap tract today can suppress a literary gem tomorrow. All it need do is to incite a lascivious thought or arouse a lustful desire. The list of books that judges or juries can place in that category is endless.

I would give the broad sweep of the First Amendment full support. I have the same confidence in the ability of our people to reject noxious literature as I have in their capacity to sort out the true from the false in theology, economics, politics, or any other field.

RESPONSE

FROM *THE COMMONWEAL*, JULY 12, 1957, "OBSCENITY AND FREEDOM"

. . . Freedom of the press is vital to the health of a democracy; infringement of it can never be other than dangerous and must be guarded against at almost all costs. On the other hand, the flood of obscene literature which increasingly threatens and affronts public decency is also an evil to be guarded against.

Is this a stalemate, with freedom to publish and disseminate obscene writings the inevitable price of freedom of speech in other areas, with suffering the abuse of a right the necessary corollary to the protection of a right itself?

Rather than a stalemate, it is a question of balance. Public decency must be safeguarded without violating the rights of individuals. Individual cases involving obscenity must be dealt with according to specific juridical procedure, especially that of jury trial, and the working consensus arrived at without imposing an arbitrary single standard on the pluralist community. In most instances, we suspect, the consensus will be arrived at fairly easily. In the others, the borderline cases, we must rely on the machinery of American justice.

Such a course does not appeal to the zealots of either camp—those who demand freedom at any cost and those who will have protection at any cost. It seems to be the only course, however, for those who value freedom, art, *and* decency. That which is clearly obscenity, in the eyes of many, may be permitted to circulate in this country for a perilously long time, perhaps always. Serious works of art may be demeaned and suppressed, to our considerable detriment. But we can have faith that freedom will not be lost, art will not be fettered for long, and indecency will not flourish without check.

26

NAACP v. ALABAMA EX REL. PATTERSON
357 U.S. 449 (1958)

In 1956 the Alabama attorney general sued the National Association for the Advancement of Colored People in an effort to drive it from the state. Based in New York, the NAACP had been active in Alabama since 1918. It had never qualified to operate in the state, however, as the attorney general said it must do under a statute requiring that a non-Alabama corporation file its corporate charter and designate a place of business and an agent before doing business in the state. The state argued that the citizens of Alabama would suffer "irreparable injury" if the NAACP were to continue its activities without complying with the qualification statute. These activities included organizing bus boycotts in Montgomery and helping students try to desegregate the state university.

The NAACP considered itself exempt from the qualification statute and argued that it was protected from the state's demands by the First Amendment. The organization eventually agreed to comply with the statute and provided most of the materials that the court had ordered it to produce, but it withheld its membership list on First Amendment grounds. The NAACP was held in contempt and fined $100,000. The Alabama Supreme Court declined to review the case, but the U.S. Supreme Court, with Justice Harlan writing, voted unanimously to reverse.

NAACP v. *Alabama* was the first of several cases in which the Court, against the efforts of Southern states to curb the activities of the NAACP, asserted a constitutional "right of association." This right is not mentioned in the Constitution. But for the Court it seemed to derive from the other First Amendment guarantees and was in any event an "indispensable" constitutional liberty. As in other cases since *American Communications Assn.* v. *Douds* (1950), the Court sought in *NAACP* v. *Alabama* to determine the proper balance between individual and societal rights. Alabama, the Court concluded, had failed to show why its need for the NAACP's membership list was strong enough to outweigh the harm to associational rights likely to result from compelled disclosure.

Opinion of the Court: **Harlan**, Black, Douglas, Frankfurter, Burton, Clark, Warren, Brennan, Whittaker.

NAACP v. *Alabama ex rel. Patterson* was decided on June 30, 1958.

JUSTICE HARLAN DELIVERED THE OPINION OF THE COURT . . .

We . . . reach petitioner's claim that the production order in the state litigation trespasses upon fundamental freedoms protected by the Due Process Clause of the Fourteenth Amendment. Petitioner argues that in view of the facts and circumstances shown in the record, the effect of compelled disclosure of the membership lists will be to abridge the rights of its rank-and-file members to engage in lawful association in support of their common beliefs. It contends that governmental action which, although not directly suppressing association, nevertheless carries this consequence, can be justified only upon some overriding valid interest of the State.

Effective advocacy of both public and private points of view, particularly controversial ones, is undeniably enhanced by group association, as this Court has more than once recognized by remarking upon the close nexus between the freedoms of speech and assembly. *De-Jonge* v. *Oregon* [1937]; *Thomas* v. *Collins* [1945]. It is beyond debate that freedom to engage in association for the advancement of beliefs and ideas is an inseparable aspect of the "liberty" assured by the Due Process Clause of the Fourteenth Amendment, which embraces freedom of speech. See *Gitlow* v. *New York* [1925]. . . . Of course, it is immaterial whether the beliefs sought to be advanced by association pertain to political, economic, religious, or cultural matters, and state action which may have the effect of curtailing the freedom to associate is subject to the closest scrutiny.

The fact that Alabama, so far as is relevant to the validity of the contempt judgment presently under review, has taken no direct action . . . to restrict the right of petitioner's members to associate freely, does not end inquiry into the effect of the production order. See *American Communications Assn.* v. *Douds* [1950]. In the domain of these indispensable liberties, whether of speech, press, or association, the decisions of this Court recognize that abridgment of such rights, even though unintended, may inevitably follow from varied forms of governmental action. Thus in *Douds*, the Court stressed that the legislation there challenged, which on its face sought to regulate labor unions and to secure stability in interstate commerce, would have the practical effect "of discouraging" the exercise of constitutionally protected political rights, and it upheld the statute only after concluding that the reasons advanced for its enactment were constitutionally sufficient to justify its possible deterrent effect upon such freedoms. . . .

It is hardly a novel perception that compelled disclosure of affiliation with groups engaged in advocacy may constitute as effective a restraint on freedom of association as the forms of governmental action in the cases above were thought likely to produce upon the particular constitutional rights there involved. This Court has recognized the vital relationship between freedom to associate and privacy in one's associations. When referring to the varied forms of governmental action which might interfere with freedom of assembly, it said in *Douds*: "A requirement that adherents of particular religious faiths or political parties wear identifying armbands, for example, is obviously of this nature." Compelled disclosure of membership in an organization engaged in advocacy of particular beliefs is of the same order. Inviolability of privacy in group association may in many circumstances be indispensable to preservation of freedom of association, particularly where a group espouses dissident beliefs. . . .

We think that the production order, in the respects here drawn in question, must be regarded as entailing the likelihood of a substantial restraint upon the exercise by petitioner's members of their right to freedom of association. Petitioner has made an uncontroverted showing that on past occasions revelation of the identity of its rank-and-file members has exposed these members to economic reprisal, loss of employment, threat of physical coercion, and other manifestations of public hostility. Under these circumstances, we think it apparent that compelled disclosure of petitioner's Alabama membership is likely to affect adversely the ability of petitioner and its members to pursue their collective effort to foster beliefs which they admittedly have the right to advocate, in that it may induce members to withdraw from the Association and dissuade others from joining it because of fear of exposure of their beliefs shown through their associations and of the consequences of this exposure.

It is not sufficient to answer, as the State does here, that whatever repressive effect compulsory disclosure of names of petitioner's members may have upon participation by Alabama citizens in petitioner's activities follows not from state action but from private community pressures. The crucial factor is the interplay of governmental and private action, for it is only after the initial exertion of state power represented by the production order that private action takes hold.

We turn to the final question whether Alabama has demonstrated an interest in obtaining the disclosures it seeks from petitioner which is sufficient to justify the deterrent effect which we have concluded these disclosures may well have on the free exercise by petitioner's members of their constitutionally protected right of association. . . . It is not of moment that the State has here acted solely through its judicial branch, for whether legislative or judicial, it is still the application of state power which we are asked to scrutinize.

It is important to bear in mind that petitioner asserts no right to absolute immunity from state investigation, and no right to disregard Alabama's laws. As shown by its substantial compliance with the production order, petitioner does not deny Alabama's right to obtain from it such information as the State desires concerning the purposes of the Association and its activities within the State. Petitioner has not objected to divulging the identity of its members who are employed by or hold official positions with it. It has urged the rights solely of its ordinary rank-and-file members. . . .

Whether there was "justification" in this instance turns solely on the substantiality of Alabama's interest in obtaining the membership lists. During the course of a hearing before the Alabama Circuit Court on a motion of petitioner to set aside the production order, the State Attorney General presented at length, under examination by petitioner, the State's reason for requesting the membership lists. The exclusive purpose was to determine whether petitioner was conducting intrastate business in violation of the Alabama foreign corporation registration statute, and the membership lists were expected to help resolve this question. The issues in the litigation commenced by Alabama by its bill in equity were whether the character of petitioner and its activities in Alabama had been such as to make petitioner subject to the registration statute, and whether the extent of petitioner's activities without qualifying suggested its permanent ouster from the State. Without intimating the slightest view upon the merits of these issues, we are unable to perceive that the disclosure of the names of petitioner's rank-and-file members has a substantial bearing on either of them. . . .

We hold that the immunity from state scrutiny of membership lists which the Association claims on behalf of its members is here so related to the right of the members to pursue their lawful private interests privately and to associate freely with others in so doing as to come within the protection of the Fourteenth Amendment. And we conclude that Alabama has fallen short of showing a controlling justification for the deterrent effect on the free enjoyment of the right to associate which disclosure of membership lists is likely to have. Accordingly, the judgment of civil contempt and the $100,000 fine which resulted from petitioner's refusal to comply with the production order in this respect must fall. . . .

REVERSED.

RESPONSE

FROM NATIONAL ASSOCIATION FOR THE ADVANCEMENT OF COLORED PEOPLE PRESS RELEASE, JUNE 30, 1958

Today's Supreme Court decision in the Alabama case validates the NAACP policy of with-holding the names of members and contributors as a protective measure against official and unofficial persecution. In the light of this ruling we expect to resume our activity in Alabama in the near future.

This decision—along with one handed down an January 21 by a three-judge federal court in Virginia invalidating three new laws of that state which would require filing of membership lists by the NAACP—should give pause to the persistent and systematic harassment of the Association which has been widespread in certain Southern states.

While we do not anticipate an immediate end to persecution of the NAACP in the South, we believe that these decisions underscore the fact that efforts to destroy the Association as an effective force through punitive legislative and judicial action have failed.

BARENBLATT V. UNITED STATES

360 U.S. 109 (1959)

The House Un-American Activities Committee, formed in 1938 and disbanded in 1957, mainly investigated the domestic activities of the Communist Party. It held more than 200 public hearings and subpoenaed more than 3,000 persons. In 1956, during its inquiry into alleged Communist infiltration into higher education, the committee subpoenaed Lloyd Barenblatt because he allegedly had been a member of a Communist club while he was a graduate student and then a teaching fellow at the University of Michigan in the late 1940s. Barenblatt refused to answer the committee's questions as to whether he was then or had ever been a member of the Communist Party. Instead he filed a statement detailing his constitutional objections to the investigation, including his view that the First Amendment precluded legislative inquiries into his political beliefs and associations. Charged with contempt of court, Barenblatt was convicted, fined $250, and sentenced to six months in prison. He appealed on First Amendment grounds. The U.S. Court of Appeals for the District of Columbia upheld his conviction, as did the Supreme Court, with Justice Harlan writing for the five-man majority.

Barenblatt was another "balancing" case that fractured the Court. Having examined "the competing public and private interests at stake," Justice Harlan found those of the government (which boiled down to "self-preservation") weightier than Barenblatt's. In a dissent joined by Justices Warren and Douglas, Justice Black was sharply critical of not only the majority's holding but also its approach to the First Amendment. "To apply the Court's balancing test under such circumstances," he wrote, "is to read the First Amendment to say 'Congress shall pass no law abridging freedom of speech, press, assembly, and petition, unless Congress and the Supreme Court reach the joint conclusion that on balance the interest of the Government in stifling these freedoms is greater than the interest of the people in having them exercised.' This is closely akin to the notion that neither the First Amendment nor any other provision of the Bill of Rights should be enforced unless the Court believes it is *reasonable* to do so."

Barenblatt was not the only case of its kind to reach the Supreme Court. During the 1940s and 1950s, as not only Congress but also state legislatures investigated matters involving apparent threats to internal security, refusals to testify led to contempt citations—and litigation. Before *Barenblatt*, the Court imposed procedural limitations on the conduct of these legislative probes and, in *Sweezy* v. *New Hampshire* (1957), even held that a state legislative inquiry violated the First Amendment. *Barenblatt* thus seemed to mark a major change of direction for the Court, inasmuch as it sustained HUAC's authority against a First Amendment challenge. But as the years passed the Court did not again declare in reviewing a contempt conviction that "the balance between the individual and the governmental interests . . . must be struck in favor of the latter." To the contrary, "individual interests" prevailed, though typically the Court did not base its decisions on the First Amendment.

Opinion of the Court: **Harlan**, Frankfurter, Clark, Whittaker, Stewart. Dissenting opinions: **Black**, Warren, Douglas; **Brennan**.

Barenblatt v. *United States* was decided on June 8, 1959.

JUSTICE HARLAN DELIVERED THE OPINION OF THE COURT . . .

Once more the Court is required to resolve the conflicting constitutional claims of congressional power and of an individual's right to resist its exercise. The congressional power in question concerns the internal process of Congress in moving within its legislative domain; it involves the utilization of its committees to secure "testimony needed to enable it efficiently to exercise a legislative function belonging to it under the Constitution." *McGrain* v. *Daugherty* [1927]. The power of inquiry has been employed by Congress throughout our history, over the whole range of the national interests concerning which Congress might legislate or decide upon due investigation not to legislate; it has similarly been utilized in determining what to appropriate from the national purse, or whether to appropriate. The scope of the power of inquiry, in short, is as penetrating and far-reaching as the potential power to enact and appropriate under the Constitution.

Broad as it is, the power is not, however, without limitations. Since Congress may only investigate into those areas in which it may potentially legislate or appropriate, it cannot inquire into matters which are within the exclusive province of one of the other branches of the Government. . . . And the Congress, in common with all branches of the Government, must exercise its powers subject to the limitations placed by the Constitution on governmental action, more particularly in the context of this case the relevant limitations of the Bill of Rights. . . .

The precise constitutional issue confronting us is whether the Subcommittee's inquiry into petitioner's past or present membership in the Communist Party transgressed the provisions of the First Amendment, which of course reach and limit congressional investigations. . . .

The Court's past cases establish sure guides to decision. Undeniably, the First Amendment in some circumstances protects an individual from being compelled to disclose his associational relationships. However, the protections of the First Amendment, unlike a proper claim of the privilege against self-incrimination under the Fifth Amendment, do not afford a witness the right to resist inquiry in all circumstances. Where First Amendment rights are asserted to bar governmental interrogation, resolution of the issue always involves a balancing by the courts of the competing private and public interests at stake in the particular circumstances shown. . . .

The first question is whether this investigation was related to a valid legislative purpose, for Congress may not constitutionally require an individual to disclose his political relationships or other private affairs except in relation to such a purpose. . . .

That Congress has wide power to legislate in the field of Communist activity in this Country, and to conduct appropriate investigations in aid thereof, is hardly debatable. The existence of such power has never been questioned by this Court, and it is sufficient to say, without particularization, that Congress has enacted or considered in this field a wide range of legislative measures, not a few of which have stemmed from recommendations of the very Committee whose actions have been drawn in question here. In the last analysis this power rests on the right of self-preservation, "the ultimate value of any society." *Dennis* v. *United States* [1951]. Justification for its exercise in turn rests on the long and widely accepted view that the tenets of the Communist Party include the ultimate overthrow of the Government of the United States by force and violence, a view which has been given formal expression by the Congress.

On these premises, this Court in its constitutional adjudications has consistently refused to view the Communist Party as an ordinary political party, and has upheld federal legislation aimed at the Communist problem which in a different context would certainly have raised constitutional issues of the gravest character. . . . On the same premises this Court has upheld under the Fourteenth Amendment state legislation requiring those occupying or seeking public office to disclaim knowing membership in any organization advocating overthrow of the Government by force and violence, which legislation none can avoid seeing was aimed at membership in the Communist Party. . . . To suggest that because the Communist Party may also sponsor peaceable political reforms the constitutional issues before us should now be judged as if that Party were just an ordinary political party from the standpoint of national security, is to ask this Court to blind itself to world affairs which have determined the whole course of our national policy since the close of World War II. . . .

Nor can we accept the further contention that this investigation should not be deemed to have been in furtherance of a legislative purpose because the true objective of the Committee and of the Congress was purely "exposure." So long as Congress acts in pursuance of its constitutional power, the Judiciary lacks authority to intervene on the basis of the motives which spurred the exercise of that power. . . .

We conclude that the balance between the individual and the governmental interests here at stake must be struck in favor of the latter, and that therefore the provisions of the First Amendment have not been offended.

We hold that petitioner's conviction for contempt of Congress discloses no infirmity, and that the judgment of the Court of Appeals must be
AFFIRMED.

JUSTICE BLACK, DISSENTING . . .

The First Amendment says in no equivocal language that Congress shall pass no law abridging freedom of speech, press, assembly, or petition. The activities of this Committee, authorized by Congress, do precisely that, through exposure, obloquy, and public scorn. . . . The Court does not really deny this fact but relies on a combination of three reasons for permitting the infringement: (A) The notion that despite the First Amendment's command Congress can abridge speech and association if this Court decides that the governmental interest in abridging speech is greater than an individual's interest in exercising that freedom, (B) the Government's right to "preserve itself," (C) the fact that the Committee is only after Communists or suspected Communists in this investigation.

(A) I do not agree that laws directly abridging First Amendment freedoms can be justified by a congressional or judicial balancing process. There are, of course, cases suggesting that a law which primarily regulates conduct but which might also indirectly affect speech can be upheld if the effect on speech is minor in relation to the need for control of the conduct. . . . But we did not . . . even remotely suggest that a law directly aimed at curtailing speech and political persuasion could be saved through a balancing process. Neither these cases, nor any others, can be read as allowing legislative bodies to pass laws abridging freedom of speech, press, and association merely because of hostility to views peacefully expressed in a place where the speaker had a right to be.

To apply the Court's balancing test under such circumstances is to read the First Amendment to say "Congress shall pass no law abridging freedom of speech, press, assembly, and petition, unless Congress and the Supreme Court reach the joint conclusion that on balance the interest of the Government in stifling these freedoms is greater than the interest of the people in having them exercised." This is closely akin to the notion that neither the First Amendment nor any other provision of the Bill of Rights should be enforced unless the Court believes it is *reasonable* to do so. Not only does this violate the genius of our *written* Constitution, but it runs expressly counter to the injunction to Court and Congress made by Madison when he introduced the Bill of Rights. "If they [the first ten amendments] are incorporated into the Constitution, independent tribunals of justice will consider themselves in a peculiar manner the guardians of those rights; they will be an impenetrable bulwark against every assumption of power in the Legislative or Executive; they will be naturally led to resist every encroachment upon rights expressly stipulated for in the Constitution by the declaration of rights." Unless we return to this view of our judicial function, unless we once again accept the notion that the Bill of Rights means what it says and that this Court must enforce that meaning, I am of the opinion that our great charter of liberty will be more honored in the breach than in the observance.

But even assuming what I cannot assume, that some balancing is proper in this case, I feel that the Court after stating the test ignores it completely. At most it balances the right of the Government to preserve itself, against Barenblatt's right to refrain from revealing Communist affiliations. Such a balance, however, mistakes the factors to be weighed. In the first place, it completely leaves out the real interest in Barenblatt's silence, the interest of the people as a whole in being able to join organizations, advocate causes, and make political "mistakes" without later being subjected to governmental penalties for having dared to think for themselves. It is this right, the right to err politically, which keeps us strong as a Nation. For no number of laws against communism can have as much effect as the personal conviction which comes from having heard its arguments and rejected them, or from having once accepted its tenets and later recognized their worthlessness. Instead, the obloquy which results from investigations such as this not only stifles "mistakes" but prevents all but the most courageous from hazarding any views which might at some later time become disfavored. This result, whose importance cannot be overestimated, is doubly crucial when it affects the universities, on which we must largely rely for the experimentation and development of new ideas essential to our country's welfare. It is these interests of society, rather than Barenblatt's own right to silence, which I think the Court should put on the balance against the demands of the Government, if any balancing process is to be tolerated. Instead they are not mentioned, while on the other side the demands of the Government are vastly overstated and called "self preservation." It is admitted that this Committee can only seek information for the purpose of suggesting laws, and that Congress's power to make laws in the realm of speech and association is quite limited, even on the Court's test. Its interest in making such laws in the field of education, primarily a state function, is clearly narrower still. Yet the Court styles this attenuated interest self-preservation and allows it to overcome the need our country has to let us all think, speak, and associate politically as we like and without fear of reprisal. Such a result reduces "balancing" to a mere play on words. . . .

(B) Moreover, I cannot agree with the Court's notion that First Amendment freedoms must be abridged in order to "preserve" our country. That notion rests on the unarticulated premise that this Nation's security hangs upon its power to punish people because of what they think, speak, or write about, or because of those with whom they associate for political purposes. The Government, in its brief, virtually admits this position when it speaks of the "communication of unlawful ideas." I challenge this premise, and deny that ideas can be proscribed under our Constitution. I agree that despotic governments cannot exist without stifling the voice of opposition to their oppressive practices. The First Amendment means to me, however, that the only constitutional way our Government can preserve itself is to leave its people the fullest possible freedom to praise, criticize, or discuss, as they see fit, all governmental policies and to suggest, if they desire, that even its most fundamental postulates are bad and should be changed. . . . On that premise this land was created, and on that premise it has grown to greatness. Our Constitution assumes that the common sense of the people and their attachment to our country will enable them, after free discussion, to withstand ideas that are wrong. To say that our patriotism must be protected against false ideas by means other than these is, I think, to make a baseless charge. Unless we can rely on these qualities—if, in short, we begin to punish speech—we cannot honestly proclaim ourselves to be a free Nation and we have lost what the Founders of this land risked their lives and their sacred honor to defend.

(C) The Court implies, however, that the ordinary rules and requirements of the Constitution do not apply because the Committee is merely after Communists and they do not constitute a political party but only a criminal gang. . . . By accepting this charge and allowing it to support treatment of the Communist Party and its members which would violate the Constitution if applied to other groups, the Court, in effect, declares that Party outlawed. It has been only a few years since there was a practically unanimous feeling throughout the country and in our courts that this could not be done in our free land. Of course it has always been recognized that members of the Party who, either individually or in combination, commit acts in violation of valid laws can be prosecuted. But the Party as a whole and innocent members of it could not be attainted merely because it had some illegal aims and because some of its members were lawbreakers. . . .

. . . Today, Communists or suspected Communists have been denied an opportunity to work as government employees, lawyers, doctors, teachers, pharmacists, veterinarians, subway conductors, industrial workers, and in just about any other job. . . . In today's holding they are singled out and, as a class, are subjected to inquisitions which the Court suggests would be unconstitutional but for the fact of "Communism.". . .

RESPONSES

**FROM THE *EVENING STAR*, WASHINGTON, D.C., JUNE 10, 1959,
"SLIGHT TURN TO THE RIGHT"**

Justice Black's dissenting opinion in the case of Lloyd Barenblatt suggests that the Supreme Court has ridden roughshod over the First Amendment and the liberties which it safeguards. We do not believe, however, that the majority ruling (5 to 4) in the Barenblatt case supports any such extreme interpretation. . . .

The essential fact is that nothing in this decision prevents Barenblatt from belonging to the Communist Party. Nothing in it prevents him from expounding Communist doctrine to all who will listen. He is free to associate with whomever he pleases. All the decision holds is that he must choose between facing punishment for contempt and giving a truthful answer when asked, in a proper setting, whether he is a Communist.

The dissenting opinion objects to this on the ground that to ask the question, or to require an answer, is to subject him to "punishment" in the form of public scorn and contempt. This is true. But what is the alternative? Does the Constitution immunize a Communist, or the holder of some other unpopular belief, from public repudiation? Does a person—any teacher, editor, or preacher—have a *constitutional* right to be a "secret" Communist and exert his influence accordingly? Perhaps he does. But it seems to us that this distorts the intent of the First Amendment. Our forefathers who were to draft the Constitution held beliefs which were despised by the British Crown and by the American Tories. But they were willing to stand publicly on their beliefs and pledge to each other "our lives, our fortunes, and our sacred honor."

When Patrick Henry sounded his call for liberty or death, he did not claim any right to conceal the fact that he advocated rebellion. Thomas Jefferson was not wearing a mask when he drafted the Declaration of Independence. They and their associates might have suffered greatly for expressing their views. But they were willing to stand up and be counted, and we do not think they intended the Constitution, for which they risked everything, to confer any privileged, secret status on those who, in this day and age, would overthrow our form of government if they could.

FROM *THE NEW REPUBLIC*, JUNE 22, 1959, "BARENBLATT CASE"

Dissenting from the Supreme Court opinion of June 8 which upheld the contempt conviction of former Vassar College instructor Lloyd Barenblatt for refusing to tell the House Un-American Activities Committee whether or not he was a Communist, Chief Justice Warren and Justices Black, Douglas, and Brennan adopted the proposition that Congress lacks the power under the Constitution to investigate individual Communist affiliations, when its dominant motive in conducting such an investigation is—as all the world knows—"exposure purely for the sake of exposure." In view of the disreputable behavior of the Congressional committee in question, this opinion of the dissenters evokes understandable sympathy. And yet, inquiry into the motives of Congressional action is extremely treacherous business for the judiciary to engage in. Moreover, the broad power of the legislature to investigate with a view to not passing laws, and in investigating to expose, is one of the foundations of our form of government, and not at all the recent pestiferous invention of the late Joseph McCarthy.

But in the *Barenblatt* case, as in the *Watkins* case of 1957, the Court could have reached the opposite result *without* attempting to restrict the scope of Congressional investigating power. It is too bad the Court did not see fit to do so, and elected rather to emasculate to a substantial extent the beneficial doctrine it announced in *Watkins*. In that case the Court said among other things that, broad and necessary as the powers of inquiry of each House of Congress may be, it must be each House as a whole that decides when to investigate what. It could not be said that the House of Representatives had made a responsible decision to investigate Communism among teachers or labor leaders when a generation ago it empowered the House Un-American Activities Committee to look into so open-ended, almost wholly undefined a thing as "Un-American propaganda." If Congress is to delegate great power to one of its own committees, it should, as much as when it delegates to an administrative agency, speak in more precise, or at least in more comprehensible, terms than that. It isn't that Congress doesn't have the power; it is that *Congress* has not exercised it.

28

EDWARDS V. SOUTH CAROLINA
372 U.S. 229 (1963)

In March 1961 some 200 black high school and college students walked to the grounds of the state capitol in Columbia, South Carolina, to protest racial discrimination and seek repeal of discriminatory laws. Police met the students as they entered the grounds and informed them of their right to be there as long as they were peaceful. For almost an hour the students walked around the area, carrying placards saying "I Am Proud to Be a Negro" and "Down with Segregation." During this time a crowd of 200 to 300 persons gathered, evidently out of curiosity. There was no trouble, real or threatened, and police protection appeared sufficient to prevent any foreseeable disorder. Nonetheless, after the crowd had gathered, police told the students they had to disperse within fifteen minutes or be arrested. Instead of leaving, the students sang "The Star Spangled Banner" and other patriotic and religious songs while stamping their feet and clapping their hands. After fifteen minutes had passed, they were arrested for breach of the peace and then convicted. The South Carolina Supreme Court affirmed the convictions, but the U.S. Supreme Court, by a vote of 8 to 1, reversed on First Amendment grounds.

Edwards was a case about "expressive conduct"—specifically, a civil rights demonstration—and it affirmed the proposition that the grounds of a state capitol, like public streets and parks, are among the public forums where First Amendment rights may be exercised. Such speech is subject to regulations regarding time, place, and manner, but in *Edwards* the Court was not presented with any issue arising from such a regulation. Instead, the Court considered whether South Carolina had used the criminal law to deny speech on account of its content. The problem the Court found was that the demonstrators had been convicted under a vague statute "upon evidence which showed no more than that the opinions which they were peacefully expressing were sufficiently opposed to the views of the majority of the community to attract a crowd and necessitate police protection." The Constitution, the Court held, "does not permit a State to make criminal the peaceful expression of unpopular views." Though Justice Stewart's majority opinion did not apply the clear-and-present-danger test, it was apparent that the majority did not think the petitioners in *Edwards* had threatened any such danger. The majority cited these words from the Court's decision in *Terminiello* v. *Chicago* (1949): "Speech . . . is . . . protected against censorship or punishment, unless shown likely to produce a clear and present danger of a serious substantive evil that rises far above public inconvenience, annoyance, or unrest."

In dissent, Justice Clark applied the clear-and-present-danger test and found that indeed "a dangerous disturbance was imminent."

Opinion of the Court: **Stewart**, Black, Douglas, Warren, Harlan, Brennan, White, Goldberg. Dissenting opinion: **Clark**.

Edwards v. *South Carolina* was decided on February 25, 1963.

OPINION

JUSTICE STEWART DELIVERED THE OPINION OF THE COURT . . .

The petitioners contend that there was a complete absence of any evidence of the commission of [breach of the peace], and that they were thus denied one of the most basic elements of due process of law. . . . Whatever the merits of this contention, we need not pass upon it in the present case. The state courts have held that the petitioners' conduct constituted breach of the peace under state law, and we may accept their decision as binding upon us to that extent. But it nevertheless remains our duty in a case such as this to make an independent examination of the whole record. . . . And it is clear to us that in arresting, convicting, and punishing the petitioners under the circumstances disclosed by this record, South Carolina infringed the petitioners' constitutionally protected rights of free speech, free assembly, and freedom to petition for redress of their grievances.

It has long been established that these First Amendment freedoms are protected by the Fourteenth Amendment from invasion by the States. *Gitlow* v. *New York* [1925]; *Whitney* v. *California* [1927]; *Stromberg* v. *California* [1931]; *DeJonge* v. *Oregon* [1937]; *Cantwell* v. *Connecticut* [1940]. The circumstances in this case reflect an exercise of these basic constitutional rights in their most pristine and classic form. The petitioners felt aggrieved by laws of South Carolina which allegedly "prohibited Negro privileges in this State." They peaceably assembled at the site of the State Government and there peaceably expressed their grievances "to the citizens of South Carolina, along with the Legislative Bodies of South Carolina." Not until they were told by police officials that they must disperse on pain of arrest did they do more. Even then, they but sang patriotic and religious songs after one of their leaders had delivered a "religious harangue." There was no violence or threat of violence on their part, or on the part of any member of the crowd watching them. Police protection was "ample."

This, therefore, was a far cry from the situation in *Feiner* v. *New York* [1951], where two policemen were faced with a crowd which was "pushing, shoving and milling around," . . . where at least one member of the crowd "threatened violence if the police did not act," . . . where "the crowd was pressing closer around petitioner and the officer," . . . and where "the speaker passes the bounds of argument or persuasion and undertakes incitement to riot." And the record is barren of any evidence of "fighting words." See *Chaplinsky* v. *New Hampshire* [1942].

We do not review in this case criminal convictions resulting from the evenhanded application of a precise and narrowly drawn regulatory statute evincing a legislative judgment that certain specific conduct be limited or proscribed. If, for example, the petitioners had been convicted upon evidence that they had violated a law regulating traffic, or had disobeyed a law reasonably limiting the periods during which the State House grounds were open to the public, this would be a different case. These petitioners were convicted of an offense so generalized as to be, in the words of the South Carolina Supreme Court, "not susceptible of exact definition." And they were convicted upon evidence which showed no more than that the opinions which they were peaceably expressing were sufficiently opposed to the views of the majority of the community to attract a crowd and necessitate police protection.

The Fourteenth Amendment does not permit a State to make criminal the peaceful expression of unpopular views. "[A] function of free speech under our system of government is to invite dispute. It may indeed best serve its high purpose when it induces a condition of unrest, creates dissatisfaction with conditions as they are, or even stirs people to anger. Speech is often provocative and challenging. It may strike at prejudices and preconceptions and have profound unsettling effects as it presses for acceptance of an idea. That is why freedom of speech . . . is . . . protected against censorship or punishment, unless shown likely to produce a clear and present danger of a serious substantive evil that rises far above public inconvenience, annoyance, or unrest. . . . There is no room under our Constitution for a more restrictive view. For the alternative would lead to standardization of ideas either by legislatures, courts, or dominant political or community groups." *Terminiello* v. *Chicago* [1949]. As in the *Terminiello* case, the courts of South Carolina have defined a criminal offense so as to permit conviction of the petitioners if their speech "stirred people to anger, invited public dispute, or brought about a condition of unrest. A conviction resting on any of those grounds may not stand."

As Chief Justice Hughes wrote in *Stromberg*, "The maintenance of the opportunity for free political discussion to the end that government may be responsive to the will of the people and that changes may be obtained by lawful means, an opportunity essential to the security of the Republic, is a fundamental principle of our constitutional system. A statute which upon its face, and as authoritatively construed, is so vague and indefinite as to permit the punishment of the fair use of this opportunity is repugnant to the guaranty of liberty contained in the Fourteenth Amendment. . . ."

For these reasons we conclude that these criminal convictions cannot stand.

REVERSED.

NEW YORK TIMES CO. V. SULLIVAN
376 U.S. 254 (1964)

On March 29, 1960, civil rights leaders published a full-page ad in the *New York Times* alleging an "unprecedented wave of terror" against those pressing for desegregation—black students, Dr. Martin Luther King, Jr., and their white allies. The ad, which concluded with an appeal for funds, illustrated this "wave of terror" by describing certain events in Montgomery, Alabama. A Montgomery city commissioner named L. B. Sullivan claimed that the ad defamed him even though it did not mention him by name. The ad contained some errors, most of which were minor factual ones, and the trial judge found the errors to be "libelous per se." The judge instructed the jury that the defendants—which included both the *Times* and four black Alabama clergymen listed in the ad as its endorsers—could be held liable if the jury found that the ad had been published and that what it said concerned Sullivan. The jury returned a verdict for Sullivan in the amount of $500,000 against all the defendants. The Alabama Supreme Court affirmed the judgment, but the U.S. Supreme Court voted unanimously to reverse.

Before *Sullivan* the law of defamation had been a matter decided by the states and, according to the Supreme Court, did not ordinarily raise any constitutional issues. With few exceptions, the law in the states defined libel in broad terms and favored plaintiffs. As a general matter, defendants could "prove their innocence" by demonstrating the truth of the allegedly false utterance. In some states defendants were allowed to invoke the "privilege" of "fair comment" in behalf of libelous opinions—though usually not in behalf of libelous facts; defendants were denied such privileges, however, if they were guilty of malice toward those claiming injury.

Sullivan fundamentally changed the law of libel. The Court, with Justice Brennan writing, said that the defense of truth traditionally available to defendants was inadequate to protect First Amendment values, and made it clear that the defendant's privilege in cases of libel of public officials had to be much broader than it was in most states. The holding in the case was that public officials may recover damages in a libel action concerning their official conduct only if they can prove by clear and convincing evidence "actual malice," i.e., "that the statement was made with . . . knowledge that it was false or with reckless disregard of whether it was false or not."

Later libel cases have shown that *Sullivan* was by no means the final word on these matters. But the case remains enormously significant, and not simply because it nationalized and revolutionized the law of libel. For in *Sullivan* the Court also set forth, perhaps more clearly than it has in any other case, the libertarian understanding that has informed its approach to many First Amendment questions. "We consider this case," the Court said, "against the background of a profound national commitment to the principle that debate on public issues should be uninhibited, robust, and wide-open, and that it may well include vehement, caustic, and sometimes unpleasantly sharp attacks on government and public officials." Erroneous statements are "inevitable in free debate," the Court continued, and such statements must be protected if freedom of expression—obviously now a very "preferred" freedom—is to survive.

In earlier years the Court had taken a different view of libel and indeed a different approach to the First Amendment generally. In *Chaplinsky* v. *New Hampshire* (1942), the Court had said that libelous utterances are no essential part of any exposition of ideas and are not protected by the First Amendment. It reiterated this position in *Beauharnais* v. *Illinois* (1952). Had the Court followed this doctrine and held for Commissioner Sullivan, the decision would have encouraged other public officials opposed to desegregation and equal rights to bring libel suits in hopes of thwarting the civil-rights movement. *New York Times Co.* v. *Sullivan* had the effect of denying to these officials a powerful means of counterattack.

Opinion of the Court: **Brennan**, Warren, Clark, Harlan, Stewart, White. Concurring opinions: **Black**, Douglas; **Goldberg**, Douglas.

New York Times Co. v. *Sullivan* was decided on March 9, 1964.

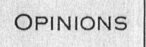

OPINIONS

JUSTICE BRENNAN DELIVERED THE OPINION OF THE COURT . . .

We are required in this case to determine for the first time the extent to which the constitutional protections for speech and press limit a State's power to award damages in a libel action brought by a public official against critics of his official conduct. . . .

Under Alabama law as applied in this case, a publication is "libelous per se" if the words "tend to injure a person . . . in his reputation" or to "bring [him] into public contempt"; the trial court stated that the standard was met if the words are such as to "injure him in his public office, or impute misconduct to him in his office, or want of official integrity, or want of fidelity to a public trust. . . ." The jury must find that the words were published "of and concerning" the plaintiff, but where the plaintiff is a public official his place in the governmental hierarchy is sufficient evidence to support a finding that his reputation has been affected by statements that reflect upon the agency of which he is in charge. Once "libel per se" has been established, the defendant has no defense as to stated facts unless he can persuade the jury that they were true in all their particulars. . . . Unless he can discharge the burden of proving truth, general damages are presumed, and may be awarded without proof of pecuniary injury. A showing of actual malice is apparently a prerequisite to recovery of punitive damages, and the defendant may in any event forestall a punitive award by a retraction meeting the statutory requirements. Good motives and belief in truth do not negate an inference of malice, but are relevant only in mitigation of punitive damages if the jury chooses to accord them weight. . . .

The question before us is whether this rule of liability, as applied to an action brought by a public official against critics of his official conduct, abridges the freedom of speech and of the press that is guaranteed by the First and Fourteenth Amendments.

Respondent relies heavily, as did the Alabama courts, on statements of this Court to the effect that the Constitution does not protect libelous publications. Those statements do not foreclose our inquiry here. None of the cases sustained the use of libel laws to impose sanctions upon expression critical of the official conduct of public officials. . . . In *Beauharnais* v. *Illinois* [1950], the Court sustained an Illinois criminal libel statute as applied to a publication held to be both defamatory of a racial group and "liable to cause violence and disorder." But the Court was careful to note that it "retains and exercises authority to nullify action which encroaches on freedom of utterance under the guise of punishing libel"; for "public men, are, as it were, public property," and "discussion cannot be denied and the right, as well as the duty, of criticism must not be stifled." . . . [W]e are compelled by neither precedent nor policy to give any more weight to the epithet "libel" than we have to other "mere labels" of state law. *NAACP* v. *Button* [1963]. Like insurrection, contempt, advocacy of unlawful acts, breach of the peace, obscenity, solicitation of legal business, and the various other formulae for the repression of expression that have been challenged in this court, libel can claim no talismanic immunity from constitutional limitations. It must be measured by standards that satisfy the First Amendment.

The general proposition that freedom of expression upon public questions is secured by the First Amendment has long been settled by our decisions. The constitutional safeguard, we have said, "was fashioned to assure unfettered interchange of ideas for the bringing about of political and social changes desired by the people." *Roth* v. *United States* [1957]. "The maintenance of the opportunity for free political discussion to the end that government may be responsive to the will of the people and that changes may be obtained by lawful means, an opportunity essential to the security of the Republic, is a fundamental principle of our constitutional system." *Stromberg* v. *California* [1931]. . . .

Thus we consider this case against the background of a profound national commitment to the principle that debate on public issues should be uninhibited, robust, and wide-open, and that it may well include vehement, caustic, and sometimes unpleasantly sharp attacks on government and public officials. . . . The present advertisement, as an expression of grievance and protest on one of the major public issues of our time, would seem clearly to qualify for the constitutional protection. The question is whether it forfeits that protection by the falsity of some of its factual statements and by its alleged defamation of respondent.

Authoritative interpretations of the First Amendment guarantees have consistently refused to recognize an exception for any test of truth—whether administered by judges, juries, or administrative officials—and especially one that puts the burden of proving truth on the speaker. . . .

. . . [E]rroneous statement is inevitable in free debate, and . . . must be protected if the freedoms of expression are to have the "breathing space" that they "need . . . to survive." *Button.* . . .

Injury to official reputation affords no more warrant for repressing speech that would otherwise be free than does factual error. . . . Criticism of . . . official conduct does not lose its constitutional protection merely because it is effective criticism and hence diminishes . . . official reputations.

If neither factual error nor defamatory content suffices to remove the constitutional shield from criticism of official conduct, the combination of the two elements is no less inadequate. This is the lesson to be drawn from the great controversy over the Sedition Act of 1798, . . . which first crystallized a national awareness of the central meaning of the First Amendment. . . . That statute made it a crime, punishable by a $5,000 fine and five years in prison, "if any person shall write, print, utter, or publish . . . any false, scandalous, and malicious writing or writings against the government of the United States, or either house of the Congress. . ., or the President . . ., with intent to defame . . . or to bring them, or either of them, into contempt or disrepute; or to excite against them, or either or any of them, the hatred of the good people of the United States." The Act allowed the defendant the defense of truth, and provided that the jury were to be judges both of the law and the facts. Despite these qualifications, the Act was vigorously condemned as unconstitutional in an attack joined in by Jefferson and Madison.

Although the Sedition Act was never tested in this Court, the attack upon its validity has carried the day in the court of history. Fines levied in its prosecution were repaid by Act of Congress on the ground that it was unconstitutional. . . . The invalidity of the Act has also been assumed by Justices of this Court. See Holmes, J., dissenting and joined by Brandeis, J., in *Abrams* v. *United States* [1919]; Jackson, J., dissenting in *Beauharnais* v. *Illinois* [1952]. . . . These views reflect a broad consensus that the Act, because of the restraint it imposed upon criticism of government and public officials, was inconsistent with the First Amendment.

There is no force in respondent's argument that the constitutional limitations implicit in the history of the Sedition Act apply only to Congress and not to the States. It is true that the First Amendment was originally addressed only to action by the Federal Government, and that Jefferson, for one, while denying the power of Congress "to controul the freedom of the press," recognized such a power in the States. . . . But this distinction was eliminated with the adoption of the Fourteenth Amendment and the application to the States of the First Amendment's restrictions. See, e.g., *Gitlow* v. *New York* [1925]. . . .

What a State may not constitutionally bring about by means of a criminal statute is likewise beyond the reach of its civil law of libel. The fear of damage awards under a rule such as that invoked by the Alabama courts here may be markedly more inhibiting than the fear of prosecution under a criminal statute. . . . Alabama, for example, has a criminal libel law which subjects to prosecution "any person who speaks, writes, or prints of and concerning another any accusation falsely and maliciously importing the commission by such person of a felony, or any other indictable offense involving moral turpitude," and which allows as punishment upon conviction a fine not exceeding $500 and a prison sentence of six months. . . . Presumably a person charged with violation of this statute enjoys ordinary criminal-law safeguards such as the requirements of an indictment and of proof beyond a reasonable doubt. These safeguards are not available to the defendant in a civil action. The judgment awarded in this case—without the need for any proof of actual pecuniary loss— was one thousand times greater than the maximum fine provided by the Alabama criminal statute, and one hundred times greater than that provided by the Sedition Act. And since there is no double-jeopardy limitation applicable to civil lawsuits, this is not the only judgment that may be awarded against petitioners for the same publication. Whether or not a newspaper can survive a succession of such judgments, the pall of fear and timidity imposed upon those who would give voice to public criticism is an atmosphere in which the First Amendment freedoms cannot survive. . . .

The state rule of law is not saved by its allowance of the defense of truth. . . . A rule compelling the critic of official conduct to guarantee the truth of all his factual assertions—and to do so on pain of libel judgments virtually unlimited in amount—leads to . . . "self-censorship."

Allowance of the defense of truth, with the burden of proving it on the defendant, does not mean that only false speech will be deterred. . . . Under such a rule, would-be critics of official conduct may be deterred from voicing their criticism, even though it is believed to be true and even though it is in fact true, because of doubt whether it can be proved in court or fear of the expense of having to do so. . . . The rule thus dampens the vigor and limits the variety of public debate. It is inconsistent with the First and Fourteenth Amendments.

The constitutional guarantees require, we think, a federal rule that prohibits a public official from recovering damages for a defamatory falsehood relating to his official conduct unless he proves that the statement was made with "actual malice"—that is, with knowledge that it was false or with reckless disregard of whether it was false or not. . . .

We hold today that the Constitution delimits a State's power to award damages for libel in actions brought by public officials against critics of their official conduct. Since this is such an action, the rule requiring proof of actual malice is applicable. While Alabama law apparently requires proof of actual malice for an award of punitive damages, where general damages are concerned malice is "presumed." Such a presumption is inconsistent with the federal rule. . . . Since the trial judge did not instruct the jury to differentiate between general and punitive damages, it may be that the verdict was wholly an award of one or the other. But it is impossible to know, in view of the general verdict returned. Because of this uncertainty, the judgment must be reversed and the case remanded. . . .

Since respondent may seek a new trial, we deem that considerations of effective judicial administration require us to review the evidence in the present record to determine whether it could constitutionally support a judgment for respondent. . . . Applying these standards, we consider that the proof presented to show actual malice lacks the convincing clarity which the constitutional standard demands, and hence that it would not constitutionally sustain the judgment for respondent under the proper rule of law. . . .

REVERSED and remanded.

JUSTICE BLACK, CONCURRING . . .

I concur in reversing this half-million-dollar judgment against the New York Times Company and the four individual defendants. . . . Unlike the Court, . . . I vote to reverse exclusively on the ground that the *Times* and the individual defendants had an absolute, unconditional constitutional right to publish in the *Times* advertisement their criticisms of the Montgomery agencies and officials. . . .

The half-million-dollar verdict does give dramatic proof, however, that state libel laws threaten the very existence of an American press virile enough to publish unpopular views on public affairs and bold enough to criticize the conduct of public officials. The factual background of this case emphasizes the imminence and enormity of that threat. One of the acute and highly emotional issues in this country arises out of efforts of many people, even including some public officials, to continue state-commanded segregation of races in the public schools and other public places, despite our several holdings that such a state practice is forbidden by the Fourteenth Amendment. Montgomery is one of the localities in which widespread hostility to desegregation has been manifested. This hostility has sometimes extended itself to persons who favor desegregation, particularly to so-called "outside agitators," a term which can be made to fit papers like the *Times*, which is published in New York. The scarcity of testimony to show that Commissioner Sullivan suffered any actual damages at all suggests that these feelings of hostility had at least as much to do with rendition of this half-million-dollar verdict as did an appraisal of damages. Viewed realistically, this record lends support to an inference that instead of being damaged Commissioner Sullivan's political, social, and financial prestige has likely been enhanced by the *Times'* publication. . . .

In my opinion the Federal Constitution has dealt with this deadly danger to the press in the only way possible without leaving the free press open to destruction—by granting the press an absolute immunity for criticism of the way public officials do their public duty. . . . Stopgap measures like those the Court adopts are in my judgment not enough. This record certainly does not indicate that any different verdict would have been rendered here whatever the Court had charged the jury about "malice," "truth," "good motives," "justifiable ends," or any other legal formulas which in theory would protect the press. Nor does the record indicate that any of these legalistic words would have caused the courts below to set aside or to reduce the half-million-dollar verdict in any amount. . . .

We would, I think, more faithfully interpret the First Amendment by holding that at the very least it leaves the people and the press free to criticize officials and discuss public affairs with impunity. This Nation of ours elects many of its important officials; so do the States, the municipalities, the counties, and even many precincts. These officials are responsible to the people for the way they perform their duties. While our Court has held that some kinds of speech and writings, such as "obscenity," *Roth* v. *United States* [1957], and "fighting words," *Chaplinsky* v. *New Hampshire* [1942], are not expression within the protection of the First Amendment, freedom to discuss public affairs and public officials is unquestionably, as the Court today holds, the kind of speech the First Amendment was primarily designed to keep within the area of free discussion. To punish the exercise of this right to discuss public affairs or to penalize it through libel judgments is to abridge or shut off discussion of the very kind most needed. This Nation, I suspect, can live in peace without libel suits based on public discussions of public affairs and public officials. But I doubt that a country can live in freedom where its people can be made to suffer physically or financially for criticizing their government, its actions, or its officials. . . . An unconditional right to say what one pleases about public affairs is what I consider to be the minimum guarantee of the First Amendment.

I regret that the Court has stopped short of this holding indispensable to preserve our free press from destruction.

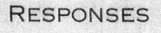

RESPONSES

FROM THE *NEW YORK TIMES*, MARCH 10, 1964, "FREE PRESS AND FREE PEOPLE"

The unanimous decision of the Supreme Court yesterday in a case involving this newspaper is a victory of first importance in the long—and never-ending—struggle for the rights of a free press. But it is more than that. It is also a vindication of the right of a free people to have unimpeded access to the news and to fair comment on the news. . . .

What the decision means is that in presenting the news or additional comment on the news, as well as in editorial-type advertisements, the freedom to criticize that is absolutely vital to an unfettered press is protected, subject only to the reasonable limitation that the criticism be made in good faith and not maliciously. . . .

It is an increasingly important function of the press—and must be, if the press is to live up to its proper responsibilities—to encourage the free give-and-take of ideas and, above all, to be free to express criticism of public officials and public policies. This is all part of the lifeblood of a democracy. In its landmark decision yesterday, the Supreme Court of the United States has struck a solid blow not only for the freedom of the press but for the prerogatives of a free people.

FROM *THE NEW REPUBLIC*, MARCH 9, 1964, "IMMUNITY FROM CRITICISM"

Twice in the nineteenth century the South decided that it had found exactly the race policies it wanted; and both times, as the historian C. Vann Woodward reminds us, the South then closed its mind. "The debate was over. Dissent was ground down or smashed. Conformity was demanded of all." This is what happened over the slavery issue in the early 1830s. The same thing happened again over segregation around the turn of the century. A somewhat similar attitude began to manifest itself in the mid-1950s, in reaction to the Supreme Court's desegregation decision. But there is a highly significant difference this time, which the Court has emphasized in the *New York Times* libel case.

The big difference is that the South cannot now in any real measure seal itself off from national public opinion, from the national press, magazines, radio and TV. Not unnaturally, there was an attempt in Alabama to demand immunity from these national media also, and it was this attempt that the Supreme Court has struck down. . . . Freedoms of expression, the court said, quoting an earlier case, "must have the breathing space that they need to survive." Although the principle now laid down is fresh, it long ago, as Justice Brennan said, "carried the day in the courts of history."

It should be noted that the right to make vigorous and relatively free-swinging attacks on public officials, which the courts have now safeguarded, is not altogether without limit. To be immune from suits, an attack must relate to the official's conduct of public business, not to his private affairs. This was conceded even by Justice Goldberg, who, like Justices Black and Douglas, would have granted an immunity broader than that defined by the majority of the court. The making of knowingly false statements is not protected.

FROM THE *EVENING STAR*, WASHINGTON, D.C., MARCH 10, 1964, "NEW LIBEL TEST"

In a unanimous opinion of far-reaching import, the Supreme Court has radically altered the law of libel.

For the first time the court has held that the First Amendment's guarantees of free press and free speech confer an immunity from the normal libel or slander suit involving statements made about public officials. In the court's words, the Constitution "prohibits a public official from recovering damages for a defamatory falsehood relating to his official conduct unless he proves the statement was made with actual malice—that is, with the knowledge that it was false or with reckless disregard of whether it was false or not."

As a practical matter, this means that a public official, except in the most extreme cases, has no legal protection against statements concerning his official conduct which are false and damaging to his reputation. . . .

This decision came in the case of a libel suit against the *New York Times* and four Negro ministers for an advertisement that allegedly libeled an Alabama official. The jury returned a damage award of $500,000 and this was upheld by the Alabama appellate courts. Clearly, this was a punitive, intimidatory award which bore no relation to any damage, real or fancied, suffered by the plaintiff, who was not even named in the ad.

This, however, was an extreme case which had its roots in racial prejudice. But the sweep of the principle laid down by the court is not limited to such cases. The immunity which is conferred applies to all manner of statements and publications, and consequently, or so it seems to us, imposes the very highest standard of responsibility on the press and on individuals.

It may now be possible, for example, to falsely accuse a public official of stealing public funds, and not be liable to him for damages. This is a freedom which the court holds to be necessary to full and uninhibited discussion and debate of public affairs. But it is also a freedom, especially in the case of the press, which must be exercised with much care and restraint.

LAMONT V. POSTMASTER GENERAL
381 U.S. 301 (1965)

A 1962 federal statute directed the Postmaster General to detain and deliver only upon the addressee's request unsealed foreign mail that the government judged to be "communist political propaganda." The Post Office implemented the law by notifying an addressee of such mail and awaiting a response. Corliss Lamont in New York and Leif Heilberg in San Francisco received such notice but chose not to respond. Instead they sued the Post Master, contending that the statute violated their First Amendment rights. In Lamont's case, the district court held that the issue was not ripe for decision. In Heilberg's, the district court reached the merits of the issue and agreed with the plaintiff. Taking the appeals in the two cases, the Supreme Court unanimously held that the law was unconstitutional.

The Court did not invoke the clear-and-present-danger test in deciding the cases, nor did it engage—explicitly, at least—in First Amendment balancing. The Court found objectionable the burden the government placed on an addressee to request mail that was being held by the Post Office. "The regime of this Act," wrote Justice Douglas for the Court, quoting *New York Times* v. *Sullivan* (1964), "is at war with the 'uninhibited, robust, and wide-open' debate . . . contemplated by the First Amendment."

In *Lamont* the Court for the first time voided a federal statute on free-speech grounds. *Lamont* came thirty-four years after *Stromberg* v. *California* (1931), the first case in which the Court found a state law in violation of the free speech clause.

Opinion of the Court: **Douglas**, Black, Clark, Stewart, Warren. Concurring opinion: **Brennan**, Goldberg. Concurring in the judgment of the Court on the grounds set forth in the concurring opinion: **Harlan**. Not participating: White.

Lamont v. *Postmaster General* was decided on May 24, 1965.

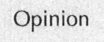

Opinion

JUSTICE DOUGLAS DELIVERED THE OPINION OF THE COURT . . .

We conclude that the Act as construed and applied is unconstitutional because it requires an official act (viz., returning the reply card) as a limitation on the unfettered exercise of the addressee's First Amendment rights. . . .

We struck down in *Murdock* v. *Pennsylvania* [1940] a flat license tax on the exercise of First Amendment rights. A registration requirement imposed on a labor union organizer before making a speech met the same fate in *Thomas* v. *Collins* [1945]. A municipal licensing system for those distributing literature was held invalid in *Lovell* v. *Griffin* [1938]. . . .

Here the Congress—expressly restrained by the First Amendment from "abridging" freedom of speech and of press—is the actor. The Act sets administrative officials astride the flow of mail to inspect it, appraise it, write the addressee about it, and await a response before dispatching the mail. Just as the licensing or taxing authorities in the *Lovell*, *Thomas*, and *Murdock* cases sought to control the flow of ideas to the public, so here federal agencies regulate the flow of mail. We do not have here . . . any question concerning the extent to which Congress may classify the mail and fix the charges for its carriage. Nor do we reach the question whether the standard here applied could pass constitutional muster. Nor do we deal with the right of Customs to inspect material from abroad for contraband. We rest on the narrow ground that the addressee in order to receive his mail must request in writing that it be delivered. This amounts in our judgment to an unconstitutional abridgment of the addressee's First Amendment rights. The addressee carries an affirmative obligation which we do not think the Government may impose on him. This requirement is almost certain to have a deterrent effect, especially as respects those who have sensitive positions. Their livelihood may be dependent on a security clearance. Public officials, like schoolteachers who have no tenure, might think they would invite disaster if they read what the Federal Government says contains the seeds of treason. Apart from them, any addressee is likely to feel some inhibition in sending for literature which federal officials have condemned as "communist political propaganda." The regime of this Act is at war with the "uninhibited, robust, and wide-open" debate and discussion that are contemplated by the First Amendment. *New York Times Co.* v. *Sullivan*.

We reverse the judgment in [*Lamont*] and affirm that in [*Heilberg*].

JUSTICE BRENNAN, CONCURRING . . .

It is true that the First Amendment contains no specific guarantee of access to publications. However, the protection of the Bill of Rights goes beyond the specific guarantees to protect from congressional abridgment those equally fundamental personal rights necessary to make the express guarantees fully meaningful. . . . I think the right to receive publications is such a fundamental right. The dissemination of ideas can accomplish nothing if otherwise willing addressees are not free to receive and consider them. It would be a barren marketplace of ideas that had only sellers and no buyers.

Even if we were to accept the characterization of this statute as a regulation not intended to control the content of speech, but only incidentally limiting its unfettered exercise, . . . we "have consistently held that only a compelling [governmental] interest in the regulation of a subject within [governmental] constitutional power to regulate can justify limiting First Amendment freedoms." *NAACP* v. *Button* [1963]. The Government's brief expressly disavows any support for this statute "in large public interests such as would be needed to justify a true restriction upon freedom of expression or inquiry." Rather the Government argues that, since an addressee taking the trouble to return the card can receive the publication named in it, only inconvenience and not an abridgment is involved. But inhibition as well as prohibition against the exercise of precious First Amendment rights is a power denied to government. . . .

UNITED STATES V. ROBEL
389 U.S. 258 (1967)

In 1950 Congress passed the Internal Security Act of 1950, also known as the McCarran Act, in order to expose the Communist Party in the United States. Title I created the Subversive Activities Control Board and authorized it to compel Communist-dominated organizations to register with the Attorney General. Registered organizations were required to disclose the names of their officers and source of funds, and members of such organizations could be denied passports and the right to work in defense plants. In *Communist Party* v. *Subversive Activities Control Board* (1961), the Supreme Court sustained the board's registration authority, but in *Aptheker* v. *Secretary of State* (1964) the Court ruled that the denial of passports to party members violated the Fifth Amendment. Three years later in *Robel* the Court addressed the constitutionality of the ban on working in defense facilities.

The case came from the state of Washington. Edward Robel, a member of the Communist Party, worked as a machinist at a shipyard in Seattle that the Secretary of Defense had officially designated a defense facility. Robel was indicted for continuing to work at the shipyard while a party member, but the district court dismissed the case. The government then appealed directly to the Supreme Court, which held 6 to 2 that the law abridged the First Amendment right of association.

Robel was only the second case—after *Lamont* v. *Postmaster* (1965)—in which the Court held a law of Congress unconstitutional on First Amendment grounds. As in some other cases in the 1960s, the Court did not use (or appear to use) the balancing test with which it had frequently analyzed First Amendment claims since the early 1950s. Indeed, for the first time it explicitly rejected the balancing approach, doing so in footnote 20 of the opinion written by Chief Justice Warren. The Court held that in pursuit of a "concededly legitimate legislative goal" Congress must use means having a "less drastic" impact on activities protected by the First Amendment.

As a result of *Aptheker, Robel,* and other judicial decisions, the McCarran Act was effectively nullified. The Subversive Activities Control Board lost support in Congress and was terminated in 1973.

Opinion of the Court: **Warren**, Black, Douglas, Stewart, Fortas. Concurring opinion: **Brennan**. Dissenting opinion: **White**, Harlan. Not participating: Marshall.

United States v. *Robel* was decided on December 11, 1967.

> OPINIONS

CHIEF JUSTICE WARREN DELIVERED THE OPINION OF THE COURT . . .

This appeal draws into question the constitutionality of 5 (a) (1) (D) of the Subversive Activities Control Act of 1950. . . .

. . . We . . . cannot agree with the Government's characterization of the essential issue in this case. It is true that the specific disability imposed by 5 (a) (1) (D) is to limit the employment opportunities of those who fall within its coverage, and such a limitation is not without serious constitutional implications. . . . But the operative fact upon which the job disability depends is the exercise of an individual's right of association, which is protected by the provisions of the First Amendment. . . .

The Government seeks to defend the statute on the ground that it was passed pursuant to Congress' war power. The Government argues that this Court has given broad deference to the exercise of that constitutional power by the national legislature. That argument finds support in a number of decisions of this Court. However, the phrase "war power" cannot be invoked as a talismanic incantation to support any exercise of congressional power which can be brought within its ambit. . . . More specifically in this case, the Government asserts that 5 (a) (1) (D) is an expression "of the growing concern shown by the executive and legislative branches of government over the risks of internal subversion in plants on which the national defense depend[s]." Yet, this concept of "national defense" cannot be deemed an end in itself, justifying any exercise of legislative power designed to promote such a goal. Implicit in the term "national defense" is the notion of defending those values and ideals which set this Nation apart. For almost two centuries, our country has taken singular pride in the democratic ideals enshrined in its Constitution, and the most cherished of those ideals have found expression in the First Amendment. It would indeed be ironic if, in the name of national defense, we would sanction the subversion of one of those liberties—the freedom of association—which makes the defense of the Nation worthwhile.

When Congress' exercise of one of its enumerated powers clashes with those individual liberties protected by the Bill of Rights, it is our "delicate and difficult task" to determine whether the resulting restriction on freedom can be tolerated. . . . The Government emphasizes that the purpose of 5 (a) (1) (D) is to reduce the threat of sabotage and espionage in the Nation's defense plants. The Government's interest in such a prophylactic measure is not insubstantial. But it cannot be doubted that the means chosen to implement that governmental purpose in this instance cut deeply into the right of association. Section 5 (a) (1) (D) put appellee to the choice of surrendering his organizational affiliation, regardless of whether his membership threatened the security of a defense facility, or giving up his job. When appellee refused to make that choice, he became subject to a possible criminal penalty of five years' imprisonment and a $10,000 fine. The statute quite literally establishes guilt by association alone, without any need to establish that an individual's association poses the threat feared by the Government in proscribing it. The inhibiting effect on the exercise of First Amendment rights is clear.

It has become axiomatic that "[p]recision of regulation must be the touchstone in an area so closely touching our most precious freedoms." *NAACP* v. *Button* [1963]. . . . Such precision is notably lacking in 5 (a) (1) (D). That statute casts its net across a broad range of associational activities, indiscriminately trapping membership which can be constitutionally punished and membership which cannot be so proscribed. It is made irrelevant to the statute's operation that an individual may be a passive or inactive member of a designated organization, that he may be unaware of the organization's unlawful aims, or that he may disagree with those unlawful aims. It is also made irrelevant that an individual who is subject to the penalties of 5 (a) (1) (D) may occupy a nonsensitive position in a defense facility. Thus, 5 (a) (1) (D) contains the fatal defect of overbreadth because it seeks to bar employment both for association which may be proscribed and for association which may not be proscribed consistently with First Amendment rights. . . . This the Constitution will not tolerate.

We are not unmindful of the congressional concern over the danger of sabotage and espionage in national defense industries, and nothing we hold today should be read to deny Congress the power under narrowly drawn legislation to keep from sensitive positions in defense facilities those who would use their positions to disrupt the Nation's production facilities. We have recognized that, while the Constitution protects against invasions of individual rights, it does not withdraw from the Government the power to safeguard its vital interests. . . . Our decision today simply recognizes that, when legitimate legislative concerns are expressed in a statute which imposes a substantial burden on protected First Amendment activities, Congress must achieve its goal by means which have a "less drastic" impact on the continued vitality of First Amendment freedoms. [Footnote 20; see below.] The Constitution and the basic position of First Amendment rights in our democratic fabric demand nothing less.

AFFIRMED.

Footnote 20. It has been suggested that this case should be decided by "balancing" the governmental interests expressed in 5 (a) (1) (D) against the First Amendment rights asserted by the appellee. This we decline to do. We recognize that both interests are substantial, but we deem it inappropriate for this Court to label one as being more important or more substantial than the other. Our inquiry is more circumscribed. Faced with a clear conflict between a federal statute enacted in the interests of national security and an individual's exercise of his First Amendment rights, we have confined our analysis to whether Congress has adopted a constitutional means in achieving its concededly legitimate legislative goal. In making this determination we have found it necessary to measure the validity of the means adopted by Congress against both the goal it has sought to achieve and the specific prohibitions of the First Amendment. But we have in no way "balanced" those respective interests. We have ruled only that the Constitution requires that the conflict between congressional power and individual rights be accommodated by legislation drawn more narrowly to avoid the conflict. There is, of course, nothing novel in that analysis. Such a course of adjudication was enunciated by Chief Justice Marshall when he declared: "Let the end be legitimate, let it be within the scope of the constitution, and all means which are appropriate, which are plainly adapted to that end, which are not prohibited, but consist with the letter and spirit of the constitution, are constitutional." *M'Culloch* v. *Maryland* [1819]. . . . In this case, the means chosen by Congress are contrary to the "letter and spirit" of the First Amendment.

JUSTICE WHITE, DISSENTING . . .

The Court holds that because of the First Amendment a member of the Communist Party who knows that the Party has been held to be a Communist-action organization may not be barred from employment in defense establishments important to the security of the Nation. It therefore refuses to enforce the contrary judgments of the Legislative and Executive Branches of the Government. Respectfully disagreeing with this view, I dissent.

The constitutional right found to override the public interest in national security defined by Congress is the right of association, here the right of appellee Robel to remain a member of the Communist Party after being notified of its adjudication as a Communist-action organization. Nothing in the Constitution requires this result. The right of association is not mentioned in the Constitution. It is a judicial construct appended to the First Amendment rights to speak freely, to assemble, and to petition for redress of grievances. While the right of association has deep roots in history and is supported by the inescapable necessity for group action in a republic as large and complex as ours, it has only recently blossomed as the controlling factor in constitutional litigation; its contours as yet lack delineation. Although official interference with First Amendment rights has drawn close scrutiny, it is now apparent that the right of association is not absolute and is subject to significant regulation by the State. . . .

The relevant cases uniformly reveal the necessity for accommodating the right of association and the public interest. *NAACP* v. *Alabama* [1958], which contained the first substantial discussion of the right in an opinion of this Court, exemplifies the judicial approach. There, after noting the impact of official action on the right to associate, the Court inquired "whether Alabama has demonstrated an interest in obtaining the disclosures it seeks from petitioner which is sufficient to justify the deterrent effect which we have concluded these disclosures may well have on the free exercise by petitioner's members of their constitutionally protected right of association." . . .

Nor does the Court mandate a different course in this case. Apparently "active" members of the Communist Party who have demonstrated their commitment to the illegal aims of the Party may be barred from defense facilities. This exclusion would have the same deterrent effect upon associational rights as the statute before us, but the governmental interest in security would override that effect. Also, the Court would seem to permit barring appellee, although not an "active" member of the Party, from employment in "sensitive" positions in the defense establishment. Here, too, the interest in anticipating and preventing espionage or sabotage would outweigh the deterrent impact of job disqualification. If I read the Court correctly, associating with the Communist Party may at times be deterred by barring members from employment and nonmembership may at times be imposed as a condition of engaging in defense work. In the case before us the Court simply disagrees with the Congress and the Defense Department, ruling that Robel does not present a sufficient danger to the national security to require him to choose between membership in the Communist Party and his employment in a defense facility. Having less confidence than the majority in the prescience of this remote body when dealing with threats to the security of the country, I much prefer the judgment of Congress and the Executive Branch that the interest of appellee in remaining a member of the Communist Party, knowing that it has been adjudicated a Communist-action organization, is less substantial than the public interest in excluding him from employment in critical defense industries.

The national interest asserted by the Congress is real and substantial. After years of study, Congress prefaced the Subversive Activities Control Act of 1950 . . . with its findings that there exists an international Communist movement which by treachery, deceit, espionage, and sabotage seeks to overthrow existing governments; that the movement operates in this country through Communist-action organizations which are under foreign domination and control and which seek to overthrow the Government by any necessary means, including force and violence; that the Communist movement in the United States is made up of thousands of adherents, rigidly disciplined, operating in secrecy, and employing espionage and sabotage tactics in form and manner evasive of existing laws. Congress therefore, among other things, defined the characteristics of Communist-action organizations, provided for their adjudication by the SACB, and decided that the security of the United States required the exclusion of Communist-action organization members from employment in certain defense facilities. . . .

Against this background protective measures were clearly appropriate. . . .

The statute does not prohibit membership in the Communist Party. Nor are appellee and other Communists excluded from all employment in the United States, or even from all defense plants. The touchstones for exclusion are the requirements of national security, and the facilities designated under this standard amount to only about one percent of all the industrial establishments in the United States.

It is this impact on associational rights, although specific and minimal, which the Court finds impermissible. But as the statute's dampening effect on associational rights is to be weighed against the asserted and obvious government interest in keeping members of Communist-action groups from defense facilities, it would seem important to identify what interest Robel has in joining and remaining a member of a group whose primary goals he may not share. We are unenlightened, however, by the opinion of the Court or by the record in this case, as to the purposes which Robel and others like him may have in associating with the Party. The legal aims and programs of the Party are not identified or appraised nor are Robel's activities as a member of the Party. The Court is left with a vague and formless concept of associational rights and its own notions of what constitutes an unreasonable risk to defense facilities. . . .

The Court's motives are worthy. It seeks the widest bounds for the exercise of individual liberty consistent with the security of the country. In so doing it arrogates to itself an independent judgment of the requirements of national security. These are matters about which judges should be wary.

UNITED STATES V. O'BRIEN
391 U.S. 367 (1968)

David Paul O'Brien burned his Selective Service registration certificate on the steps of the South Boston Courthouse and was subsequently charged with violating a 1965 amendment to the Selective Service Act that outlawed destruction of draft cards. In district court, O'Brien said that he burned his card in order to influence others to adopt his anti-war views, and that the 1965 amendment abridged his right to free speech. The district court rejected O'Brien's constitutional argument, and he was convicted and sentenced. Although the U.S. Court of Appeals for the Second Circuit sustained his conviction on other statutory grounds, it found the 1965 amendment unconstitutional. The Supreme Court disagreed; it held the law constitutional and reinstated the judgment and sentence of the district court.

In *O'Brien,* a symbolic speech case, the Court said that "when 'speech' and 'nonspeech' elements are combined in the same course of conduct a sufficiently important governmental interest in regulating the nonspeech element can justify incidental limitations on First Amendment freedoms." The court spelled out a four-part test for assessing the constitutionality of such a regulation: it must be within the constitutional power of the government; it must further a substantial governmental interest; this interest must not be related to the suppression of free speech; and the restriction of free speech must be no greater than is essential to the furthering of the governmental interest.

O'Brien's four-part test has been applied in symbolic-speech cases as well as in cases involving restrictions of time, place, and manner.

Opinion of the Court: **Warren**, Black, Harlan, Brennan, Stewart, White. Concurring opinion: **Harlan**. Dissenting opinion: **Douglas**. Not participating: Marshall.

United States v. *O'Brien* was decided on May 27, 1968.

Opinion

CHIEF JUSTICE WARREN DELIVERED THE OPINION OF THE COURT . . .

By the 1965 Amendment, Congress added to 12 (b) (3) of the 1948 Act the provision here at issue, subjecting to criminal liability not only one who "forges, alters, or in any manner changes" but also one who "knowingly destroys, [or] knowingly mutilates" a certificate. We note at the outset that the 1965 Amendment plainly does not abridge free speech on its face, and we do not understand O'Brien to argue otherwise. Amended 12 (b) (3) on its face deals with conduct having no connection with speech. It prohibits the knowing destruction of certificates issued by the Selective Service System, and there is nothing necessarily expressive about such conduct. The Amendment does not distinguish between public and private destruction, and it does not punish only destruction engaged in for the purpose of expressing views. Compare *Stromberg* v. *California* [1931]. A law prohibiting destruction of Selective Service certificates no more abridges free speech on its face than a motor vehicle law prohibiting the destruction of drivers' licenses, or a tax law prohibiting the destruction of books and records.

O'Brien nonetheless argues that the 1965 Amendment is unconstitutional in its application to him, and is unconstitutional as enacted because what he calls the "purpose" of Congress was "to suppress freedom of speech." We consider these arguments separately.

O'Brien first argues that the 1965 Amendment is unconstitutional as applied to him because his act of burning his registration certificate was protected "symbolic speech" within the First Amendment. His argument is that the freedom of expression which the First Amendment guarantees includes all modes of "communication of ideas by conduct," and that his conduct is within this definition because he did it in "demonstration against the war and against the draft."

We cannot accept the view that an apparently limitless variety of conduct can be labeled "speech" whenever the person engaging in the conduct intends thereby to express an idea. However, even on the assumption that the alleged communicative element in O'Brien's conduct is sufficient to bring into play the First Amendment, it does not necessarily follow that the destruction of a registration certificate is constitutionally protected activity. This Court has held that when "speech" and "nonspeech" elements are combined in the same course of conduct, a sufficiently important governmental interest in regulating the nonspeech element can justify incidental limitations on First Amendment freedoms. To characterize the quality of the governmental interest which must appear, the Court has employed a variety of descriptive terms: compelling; substantial; subordinating; paramount; cogent; strong. Whatever imprecision inheres in these terms, we think it clear that a government regulation is sufficiently justified if it is within the constitutional power of the Government; if it furthers an important or substantial governmental interest; if the governmental interest is unrelated to the suppression of free expression; and if the incidental restriction on alleged First Amendment freedoms is no greater than is essential to the furtherance of that interest. We find that the 1965 Amendment to 12 (b) (3) of the Universal Military Training and Service Act meets all of these requirements, and consequently that O'Brien can be constitutionally convicted for violating it.

The constitutional power of Congress to raise and support armies and to make all laws necessary and proper to that end is broad and sweeping. . . . The power of Congress to classify and conscript manpower for military service is "beyond question." . . . Pursuant to this power, Congress may establish a system of registration for individuals liable for training and service, and may require such individuals within reason to cooperate in the registration system. The issuance of certificates indicating the registration and eligibility classification of individuals is a legitimate and substantial administrative aid in the functioning of this system. And legislation to insure the continuing availability of issued certificates serves a legitimate and substantial purpose in the system's administration.

O'Brien's argument to the contrary is necessarily premised upon his unrealistic characterization of Selective Service certificates. He essentially adopts the position that such certificates are so many pieces of paper designed to notify registrants of their registration or classification, to be retained or tossed in the wastebasket according to the convenience or taste of the registrant. Once the registrant has received notification, according to this view, there is no reason for him to retain the certificates. O'Brien notes that most of the information on a registration certificate serves no notification purpose at all; the registrant hardly needs to be told his address and physical characteristics. We agree that the registration certificate contains much information of which the registrant needs no notification. This circumstance, however, does not lead to the conclusion that the certificate serves no purpose, but that, like the classification certificate, it serves purposes in addition to initial notification. Many of these purposes would be defeated by the certificates' destruction or mutilation. Among these are:

1. The registration certificate serves as proof that the individual described thereon has registered for the draft. The classification certificate shows the eligibility classification of a named but undescribed individual. Voluntarily displaying the two certificates is an easy and painless way for a young man to dispel a question as to whether he might be delinquent in his Selective Service obligations. Correspondingly, the availability of the certificates for such display relieves the Selective Service System of the administrative burden it would otherwise have in verifying the registration and classification of all suspected delinquents. Further, since both certificates are in the nature of "receipts" attesting that the registrant has done what the law requires, it is in the interest of the just and efficient administration of the system that they be continually available, in the event, for example, of a mix-up in the registrant's file. Additionally, in a time of national crisis, reasonable availability to each registrant of the two small cards assures a rapid and uncomplicated means for determining his fitness for immediate induction, no matter how distant in our mobile society he may be from his local board.
2. The information supplied on the certificates facilitates communication between registrants and local boards, simplifying the system and benefiting all concerned. To begin with, each certificate bears the address of the registrant's local board, an item unlikely to be committed to memory. Further, each card bears the registrant's Selective Service number, and a registrant who has his number readily available so that he can communicate it to his local board when he supplies or requests information can make simpler the board's task in locating his file. Finally, a registrant's inquiry, particularly through a local board other than his own, concerning his eligibility status is frequently answerable simply on the basis of his classification certificate; whereas, if the certificate were not reasonably available and the registrant were uncertain of his classification, the task of answering his questions would be considerably complicated.
3. Both certificates carry continual reminders that the registrant must notify his local board of any change of address, and other specified changes in his status. The smooth

functioning of the system requires that local boards be continually aware of the status and whereabouts of registrants, and the destruction of certificates deprives the system of a potentially useful notice device.

4. The regulatory scheme involving Selective Service certificates includes clearly valid prohibitions against the alteration, forgery, or similar deceptive misuse of certificates. The destruction or mutilation of certificates obviously increases the difficulty of detecting and tracing abuses such as these. Further, a mutilated certificate might itself be used for deceptive purposes.

The many functions performed by Selective Service certificates establish beyond doubt that Congress has a legitimate and substantial interest in preventing their wanton and unrestrained destruction and assuring their continuing availability by punishing people who knowingly and wilfully destroy or mutilate them. And we are unpersuaded that the pre-existence of the nonpossession regulations in any way negates this interest. . . .

We think it apparent that the continuing availability to each registrant of his Selective Service certificates substantially furthers the smooth and proper functioning of the system that Congress has established to raise armies. We think it also apparent that the Nation has a vital interest in having a system for raising armies that functions with maximum efficiency and is capable of easily and quickly responding to continually changing circumstances. For these reasons, the Government has a substantial interest in assuring the continuing availability of issued Selective Service certificates.

It is equally clear that the 1965 Amendment specifically protects this substantial governmental interest. We perceive no alternative means that would more precisely and narrowly assure the continuing availability of issued Selective Service certificates than a law which prohibits their wilful mutilation or destruction. . . . The 1965 Amendment prohibits such conduct and does nothing more. In other words, both the governmental interest and the operation of the 1965 Amendment are limited to the noncommunicative aspect of O'Brien's conduct. The governmental interest and the scope of the 1965 Amendment are limited to preventing harm to the smooth and efficient functioning of the Selective Service System. When O'Brien deliberately rendered unavailable his registration certificate, he wilfully frustrated this governmental interest. For this noncommunicative impact of his conduct, and for nothing else, he was convicted.

The case at bar is therefore unlike one where the alleged governmental interest in regulating conduct arises in some measure because the communication allegedly integral to the conduct is itself thought to be harmful. In *Stromberg* [1931], for example, this Court struck down a statutory phrase which punished people who expressed their "opposition to organized government" by displaying "any flag, badge, banner, or device." Since the statute there was aimed at suppressing communication it could not be sustained as a regulation of noncommunicative conduct. . . .

In conclusion, we find that because of the Government's substantial interest in assuring the continuing availability of issued Selective Service certificates, because amended 462 (b) is an appropriately narrow means of protecting this interest and condemns only the independent noncommunicative impact of conduct within its reach, and because the noncommunicative impact of O'Brien's act of burning his registration certificate frustrated the Government's interest, a sufficient governmental interest has been shown to justify O'Brien's conviction.

O'Brien finally argues that the 1965 Amendment is unconstitutional as enacted because what he calls the "purpose" of Congress was "to suppress freedom of speech." We reject this argument because under settled principles the purpose of Congress, as O'Brien uses that term, is not a basis for declaring this legislation unconstitutional.

It is a familiar principle of constitutional law that this Court will not strike down an otherwise constitutional statute on the basis of an alleged illicit legislative motive. . . .

Inquiries into congressional motives or purposes are a hazardous matter. When the issue is simply the interpretation of legislation, the Court will look to statements by legislators for guidance as to the purpose of the legislature, because the benefit to sound decision-making in this circumstance is thought sufficient to risk the possibility of misreading Congress' purpose. It is entirely a different matter when we are asked to void a statute that is, under well-settled criteria, constitutional on its face, on the basis of what fewer than a handful of Congressmen said about it. What motivates one legislator to make a speech about a statute is not necessarily what motivates scores of others to enact it, and the stakes are sufficiently high for us to eschew guesswork. We decline to void essentially on the ground that it is unwise legislation which Congress had the undoubted power to enact and which could be reenacted in its exact form if the same or another legislator made a "wiser" speech about it. . . .

Since the 1965 Amendment to 12 (b) (3) of the Universal Military Training and Service Act is constitutional as enacted and as applied, the Court of Appeals should have affirmed the judgment of conviction entered by the District Court. Accordingly, we vacate the judgment of the Court of Appeals, and reinstate the judgment and sentence of the District Court. . . .

RED LION BROADCASTING CO. V.
FEDERAL COMMUNICATIONS COMMISSION
395 U.S. 367 (1969)

WGCB, a Pennsylvania radio station owned by the Red Lion Broadcasting Company, carried a fifteen-minute broadcast by the Reverend Billy James Hargis in which he discussed a book by Fred J. Cook entitled *Goldwater: Extremist on the Right*. Hargis said that Cook had been fired by the *New York World Telegram* for making false charges against city officials; had worked for *The Nation*, a champion of "Communist causes"; had defended Alger Hiss and attacked J. Edgar Hoover; and now had written a book "to smear and destroy Barry Goldwater." When Cook asked WGCB to give him free reply time, the station turned him down. The Federal Communications Commission ruled that WGCB, and thus its owner, Red Lion, had failed to meet its obligation under the commission's "fairness doctrine," which required that a station airing a personal attack on someone must send that person a tape, transcript, or summary of the broadcast and offer reply time. Red Lion appealed on First Amendment grounds, but the U.S. Court of Appeals for the District of Columbia Circuit declined to overturn the decision.

Meanwhile, soon after the Red Lion litigation got under way, the FCC wrote new rules clarifying the personal-attack aspect of the fairness doctrine and spelling out procedures for its application to political editorials. The Radio Television News Directors Association (RTNDA) challenged the rules on grounds of free speech and press, and the U.S. Court of Appeals for the Seventh Circuit found them unconstitutional.

Faced with this conflict in the circuits, the Supreme Court reviewed the two cases together. In an opinion by Justice White, a unanimous Court upheld the FCC's specific enforcement action against Red Lion and also the new personal-attack and political-editorial rules—in sum, the fairness doctrine. The Court elaborated the differences among various media in concluding that the finite number of broadcast frequencies meant it was "idle to posit an unabridgeable First Amendment right to broadcast comparable to the right of every individual to speak, write, or publish." If "there is to be any effective communication by radio," the Court continued, "only a few can be licensed." For this reason, government may regulate the few so that the "public interest," which "encompasses the presentation of vigorous debate of controversial issues of importance and concern to the public," is served. Indeed, the Court found that the fairness doctrine, far from abridging First Amendment rights, actually enhanced them.

The Court since *Red Lion* has continued to take the view, in effect, that the application of the First Amendment to a given medium must take into account the nature of that medium. Indeed, five years after *Red Lion*, in *Miami Herald Publishing Co.* v. *Tornillo* (1974), the Court struck down as an abridgment of the First Amendment a Florida law requiring newspapers to provide free reply space to any candidate whose character or record had been criticized in their pages. This state-imposed right of reply was similar to the one applicable to the broadcast media in *Red Lion*, but the two media were sufficiently different as to compel different outcomes.

Red Lion was fundamentally a case about the fairness doctrine, and while the decision sustained its constitutionality, that of course did not settle the question of whether it was good public policy.

Broadcasters continued to criticize the doctrine, and the scarcity rationale that underlay the Court's First Amendment reasoning in the case was called into question by the growth of cable television, which increased public access to the airwaves. In 1987 President Reagan vetoed legislation that would have codified the fairness doctrine. The FCC, expressing First Amendment concerns that the doctrine intruded on broadcasters' editorial judgment and gave the government censorship power, repealed it. But the commission did not eliminate the related personal-attack and political-editorial rules, which have remained controversial.

Opinion of the Court: **White**, Black, Warren, Brennan, Harlan, Marshall, Stewart, Fortas. Not participating: Douglas.

Red Lion Broadcasting Co. v. *Federal Communications Commission* was decided on June 9, 1969.

OPINION

JUSTICE WHITE DELIVERED THE OPINION OF THE COURT . . .

The Federal Communications Commission has for many years imposed on radio and television broadcasters the requirement that discussion of public issues be presented on broadcast stations, and that each side of those issues must be given fair coverage. This is known as the fairness doctrine, which originated very early in the history of broadcasting and has maintained its present outlines for some time. It is an obligation whose content has been defined in a long series of FCC rulings in particular cases, and which is distinct from the statutory requirement of 315 of the Communications Act that equal time be allotted all qualified candidates for public office. Two aspects of the fairness doctrine, relating to personal attacks in the context of controversial public issues and to political editorializing, were codified more precisely in the form of FCC regulations in 1967. The two cases before us now, which were decided separately below, challenge the constitutional and statutory bases of the doctrine and component rules. *Red Lion* involves the application of the fairness doctrine to a particular broadcast, and *RTNDA* [*U.S.* v. *Radio Television News*

Directors Association] arises as an action to review the FCC's 1967 promulgation of the personal attack and political editorializing regulations. . . .

The history of the emergence of the fairness doctrine and of the related legislation shows that the Commission's action in the *Red Lion* case did not exceed its authority, and that in adopting the new regulations the Commission was implementing congressional policy rather than embarking on a frolic of its own.

Before 1927, the allocation of frequencies was left entirely to the private sector, and the result was chaos. It quickly became apparent that broadcast frequencies constituted a scarce resource whose use could be regulated and rationalized only by the Government. Without government control, the medium would be of little use because of the cacophony of competing voices, none of which could be clearly and predictably heard. Consequently, the Federal Radio Commission was established to allocate frequencies among competing applicants in a manner responsive to the public "convenience, interest, or necessity."

Very shortly thereafter the Commission expressed its view that the "public interest requires ample play for the free and fair competition of opposing views, and the commission believes that the principle applies . . . to all discussions of issues of importance to the public." . . . This doctrine was applied through denial of license renewals or construction permits. . . .

After an extended period during which the licensee was obliged not only to cover and to cover fairly the views of others, but also to refrain from expressing his own personal views . . . the latter limitation on the licensee was abandoned and the doctrine developed into its present form. There is a twofold duty laid down by the FCC's decisions and described by the 1949 Report on Editorializing by Broadcast Licensees. The broadcaster must give adequate coverage to public issues, and coverage must be fair in that it accurately reflects the opposing views. . . . This must be done at the broadcaster's own expense if sponsorship is unavailable. . . . Moreover, the duty must be met by programming obtained at the licensee's own initiative if available from no other source. . . . The Federal Radio Commission had imposed these two basic duties on broadcasters since the outset, . . . and in particular respects the personal attack rules and regulations at issue here have spelled them out in greater detail.

When a personal attack has been made on a figure involved in a public issue, both the doctrine of . . . *Red Lion*, and . . . the 1967 regulations at issue in *RTNDA* require that the individual attacked himself be offered an opportunity to respond. Likewise, where one candidate is endorsed in a political editorial, the other candidates must themselves be offered reply time to use personally or through a spokesman. . . .

The statutory authority of the FCC to promulgate these regulations derives from the mandate to the "Commission from time to time, as public convenience, interest, or necessity requires" to promulgate "such rules and regulations and prescribe such restrictions and conditions . . . as may be necessary to carry out the provisions of this chapter. . . ." The Commission is specifically directed to consider the demands of the public interest in the course of granting licenses . . . and modifying them. Moreover, the FCC has included among the conditions of the Red Lion license itself the requirement that operation of the station be carried out in the public interest. . . . This mandate to the FCC to assure that broadcasters operate in the public interest . . . is broad enough to encompass these regulations. . . .

The broadcasters challenge the fairness doctrine and its specific manifestations in the personal attack and political editorial rules on conventional First Amendment grounds, alleging that the rules abridge their freedom of speech and press. Their contention is that the First Amendment protects their desire to use their allotted frequencies continuously to broadcast whatever they choose, and to exclude whomever they choose from ever using that frequency. No man may be prevented from saying or publishing what he thinks, or from refusing in his speech or other utterances to give equal weight to the views of his opponents. This right, they say, applies equally to broadcasters.

Although broadcasting is clearly a medium affected by a First Amendment interest, . . . differences in the characteristics of new media justify differences in the First Amendment standards applied to them. *Burstyn* v. *Wilson* [1952]. For example, the ability of new technology to produce sounds more raucous than those of the human voice justifies restrictions on the sound level, and on the hours and places of use, of sound trucks so long as the restrictions are reasonable and applied without discrimination. *Kovacs* v. *Cooper* [1949].

Just as the Government may limit the use of sound-amplifying equipment potentially so noisy that it drowns out civilized private speech, so may the Government limit the use of broadcast equipment. The right of free speech of a broadcaster, the user of a sound truck, or any other individual does not embrace a right to snuff out the free speech of others. . . .

. . . [T]he reach of radio signals is incomparably greater than the range of the human voice, and the problem of interference is a massive reality. The lack of know-how and equipment may keep many from the air, but only a tiny fraction of those with resources and intelligence can hope to communicate by radio at the same time if intelligible communication is to be had, even if the entire radio spectrum is utilized in the present state of commercially acceptable technology.

It was this fact, and the chaos which ensued from permitting anyone to use any frequency at whatever power level he wished, which made necessary the enactment of the Radio Act of 1927 and the Communications Act of 1934. . . . It was this reality which at the very least necessitated first the division of the radio spectrum into portions reserved respectively for public broadcasting and for other important radio uses such as amateur operation, aircraft, police, defense, and navigation; and then the subdivision of each portion, and assignment of specific frequencies to individual users or groups of users. Beyond this, however, because the frequencies reserved for public broadcasting were limited in number, it was essential for the Government to tell some applicants that they could not broadcast at all because there was room for only a few.

Where there are substantially more individuals who want to broadcast than there are frequencies to allocate, it is idle to posit an unabridgeable First Amendment right to broadcast comparable to the right of every individual to speak, write, or publish. If 100 persons want broadcast licenses but there are only 10 frequencies to allocate, all of them may have the same "right" to a license; but if there is to be any effective communication by radio, only a few can be licensed and the rest must be barred from the airwaves. It would be strange if the First Amendment, aimed at protecting and furthering communications, prevented the Government from making radio communication possible by requiring licenses to broadcast and by limiting the number of licenses so as not to overcrowd the spectrum.

This has been the consistent view of the Court. Congress unquestionably has the power to grant and deny licenses and to eliminate existing stations. . . . No one has a First Amendment right to a license or to monopolize a radio frequency; to deny a station license because "the public interest" requires it "is not a denial of free speech." *National Broadcasting Co.* v. *United States* [1943].

By the same token, as far as the First Amendment is concerned those who are licensed stand no better than those to whom licenses are refused. A license permits broadcasting, but the licensee has no constitutional right to be the one who holds the license or to monopolize a radio frequency to the exclusion of his fellow citizens. There is nothing in the First Amendment which prevents the Government from requiring a licensee to share his frequency with others and to conduct himself as a proxy or fiduciary with obligations to present those views and voices which are representative of his community and which would otherwise, by necessity, be barred from the airwaves.

This is not to say that the First Amendment is irrelevant to public broadcasting. On the contrary, it has a major role to play. . . . Because of the scarcity of radio frequencies, the Government is permitted to put restraints on licensees in favor of others whose views should be expressed on this unique medium. But the people as a whole retain their interest in free speech by radio and their collective right to have the medium function consistently with the ends and purposes of the First Amendment. It is the right of the viewers and listeners, not the right of the broadcasters, which is paramount. . . . It is the purpose of the First Amendment to preserve an uninhibited market-place of ideas in which truth will ultimately prevail, rather than to countenance monopolization of that market, whether it be by the Government itself or a private licensee. . . . It is the right of the public to receive suitable access to social, political, esthetic, moral, and other ideas and experiences which is crucial here. That right may not constitutionally be abridged either by Congress or by the FCC.

Rather than confer frequency monopolies on a relatively small number of licensees, in a Nation of 200,000,000, the Government could surely have decreed that each frequency should be shared among all or some of those who wish to use it, each being assigned a portion of the broadcast day or the broadcast week. The ruling and regulations at issue here do not go quite so far. They assert that under specified circumstances, a licensee must offer to make available a reasonable amount of broadcast time to those who have a view different from that which has already been expressed on his station. The expression of a political endorsement, or of a personal attack while dealing with a controversial public issue, simply triggers this time sharing. As we have said, the First Amendment confers no right on licensees to prevent others from broadcasting on "their" frequencies and no right to an unconditional monopoly of a scarce resource which the Government has denied others the right to use.

In terms of constitutional principle, and as enforced sharing of a scarce resource, the personal attack and political editorial rules are indistinguishable from the equal-time provision of 315 [of the Communications Act], a specific enactment of Congress requiring stations to set aside reply time under specified circumstances and to which the fairness doctrine and these constituent regulations are important complements. That provision, which has been part of the law since 1927, . . . has been held valid by this Court as an obligation of the licensee relieving him of any power in any way to prevent or censor the broadcast, and thus insulating him from liability for defamation. The constitutionality of the statute under the First Amendment was unquestioned. . . .

Nor can we say that it is inconsistent with the First Amendment goal of producing an informed public capable of conducting its own affairs to require a broadcaster to permit answers to personal attacks occurring in the course of discussing controversial issues, or to require that the political opponents of those endorsed by the station be given a chance to communicate with the public. Otherwise, station owners and a few networks would have unfettered power to make time available only to the highest bidders, to communicate only their own views on public issues, people, and candidates, and to permit on the air only those with whom they agreed. There is no sanctuary in the First Amendment for unlimited private censorship operating in a medium not open to all. . . .

It is strenuously argued, however, that if political editorials or personal attacks will trigger an obligation in broadcasters to afford the opportunity for expression to speakers who need not pay for time and whose views are unpalatable to the licensees, then broadcasters will be irresistibly forced to self-censorship and their coverage of controversial public issues will be eliminated or at least rendered wholly ineffective. Such a result would indeed be a serious matter, for should licensees actually eliminate their coverage of controversial issues, the purposes of the doctrine would be stifled.

. . . [This] possibility is at best speculative. The communications industry, and in particular the networks, have taken pains to present controversial issues in the past, and even now they do not assert that they intend to abandon their efforts in this regard. . . . [I]f experience with the administration of these doctrines indicates that they have the net effect of reducing rather than enhancing the volume and quality of coverage, there will be time enough to reconsider the constitutional implications. The fairness doctrine in the past has had no such overall effect.

That this will occur now seems unlikely, however, since if present licensees should suddenly prove timorous, the Commission is not powerless to insist that they give adequate and fair attention to public issues. It does not violate the First Amendment to treat licensees given the privilege of using scarce radio frequencies as proxies for the entire community, obligated to give suitable time and attention to matters of great public concern. To condition the granting or renewal of licenses on a willingness to present representative community views on controversial issues is consistent with the ends and purposes of those constitutional provisions forbidding the abridgment of freedom of speech and freedom of the press. Congress need not stand idly by and permit those with licenses to ignore the problems which beset the people or to exclude from the airways anything but their own views of fundamental questions. The statute, long administrative practice, and cases are to this effect. . . .

The litigants embellish their First Amendment arguments with the contention that the regulations are so vague that their duties are impossible to discern. Of this point it is enough to say that, judging the validity of the regulations on their face as they are presented here, we cannot conclude that the FCC has been left a free hand to vindicate its own idiosyncratic conception of the public interest or of the requirements of free speech. Past adjudications by the FCC give added precision to the regulations; there was nothing vague about the FCC's specific ruling in *Red Lion* that Fred Cook should be provided an opportunity to reply. The regulations at issue in *RTNDA* could be employed in precisely the same way as the fairness doctrine was in *Red Lion*. Moreover, the FCC itself has recognized that the applicability of its regulations to situations beyond the scope of past cases may be questionable, . . . and will not impose sanctions in such cases without warning. We need not approve every aspect of the fairness doctrine to decide these cases, and we will not now pass upon the constitutionality of these regulations by envisioning the most extreme applications conceivable . . ., but will deal with those problems if and when they arise.

We need not and do not now ratify every past and future decision by the FCC with regard to programming. There is no question here of the Commission's refusal to permit the broadcaster to carry a particular program or to publish his own views; of a discriminatory refusal to require the licensee to broadcast certain views which have been denied access to the airwaves; of government censorship of a particular program . . .; or of the official government view dominating public broadcasting. Such questions would raise more serious First Amendment issues. But we do hold that the Congress and the Commission do not violate the First Amendment when they require a radio or television station to give reply time to answer personal attacks and political editorials. . . .

. . . [W]e hold the regulations and ruling at issue here are both authorized by statute and constitutional. The judgment of the Court of Appeals in *Red Lion* is affirmed and that in *RTNDA* reversed and the cases remanded for proceedings consistent with this opinion.

TINKER V. DES MOINES INDEPENDENT COMMUNITY SCHOOL DISTRICT
393 U.S. 503 (1969)

In December 1965, three Des Moines, Iowa, teenagers—siblings John and Mary Beth Tinker and Christopher Eckhardt—decided to protest the war in Vietnam by wearing black armbands to school. Aware of their plan, school authorities adopted a regulation banning such armbands. The students wore them anyway and were suspended. They complained in federal court that the school had violated their free speech rights. Although the lower courts sided with the school authorities, the students prevailed in the Supreme Court.

Previous decisions, including *West Virginia State Board of Education* v. *Barnette* (1943), had established that students in public schools were entitled to some constitutional protections. In *Tinker*, the Court for the first time set forth standards for safeguarding public school students' free speech rights. The case involved non-verbal expression or "symbolic speech," which the Court first recognized as meriting protection in *Stromberg* v. *California* (1931).

Justice Fortas, writing for the Court, found that the students' wearing of armbands had not created any disorder or disturbance, and that the mere "fear of a disturbance" could not justify the regulation at issue. Fortas further noted that the schools, while permitting students to wear other political symbols, such as campaign buttons, had through the regulation at issue targeted a specific view on a single subject. That kind of prohibition, he said, was "not constitutionally permissible."

In dissent, Justice Black read the record differently, finding that "the armbands did exactly what the elected school officials and principals foresaw they would, that is, took the students' minds off their classwork and diverted them to thoughts about the highly emotional subject of the Vietnam war. . . . [I]f the time has come when pupils of state-supported schools . . . can defy . . . orders of school officials to keep their minds on their own school work, it is the beginning of a new revolutionary era of permissiveness . . . fostered by the judiciary."

Opinion of the Court: **Fortas**, Warren, Douglas, Brennan, Stewart, White, Marshall. Concurring opinions: **Stewart**; **White**. Dissenting opinions: **Black**; **Harlan**.

Tinker v. *Des Moines Independent Community School District* was decided on February 24, 1969.

OPINIONS

JUSTICE FORTAS DELIVERED THE OPINION OF THE COURT . . .

The District Court recognized that the wearing of an armband for the purpose of expressing certain views is the type of symbolic act that is within the Free Speech Clause of the First Amendment. . . . As we shall discuss, the wearing of armbands in the circumstances of this case was entirely divorced from actually or potentially disruptive conduct by those participating in it. It was closely akin to "pure speech" which, we have repeatedly held, is entitled to comprehensive protection under the First Amendment. . . .

First Amendment rights, applied in light of the special characteristics of the school environment, are available to teachers and students. It can hardly be argued that either students or teachers shed their constitutional rights to freedom of speech or expression at the schoolhouse gate. This has been the unmistakable holding of this Court for almost fifty years. In *Meyer* v. *Nebraska* [1923] and *Bartels* v. *Iowa* [1923], this Court . . . held that the Due Process Clause of the Fourteenth Amendment prevents States from forbidding the teaching of a foreign language to young students. Statutes to this effect, the Court held, unconstitutionally interfere with the liberty of teacher, student, and parent. . . .

In *West Virginia State Board of Education* v. *Barnette* [1943], this Court held that under the First Amendment, the student in public school may not be compelled to salute the flag. . . . On the other hand, the Court has repeatedly emphasized the need for affirming the comprehensive authority of the States and of school officials, consistent with fundamental constitutional safeguards, to prescribe and control conduct in the schools. . . . Our problem lies in the area where students in the exercise of First Amendment rights collide with the rules of the school authorities.

The problem posed by the present case does not relate to regulation of the length of skirts or the type of clothing, to hair style, or deportment. . . . It does not concern aggressive, disruptive action or even group demonstrations. Our problem involves direct, primary First Amendment rights akin to "pure speech."

The school officials banned and sought to punish petitioners for a silent, passive expression of opinion, unaccompanied by any disorder or disturbance on the part of petitioners. There is here no evidence whatever of petitioners' interference, actual or nascent, with the schools' work or of collision with the rights of other students to be secure and to be let alone. Accordingly, this case does not concern speech or action that intrudes upon the work of the school or the rights of other students.

Only a few of the 18,000 students in the school system wore the black armbands. Only five students were suspended for wearing them. There is no indication that the work of the schools or any class was disrupted. Outside the classrooms, a few students made hostile remarks to the children wearing armbands, but there were no threats or acts of violence on school premises.

The District Court concluded that the action of the school authorities was reasonable because it was based upon their fear of a disturbance from the wearing of the armbands. But, in our system, undifferentiated fear or apprehension of disturbance is not enough to overcome the right to freedom of expression. Any departure from absolute regimentation may cause trouble. Any variation from the majority's opinion may inspire fear. Any word spoken, in class, in the lunchroom, or on the campus, that deviates from the views of another person may start an argument or cause a disturbance. But our Constitution says we must take this risk . . . and our history says that it is this sort of hazardous freedom—this kind of openness—that is the basis of our national strength and of the independence and vigor of Americans who grow up and live in this relatively permissive, often disputatious, society.

In order for the State in the person of school officials to justify prohibition of a particular expression of opinion, it must be able to show that its action was caused by something more than a mere desire to avoid the discomfort and unpleasantness that always accompany an unpopular viewpoint. . . .

In the present case, the District Court made no such finding, and our independent examination of the record fails to yield evidence that the school authorities had reason to anticipate that the wearing of the armbands would substantially interfere with the work of the school or impinge upon the rights of other students. . . .

On the contrary, the action of the school authorities appears to have been based upon an urgent wish to avoid the controversy which might result from the expression, even by the silent symbol of armbands, of opposition to this Nation's part in the conflagration in Vietnam. . . .

It is also relevant that the school authorities did not purport to prohibit the wearing of all symbols of political or controversial significance. The record shows that students in some of the schools wore buttons relating to national political campaigns, and some even wore the Iron Cross, traditionally a symbol of Nazism. The order prohibiting the wearing of armbands did not extend to these. Instead, a particular symbol—black armbands worn to exhibit opposition to this Nation's involvement in Vietnam—was singled out for prohibition. Clearly, the prohibition of expression of one particular opinion, at least without evidence that it is necessary to avoid material and substantial interference with schoolwork or discipline, is not constitutionally permissible.

In our system, state-operated schools may not be enclaves of totalitarianism. School officials do not possess absolute authority over their students. Students in school as well as out of school are "persons" under our Constitution. They are possessed of fundamental rights which the State must respect, just as they themselves must respect their obligations to the State. In our system, students may not be regarded as closed-circuit recipients of only that which the State chooses to communicate. They may not be confined to the expression of those sentiments that are officially approved. In the absence of a specific showing of constitutionally valid reasons to regulate their speech, students are entitled to freedom of expression of their views. . . .

The principle of these cases is not confined to the supervised and ordained discussion which takes place in the classroom. The principal use to which the schools are dedicated is to accommodate students during prescribed hours for the purpose of certain types of activities. Among those activities is personal intercommunication among the students. This is not only an inevitable part of the process of attending school; it is also an important part of the educational process. A student's rights, therefore, do not embrace merely the classroom hours. . . . But conduct by the student, in class or out of it, which for any reason—whether it stems from time, place, or type of behavior—materially disrupts classwork or involves substantial disorder or invasion of the rights of others is, of course, not immunized by the constitutional guarantee of freedom of speech. . . .

As we have discussed, the record does not demonstrate any facts which might reasonably have led school authorities to forecast substantial disruption of or material interference with school activities, and no disturbances or disorders on the school premises in fact occurred. These petitioners merely went about their ordained rounds in school. Their deviation consisted only in wearing on their sleeve a band of black cloth, not more than two inches wide. They wore it to exhibit their disapproval of the Vietnam hostilities and their advocacy of a truce, to make their views known, and, by their example, to influence others to adopt them. They neither interrupted school activities nor sought to intrude in the school affairs or the lives of others. They caused discussion outside of the classrooms, but no interference with work and no disorder. In the circumstances, our Constitution does not permit officials of the State to deny their form of expression. . . .

REVERSED and remanded.

JUSTICE BLACK, DISSENTING . . .

The Court's holding in this case ushers in what I deem to be an entirely new era in which the power to control pupils by the elected "officials of state supported public schools" in the United States is in ultimate effect transferred to the Supreme Court. . . .

As I read the Court's opinion it relies upon the following grounds for holding unconstitutional the judgment of the Des Moines school officials and the two courts below. First, the Court concludes that the wearing of armbands is "symbolic speech" which is "akin to 'pure speech'" and therefore protected by the First and Fourteenth Amendments. Secondly, the Court decides that the public schools are an appropriate place to exercise "symbolic speech." Finally, the Court arrogates to itself, rather than to the State's elected officials charged with running the schools, the decision as to which school disciplinary regulations are "reasonable."

Assuming that the Court is correct in holding that the conduct of wearing armbands for the purpose of conveying political ideas is protected by the First Amendment, . . . the crucial remaining questions are whether students and teachers may use the schools at their whim as a platform for the exercise of free speech—"symbolic" or "pure"—and whether the courts will allocate to themselves the function of deciding how the pupils' school day will be spent. While I have always believed that under the First and Fourteenth Amendments neither the State nor the Federal Government has any authority to regulate or censor the content of speech, I have never believed that any person has a right to give speeches or engage in demonstrations where he pleases and when he pleases. . . .

While the record does not show that any of these armband students shouted, used profane language, or were violent in any manner, detailed testimony by some of them shows their armbands caused comments, warnings by other students, the poking of fun at them, and a warning by an older football player that other, nonprotesting students had better let them alone. There is also evidence that a teacher of mathematics had his lesson period practically "wrecked" chiefly by disputes with Mary Beth Tinker, who wore her armband for her "demonstration." Even a casual reading of the record shows that this armband did divert students' minds from their regular lessons, and that talk, comments, etc., made John Tinker "self-conscious" in attending school with his armband. While the absence of obscene remarks or boisterous and loud disorder perhaps justifies the Court's statement that the few armband students did not actually "disrupt" the classwork, I think the record overwhelmingly shows that the armbands did exactly what the elected school officials and principals foresaw they would, that is, took the students' minds off their classwork and diverted them to thoughts about the highly emotional subject of the Vietnam war. And I repeat that if the time has come when pupils of state-supported schools, kindergartens, grammar schools, or high schools, can defy and flout orders of school officials to keep their minds on their own schoolwork, it is the beginning of a new revolutionary era of permissiveness in this country fostered by the judiciary. . . .

In my view, teachers in state-controlled public schools are hired to teach there. . . . Certainly a teacher is not paid to go into school and teach subjects the State does not hire him to teach as a part of its selected curriculum. Nor are public school students sent to the schools at public expense to broadcast political or any other views to educate and inform the public. The original idea of schools, which I do not believe is yet abandoned as worthless or out of date, was that children had not yet reached the point of experience and wisdom which enabled them to teach all of their elders. It may be that the Nation has outworn the old-fashioned slogan that "children are to be seen not heard," but one may, I hope, be permitted to harbor the thought that taxpayers send children to school on the premise that at their age they need to learn, not teach. . . .

Change has been said to be truly the law of life, but sometimes the old and the tried and true are worth holding. The schools of this Nation have undoubtedly contributed to giving us tranquility and to making us more law-abiding people. Uncontrolled and uncontrollable liberty is an enemy to domestic peace. We cannot close our eyes to the fact that some of the country's greatest problems are crimes committed by the youth, too many of school age. School discipline, like parental discipline, is an integral and important part of training our children to be good citizens—to be better citizens. Here a very small number of students have crisply and summarily refused to obey a school order designed to give pupils who want to learn the opportunity to do so. One does not need to be a prophet or the son of a prophet to know that after the Court's holding today some students in Iowa schools and indeed in all schools will be ready, able, and willing to defy their teachers on practically all orders. This is the more unfortunate for the schools since groups of students all over the land are already running loose, conducting break-ins, sit-ins, lie-ins, and smash-ins. Many of these student groups, as is all too familiar to all who read the newspapers and watch the television news programs, have already engaged in rioting, property seizures, and destruction. They have picketed schools to force students not to cross their picket lines and have too often violently attacked earnest but frightened students who wanted an education that the pickets did not want them to get. Students engaged in such activities are apparently confident that they know far more about how to operate public school systems than do their parents, teachers, and elected school officials. It is no answer to say that the particular students here have not yet reached such high points in their demands to attend classes in order to exercise their political pressures. Turned loose with lawsuits for damages and injunctions against their teachers as they are here, it is nothing but wishful thinking to imagine that young, immature students will not soon believe it is their right to control the schools rather than the right of the States that collect the taxes to hire the teachers for the benefit of the pupils. This case, therefore, wholly without constitutional reasons in my judgment, subjects all the public schools in the country to the whims and caprices of their loudest-mouthed, but maybe not their brightest, students. I, for one, am not fully persuaded that school pupils are wise enough, even with this Court's expert help from Washington, to run the 23,390 public school systems in our fifty States. I wish, therefore, wholly to disclaim any purpose on my part to hold that the Federal Constitution compels the teachers, parents, and elected school officials to surrender control of the American public school system to public school students. I dissent.

RESPONSES

FROM THE *EVENING STAR*, WASHINGTON, D.C., FEBRUARY 26, 1969, "THE COURT AND THE KIDS"

The Supreme Court has displayed something short of supreme wisdom in its ruling upholding the right of children to stage protests in public schools and to demonstrate in favor of their political beliefs. The seven-judge majority carefully pointed out that the permissiveness was limited to peaceful demonstrations. They piously asserted that their ruling was in no way related to miniskirts and long hair. They were, they said, only doing right by the Constitution. And they turned to other business, leaving the country's school authorities holding a large can of worms. . . .

No particular legal expertise is required to see how wide a door has been opened. Any minute now some miniskirted teenie-bopper or long-haired adolescent will come up with a high-minded cause for which they must speak up—symbolically—by displaying their thighs or hiding their ears. What hope remains of editing the garbage out of student publications when a hyper-sensitive pre-teen author holds "John F. Tinker et al. v. Des Moines Independent Community School District et al." over the faculty's head? What hope remains for discipline in general when school authorities are required to wait for the riot to start before lifting a finger? What expectation can there be that our universities will some day regain their sanity when the grade schools offer primary training in protest?

The general subject of student protests raises fine constitutional points that cannot lightly be dismissed by the disciplinarians or taken completely for granted by the libertarians. And now the Supreme Court—Justices Harlan and Black excepted—has compounded the complexity of the debate by its implicit assumption that the full protection of the United States Constitution starts at the birth of a United States citizen.

Just where that protection should begin is a suitable subject for discussion—perhaps 18 might be about right. But one thing should be clear to the most isolated legal theorists: Infants are not prepared for freedom, and one of the duties of society is to provide preparation through discipline.

Man is a social animal through necessity, not through instinct. Unlike the bee or the wolf, he must be taught that the rights and needs of others must be respected, sometimes at the expense of his natural inclination to self-indulgence. Sometimes it is necessary for teachers to curb the freedom of those shrill and demanding voices. Sometimes it is necessary for parents to indulge in cruel and unusual punishments to bring those burgeoning little egos under control. And even the justices of the Supreme Court should be wise enough to know it.

FROM THE *NEW YORK TIMES*, FEBRUARY 26, 1969, "ARMBANDS YES, MINISKIRTS NO"

The majority of the justices felt—we think, rightly—that a line could and should be drawn between expression and disorderly excess. A close reading of the fact and decision shows that there is no license given here to riot, to interfere with classroom work, or to substitute the Court for the thousands of school boards.

Freedom of expression—in an open manner by those holding minority or unpopular views—is part of the vigor and strength of our schools and society. So long as it does not obstruct the right of others in the classroom or on campus, it must be allowed in this country. If dissent ever has to go underground, America will be in real trouble.

BRANDENBURG V. OHIO
395 U.S. 444 (1969)

Clarence Brandenburg, a Ku Klux Klan leader in Ohio, organized a Klan rally in Hamilton County. There Brandenburg gave a speech in which he said, in part: "We're not a revengent [sic] organization, but if our President, our Congress, our Supreme Court, continues to suppress the white, Caucasian race, it's possible that there might have to be some revengeance taken." Brandenburg also offered his opinion that "the nigger should be returned to Africa, the Jew returned to Israel."

There was television coverage of the rally, and Brandenburg's remarks drew the interest of state authorities, who proceeded to prosecute him for advocating racial strife in violation of the Ohio Criminal Syndicalism Statute. Enacted in 1919, this law was similar to other state syndicalism laws of that era. Indeed, it was virtually identical to the California law that the Court had sustained in *Whitney* v. *California* (1927). Brandenburg appealed his conviction, contending that the Ohio law abridged his First Amendment right to free speech. He lost in the Ohio courts but won in the Supreme Court.

In *Brandenburg* the Court explicitly overruled *Whitney* and elaborated a new test for judging the constitutionality of speech advocating illegal action. Under the "clear and present danger" test, originally formulated for use in a case like *Brandenburg* but unmentioned in the Court's decision, subversive speech could be punished if it had a "tendency" to promote lawlessness (*Schenck* v. *United States*, 1919) or if it was part of a broader, dangerous movement like the Communist Party (*Dennis* v. *United States*, 1951). Under *Brandenburg*, such speech may be punished only if it "is directed to inciting or producing imminent lawless action and is likely to incite or produce such action." *Brandenburg's* "direct incitement" test promised greater First Amendment protection for political speech previously subject to punishment. The opinion was rendered *per curiam*, "by the court," and therefore not attributed to any justice. Such opinions may be rendered by the whole Court or a majority. Here the entire Court was in agreement.

Opinion of the Court (*per curiam*): Warren, Black, Douglas, Harlan, Brennan, Stewart, White, Fortas, Marshall. Concurring opinions: **Black**; **Douglas**, Black.

Brandenburg v. *Ohio* was decided on June 9, 1969.

OPINIONS

PER CURIAM . . .

The Ohio Criminal Syndicalism Statute was enacted in 1919. From 1917 to 1920, identical or quite similar laws were adopted by twenty states and two territories. . . . In 1927, this Court sustained the constitutionality of California's Criminal Syndicalism Act, . . . the text of which is quite similar to that of the laws of Ohio. *Whitney* v. *California* [1927]. The Court upheld the statute on the ground that, without more, "advocating" violent means to effect political and economic change involves such danger to the security of the State that the State may outlaw it. . . . But *Whitney* has been thoroughly discredited by later decisions. See *Dennis* v. *United States* [1951]. These later decisions have fashioned the principle that the constitutional guarantees of free speech and free press do not permit a State to forbid or proscribe advocacy of the use of force or of law violation except where such advocacy is directed to inciting or producing imminent lawless action and is likely to incite or produce such action. . . . A statute which fails to draw this distinction impermissibly intrudes upon the freedoms guaranteed by the First and Fourteenth Amendments. It sweeps within its condemnation speech which our Constitution has immunized from governmental control. . . .

Measured by this test, Ohio's Criminal Syndicalism Act cannot be sustained. The Act punishes persons who "advocate or teach the duty, necessity, or propriety" of violence "as a means of accomplishing industrial or political reform"; or who publish or circulate or display any book or paper containing such advocacy; or who "justify" the commission of violent acts "with intent to exemplify, spread or advocate the doctrines of criminal syndicalism"; or who "voluntarily assemble" with a group formed "to teach or advocate the doctrines of criminal syndicalism." Neither the indictment nor the trial judge's instructions to the jury in any way refined the statute's bald definition of the crime in terms of mere advocacy not distinguished from incitement to imminent lawless action.

Accordingly, we are here confronted with a statute which, by its own words and as applied, purports to punish mere advocacy and to forbid, on pain of criminal punishment, assembly with others merely to advocate the described type of action. Such a statute falls within the condemnation of the First and Fourteenth Amendments. The contrary teaching of *Whitney* v. *California* cannot be supported, and that decision is therefore . . .

REVERSED.

JUSTICE DOUGLAS, CONCURRING . . .

While I join the opinion of the court, I desire to enter a caveat. . . . I see no place in the regime of the First Amendment for any "clear and present danger" test, whether strict and tight as some would make it, or free-wheeling as the Court in *Dennis* rephrased it.

When one reads the opinions closely and sees when and how the "clear and present danger" test has been applied, great misgivings are aroused. First, the threats were often loud but always puny and made serious only by judges so wedded to the status quo that critical analysis made them nervous. Second, the test was so twisted and perverted in *Dennis* as to make the trial of those teachers of Marxism an all-out political trial which was part and parcel of the cold war that has eroded substantial parts of the First Amendment.

Action is often a method of expression and within the protection of the First Amendment. . . .

. . . I think that all matters of belief are beyond the reach of subpoenas or the probings of investigators. That is why the invasions of privacy made by investigating committees were notoriously unconstitutional. That is the deep-seated fault in the infamous loyalty-security hearing which, since 1947 when President Truman launched them, have processed 20,000,000 men and women. Those hearings were primarily concerned with one's thoughts, ideas, beliefs, and convictions. They were the most blatant violations of the First Amendment we have ever known.

The line between what is permissible and not subject to control and what may be made impermissible and subject to regulations is the line between ideas and overt acts.

The example usually given by those who would punish speech is the case of one who falsely shouts fire in a crowded theater.

That is, however, a classic case where speech is brigaded with action. . . . They are indeed inseparable and a prosecution can be launched for the overt acts actually caused. Apart from rare instances of that kind, speech is, I think, immune from prosecution. Certainly there is no constitutional line between advocacy of abstract ideas . . . and advocacy of political action. . . . The quality of advocacy turns on the depth of the conviction; and government has no power to invade that sanctuary of belief and conscience.

36

Cohen v. California
403 U.S. 15 (1971)

Walking through a corridor of the Los Angeles County Courthouse, Paul Robert Cohen wore a jacket bearing the words "Fuck the Draft." He was arrested for violating a state law against disturbing the peace by "offensive conduct." At trial, Cohen said he wore the jacket to inform the public of his opposition to the Vietnam War and the draft. He was convicted and sentenced to thirty days in prison. Appealing on First Amendment grounds, Cohen lost in the California courts but won in the U.S. Supreme Court.

In *Chaplinsky* v. *New Hampshire* (1942), the Court said that the "lewd and obscene, the profane, the libelous," and insulting or "fighting" words were not protected by the First Amendment because they failed to contribute to "the exposition of ideas" and lacked any "social value" in search for truth. In *Cohen*, the Court, with Justice Harlan writing, found that the words at issue in the case—"Fuck the Draft"—could not be placed in any of *Chaplinsky's* unprotected categories. The Court said that the words were neither obscene nor insulting; insulting or fighting words, the Court explained, must be directed at someone in particular, and Cohen's words were not.

The Court also rejected the notion that states could act as "guardians of public morality." There was no principle, it said, by which to distinguish "this from any other offensive word," and it is "often true that one man's vulgarity is another's lyric."

Whether the majority understood "Fuck the Draft" as a lyric or a vulgarity, it was certain that these words conveyed not only "ideas capable of relatively precise, detaching explication, but otherwise inexpressible emotions as well." The Court emphasized that the Constitution must be solicitous of both the cognitive and emotive aspects of speech.

Cohen expanded the definition of protected speech by diminishing *Chaplinsky* and embracing a theory of moral relativism that effectively prevented the states from maintaining standards of public discourse.

Opinion of the Court: **Harlan**, Douglas, Brennan, Stewart, Marshall. Dissenting opinion: **Blackmun**, Burger, Black, and White, in part.

Cohen v. *California* was decided on June 7, 1971.

OPINIONS

JUSTICE HARLAN DELIVERED THE OPINION OF THE COURT . . .

. . . [T]he issue flushed by this case stands out in bold relief. It is whether California can excise, as "offensive conduct," one particular scurrilous epithet from the public discourse, either upon the theory of the court below that its use is inherently likely to cause violent reaction or upon a more general assertion that the States, acting as guardians of public morality, may properly remove this offensive word from the public vocabulary.

The rationale of the California court is plainly untenable. At most it reflects an "undifferentiated fear or apprehension of disturbance [which] is not enough to overcome the right to freedom of expression." *Tinker* v. *Des Moines Independent Community School District* [1969]. We have been shown no evidence that substantial numbers of citizens are standing ready to strike out physically at whoever may assault their sensibilities with execrations like that uttered by Cohen. There may be some persons about with such lawless and violent proclivities, but that is an insufficient base upon which to erect, consistently with constitutional values, a governmental power to force persons who wish to ventilate their dissident views into avoiding particular forms of expression. The argument amounts to little more than the self-defeating proposition that to avoid physical censorship of one who has not sought to provoke such a response by a hypothetical coterie of the violent and lawless, the States may more appropriately effectuate that censorship themselves. . . .

Admittedly, it is not so obvious that the First and Fourteenth Amendments must be taken to disable the States from punishing public utterance of this unseemly expletive in order to maintain what they regard as a suitable level of discourse within the body politic. We think, however, that examination and reflection will reveal the shortcomings of a contrary viewpoint.

At the outset, we cannot overemphasize that, in our judgment, most situations where the State has a justifiable interest in regulating speech will fall within one or more of the various established exceptions . . . to the usual rule that governmental bodies may not prescribe the form or content of individual expression. Equally important to our conclusion is the constitutional backdrop against which our decision must be made. The constitutional right of free expression is powerful medicine in a society as diverse and populous as ours. It is designed and intended to remove governmental restraints from the arena of public discussion, putting the decision as to what views shall be voiced largely into the hands of each of us, in the hope that use of such freedom will ultimately produce a more capable citizenry and more perfect polity and in the belief that no other approach would comport with the premise of individual dignity and choice upon which our political system rests. . . .

To many, the immediate consequence of this freedom may often appear to be only verbal tumult, discord, and even offensive utterance. These are, however, within established limits, in truth necessary side effects of the broader enduring values which the process of open debate permits us to achieve. That the air may at times seem filled with verbal cacophony is, in this sense, not a sign of weakness but of strength. We cannot lose sight of the fact that, in what otherwise might seem a trifling and annoying instance of individual distasteful abuse of a privilege, these fundamental societal values are truly implicated. . . .

Against this perception of the constitutional policies involved, we discern certain more particularized considerations that peculiarly call for reversal of this conviction. First, the principle contended for by the State seems inherently boundless: How is one to distinguish this from any other offensive word? Surely the State has no right to cleanse public debate to the point where it is grammatically palatable to the most squeamish among us. Yet no readily ascertainable general principle exists for stopping short of that result were we to affirm the judgment below. For, while the particular four-letter word being litigated here is perhaps more distasteful than most others of its genre, it is nevertheless often true that one man's vulgarity is another's lyric. Indeed, we think it is largely because governmental officials cannot make principled distinctions in this area that the Constitution leaves matters of taste and style so largely to the individual.

Additionally, we cannot overlook the fact, because it is well illustrated by the episode involved here, that much linguistic expression serves a dual communicative function: it conveys not only ideas capable of relatively precise, detached explication, but otherwise inexpressible emotions as well. In fact, words are often chosen as much for their emotive as their cognitive force. We cannot sanction the view that the Constitution, while solicitous of the cognitive content of individual speech, has little or no regard for that emotive function which, practically speaking, may often be the more important element of the overall message sought to be communicated. . . .

Finally, and in the same vein, we cannot indulge the facile assumption that one can forbid particular words without also running a substantial risk of suppressing ideas in the process. Indeed, governments might soon seize upon the censorship of particular words as a convenient guise for banning the expression of unpopular views. We have been able . . . to discern little social benefit that might result from running the risk of opening the door to such grave results.

It is, in sum, our judgment that, absent a more particularized and compelling reason for its actions, the State may not, consistently with the First and Fourteenth Amendments, make the simple public display here involved of this single four-letter expletive a criminal offense. Because that is the only arguably sustainable rationale for the conviction here at issue, the judgment below must be

REVERSED.

JUSTICE BLACKMUN, DISSENTING . . .

Cohen's absurd and immature antic, in my view, was mainly conduct and little speech. . . . The California Court of Appeal appears so to have described it, . . . and I cannot characterize it otherwise. Further, the case appears to me to be well within the sphere of *Chaplinsky* v. *New Hampshire* [1942], where Justice Murphy, a known champion of First Amendment freedoms, wrote for a unanimous bench. As a consequence, this Court's agonizing over First Amendment values seem misplaced and unnecessary.

37

NEW YORK TIMES CO. V. UNITED STATES
403 U.S. 713 (1971)

On June 13, 1971, the *New York Times* began publishing excerpts from a classified Defense Department study of U.S. involvement in Indochina known as the "Pentagon Papers." When the *Times* ignored a Justice Department request to stop, the Attorney General won a lower court order temporarily restraining publication. By June 19, the *Washington Post*, which also had begun to publish the papers, found itself under a restraining order as well. With the government pressing for permanent restraints and the newspapers resisting on free press grounds, the cases quickly came to the Supreme Court. The justices heard argument on June 26, and four days later the Court held against the government by a vote of 6 to 3.

New York Times Co. v. *United States* was a prior-restraint case, and it concerned the first effort ever by the Justice Department to block publication of a news story. In a brief *per curiam* opinion, the Court said it agreed with the lower courts that the government had not met the "heavy" burden of showing why restraint was justified. The Court's opinion did not explain what this showing would have to be, or suggest whether the newspapers could be prosecuted or sanctioned subsequent to publication. But there was no lack of individual opinion on such matters: the case generated no fewer than nine additional opinions, including three dissents.

Though unimportant doctrinally, *New York Times Co.* v. *United States* had enormous political significance. The decision protected the press in its effort to penetrate government secrecy. It also lent credence to the idea of the press as the people's "watchdog" against official wrongdoing. Together with *New York Times Co.* v. *Sullivan* (1964), the decision ensured a more powerful role for the media in public life.

Opinion of the Court (*per curiam*): Black, Douglas, Brennan, Stewart, White, Marshall. Concurring opinions: **Black,** Douglas; **Douglas,** Black; **Brennan**; **Stewart**, White; **White**, Stewart; **Marshall.** Dissenting opinions: **Burger**; **Harlan**, Burger, Blackmun; **Blackmun**.

New York Times Co. v. *United States* was decided on June 30, 1971.

OPINIONS

PER CURIAM . . .

We granted certiorari in these cases in which the United States seeks to enjoin the *New York Times* and the *Washington Post* from publishing the contents of a classified study entitled "History of U.S. Decision-Making Process on Viet Nam Policy."

"Any system of prior restraints of expression comes to this Court bearing a heavy presumption against its constitutional validity." *Bantam Books, Inc.* v. *Sullivan* [1963]; see also *Near* v. *Minnesota* [1931]. The Government "thus carries a heavy burden of showing justification for the imposition of such a restraint." *Organization for a Better Austin* v. *Keefe* [1971]. The District Court for the Southern District of New York in the *New York Times* case and the District Court for the District of Columbia and the Court of Appeals for the District of Columbia Circuit in the *Washington Post* case held that the Government had not met that burden. We agree.

The judgment of the Court of Appeals for the District of Columbia Circuit is therefore affirmed. The order of the Court of Appeals for the Second Circuit is reversed, and the case is remanded with directions to enter a judgment affirming the judgment of the District Court for the Southern District of New York. The stays entered June 25, 1971, by the Court are vacated. The judgments shall issue forthwith.

JUSTICE BLACK, CONCURRING . . .

I adhere to the view that the Government's case against the *Washington Post* should have been dismissed and that the injunction against the *New York Times* should have been vacated without oral argument when the cases were first presented to this Court. I believe that every moment's continuance of the injunctions against these newspapers amounts to a flagrant, indefensible, and continuing violation of the First Amendment. . . .

In the First Amendment the Founding Fathers gave the free press the protection it must have to fulfill its essential role in our democracy. The press was to serve the governed, not the governors. The Government's power to censor the press was abolished so that the press would remain forever free to censure the Government. The press was protected so that it could bare the secrets of government and inform the people. Only a free and unrestrained press can effectively expose deception in government. And paramount among the responsibilities of a free press is the duty to prevent any part of the government from deceiving the people and sending them off to distant lands to die of foreign fevers and foreign shot and shell. In my view, far from deserving condemnation for their courageous reporting, the *New York Times*, the *Washington Post*, and other newspapers should be commended for serving the purpose that the Founding Fathers saw so clearly. In revealing the workings of government that led to the Vietnam war, the newspapers nobly did precisely that which the Founders hoped and trusted they would do. . . .

. . . [W]e are asked to hold that despite the First Amendment's emphatic command, the Executive Branch, the Congress, and the Judiciary can make laws enjoining publication of current news and abridging freedom of the press in the name of "national security." The Government does not even attempt to rely on any act of Congress. Instead it makes the bold and dangerously far-reaching contention that the courts should take it upon themselves to "make" a law abridging freedom of the press in the name of equity, presidential power, and national security, even when the representatives of the people in Congress have adhered to the command of the First Amendment and refused to make such a law. To find that the President has "inherent power" to halt the publication of news by resort to the courts would wipe out the First Amendment and destroy the fundamental liberty and security of the very people the Government hopes to make "secure." No one can read the history of the adoption of the First Amendment without being convinced beyond any doubt that it was injunctions like those sought here that Madison and his collaborators intended to outlaw in this Nation for all time.

The word "security" is a broad, vague generality whose contours should not be invoked to abrogate the fundamental law embodied in the First Amendment. The guarding of military and diplomatic secrets at the expense of informed representative government provides no real security for our Republic. The Framers of the First Amendment, fully aware of both the need to defend a new nation and the abuses of the English and Colonial governments, sought to give this new society strength and security by providing that freedom of speech, press, religion, and assembly should not be abridged. . . .

JUSTICE BRENNAN, CONCURRING . . .

I write separately in these cases only to emphasize what should be apparent: that our judgments in the present cases may not be taken to indicate the propriety, in the future, of issuing temporary stays and restraining orders to block the publication of material sought to be suppressed by the Government. So far as I can determine, never before has the United States sought to enjoin a newspaper from publishing information in its possession. The relative novelty of the questions presented, the necessary haste with which decisions were reached, the magnitude of the interests asserted, and the fact that all the parties have concentrated their arguments upon the question whether permanent restraints were proper may have justified at least some of the restraints heretofore imposed in these cases. Certainly it is difficult to fault the several courts below for seeking to assure that the issues here involved were preserved for ultimate review by this Court. But even if it be assumed that some of the interim restraints were proper in the two cases before us, that assumption has no bearing upon the propriety of similar judicial action in the future. To begin with, there has now been ample time for reflection and judgment; whatever values there may be in the preservation of novel questions for appellate review may not support any restraints in the future. More important, the First Amendment stands as an absolute bar to the imposition of judicial restraints in circumstances of the kind presented by these cases.

The error that has pervaded these cases from the outset was the granting of any injunctive relief whatsoever, interim or otherwise. The entire thrust of the Government's claim throughout these cases has been that publication of the material sought to be enjoined "could," or "might," or "may" prejudice the national interest in various ways. But the First Amendment tolerates absolutely no prior judicial restraints of the press predicated upon surmise or conjecture that untoward consequences may result. Our cases, it is true, have indicated that there is a single, extremely narrow class of cases in which the First Amendment's ban on prior judicial restraint may be overridden. Our cases have thus far indicated that such cases may arise only when the Nation "is at war," *Schenck* v. *United States* [1919], during which times "[n]o one would question but that a government might prevent actual obstruction to its recruiting service or the publication of the sailing dates of transports or the number and location of troops." *Near* v. *Minnesota* [1931]. Even if the present world situation were assumed to be tantamount to a time of war, or if the power of presently available armaments would justify even in peacetime the suppression of information that would set in motion a nuclear holocaust, in neither of these actions has the Government presented or even alleged that publication of items from or based upon the material at issue would cause the happening of an event of that nature. . . . Thus, only governmental allegation and proof that publication must inevitably, directly, and immediately cause the occurrence of an event kindred to imperiling the safety of a transport already at sea can support even the issuance of an interim restraining order. In no event may mere conclusions be sufficient: for if the Executive Branch seeks judicial aid in preventing publication, it must inevitably submit the basis upon which that aid is sought to scrutiny by the judiciary. And therefore, every restraint issued in this case, whatever its form, has violated the First Amendment—and not less so because that restraint was justified as necessary to afford the courts an opportunity to examine the claim more thoroughly. Unless and until the Government has clearly made out its case, the First Amendment commands that no injunction may issue.

JUSTICE STEWART, CONCURRING . . .

In the absence of the governmental checks and balances present in other areas of our national life, the only effective restraint upon executive policy and power in the areas of national defense and international affairs may lie in an enlightened citizenry—in an informed and critical public opinion which alone can here protect the values of democratic government. For this reason, it is perhaps here that a press that is alert, aware, and free most vitally serves the basic purpose of the First Amendment. For without an informed and free press there cannot be an enlightened people.

Yet it is elementary that the successful conduct of international diplomacy and the maintenance of an effective national defense require both confidentiality and secrecy. Other nations can hardly deal with this Nation in an atmosphere of mutual trust unless they can be assured that their confidences will be kept. And within our own executive departments, the development of considered and intelligent international policies would be impossible if those charged with their formulation could not communicate with each other freely, frankly, and in confidence. In the area of basic national defense the frequent need for absolute secrecy is, of course, self-evident.

I think there can be but one answer to this dilemma, if dilemma it be. The responsibility must be where the power is. If the Constitution gives the Executive a large degree of unshared power in the conduct of foreign affairs and the maintenance of our national defense, then under the Constitution the Executive must have the largely unshared duty to determine and preserve the degree of internal security necessary to exercise that power successfully. It is an awesome responsibility, requiring judgment and wisdom of a high order. I should suppose that moral, political, and practical considerations would dictate that a very first principle of that wisdom would be an insistence upon avoiding secrecy for its own sake. For when everything is classified, then nothing is classified, and the system becomes one to be disregarded by the cynical or the careless, and to be manipulated by those intent on self-protection or self-promotion. I should suppose, in short, that the hallmark of a truly effective internal security system would be the maximum possible disclosure, recognizing that secrecy can best be preserved only when credibility is truly maintained. But be that as it may, it is clear to me that it is the constitutional duty of the Executive—as a matter of sovereign prerogative and not as a matter of law as the courts know law—through the promulgation and enforcement of executive regulations, to protect the confidentiality necessary to carry out its responsibilities in the fields of international relations and national defense.

This is not to say that Congress and the courts have no role to play. Undoubtedly Congress has the power to enact specific and appropriate criminal laws to protect government property and preserve government secrets. Congress has passed such laws, and several of them are of very colorable relevance to the apparent circumstances of these cases. And if a criminal prosecution is instituted, it will be the responsibility of the courts to decide the applicability of the criminal law under which the charge is brought. . . .

But in the cases before us we are asked neither to construe specific regulations nor to apply specific laws. We are asked, instead, to perform a function that the Constitution gave to the Executive, not the Judiciary. We are asked, quite simply, to prevent the publication by two newspapers of material that the Executive Branch insists should not, in the national interest, be published. I am convinced that the Executive is correct with respect to some of the documents involved. But I cannot say that disclosure of any of them will surely result in direct, immediate, and irreparable damage to our Nation or its people. That being so, there can under the First Amendment be but one judicial resolution of the issues before us. I join the judgments of the Court.

JUSTICE WHITE, CONCURRING . . .

The Government's position is simply stated: The responsibility of the Executive for the conduct of the foreign affairs and for the security of the Nation is so basic that the President is entitled to an injunction against publication of a newspaper story whenever he can convince a court that the information to be revealed threatens "grave and irreparable" injury to the public interest; and the injunction should issue whether or not the material to be published is classified, whether or not publication would be lawful under relevant criminal statutes enacted by Congress, and regardless of the circumstances by which the newspaper came into possession of the information.

At least in the absence of legislation by Congress, based on its own investigations and findings, I am quite unable to agree that the inherent powers of the Executive and the courts reach so far as to authorize remedies having such sweeping potential for inhibiting publications by the press. . . .

. . . [T]erminating the ban on publication of the relatively few sensitive documents the Government now seeks to suppress does not mean that the law either requires or invites newspapers or others to publish them or that they will be immune from criminal action if they do. Prior restraints require an unusually heavy justification under the First Amendment; but failure by the Government to justify prior restraints does not measure its constitutional entitlement to a conviction for criminal publication. That the Government mistakenly chose to proceed by injunction does not mean that it could not successfully proceed in another way. . . .

. . . Congress has addressed itself to the problems of protecting the security of the country and the national defense from unauthorized disclosure of potentially damaging information. . . . It has not, however, authorized the injunctive remedy against threatened publication. It has apparently been satisfied to rely on criminal sanctions and their deterrent effect on the responsible as well as the irresponsible press. . . .

CHIEF JUSTICE BURGER, DISSENTING . . .

. . . In these cases, the imperative of a free and unfettered press comes into collision with another imperative, the effective functioning of a complex modern government and specifically the effective exercise of certain constitutional powers of the Executive. Only those who view the First Amendment as an absolute in all circumstances—a view I respect, but reject—can find such cases as these to be simple or easy.

These cases are not simple for another and more immediate reason. We do not know the facts of the cases. No District Judge knew all the facts. No Court of Appeals judge knew all the facts. No member of this Court knows all the facts.

Why are we in this posture, in which only those judges to whom the First Amendment is absolute and permits of no restraint in any circumstances or for any reason, are really in a position to act?

I suggest we are in this posture because these cases have been conducted in unseemly haste. . . . The prompt setting of these cases reflects our universal abhorrence of prior restraint. But prompt judicial action does not mean unjudicial haste.

Here, moreover, the frenetic haste is due in large part to the manner in which the *Times* proceeded from the date it obtained the purloined documents. It seems reasonably clear now that the haste precluded reasonable and deliberate judicial treatment of these cases and was not warranted. The precipitate action of this Court aborting trials not yet completed is not the kind of judicial conduct that ought to attend the disposition of a great issue.

The newspapers make a derivative claim under the First Amendment; they denominate this right as the public "right to know"; by implication, the *Times* asserts a sole trusteeship of that right by virtue of its journalistic "scoop." The right is asserted as an absolute. Of course, the First Amendment right itself is not an absolute, as Justice Holmes so long ago pointed out in his aphorism concerning the right to shout "fire" in a crowded theater if there was no fire. . . . An issue of this importance should be tried and heard in a judicial atmosphere conducive to thoughtful, reflective deliberation, especially when haste, in terms of hours, is unwarranted in light of the long period the *Times*, by its own choice, deferred publication.

It is not disputed that the *Times* has had unauthorized possession of the documents for three to four months, during which it has had its expert analysts studying them, presumably digesting them and preparing the material for publication. During all of this time, the *Times*, presumably in its capacity as trustee of the public's "right to know," has held up publication for purposes it considered proper, and thus public knowledge was delayed. No doubt this was for a good reason; the analysis of 7,000 pages of complex material drawn from a vastly greater volume of material would inevitably take time, and the writing of good news stories takes time. But why should the United States Government, from whom this information was illegally acquired by someone, along with all the counsel, trial judges, and appellate judges, be placed under needless pressure? After these months of deferral, the alleged "right to know" has somehow and suddenly become a right that must be vindicated instanter.

Would it have been unreasonable, since the newspaper could anticipate the Government's objections to release of secret material, to give the Government an opportunity to review the entire collection and determine whether agreement could be reached on publication? Stolen or not, if security was not in fact jeopardized, much of the material could no doubt have been declassified, since it spans a period ending in 1968. With such an approach—one that great newspapers have in the past practiced and stated editorially to be the duty of an honorable press—the newspapers and Government might well have narrowed the area of disagreement as to what was and was not publishable, leaving the remainder to be resolved in orderly litigation, if necessary. To me it is hardly believable that a newspaper long regarded as a great institution in American life would fail to perform one of the basic and simple duties of every citizen with respect to the discovery or possession of stolen property or secret government documents. That duty, I had thought—perhaps naïvely—was to report forthwith, to responsible public officers. This duty rests on taxi drivers, Justices, and the *New York Times*. The course followed by the *Times*, whether so calculated or not, removed any possibility of orderly litigation of the issues. If the action of the judges up to now has been correct, that result is sheer happenstance. . . .

We all crave speedier judicial processes, but when judges are pressured as in these cases, the result is a parody of the judicial function.

JUSTICE HARLAN, WITH WHOM CHIEF JUSTICE BURGER AND JUSTICE BLACKMUN JOIN, DISSENTING . . .

Forced as I am to reach the merits of these cases, I dissent from the opinion and judgments of the Court. Within the severe limitations imposed by the time constraints under which I have been required to operate, I can only state my reasons in telescoped form, even though in different circumstances I would have felt constrained to deal with the cases in the fuller sweep indicated above [in paragraphs omitted here suggesting seven questions].

It is a sufficient basis for affirming the Court of Appeals for the Second Circuit in the *Times* litigation to observe that its order must rest on the conclusion that because of the time elements the Government had not been given an adequate opportunity to present its case to the District Court. At the least this conclusion was not an abuse of discretion.

In the *Post* litigation the Government had more time to prepare; this was apparently the basis for the refusal of the Court of Appeals for the District of Columbia Circuit on rehearing to conform its judgment to that of the Second Circuit. But I think there is another and more fundamental reason why this judgment cannot stand—a reason which also furnishes an additional ground for not reinstating the judgment of the District Court in the *Times* litigation, set aside by the Court of Appeals. It is plain to me that the scope of the judicial function in passing upon the activities of the Executive Branch of the Government in the field of foreign affairs is very narrowly restricted. This view is, I think, dictated by the concept of separation of powers upon which our constitutional system rests.

In a speech on the floor of the House of Representatives, Chief Justice John Marshall, then a member of that body, stated: "The President is the sole organ of the nation in its external relations, and its sole representative with foreign nations.". . .

From that time, shortly after the founding of the Nation, to this, there has been no substantial challenge to this description of the scope of executive power. . . .

From this constitutional primacy in the field of foreign affairs, it seems to me that certain conclusions necessarily follow. Some of these were stated concisely by President Washington, declining the request of the House of Representatives for the papers leading up to the negotiation of the Jay Treaty:

> The nature of foreign negotiations requires caution, and their success must often depend on secrecy; and even when brought to a conclusion a full disclosure of all the measures, demands, or eventual concessions which may have been proposed or contemplated would be extremely impolitic; for this might have a pernicious influence on future negotiations, or produce immediate inconveniences, perhaps danger and mischief, in relation to other powers. . . .

The power to evaluate the "pernicious influence" of premature disclosure is not, however, lodged in the Executive alone. I agree that, in performance of its duty to protect the values of the First Amendment against political pressures, the judiciary must review the initial Executive determination to the point of satisfying itself that the subject matter of the dispute does lie within the proper compass of the President's foreign relations power. Constitutional considerations forbid "a complete abandonment of judicial control." Cf. *United States* v. *Reynolds* [1953]. Moreover, the judiciary may properly insist that the determination that disclosure of the subject matter would irreparably impair the national security be made by the head of the Executive Department concerned—here the Secretary of State or the Secretary of Defense—after actual personal consideration by that officer. This safeguard is required in the analogous area of executive claims of privilege for secrets of state. . . .

But in my judgment the judiciary may not properly go beyond these two inquiries and redetermine for itself the probable impact of disclosure on the national security.

Even if there is some room for the judiciary to override the executive determination, it is plain that the scope of review must be exceedingly narrow. I can see no indication in the opinions of either the District Court or the Court of Appeals in the *Post* litigation that the conclusions of the Executive were given even the deference owing to an administrative agency, much less that owing to a co-equal branch of the Government operating within the field of its constitutional prerogative.

Accordingly, I would vacate the judgment of the Court of Appeals for the District of Columbia Circuit on this ground and remand the case for further proceedings in the District Court. Before the commencement of such further proceedings, due opportunity should be afforded the Government for procuring from the Secretary of State or the Secretary of Defense or both an expression of their views on the issue of national security. The ensuing review by the District Court should be in accordance with the views expressed in this opinion. And for the reasons stated above I would affirm the judgment of the Court of Appeals for the Second Circuit.

Pending further hearings in each case conducted under the appropriate ground rules, I would continue the restraints on publication. I cannot believe that the doctrine prohibiting prior restraints reaches to the point of preventing courts from maintaining the status quo long enough to act responsibly in matters of such national importance as those involved here.

RESPONSES

FROM THE *NEW YORK TIMES*, JULY 1, 1971, "AN ENLIGHTENED PEOPLE"

The historic decision of the Supreme Court in the case of the United States Government vs. the *New York Times* and the *Washington Post* is a ringing victory for freedom under law. By lifting the restraining order that had prevented this and other newspapers from publishing the hitherto secret Pentagon Papers, the nation's highest tribunal strongly reaffirmed the guarantee of the people's right to know, implicit in the First Amendment to the Constitution of the United States.

This was the essence of what the *New York Times* and other newspapers were fighting for, and this is the essence of the Court's majority opinions. The basic question, which goes to the very core of the American political system, involved the weighing by the Court of the First Amendment's guarantee of freedom against the Government's power to restrict that freedom in the name of national security. The Supreme Court did not hold that the First Amendment gave an absolute right to publish anything under all circumstances. Nor did the *Times* seek that right. What the *Times* sought, and what the Court upheld, was the right to publish these particular documents at this particular time without prior Government restraint.

The crux of the problem lay indeed in this question of prior restraint. For the first time in the history of the United States, the Federal Government had sought through the courts to prevent publication of material that it maintained would do "irreparable injury" to the national security if spread before the public. The *Times*, supported in this instance by the overwhelming majority of the American press, held on the contrary that it was in the national interest to publish this information, which was of historic rather than current operational nature.

If the documents had involved troop movements, ship sailings, imminent military plans, the case might have been quite different; and in fact the *Times* would not have endeavored to publish such material. But this was not the case; the documents and accompanying analysis are historic, in no instance going beyond 1968 and incapable in 1971 of harming the life of a single human being or interfering with any current military operation. The majority of the Court clearly recognized that embarrassment of public officials in the past—or even in the present—is insufficient reason to overturn what Justice White described as the "concededly extraordinary protection against prior restraint under our constitutional system."

So far as the Government's classification of the material is concerned, it is quite true, as some of our critics have observed, that "no one elected the *Times*" to declassify it. But it is also true, as the Court implicitly recognizes, that the public interest is not served by classification and retention in secret form of vast amounts of information, 99.5 percent of which a retired senior civil servant recently testified "could not be prejudicial to the defense interests of the nation."

Out of this case should surely come a total revision of governmental procedures and practice in the entire area of classification of documents. Everyone who has ever had anything to do with such documents knows that for many years the classification procedures have been hopelessly muddled by inertia, timidity, and sometimes even stupidity and venality.

Beyond all this, one may hope that the entire exercise will induce the present Administration to re-examine its own attitudes toward secrecy, suppression, and restriction of the liberties of free man in a free society. The issue the Supreme Court decided yesterday touched the heart of this republic; and we fully realize that this is not so much a victory for any particular newspaper as it is for the basic principles on which the American form of government rests. This is really the profound message of yesterday's decision, in which this newspaper rejoices with humility and with the consciousness that the freedom thus reaffirmed carries with it, as always, the reciprocal obligation to present the truth to the American public so far as it can be determined. That is, in fact, why the Pentagon materials had to be published. It is only with the fullest possible understanding of the facts and of the background of any policy decision that the American people can be expected to play the role required of them in this democracy.

It would be well for the present Administration, in the light of yesterday's decision, to reconsider with far more care and understanding than it has in the past, the fundamental importance of individual freedoms—including especially freedom of speech, of the press, of assembly—to the life of the American democracy. "Without an informed and free press," as Justice Stewart said, "there cannot be an enlightened people."

FROM THE *EVENING STAR*, WASHINGTON, D.C., JULY 1, 1971, "THE COURT AND THE PRESS"

Yesterday's Supreme Court ruling denying the government's attempt to prevent the publication of the Pentagon Papers has been hailed by much of the press as a landmark decision. Such a reaction, following two weeks of suspense, is understandable. It is, however, somewhat inaccurate.

The court established no important legal precedent. It enunciated no novel interpretation of the Constitution. It initiated no abrupt change in the relationship between the government and the press. But the 6-to-3 ruling did accomplish something of equal importance. It rejected the landmark ruling sought by the government. It declined the opportunity to limit the constitutional guarantee of a free press. It did not give the executive branch a right to restrain the publication of any material it determines on its own authority to be detrimental to national security.

The ruling did not, conversely, break new ground by dismissing the possibility of prior restraint under any circumstances. Two of the Justices—Douglas and Black—in their individual opinions hold the view that the First Amendment is absolute. But the majority, including the three dissenters, stuck with the precedent established by three prior Supreme Court decisions. The First Amendment, according to these previous interpretations, is presumed to bar prior restraint of publication. But it is recognized that, under extreme circumstances of clear and immediate danger to the survival of the nation or its citizens, the right to publish may be abridged. The government's bid for such restraint will still, as a result of yesterday's ruling, come to the court "bearing a heavy presumption against its constitutional validity.". . .

The press . . . should see the decision as something more than a cause for celebration. The reaffirmation of the right to publish free of interference is an occasion for sober reconsideration of the responsibility that goes with that right. And it should be noted, too, that the concept of press responsibility is no more abstract than that of press freedom.

Five of the justices in their separate opinions yesterday specifically mentioned the possibility of criminal prosecution, and Justice White came close to inviting the government to bring criminal charges in the present case. That statement of the potential consequences of publication, gratuitously included in the opinions of a majority of the present court, should serve to reassure the public and the government—and to remind the press—that freedom and irresponsibility are quite separate items.

38

BRANZBURG V. HAYES

408 U.S. 665 (1972)

In *Branzburg* the Supreme Court reviewed three cases in which journalists had refused to testify before grand juries. Paul Branzburg of the *Louisville Courier-Journal* declined to tell a Kentucky grand jury the names of persons he had written about who were involved in making or using illegal drugs. Television journalist Paul Pappas refused to answer a Massachusetts grand jury's questions about what had taken place inside Black Panther headquarters in New Bedford during his visit there. And Earl Caldwell, a *New York Times* reporter who had extensively covered the Black Panthers, declined to appear before a federal grand jury investigating their activities.

Each of these cases involved the confidentiality of the news-gathering process, and the argument pressed by Branzburg, Pappas, and Caldwell was that under the First Amendment they could not be compelled to violate such confidentiality in grand-jury testimony. This argument was rejected by the state courts in the *Branzburg* and *Pappas* cases. In *Caldwell*, the U.S. Court of Appeals for the Ninth Circuit reversed a contempt order against the journalist and found that the First Amendment extends to journalists a qualified right to refuse to testify. Considering the three cases together, the U.S. Supreme Court by a vote of 5 to 4 disagreed with the Ninth Circuit and ruled that the First Amendment does *not* include a testimonial privilege for journalists. "We see no reason to hold," wrote Justice White for the Court, "that these reporters, any more than other citizens, should be excused from furnishing information that may help the grand jury in arriving at its initial determinations."

Branzburg was a case of first impression: never before had the Court been asked to decide whether the First Amendment contains a testimonial privilege for reporters. The majority that held against such a privilege was not a firm one, since one of its five members, Justice Powell, filed a concurring opinion endorsing a qualified privilege. Inasmuch as the four justices in dissent also argued for a qualified privilege, lower courts have often construed *Branzburg* as in fact recognizing such a privilege.

Branzburg explicitly acknowledged the role of the states and Congress in creating by statute a reporter's privilege. More than two dozen states now have some type of journalists' "shield law," as it is called. There is no such federal law.

Opinion of the Court: **White**, Burger, Blackmun, Powell, Rehnquist. Concurring opinion: **Powell**. Dissenting opinions: **Douglas**; **Stewart**, Brennan, Marshall.

Branzburg v. *Hayes* was decided on June 29, 1972.

OPINIONS

JUSTICE WHITE DELIVERED THE OPINION OF THE COURT . . .

The issue in these cases is whether requiring newsmen to appear and testify before state or federal grand juries abridges the freedom of speech and press guaranteed by the First Amendment. We hold that it does not. . . .

Petitioners Branzburg and Pappas and respondent Caldwell press First Amendment claims that may be simply put: that to gather news it is often necessary to agree either not to identify the source of information published or to publish only part of the facts revealed, or both; that if the reporter is nevertheless forced to reveal these confidences to a grand jury, the source so identified and other confidential sources of other reporters will be measurably deterred from furnishing publishable information, all to the detriment of the free flow of information protected by the First Amendment. Although the newsmen in these cases do not claim an absolute privilege against official interrogation in all circumstances, they assert that the reporter should not be forced either to appear or to testify before a grand jury or at trial until and unless sufficient grounds are shown for believing that the reporter possesses information relevant to a crime the grand jury is investigating, that the information the reporter has is unavailable from other sources, and that the need for the information is sufficiently compelling to override the claimed invasion of First Amendment interests occasioned by the disclosure. . . . The heart of the claim is that the burden on news gathering resulting from compelling reporters to disclose confidential information outweighs any public interest in obtaining the information.

We do not question the significance of free speech, press, or assembly to the country's welfare. Nor is it suggested that news gathering does not qualify for First Amendment protection; without some protection for seeking out the news, freedom of the press could be eviscerated. But these cases involve no intrusions upon speech or assembly, no prior restraint or restriction on what the press may publish, and no express or implied command that the press publish what it prefers to withhold. No exaction or tax for the privilege of publishing, and no penalty, civil or criminal, related to the content of published material is at issue here. The use of confidential sources by the press is not forbidden or restricted; reporters remain free to seek news from any source by means within the law. No attempt is made to require the press to publish its sources of information or indiscriminately to disclose them on request.

The sole issue before us is the obligation of reporters to respond to grand jury subpoenas as other citizens do and to answer questions relevant to an investigation into the commission of crime. Citizens generally are not constitutionally immune from grand jury subpoenas; and neither the First Amendment nor any other constitutional provision protects the average citizen from disclosing to a grand jury information that he has received in confidence. The claim is, however, that reporters are exempt from these obligations because if forced to respond to subpoenas and identify their sources or disclose other confidences, their informants will refuse or be reluctant to furnish newsworthy information in the future. This asserted burden on news gathering is said to make compelled testimony from newsmen constitutionally suspect and to require a privileged position for them.

It is clear that the First Amendment does not invalidate every incidental burdening of the press that may result from the enforcement of civil or criminal statutes of general applicability. . . .

It has generally been held that the First Amendment does not guarantee the press a constitutional right of special access to information not available to the public generally. . . .

Despite the fact that news gathering may be hampered, the press is regularly excluded from grand jury proceedings, our own conferences, the meetings of other official bodies gathered in executive session, and the meetings of private organizations. Newsmen have no constitutional right of access to the scenes of crime or disaster when the general public is excluded, and they may be prohibited from attending or publishing information about trials if such restrictions are necessary to assure a defendant a fair trial before an impartial tribunal. . . .

It is thus not surprising that the great weight of authority is that newsmen are not exempt from the normal duty of appearing before a grand jury and answering questions relevant to a criminal investigation. . . .

A number of States have provided newsmen a statutory privilege of varying breadth, but the majority have not done so, and none has been provided by federal statute. Until now the only testimonial privilege for unofficial witnesses that is rooted in the Federal Constitution is the Fifth Amendment privilege against compelled self-incrimination. We are asked to create another by interpreting the First Amendment to grant newsmen a testimonial privilege that other citizens do not enjoy. This we decline to do. Fair and effective law enforcement aimed at providing security for the person and property of the individual is a fundamental function of government, and the grand jury plays an important, constitutionally mandated role in this process. On the records now before us, we perceive no basis for holding that the public interest in law enforcement and in ensuring effective grand jury proceedings is insufficient to override the consequential, but uncertain, burden on news gathering that is said to result from insisting that reporters, like other citizens, respond to relevant questions put to them in the course of a valid grand jury investigation or criminal trial.

This conclusion itself involves no restraint on what newspapers may publish or on the type or quality of information reporters may seek to acquire, nor does it threaten the vast bulk of confidential relationships between reporters and their sources. Grand juries address themselves to the issues of whether crimes have been committed and who committed them. Only where news sources themselves are implicated in crime or possess information relevant to the grand jury's task need they or the reporter be concerned about grand jury subpoenas. Nothing before us indicates that a large number or percentage of all confidential news sources falls into either category and would in any way be deterred by our holding that the Constitution does not, as it never has, exempt the newsman from performing the citizen's normal duty of appearing and furnishing information relevant to the grand jury's task. . . .

The argument that the flow of news will be diminished by compelling reporters to aid the grand jury in a criminal investigation is not irrational, nor are the records before us silent on the matter. But we remain unclear how often and to what extent informers are actually deterred from furnishing information when newsmen are forced to testify before a grand jury. The available data indicate that some newsmen rely a great deal on confidential sources and that some informants are particularly sensitive to the threat of exposure and may be silenced if it is held by this Court that, ordinarily, newsmen must testify pursuant to subpoenas, but the evidence fails to demonstrate that there would be a significant constriction of the flow of news to the public if this Court reaffirms the prior common-law and constitutional rule regarding the testimonial obligations of newsmen. Estimates of the inhibiting effect of such subpoenas on the willingness of informants to make disclosures to newsmen are widely divergent and to a great extent speculative. It would be difficult to canvass the views of the informants themselves; surveys of reporters on this topic are chiefly opinions of predicted informant behavior and must be viewed in the light of the professional self-interest of the interviewees. . . .

We are admonished that refusal to provide a First Amendment reporter's privilege will undermine the freedom of the press to collect and disseminate news. But this is not the lesson history teaches us. . . . [T]he common law recognized no such privilege, and the constitutional argument was not even asserted until 1958. From the beginning of our country the press has operated without constitutional protection for press informants, and the press has flourished. The existing constitutional rules have not been a serious obstacle to either the development or retention of confidential news sources by the press.

It is said that currently press subpoenas have multiplied, that mutual distrust and tension between press and officialdom have increased, that reporting styles have changed, and that there is now more need for confidential sources, particularly where the press seeks news about minority cultural and political groups or dissident organizations suspicious of the law and public officials. These developments, even if true, are treacherous grounds for a far-reaching interpretation of the First Amendment fastening a nationwide rule on courts, grand juries, and prosecuting officials everywhere. . . .

The argument for such a constitutional privilege rests heavily on those cases holding that the infringement of protected First Amendment rights must be no broader than necessary to achieve a permissible governmental purpose. . . . [The opinion refers here to an earlier footnote citing *Freedman* v. *Maryland* (1965) and three other cases.]

The requirements of those cases [the opinion refers here to an earlier footnote citing *NAACP* v. *Button* (1963) and five other cases] . . . that a State's interest must be "compelling" or "paramount" to justify even an indirect burden on First Amendment rights, are met here. . . .

Similar considerations dispose of the reporters' claims that preliminary to requiring their grand jury appearance, the State must show that a crime has been committed and that they possess relevant information not available from other sources, for only the grand jury itself can make this determination. The role of the grand jury as an important instrument of effective law enforcement necessarily includes an investigatory function with respect to determining whether a crime has been committed and who committed it. To this end it must call witnesses, in the manner best suited to perform its task. . . .

We see no reason to hold that these reporters, any more than other citizens, should be excused from furnishing information that may help the grand jury in arriving at its initial determinations.

The privilege claimed here is conditional, not absolute; given the suggested preliminary showings and compelling need, the reporter would be required to testify. Presumably, such a rule would reduce the instances in which reporters could be required to appear, but predicting in advance when and in what circumstances they could be compelled to do so would be difficult. Such a rule would also have implications for the issuance of compulsory process to reporters at civil and criminal trials and at legislative hearings. If newsmen's confidential sources are as sensitive as they are claimed to be, the prospect of being unmasked whenever a judge determines the situation justifies it is hardly a satisfactory solution to the problem. For them, it would appear that only an absolute privilege would suffice.

We are unwilling to embark the judiciary on a long and difficult journey to such an uncertain destination. The administration of a constitutional newsman's privilege would present practical and conceptual difficulties of a high order. Sooner or later, it would be necessary to define those categories of newsmen who qualified for the privilege, a questionable procedure in light of the traditional doctrine that liberty of the press is the right of the lonely pamphleteer who uses carbon paper or a mimeograph just as much as of the large metropolitan publisher who utilizes the latest photocomposition methods. . . . Freedom of the press is a "fundamental personal right" which "is not confined to newspapers and periodicals. It necessarily embraces pamphlets and leaflets. . . . The press in its historic connotation comprehends every sort of publication which affords a vehicle of information and opinion." *Lovell* v. *Griffin* [1938]. . . . The informative function asserted by representatives of the organized press in the present cases is also performed by lecturers, political pollsters, novelists, academic researchers, and dramatists. Almost any author may quite accurately assert that he is contributing to the flow of information to the public, that he relies on confidential sources of information, and that these sources will be silenced if he is forced to make disclosures before a grand jury.

In each instance where a reporter is subpoenaed to testify, the courts would also be embroiled in preliminary factual and legal determinations with respect to whether the proper predicate had been laid for the reporter's appearance: Is there probable cause to believe a crime has been committed? Is it likely that the reporter has useful information gained in confidence? Could the grand jury obtain the information elsewhere? Is the official interest sufficient to outweigh the claimed privilege?

Thus, in the end, by considering whether enforcement of a particular law served a "compelling" governmental interest, the courts would be inextricably involved in distinguishing between the value of enforcing different criminal laws. By requiring testimony from a reporter in investigations involving some crimes but not in others, they would be making a value judgment that a legislature had declined to make, since in each case the criminal law involved would represent a considered legislative judgment, not constitutionally suspect, of what conduct is liable to criminal prosecution. The task of judges, like other officials outside the legislative branch, is not to make the law but to uphold it in accordance with their oaths.

At the federal level, Congress has freedom to determine whether a statutory newsman's privilege is necessary and desirable and to fashion standards and rules as narrow or broad as deemed necessary to deal with the evil discerned and, equally important, to refashion those rules as experience from time to time may dictate. There is also merit in leaving state legislatures free, within First Amendment limits, to fashion their own standards in light of the conditions and problems with respect to the relations between law enforcement officials and press in their own areas. . . .

In addition, there is much force in the pragmatic view that the press has at its disposal powerful mechanisms of communication and is far from helpless to protect itself from harassment or substantial harm. Furthermore, if what the newsmen urged in these cases is true—that law enforcement cannot hope to gain and may suffer from subpoenaing newsmen before grand juries—prosecutors will be loath to risk so much for so little. Thus, at the federal level the Attorney General has already fashioned a set of rules for federal officials in connection with subpoenaing members of the press to testify before grand juries or at criminal trials. These rules are a major step in the direction the reporters herein desire to move. They may prove wholly sufficient to resolve the bulk of disagreements and controversies between press and federal officials.

Finally, as we have earlier indicated, news gathering is not without its First Amendment protections, and grand jury investigations if instituted or conducted other than in good faith, would pose wholly different issues for resolution under the First Amendment. Official harassment of the press undertaken not for purposes of law enforcement but to disrupt a reporter's relationship with his news sources would have no justification. Grand juries are subject to judicial control and subpoenas to motions to quash. We do not expect courts will forget that grand juries must operate within the limits of the First Amendment as well as the Fifth. . . .

JUSTICE POWELL, CONCURRING . . .

I add this brief statement to emphasize what seems to me to be the limited nature of the Court's holding. The Court does not hold that newsmen, subpoenaed to testify before a grand jury, are without constitutional rights with respect to the gathering of news or in safeguarding their sources. Certainly, we do not hold, as suggested in Justice Stewart's dissenting opinion, that state and federal authorities are free to "annex" the news media as "an investigative arm of government." The solicitude repeatedly shown by this Court for First Amendment freedoms should be sufficient assurance against any such effort, even if one seriously believed that the media—properly free and untrammeled in the fullest sense of these terms—were not able to protect themselves.

As indicated in the concluding portion of the opinion, the Court states that no harassment of newsmen will be tolerated. If a newsman believes that the grand jury investigation is not being conducted in good faith he is not without remedy. Indeed, if the newsman is called upon to give information bearing only a remote and tenuous relationship to the subject of the investigation, or if he has some other reason to believe that his testimony implicates confidential source relationships without a legitimate need of law enforcement, he will have access to the court on a motion to quash and an appropriate protective order may be entered. The asserted claim to privilege should be judged on its facts by the striking of a proper balance between freedom of the press and the obligation of all citizens to give relevant testimony with respect to criminal conduct. The balance of these vital constitutional and societal interests on a case-by-case basis accords with the tried and traditional way of adjudicating such questions.

In short, the courts will be available to newsmen under circumstances where legitimate First Amendment interests require protection.

JUSTICE STEWART, DISSENTING . . .

The Court's crabbed view of the First Amendment reflects a disturbing insensitivity to the critical role of an independent press in our society. . . . [T]he Court in these cases holds that a newsman has no First Amendment right to protect his sources when called before a grand jury. The Court thus invites state and federal authorities to undermine the historic independence of the press by attempting to annex the journalistic profession as an investigative arm of government. Not only will this decision impair performance of the press' constitutionally protected functions, but it will, I am convinced, in the long run harm rather than help the administration of justice. . . .

The reporter's constitutional right to a confidential relationship with his source stems from the broad societal interest in a full and free flow of information to the public. It is this basic concern that underlies the Constitution's protection of a free press. . . .

Enlightened choice by an informed citizenry is the basic ideal upon which an open society is premised, and a free press is thus indispensable to a free society. Not only does the press enhance personal self-fulfillment by providing the people with the widest possible range of fact and opinion, but it also is an incontestable precondition of self-government. . . . As private and public aggregations of power burgeon in size and the pressures for conformity necessarily mount, there is obviously a continuing need for an independent press to disseminate a robust variety of information and opinion through reportage, investigation, and criticism, if we are to preserve our constitutional tradition of maximizing freedom of choice by encouraging diversity of expression.

In keeping with this tradition, we have held that the right to publish is central to the First Amendment and basic to the existence of constitutional democracy. . . .

A corollary of the right to publish must be the right to gather news. The full flow of information to the public protected by the free-press guarantee would be severely curtailed if no protection whatever were afforded to the process by which news is assembled and disseminated. . . .

No less important to the news dissemination process is the gathering of information. News must not be unnecessarily cut off at its source, for without freedom to acquire information the right to publish would be impermissibly compromised. Accordingly, a right to gather news, of some dimensions, must exist. . . .

The right to gather news implies, in turn, a right to a confidential relationship between a reporter and his source. This proposition follows as a matter of simple logic once three factual predicates are recognized: (1) newsmen require informants to gather news; (2) confidentiality—the promise or understanding that names or certain aspects of communications will be kept off the record—is essential to the creation and maintenance of a news-gathering relationship with informants; and (3) an unbridled subpoena power—the absence of a constitutional right protecting, in any way, a confidential relationship from compulsory process—will either deter sources from divulging information or deter reporters from gathering and publishing information.

It is obvious that informants are necessary to the news-gathering process as we know it today. If it is to perform its constitutional mission, the press must do far more than merely print public statements or publish prepared handouts. . . .

It is equally obvious that the promise of confidentiality may be a necessary prerequisite to a productive relationship between a newsman and his informants. An officeholder may fear his superior; a member of the bureaucracy, his associates; a dissident, the scorn of majority opinion. All may have information valuable to the public discourse, yet each may be willing to relate that information only in confidence to a reporter whom he trusts, either because of excessive caution or because of a reasonable fear of reprisals or censure for unorthodox views. The First Amendment concern must not be with the motives of any particular news source, but rather with the conditions in which informants of all shades of the spectrum may make information available through the press to the public. . . .

Finally, and most important, when governmental officials possess an unchecked power to compel newsmen to disclose information received in confidence, sources will clearly be deterred from giving information, and reporters will clearly be deterred from publishing it, because uncertainty about exercise of the power will lead to "self-censorship." The uncertainty arises, of course, because the judiciary has traditionally imposed virtually no limitations on the grand jury's broad investigatory powers. . . .

After today's decision, the potential informant can never be sure that his identity or off-the-record communications will not subsequently be revealed through the compelled testimony of a newsman. A public-spirited person inside government, who is not implicated in any crime, will now be fearful of revealing corruption or other governmental wrongdoing, because he will now know he can subsequently be identified by use of compulsory process. The potential source must, therefore, choose between risking exposure by giving information or avoiding the risk by remaining silent.

The reporter must speculate about whether contact with a controversial source or publication of controversial material will lead to a subpoena. In the event of a subpoena, under today's decision, the newsman will know that he must choose between being punished for contempt if he refuses to testify, or violating his profession's ethics and impairing his resourcefulness as a reporter if he discloses confidential information. . . .

Posed against the First Amendment's protection of the newsman's confidential relationships in these cases is society's interest in the use of the grand jury to administer justice fairly and effectively. . . .

Yet the longstanding rule making every person's evidence available to the grand jury is not absolute. The rule has been limited by the Fifth Amendment, the Fourth Amendment, and the evidentiary privileges of the common law. . . .

In striking the proper balance between the public interest in the efficient administration of justice and the First Amendment guarantee of the fullest flow of information, we must begin with the basic proposition that because of their "delicate and vulnerable" nature . . . and their transcendent importance for the just functioning of our society, First Amendment rights require special safeguards.

This Court has erected such safeguards when government, by legislative investigation or other investigative means, has attempted to pierce the shield of privacy inherent in freedom of association. . . .

Thus, when an investigation impinges on First Amendment rights, the government must not only show that the inquiry is of "compelling and overriding importance" but it must also "convincingly" demonstrate that the investigation is "substantially related" to the information sought. . . .

I believe the safeguards developed in our decisions involving governmental investigations must apply to the grand jury inquiries in these cases. . . .

Accordingly, when a reporter is asked to appear before a grand jury and reveal confidences, I would hold that the government must (1) show that there is probable cause to believe that the newsman has information that is clearly relevant to a specific probable violation of law; (2) demonstrate that the information sought cannot be obtained by alternative means less destructive of First Amendment rights; and (3) demonstrate a compelling and overriding interest in the information. . . .

RESPONSE

FROM THE *NEW YORK TIMES*, JULY 15, 1972, ". . . LOSS FOR THE PUBLIC"

In the cases involving three newsmen—including a reporter for the *New York Times*—who maintained their right to protect their sources of information, the Court's majority seemed oblivious of the chilling effect of its decision on the press's freedom to investigate, to expose, without fear of governmental sanctions. The decision is an assault on the public's right to know. By forcing newsmen to reveal their sources of information to a grand jury, the Court is in fact undermining the whole basis of the confidential relationship between a reporter and his sources, which is the only basis on which much information of vital importance to the public can ever be revealed.

It is the public, rather than the media or the reporters, that will be the principal victim of this amazingly constricted viewpoint of the Court. For it will be infinitely more difficult henceforth to obtain and publish information involving criminal matters that, perhaps for ulterior motives, governmental bodies may wish to conceal. . . .

The newsmen did not claim "an absolute privilege against official interrogation in all circumstances"—after all, newsmen do have the normal obligations of citizenship—but they did claim, and are now denied, protection against grand jury questioning except when there was special reason to believe that they possessed relevant information for which there was "compelling" need. In eighteen states including New York, reporters have this special and needed right to the privacy of communications; and Justice Powell's "enigmatic" opinion, concurring with the majority, specifically notes that newsmen do have constitutional rights "in safeguarding their sources," and that governmental authorities are not free to "annex" the news media as "an investigative arm of government."

Yet the purport of the prevailing opinion raises exactly this danger, especially insofar as two of the three cases themselves involved reportorial activities with such an unpopular and suspect group as the Black Panthers, and the third was concerned with the equally unpopular and generally suspect "drug culture." Obviously the decision opens a way to fishing expeditions on the part of grand juries and prosecuting attorneys, at the expense of a newsman's ability to maintain independent and confidential relationships with persons in possession of useful information who fear loss of jobs, harassment, or other reprisals if their identity is disclosed.

MILLER V. CALIFORNIA
413 U.S. 15 (1973)

PARIS ADULT THEATRE I V. SLATON
413 U.S. 49 (1973)

Defendant Miller used a mass mailing campaign to advertise books containing pictures and drawings of men and women in groups of two or more engaging in a variety of sexual activities, with genitals often prominently displayed. Miller was convicted of violating a California law prohibiting the mailing of unsolicited obscene materials. A state appeals court sustained the conviction.

In Georgia, meanwhile, law-enforcement authorities sued under Georgia civil law to enjoin the showing of allegedly obscene films by the two Paris Adult Theatres. The trial judge dismissed the complaints, finding the films obscene yet "constitutionally permissible." The Georgia Supreme Court reversed, holding that "the sale and delivery of obscene material to willing adults is not protected by the First Amendment."

Deciding *Miller* and *Paris Adult Theatre* together, the Supreme Court vacated the judgments in both and sent the cases back to the lower courts, with guidance as to how they should be reviewed. It is the guidance that the Court provided in these cases that makes them significant, for the Court finally clarified the mess that its obscenity standards had become in the sixteen years since it first directly addressed the subject in *Roth* v. *United States*. There, having affirmed the traditional view that obscenity lacks First Amendment protection, the Court for the first time set forth a test for identifying obscenity. Obscenity is "utterly without redeeming social importance," the *Roth* Court announced, and material is obscene if "to the average person, applying contemporary community standards, the dominant theme of the material taken as a whole appeals to prurient interest."

Later cases found the Court grappling with questions arising from this test—concerning the definition of "community," the determination of the community's standards, and the meaning of "prurient interest." In these cases no five justices were ever able to agree on standards for distinguishing obscene from non-obscene materials, and the Court usually voted to lift the restriction at issue. The most famous (or infamous) of these decisions came in 1966, when in *Memoirs of a Woman of Pleasure* v. *Massachusetts* the Court overturned the obscenity prosecution of *Fanny Hill*, which for several centuries had been routinely banned as pornographic. Regarding the book as having "some minimal literary value," the Court concluded that it was not utterly without redeeming social importance—that, in other words, it was not obscene.

As the Court moved in this more libertarian direction, it seemed by the late sixties that it might repudiate the distinction at the heart of its obscenity jurisprudence—that between "protected" and "unprotected" materials. But with the composition of the Court changing in the early 1970s, this was not to be. The Court split identically in *Miller* and *Paris Adult Theatre*, with the four new justices (Burger, Blackmun, Powell, and Rehnquist) joining Justice White to constitute the same majority of five in each case. These justices reaffirmed the basic holding of *Roth* that obscenity lacks First Amendment protection. In *Miller* they articulated new standards for identifying obscenity: material is obscene if "(a) the average person, applying contemporary community standards, would find that the work, taken as a whole, appeals to the prurient interest; (b) the work depicts or describes, in a patently offensive way, sexual conduct specifically defined by the applicable state law; and (c) the work, taken as a whole, lacks serious literary, artistic, political, or scientific value." In *Paris Adult Theatre* the five confirmed that obscenity regulations should be subjected to the deferential analysis the Court employs in cases not involving constitutional rights. Necessarily, this judgment rejected the contention that such regulations merited strict scrutiny.

Justice Douglas's dissent in *Miller* and Justice Brennan's dissent in *Paris Adult Theatre* revealed the split within the Court—and indeed the paths not taken. Justice Douglas argued that not the justices but the people, through a constitutional amendment, are the ones who must place restraints on obscenity, if there are to be any. And Justice Brennan, who had written the Court's opinion in *Roth*, argued that the imprecision of the Court's obscenity standards since *Roth* had created such a danger for First Amendment rights that the effort to distinguish between protected and unprotected materials must be abandoned. Brennan would have permitted government regulation of obscenity only in cases of distribution to juveniles or "obtrusive exposure to unconsenting adults."

Rejecting these more libertarian positions, *Miller* and *Paris Adult Theatre* emphasized the right of the people "to maintain a decent society." Yet the cases made clear that the people could exercise this right and be confident of success only against obscenity narrowly defined—as hard-core pornography. The record since *Miller* shows that only very explicit works have been declared obscene.

Miller. Opinion of the Court: **Burger**, White, Blackmun, Powell, Rehnquist. Dissenting opinions: **Douglas**; **Brennan**, Stewart, Marshall.

Paris Adult Theatre. Opinion of the Court: **Burger**, White, Blackmun, Powell, Rehnquist. Dissenting opinions: **Douglas**; **Brennan**, Stewart, Marshall.

Miller v. *California* and *Paris Adult Theatre* v. *Slaton* were decided on June 21, 1973.

OPINIONS

MILLER V. CALIFORNIA

CHIEF JUSTICE BURGER DELIVERED THE OPINION OF THE COURT . . .

This much has been categorically settled by the Court, that obscene material is unprotected by the First Amendment. . . . We acknowledge, however, the inherent dangers of undertaking to regulate any form of expression. State statutes designed to regulate obscene materials must be carefully limited. . . . As a result, we now confine the permissible scope of such regulation to works which depict or describe sexual conduct. That conduct must be specifically defined by the applicable state law, as written or authoritatively construed. A state offense must also be limited to works which, taken as a whole, appeal to the prurient interest in sex, which portray sexual conduct in a patently offensive way, and which, taken as a whole, do not have serious literary, artistic, political, or scientific value.

The basic guidelines for the trier of fact must be: (a) whether "the average person, applying contemporary community standards" would find that the work, taken as a whole, appeals to the prurient interest . . . ; (b) whether the work depicts or describes, in a patently offensive way, sexual conduct specifically defined by the applicable state law; and (c) whether the work, taken as a whole, lacks serious literary, artistic, political, or scientific value. . . . If a state law that regulates obscene material is thus limited, as written or construed, the First Amendment values applicable to the States through the Fourteenth Amendment are adequately protected by the ultimate power of appellate courts to conduct an independent review of constitutional claims when necessary. . . .

We emphasize that it is not our function to propose regulatory schemes for the States. That must await their concrete legislative efforts. It is possible, however, to give a few plain examples of what a state statute could define for regulation under part (b) of the standard announced in this opinion:

(a) Patently offensive representations or descriptions of ultimate sexual acts, normal or perverted, actual or simulated.
(b) Patently offensive representations or descriptions of masturbation, excretory functions, and lewd exhibition of the genitals.

Sex and nudity may not be exploited without limit by films or pictures exhibited or sold in places of public accommodation any more than live sex and nudity can be exhibited or sold without limit in such public places. At a minimum, prurient, patently offensive depiction or description of sexual conduct must have serious literary, artistic, political, or scientific value to merit First Amendment protection. . . . For example, medical books for the education of physicians and related personnel necessarily use graphic illustrations and descriptions of human anatomy. In resolving the inevitably sensitive questions of fact and law, we must continue to rely on the jury system, accompanied by the safeguards that judges, rules of evidence, presumption of innocence, and other protective features provide, as we do with rape, murder, and a host of other offenses against society and its individual members.

Justice Brennan, author of the opinions of the Court, or the plurality opinions, in *Roth* v. *United States* [1957], *Jacobellis* v. *Ohio* [1964], *Ginzburg* v. *United States* [1966], *Mishkin* v. *New York* [1966], and *Memoirs* v. *Massachusetts* [1966], has abandoned his former position and now maintains that no formulation of this Court, the Congress, or the States can adequately distinguish obscene material unprotected by the First Amendment from protected expression. *Paris Adult Theatre I* v. *Slaton* (Brennan, J., dissenting). Paradoxically, Justice Brennan indicates that suppression of unprotected obscene material is permissible to avoid exposure to unconsenting adults, as in this case, and to juveniles, although he gives no indication of how the division between protected and nonprotected materials may be drawn with greater precision for these purposes than for regulation of commercial exposure to consenting adults only. . . .

Under the holdings announced today, no one will be subject to prosecution for the sale or exposure of obscene materials unless these materials depict or describe patently offensive "hard core" sexual conduct specifically defined by the regulating state law, as written or construed. We are satisfied that these specific prerequisites will provide fair notice to a dealer in such materials that his public and commercial activities may bring prosecution. . . . If the inability to define regulated materials with ultimate, god-like precision altogether removes the power of the States or the Congress to regulate, then "hard core" pornography may be exposed without limit to the juvenile, the passerby, and the consenting adult alike, as, indeed, Justice Douglas contends. . . .

It is certainly true that the absence, since *Roth*, of a single majority view of this Court as to proper standards for testing obscenity has placed a strain on both state and federal courts. But today, for the first time since *Roth* was decided in 1957, a majority of this Court has agreed on concrete guidelines to isolate "hard core" pornography from expression protected by the First Amendment. Now we may . . . attempt to provide positive guidance to federal and state courts alike.

This may not be an easy road, free from difficulty. But no amount of "fatigue" should lead us to adopt a convenient "institutional" rationale—an absolutist, "anything goes" view of the First Amendment—because it will lighten our burdens. . . .

Under a National Constitution, fundamental First Amendment limitations on the powers of the States do not vary from community to community, but this does not mean that there are, or should or can be, fixed, uniform national standards of precisely what appeals to the "prurient interest" or is "patently offensive." These are essentially questions of fact, and our Nation is simply too big and too diverse for this Court to reasonably expect that such standards could be articulated for all fifty States in a single formulation, even assuming the prerequisite consensus exists. When triers of fact are asked to decide whether "the average person, applying contemporary community standards" would consider certain materials "prurient," it would be unrealistic to require that the answer be based on some abstract formulation. The adversary system, with lay jurors as the usual ultimate factfinders in criminal prosecutions, has historically permitted triers of fact to draw on the standards of their community, guided always by limiting instructions on the law. To require a State to structure obscenity proceedings around evidence of a national "community standard" would be an exercise in futility. . . .

It is neither realistic nor constitutionally sound to read the First Amendment as requiring that the people of Maine or Mississippi accept public depiction of conduct found tolerable in Las Vegas, or New York City. . . . People in different States vary in their tastes and attitudes, and this diversity is not to be strangled by the absolutism of imposed uniformity. As the Court made clear in *Mishkin*, the primary concern with requiring a jury to apply the standard of "the average person, applying contemporary community standards" is to be certain that, so far as material is not aimed at a deviant group, it will be judged by its impact on an average person, rather than a particularly susceptible or sensitive person—or indeed a totally insensitive one. . . . We hold that the requirement that the jury evaluate the materials with reference to "contemporary standards of the State of California" serves this protective purpose and is constitutionally adequate.

The dissenting Justices sound the alarm of repression. But, in our view, to equate the free and robust exchange of ideas and political debate with commercial exploitation of obscene material demeans the grand conception of the First Amendment and its high purposes in the historic struggle for freedom. . . . The First Amendment protects works which, taken as a whole, have serious literary, artistic, political, or scientific value, regardless of whether the government or a majority of the people approve of the ideas these works represent. . . . But the public portrayal of hard-core sexual conduct for its own sake, and for the ensuing commercial gain, is a different matter.

There is no evidence, empirical or historical, that the stern nineteenth-century American censorship of public distribution and display of material relating to sex . . . in any way limited or affected expression of serious literary, artistic, political, or scientific ideas. On the contrary, it is beyond any question that the era following Thomas Jefferson to Theodore Roosevelt was an "extraordinarily vigorous period," not just in economics and politics, but in belles lettres and in "the outlying fields of social and political philosophies." [V. Carrington, *Main Currents in American Thought*.] We do not see the harsh hand of censorship of ideas—good or bad, sound or unsound—and "repression" of political liberty lurking in every state regulation of commercial exploitation of human interest in sex.

Justice Brennan finds "it is hard to see how state-ordered regimentation of our minds can ever be forestalled." *Paris Adult Theatre I* (Brennan, J., dissenting). These doleful anticipations assume that courts cannot distinguish commerce in ideas, protected by the First Amendment, from commercial exploitation of obscene material. Moreover, state regulation of hard-core pornography so as to make it unavailable to nonadults, a regulation which Justice Brennan finds constitutionally permissible, has all the elements of "censorship" for adults; indeed even more rigid enforcement techniques may be called for with such dichotomy of regulation. . . . One can concede that the "sexual revolution" of recent years may have had useful byproducts in striking layers of prudery from a subject long irrationally kept from needed ventilation. But it does not follow that no regulation of patently offensive "hard core" materials is needed or permissible; civilized people do not allow unregulated access to heroin because it is a derivative of medicinal morphine.

In sum, we (a) reaffirm the *Roth* holding that obscene material is not protected by the First Amendment; (b) hold that such material can be regulated by the States, subject to the specific safeguards enunciated above, without a showing that the material is "utterly without redeeming social value"; and (c) hold that obscenity is to be determined by applying "contemporary community standards" . . . not "national standards." The judgment of the Appellate Department of the Superior Court, Orange County, California, is vacated and the case remanded to that court for further proceedings not inconsistent with the First Amendment standards established by this opinion. . . .

JUSTICE DOUGLAS, DISSENTING.

Today the Court retreats from the earlier formulations of the constitutional test and undertakes to make new definitions. This effort, like the earlier ones, is earnest and well intentioned. The difficulty is that we do not deal with constitutional terms, since "obscenity" is not mentioned in the Constitution or Bill of Rights. And the First Amendment makes no such exception from "the press" which it undertakes to protect, nor, as I have said on other occasions, is an exception necessarily implied, for there was no recognized exception to the free press at the time the Bill of Rights was adopted which treated "obscene" publications differently from other types of papers, magazines, and books. So there are no constitutional guidelines for deciding what is and what is not "obscene." The Court is at large because we deal with tastes and standards of literature. What shocks me may be sustenance for my neighbor. What causes one person to boil up in rage over one pamphlet or movie may reflect only his neurosis, not shared by others. We deal here with a regime of censorship which, if adopted, should be done by constitutional amendment after full debate by the people. . . .

The idea that the First Amendment permits government to ban publications that are "offensive" to some people puts an ominous gloss on freedom of the press. That test would make it possible to ban any paper or any journal or magazine in some benighted place. The First Amendment was designed "to invite dispute," to induce "a condition of unrest," to "create dissatisfaction with conditions as they are," and even to stir "people to anger." *Terminiello* v. *Chicago* [1949]. The idea that the First Amendment permits punishment for ideas that are "offensive" to the particular judge or jury sitting in judgment is astounding. No greater leveler of speech or literature has ever been designed. To give the power to the censor, as we do today, is to make a sharp and radical break with the traditions of a free society. The First Amendment was not fashioned as a vehicle for dispensing tranquilizers to the people. Its prime function was to keep debate open to "offensive" as well as to "staid" people. The tendency throughout history has been to subdue the individual and to exalt the power of government. The use of the standard "offensive" gives authority to government that cuts the very vitals out of the First Amendment. As is intimated by the Court's opinion, the materials before us may be garbage. But so is much of what is said in political campaigns, in the daily press, on TV, or over the radio. By reason of the First Amendment—and solely because of it—speakers and publishers have not been threatened or subdued because their thoughts and ideas may be "offensive" to some. . . .

If there are to be restraints on what is obscene, then a constitutional amendment should be the way of achieving the end. There are societies where religion and mathematics are the only free segments. It would be a dark day for America if that were our destiny. But the people can make it such if they choose to write obscenity into the Constitution and define it.

We deal with highly emotional, not rational, questions. To many the Song of Solomon is obscene. I do not think we, the judges, were ever given the constitutional power to make definitions of obscenity. If it is to be defined, let the people debate and decide by a constitutional amendment what they want to ban as obscene and what standards they want the legislatures and the courts to apply. Perhaps the people will decide that the path towards a mature, integrated society requires that all ideas competing for acceptance must have no censor. Perhaps they will decide otherwise. Whatever the choice, the courts will have some guidelines. Now we have none except our own predilections.

PARIS ADULT THEATRE I V. SLATON

CHIEF JUSTICE BURGER DELIVERED THE OPINION OF THE COURT . . .

We categorically disapprove the theory, apparently adopted by the trial judge, that obscene, pornographic films acquire constitutional immunity from state regulation simply because they are exhibited for consenting adults only. This holding was properly rejected by the Georgia Supreme Court. Although we have often pointedly recognized the high importance of the state interest in regulating the exposure of obscene materials to juveniles and unconsenting adults, . . . this Court has never declared these to be the only legitimate state interests permitting regulation of obscene material. The States have a long-recognized legitimate interest in regulating the use of obscene material in local commerce and in all places of public accommodation, as long as these regulations do not run afoul of specific constitutional prohibitions. . . .

In particular, we hold that there are legitimate state interests at stake in stemming the tide of commercialized obscenity, even assuming it is feasible to enforce effective safeguards against exposure to juveniles and to passersby. Rights and interests "other than those of the advocates are involved." *Breard* v. *Alexandria* [1951]. These include the interest of the public in the quality of life and the total community environment, the tone of commerce in the great city centers, and, possibly, the public safety itself. The Hill-Link Minority Report of the Commission on Obscenity and Pornography indicates that there is at least an arguable correlation between obscene material and crime. Quite apart from sex crimes, however, there remains one problem of large proportions aptly described by Professor Bickel:

> It concerns the tone of the society, the mode, or to use terms that have perhaps greater currency, the style and quality of life, now and in the future. A man may be entitled to read an obscene book in his room, or expose himself indecently there. . . . We should protect his privacy. But if he demands a right to obtain the books and pictures he wants in the market, and to foregather in public places—discreet, if you will, but accessible to all—with others who share his tastes, then to grant him his right is to affect the world about the rest of us, and to impinge on other privacies. Even supposing that each of us can, if he wishes, effectively avert the eye and stop the ear (which, in truth, we cannot), what is commonly read and seen and heard and done intrudes upon us all, want it or not. 22 *The Public Interest* 25–26 (Winter 1971). . . .

As Chief Justice Warren stated, there is a "right of the Nation and of the States to maintain a decent society. . . ." *Jacobellis* v. *Ohio* [1964] (dissenting opinion). . . .

But, it is argued, there are no scientific data which conclusively demonstrate that exposure to obscene material adversely affects men and women or their society. It is urged on behalf of the petitioners that, absent such a demonstration, any kind of state regulation is "impermissible." We reject this argument. It is not for us to resolve empirical uncertainties underlying state legislation, save in the exceptional case where that legislation plainly impinges upon rights protected by the Constitution itself. . . . Although there is no conclusive proof of a connection between antisocial behavior and obscene material, the legislature of Georgia could quite reasonably determine that such a connection does or might exist. In deciding *Roth*, this Court implicitly accepted that a legislature could legitimately act on such a conclusion to protect "the social interest in order and morality." . . .

From the beginning of civilized societies, legislators and judges have acted on various unprovable assumptions. Such assumptions underlie much lawful state regulation of commercial and business affairs. . . . The same is true of the federal securities and antitrust laws and a host of federal regulations. . . . On the basis of these assumptions both Congress and state legislatures have, for example, drastically restricted associational rights by adopting antitrust laws, and have strictly regulated public expression by issuers of and dealers in securities, profit sharing "coupons," and "trading stamps," commanding what they must and must not publish and announce. . . . Understandably those who entertain an absolutist view of the First Amendment find it uncomfortable to explain why rights of association, speech, and press should be severely restrained in the marketplace of goods and money, but not in the marketplace of pornography.

Likewise, when legislatures and administrators act to protect the physical environment from pollution and to preserve our resources of forests, streams, and parks, they must act on such imponderables as the impact of a new highway near or through an existing park or wilderness area. . . . The fact that a congressional directive reflects unprovable assumptions about what is good for the people, including imponderable aesthetic assumptions, is not a sufficient reason to find that statute unconstitutional.

If we accept the unprovable assumption that a complete education requires the reading of certain books . . . and the well nigh universal belief that good books, plays, and art lift the spirit, improve the mind, enrich the human personality, and develop character, can we then say that a state legislature may not act on the corollary assumption that commerce in obscene books, or public exhibitions focused on obscene conduct, have a tendency to exert a corrupting and debasing impact leading to antisocial behavior? . . . The sum of experience, including that of the past two decades, affords an ample basis for legislatures to conclude that a sensitive, key relationship of human existence, central to family life, community welfare, and the development of human personality, can be debased and distorted by crass commercial exploitation of sex. Nothing in the Constitution prohibits a State from reaching such a conclusion and acting on it legislatively simply because there is no conclusive evidence or empirical data.

It is argued that individual "free will" must govern, even in activities beyond the protection of the First Amendment and other constitutional guarantees of privacy, and that government cannot legitimately impede an individual's desire to see or acquire obscene plays, movies, and books. We do indeed base our society on certain assumptions that people have the capacity for free choice. Most exercises of individual free choice—those in politics, religion, and expression of ideas—are explicitly protected by the Constitution. Totally unlimited play for free will, however, is not allowed in our or any other society. We have just noted, for example, that neither the First Amendment nor "free will" precludes States from having "blue sky" laws to regulate what sellers of securities may write or publish about their wares. . . . Such laws are to protect the weak, the uninformed, the unsuspecting, and the gullible from the exercise of their own volition. Nor do modern societies leave disposal of garbage and sewage up to the individual "free will," but impose regulation to protect both public health and the appearance of public places. States are told by some that they must await a "laissez-faire" market solution to the obscenity-pornography problem, paradoxically "by people who have never otherwise had a kind word to say for laissez-faire," particularly in solving urban, commercial, and environmental pollution problems. See I. Kristol, *On the Democratic Idea in America* 37 (1972).

The States, of course, may follow such a "laissez-faire" policy and drop all controls on commercialized obscenity, if that is what they prefer, just as they can ignore consumer protection in the marketplace, but nothing in the Constitution compels the States to do so with regard to matters falling within state jurisdiction. . . .

It is asserted, however, that standards for evaluating state commercial regulations are inapposite in the present context, as state regulation of access by consenting adults to obscene material violates the constitutionally protected right to privacy enjoyed by petitioners' customers. Even assuming that petitioners have vicarious standing to assert potential customers' rights, it is unavailing to compare a theater open to the public for a fee, with the private home of *Stanley* v. *Georgia* [1969] and the marital bedroom of *Griswold* v. *Connecticut* [1965]. This Court, has, on numerous occasions, refused to hold that commercial ventures such as a motion-picture house are "private" for the purpose of civil rights litigation and civil rights statutes. . . . The Civil Rights Act of 1964 specifically defines motion-picture houses and theaters as places of "public accommodation" covered by the Act as operations affecting commerce.

Our prior decisions recognizing a right to privacy guaranteed by the Fourteenth Amendment included "only personal rights that can be deemed 'fundamental' or 'implicit in the concept of ordered liberty.' *Palko* v. *Connecticut* [1937]." *Roe* v. *Wade* [1973]. This privacy right encompasses and protects the personal intimacies of the home, the family, marriage, motherhood, procreation, and child rearing. . . . Nothing, however, in this Court's decisions intimates that there is any "fundamental" privacy right "implicit in the concept of ordered liberty" to watch obscene movies in places of public accommodation. . . .

It is also argued that the State has no legitimate interest in "control [of] the moral content of a person's thoughts," *Stanley*, and we need not quarrel with this. But we reject the claim that the State of Georgia is here attempting to control the minds or thoughts of those who patronize theaters. Preventing unlimited display or distribution of obscene material, which by definition lacks any serious literary, artistic, political, or scientific value as communication, *Miller* v. *California* [1973], is distinct from a control of reason and the intellect. . . . Where communication of ideas, protected by the First Amendment, is not involved, or the particular privacy of the home protected by *Stanley*, or any of the other "areas or zones" of constitutionally protected privacy, the mere fact that, as a consequence, some human "utterances" or "thoughts" may be incidentally affected does not bar the State from acting to protect legitimate state interests. . . . The fantasies of a drug addict are his own and beyond the reach of government, but government regulation of drug sales is not prohibited by the Constitution. . . .

Finally, petitioners argue that conduct which directly involves "consenting adults" only has, for that sole reason, a special claim to constitutional protection. Our Constitution establishes a broad range of conditions on the exercise of power by the States, but for us to say that our Constitution incorporates the proposition that conduct involving consenting adults only is always beyond state regulation, is a step we are unable to take. Commercial exploitation of depictions, descriptions, or exhibitions of obscene conduct on commercial premises open to the adult public falls within a State's broad power to regulate commerce and protect the public environment. The issue in this context goes beyond whether someone, or even the majority, considers the conduct depicted as "wrong" or "sinful." The States have the power to make a morally neutral judgment that public exhibition of obscene material, or commerce in such material, has a tendency to injure the community as a whole, to endanger the public safety, or to jeopardize, in Chief Justice Warren's words, the States' "right . . . to maintain a decent society." *Jacobellis* (dissenting opinion).

To summarize, we have today reaffirmed the basic holding of *Roth* v. *United States* that obscene material has no protection under the First Amendment. . . . We have directed our holdings, not at thoughts or speech, but at depiction and description of specifically defined sexual conduct that States may regulate within limits designed to prevent infringement of First Amendment rights. We have also reaffirmed the holdings of *United States* v. *Reidel* [1971] and *United States* v. *Thirty-seven Photographs* [1971] that commerce in obscene material is unprotected by any constitutional doctrine of privacy. . . . In this case we hold that the States have a legitimate interest in regulating commerce in obscene material and in regulating exhibition of obscene material in places of public accommodation, including so-called "adult" theaters from which minors are excluded. In light of these holdings, nothing precludes the State of Georgia from the regulation of the allegedly obscene material exhibited in Paris Adult Theatre I or II, provided that the applicable Georgia law, as written or authoritatively interpreted by the Georgia courts, meets the First Amendment standards set forth in *Miller*. The judgment is vacated and the case remanded to the Georgia Supreme Court for further proceedings not inconsistent with this opinion and *Miller*. . . .

JUSTICE BRENNAN, DISSENTING.

This case requires the Court to confront once again the vexing problem of reconciling state efforts to suppress sexually oriented expression with the protections of the First Amendment, as applied to the States through the Fourteenth Amendment. No other aspect of the First Amendment has, in recent years, demanded so substantial a commitment of our time, generated such disharmony of views, and remained so resistant to the formulation of stable and manageable standards. I am convinced that the approach initiated sixteen years ago in *Roth*, and culminating in the Court's decision today, cannot bring stability to this area of the law without jeopardizing fundamental First Amendment values, and I have concluded that the time has come to make a significant departure from that approach. . . .

. . . The essence of our problem in the obscenity area is that we have been unable to provide "sensitive tools" to separate obscenity from other sexually oriented but constitutionally protected speech, so that efforts to suppress the former do not spill over into the suppression of the latter. The attempt, as the late Justice Harlan observed, has only "produced a variety of views among the members of the Court unmatched in any other course of constitutional adjudication." *Interstate Circuit, Inc.* v. *Dallas* (1968) (separate opinion).

To be sure, five members of the Court did agree in *Roth* that obscenity could be determined by asking "whether to the average person, applying contemporary community standards, the dominant theme of the material taken as a whole appeals to prurient interest." But agreement on that test—achieved in the abstract and without reference to the particular material before the Court . . . was, to say the least, short lived. . . .

The view that, until today, enjoyed the most, but not majority, support was an interpretation of *Roth* . . . adopted by Chief Justice Warren, Justice Fortas, and the author of this opinion in *Memoirs* v. *Massachusetts* [1966]. We expressed the view that Federal or State Governments could control the distribution of material where "three elements . . . coalesce: it must be established that (a) the dominant theme of the material taken as a whole appeals to a prurient interest in sex; (b) the material is patently offensive because it affronts contemporary community standards relating to the description or representation of sexual matters; and (c) the material is utterly without redeeming social value." Even this formulation, however, concealed differences of opinion. . . . Moreover, it did not provide a definition covering all situations. . . . Nor, finally, did it ever command a majority of the Court. . . .

In the face of this divergence of opinion the Court began the practice in *Redrup* v. *New York* [1967], of *per curiam* reversals of convictions for the dissemination of materials that at least five members of the Court, applying their separate tests, deemed not to be obscene. This approach capped the attempt in *Roth* to separate all forms of sexually oriented expression into two categories—the one subject to full governmental suppression and the other beyond the reach of governmental regulation to the same extent as any other protected form of speech or press. Today a majority of the Court offers a slightly altered formulation of the basic *Roth* test, while leaving entirely unchanged the underlying approach.

Our experience with the *Roth* approach has certainly taught us that the outright suppression of obscenity cannot be reconciled with the fundamental principles of the First and Fourteenth Amendments. For we have failed to formulate a standard that sharply distinguishes protected from unprotected speech, and out of necessity, we have resorted to the *Redrup* approach, which resolves cases as between the parties, but offers only the most obscure guidance to legislation, adjudication by other courts, and primary conduct. By disposing of cases through summary reversal or denial of certiorari we have deliberately and effectively obscured the rationale underlying the decisions. It comes as no surprise that judicial attempts to follow our lead conscientiously have often ended in hopeless confusion.

Of course, the vagueness problem would be largely of our own creation if it stemmed primarily from our failure to reach a consensus on any one standard. But after sixteen years of experimentation and debate I am reluctantly forced to the conclusion that none of the available formulas, including the one announced today, can reduce the vagueness to a tolerable level while at the same time striking an acceptable balance between the protections of the First and Fourteenth Amendments, on the one hand, and on the other the asserted state interest in regulating the dissemination of certain sexually oriented materials. Any effort to draw a constitutionally acceptable boundary on state power must resort to such indefinite concepts as "prurient interest," "patent offensiveness," "serious literary value," and the like. The meaning of these concepts necessarily varies with the experience, outlook, and even idiosyncrasies of the person defining them. Although we have assumed that obscenity does exist and that we "know it when [we] see it," *Jacobellis* (Stewart, J., concurring), we are manifestly unable to describe it in advance except by reference to concepts so elusive that they fail to distinguish clearly between protected and unprotected speech. . . .

The vagueness of the standards in the obscenity area produces a number of separate problems, and any improvement must rest on an understanding that the problems are to some extent distinct. First, a vague statute fails to provide adequate notice to persons who are engaged in the type of conduct that the statute could be thought to proscribe. . . .

In addition to problems that arise when any criminal statute fails to afford fair notice of what it forbids, a vague statute in the areas of speech and press creates a second level of difficulty. We have indicated that "stricter standards of permissible statutory vagueness may be applied to a statute having a potentially inhibiting effect on speech; a man may the less be required to act at his peril here, because the free dissemination of ideas may be the loser." *Smith* v. *California* [1959]. . . .

To implement this general principle, and recognizing the inherent vagueness of any definition of obscenity, we have held that the definition of obscenity must be drawn as narrowly as possible so as to minimize the interference with protected expression. . . .

. . . [A] vague statute in this area creates a third, although admittedly more subtle, set of problems. These problems concern the institutional stress that inevitably results where the line separating protected from unprotected speech is excessively vague. . . .

As a result of our failure to define standards with predictable application to any given piece of material, there is no probability of regularity in obscenity decisions by state and lower federal courts. That is not to say that these courts have performed badly in this area or paid insufficient attention to the principles we have established. The problem is, rather, that one cannot say with certainty that material is obscene until at least five members of this Court, applying inevitably obscure standards, have pronounced it so. The number of obscenity cases on our docket gives ample testimony to the burden that has been placed upon this Court.

But the sheer number of the cases does not define the full extent of the institutional problem. For, quite apart from the number of cases involved and the need to make a fresh constitutional determination in each case, we are tied to the "absurd business of perusing and viewing the miserable stuff that pours into the Court . . . ." *Interstate Circuit, Inc.* (separate opinion of Harlan, J.). . . .

Moreover, we have managed the burden of deciding scores of obscenity cases by relying on *per curiam* reversals or denials of certiorari—a practice which conceals the rationale of decision and gives at least the appearance of arbitrary action by this Court. . . . More important, . . . the practice effectively censors protected expression by leaving lower court determinations of obscenity intact even though the status of the allegedly obscene material is entirely unsettled until final review here. In addition, the uncertainty of the standards creates a continuing source of tension between state and federal courts, since the need for an independent determination by this Court seems to render superfluous even the most conscientious analysis by state tribunals. And our inability to justify our decisions with a persuasive rationale—or indeed, any rationale at all—necessarily creates the impression that we are merely second-guessing state court judges.

The severe problems arising from the lack of fair notice, from the chill on protected expression, and from the stress imposed on the state and federal judicial machinery persuade me that a significant change in direction is urgently required. . . .

Our experience since *Roth* requires us not only to abandon the effort to pick out obscene materials on a case-by-case basis, but also to reconsider a fundamental postulate of *Roth*: that there exists a definable class of sexually oriented expression that may be totally suppressed by the Federal and State Governments. Assuming that such a class of expression does in fact exist, I am forced to conclude that the concept of "obscenity" cannot be defined with sufficient specificity and clarity to provide fair notice to persons who create and distribute sexually oriented materials, to prevent substantial erosion of protected speech as a byproduct of the attempt to suppress unprotected speech, and to avoid very costly institutional harms. Given these inevitable side effects of state efforts to suppress what is assumed to be unprotected speech, we must scrutinize with care the state interest that is asserted to justify the suppression. For in the absence of some very substantial interest in suppressing such speech, we can hardly condone the ill effects that seem to flow inevitably from the effort. . . .

Because we assumed—incorrectly, as experience has proved—that obscenity could be separated from other sexually oriented expression without significant costs either to the First Amendment or to the judicial machinery charged with the task of safeguarding First Amendment freedoms, we had no occasion in *Roth* to probe the asserted state interest in curtailing unprotected, sexually oriented speech. Yet, as we have increasingly come to appreciate the vagueness of the concept of obscenity, we have begun to recognize and articulate the state interests at stake. . . .

The opinions in *Redrup* and *Stanley* reflected our emerging view that the state interests in protecting children and in protecting unconsenting adults may stand on a different footing from the other asserted state interests. . . .

But, whatever the strength of the state interests in protecting juveniles and unconsenting adults from exposure to sexually oriented materials, those interests cannot be asserted in defense of the holding of the Georgia Supreme Court in this case. That court assumed for the purposes of its decision that the films in issue were exhibited only to persons over the age of 21 who viewed them willingly and with prior knowledge of the nature of their contents. And on that assumption the state court held that the films could still be suppressed. The justification for the suppression must be found, therefore, in some independent interest in regulating the reading and viewing habits of consenting adults. . . .

. . . The traditional description of state police power does embrace the regulation of morals as well as the health, safety, and general welfare of the citizenry. . . . And much legislation—compulsory public education laws, civil rights laws, even the abolition of capital punishment—is grounded, at least in part, on a concern with the morality of the community. But the State's interest in regulating morality by suppressing obscenity, while often asserted, remains essentially unfocused and ill defined. And, since the attempt to curtail unprotected speech necessarily spills over into the area of protected speech, the effort to serve this speculative interest through the suppression of obscene material must tread heavily on rights protected by the First Amendment. . . .

Like the proscription of abortions, the effort to suppress obscenity is predicated on unprovable, although strongly held, assumptions about human behavior, morality, sex, and religion. The existence of these assumptions cannot validate a statute that substantially undermines the guarantees of the First Amendment, any more than the existence of similar assumptions on the issue of abortion can validate a statute that infringes the constitutionally protected privacy interests of a pregnant woman.

If, as the Court today assumes, "a state legislature may . . . act on the . . . assumption that commerce in obscene books, or public exhibitions focused on obscene conduct, have a tendency to exert a corrupting and debasing impact leading to antisocial behavior," then it is hard to see how state-ordered regimentation of our minds can ever be forestalled. For if a State, in an effort to maintain or create a particular moral tone, may prescribe what its citizens cannot read or cannot see, then it would seem to follow that in pursuit of that same objective a State could decree that its citizens must read certain books or must view certain films. . . . However laudable its goal—and that is obviously a question on which reasonable minds may differ—the State cannot proceed by means that violate the Constitution. . . .

In short, while I cannot say that the interests of the State—apart from the question of juveniles and unconsenting adults—are trivial or nonexistent, I am compelled to conclude that these interests cannot justify the substantial damage to constitutional rights and to this Nation's judicial machinery that inevitably results from state efforts to bar the distribution even of unprotected material to consenting adults. . . . I would hold, therefore, that at least in the absence of distribution to juveniles or obtrusive exposure to unconsenting adults, the First and Fourteenth Amendments prohibit the State and Federal Governments from attempting wholly to suppress sexually oriented materials on the basis of their allegedly "obscene" contents. Nothing in this approach precludes those governments from taking action to serve what may be strong and legitimate interests through regulation of the manner of distribution of sexually oriented material. . . .

RESPONSES

FROM THE *LOS ANGELES TIMES*, JUNE 24, 1973, "THE MUDDIED WATERS OF OBSCENITY"

The new Supreme Court decision on obscenity is not helpful. It fails once again to provide clearer standards by which unacceptable materials are to be judged. And it invites more confusion by providing that each local community shall have broad discretion in setting its own standards of acceptability.

Until this decision, legal action had been restrained by earlier court requirements that, to be found illegal and beyond the protection of the First Amendment, materials had to be judged prurient and "utterly without redeeming social importance." In practice, that has meant that there was only limited police action and that the purveyors of pornography were free to carry on their operations so long as they did not intrude on the unwilling public or offer their products to minors.

That had seemed to us a sensible approach, consonant with the general acceptance of freedom of sexual activity by consenting adults within the bounds of reasonable privacy. . . .

By its decision, the court attaches an undeserved consequence to pornography even while acknowledging that there is no conclusive proof of a connection between obscene products and public safety. The court offers new and ambiguous words, such as "hard-core" and "patently offensive," to add to the already confused search for more precise definitions. There has been no agreement on definitions because there can be no agreement on the gray areas that inevitably come between black and white.

Chief Justice Warren E. Burger, in the majority opinion, recognized "that the 'sexual revolution' of recent years may have had useful byproducts of striking layers of prudery from a subject long irrationally kept from needed ventilation," but he insisted that "it does not follow that no regulation of patently offensive 'hard-core' materials is needed or permissible."

In the decision, however, the remedy encouraged is not regulation but prohibition.

FROM THE *WASHINGTON POST*, JUNE 24, 1973,
"CENSORSHIP, OBSCENITY AND A MATURE PEOPLE"

While freely acknowledging that the legal situation prior to the recent decisions was far from satisfactory, we think the Court is moving in the wrong direction. Censorship and the business of legislating morality are at best dangerous and imprecise exercises in a democracy. Prior to the recent decisions, the Supreme Court had failed so badly in attempting to construct clear guidelines as to what was and what was not obscene that it had to decide, in effect, on a case-by-case basis what obscenity was and what it was not. It had become the country's ultimate board of censure.

The problem has been that the question of what is obscene is a very emotional and a very personal question. Justice Douglas put it well when he said, "What shocks me may be sustenance for my neighbor." Another justice, in trying to come to terms with the problem, said, "I could never succeed [in defining it] intelligibly," but "I know it when I see it." But if the justices were struggling, at least the local censor had some notion that there was some kind of national check on their discretion. The new decisions have the double failure of loosening the check on zealous local censors while giving them different, but no better, guidance as to what is obscene. . . .

The fact is that there really is very little sense in trying to censor what adult Americans are willing to buy or pay to see. There is no question but that much that would strike us as obscene has been moving around and freely available under the old rules. And there is some risk in this. But judging from the Danish experience, the risk is perhaps not as great as we might fear. In any case, the danger has to be balanced against the dangers inherent in a free society in permitting judges or anyone else to entangle themselves in the dangerous and virtually impossible business of deciding what is offensive and what is not and of deciding what other people may or may not see or read.

FROM THE *BOSTON HERALD AMERICAN*, JUNE 26, 1973

The U.S. Supreme Court resorted to some old-fashioned American pragmatic thinking in its decision last week redefining obscenity. In effect, the court told purveyors of pornography they are going to be forced to prove their product's value in the local marketplace, like anyone else, with all the risks that entails.

That means the free ride is ended. No longer will pornography be protected by the broad sweep of constitutional immunity provided by an abstract definition drawn by the court back in 1957. From now on it must stand or fall in its ability to meet local community standards rather than hypothetical criteria of what constitutes obscenity throughout the country.

This strikes contrary to the contrived permissiveness which has clouded the controversial issue for the past decade and a half; and already the cry is being raised that it is a violation of the freedom of expression.

Nonsense! It's a return to reality and morality, which will permit ordinary men and women to make for themselves judgments on what they consider good for their community, without having the theoretical hypothesizing of so-called experts imposed on them. What is closer to the truth is that the court has at last recognized the everyday fact that what is acceptable in New York or Los Angeles, may not be permitted in Boston. And that is the way it should be, because as everyone knows the mores of the communities are different.

FROM THE *WALL STREET JOURNAL*, JUNE 27, 1973, "ON PORNOGRAPHY"

The latest Supreme Court decision on pornography is being praised and damned as the turning point in the contest between antipornography forces and anticensorship forces. Our guess is that it will instead prove to be one more inconclusive skirmish in the court's ongoing effort to set standards when a powerful element of society believes there should be no standards.

The social divisions on pornography parallel so many others in American life. On one side are the proponents of the traditional culture, as we have called them, the bedrock Americans.

On the other side are what we have called the cosmopolitan Americans, numerically smaller but immensely powerful because they are articulate, leisured, and entirely persuaded of the righteousness of their beliefs. The battle between the two groups over pornography has little to do with the arguments either offers, and much to do with the vision of society each holds.

As we listen to the debate, our most powerful feeling is a growing impatience with the arguments of the cosmopolitan forces, which is to say all of the standard and supposedly self-evident arguments against banning anything on the grounds of obscenity. That is by no means to say we are persuaded by the ostensible arguments on the other side, that pornography leads to rape and so on. But the debate after all is not over whether it is wise to ban pornography, but over whether majorities can be prevented from banning it through their duly constituted governments. Surely arguments for setting aside majority rule ought to be serious ones.

Yet how often does anyone look hard at the basic legal position of the absolutist anti-censorship position? The late Justice Black and Justice Douglas have argued that the First Amendment says "Congress shall make *no law*. . . ." But to be completely literal, it says "*Congress* shall make no law. . . ." This applies to the states as well, the court decided in 1931, because the Fourteenth Amendment says that no state shall deprive anyone of "liberty" without the due process of law. Surely, the court held, liberty means freedom of speech.

Now, we think the 1931 decision makes eminent sense. But if we are to interpret "liberty" in its broadest historical sense, we must interpret freedom of speech in the same way. Historically and traditionally this is to exclude obscenity; even the 1931 decision said that of course obscenity is subject to prior restraint. The point is that the anticensorship Justices cavalierly have interpreted the Constitution both ways, loosely or literally, as it suited the end they sought to reach.

Quite similarly, take the even more fundamental argument that banning *Deep Throat* inevitably leads to banning *Ulysses* and probably the Socialist Party platform. Yet from 1776 to 1931 and beyond our political liberties somehow evolved and flourished despite obscenity laws. Similarly, most of the world's democracies today somehow survive with the censorship of sexual materials.

On a more practical level, take the problem of definition. Laws against obscenity cannot be enforced, it is argued, because the term simply cannot be defined by courts that every day define hundreds of terms such as "due process of law," "negligence," or "reasonable man." The actual problem is that any definition will include an element of the arbitrary, and the cosmopolitan Americans are ready to use their vast skills to seize any such element to discredit any such definition that is offered. It is already happening again with the one offered last week.

That we find these arguments increasingly tiresome does not mean we totally reject the view of society for which they stand as surrogates. Certainly we share the rebellion of the cosmopolitan Americans against the Victorianism and Comstockery that are also a part of our historical heritage. Given that heritage, surely an element of sexual liberation is a useful corrective. Beyond that, there is something appealing in the vision of a society without inhibiting social codes. Tolerating the exploitation of sex, it can persuasively be argued, is a small price to pay to maximize human choice.

Yet we think there is a more enduring truth in the contrary view that any society must set some standards; that even if it cannot effectively ban pornography, for example, it has to express a view of right and wrong. We find that few of those who adopt Justice Douglas's absolutist position are willing to carry it to the logical extreme he does, saying society has no interest that allows it to prevent the torture of willing masochists. Shall we put this on stage? A ticket to watch a suicide, anyone? And once the principle of standards is accepted, the entire position of cosmopolitan Americans needs to be rethought; they are prepared only to discuss whether to draw a line, and have never thought about the question of where to draw it.

With enough will, these two visions of society can be more or less reconciled in any number of ways. In last week's decision, the court majority in effect sought to reconcile them through emphasis on local option. We find much to be said for regulating pornography through something like zoning laws. But no such effort will withstand the concerted attack of the most literate and articulate elements of society; no solution can work unless there is some minimum of social consensus behind the legal provisions.

So long as that consensus is lacking, neither last week's Supreme Court decision nor any conceivable legal formulation will end the controversy, or ease its effect in aggravating the dangerous social division that underlies it. The first step towards consensus, it seems to us, is for the cosmopolitan Americans to recognize that their case is not nearly as strong as they tend to assume, that the issue is not entirely one-sided, and that perhaps after all some degree of compromise would not spell the end of civilization.

MIAMI HERALD PUBLISHING CO. V. TORNILLO
418 U.S. 241 (1974)

The *Miami Herald* published editorials critical of Pat Tornillo's candidacy for the Florida House of Representatives, and Tornillo insisted that the *Herald* print verbatim his reply. When the paper refused, Tornillo sued in Circuit Court, Dade County, seeking relief under Florida's "right of reply" statute. Under that law, enacted in 1913, if a newspaper criticized the personal character or official record of a candidate for office, the candidate could demand that the paper print his reply at its own expense. The *Herald* argued that the statute violated the free press clause; the Circuit Court agreed and struck down the law. Tornillo succeeded in his appeal to the Florida Supreme Court, but the U.S. Supreme Court, in a unanimous decision, reversed the state court's judgment by holding that the right-of-reply law was a clear violation of the First Amendment.

In the *Red Lion* case decided five years earlier, the Court had sustained regulations in news broadcasting that effectively established a right of reply. In *Tornillo*, the Court did not attempt to explain the result in *Red Lion*; in fact, it did not even mention that decision. The different outcome in *Tornillo* may have reflected the Court's understanding of the differences between print and broadcast media. In any event, *Tornillo* made it emphatically clear that newspapers, at least, enjoy a constitutional liberty that states may not abridge through right-of-reply requirements.

"The Florida statute fails to clear the barriers of the First Amendment," wrote Chief Justice Burger for the Court, "because of its intrusion into the function of editors. . . . The choice of material to go into a newspaper, and the decisions made as to limitations on the size and content of the paper, and treatment of public issues and public officials—whether fair or unfair—constitute the exercise of editorial control and judgment."

Opinion of the Court: **Burger**, Douglas, Brennan, Stewart, White, Marshall, Blackmun, Powell, Rehnquist. Concurring statement: **Brennan**, Rehnquist. Concurring opinion: **White**.

Miami Herald Publishing Co. v. *Tornillo* was decided on June 25, 1974.

OPINIONS

CHIEF JUSTICE BURGER DELIVERED THE OPINION OF THE COURT.

The issue in this case is whether a state statute granting a political candidate a right to equal space to reply to criticism and attacks on his record by a newspaper violates the guarantees of a free press. . . .

The appellee and supporting advocates of an enforceable right of access to the press vigorously argue that government has an obligation to ensure that a wide variety of views reach the public. . . . It is urged that at the time the First Amendment to the Constitution was ratified in 1791 as part of our Bill of Rights the press was broadly representative of the people it was serving. While many of the newspapers were intensely partisan and narrow in their views, the press collectively presented a broad range of opinions to readers. Entry into publishing was inexpensive; pamphlets and books provided meaningful alternatives to the organized press for the expression of unpopular ideas and often treated events and expressed views not covered by conventional newspapers. A true marketplace of ideas existed in which there was relatively easy access to the channels of communication.

Access advocates submit that although newspapers of the present are superficially similar to those of 1791, the press of today is in reality very different from that known in the early years of our national existence. In the past half century a communications revolution has seen the introduction of radio and television into our lives, the promise of a global community through the use of communications satellites, and the specter of a "wired" nation by means of an expanding cable television network with two-way capabilities. The printed press, it is said, has not escaped the effects of this revolution. Newspapers have become big business, and there are far fewer of them to serve a larger literate population. Chains of newspapers, national newspapers, national wire and news services, and one-newspaper towns are the dominant features of a press that has become noncompetitive and enormously powerful and influential in its capacity to manipulate popular opinion and change the course of events. Major metropolitan newspapers have collaborated to establish news services national in scope. Such national news organizations provide syndicated "interpretive reporting" as well as syndicated features and commentary, all of which can serve as part of the new school of "advocacy journalism."

The elimination of competing newspapers in most of our large cities, and the concentration of control of media that results from the only newspaper's being owned by the same interests which own a television station and a radio station, are important components of this trend toward concentration of control of outlets to inform the public.

The result of these vast changes has been to place in a few hands the power to inform the American people and shape public opinion. Much of the editorial opinion and commentary that is printed is that of syndicated columnists distributed nationwide, and as a result, we are told, on national and world issues there tends to be a homogeneity of editorial opinion, commentary, and interpretive analysis. The abuses of bias and manipulative reportage are, likewise, said to be the result of the vast accumulations of unreviewable power in the modern media empires. In effect, it is claimed, the public has lost any ability to respond or to contribute in a meaningful way to the debate on issues. The monopoly of the means of communication allows for little or no critical analysis of the media except in professional journals of very limited readership. . . .

The obvious solution, which was available to dissidents at an earlier time when entry into publishing was relatively inexpensive, today would be to have additional newspapers. But the same economic factors which have caused the disappearance of vast numbers of metro-politan newspapers have made entry into the marketplace of ideas served by the print media almost impossible. It is urged that the claim of newspapers to be "surrogates for the public" carries with it a concomitant fiduciary obligation to account for that stewardship. From this premise it is reasoned that the only effective way to insure fairness and accuracy and to pro-vide for some accountability is for government to take affirmative action. The First Amend-ment interest of the public in being informed is said to be in peril because the "marketplace of ideas" is today a monopoly controlled by the owners of the market.

Proponents of enforced access to the press take comfort from language in several of this Court's decisions which suggests that the First Amendment acts as a sword as well as a shield, that it imposes obligations on the owners of the press in addition to protecting the press from government regulation. . . .

In *New York Times Co.* v. *Sullivan* [1964], the Court spoke of "a profound national com-mitment to the principle that debate on public issues should be uninhibited, robust, and wide-open." It is argued that the "uninhibited, robust" debate is not "wide-open" but open only to a monopoly in control of the press. . . .

However much validity may be found in these arguments, at each point the implementa-tion of a remedy such as an enforceable right of access necessarily calls for some mechanism, either governmental or consensual. If it is governmental coercion, this at once brings about a confrontation with the express provisions of the First Amendment and the judicial gloss on that Amendment developed over the years. . . .

. . . [T]he Court has expressed sensitivity as to whether a restriction or requirement con-stituted the compulsion exerted by government on a newspaper to print that which it would not otherwise print. The clear implication has been that any such a compulsion to publish that which "'reason' tells them should not be published" is unconstitutional. A responsible press is an undoubtedly desirable goal, but press responsibility is not mandated by the Constitution and like many other virtues it cannot be legislated.

Appellee's argument that the Florida statute does not amount to a restriction of appellant's right to speak because "the statute in question here has not prevented the *Miami Herald* from saying anything it wished" begs the core question. Compelling editors or publishers to pub-lish that which "'reason' tells them should not be published" is what is at issue in this case. The Florida statute operates as a command in the same sense as a statute or regulation for-bidding appellant to publish specified matter. Governmental restraint on publishing need not fall into familiar or traditional patterns to be subject to constitutional limitations on govern-mental powers. *Grosjean* v. *American Press Co.* [1936]. The Florida statute exacts a penalty on the basis of the content of a newspaper. The first phase of the penalty resulting from the compelled printing of a reply is exacted in terms of the cost in printing and composing time and materials and in taking up space that could be devoted to other material the newspaper may have preferred to print. It is correct, as appellee contends, that a newspaper is not sub-ject to the finite technological limitations of time that confront a broadcaster, but it is not cor-rect to say that, as an economic reality, a newspaper can proceed to infinite expansion of its column space to accommodate the replies that a government agency determines or a statute commands the readers should have available.

Faced with the penalties that would accrue to any newspaper that published news or commentary arguably within the reach of the right-of-access statute, editors might well conclude that the safe course is to avoid controversy. Therefore, under the operation of the Florida statute, political and electoral coverage would be blunted or reduced. . . .

Even if a newspaper would face no additional costs to comply with a compulsory access law and would not be forced to forgo publication of news or opinion by the inclusion of a reply, the Florida statute fails to clear the barriers of the First Amendment because of its intrusion into the function of editors. A newspaper is more than a passive receptacle or conduit for news, comment, and advertising. The choice of material to go into a newspaper, and the decisions made as to limitations on the size and content of the paper, and treatment of public issues and public officials—whether fair or unfair—constitute the exercise of editorial control and judgment. It has yet to be demonstrated how governmental regulation of this crucial process can be exercised consistent with First Amendment guarantees of a free press as they have evolved to this time. Accordingly, the judgment of the Supreme Court of Florida is
REVERSED.

JUSTICE WHITE, CONCURRING.

The Court today holds that the First Amendment bars a State from requiring a newspaper to print the reply of a candidate for public office whose personal character has been criticized by that newspaper's editorials. According to our accepted jurisprudence, the First Amendment erects a virtually insurmountable barrier between government and the print media so far as government tampering, in advance of publication, with news and editorial content is concerned. . . . A newspaper or magazine is not a public utility subject to "reasonable" governmental regulation in matters affecting the exercise of journalistic judgment as to what shall be printed. . . .

Of course, the press is not always accurate, or even responsible, and may not present full and fair debate on important public issues. But the balance struck by the First Amendment with respect to the press is that society must take the risk that occasionally debate on vital matters will not be comprehensive and that all viewpoints may not be expressed. . . .

To justify this statute, Florida advances a concededly important interest of ensuring free and fair elections by means of an electorate informed about the issues. But prior compulsion by government in matters going to the very nerve center of a newspaper—the decision as to what copy will or will not be included in any given edition—collides with the First Amendment. . . .

The constitutionally obnoxious feature of [the law] is not that the Florida Legislature may also have placed a high premium on the protection of individual reputational interests; for government certainly has "a pervasive and strong interest in preventing and redressing attacks upon reputation." *Rosenblatt* v. *Baer* [1966]. Quite the contrary, this law runs afoul of the elementary First Amendment proposition that government may not force a newspaper to print copy which, in its journalistic discretion, it chooses to leave on the newsroom floor. Whatever power may reside in government to influence the publishing of certain narrowly circumscribed categories of material, . . . we have never thought that the First Amendment permitted public officials to dictate to the press the contents of its news columns or the slant of its editorials.

But though a newspaper may publish without government censorship, it has never been entirely free from liability for what it chooses to print. . . . Among other things, the press has not been wholly at liberty to publish falsehoods damaging to individual reputation. At least until today, we have cherished the average citizen's reputation interest enough to afford him a fair chance to vindicate himself in an action for libel characteristically provided by state law. He has been unable to force the press to tell his side of the story or to print a retraction, but he has had at least the opportunity to win a judgment if he has been able to prove the falsity of the damaging publication, as well as a fair chance to recover reasonable damages for his injury.

Reaffirming the rule that the press cannot be forced to print an answer to a personal attack made by it, however, throws into stark relief the consequences of the new balance forged by the Court in the companion case also announced today. [*Gertz* v. *Welch*] goes far toward eviscerating the effectiveness of the ordinary libel action, which has long been the only potent response available to the private citizen libeled by the press. Under *Gertz*, the burden of proving liability is immeasurably increased, proving damages is made exceedingly more difficult, and vindicating reputation by merely proving falsehood and winning a judgment to that effect are wholly foreclosed. Needlessly, in my view, the Court trivializes and denigrates the interest in reputation by removing virtually all the protection the law has always afforded. . . .

One need not think less of the First Amendment to sustain reasonable methods for allowing the average citizen to redeem a falsely tarnished reputation. Nor does one have to doubt the genuine decency, integrity, and good sense of the vast majority of professional journalists to support the right of any individual to have his day in court when he has been falsely maligned in the public press. The press is the servant, not the master, of the citizenry, and its freedom does not carry with it an unrestricted hunting license to prey on the ordinary citizen. . . .

To me it is a near absurdity to so deprecate individual dignity, as the Court does in *Gertz*, and to leave the people at the complete mercy of the press, at least in this stage of our history when the press, as the majority in this case so well documents, is steadily becoming more powerful and much less likely to be deterred by threats of libel suits.

BUCKLEY V. VALEO
424 U.S. 1 (1976)

In the early 1900s Congress first passed laws designed to regulate funding of political campaigns. Badly drafted, these laws went mostly unenforced. In 1971 Congress returned to the issue and enacted the Federal Election Campaign Act (FECA), which established disclosure requirements concerning the amounts, sources, and uses of campaign funds. The new law helped expose the abuses of Watergate and led to additional regulations, passed in 1974 amendments to FECA. Hoping to be free of these requirements during the 1976 campaign, various federal officeholders and candidates mounted a comprehensive challenge to FECA in a lawsuit filed in federal court in Washington, D.C. The controversy was soon transmitted to the Court of Appeals, which in large measure sustained the law. In a lengthy *per curiam* opinion (one issued "by the court" instead of by an individual justice), the Supreme Court rendered a mixed verdict that effectively rewrote the statute. The Court sustained FECA's individual contribution limits, its disclosure and reporting provisions, and the public financing scheme it established. But the Court struck down the law's limitations on campaign expenditures, on independent expenditures by individuals and groups, and on expenditures from a candidate's own personal funds. It also found invalid the FECA provisions under which members of the Federal Election Commission were to be appointed.

While the *Buckley* plaintiffs challenged FECA on a variety of grounds, First Amendment concerns radiated throughout most of their complaint. The Court's decisions on FECA's limits on contributions and expenditures, and on its provisions compelling disclosure of campaign contributions, mainly involved issues of free speech and association. Indeed, it was *Buckley's* probe of the extent of protection afforded political activities by the First Amendment that made it a landmark case. Significantly, in holding unconstitutional FECA's several limitations on expenditures, the Court rejected the argument that campaign funding is mainly conduct and not speech and thus subject to a more deferential standard of review.

Two years after *Buckley*, in *First National Bank of Boston* v. *Bellotti*, the Court struck down a Massachusetts law banning corporations from spending to influence the outcome of a ballot referendum. *Bellotti* established the free speech rights of corporations; specifically, the Court held that a campaign expenditure by a corporation is speech meriting the same First Amendment protection as an individual's expenditure.

Opinion of the Court (*per curiam*): Burger, Brennan, Stewart, White, Marshall, Blackmun, Powell, Rehnquist. Concurring in part and dissenting in part: **Burger**; **White**; **Marshall**; **Blackmun**; **Powell**; **Rehnquist**. Not participating: Stevens.
Buckley v. *Valeo* was decided on January 30, 1976.

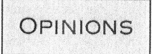

PER CURIAM . . .

. . . The statutes at issue, summarized in broad terms, contain the following provisions: (a) individual political contributions are limited to $1,000 to any single candidate per election, with an overall annual limitation of $25,000 by any contributor; independent expenditures by individuals and groups "relative to a clearly identified candidate" are limited to $1,000 a year; campaign spending by candidates for various federal offices and spending for national conventions by political parties are subject to prescribed limits; (b) contributions and expenditures above certain threshold levels must be reported and publicly disclosed; (c) a system for public funding of Presidential campaign activities is established by Subtitle H of the Internal Revenue Code; and (d) a Federal Election Commission is established to administer and enforce the legislation. . . .

I. Contribution and Expenditure Limitations . . .

A. General Principles

The Act's contribution and expenditure limitations operate in an area of the most fundamental First Amendment activities. Discussion of public issues and debate on the qualifications of candidates are integral to the operation of the system of government established by our Constitution. The First Amendment affords the broadest protection to such political expression in order "to assure [the] unfettered interchange of ideas for the bringing about of political and social changes desired by the people." *Roth* v. *United States* [1957]. . . .
. . . Appellees contend that what the Act regulates is conduct, and that its effect on speech and association is incidental at most. Appellants respond that contributions and expenditures are at the very core of political speech, and that the Act's limitations thus constitute restraints on First Amendment liberty that are both gross and direct.
In upholding the constitutional validity of the Act's contribution and expenditure provisions on the ground that those provisions should be viewed as regulating conduct, not speech, the Court of Appeals relied upon *United States* v. *O'Brien* [1968]. . . . The *O'Brien* case involved a defendant's claim that the First Amendment prohibited his prosecution for burning his draft card because his act was "'symbolic speech'" engaged in as a "'demonstration against the war and against the draft.'" On the assumption that "the alleged communicative element in O'Brien's conduct [was] sufficient to bring into play the First Amendment," the Court sustained the conviction because it found "a sufficiently important governmental interest in reg-

ulating the nonspeech element" that was "unrelated to the suppression of free expression" and that had an "incidental restriction on alleged First Amendment freedoms . . . no greater than [was] essential to the furtherance of that interest." The Court expressly emphasized that *O'Brien* was not a case "where the alleged governmental interest in regulating conduct arises in some measure because the communication allegedly integral to the conduct is itself thought to be harmful."

We cannot share the view that the present Act's contribution and expenditure limitations are comparable to the restrictions on conduct upheld in *O'Brien*. The expenditure of money simply cannot be equated with such conduct as destruction of a draft card. Some forms of communication made possible by the giving and spending of money involve speech alone, some involve conduct primarily, and some involve a combination of the two. Yet this Court has never suggested that the dependence of a communication on the expenditure of money operates itself to introduce a nonspeech element or to reduce the exacting scrutiny required by the First Amendment. . . .

Even if the categorization of the expenditure of money as conduct were accepted, the limitations challenged here would not meet the *O'Brien* test because the governmental interests advanced in support of the Act involve "suppressing communication." . . .

Nor can the Act's contribution and expenditure limitations be sustained, as some of the parties suggest, by reference to the constitutional principles reflected in [the Court's time, place, and manner cases]. Those cases stand for the proposition that the government may adopt reasonable time, place, and manner regulations, which do not discriminate among speakers or ideas, in order to further an important governmental interest unrelated to the restriction of communication. . . . The critical difference between this case and those . . . cases is that the present Act's contribution and expenditure limitations impose direct quantity restrictions on political communication and association by persons, groups, candidates, and political parties in addition to any reasonable time, place, and manner regulations otherwise imposed.

A restriction on the amount of money a person or group can spend on political communication during a campaign necessarily reduces the quantity of expression by restricting the number of issues discussed, the depth of their exploration, and the size of the audience reached. This is because virtually every means of communicating ideas in today's mass society requires the expenditure of money. . . .

The expenditure limitations contained in the Act represent substantial rather than merely theoretical restraints on the quantity and diversity of political speech. The $1,000 ceiling on spending "relative to a clearly identified candidate" would appear to exclude all citizens and groups except candidates, political parties, and the institutional press from any significant use of the most effective modes of communication. Although the Act's limitations on expenditures by campaign organizations and political parties provide substantially greater room for discussion and debate, they would have required restrictions in the scope of a number of past congressional and Presidential campaigns and would operate to constrain campaigning by candidates who raise sums in excess of the spending ceiling.

By contrast with a limitation upon expenditures for political expression, a limitation upon the amount that any one person or group may contribute to a candidate or political committee entails only a marginal restriction upon the contributor's ability to engage in free communication. A contribution serves as a general expression of support for the candidate and his views, but does not communicate the underlying basis for the support. The quantity of communication by the contributor does not increase perceptibly with the size of his contribution, since the expression rests solely on the undifferentiated, symbolic act of contributing. At most, the size of the contribution provides a very rough index of the intensity of the contributor's support for the candidate. A limitation on the amount of money a person may give to a candidate or campaign organization thus involves little direct restraint on his political communication, for it permits the symbolic expression of support evidenced by a contribution but does not in any way infringe the contributor's freedom to discuss candidates and issues. While contributions may result in political expression if spent by a candidate or an association to present views to the voters, the transformation of contributions into political debate involves speech by someone other than the contributor.

. . . The overall effect of the Act's contribution ceilings is merely to require candidates and political committees to raise funds from a greater number of persons and to compel people who would otherwise contribute amounts greater than the statutory limits to expend such funds on direct political expression, rather than to reduce the total amount of money potentially available to promote political expression.

The Act's contribution and expenditure limitations also impinge on protected associational freedoms. . . .

In sum, although the Act's contribution and expenditure limitations both implicate fundamental First Amendment interests, its expenditure ceilings impose significantly more severe restrictions on protected freedoms of political expression and association than do its limitations on financial contributions.

B. Contribution Limitations . . .

. . . [T]he primary First Amendment problem raised by the Act's contribution limitations is their restriction of one aspect of the contributor's freedom of political association. . . . Even a "'significant interference' with protected rights of political association" may be sustained if the State demonstrates a sufficiently important interest and employs means closely drawn to avoid unnecessary abridgment of associational freedoms. *Cousins* v. *Wigoda* [1972]. . . .

Appellees argue that the Act's restrictions on large campaign contributions are justified by three governmental interests. According to the parties and amici, the primary interest served by the limitations and, indeed, by the Act as a whole, is the prevention of corruption and the appearance of corruption spawned by the real or imagined coercive influence of large financial contributions on candidates' positions and on their actions if elected to office. Two "ancillary" interests underlying the Act are also allegedly furthered by the $1,000 limits on contributions. First, the limits serve to mute the voices of affluent persons and groups in the election process and thereby to equalize the relative ability of all citizens to affect the outcome of elections. Second, it is argued, the ceilings may to some extent act as a brake on the skyrocketing cost of political campaigns and thereby serve to open the political system more widely to candidates without access to sources of large amounts of money.

It is unnecessary to look beyond the Act's primary purpose—to limit the actuality and appearance of corruption resulting from large individual financial contributions—in order to find a constitutionally sufficient justification for the $1,000 contribution limitation. Under a system of private financing of elections, a candidate lacking immense personal or family wealth must depend on financial contributions from others to provide the resources necessary to conduct a successful campaign. The increasing importance of the communications media and sophisticated mass-mailing and polling operations to effective campaigning make the raising of large sums of money an ever more essential ingredient of an effective candidacy. To the extent that large contributions are given to secure a political quid pro quo from current and potential office holders, the integrity of our system of representative democracy is undermined. Although the scope of such pernicious practices can never be reliably ascertained, the deeply disturbing examples surfacing after the 1972 election demonstrate that the problem is not an illusory one.

Of almost equal concern as the danger of actual quid pro quo arrangements is the impact of the appearance of corruption stemming from public awareness of the opportunities for abuse inherent in a regime of large individual financial contributions. . . .

Appellants contend that the contribution limitations must be invalidated because bribery laws and narrowly drawn disclosure requirements constitute a less restrictive means of dealing with "proven and suspected quid pro quo arrangements." But . . . Congress was surely entitled to conclude that disclosure was only a partial measure, and that contribution ceilings were a necessary legislative concomitant to deal with the reality or appearance of corruption inherent in a system permitting unlimited financial contributions, even when the identities of the contributors and the amounts of their contributions are fully disclosed.

The Act's $1,000 contribution limitation focuses precisely on the problem of large campaign contributions—the narrow aspect of political association where the actuality and potential for corruption have been identified—while leaving persons free to engage in independent political expression, to associate actively through volunteering their services, and to assist to a limited but nonetheless substantial extent in supporting candidates and committees with financial resources. Significantly, the Act's contribution limitations in themselves do not undermine to any material degree the potential for robust and effective discussion of candidates and campaign issues by individual citizens, associations, the institutional press, candi-.dates, and political parties.

We find that, under the rigorous standard of review established by our prior decisions, the weighty interests served by restricting the size of financial contributions to political candidates are sufficient to justify the limited effect upon First Amendment freedoms caused by the $1,000 contribution ceiling. . . .

C. Expenditure Limitations . . .

Section 608 (e) (1) provides that "[n]o person may make any expenditure . . . relative to a clearly identified candidate during a calendar year which, when added to all other expenditures made by such person during the year advocating the election or defeat of such candidate, exceeds $1,000." . . .

. . . [T]he constitutionality of 608 (e) (1) turns on whether the governmental interests advanced in its support satisfy the exacting scrutiny applicable to limitations on core First Amendment rights of political expression.

We find that the governmental interest in preventing corruption and the appearance of corruption is inadequate to justify 608 (e) (1)'s ceiling on independent expenditures. First, assuming, *arguendo*, that large independent expenditures pose the same dangers of actual or apparent quid pro quo arrangements as do large contributions, 608 (e) (1) does not provide an answer that sufficiently relates to the elimination of those dangers. Unlike the contribution limitations' total ban on the giving of large amounts of money to candidates, 608 (e) (1) prevents only some large expenditures. So long as persons and groups eschew expenditures that in express terms advocate the election or defeat of a clearly identified candidate, they are free to spend as much as they want to promote the candidate and his views. . . . It would naïvely underestimate the ingenuity and resourcefulness of persons and groups desiring to buy influence to believe that they would have much difficulty devising expenditures that skirted the restriction on express advocacy of election or defeat but nevertheless benefited the candidate's campaign. . . .

Second, . . . the independent advocacy restricted by the provision does not presently appear to pose dangers of real or apparent corruption comparable to those identified with large campaign contributions. . . . Section 608 (b)'s contribution ceilings rather than 608 (e) (1)'s independent expenditure limitation prevent attempts to circumvent the Act through prearranged or coordinated expenditures amounting to disguised contributions. . . .

While the independent expenditure ceiling . . . fails to serve any substantial governmental interest in stemming the reality or appearance of corruption in the electoral process, it heavily burdens core First Amendment expression. For the First Amendment right to "'speak one's mind . . . on all public institutions'" includes the right to engage in "'vigorous advocacy' no less than 'abstract discussion.'" *New York Times Co.* v. *Sullivan* [1964], quoting *Bridges* v. *California* [1941], and *NAACP* v. *Button* [1958]. Advocacy of the election or defeat of candidates for federal office is no less entitled to protection under the First Amendment than the discussion of political policy generally or advocacy of the passage or defeat of legislation.

It is argued, however, that the ancillary governmental interest in equalizing the relative ability of individuals and groups to influence the outcome of elections serves to justify the limitation on express advocacy of the election or defeat of candidates imposed by 608 (e) (1)'s expenditure ceiling. But the concept that government may restrict the speech of some elements of our society in order to enhance the relative voice of others is wholly foreign to the First Amendment. . . . The First Amendment's protection against governmental abridgment of free expression cannot properly be made to depend on a person's financial ability to engage in public discussion. . . .

For the reasons stated, we conclude that 608 (e) (1)'s independent expenditure limitation is unconstitutional under the First Amendment. . . .

The Act also sets limits on expenditures by a candidate "from his personal funds, or the personal funds of his immediate family, in connection with his campaigns during any calendar year." 608 (a) (1). . . .

The ceiling on personal expenditures by candidates on their own behalf, like the limitations on independent expenditures contained in 608 (e) (1), imposes a substantial restraint on the ability of persons to engage in protected First Amendment expression. The candidate, no less than any other person, has a First Amendment right to engage in the discussion of public issues and vigorously and tirelessly to advocate his own election and the election of other candidates. . . . Section 608 (a)'s ceiling on personal expenditures by a candidate in furtherance of his own candidacy thus clearly and directly interferes with constitutionally protected freedoms.

The primary governmental interest served by the Act—the prevention of actual and apparent corruption of the political process—does not support the limitation on the candidate's expenditure of his own personal funds. . . . Indeed, the use of personal funds reduces the candidate's dependence on outside contributions and thereby counteracts the coercive pressures and attendant risks of abuse to which the Act's contribution limitations are directed.

The ancillary interest in equalizing the relative financial resources of candidates competing for elective office, therefore, provides the sole relevant rationale for 608 (a)'s expenditure ceiling. That interest is clearly not sufficient to justify the provision's infringement of fundamental First Amendment rights. First, the limitation may fail to promote financial equality among candidates. A candidate who spends less of his personal resources on his campaign may nonetheless outspend his rival as a result of more successful fundraising efforts. Indeed, a candidate's personal wealth may impede his efforts to persuade others that he needs their financial contributions or volunteer efforts to conduct an effective campaign. Second, and more fundamentally, the First Amendment simply cannot tolerate 608 (a)'s restriction upon the freedom of a candidate to speak without legislative limit on behalf of his own candidacy. We therefore hold that 608 (a)'s restriction on a candidate's personal expenditures is unconstitutional.

Section 608 (c) places limitations on overall campaign expenditures by candidates seeking nomination for election and election to federal office. . . .

No governmental interest that has been suggested is sufficient to justify the restriction on the quantity of political expression imposed by 608 (c)'s campaign expenditure limitations. The major evil associated with rapidly increasing campaign expenditures is the danger of candidate dependence on large contributions. The interest in alleviating the corrupting influence of large contributions is served by the Act's contribution limitations and disclosure provisions rather than by 608 (c)'s campaign expenditure ceilings. . . .

The campaign expenditure ceilings appear to be designed primarily to serve the governmental interests in reducing the allegedly skyrocketing costs of political campaigns. . . . [But] the mere growth in the cost of federal election campaigns in and of itself provides no basis for governmental restrictions on the quantity of campaign spending and the resulting limitation on the scope of federal campaigns. The First Amendment denies government the power to determine that spending to promote one's political views is wasteful, excessive, or unwise. In the free society ordained by our Constitution it is not the government, but the people—individually as citizens and candidates and collectively as associations and political committees—who must retain control over the quantity and range of debate on public issues in a political campaign.

For these reasons we hold that 608 (c) is constitutionally invalid.

In sum, the provisions of the Act that impose a $1,000 limitation on contributions to a single candidate, 608 (b) (1), a $5,000 limitation on contributions by a political committee to a single candidate, 608 (b) (2), and a $25,000 limitation on total contributions by an individual during any calendar year, 608 (b) (3), are constitutionally valid. These limitations, along with the disclosure provisions, constitute the Act's primary weapons against the reality or appearance of improper influence stemming from the dependence of candidates on large campaign contributions. The contribution ceilings thus serve the basic governmental interest in safeguarding the integrity of the electoral process without directly impinging upon the rights of individual citizens and candidates to engage in political debate and discussion. By contrast, the First Amendment requires the invalidation of the Act's independent expenditure ceiling, 608 (e) (1), its limitation on a candidate's expenditures from his own personal funds, 608 (a), and its ceilings on overall campaign expenditures, 608 (c). These provisions place substantial and direct restrictions on the ability of candidates, citizens, and associations to engage in protected political expression, restrictions that the First Amendment cannot tolerate.

II. Reporting and Disclosure Requirements

Unlike the limitations on contributions and expenditures imposed by 18 U.S.C. 608, the disclosure requirements of the Act are not challenged by appellants as per se unconstitutional restrictions on the exercise of First Amendment freedoms of speech and association. Indeed, appellants argue that "narrowly drawn disclosure requirements are the proper solution to virtually all of the evils Congress sought to remedy." The particular requirements embodied in the Act are attacked as overbroad—both in their application to minor-party and independent candidates and in their extension to contributions as small as $11 or $101. Appellants also challenge the provision for disclosure by those who make independent contributions and expenditures, 434 (e). The Court of Appeals found no constitutional infirmities in the provisions challenged here. We affirm the determination on overbreadth and hold that 434 (e), if narrowly construed, also is within constitutional bounds. . . .

A. General Principles

Unlike the overall limitations on contributions and expenditures, the disclosure requirements impose no ceiling on campaign-related activities. But we have repeatedly found that compelled disclosure, in itself, can seriously infringe on privacy of association and belief guaranteed by the First Amendment. . . .

We long have recognized that significant encroachments on First Amendment rights of the sort that compelled disclosure imposes cannot be justified by a mere showing of some legitimate governmental interest. Since *NAACP* v. *Alabama* [1958] we have required that the subordinating interests of the State must survive exacting scrutiny. We also have insisted that there be a "relevant correlation" or "substantial relation" between the governmental interest and the information required to be disclosed. . . .

The strict test established by *NAACP* v. *Alabama* is necessary because compelled disclosure has the potential for substantially infringing the exercise of First Amendment rights. But we have acknowledged that there are governmental interests sufficiently important to outweigh the possibility of infringement, particularly when the "free functioning of our national institutions" is involved. *Communist Party* v. *Subversive Activities Control Bd.* [1961].

The governmental interests sought to be vindicated by the disclosure requirements are of this magnitude. They fall into three categories. First, disclosure provides the electorate with information "as to where political campaign money comes from and how it is spent by the candidate" in order to aid the voters in evaluating those who seek federal office. It allows voters to place each candidate in the political spectrum more precisely than is often possible solely on the basis of party labels and campaign speeches. The sources of a candidate's financial support also alert the voter to the interests to which a candidate is most likely to be responsive and thus facilitate predictions of future performance in office.

Second, disclosure requirements deter actual corruption and avoid the appearance of corruption by exposing large contributions and expenditures to the light of publicity. . . .

Third, and not least significant, recordkeeping, reporting, and disclosure requirements are an essential means of gathering the data necessary to detect violations of the contribution limitations described above. . . .

B. Application to Minor Parties and Independents

Appellants contend that the Act's requirements are overbroad insofar as they apply to contributions to minor parties and independent candidates because the governmental interest in this information is minimal and the danger of significant infringement on First Amendment rights is greatly increased. . . .

In *NAACP* v. *Alabama* the organization had "made an uncontroverted showing that on past occasions revelation of the identity of its rank-and-file members [had] exposed these members to economic reprisal, loss of employment, threat of physical coercion, and other manifestations of public hostility," and the State was unable to show that the disclosure it sought had a "substantial bearing" on the issues it sought to clarify. . . .

. . . No record of harassment on a similar scale was found in this case. We agree with the Court of Appeals' conclusion that *NAACP* v. *Alabama* is inapposite where, as here, any serious infringement on First Amendment rights brought about by the compelled disclosure of contributors is highly speculative. . . .

CHIEF JUSTICE BURGER, CONCURRING IN PART AND DISSENTING IN PART.

For reasons set forth more fully later, I dissent from those parts of the Court's holding sustaining the statutory provisions (a) for disclosure of small contributions, (b) for limitations on contributions, and (c) for public financing of Presidential campaigns. In my view, the Act's disclosure scheme is impermissibly broad and violative of the First Amendment as it relates to reporting contributions in excess of $10 and $100. The contribution limitations infringe on First Amendment liberties and suffer from the same infirmities that the Court correctly sees in the expenditure ceilings. . . .

. . . [N]o legitimate public interest has been shown in forcing the disclosure of modest contributions that are the prime support of new, unpopular, or unfashionable political causes. There is no realistic possibility that such modest donations will have a corrupting influence especially on parties that enjoy only "minor" status. Major parties would not notice them; minor parties need them. . . . In any event, the dangers to First Amendment rights here are too great. Flushing out the names of supporters of minority parties will plainly have a deterrent effect on potential contributors. . . .

I agree fully with that part of the Court's opinion that holds unconstitutional the limitations the Act puts on campaign expenditures which "place substantial and direct restrictions on the ability of candidates, citizens, and associations to engage in protected political expression, restrictions that the First Amendment cannot tolerate." Yet when it approves similarly stringent limitations on contributions, the Court ignores the reasons it finds so persuasive in the context of expenditures. For me contributions and expenditures are two sides of the same First Amendment coin.

By limiting campaign contributions, the Act restricts the amount of money that will be spent on political activity—and does so directly. . . .

The Court's attempt to distinguish the communication inherent in political contributions from the speech aspects of political expenditures simply "will not wash." We do little but engage in word games unless we recognize that people—candidates and contributors—spend money on political activity because they wish to communicate ideas, and their constitutional interest in doing so is precisely the same whether they or someone else utters the words.

The Court attempts to make the Act seem less restrictive by casting the problem as one that goes to freedom of association rather than freedom of speech. I have long thought freedom of association and freedom of expression were two peas from the same pod. The contribution limitations of the Act impose a restriction on certain forms of associational activity that are for the most part, as the Court recognizes, harmless in fact. And the restrictions are hardly incidental in their effect upon particular campaigns. Judges are ill-equipped to gauge the precise impact of legislation, but a law that impinges upon First Amendment rights requires us to make the attempt. It is not simply speculation to think that the limitations on contributions will foreclose some candidacies. The limitations will also alter the nature of some electoral contests drastically.

At any rate, the contribution limits are a far more severe restriction on First Amendment activity than the sort of "chilling" legislation for which the Court has shown such extraordinary concern in the past. See, e.g., *Cohen* v. *California* [1971]. . . .

JUSTICE WHITE, CONCURRING IN PART AND DISSENTING IN PART . . .

. . . I dissent . . . from the Court's view that the expenditure limitations of 18 U.S.C. 608 (c) and (e) (1970 ed., Supp. IV) violate the First Amendment. . . .

Since the contribution and expenditure limitations are neutral as to the content of speech and are not motivated by fear of the consequences of the political speech of particular candidates or of political speech in general, this case depends on whether the nonspeech interests of the Federal Government in regulating the use of money in political campaigns are sufficiently urgent to justify the incidental effects that the limitations visit upon the First Amendment interests of candidates and their supporters. . . .

. . . The Court . . . accepts the congressional judgment that the evils of unlimited contributions are sufficiently threatening to warrant restriction regardless of the impact of the limits on the contributor's opportunity for effective speech and in turn on the total volume of the candidate's political communications by reason of his inability to accept large sums from those willing to give.

. . . Congress was plainly of the view that these expenditures also have corruptive potential; but the Court strikes down the provision, strangely enough claiming more insight as to what may improperly influence candidates than is possessed by the majority of Congress that passed this bill and the President who signed it. Those supporting the bill undeniably included many seasoned professionals who have been deeply involved in elective processes and who have viewed them at close range over many years.

It would make little sense to me, and apparently made none to Congress, to limit the amounts an individual may give to a candidate or spend with his approval but fail to limit the amounts that could be spent on his behalf. Yet the Court permits the former while striking down the latter limitation. . . .

RESPONSES

FROM THE *WASHINGTON POST,* FEBRUARY 2, 1976, "CAMPAIGN FINANCE: SECOND THOUGHTS"

One function of the Supreme Court is to provide a sober second thought about laws and policies adopted in times of stress. The Court has met this reflective obligation with impressive care in its decision on the 1974 campaign financing law, Congress's complex attempt to reduce the corrosive influence of money in politics. In upholding many parts of the law and striking down others, the Court has established a legal framework for this year's campaigns. It has also emphasized some constitutional issues which the advocates of regulation, including ourselves, may not have paid enough attention to in the first post-Watergate clamor for controls.

The most important aspects of the ruling define how far the regulation of campaign spending may reach without running into the First Amendment's guarantee of free political expression. The Court emphatically upheld detailed disclosure of the sources and uses of campaign funds. A majority also approved limits on contributions to presidential and congressional campaigns, but rejected ceilings on spending as an interference with free speech. This means that candidates are free to spend as much as they can raise from their own funds or contributions that do not exceed the limits. It also means individuals and groups may not give huge amounts to candidates, but may spend whatever they want to independently. The only private political outlays Congress may constitutionally limit, the Court concluded, are those involving some transaction between a candidate and a supporter—a contribution, a loan, a prearrangement, or a deal. Those are the areas in which corruption and the appearance of corruption most readily arise.

Full disclosure and contributions limits should do much to combat the excessive or improper influence of monied interests. But serious problems remain. Without spending ceilings, some well-financed candidates may still be able to drown their opposition in a flood of advertising, mailings, and telephone appeals. Wealthy candidates will at least have an initial edge over those who have to solicit large numbers of small contributions. Moreover, in practice the distinction between "coordinated" and "independent" spending will be hard to make; groups backing candidates are likely to launch lavish "independent" drives to get around the contributions limits.

Many opponents of unchecked spending view these possibilities as loopholes opened by the Court. But one man's loophole is another man's liberty. To the Court, these are fundamental aspects of freedom which, however troubling in some ways, may not be abridged. "The First Amendment," the Court said, "denies the government the power to determine that spending to promote one's political views is wasteful, excessive, or unwise." The Constitution leaves such judgments to the people. In our view this is persuasive: which is another way of saying that the Court's well-reasoned opinion has afflicted us with some sober second thoughts about our advocacy of spending controls.

FROM THE *WALL STREET JOURNAL,* FEBRUARY 2, 1976, "THE HALF-DEAD MONSTER"

The United States Supreme Court has administered a semi-fatal blow to that malformed product of "post-Watergate morality," the 1974 Federal Election Campaign Act. But the remains of the law will probably act like the Frankenstein's monster it truly is. It will be awfully hard to kill, and the more you wound it, the more havoc it will wreak.

It seems to us the court was absolutely right in overthrowing the keystone of the law, a blatantly unconstitutional limit on campaign expenditures. This limit applied not only to the campaigner's own spending, but to money outlays by other individuals or groups "relative to a clearly identified candidate." In other words, if Stewart Mott wanted to plug Nelson Rockefeller as a presidential candidate, as the GM heir did on his own in 1968, he would have been allowed to spend only $1,000, scarcely enough to buy one corner of a page in the *New York Times.*

Obviously, as the Supreme Court found, this part of the law substantially restricted Mr. Mott's right to political expression, but the court also somehow concluded that this right did not include the right to give unlimited contributions to a candidate. In the confusion of partial concurrences and dissents, the Justices managed to draw a fine line between buying an ad to praise someone and handing him money directly so he could praise himself. But if the court didn't kill the monster, at least it dealt a crippling blow.

FROM THE *NEW YORK TIMES*, FEBRUARY 4, 1976, "CAMPAIGNS UNLIMITED"

By abolishing all restraints on political expenditures by individuals and organizations, the Supreme Court in its decision last week opened wide the doors to a return of the evils that the 1974 Federal Campaign Reform Law was intended to prevent.

The Court upheld the limit of $1,000 on individual contributions to a candidate but probably rendered the limit a nullity by permitting a contributor to spend unlimited amounts on behalf of a specific candidate as long as he did not coordinate his expenditures with the candidate's own campaign committee.

The Court tries to deal with this seeming contradiction in two ways. On practical grounds, it argues that "such independent expenditures may well provide little assistance to the candidate's campaign and indeed may prove counterproductive." Yet few big contributors are likely to share this view. If they place newspaper or television advertisements or rent space on a thousand billboards carrying the message, "Elect Candidate Jones," most will be reasonably sure that Mr. Jones will not consider their efforts "counterproductive" or of "little assistance."

Secondly, the Court notes that, if such expenditures can be shown to be controlled or coordinated by the candidate, they should be treated as if they were direct contributions and be subject to the $1,000 limit. But can control or coordination be proved? That will be difficult at best; it will be impossible unless there exists a Federal Election Commission with a large, well-trained staff capable of policing this gray area.

VIRGINIA PHARMACY BOARD V. VIRGINIA CONSUMER COUNCIL

425 U.S. 748 (1976)

The Virginia Consumer Council brought suit against the Virginia State Board of Pharmacy, challenging a 1968 state law that said it was unprofessional conduct for a licensed pharmacist to advertise prices of prescription drugs. The council claimed that the First Amendment entitled users of prescription drugs to information about drug prices and that to prohibit pharmacists from providing that information through advertising and other promotional means was unconstitutional. The three-judge district court agreed, and the Supreme Court, by a vote of 7 to 1, affirmed.

In *Virginia Pharmacy Board* the Court for the first time held that commercial speech is entitled to First Amendment protection. The Court first spoke to this question in *Valentine* v. *Chrestensen* (1942), observing that the First Amendment does not protect commercial advertising. In subsequent cases the Court reiterated its view that the First Amendment protects communications unless they are "purely commercial." In the first half of the seventies, however, the Court relaxed its attachment to the "commercial speech exception," as it was called, and indeed rejected an argument for it in *Bigelow* v. *Virginia* (1975). In *Virginia Pharmacy Board* the Court, completing its departure from *Valentine*, denied that there was any such exception. "Our question," wrote Justice Blackmun for the majority, "is whether speech which does 'no more than propose a commercial transaction' . . . is so removed from any 'exposition of ideas,' and from 'truth, science, morality, and arts in general, in its diffusion of liberal sentiments on the administration of Government,' that it lacks all protection. Our answer is that it is not."

Since *Virginia Pharmacy Board* the Court has continued to provide some protection for commercial speech, but less than for non-commercial speech. For example, in assessing the interest of government in regulating protected speech, the Court requires that this interest be "compelling" in the case of non-commercial speech but only "substantial" for commercial speech. Also, when government does regulate commercial speech, the Court does not direct it to use the means "least restrictive" of expression, a requirement often imposed in cases of non-commercial speech.

Opinion of the Court: **Blackmun**, Burger, Brennan, Stewart, White, Marshall, Powell. Concurring opinions: **Burger**; **Stewart**. Dissenting opinion: **Rehnquist**. Not participating: Stevens.

Virginia Pharmacy Board v. *Virginia Consumer Council* was decided on May 24, 1976.

OPINIONS

JUSTICE BLACKMUN DELIVERED THE OPINION OF THE COURT . . .

The appellants contend that the advertisement of prescription drug prices is outside the protection of the First Amendment because it is "commercial speech." There can be no question that in past decisions the Court has given some indication that commercial speech is unprotected. In *Valentine* v. *Chrestensen* [1942], the Court upheld a New York statute that prohibited the distribution of any "handbill, circular . . . or other advertising matter whatsoever in or upon any street." The Court concluded that, although the First Amendment would forbid the banning of all communication by handbill in the public thoroughfares, it imposed "no such restraint on government as respect purely commercial advertising." Further support for a "commercial speech" exception to the First Amendment may perhaps be found in *Breard* v. *Alexandria* [1951], where the Court upheld a conviction for violation of an ordinance prohibiting door-to-door solicitation of magazine subscriptions. The Court reasoned: "The selling . . . brings into the transaction a commercial feature." . . . Moreover, the Court several times has stressed that communications to which First Amendment protection was given were not "purely commercial." *New York Times Co.* v. *Sullivan* [1964]; *Thomas* v. *Collins* [1945]; *Murdock* v. *Pennsylvania* [1943]; *Jamison* v. *Texas* [1943].

Since the decision in *Breard*, however, the Court has never denied protection on the ground that the speech in issue was "commercial speech." That simplistic approach, which by then had come under criticism or was regarded as of doubtful validity by Members of the Court, was avoided in *Pittsburgh Press Co.* v. *Human Relations Comm'n* [1973]. There the Court upheld an ordinance prohibiting newspapers from listing employment advertisements in columns according to whether male or female employees were sought to be hired. The Court, to be sure, characterized the advertisements as "classic examples of commercial speech," and a newspaper's printing of the advertisements as of the same character. The Court, however, upheld the ordinance on the ground that the restriction it imposed was permissible because the discriminatory hirings proposed by the advertisements, and by their newspaper layout, were themselves illegal.

Last term, in *Bigelow* v. *Virginia* (1975), the notion of unprotected "commercial speech" all but passed from the scene. We reversed a conviction for violation of a Virginia statute that made the circulation of any publication to encourage or promote the processing of an abortion in Virginia a misdemeanor. The defendant had published in his newspaper the availability of abortions in New York. The advertisement in question, in addition to announcing that abortions were legal in New York, offered the services of a referral agency in that State. We rejected the contention that the publication was unprotected because it was commercial. *Chrestensen*'s continued validity was questioned, and its holding was described as "distinctly a limited one" that merely upheld "a reasonable regulation of the manner in which commercial advertising could be distributed." We concluded that "the Virginia courts erred in their assumptions that advertising, as such, was entitled to no First Amendment protection," and we observed that the "relationship of speech to the marketplace of products or of services does not make it valueless in the marketplace of ideas."

Some fragment of hope for the continuing validity of a "commercial speech" exception arguably might have persisted because of the subject matter of the advertisement in *Bigelow*. We noted that in announcing the availability of legal abortions in New York, the advertisement "did more than simply propose a commercial transaction. It contained factual material of clear 'public interest.'" And, of course, the advertisement related to activity with which, at least in some respects, the State could not interfere. See *Roe* v. *Wade* [1973]; *Doe* v. *Bolton* [1973]. Indeed, we observed: "We need not decide in this case the precise extent to which the First Amendment permits regulation of advertising that is related to activities the State may legitimately regulate or even prohibit."

Here, in contrast, the question whether there is a First Amendment exception for "commercial speech" is squarely before us. Our pharmacist does not wish to editorialize on any subject, cultural, philosophical, or political. He does not wish to report any particularly newsworthy fact, or to make generalized observations even about commercial matters. The "idea" he wishes to communicate is simply this: "I will sell you the X prescription drug at the Y price." Our question, then, is whether this communication is wholly outside the protection of the First Amendment.

We begin with several propositions that already are settled or beyond serious dispute. It is clear, for example, that speech does not lose its First Amendment protection because money is spent to project it, as in a paid advertisement of one form or another. *Buckley* v. *Valeo* [1976]. . . . Speech likewise is protected even though it is carried in a form that is "sold" for profit, *Smith* v. *California* [1959] (books); *Joseph Burstyn, Inc.* v. *Wilson* [1952] (motion pictures); *Murdock* v. *Pennsylvania* [1943] (religious literature), and even though it may involve a solicitation to purchase or otherwise pay or contribute money. . . .

If there is a kind of commercial speech that lacks all First Amendment protection, therefore, it must be distinguished by its content. Yet the speech whose content deprives it of protection cannot simply be speech on a commercial subject. No one would contend that our pharmacist may be prevented from being heard on the subject of whether, in general, pharmaceutical prices should be regulated, or their advertisement forbidden. Nor can it be dispositive that a commercial advertisement is noneditorial, and merely reports a fact. Purely factual matter of public interest may claim protection. . . .

Our question is whether speech which does "no more than propose a commercial transaction," *Pittsburgh Press Co.*, is so removed from any "exposition of ideas," *Chaplinsky* v. *New Hampshire* [1942], and from "'truth, science, morality, and arts in general, in its diffusion of liberal sentiments on the administration of Government,'" *Roth* v. *United States* [1957], that it lacks all protection. Our answer is that it is not.

Focusing first on the individual parties to the transaction that is proposed in the commercial advertisement, we may assume that the advertiser's interest is a purely economic one. That hardly disqualifies him from protection under the First Amendment. The interests of the contestants in a labor dispute are primarily economic, but it has long been settled that both the employee and the employer are protected by the First Amendment when they express themselves on the merits of the dispute in order to influence its outcome. . . .

As to the particular consumer's interest in the free flow of commercial information, that interest may be as keen, if not keener by far, than his interest in the day's most urgent political debate. Appellees' case in this respect is a convincing one. Those whom the suppression of prescription drug price information hits the hardest are the poor, the sick, and particularly the aged. A disproportionate amount of their income tends to be spent on prescription drugs; yet they are the least able to learn, by shopping from pharmacist to pharmacist, where their scarce dollars are best spent. When drug prices vary as strikingly as they do, information as to who is charging what becomes more than a convenience. It could mean the alleviation of physical pain or the enjoyment of basic necessities.

Generalizing, society also may have a strong interest in the free flow of commercial information. Even an individual advertisement, though entirely "commercial," may be of general public interest. . . . Obviously, not all commercial messages contain the same or even a very great public interest element. There are few to which such an element, however, could not be added. Our pharmacist, for example, could cast himself as a commentator on store-to-store disparities in drug prices, giving his own and those of a competitor as proof. We see little point in requiring him to do so, and little difference if he does not.

Moreover, there is another consideration that suggests that no line between publicly "interesting" or "important" commercial advertising and the opposite kind could ever be drawn. Advertising, however tasteless and excessive it sometimes may seem, is nonetheless dissemination of information as to who is producing and selling what product, for what reason, and at what price. So long as we preserve a predominantly free enterprise economy, the allocation of our resources in large measure will be made through numerous private economic decisions. It is a matter of public interest that those decisions, in the aggregate, be intelligent and well informed. To this end, the free flow of commercial information is indispensable. . . . And if it is indispensable to the proper allocation of resources in a free enterprise system, it is also indispensable to the formation of intelligent opinions as to how that system ought to be regulated or altered. Therefore, even if the First Amendment were thought to be primarily an instrument to enlighten public decisionmaking in a democracy, we could not say that the free flow of information does not serve that goal.

Arrayed against these substantial individual and societal interests are a number of justifications for the advertising ban. These have to do principally with maintaining a high degree of professionalism on the part of licensed pharmacists. Indisputably, the State has a strong interest in maintaining that professionalism. . . .

Price advertising, it is argued, will place in jeopardy the pharmacist's expertise and, with it, the customer's health. . . .

The strength of these proffered justifications is greatly undermined by the fact that high professional standards, to a substantial extent, are guaranteed by the close regulation to which pharmacists in Virginia are subject. And this case concerns the retail sale by the pharmacist more than it does his professional standards. Surely, any pharmacist guilty of professional dereliction that actually endangers his customer will promptly lose his license. At the same time, we cannot discount the Board's justifications entirely. The Court regarded justifications of this type sufficient to sustain the advertising bans challenged on due process and equal protection grounds. . . .

The challenge now made, however, is based on the First Amendment. This casts the Board's justifications in a different light, for on close inspection it is seen that the State's protectiveness of its citizens rests in large measure on the advantages of their being kept in ignorance. The advertising ban does not directly affect professional standards one way or the other. It affects them only through the reactions it is assumed people will have to the free flow of drug price information. . . .

It appears to be feared that if the pharmacist who wishes to provide low cost, and assertedly low quality, services is permitted to advertise, he will be taken up on his offer by too many unwitting customers. They will choose the low-cost, low-quality service and drive the "professional" pharmacist out of business. They will respond only to costly and excessive advertising, and end up paying the price. They will go from one pharmacist to another, following the discount, and destroy the pharmacist-customer relationship. They will lose respect for the profession because it advertises. All this is not in their best interests, and all this can be avoided if they are not permitted to know who is charging what.

There is, of course, an alternative to this highly paternalistic approach. That alternative is to assume that this information is not in itself harmful, that people will perceive their own best interests if only they are well enough informed, and that the best means to that end is to open the channels of communication rather than to close them. If they are truly open, nothing prevents the "professional" pharmacist from marketing his own assertedly superior product, and contrasting it with that of the low-cost, high-volume prescription drug retailer. But the choice among these alternative approaches is not ours to make or the Virginia General Assembly's. It is precisely this kind of choice, between the dangers of suppressing information, and the dangers of its misuse if it is freely available, that the First Amendment makes for us. Virginia is free to require whatever professional standards it wishes of its pharmacists; it may subsidize them or protect them from competition in other ways. . . . But it may not do so by keeping the public in ignorance of the entirely lawful terms that competing pharmacists are offering. In this sense, the justifications Virginia has offered for suppressing the flow of prescription drug price information, far from persuading us that the flow is not protected by the First Amendment, have reinforced our view that it is. We so hold.

In concluding that commercial speech, like other varieties, is protected, we of course do not hold that it can never be regulated in any way. Some forms of commercial speech regulation are surely permissible. We mention a few only to make clear that they are not before us and therefore are not foreclosed by this case.

There is no claim, for example, that the prohibition on prescription drug price advertising is a mere time, place, and manner restriction. We have often approved restrictions of that kind provided that they are justified without reference to the content of the regulated speech, that they serve a significant governmental interest, and that in so doing they leave open ample alternative channels for communication of the information. . . . Whatever may be the proper bounds of time, place, and manner restrictions on commercial speech, they are plainly exceeded by this Virginia statute, which singles out speech of a particular content and seeks to prevent its dissemination completely.

Nor is there any claim that prescription drug price advertisements are forbidden because they are false or misleading in any way. Untruthful speech, commercial or otherwise, has never been protected for its own sake. . . . Obviously, much commercial speech is not provably false, or even wholly false, but only deceptive or misleading. We foresee no obstacle to a State's dealing effectively with this problem. The First Amendment, as we construe it today, does not prohibit the State from insuring that the stream of commercial information flow cleanly as well as freely. . . .

Also, there is no claim that the transactions proposed in the forbidden advertisements are themselves illegal in any way. . . . Finally, the special problems of the electronic broadcast media are likewise not in this case. . . .

What is at issue is whether a State may completely suppress the dissemination of concededly truthful information about entirely lawful activity, fearful of that information's effect upon its disseminators and its recipients. Reserving other questions, we conclude that the answer to this one is in the negative.

The judgment of the District Court is
AFFIRMED.

JUSTICE STEWART, CONCURRING . . .

The Court's determination that commercial advertising of the kind at issue here is not "wholly outside the protection of" the First Amendment indicates by its very phrasing that there are important differences between commercial price and product advertising, on the one hand, and ideological communication on the other. . . . Ideological expression, be it oral, literary, pictorial, or theatrical, is integrally related to the exposition of thought—thought that may shape our concepts of the whole universe of man. Although such expression may convey factual information relevant to social and individual decisionmaking, it is protected by the Constitution, whether or not it contains factual representations and even if it includes inaccurate assertions of fact. Indeed, disregard of the "truth" may be employed to give force to the underlying idea expressed by the speaker. "Under the First Amendment there is no such thing as a false idea," and the only way that ideas can be suppressed is through "the competition of other ideas," *Gertz* v. *Robert Welch, Inc.* [1974].

Commercial price and product advertising differs markedly from ideological expression because it is confined to the promotion of specific goods or services. The First Amendment protects the advertisement because of the "information of potential interest and value" conveyed, *Bigelow,* rather than because of any direct contribution to the interchange of ideas. . . . Since the factual claims contained in commercial price or product advertisements relate to tangible goods or services, they may be tested empirically and corrected to reflect the truth without in any manner jeopardizing the free dissemination of thought. Indeed, the elimination of false and deceptive claims serves to promote the one facet of commercial price and product advertising that warrants First Amendment protection—its contribution to the flow of accurate and reliable information relevant to public and private decisionmaking.

JUSTICE REHNQUIST, DISSENTING . . .

The Court speaks of the consumer's interest in the free flow of commercial information, particularly in the case of the poor, the sick, and the aged. It goes on to observe that "society also may have a strong interest in the free flow of commercial information." One need not disagree with either of these statements in order to feel that they should presumptively be the concern of the Virginia Legislature, which sits to balance these and other claims in the process of making laws such as the one here under attack. The Court speaks of the importance in a "predominantly free enterprise economy" of intelligent and well-informed decisions as to allocation of resources. While there is again much to be said for the Court's observation as a matter of desirable public policy, there is certainly nothing in the United States Constitution which requires the Virginia Legislature to hew to the teachings of Adam Smith in its legislative decisions regulating the pharmacy profession. . . .

The Court addresses itself to the valid justifications which may be found for the Virginia statute, and apparently discounts them because it feels they embody a "highly paternalistic approach." It concludes that the First Amendment requires that channels of advertising communication with respect to prescription drugs must be opened, and that Virginia may not keep "the public in ignorance of the entirely lawful terms that competing pharmacists are offering."

The Court concedes that legislatures may prohibit false and misleading advertisements, and may likewise prohibit advertisements seeking to induce transactions which are themselves illegal. In a final footnote the opinion tosses a bone to the traditionalists in the legal and medical professions by suggesting that because they sell services rather than drugs the holding of this case is not automatically applicable to advertising in those professions. But if the sole limitation on permissible state proscription of advertising is that it may not be false or misleading, surely the difference between pharmacists' advertising and lawyers' and doctors' advertising can be only one of degree and not of kind. I cannot distinguish between the public's right to know the price of drugs and its right to know the price of title searches or physical examinations or other professional services for which standardized fees are charged. . . .

There are undoubted difficulties with an effort to draw a bright line between "commercial speech" on the one hand and "protected speech" on the other, and the Court does better to face up to these difficulties than to attempt to hide them under labels. In this case, however, the Court has unfortunately substituted for the wavering line previously thought to exist between commercial speech and protected speech a no more satisfactory line of its own— that between "truthful" commercial speech, on the one hand, and that which is "false and misleading" on the other. The difficulty with this line is not that it wavers, but on the contrary that it is simply too Procrustean to take into account the congeries of factors which I believe could, quite consistently with the First and Fourteenth Amendments, properly influence a legislative decision with respect to commercial advertising.

The Court insists that the rule it lays down is consistent even with the view that the First Amendment is "primarily an instrument to enlighten public decisionmaking in a democracy." I had understood this view to relate to public decisionmaking as to political, social, and other public issues, rather than the decision of a particular individual as to whether to purchase one or another kind of shampoo. It is undoubtedly arguable that many people in the country regard the choice of shampoo as just as important as who may be elected to local, state, or national political office, but that does not automatically bring information about competing shampoos within the protection of the First Amendment. . . .

In the case of "our" hypothetical pharmacist, he may now presumably advertise not only the prices of prescription drugs, but may attempt to energetically promote their sale so long as he does so truthfully. Quite consistently with Virginia law requiring prescription drugs to be available only through a physician, "our" pharmacist might run any of the following representative advertisements in a local newspaper: "Pain getting you down? Insist that your physician prescribe Demerol. You pay a little more than for aspirin, but you get a lot more relief." "Can't shake the flu? Get a prescription for Tetracycline from your doctor today." "Don't spend another sleepless night. Ask your doctor to prescribe Seconal without delay."

Unless the State can show that these advertisements are either actually untruthful or misleading, it presumably is not free to restrict in any way commercial efforts on the part of those who profit from the sale of prescription drugs to put them in the widest possible circulation. But such a line simply makes no allowance whatever for what appears to have been a considered legislative judgment in most States that while prescription drugs are a necessary and vital part of medical care and treatment, there are sufficient dangers attending their widespread use that they simply may not be promoted in the same manner as hair creams, deodorants, and toothpaste. The very real dangers that general advertising for such drugs might create in terms of encouraging, even though not sanctioning, illicit use of them by individuals for whom they have not been prescribed, or by generating patient pressure upon physicians to prescribe them, are simply not dealt with in the Court's opinion. If prescription drugs may be advertised, they may be advertised on television during family viewing time. Nothing we know about the acquisitive instincts of those who inhabit every business and profession to a greater or lesser extent gives any reason to think that such persons will not do everything they can to generate demand for these products in much the same manner and to much the same degree as demand for other commodities has been generated.

Both Congress and state legislatures have by law sharply limited the permissible dissemination of information about some commodities because of the potential harm resulting from those commodities, even though they were not thought to be sufficiently demonstrably harmful to warrant outright prohibition of their sale. Current prohibitions on television advertising of liquor and cigarettes are prominent in this category, but apparently under the Court's holding so long as the advertisements are not deceptive they may no longer be prohibited.

This case presents a fairly typical First Amendment problem—that of balancing interests in individual free speech against public welfare determinations embodied in a legislative enactment. As the Court noted in *American Communications Assn.* v. *Douds* [1950]:

[L]egitimate attempts to protect the public, not from the remote possible effects of noxious ideologies, but from the present excesses of direct, active conduct, are not presumptively bad because they interfere with and, in some of its manifestations, restrain the exercise of First Amendment rights.

Here the rights of the appellees seem to me to be marginal at best. There is no ideological content to the information which they seek and it is freely available to them—they may even publish it if they so desire. The only persons directly affected by this statute are not parties to this lawsuit. On the other hand, the societal interest against the promotion of drug use for every ill, real or imaginary, seems to me extremely strong. I do not believe that the First Amendment mandates the Court's "open door policy" toward such commercial advertising.

RESPONSE

FROM THE *WALL STREET JOURNAL*, MAY 27, 1976, "ELEVATING 'COMMERCIAL SPEECH'"

The Supreme Court went a long way towards correcting a puzzling legal anomaly this week when it struck down a Virginia law that bars advertising of prescription drug prices. The decision gave "commercial speech," or advertising, a large measure of protection under the First Amendment, something it has not had in the past.

This case opens up a rich lode for groups with a genuine interest in protecting consumers from anti-competitive practices. During all those years when commercial speech was held to be unworthy of the Constitution's guarantee of freedom, any number of state laws have sprung up forbidding price advertising of such things as eyeglasses, funeral services, or what have you. They deserve to be eliminated.

The High Court's Monday decision did not go as far as it might have. It has reserved for another day any definitive ruling on whether the right to advertise freely extends to doctors and lawyers. Medical societies and bar associations have for years restricted their members from promoting their services with the result that clients often have little idea of what they will be charged until they are in the practitioner's office. Also, fee schedules are frequently uniform in a community. It can be hoped that consumerists will continue to press the court to break down these remaining barriers to competition.

It is in fact hard to see why the legal doctrine separating commercial speech from other varieties ever came into being at all. The definitive ruling to that effect dates back to 1942 when the High Court upheld New York City's action in barring a local entrepreneur from distributing handbills advertising his exhibition of a submarine moored at a local pier. The court held simply that the Constitution places no restraint on the right of government to proscribe "purely commercial advertising," but it gave little explanation of how it reached that conclusion.

No doubt the courts' historical ambivalence towards the rights of advertisers has reflected in part a public ambivalence. The uninhibited hawking of wares in the marketplace often intrudes on public sensibilities and has been generally held in low esteem among intellectuals. The decisions to exclude it from free speech protections have no doubt grown partly out of a desire by courts not to further complicate the already difficult issue of what is, and is not, protected under the First Amendment. Interestingly, pornography seemingly has gotten more protection in recent years than advertising.

This fear that advertising might "pollute" the free speech right is largely irrational but has been allowed to stand in the absence of any strong movement to dislodge it. The movement has come as more and more economic research has focused on the public cost of bans on price advertising and as consumer groups have set out to contest the issue. No doubt the High Court was strongly influenced in its Monday decision by studies which estimate consumer costs to range from $130 million to $380 million because of the barriers that thirty states have erected against prescription drug advertising.

Advertising barriers usually are defended on grounds that price competition would lower professional standards in fields where a high level of professionalism is required. The court is obviously prepared to consider this argument on behalf of bans on price advertising by attorneys and doctors. But even here, it is difficult to see what relationship exists between price advertising and professional integrity. Certainly there are a good many industries that affect human life that impose no special risks on consumers merely because they advertise the prices of their products and services.

More than likely the converse is true. The more information the public has the more likely it is to accurately judge who is the quack and who the honest and expert practitioner. The Supreme Court has opened the door to the supply of fuller information. It can be hoped that it will not draw back from its affirmation that free and open exchange of market information ultimately is the best bet for protecting the consumer's best interests.

ZURCHER V. STANFORD DAILY

436 U.S. 547 (1978)

Demonstrators seized and occupied the administrative offices of Stanford University Hospital. When officers of the Palo Alto Police Department tried to break through barricaded doors, they were attacked by a group of demonstrators armed with sticks and clubs. Nine officers were injured. The *Stanford Daily*, the student newspaper at Stanford University, published articles and photographs about these events. The local district attorney obtained a warrant and searched the *Daily's* offices for any negatives, films, and pictures. Police found no photographs other than those already published but did read some notes and correspondence.

The *Stanford Daily*, which was not accused of any crime, sued the police in federal district court, contending that the search violated the First Amendment's free press clause and the Fourth Amendment's protection against unreasonable searches. The court ruled (1) that the Fourth Amendment prohibits a warrant to search for materials in the hands of an innocent party unless there is probable cause to believe that a subpoena is impractical and (2) that only in exceptional circumstances may a newspaper be the innocent object of such a search. The search of the *Daily* was, the court said, illegal. The U.S. Court of Appeals for the Ninth Circuit adopted the opinion of the district court. But the Supreme Court, by a vote of 5 to 3, reversed, holding that the First Amendment does not forbid the search of a third party when it is a newspaper, and that the Fourth Amendment adequately protects media institutions when they become objects of a search.

The Court's view of this novel issue—whether the Constitution mandates special treatment for searches of press offices—provoked sharp criticism from the news media. As a result, Congress in 1980 passed legislation limiting newsroom searches to circumstances where subpoenas have proved ineffective or where probable cause exists to suspect journalists of wrongdoing.

Opinion of the Court: **White**, Burger, Blackmun, Powell, Rehnquist. Concurring opinion: **Powell**. Dissenting opinions: **Stewart**, Marshall; **Stevens**. Not participating: Brennan.

Zurcher v. *Stanford Daily* was decided on May 31, 1978.

OPINIONS

JUSTICE WHITE DELIVERED THE OPINION OF THE COURT . . .

The District Court held, and respondents assert here, that whatever may be true of third-party searches generally, where the third party is a newspaper, there are additional factors derived from the First Amendment that justify a nearly per se rule forbidding the search warrant and permitting only the subpoena. . . . The general submission is that searches of newspaper offices for evidence of crime reasonably believed to be on the premises will seriously threaten the ability of the press to gather, analyze, and disseminate news. This is said to be true for several reasons: First, searches will be physically disruptive to such an extent that timely publication will be impeded. Second, confidential sources of information will dry up, and the press will also lose opportunities to cover various events because of fears of the participants that press files will be readily available to the authorities. Third, reporters will be deterred from recording and preserving their recollections for future use if such information is subject to seizure. Fourth, the processing of news and its dissemination will be chilled by the prospects that searches will disclose internal editorial deliberations. Fifth, the press will resort to self-censorship to conceal its possession of information of potential interest to the police.

It is true that the struggle from which the Fourth Amendment emerged "is largely a history of conflict between the Crown and the press," *Stanford* v. *Texas* [1965], and that in issuing warrants and determining the reasonableness of a search, state and federal magistrates should be aware that "unrestricted power of search and seizure could also be an instrument for stifling liberty of expression." *Marcus* v. *Search Warrant* [1961]. Where the materials sought to be seized may be protected by the First Amendment, the requirements of the Fourth Amendment must be applied with "scrupulous exactitude." *Stanford*. "A seizure reasonable as to one type of material in one setting may be unreasonable in a different setting or with respect to another kind of material." *Roaden* v. *Kentucky* [1973]. Hence, in *Stanford*, the Court invalidated a warrant authorizing the search of a private home for all books, records, and other materials relating to the Communist Party, on the ground that whether or not the warrant would have been sufficient in other contexts, it authorized the searchers to rummage among and make judgments about books and papers and was the functional equivalent of a general warrant, one of the principal targets of the Fourth Amendment. Where presumptively protected materials are sought to be seized, the warrant requirement should be administered to leave as little as possible to the discretion or whim of the officer in the field.

Similarly, where seizure is sought of allegedly obscene materials, the judgment of the arresting officer alone is insufficient to justify issuance of a search warrant or a seizure without a warrant incident to arrest. The procedure for determining probable cause must afford an opportunity for the judicial officer to "focus searchingly on the question of obscenity." *Marcus*. . . .

Neither the Fourth Amendment nor the cases requiring consideration of First Amendment values in issuing search warrants, however, call for imposing the regime ordered by the District Court. Aware of the long struggle between Crown and press and desiring to curb unjustified official intrusions, the Framers took the enormously important step of subjecting searches to the test of reasonableness and to the general rule requiring search warrants issued by neutral magistrates. They nevertheless did not forbid warrants where the press was involved, did not require special showings that subpoenas would be impractical, and did not insist that the owner of the place to be searched, if connected with the press, must be shown to be implicated in the offense being investigated. Further, the prior cases do no more than insist that the courts apply the warrant requirements with particular exactitude when First Amendment interests would be endangered by the search. As we see it, no more than this is required where the warrant requested is for the seizure of criminal evidence reasonably believed to be on the premises occupied by a newspaper. Properly administered, the preconditions for a warrant—probable cause, specificity with respect to the place to be searched and the things to be seized, and overall reasonableness—should afford sufficient protection against the harms that are assertedly threatened by warrants for searching newspaper offices.

There is no reason to believe, for example, that magistrates cannot guard against searches of the type, scope, and intrusiveness that would actually interfere with the timely publication of a newspaper. Nor, if the requirements of specificity and reasonableness are properly applied, policed, and observed, will there be any occasion or opportunity for officers to rummage at large in newspaper files or to intrude into or to deter normal editorial and publication decisions. The warrant issued in this case authorized nothing of this sort. Nor are we convinced, any more than we were in *Branzburg* v. *Hayes* [1972], that confidential sources will disappear and that the press will suppress news because of fears of warranted searches. Whatever incremental effect there may be in this regard if search warrants, as well as subpoenas, are permissible in proper circumstances, it does not make a constitutional difference in our judgment.

The fact is that respondents and amici have pointed to only a very few instances in the entire United States since 1971 involving the issuance of warrants for searching newspaper premises. This reality hardly suggests abuse; and if abuse occurs, there will be time enough to deal with it. Furthermore, the press is not only an important, critical, and valuable asset to society, but it is not easily intimidated—nor should it be.

Respondents also insist that the press should be afforded opportunity to litigate the State's entitlement to the material it seeks before it is turned over or seized and that whereas the search warrant procedure is defective in this respect, resort to the subpoena would solve the problem. . . . But presumptively protected materials are not necessarily immune from seizure under warrant for use at a criminal trial. Not every such seizure, and not even most, will impose a prior restraint. . . . And surely a warrant to search newspaper premises for criminal evidence such as the one issued here for news photographs taken in a public place carries no realistic threat of prior restraint or of any direct restraint whatsoever on the publication of the *Daily* or on its communication of ideas. The hazards of such warrants can be avoided by a neutral magistrate carrying out his responsibilities under the Fourth Amendment, for he has ample tools at his disposal to confine warrants to search within reasonable limits.

We note finally that if the evidence sought by warrant is sufficiently connected with the crime to satisfy the probable-cause requirement, it will very likely be sufficiently relevant to justify a subpoena and to withstand a motion to quash. Further, Fifth Amendment and state shield-law objections that might be asserted in opposition to compliance with a subpoena are largely irrelevant to determining the legality of a search warrant under the Fourth Amendment. Of course, the Fourth Amendment does not prevent or advise against legislative or executive efforts to establish nonconstitutional protections against possible abuses of the search warrant procedure, but we decline to reinterpret the Amendment to impose a general constitutional barrier against warrants to search newspaper premises, to require resort to subpoenas as a general rule, or to demand prior notice and hearing in connection with the issuance of search warrants.

We accordingly reject the reasons given by the District Court and adopted by the Court of Appeals for holding the search for photographs at the *Stanford Daily* to have been unreasonable within the meaning of the Fourth Amendment and in violation of the First Amendment. Nor has anything else presented here persuaded us that the Amendments forbade this search. It follows that the judgment of the Court of Appeals is

REVERSED.

JUSTICE STEWART, DISSENTING . . .

It seems to me self-evident that police searches of newspaper offices burden the freedom of the press. The most immediate and obvious First Amendment injury caused by such a visitation by the police is physical disruption of the operation of the newspaper. Policemen occupying a newsroom and searching it thoroughly for what may be an extended period of time will inevitably interrupt its normal operations, and thus impair or even temporarily prevent the processes of newsgathering, writing, editing, and publishing. By contrast, a subpoena would afford the newspaper itself an opportunity to locate whatever material might be requested and produce it.

But there is another and more serious burden on a free press imposed by an unannounced police search of a newspaper office: the possibility of disclosure of information received from confidential sources, or of the identity of the sources themselves. Protection of those sources is necessary to ensure that the press can fulfill its constitutionally designated function of informing the public, because important information can often be obtained only by an assurance that the source will not be revealed. . . .

Today the Court does not question the existence of this constitutional protection, but says only that it is not "convinced . . . that confidential sources will disappear and that the press will suppress news because of fears of warranted searches." . . . This facile conclusion seems to me to ignore common experience. It requires no blind leap of faith to understand that a person who gives information to a journalist only on condition that his identity will not be revealed will be less likely to give that information if he knows that, despite the journalist's assurance, his identity may in fact be disclosed. And it cannot be denied that confidential information may be exposed to the eyes of police officers who execute a search warrant by rummaging through the files, cabinets, desks, and wastebaskets of a newsroom. Since the indisputable effect of such searches will thus be to prevent a newsman from being able to promise confidentiality to his potential sources, it seems obvious to me that a journalist's access to information, and thus the public's, will thereby be impaired.

A search warrant allows police officers to ransack the files of a newspaper, reading each and every document until they have found the one named in the warrant, while a subpoena would permit the newspaper itself to produce only the specific documents requested. A search, unlike a subpoena, will therefore lead to the needless exposure of confidential information completely unrelated to the purpose of the investigation. The knowledge that police officers can make an unannounced raid on a newsroom is thus bound to have a deterrent effect on the availability of confidential news sources. The end result, wholly inimical to the First Amendment, will be a diminishing flow of potentially important information to the public. . . .

The decisions of this Court establish that a prior adversary judicial hearing is generally required to assess in advance any threatened invasion of First Amendment liberty. A search by police officers affords no timely opportunity for such a hearing, since a search warrant is ordinarily issued ex parte upon the affidavit of a policeman or prosecutor. There is no opportunity to challenge the necessity for the search until after it has occurred and the constitutional protection of the newspaper has been irretrievably invaded.

On the other hand, a subpoena would allow a newspaper, through a motion to quash, an opportunity for an adversary hearing with respect to the production of any material which a prosecutor might think is in its possession. . . .

. . . If, in the present litigation, the *Stanford Daily* had been served with a subpoena, it would have had an opportunity to demonstrate to the court what the police ultimately found to be true—that the evidence sought did not exist. The legitimate needs of government thus would have been served without infringing the freedom of the press.

Perhaps as a matter of abstract policy a newspaper office should receive no more protection from unannounced police searches than, say, the office of a doctor or the office of a bank. But we are here to uphold a Constitution. And our Constitution does not explicitly protect the practice of medicine or the business of banking from all abridgment by government. It does explicitly protect the freedom of the press.

RICHMOND NEWSPAPERS, INC. V. VIRGINIA
478 U.S. 555 (1980)

A second-degree murder conviction was overturned by the Virginia Supreme Court on grounds that evidence against the accused had been improperly admitted. The retrial ended in a mistrial, and then another retrial met the same fate, apparently because a prospective juror had read newspaper accounts of the previous trials and had told others in the jury pool about it. At the start of the fourth trial, with reporters for the Richmond newspapers attending, the lawyer for the accused moved that the proceedings be closed to the public. The prosecution had no objection to this request, and the trial judge, concerned about ensuring fairness to the defendant, proceeded to clear the courtroom of all but those scheduled to testify. Lawyers for the Richmond papers failed to persuade the judge to vacate his closure order. Suing for access to the trial, the newspapers were rebuffed by the Virginia Supreme Court but prevailed in the U.S. Supreme Court, 7 to 1.

Richmond Newspapers was by no means the first Supreme Court case involving conflicts between a defendant's right to a fair trial and the right to obtain and publish information about the accused and his trial. In *Nebraska Press Association* v. *Stuart* (1976), the Court held that a state judge's order barring the press from reporting about the trial of a mass murderer—an order issued to guard against prejudicial publicity—violated the First Amendment ban on prior restraint. The Court did not decide, however, whether the First Amendment actually guarantees a right of the public to attend trials. Nor did it do so three years later in *Gannett Co.* v. *DePasquale* (1979). Indeed, in the latter case, the Court, declining to address the First Amendment issue, held that the Sixth Amendment's guarantee to the accused of a public trial does not bestow upon the public or the press a right of access to a pretrial hearing—a ruling that alarmed the news media.

In *Richmond Newspapers* the Court could not avoid the question that the press now vigorously petitioned it to answer in the affirmative—whether the First Amendment provides a right of access to the courts. The Court's declaration of this right in the context of this particular case left unresolved key questions, such as whether the right of access to trials extends to pretrial hearings, and to civil as well as criminal trials. During the 1980s the Court issued rulings effectively extending the right to pretrial hearings. It has yet to rule on the right of access to civil trials.

In his opinion announcing the Court's judgment, Chief Justice Burger, joined by Justices White and Stevens, argued from history in concluding that trials are presumptively open to the public and therefore the press. Justice Brennan, joined by Justice Marshall, made a different argument—that the First Amendment has "a structural role to play in securing and fostering our republican system of self-government," a role that requires a right of access to trials. *Richmond Newspapers* thus did not provide the majority rationale necessary for principled applications in other contexts in which access might be sought. Nor did it set forth a standard for determining when the government's (or the defendant's) interests might outweigh the public right of access. The Court has since made clear that any denial of access must pass the very stringent test of being "narrowly tailored" in order to serve "a compelling governmental interest."

Judgment of the Court: **Burger**, White, Stevens. Concurring opinions: **White**; **Stevens**. Concurring in the judgment: **Brennan**, Marshall; **Stewart**; **Blackmun**. Dissenting opinion: **Rehnquist**. Not participating: Powell.

Richmond Newspapers, Inc. v. *Virginia* was decided on July 2, 1980.

CHIEF JUSTICE BURGER ANNOUNCED THE JUDGMENT OF THE COURT AND DELIVERED AN OPINION IN WHICH JUSTICE WHITE AND JUSTICE STEVENS JOINED.

The narrow question presented in this case is whether the right of the public and press to attend criminal trials is guaranteed under the United States Constitution. . . .

We begin consideration of this case by noting that the precise issue presented here has not previously been before this Court for decision. In *Gannett Co.* v. *DePasquale* [1979], the Court was not required to decide whether a right of access to trials, as distinguished from hearings on pretrial motions, was constitutionally guaranteed. The Court held that the Sixth Amendment's guarantee to the accused of a public trial gave neither the public nor the press an enforceable right of access to a pretrial suppression hearing. . . . Moreover, the Court did not decide whether the First and Fourteenth Amendments guarantee a right of the public to attend trials. . . .

In prior cases the Court has treated questions involving conflicts between publicity and a defendant's right to a fair trial; as we observed in *Nebraska Press Assn.* v. *Stuart* [1976], "[t]he problems presented by this [conflict] are almost as old as the Republic." . . . But here for the first time the Court is asked to decide whether a criminal trial itself may be closed to the public upon the unopposed request of a defendant, without any demonstration that closure is required to protect the defendant's superior right to a fair trial, or that some other overriding consideration requires closure.

The origins of the proceeding which has become the modern criminal trial in Anglo-American justice can be traced back beyond reliable historical records. We need not here review all details of its development, but a summary of that history is instructive. What is significant for present purposes is that throughout its evolution, the trial has been open to all who cared to observe.

In the days before the Norman Conquest, cases in England were generally brought before moots, such as the local court of the hundred or the county court, which were attended by the freemen of the community. . . . Somewhat like modern jury duty, attendance at these early meetings was compulsory on the part of the freemen, who were called upon to render judgment. . . .

With the gradual evolution of the jury system in the years after the Norman Conquest, . . . the duty of all freemen to attend trials to render judgment was relaxed, but there is no indication that criminal trials did not remain public. . . .

From these early times, although great changes in courts and procedure took place, one thing remained constant: the public character of the trial at which guilt or innocence was decided. Sir Thomas Smith, writing in 1565 about "the definitive proceedings in causes criminall," explained that, while the indictment was put in writing as in civil law countries:

> All the rest is done openlie in the presence of the Judges, the Justices, the enquest, the prisoner, and so manie as will or can come so neare as to heare it, and all depositions and witnesses given aloude, that all men may heare from the mouth of the depositors and witnesses what is saide. . . .

Three centuries later, Sir Frederick Pollock was able to state of the "rule of publicity" that, "[h]ere we have one tradition, at any rate, which has persisted through all changes." . . .

We have found nothing to suggest that the presumptive openness of the trial, which English courts were later to call "one of the essential qualities of a court of justice," . . . was not also an attribute of the judicial systems of colonial America. In Virginia, for example, such records as there are of early criminal trials indicate that they were open, and nothing to the contrary has been cited. . . .

In some instances, the openness of trials was explicitly recognized as part of the fundamental law of the Colony. . . .

As we have shown, . . . the historical evidence demonstrates conclusively that at the time when our organic laws were adopted, criminal trials both here and in England had long been presumptively open. This is no quirk of history; rather, it has long been recognized as an indispensable attribute of an Anglo-American trial. Both Hale in the seventeenth century and Blackstone in the eighteenth saw the importance of openness to the proper functioning of a trial; it gave assurance that the proceedings were conducted fairly to all concerned, and it discouraged perjury, the misconduct of participants, and decisions based on secret bias or partiality. . . .

People in an open society do not demand infallibility from their institutions, but it is difficult for them to accept what they are prohibited from observing. When a criminal trial is conducted in the open, there is at least an opportunity both for understanding the system in general and its workings in a particular case. . . .

In earlier times, both in England and America, attendance at court was a common mode of "passing the time." . . . With the press, cinema, and electronic media now supplying the representations or reality of the real life drama once available only in the courtroom, attendance at court is no longer a widespread pastime. . . . Instead of acquiring information about trials by firsthand observation or by word of mouth from those who attended, people now acquire it chiefly through the print and electronic media. In a sense, this validates the media claim of functioning as surrogates for the public. While media representatives enjoy the same right of access as the public, they often are provided special seating and priority of entry so that they may report what people in attendance have seen and heard. . . .

From this unbroken, uncontradicted history, supported by reasons as valid today as in centuries past, we are bound to conclude that a presumption of openness inheres in the very nature of a criminal trial under our system of justice. This conclusion is hardly novel; without a direct holding on the issue, the Court has voiced its recognition of it in a variety of contexts over the years. . . .

Despite the history of criminal trials being presumptively open since long before the Constitution, the State presses its contention that neither the Constitution nor the Bill of Rights contains any provision which by its terms guarantees to the public the right to attend criminal trials. Standing alone, this is correct, but there remains the question whether, absent an explicit provision, the Constitution affords protection against exclusion of the public from criminal trials.

The First Amendment, in conjunction with the Fourteenth, prohibits governments from "abridging the freedom of speech, or of the press; or the right of the people peaceably to assemble, and to petition the Government for a redress of grievances." These expressly guaranteed freedoms share a common core purpose of assuring freedom of communication on matters relating to the functioning of government. Plainly it would be difficult to single out any aspect of government of higher concern and importance to the people than the manner in which criminal trials are conducted; as we have shown, recognition of this pervades the centuries-old history of open trials and the opinions of this Court. . . .

The Bill of Rights was enacted against the backdrop of the long history of trials being presumptively open. Public access to trials was then regarded as an important aspect of the process itself; the conduct of trials "before as many of the people as chuse to attend" was regarded as one of "the inestimable advantages of a free English constitution of government." . . . In guaranteeing freedoms such as those of speech and press, the First Amendment can be read as protecting the right of everyone to attend trials so as to give meaning to those explicit guarantees. "[T]he First Amendment goes beyond protection of the press and the self-expression of individuals to prohibit government from limiting the stock of information from which members of the public may draw." *First National Bank of Boston* v. *Bellotti* [1978]. Free speech carries with it some freedom to listen. "In a variety of contexts this Court has referred to a First Amendment right to 'receive information and ideas.'" *Kleindienst* v. *Mandel* [1972]. What this means in the context of trials is that the First Amendment guarantees of speech and press, standing alone, prohibit government from summarily closing courtroom doors which had long been open to the public at the time that Amendment was adopted. . . .

The right of access to places traditionally open to the public, as criminal trials have long been, may be seen as assured by the amalgam of the First Amendment guarantees of speech and press; and their affinity to the right of assembly is not without relevance. From the outset, the right of assembly was regarded not only as an independent right but also as a catalyst to augment the free exercise of the other First Amendment rights with which it was deliberately linked by the draftsmen. "The right of peaceable assembly is a right cognate to those of free speech and free press and is equally fundamental." *DeJonge* v. *Oregon* [1937]. People assemble in public places not only to speak or to take action, but also to listen, observe, and learn. . . . Subject to the traditional time, place, and manner restrictions, see, e.g., *Cox* v. *New Hampshire* [1941], . . . streets, sidewalks, and parks are places traditionally open, where First Amendment rights may be exercised; a trial courtroom also is a public place where the people generally—and representatives of the media—have a right to be present, and where their presence historically has been thought to enhance the integrity and quality of what takes place.

The State argues that the Constitution nowhere spells out a guarantee for the right of the public to attend trials, and that accordingly no such right is protected. The possibility that such a contention could be made did not escape the notice of the Constitution's draftsmen; they were concerned that some important rights might be thought disparaged because not specifically guaranteed. It was even argued that because of this danger no Bill of Rights should be adopted. . . .

But arguments such as the State makes have not precluded recognition of important rights not enumerated. Notwithstanding the appropriate caution against reading into the Constitution rights not explicitly defined, the Court has acknowledged that certain unarticulated rights are implicit in enumerated guarantees. For example, the rights of association and of privacy, the right to be presumed innocent, and the right to be judged by a standard of proof beyond a reasonable doubt in a criminal trial, as well as the right to travel, appear nowhere in the Constitution or Bill of Rights. Yet these important but unarticulated rights have nonetheless been found to share constitutional protection in common with explicit guarantees. The concerns expressed by Madison and others have thus been resolved; fundamental rights, even though not expressly guaranteed, have been recognized by the Court as indispensable to the enjoyment of rights explicitly defined.

We hold that the right to attend criminal trials is implicit in the guarantees of the First Amendment; without the freedom to attend such trials, which people have exercised for centuries, important aspects of freedom of speech and "of the press could be eviscerated." *Branzburg* v. *Hayes* [1972].

Having concluded there was a guaranteed right of the public under the First and Fourteenth Amendments to attend the trial of [the accused man] Stevenson's case, we return to the closure order challenged by appellants. The Court in *Gannett* made clear that although the Sixth Amendment guarantees the accused a right to a public trial, it does not give a right to a private trial. Despite the fact that this was the fourth trial of the accused, the trial judge made no findings to support closure; no inquiry was made as to whether alternative solutions would have met the need to ensure fairness; there was no recognition of any right under the Constitution for the public or press to attend the trial. In contrast to the pretrial proceeding dealt with in *Gannett*, there exist in the context of the trial itself various tested alternatives to satisfy the constitutional demands of fairness. . . . There was no suggestion that any problems with witnesses could not have been dealt with by their exclusion from the courtroom or their sequestration during the trial. . . . Nor is there anything to indicate that sequestration of the jurors would not have guarded against their being subjected to any improper information. All of the alternatives admittedly present difficulties for trial courts, but none of the factors relied on here was beyond the realm of the manageable. Absent an overriding interest articulated in findings, the trial of a criminal case must be open to the public. Accordingly, the judgment under review is

REVERSED.

JUSTICE BRENNAN, CONCURRING IN THE JUDGMENT . . .

While freedom of expression is made inviolate by the First Amendment, and, with only rare and stringent exceptions, may not be suppressed, . . . the First Amendment has not been viewed by the Court in all settings as providing an equally categorical assurance of the correlative freedom of access to information. . . . Yet the Court has not ruled out a public access component to the First Amendment in every circumstance. Read with care and in context, our decisions must therefore be understood as holding only that any privilege of access to governmental information is subject to a degree of restraint dictated by the nature of the information and countervailing interests in security or confidentiality. . . . These cases neither comprehensively nor absolutely deny that public access to information may at times be implied by the First Amendment and the principles which animate it.

The Court's approach in right-of-access cases simply reflects the special nature of a claim of First Amendment right to gather information. Customarily, First Amendment guarantees are interposed to protect communication between speaker and listener. When so employed against prior restraints, free speech protections are almost insurmountable. . . . But the First Amendment embodies more than a commitment to free expression and communicative interchange for their own sakes; it has a structural role to play in securing and fostering our republican system of self-government. . . . Implicit in this structural role is not only "the principle that debate on public issues should be uninhibited, robust, and wide-open," *New York Times Co.* v. *Sullivan* [1964], but also the antecedent assumption that valuable public debate—as well as other civic behavior—must be informed. The structural model links the First Amendment to that process of communication necessary for a democracy to survive, and thus entails solicitude not only for communication itself, but also for the indispensable conditions of meaningful communication.

However, . . . it must be invoked with discrimination and temperance. For so far as the participating citizen's need for information is concerned, "[t]here are few restrictions on action which could not be clothed by ingenious argument in the garb of decreased data flow." *Zemel* v. *Rusk* [1965]. An assertion of the prerogative to gather information must accordingly be assayed by considering the information sought and the opposing interests invaded.

This judicial task is as much a matter of sensitivity to practical necessities as it is of abstract reasoning. But at least two helpful principles may be sketched. First, the case for a right of access has special force when drawn from an enduring and vital tradition of public entree to particular proceedings or information. . . . Such a tradition commands respect in part because the Constitution carries the gloss of history. More importantly, a tradition of accessibility implies the favorable judgment of experience. Second, the value of access must be measured in specifics. Analysis is not advanced by rhetorical statements that all information bears upon public issues; what is crucial in individual cases is whether access to a particular government process is important in terms of that very process.

To resolve the case before us, therefore, we must consult historical and current practice with respect to open trials, and weigh the importance of public access to the trial process itself. . . .

. . . The earliest charters of colonial government expressly perpetuated the accepted practice of public trials. . . . Subsequently framed state constitutions also prescribed open trial proceedings. . . . Today, the overwhelming majority of States secure the right to public trials. . . .

This Court too has persistently defended the public character of the trial process. . . .

Tradition, contemporaneous state practice, and this Court's own decisions manifest a common understanding that "[a] trial is a public event. What transpires in the court room is public property." *Craig* v. *Harney* [1947]. As a matter of law and virtually immemorial custom, public trials have been the essentially unwavering rule in ancestral England and in our own Nation. . . . Such abiding adherence to the principle of open trials "reflect[s] a profound judgment about the way in which law should be enforced and justice administered." . . .

Publicity serves to advance several of the particular purposes of the trial (and, indeed, the judicial) process. Open trials play a fundamental role in furthering the efforts of our judicial system to assure the criminal defendant a fair and accurate adjudication of guilt or innocence. . . . But, as a feature of our governing system of justice, the trial process serves other, broadly political, interests, and public access advances these objectives as well. To that extent, trial access possesses specific structural significance.

The trial is a means of meeting "the notion, deeply rooted in the common law, that 'justice must satisfy the appearance of justice.'" *Levine* v. *United States* [1960]. . . . For a civilization founded upon principles of ordered liberty to survive and flourish, its members must share the conviction that they are governed equitably. That necessity underlies constitutional provisions as diverse as the rule against takings without just compensation . . . and the Equal Protection Clause. It also mandates a system of justice that demonstrates the fairness of the law to our citizens. One major function of the trial, hedged with procedural protections and conducted with conspicuous respect for the rule of law, is to make that demonstration. . . .

Secrecy is profoundly inimical to this demonstrative purpose of the trial process. Open trials assure the public that procedural rights are respected, and that justice is afforded equally. Closed trials breed suspicion of prejudice and arbitrariness, which in turn spawns disrespect for law. Public access is essential, therefore, if trial adjudication is to achieve the objective of maintaining public confidence in the administration of justice. . . .

But the trial is more than a demonstrably just method of adjudicating disputes and protecting rights. It plays a pivotal role in the entire judicial process, and, by extension, in our form of government. Under our system, judges are not mere umpires, but, in their own sphere, lawmakers—a coordinate branch of government. While individual cases turn upon the controversies between parties, or involve particular prosecutions, court rulings impose official and practical consequences upon members of society at large. Moreover, judges bear responsibility for the vitally important task of construing and securing constitutional rights. Thus, so far as the trial is the mechanism for judicial factfinding, as well as the initial forum for legal decisionmaking, it is a genuine governmental proceeding.

It follows that the conduct of the trial is pre-eminently a matter of public interest. . . .

Finally, with some limitations, a trial aims at true and accurate factfinding. Of course, proper factfinding is to the benefit of criminal defendants and of the parties in civil proceedings. But other, comparably urgent, interests are also often at stake. A miscarriage of justice that imprisons an innocent accused also leaves a guilty party at large, a continuing threat to society. Also, mistakes of fact in civil litigation may inflict costs upon others than the plaintiff and defendant. Facilitation of the trial factfinding process, therefore, is of concern to the public as well as to the parties. . . .

As previously noted, resolution of First Amendment public access claims in individual cases must be strongly influenced by the weight of historical practice and by an assessment of the specific structural value of public access in the circumstances. With regard to the case at hand, our ingrained tradition of public trials and the importance of public access to the broader purposes of the trial process, tip the balance strongly toward the rule that trials be open. . . .

JUSTICE REHNQUIST, DISSENTING.

In the Gilbert and Sullivan operetta "Iolanthe," the Lord Chancellor recites:

> The Law is the true embodiment of everything that's excellent, It has no kind of fault or flaw,
> And I, my Lords, embody the Law.

It is difficult not to derive more than a little of this flavor from the various opinions supporting the judgment in this case. The opinion of the Chief Justice states:

> [H]ere for the first time the Court is asked to decide whether a criminal trial itself may be closed
> to the public upon the unopposed request of a defendant, without any demonstration that clo-

sure is required to protect the defendant's superior right to a fair trial, or that some other over-riding consideration requires closure. . . .

The opinion of Justice Brennan states:

> Read with care and in context, our decisions must therefore be understood as holding only that any privilege of access to governmental information is subject to a degree of restraint dictated by the nature of the information and countervailing interests in security or confidentiality. . . .

. . . I do not believe that either the First or Sixth Amendment, as made applicable to the States by the Fourteenth, requires that a State's reasons for denying public access to a trial, where both the prosecuting attorney and the defendant have consented to an order of closure approved by the judge, are subject to any additional constitutional review at our hands. And I most certainly do not believe that the Ninth Amendment confers upon us any such power to review orders of state trial judges closing trials in such situations. . . .

We have at present fifty state judicial systems and one federal judicial system in the United States, and our authority to reverse a decision by the highest court of the State is limited to only those occasions when the state decision violates some provision of the United States Constitution. And that authority should be exercised with a full sense that the judges whose decisions we review are making the same effort as we to uphold the Constitution. As said by Justice Jackson, concurring in the result in *Brown* v. *Allen* [1953], "we are not final because we are infallible, but we are infallible only because we are final."

The proper administration of justice in any nation is bound to be a matter of the highest concern to all thinking citizens. But to gradually rein in, as this Court has done over the past generation, all of the ultimate decisionmaking power over how justice shall be administered, not merely in the federal system but in each of the fifty States, is a task that no Court consisting of nine persons, however gifted, is equal to. Nor is it desirable that such authority be exercised by such a tiny numerical fragment of the 220 million people who compose the population of this country. In the same concurrence just quoted, Justice Jackson accurately observed that "[t]he generalities of the Fourteenth Amendment are so indeterminate as to what state actions are forbidden that this Court has found it a ready instrument, in one field or another, to magnify federal, and incidentally its own, authority over the states." . . .

However high-minded the impulses which originally spawned this trend may have been, and which impulses have been accentuated since the time Justice Jackson wrote, it is basically unhealthy to have so much authority concentrated in a small group of lawyers who have been appointed to the Supreme Court and enjoy virtual life tenure. Nothing in the reasoning of Chief Justice Marshall in *Marbury* v. *Madison* [1803] requires that this Court through ever-broadening use of the Supremacy Clause smother a healthy pluralism which would ordinarily exist in a national government embracing fifty States.

The issue here is not whether the "right" to freedom of the press conferred by the First Amendment to the Constitution overrides the defendant's "right" to a fair trial conferred by other Amendments to the Constitution; it is instead whether any provision in the Constitution may fairly be read to prohibit what the trial judge in the Virginia state-court system did in this case. Being unable to find any such prohibition in the First, Sixth, Ninth, or any other Amendment to the United States Constitution, or in the Constitution itself, I dissent.

46

NEW YORK V. FERBER
458 U.S. 747 (1982)

Paul Ferber, owner of a Manhattan bookstore offering sexually oriented materials, sold two films to an undercover officer. The films showed young boys masturbating, and Ferber was convicted under a state law banning the knowing distribution of pornography that used minors as actors or models. The New York Court of Appeals reversed Ferber's conviction, holding that the child pornography law violated the free speech guarantee of the First Amendment. The U.S. Supreme Court then reversed the New York court, voting unanimously to uphold the statute.

In *Ferber* the Court was confronted with whether under its previous holdings on obscenity the states had sufficient authority to outlaw child pornography, as almost two-thirds of them had done. The case drew from the Court new doctrine declaring child pornography a category of "unprotected speech." In defining child pornography, the Court said that it need not "appeal to the prurient interest of the average person" and need not be "patently offensive."

Ferber enabled the states to protect the "physical and psychological well-being" of children who could be exploited and harmed by participating in what the New York appeals court called "non-obscene adolescent sex." In *Osborne* v. *Ohio* (1990), the Court extended the logic of *Ferber* by sustaining a state law outlawing the possession or viewing of child pornography, even in one's own home.

Opinion of the Court: **White**, Burger, Powell, Rehnquist, O'Connor. Concurring opinion: **O'Connor**. Concurring in the judgment: **Brennan**, Marshall; **Stevens**. Concurring in the result: **Blackmun**.

New York v. *Ferber* was decided on July 2, 1982.

JUSTICE WHITE DELIVERED THE OPINION OF THE COURT . . .

At issue in this case is [Section] 263.15, defining a class D felony:

> A person is guilty of promoting a sexual performance by a child when, knowing the character and content thereof, he produces, directs or promotes any performance which includes sexual conduct by a child less than sixteen years of age.

A companion provision bans only the knowing dissemination of obscene material. 263.10. . . .

The Court of Appeals proceeded on the assumption that the standard of obscenity incorporated in 263.10, which follows the guidelines enunciated in *Miller* v. *California* [1973], constitutes the appropriate line dividing protected from unprotected expression by which to measure a regulation directed at child pornography. It was on the premise that "nonobscene adolescent sex" could not be singled out for special treatment that the court found 263.15 "strikingly underinclusive." Moreover, the assumption that the constitutionally permissible regulation of pornography could not be more extensive with respect to the distribution of material depicting children may also have led the court to conclude that a narrowing construction of 263.15 was unavailable.

The Court of Appeals' assumption was not unreasonable in light of our decisions. This case, however, constitutes our first examination of a statute directed at and limited to depictions of sexual activity involving children. We believe our inquiry should begin with the question of whether a State has somewhat more freedom in proscribing works which portray sexual acts or lewd exhibitions of genitalia by children.

In *Chaplinsky* v. *New Hampshire* [1942], the Court laid the foundation for the excision of obscenity from the realm of constitutionally protected expression:

> There are certain well-defined and narrowly limited classes of speech, the prevention and punishment of which have never been thought to raise any Constitutional problem. These include the lewd and obscene. . . . It has been well observed that such utterances are no essential part of any exposition of ideas, and are of such slight social value as a step to truth that any benefit that may be derived from them is clearly outweighed by the social interest in order and morality. . . .

Embracing this judgment, the Court squarely held in *Roth* v. *United States* [1957], that "obscenity is not within the area of constitutionally protected speech or press." The Court recognized that "rejection of obscenity as utterly without redeeming social importance" was implicit in the history of the First Amendment: The original States provided for the prosecution of libel, blasphemy, and profanity, and the "universal judgment that obscenity should be restrained [is] reflected in the international agreement of over fifty nations, in the obscenity laws of all of the forty-eight states, and in the twenty obscenity laws enacted by Congress from 1842 to 1956."

Roth was followed by fifteen years during which this Court struggled with "the intractable obscenity problem." . . . Despite considerable vacillation over the proper definition of obscenity, a majority of the Members of the Court remained firm in the position that "the States have a legitimate interest in prohibiting dissemination or exhibition of obscene material when the mode of dissemination carries with it a significant danger of offending the sensibilities of unwilling recipients or of exposure to juveniles." *Miller* v. *California* [1973]. . . .

Throughout this period, we recognized "the inherent dangers of undertaking to regulate any form of expression." *Miller*. . . . Consequently, our difficulty was not only to assure that statutes designed to regulate obscene materials sufficiently defined what was prohibited, but also to devise substantive limits on what fell within the permissible scope of regulation. In *Miller* . . . a majority of the Court agreed that a "state offense must also be limited to works which, taken as a whole, appeal to the prurient interest in sex, which portray sexual conduct in a patently offensive way, and which, taken as a whole, do not have serious literary, artistic, political, or scientific value." . . . Over the past decade, we have adhered to the guidelines expressed in *Miller*, which subsequently has been followed in the regulatory schemes of most States.

The *Miller* standard, like its predecessors, was an accommodation between the State's interests in protecting the "sensibilities of unwilling recipients" from exposure to pornographic material and the dangers of censorship inherent in unabashedly content-based laws. Like obscenity statutes, laws directed at the dissemination of child pornography run the risk of suppressing protected expression by allowing the hand of the censor to become unduly heavy. For the following reasons, however, we are persuaded that the States are entitled to greater leeway in the regulation of pornographic depictions of children.

First. It is evident beyond the need for elaboration that a State's interest in "safeguarding the physical and psychological well-being of a minor" is "compelling." *Globe Newspaper Co.* v. *Superior Court* [1982]. . . .

The prevention of sexual exploitation and abuse of children constitutes a government objective of surpassing importance. The legislative findings accompanying passage of the New York laws reflect this concern:

> [T]here has been a proliferation of exploitation of children as subjects in sexual performances. The care of children is a sacred trust and should not be abused by those who seek to profit through a commercial network based upon the exploitation of children. The public policy of the state demands the protection of children from exploitation through sexual performances. . . .

We shall not second-guess this legislative judgment. Respondent has not intimated that we do so. Suffice it to say that virtually all of the States and the United States have passed legislation proscribing the production of or otherwise combating "child pornography." The legislative judgment, as well as the judgment found in the relevant literature, is that the use of children as subjects of pornographic materials is harmful to the physiological, emotional, and mental health of the child. That judgment, we think, easily passes muster under the First Amendment.

Second. The distribution of photographs and films depicting sexual activity by juveniles is intrinsically related to the sexual abuse of children in at least two ways. First, the materials produced are a permanent record of the children's participation, and the harm to the child is exacerbated by their circulation. Second, the distribution network for child pornography must be closed if the production of material which requires the sexual exploitation of children is to be effectively controlled. Indeed, there is no serious contention that the legislature was unjustified in believing that it is difficult, if not impossible, to halt the exploitation of children by pursuing only those who produce the photographs and movies. While the production of pornographic materials is a low-profile, clandestine industry, the need to market the resulting products requires a visible apparatus of distribution. The most expeditious if not the only practical method of law enforcement may be to dry up the market for this material by imposing severe criminal penalties on persons selling, advertising, or otherwise promoting the product. Thirty-five States and Congress have concluded that restraints on the distribution of pornographic materials are required in order to effectively combat the problem, and there is a body of literature and testimony to support these legislative conclusions. . . .

Respondent does not contend that the State is unjustified in pursuing those who distribute child pornography. Rather, he argues that it is enough for the State to prohibit the distribution of materials that are legally obscene under the *Miller* test. While some States may find that this approach properly accommodates its interests, it does not follow that the First Amendment prohibits a State from going further. The *Miller* standard, like all general definitions of what may be banned as obscene, does not reflect the State's particular and more compelling interest in prosecuting those who promote the sexual exploitation of children. Thus, the question under the *Miller* test of whether a work, taken as a whole, appeals to the prurient interest of the average person bears no connection to the issue of whether a child has been physically or psychologically harmed in the production of the work. Similarly, a sexually explicit depiction need not be "patently offensive" in order to have required the sexual exploitation of a child for its production. In addition, a work which, taken on the whole, contains serious literary, artistic, political, or scientific value may nevertheless embody the hardest core of child pornography. . . . We therefore cannot conclude that the *Miller* standard is a satisfactory solution to the child pornography problem.

Third. The advertising and selling of child pornography provide an economic motive for and are thus an integral part of the production of such materials, an activity illegal throughout the Nation. . . . We note that were the statutes outlawing the employment of children in these films and photographs fully effective, and the constitutionality of these laws has not been questioned, the First Amendment implications would be no greater than that presented by laws against distribution: enforceable production laws would leave no child pornography to be marketed.

Fourth. The value of permitting live performances and photographic reproductions of children engaged in lewd sexual conduct is exceedingly modest, if not de minimis. We consider it unlikely that visual depictions of children performing sexual acts or lewdly exhibiting their genitals would often constitute an important and necessary part of a literary performance or scientific or educational work. . . . Nor is there any question here of censoring a particular literary theme or portrayal of sexual activity. The First Amendment interest is limited to that of rendering the portrayal somewhat more "realistic" by utilizing or photographing children.

Fifth. Recognizing and classifying child pornography as a category of material outside the protection of the First Amendment is not incompatible with our earlier decisions. . . . Leaving aside the special considerations when public officials are the target, *New York Times Co. v. Sullivan* [1964], a libelous publication is not protected by the Constitution. *Beauharnais v. Illinois* [1952]. Thus, it is not rare that a content-based classification of speech has been accepted because it may be appropriately generalized that within the confines of the given classification, the evil to be restricted so overwhelmingly outweighs the expressive interests, if any, at stake, that no process of case-by-case adjudication is required. When a definable class of material, such as that covered by 263.15, bears so heavily and pervasively on the welfare of children engaged in its production, we think the balance of competing interests is clearly struck and that it is permissible to consider these materials as without the protection of the First Amendment.

There are, of course, limits on the category of child pornography which, like obscenity, is unprotected by the First Amendment. As with all legislation in this sensitive area, the conduct to be prohibited must be adequately defined by the applicable state law, as written or authoritatively construed. Here the nature of the harm to be combated requires that the state offense be limited to works that visually depict sexual conduct by children below a specified age. The category of "sexual conduct" proscribed must also be suitably limited and described.

The test for child pornography is separate from the obscenity standard enunciated in *Miller*, but may be compared to it for the purpose of clarity. The *Miller* formulation is adjusted in the following respects: A trier of fact need not find that the material appeals to the prurient interest of the average person; it is not required that sexual conduct be portrayed . . . in a patently offensive manner; and the material at issue need not be considered as a whole. We note that the distribution of descriptions or other depictions of sexual conduct, not otherwise obscene, which do not involve live performance or photographic or other visual reproduction of live performances, retains First Amendment protection. As with obscenity laws, criminal responsibility may not be imposed without some element of scienter [degree of knowledge that makes one legally responsible for the consequences of his act] on the part of the defendant. . . .

Section 263.15's prohibition incorporates a definition of sexual conduct that comports with the above-stated principles. . . .

We hold that 263.15 sufficiently describes a category of material the production and distribution of which is not entitled to First Amendment protection. It is therefore clear that there is nothing unconstitutionally "underinclusive" about a statute that singles out this category of material for proscription. It also follows that the State is not barred by the First Amendment from prohibiting the distribution of unprotected materials produced outside the State. . . .

. . . The judgment of the New York Court of Appeals is reversed, and the case is remanded to that court for further proceedings not inconsistent with this opinion.

47

ROBERTS V. UNITED STATES JAYCEES
468 U.S. 609 (1984)

Although the bylaws of the United States Jaycees limited regular membership to men, two local chapters in Minnesota began admitting women as members. The national organization responded by imposing a series of sanctions on the two chapters and threatening to revoke their charters. The chapters then complained that the membership policy of the national organization violated the state's Human Rights Act, which prohibited discrimination by a "place of public accommodation" on account of, among other things, sex. The dispute ultimately took shape as a case in the federal courts in which the national Jaycees, deemed "a place of public accommodation" by the Minnesota Supreme Court, contended that application of the Minnesota Human Rights Act would infringe upon its First Amendment right of association. The Jaycees prevailed with this argument in the Eighth Circuit Court of Appeals. A unanimous Supreme Court reversed.

In *Roberts* the Court addressed the extent to which associational liberty may protect an organization against anti-discrimination measures. With Justice Brennan writing, the Court found that the Jaycees, because of the large and unselective memberships of its many chapters, had a weaker claim to associational liberty than it would have had if memberships had been small and highly selective—virtually family-like. Even so, the Jaycees did have, said the Court, "freedom of expressive association," and Minnesota could not infringe upon that freedom by requiring the organization to admit women unless this objective was a "compelling" one that could not be achieved through less restrictive means. Finding that the policy embodied in the Human Rights Act—eradicating discrimination against the state's female citizens—was just such a compelling interest, the Court said that application of the law imposed no serious burdens on the Jaycees' First Amendment rights.

Three years later in *Board of Directors of Rotary International* v. *Rotary Club of Duarte* (1987), the Court adhered to *Roberts* in sustaining enforcement of a similar California law against Rotary International, which excluded women from membership. And in 1988, in *New York State Club Association* v. *City of New York*, the Court again followed *Roberts* in rejecting a challenge to New York City's attempt to enforce its human rights law against clubs of more than 400 members that regularly served meals and were supported by non-members for trade or business purposes.

Opinion of the Court: **Brennan**, White, Marshall, Powell, Stevens. Concurring opinion: **O'Connor**, Rehnquist. Not participating: Burger, Blackmun.

Roberts v. *United States Jaycees* was decided on July 3, 1984.

OPINION

JUSTICE BRENNAN DELIVERED THE OPINION OF THE COURT . . .

Our decisions have referred to constitutionally protected "freedom of association" in two distinct senses. In one line of decisions, the Court has concluded that choices to enter into and maintain certain intimate human relationships must be secured against undue intrusion by the State because of the role of such relationships in safeguarding the individual freedom that is central to our constitutional scheme. In this respect, freedom of association receives protection as a fundamental element of personal liberty. In another set of decisions, the Court has recognized a right to associate for the purpose of engaging in those activities protected by the First Amendment—speech, assembly, petition for the redress of grievances, and the exercise of religion. The Constitution guarantees freedom of association of this kind as an indispensable means of preserving other individual liberties.

The intrinsic and instrumental features of constitutionally protected association may, of course, coincide. In particular, when the State interferes with individuals' selection of those with whom they wish to join in a common endeavor, freedom of association in both of its forms may be implicated. The Jaycees contend that this is such a case. Still, the nature and degree of constitutional protection afforded freedom of association may vary depending on the extent to which one or the other aspect of the constitutionally protected liberty is at stake in a given case. We therefore find it useful to consider separately the effect of applying the Minnesota statute to the Jaycees on what could be called its members' freedom of intimate association and their freedom of expressive association.

The Court has long recognized that, because the Bill of Rights is designed to secure individual liberty, it must afford the formation and preservation of certain kinds of highly personal relationships a substantial measure of sanctuary from unjustified interference by the State. . . . Without precisely identifying every consideration that may underlie this type of constitutional protection, we have noted that certain kinds of personal bonds have played a critical role in the culture and traditions of the Nation by cultivating and transmitting shared ideals and beliefs; they thereby foster diversity and act as critical buffers between the individual and the power of the State. . . . Moreover, the constitutional shelter afforded such relationships reflects the realization that individuals draw much of their emotional enrichment from close ties with others. Protecting these relationships from unwarranted state interference therefore safeguards the ability independently to define one's identity that is central to any concept of liberty. . . .

The personal affiliations that exemplify these considerations, and that therefore suggest some relevant limitations on the relationships that might be entitled to this sort of constitutional protection, are those that attend the creation and sustenance of a family. . . . Family relationships, by their nature, involve deep attachments and commitments to the necessarily few other individuals with whom one shares not only a special community of thoughts, experiences, and beliefs but also distinctively personal aspects of one's life. Among other things, therefore, they are distinguished by such attributes as relative smallness, a high degree of selectivity in decisions to begin and maintain the affiliation, and seclusion from others in critical aspects of the relationship. As a general matter, only relationships with these sorts of qualities are likely to reflect the considerations that have led to an understanding of freedom of association as an intrinsic element of personal liberty. Conversely, an association lacking these qualities—such as a large business enterprise—seems remote from the concerns giving rise to this constitutional protection. Accordingly, the Constitution undoubtedly imposes constraints on the State's power to control the selection of one's spouse that would not apply to regulations affecting the choice of one's fellow employees. . . .

Between these poles, of course, lies a broad range of human relationships that may make greater or lesser claims to constitutional protection from particular incursions by the State. Determining the limits of state authority over an individual's freedom to enter into a particular association therefore unavoidably entails a careful assessment of where that relationship's objective characteristics locate it on a spectrum from the most intimate to the most attenuated of personal attachments. . . . We need not mark the potentially significant points on this terrain with any precision. We note only that factors that may be relevant include size, purpose, policies, selectivity, congeniality, and other characteristics that in a particular case may be pertinent. In this case, however, several features of the Jaycees clearly place the organization outside of the category of relationships worthy of this kind of constitutional protection.

The undisputed facts reveal that the local chapters of the Jaycees are large and basically unselective groups. At the time of the state administrative hearing, the Minneapolis chapter had approximately 430 members, while the St. Paul chapter had about 400. . . . Apart from age and sex, neither the national organization nor the local chapters employ any criteria for judging applicants for membership, and new members are routinely recruited and admitted with no inquiry into their backgrounds. . . . In fact, a local officer testified that he could recall no instance in which an applicant had been denied membership on any basis other than age or sex. . . . Furthermore, despite their inability to vote, hold office, or receive certain awards, women affiliated with the Jaycees attend various meetings, participate in selected projects, and engage in many of the organization's social functions. . . . Indeed, numerous nonmembers of both genders regularly participate in a substantial portion of activities central to the decision of many members to associate with one another, including many of the organization's various community programs, awards ceremonies, and recruitment meetings. . . .

In short, the local chapters of the Jaycees are neither small nor selective. Moreover, much of the activity central to the formation and maintenance of the association involves the participation of strangers to that relationship. Accordingly, we conclude that the Jaycees chapters lack the distinctive characteristics that might afford constitutional protection to the decision of its members to exclude women. We turn therefore to consider the extent to which application of the Minnesota statute to compel the Jaycees to accept women infringes the group's freedom of expressive association.

An individual's freedom to speak, to worship, and to petition the government for the redress of grievances could not be vigorously protected from interference by the State unless a correlative freedom to engage in group effort toward those ends were not also guaranteed. . . . According protection to collective effort on behalf of shared goals is especially important in preserving political and cultural diversity and in shielding dissident expression from suppression by the majority. . . . Consequently, we have long understood as implicit in the right to engage in activities protected by the First Amendment a corresponding right to associate with others in pursuit of a wide variety of political, social, economic, educational, religious, and cultural ends. . . . In view of the various protected activities in which the Jaycees engages, . . . that right is plainly implicated in this case.

Government actions that may unconstitutionally infringe upon this freedom can take a number of forms. Among other things, government may . . . try to interfere with the internal organization or affairs of the group. . . . By requiring the Jaycees to admit women as full voting members, the Minnesota Act works [such] an infringement. . . . There can be no clearer example of an intrusion into the internal structure or affairs of an association than a regulation that forces the group to accept members it does not desire. Such a regulation may impair the ability of the original members to express only those views that brought them together. Freedom of association therefore plainly presupposes a freedom not to associate. . . .

The right to associate for expressive purposes is not, however, absolute. Infringements on that right may be justified by regulations adopted to serve compelling state interests, unrelated to the suppression of ideas, that cannot be achieved through means significantly less restrictive of associational freedoms. . . . We are persuaded that Minnesota's compelling interest in eradicating discrimination against its female citizens justifies the impact that application of the statute to the Jaycees may have on the male members' associational freedoms.

On its face, the Minnesota Act does not aim at the suppression of speech, does not distinguish between prohibited and permitted activity on the basis of viewpoint, and does not license enforcement authorities to administer the statute on the basis of such constitutionally impressible criteria. . . . Nor does the Jaycees contend that the Act has been applied in this case for the purpose of hampering the organization's ability to express its views. Instead, as the Minnesota Supreme Court explained, the Act reflects the State's strong historical commitment to eliminating discrimination and assuring its citizens equal access to publicly available goods and services. . . . That goal, which is unrelated to the suppression of expression, plainly serves compelling state interests of the highest order. . . .

By prohibiting gender discrimination in places of public accommodation, the Minnesota Act protects the State's citizenry from a number of serious social and personal harms. In the context of reviewing state actions under the Equal Protection Clause, this Court has frequently noted that discrimination based on archaic and overbroad assumptions about the relative needs and capacities of the sexes forces individuals to labor under stereotypical notions that often bear no relationship to their actual abilities. It thereby both deprives persons of their individual dignity and denies society the benefits of wide participation in political, economic, and cultural life. . . . These concerns are strongly implicated with respect to gender discrimination in the allocation of publicly available goods and services. . . .

Nor is the state interest in assuring equal access limited to the provision of purely tangible goods and services. . . . A State enjoys broad authority to create rights of public access on behalf of its citizens. . . . Like many States and municipalities, Minnesota has adopted a functional definition of public accommodations that reaches various forms of public, quasi-commercial conduct. . . . This expansive definition reflects a recognition of the changing nature of the American economy and of the importance, both to the individual and to society, of removing the barriers to economic advancement and political and social integration that have historically plagued certain disadvantaged groups, including women. . . . Thus, in explaining its conclusion that the Jaycees local chapters are "place[s] of public accommodations" within the meaning of the Act, the Minnesota court noted the various commercial programs and benefits offered to members and stated that "[l]eadership skills are 'goods,' [and] business contacts and employment promotions are 'privileges' and 'advantages.'" . . . Assuring women equal access to such goods, privileges, and advantages clearly furthers compelling state interests.

In applying the Act to the Jaycees, the State has advanced those interests through the least restrictive means of achieving its ends. Indeed, the Jaycees has failed to demonstrate that the Act imposes any serious burdens on the male members' freedom of expressive association. . . . To be sure, as the Court of Appeals noted, a "not insubstantial part" of the Jaycees' activities constitutes protected expression on political, economic, cultural, and social affairs. . . . Over the years, the national and local levels of the organization have taken public positions on a number of diverse issues, . . . and members of the Jaycees regularly engage in a variety of civic, charitable, lobbying, fundraising, and other activities worthy of constitutional protection under the First Amendment. . . . There is, however, no basis in the record for concluding that admission of women as full voting members will impede the organization's ability to engage in these protected activities or to disseminate its preferred views. The Act requires no change in the Jaycees' creed of promoting the interests of young men, and it imposes no restrictions on the organization's ability to exclude individuals with ideologies or philosophies different from those of its existing members. . . . Moreover, the Jaycees already invites women to share the group's views and philosophy and to participate in much of its training and community activities. Accordingly, any claim that admission of women as full voting members will impair a symbolic message conveyed by the very fact that women are not permitted to vote is attenuated at best.

While acknowledging that "the specific content of most of the resolutions adopted over the years by the Jaycees has nothing to do with sex," . . . the Court of Appeals nonetheless entertained the hypothesis that women members might have a different view or agenda with respect to these matters so that, if they are allowed to vote, "some change in the Jaycees' philosophical cast can reasonably be expected." It is similarly arguable that, insofar as the Jaycees is organized to promote the views of young men whatever those views happen to be, admission of women as voting members will change the message communicated by the group's speech because of the gender-based assumptions of the audience. Neither supposition, however, is supported by the record. In claiming that women might have a different attitude about such issues as the federal budget, school prayer, voting rights, and foreign relations, . . . or that the organization's public positions would have a different effect if the group were not "a purely young men's association," the Jaycees relies solely on unsupported generalizations about the relative interests and perspectives of men and women. . . . Although such generalizations may or may not have a statistical basis in fact with respect to particular positions adopted by the Jaycees, we have repeatedly condemned legal decisionmaking that relies uncritically on such assumptions. . . . In the absence of a showing far more substantial than that attempted by the Jaycees, we decline to indulge in the sexual stereotyping that underlies appellee's contention that, by allowing women to vote, application of the Minnesota Act will change the content or impact of the organization's speech. . . .

In any event, even if enforcement of the Act causes some incidental abridgment of the Jaycees' protected speech, that effect is no greater than is necessary to accomplish the state's legitimate purposes. . . .

The judgment of the Court of Appeals is
REVERSED.

RENTON V. PLAYTIME THEATRES, INC.
475 U.S. 41 (1986)

Playtime Theatres bought two theaters in downtown Renton, Washington, with the intention of showing adult films. A Renton zoning ordinance prohibited any "adult motion picture theater" from locating within 1,000 feet of a residential zone, single- or multiple-family dwelling, church, park, or school. Both theaters fell within a prohibited area. Playtime sued in federal court, challenging the ordinance on free speech grounds. It lost in district court but prevailed in the Ninth Circuit Court of Appeals. The Supreme Court then reversed, finding no constitutional defects in the ordinance.

Ten years earlier, the Court had considered the constitutionality of a Detroit ordinance that prohibited locating an adult theater within 1,000 feet of any two other such theaters or within 500 feet of any residential zone (*Young* v. *American Mini Theatres*, 1976). Five justices held the ordinance constitutional, but only four could agree on the rationale. In *Renton*, in which Justice Rehnquist wrote for a majority of six, the Court made clear that local governments have substantial latitude under the First Amendment to regulate the location of adult establishments in order to preserve the quality of life in their communities.

The majority found that the ordinance was not content-based because it did not attempt to suppress the showing of adult films. Instead, said the majority, the ordinance was content-neutral because it was aimed at mitigating the "secondary," i.e., "adverse," effects of adult theaters upon urban neighborhoods. Thus seeing the ordinance as a content-neutral time, place, and manner regulation, the majority applied the pertinent First Amendment test: whether a challenged law serves a "substantial government interest and allows for reasonable alternative avenues of communication." Preserving the quality of urban life is such an interest, the majority said, and the city's decision to concentrate adult theaters through zoning still left available 520 acres of land where they might be located.

Justice Brennan's dissent, joined by Justice Marshall, demonstrated the importance of the kind of test used to measure whether a challenged law violates the First Amendment. While contending that even as a content-neutral time, place, and manner regulation the Renton ordinance should be judged unconstitutional, Brennan said that it was in fact not such a regulation but rather a direct assault on the content of adult films; the law must therefore, he said, be subjected to the more stringent test: whether it is a precisely drawn means of serving a compelling governmental interest. Under this test, Brennan concluded, the ordinance was "patently unconstitutional."

Opinion of the Court: **Rehnquist**, Burger, White, Powell, Stevens, O'Connor. Concurring in the result: Blackmun. Dissenting opinion: **Brennan**, Marshall.
Renton v. *Playtime Theatres, Inc.* was decided on February 25, 1986.

OPINIONS

JUSTICE REHNQUIST DELIVERED THE OPINION OF THE COURT . . .

In our view, the resolution of this case is largely dictated by our decision in *Young* v. *American Mini Theatres, Inc.* [1976]. There, although five Members of the Court did not agree on a single rationale for the decision, we held that the city of Detroit's zoning ordinance, which prohibited locating an adult theater within 1,000 feet of any two other "regulated uses" or within 500 feet of any residential zone, did not violate the First and Fourteenth Amendments. . . . The Renton ordinance, like the one in *American Mini Theatres*, does not ban adult theaters altogether, but merely provides that such theaters may not be located within 1,000 feet of any residential zone, single- or multiple-family dwelling, church, park, or school. The ordinance is therefore properly analyzed as a form of time, place, and manner regulation. . . .

Describing the ordinance as a time, place, and manner regulation is, of course, only the first step in our inquiry. This Court has long held that regulations enacted for the purpose of restraining speech on the basis of its content presumptively violate the First Amendment. . . . On the other hand, so-called "content-neutral" time, place, and manner regulations are acceptable so long as they are designed to serve a substantial governmental interest and do not unreasonably limit alternative avenues of communication. . . .

At first glance, the Renton ordinance, like the ordinance in *American Mini Theatres*, does not appear to fit neatly into either the "content-based" or the "content-neutral" category. To be sure, the ordinance treats theaters that specialize in adult films differently from other kinds of theaters. Nevertheless, as the District Court concluded, the Renton ordinance is aimed not at the content of the films shown at "adult motion picture theaters," but rather at the secondary effect of such theaters on the surrounding community. The District Court found that the City Council's "predominate concerns" were with the secondary effects of adult theaters, and not with the content of adult films themselves. . . . But the Court of Appeals . . . held that this was not enough to sustain the ordinance. According to the Court of Appeals, if "a motivating factor" in enacting the ordinance was to restrict respondents' exercise of First Amendment rights the ordinance would be invalid, apparently no matter how small a part this motivating factor may have played in the City Council's decision. . . . This view of the law was rejected in *United States* v. *O'Brien* [1968], the very case that the Court of Appeals said it was applying:

It is a familiar principle of constitutional law that this Court will not strike down an otherwise constitutional statute on the basis of an alleged illicit legislative motive. . . .

. . . What motivates one legislator to make a speech about a statute is not necessarily what motivates scores of others to enact it, and the stakes are sufficiently high for us to eschew guesswork. . . .

The District Court's finding as to "predominate" intent, left undisturbed by the Court of Appeals, is more than adequate to establish that the city's pursuit of its zoning interests here was unrelated to the suppression of free expression. The ordinance by its terms is designed to prevent crime, protect the city's retail trade, maintain property values, and generally "protec[t] and preserv[e] the quality of [the city's] neighborhoods, commercial districts, and the quality of urban life," not to suppress the expression of unpopular views. . . .

In short, the Renton ordinance is completely consistent with our definition of "content-neutral" speech regulations as those that "are justified without reference to the content of the regulated speech." *Virginia Pharmacy Board* v. *Virginia Citizens Consumer Council, Inc.* [1976]. . . .

It was with this understanding in mind that, in *American Mini Theatres*, a majority of this Court decided that, at least with respect to businesses that purvey sexually explicit materials, zoning ordinances designed to combat the undesirable secondary effects of such businesses are to be reviewed under the standards applicable to "content-neutral" time, place, and manner regulations. Justice Stevens, writing for the plurality, concluded that the city of Detroit was entitled to draw a distinction between adult theaters and other kinds of theaters "without violating the government's paramount obligation of neutrality in its regulation of protected communication," noting that "[i]t is th[e] secondary effect which these zoning ordinances attempt to avoid, not the dissemination of 'offensive' speech." Justice Powell, in concurrence, elaborated:

> [The] dissent misconceives the issue in this case by insisting that it involves an impermissible time, place, and manner restriction based on the content of expression. It involves nothing of the kind. We have here merely a decision by the city to treat certain movie theaters differently because they have markedly different effects upon their surroundings. . . . Moreover, even if this were a case involving a special governmental response to the content of one type of movie, it is possible that the result would be supported by a line of cases recognizing that the government can tailor its reaction to different types of speech according to the degree to which its special and overriding interests are implicated.

The appropriate inquiry in this case, then, is whether the Renton ordinance is designed to serve a substantial governmental interest and allows for reasonable alternative avenues of communication. . . . It is clear that the ordinance meets such a standard. As a majority of this Court recognized in *American Mini Theatres*, a city's "interest in attempting to preserve the quality of urban life is one that must be accorded high respect." . . . Exactly the same vital governmental interests are at stake here.

The Court of Appeals ruled, however, that because the Renton ordinance was enacted without the benefit of studies specifically relating to "the particular problems or needs of Renton," the city's justifications for the ordinance were "conclusory and speculative." We think the Court of Appeals imposed on the city an unnecessarily rigid burden of proof. The record in this case reveals that Renton relied heavily on the experience of, and studies produced by, the city of Seattle. In Seattle, as in Renton, the adult theater zoning ordinance was aimed at preventing the secondary effects caused by the presence of even one such theater in a given neighborhood. . . .

We hold that Renton was entitled to rely on the experiences of Seattle and other cities . . . in enacting its adult theater zoning ordinance. The First Amendment does not require a city, before enacting such an ordinance, to conduct new studies or produce evidence independent of that already generated by other cities, so long as whatever evidence the city relies upon is reasonably believed to be relevant to the problem that the city addresses. That was the case here. Nor is our holding affected by the fact that Seattle ultimately chose a different method of adult theater zoning than that chosen by Renton, since Seattle's choice of a different remedy to combat the secondary effects of adult theaters does not call into question either Seattle's identification of those secondary effects or the relevance of Seattle's experience to Renton.

We also find no constitutional defect in the method chosen by Renton to further its substantial interests. Cities may regulate adult theaters by dispersing them, as in Detroit, or by effectively concentrating them, as in Renton. "It is not our function to appraise the wisdom of [the city's] decision to require adult theaters to be separated rather than concentrated in the same areas. . . . [T]he city must be allowed a reasonable opportunity to experiment with solutions to admittedly serious problems." *American Mini Theatres.* Moreover, the Renton ordinance is "narrowly tailored" to affect only that category of theaters shown to produce the unwanted secondary effects, thus avoiding the flaw that proved fatal to the regulations in *Schad v. Mount Ephraim* [1981] and *Erznoznik* v. *City of Jacksonville* [1975].

Respondents contend that the Renton ordinance is "underinclusive," in that it fails to regulate other kinds of adult businesses that are likely to produce secondary effects similar to those produced by adult theaters. On this record the contention must fail. There is no evidence that, at the time the Renton ordinance was enacted, any other adult business was located in, or was contemplating moving into, Renton. . . .

Finally, turning to the question whether the Renton ordinance allows for reasonable alternative avenues of communication, we note that the ordinance leaves some 520 acres, or more than five percent of the entire land area of Renton, open to use as adult theater sites. . . .

Respondents argue, however, that some of the land in question is already occupied by existing businesses, that "practically none" of the undeveloped land is currently for sale or lease, and that in general there are no "commercially viable" adult theater sites within the 520 acres left open by the Renton ordinance. The Court of Appeals accepted these arguments, concluded that the 520 acres was not truly "available" land, and therefore held that the Renton ordinance "would result in a substantial restriction" on speech.

We disagree with both the reasoning and the conclusion of the Court of Appeals. That respondents must fend for themselves in the real estate market, on an equal footing with other prospective purchasers and lessees, does not give rise to a First Amendment violation. And although we have cautioned against the enactment of zoning regulations that have "the effect of suppressing, or greatly restricting access to, lawful speech," *American Mini Theatres,* we have never suggested that the First Amendment compels the Government to ensure that adult theaters, or any other kinds of speech-related businesses for that matter, will be able to obtain sites at bargain prices. . . . In our view, the First Amendment requires only that Renton refrain from effectively denying respondents a reasonable opportunity to open and operate an adult theater within the city, and the ordinance before us easily meets this requirement.

In sum, we find that the Renton ordinance represents a valid governmental response to the "admittedly serious problems" created by adult theaters. . . . Renton has not used "the power to zone as a pretext for suppressing expression" . . . but rather has sought to make some areas available for adult theaters and their patrons, while at the same time preserving the quality of life in the community at large by preventing those theaters from locating in other areas. This, after all, is the essence of zoning. Here, as in *American Mini Theatres,* the city has enacted a zoning ordinance that meets these goals while also satisfying the dictates of the First Amendment. The judgment of the Court of Appeals is therefore
REVERSED.

JUSTICE BRENNAN, DISSENTING . . .

Renton's zoning ordinance selectively imposes limitations on the location of a movie theater based exclusively on the content of the films shown there. The constitutionality of the ordinance is therefore not correctly analyzed under standards applied to content-neutral time, place, and manner restrictions. But even assuming that the ordinance may fairly be characterized as content neutral, it is plainly unconstitutional under the standards established by the decisions of this Court. Although the Court's analysis is limited to cases involving "businesses that purvey sexually explicit materials," and thus does not affect our holdings in cases involving state regulation of other kinds of speech, I dissent. . . .

The fact that adult movie theaters may cause harmful "secondary" land-use effects may arguably give Renton compelling reason to regulate such establishments; it does not mean, however, that such regulations are content neutral. Because the ordinance imposes special restrictions on certain kinds of speech on the basis of content, I cannot simply accept, as the Court does, Renton's claim that the ordinance was not designed to suppress the content of adult movies. . . .

The ordinance discriminates on its face against certain forms of speech based on content. Movie theaters specializing in "adult motion pictures" may not be located within 1,000 feet of any residential zone, single- or multiple-family dwelling, church, park, or school. Other motion picture theaters, and other forms of "adult entertainment," such as bars, massage parlors, and adult bookstores, are not subject to the same restrictions. This selective treatment strongly suggests that Renton was interested not in controlling the "secondary effects" associated with adult businesses, but in discriminating against adult theaters based on the content of the films they exhibit. The Court ignores this discriminatory treatment, declaring that Renton is free "to address the potential problems created by one particular kind of adult business" and to amend the ordinance in the future to include other adult enterprises. However, because of the First Amendment interests at stake here, this one-step-at-a-time analysis is wholly inappropriate. . . .

. . . [T]he city has not justified treating adult movie theaters differently from other adult entertainment businesses. The ordinance's underinclusiveness is cogent evidence that it was aimed at the content of the films shown in adult movie theaters.

Shortly after this lawsuit commenced, the Renton City Council amended the ordinance, adding a provision explaining that its intention in adopting the ordinance had been "to promote the City of Renton's great interest in protecting and preserving the quality of its neighborhoods, commercial districts, and the quality of urban life through effective land use planning." The amended ordinance also lists certain conclusory "findings" concerning adult entertainment land uses that the Council purportedly relied upon in adopting the ordinance. The city points to these provisions as evidence that the ordinance was designed to control the secondary effects associated with adult movie theaters, rather than to suppress the content of the films they exhibit. However, the "legislative history" of the ordinance strongly suggests otherwise.

Prior to the amendment, there was no indication that the ordinance was designed to address any "secondary effects" a single adult theater might create. In addition to the suspiciously coincidental timing of the amendment, many of the City Council's "findings" do not relate to legitimate land-use concerns. As the Court of Appeals observed, "[b]oth the magistrate and the district court recognized that many of the stated reasons for the ordinance were no more than expressions of dislike for the subject matter." . . . That some residents may be offended by the content of the films shown at adult movie theaters cannot form the basis for state regulation of speech. . . .

Some of the "findings" added by the City Council do relate to supposed "secondary effects" associated with adult movie theaters. However, the Court cannot, as it does, merely accept these post hoc statements at face value. . . .

The amended ordinance states that its "findings" summarize testimony received by the City Council at certain public hearings. While none of this testimony was ever recorded or preserved, a city official reported that residents had objected to having adult movie theaters located in their community. However, the official was unable to recount any testimony as to how adult movie theaters would specifically affect the schools, churches, parks, or residences "protected" by the ordinance. The City Council conducted no studies, and heard no expert testimony, on how the protected uses would be affected by the presence of an adult movie theater, and never considered whether residents' concerns could be met by "restrictions that are less intrusive on protected forms of expression." As a result, any "findings" regarding "secondary effects" caused by adult movie theaters, or the need to adopt specific locational requirements to combat such effects, were not "findings" at all, but purely speculative conclusions. Such "findings" were not such as are required to justify the burdens the ordinance imposed upon constitutionally protected expression.

The Court holds that Renton was entitled to rely on the experiences of cities like Detroit and Seattle, which had enacted special zoning regulations for adult entertainment businesses after studying the adverse effects caused by such establishments. However, even assuming that Renton was concerned with the same problems as Seattle and Detroit, it never actually reviewed any of the studies conducted by those cities. Renton had no basis for determining if any of the "findings" made by these cities were relevant to Renton's problems or needs. Moreover, since Renton ultimately adopted zoning regulations different from either Detroit or Seattle, these "studies" provide no basis for assessing the effectiveness of the particular restrictions adopted under the ordinance. Renton cannot merely rely on the general experiences of Seattle or Detroit. . . .

In sum, the circumstances here strongly suggest that the ordinance was designed to suppress expression, even that constitutionally protected, and thus was not to be analyzed as a content-neutral time, place, and manner restriction. . . . [O]ur cases require the conclusion that the ordinance, like any other content-based restriction on speech, is constitutional "only if the [city] can show that [it] is a precisely drawn means of serving a compelling [governmental] interest." *Consolidated Edison Co.* v. *Public Service Comm'n of N. Y.* [1980]. Only this strict approach can insure that cities will not use their zoning powers as a pretext for suppressing constitutionally protected expression.

Applying this standard to the facts of this case, the ordinance is patently unconstitutional. Renton has not shown that locating adult movie theaters in proximity to its churches, schools, parks, and residences will necessarily result in undesirable "secondary effects," or that these problems could not be effectively addressed by less intrusive restrictions.

Even assuming that the ordinance should be treated like a content-neutral time, place, and manner restriction, I would still find it unconstitutional. . . .

The Court finds that the ordinance was designed to further Renton's substantial interest in "preserv[ing] the quality of urban life." . . . [T]he record here is simply insufficient to support this assertion. The city made no showing as to how uses "protected" by the ordinance would be affected by the presence of an adult movie theater. Thus, the Renton ordinance is clearly distinguishable from the Detroit zoning ordinance upheld in *American Mini Theatres*. The Detroit ordinance, which was designed to disperse adult theaters throughout the city, was supported by the testimony of urban planners and real estate experts regarding the adverse effects of locating several such businesses in the same neighborhood. . . . Here, the Renton Council was aware only that some residents had complained about adult movie theaters, and that other localities had adopted special zoning restrictions for such establishments. These are not "facts" sufficient to justify the burdens the ordinance imposed upon constitutionally protected expression.

Finally, the ordinance is invalid because it does not provide for reasonable alternative avenues of communication. The District Court found that the ordinance left 520 acres in Renton available for adult theater sites, an area comprising about five percent of the city. However, the Court of Appeals found that because much of this land was already occupied, "[l]imiting adult theater uses to these areas is a substantial restriction on speech." Many "available" sites are also largely unsuited for use by movie theaters. Again, these facts serve to distinguish this case from *American Mini Theatres*, where there was no indication that the Detroit zoning ordinance seriously limited the locations available for adult businesses. . . .

Despite the evidence in the record, the Court reasons that the fact "[t]hat respondents must fend for themselves in the real estate market, on an equal footing with other prospective purchasers and lessees, does not give rise to a First Amendment violation." However, respondents are not on equal footing with other prospective purchasers and lessees, but must conduct business under severe restrictions not imposed upon other establishments. The Court also argues that the First Amendment does not compel "the government to ensure that adult theaters, or any other kinds of speech-related businesses for that matter, will be able to obtain sites at bargain prices." However, respondents do not ask Renton to guarantee low-price sites for their businesses, but seek only a reasonable opportunity to operate adult theaters in the city. By denying them this opportunity, Renton can effectively ban a form of protected speech from its borders. The ordinance "greatly restrict[s] access to . . . lawful speech," *American Mini Theatres*, and is plainly unconstitutional.

49

BETHEL SCHOOL DIST. NO. 403 V. FRASER
478 U.S. 675 (1986)

Bethel High School in Pierce County, Washington, sponsored an educational program in self-government that included a voluntary assembly during which students nominated candidates for student elective offices. When senior Matthew Fraser spoke on behalf of his candidate, he built his speech around a graphic and explicit sexual metaphor. Teachers he consulted before giving the speech told him that it was "inappropriate" and that delivering it could have "severe consequences." Some students reacted to Fraser's speech with hoots and yells and with gestures graphically simulating the sexual activities to which he alluded; others were bewildered and embarrassed. School rules forbade "conduct which materially and substantially interferes with the educational process . . . , including the use of obscene, profane language or gestures," and Fraser was suspended for three days for violating the rules. After serving two days of his suspension and then being allowed to return to school, he sued, alleging a violation of his First Amendment free speech rights. Fraser prevailed in district court, and the U.S. Court of Appeals for the Ninth Circuit denied the school district's appeal. The Supreme Court, by a vote of 7 to 2, reversed.

In *Tinker* v. *Des Moines Independent Community School District* (1969), the Supreme Court limited the authority of school officials to restrict student speech unless it materially disrupted classroom work or produced disorder. *Tinker*, a case involving symbolic speech, led to an expansion of speech and press liberties for students. But in *Bethel* the Court declined to press *Tinker* further by establishing a First Amendment right of students to make a lewd and obscene speech in a school assembly.

Writing for the Court, Chief Justice Burger emphasized the authority of public schools to fulfill their historic mission of promoting civic virtues. "Surely," wrote Burger, "it is a highly appropriate function of public school education to prohibit the use of vulgar and offensive terms in public discourse." Speaking approvingly of the "fundamental values necessary to the maintenance of a democratic political system," Burger said that "the inculcation of these values is truly the 'work of the schools.'"

Opinion of the Court: **Burger**, White, Powell, Rehnquist, O'Connor. Concurring in the result: Blackmun. Concurring in the judgment: **Brennan**. Dissenting opinions: **Marshall**; **Stevens**.

Bethel School Dist. No. 403 v. *Fraser* was decided on July 7, 1986.

OPINIONS

CHIEF JUSTICE BURGER DELIVERED THE OPINION OF THE COURT . . .

This Court acknowledged in *Tinker* v. *Des Moines Independent Community School District* [1969] that students do not "shed their constitutional rights to freedom of speech or expression at the schoolhouse gate." The Court of Appeals read that case as precluding any discipline of Fraser for indecent speech and lewd conduct in the school assembly. That court appears to have proceeded on the theory that the use of lewd and obscene speech in order to make what the speaker considered to be a point in a nominating speech for a fellow student was essentially the same as the wearing of an armband in *Tinker* as a form of protest or the expression of a political position.

The marked distinction between the political "message" of the armbands in *Tinker* and the sexual content of the respondent's speech in this case seems to have been given little weight by the Court of Appeals. In upholding the students' right to engage in a nondisruptive, passive expression of a political viewpoint in *Tinker*, this Court was careful to note that the case "did not concern speech or action that intrudes upon the work of the schools or the rights of other students."

It is against this background that we turn to the level of First Amendment protection accorded to Fraser's utterances and actions before an official high school assembly attended by 600 students.

The role and purpose of the American public school system were well described by two historians, who stated: "[P]ublic education must prepare pupils for citizenship in the Republic. . . . It must inculcate the habits and manners of civility as values in themselves conducive to happiness and as indispensable to the practice of self-government in the community and the nation." C. Beard and M. Beard, *New Basic History of the United States* (1968). . . .

These fundamental values of "habits and manners of civility" essential to a democratic society must, of course, include tolerance of divergent political and religious views, even when the views expressed may be unpopular. But these "fundamental values" must also take into account consideration of the sensibilities of others, and, in the case of a school, the sensibilities of fellow students. The undoubted freedom to advocate unpopular and controversial views in schools and classrooms must be balanced against the society's countervailing interest in teaching students the boundaries of socially appropriate behavior. Even the most heated political discourse in a democratic society requires consideration for the personal sensibilities of the other participants and audiences.

In our Nation's legislative halls, where some of the most vigorous political debates in our society are carried on, there are rules prohibiting the use of expressions offensive to other participants in the debate. . . . Can it be that what is proscribed in the halls of Congress is beyond the reach of school officials to regulate?

The First Amendment guarantees wide freedom in matters of adult public discourse. A sharply divided Court upheld the right to express an antidraft viewpoint in a public place, albeit in terms highly offensive to most citizens. See *Cohen* v. *California* [1971]. It does not follow, however, that simply because the use of an offensive form of expression may not be prohibited to adults making what the speaker considers a political point, the same latitude must be permitted to children in a public school. . . .

Surely it is a highly appropriate function of public school education to prohibit the use of vulgar and offensive terms in public discourse. Indeed, the "fundamental values necessary to the maintenance of a democratic political system" disfavor the use of terms of debate highly offensive or highly threatening to others. Nothing in the Constitution prohibits the states from insisting that certain modes of expression are inappropriate and subject to sanctions. The inculcation of these values is truly the "work of the schools." *Tinker*. . . . The determination of what manner of speech in the classroom or in school assembly is inappropriate properly rests with the school board.

The process of educating our youth for citizenship in public schools is not confined to books, the curriculum, and the civics class; schools must teach by example the shared values of a civilized social order. Consciously or otherwise, teachers—and indeed the older students—demonstrate the appropriate form of civil discourse and political expression by their conduct and deportment in and out of class. Inescapably, like parents, they are role models. The schools, as instruments of the state, may determine that the essential lessons of civil, mature conduct cannot be conveyed in a school that tolerates lewd, indecent, or offensive speech and conduct such as that indulged in by this confused boy.

The pervasive sexual innuendo in Fraser's speech was plainly offensive to both teachers and students—indeed to any mature person. By glorifying male sexuality, and in its verbal content, the speech was acutely insulting to teenage girl students. . . .The speech could well be seriously damaging to its less mature audience, many of whom were only 14 years old and on the threshold of awareness of human sexuality. Some students were reported as bewildered by the speech and the reaction of mimicry it provoked.

This Court's First Amendment jurisprudence has acknowledged limitations on the otherwise absolute interest of the speaker in reaching an unlimited audience where the speech is sexually explicit and the audience may include children. In *Ginsberg* v. *New York* [1968], this Court upheld a New York statute banning the sale of sexually oriented material to minors, even though the material in question was entitled to First Amendment protection with respect to adults. And in addressing the question whether the First Amendment places any limit on the authority of public schools to remove books from a public school library, all Members of the Court, otherwise sharply divided, acknowledged that the school board has the authority to remove books that are vulgar. *Board of Education* v. *Pico* [1982]. These cases recognize the obvious concern on the part of parents, and school authorities acting *in loco parentis*, to protect children—especially in a captive audience—from exposure to sexually explicit, indecent, or lewd speech.

We have also recognized an interest in protecting minors from exposure to vulgar and offensive spoken language. In *FCC* v. *Pacifica Foundation* [1978] we dealt with the power of the Federal Communications Commission to regulate a radio broadcast described as "indecent but not obscene." There the Court reviewed an administrative condemnation of the radio broadcast of a self-styled "humorist" who described his own performance as being in "the words you couldn't say on the public, ah, airwaves, um, the ones you definitely wouldn't say ever." . . . The Commission concluded that "certain words depicted sexual and excretory activities in a patently offensive manner, [and] noted that they 'were broadcast at a time when children were undoubtedly in the audience.'" The Commission issued an order declaring that the radio station was guilty of broadcasting indecent language in violation of [federal law]. The

Court of Appeals set aside the Commission's determination, and we reversed, reinstating the Commission's citation of the station. We concluded that the broadcast was properly considered "obscene, indecent, or profane" within the meaning of the statute. The plurality opinion went on to reject the radio station's assertion of a First Amendment right to broadcast vulgarity. . . .

We hold that petitioner School District acted entirely within its permissible authority in imposing sanctions upon Fraser in response to his offensively lewd and indecent speech. Unlike the sanctions imposed on the students wearing armbands in *Tinker*, the penalties imposed in this case were unrelated to any political viewpoint. The First Amendment does not prevent the school officials from determining that to permit a vulgar and lewd speech such as respondent's would undermine the school's basic educational mission. A high school assembly or classroom is no place for a sexually explicit monologue directed towards an unsuspecting audience of teenage students. Accordingly, it was perfectly appropriate for the school to disassociate itself to make the point to the pupils that vulgar speech and lewd conduct is wholly inconsistent with the "fundamental values" of public school education. Justice Black, dissenting in *Tinker*, made a point that is especially relevant in this case: "I wish therefore . . . to disclaim any purpose . . . to hold that the Federal Constitution compels the teachers, parents, and elected school officials to surrender control of the American public school system to public school students." . . .

The judgment of the Court of Appeals for the Ninth Circuit is
REVERSED.

JUSTICE BRENNAN, CONCURRING IN THE JUDGMENT . . .

The Court today reaffirms the unimpeachable proposition that students do not "'shed their constitutional rights to freedom of speech or expression at the schoolhouse gate'" [quoting *Tinker*]. If respondent had given the same speech outside of the school environment, he could not have been penalized simply because government officials considered his language to be inappropriate, see *Cohen* v. *California* [1971]; the Court's opinion does not suggest otherwise. Moreover, despite the Court's characterizations, the language respondent used is far removed from the very narrow class of "obscene" speech which the Court has held is not protected by the First Amendment. *Ginsberg* [1968]; *Roth* v. *United States* [1957]. It is true, however, that the State has interests in teaching high school students how to conduct civil and effective public discourse and in avoiding disruption of educational school activities. Thus, the Court holds that under certain circumstances, high school students may properly be reprimanded for giving a speech at a high school assembly which school officials conclude disrupted the school's educational mission. Respondent's speech may well have been protected had he given it in school but under different circumstances, where the school's legitimate interests in teaching and maintaining civil public discourse were less weighty.

In the present case, school officials sought only to ensure that a high school assembly proceed in an orderly manner. There is no suggestion that school officials attempted to regulate respondent's speech because they disagreed with the views he sought to express. . . . Nor does this case involve an attempt by school officials to ban written materials they consider "inappropriate" for high school students, . . . or to limit what students should hear, read, or learn about. Thus, the Court's holding concerns only the authority that school officials have to restrict a high school student's use of disruptive language in a speech given to a high school assembly. . . .

AIRPORT COMMISSIONERS V. JEWS FOR JESUS, INC.

482 U.S. 569 (1987)

A representative of Jews for Jesus, a nonprofit religious corporation, was distributing free literature on a pedestrian walkway in the terminal of Los Angeles International Airport (LAX) when he was stopped by a security officer. The officer informed him that he was in violation of a resolution passed by the airport commissioners declaring that the Central Terminal Area was "not open for First Amendment activities by any individual and/or entity." Told that he could face legal action if he continued to distribute his literature, the man left the airport. Jews for Jesus then challenged the resolution in federal court, prevailing up through the Ninth Circuit Court of Appeals. A unanimous Supreme Court held the resolution unconstitutional on its face.

The Court, with Justice O'Connor writing, invoked the First Amendment "overbreadth" doctrine, under which a law is unconstitutional on its face if it is so broadly written that it would restrict protected as well as unprotected speech. Inasmuch as the resolution flatly banned all "First Amendment activities," the Court expended few words in concluding that it was indeed overbroad.

Opinion of the Court: **O'Connor**, Rehnquist, Brennan, White, Marshall, Blackmun, Powell, Stevens, Scalia. Concurring opinion: **White**, Rehnquist.

Airport Commissioners v. *Jews for Jesus, Inc.,* was decided on June 15, 1987.

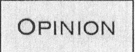

OPINION

JUSTICE O'CONNOR DELIVERED THE OPINION OF THE COURT . . .

Under the First Amendment overbreadth doctrine, an individual whose own speech or conduct may be prohibited is permitted to challenge a statute on its face "because it also threatens others not before the court—those who desire to engage in legally protected expression but who may refrain from doing so rather than risk prosecution or undertake to have the law declared partially invalid." *Brockett* v. *Spokane Arcades, Inc.* [1985]. A statute may be invalidated on its face, however, only if the overbreadth is "substantial." . . . The requirement that the overbreadth be substantial arose from our recognition that application of the overbreadth doctrine is "manifestly, strong medicine," *Broadrick* v. *Oklahoma* [1973], and that "there must be a realistic danger that the statute itself will significantly compromise recognized First Amendment protections of parties not before the Court for it to be facially challenged on overbreadth grounds." *City Council of Los Angeles* v. *Taxpayers for Vincent* [1984].

On its face, the resolution at issue in this case reaches the universe of expressive activity, and, by prohibiting all protected expression, purports to create a virtual "First Amendment Free Zone" at LAX. The resolution does not merely regulate expressive activity in the Central Terminal Area that might create problems such as congestion or the disruption of the activities of those who use LAX. Instead, the resolution expansively states that LAX "is not open for First Amendment activities by any individual and/or entity," and that "any individual and/or entity [who] seeks to engage in First Amendment activities within the Central Terminal Area . . . shall be deemed to be acting in contravention of the stated policy of the Board of Airport Commissioners." . . . The resolution therefore does not merely reach the activity of respondents at LAX; it prohibits even talking and reading, or the wearing of campaign buttons or symbolic clothing. Under such a sweeping ban, virtually every individual who enters LAX may be found to violate the resolution by engaging in some "First Amendment activit[y]." We think it obvious that such a ban cannot be justified even if LAX were a nonpublic forum because no conceivable governmental interest would justify such an absolute prohibition of speech.

Additionally, we find no apparent saving construction of the resolution. The resolution expressly applies to all "First Amendment activities," and the words of the resolution simply leave no room for a narrowing construction. In the past the Court sometimes has used either abstention or certification when, as here, the state courts have not had the opportunity to give the statute under challenge a definite construction. . . . Neither option, however, is appropriate in this case because California has no certification procedure, and the resolution is not "fairly subject to an interpretation which will render unnecessary or substantially modify the federal constitutional question." *Harmon* v. *Forssenius* [1965]. The difficulties in adopting a limiting construction of the resolution are not unlike those found in *Baggett* v. *Bullitt* [1964]. At issue in *Baggett* was the constitutionality of several statutes requiring loyalty oaths. The *Baggett* Court concluded that abstention would serve no purpose given the lack of any limiting construction, and held the statutes unconstitutional on their face under the First Amendment overbreadth doctrine. We observed that the challenged loyalty oath was not "open to one or a few interpretations, but to an indefinite number," and concluded that "[i]t is fictional to believe that anything less than extensive adjudications, under the impact of a variety of factual situations, would bring the oath within the bounds of permissible constitutional certainty." Here too, it is difficult to imagine that the resolution could be limited by anything less than a series of adjudications, and the chilling effect of the resolution on protected speech in the meantime would make such a case-by-case adjudication intolerable.

The petitioners suggest that the resolution is not substantially overbroad because it is intended to reach only expressive activity unrelated to airport-related purposes. Such a limiting construction, however, is of little assistance in substantially reducing the overbreadth of the resolution. Much nondisruptive speech—such as the wearing of a T-shirt or button that contains a political message—may not be "airport related," but is still protected speech even in a nonpublic forum. See *Cohen* v. *California* [1971]. Moreover, the vagueness of this suggested construction itself presents serious constitutional difficulty. The line between airport-related speech and nonairport-related speech is, at best, murky. The petitioners, for example, suggest that an individual who reads a newspaper or converses with a neighbor at LAX is engaged in permitted "airport-related" activity because reading or conversing permits the traveling public to "pass the time." We presume, however, that petitioners would not so categorize the activities of a member of a religious or political organization who decides to "pass the time" by distributing leaflets to fellow travelers. In essence, the result of this vague limiting construction would be to give LAX officials alone the power to decide in the first instance whether a given activity is airport related. Such a law that "confers on police a virtually unrestrained power to arrest and charge persons with a violation" of the resolution is unconstitutional because "[t]he opportunity for abuse, especially where a statute has received a virtually open-ended interpretation, is self-evident." *Lewis* v. *City of New Orleans* [1974] (Powell, J., concurring). . . .

We conclude that the resolution is substantially overbroad, and is not fairly subject to a limiting construction. Accordingly, we hold that the resolution violates the First Amendment. The judgment of the Court of Appeals is

AFFIRMED.

HUSTLER MAGAZINE V. FALWELL
485 U.S. 46 (1988)

Hustler magazine published a parody of minister Jerry Falwell (founder of the Moral Majority) in which he was depicted as a drunk in an incestuous relationship with his mother in an outhouse. Falwell sued in federal court, seeking damages for libel and intentional infliction of emotional distress. Although the jury found the parody was not libelous, it did award damages on the emotional-distress claim. The U.S. Court of Appeals for the Fourth Circuit upheld the award, but the Supreme Court, by a vote of 8 to 0, reversed.

In *Falwell* the Court was asked to embrace a novel theory—that speech that (a) is intended to inflict emotional distress, (b) is outrageous, and (c) does in fact inflict serious emotional distress is without First Amendment protection, regardless of whether it is fact or opinion, or true or false. In rejecting this theory, which contemplated an exception to the principles of *New York Times Co.* v. *Sullivan* (1964), the Court expressed doubt whether there was any principled standard by which one could distinguish "outrageous" caricatures from "more traditional political cartoons." "Outrageousness" in political discourse, the Court observed, "has an inherent subjectiveness about it which would allow a jury to impose liability on the basis of the jurors' tastes or views, or perhaps on the basis of their dislike of a particular expression."

Reiterating the principles of *New York Times*, the Court held that a public figure or official may not recover for intentional infliction of emotional distress resulting from a publication unless the publication contains a false statement of fact that was made with actual malice, i.e., with knowledge of falsity or reckless disregard for truth or falsity.

Opinion of the Court: **Rehnquist**, Brennan, Marshall, Blackmun, Stevens, O'Connor, Scalia. Concurring in the judgment: **White**. Not participating: Kennedy.

Hustler Magazine v. *Falwell* was decided on February 24, 1988.

OPINION

CHIEF JUSTICE REHNQUIST DELIVERED THE OPINION OF THE COURT . . .

This case presents us with a novel question involving First Amendment limitations upon a State's authority to protect its citizens from the intentional infliction of emotional distress. We must decide whether a public figure may recover damages for emotional harm caused by the publication of an ad parody offensive to him, and doubtless gross and repugnant in the eyes of most. Respondent would have us find that a State's interest in protecting public figures from emotional distress is sufficient to deny First Amendment protection to speech that is patently offensive and is intended to inflict emotional injury, even when that speech could not reasonably have been interpreted as stating actual facts about the public figure involved. This we decline to do.

At the heart of the First Amendment is the recognition of the fundamental importance of the free flow of ideas and opinions on matters of public interest and concern. "[T]he freedom to speak one's mind is not only an aspect of individual liberty—and thus a good unto itself— but also is essential to the common quest for truth and the vitality of society as a whole." *Bose Corp.* v. *Consumers Union of United States, Inc.* [1984]. We have therefore been particularly vigilant to ensure that individual expressions of ideas remain free from governmentally imposed sanctions. The First Amendment recognizes no such thing as a "false" idea. *Gertz* v. *Robert Welch, Inc.* [1974]. As Justice Holmes wrote, "when men have realized that time has upset many fighting faiths, they may come to believe even more than they believe the very foundations of their own conduct that the ultimate good desired is better reached by free trade in ideas—that the best test of truth is the power of the thought to get itself accepted in the competition of the market. . . ." *Abrams* v. *United States* [1919] (dissenting opinion).

The sort of robust political debate encouraged by the First Amendment is bound to produce speech that is critical of those who hold public office or those public figures who are "intimately involved in the resolution of important public questions or, by reason of their fame, shape events in areas of concern to society at large." *Associated Press* v. *Walker*, decided with *Curtis Publishing Co.* v. *Butts* [1967] (Warren, C. J., concurring in result). Justice Frankfurter put it succinctly in *Baumgartner* v. *United States* [1944] when he said that "[o]ne of the prerogatives of American citizenship is the right to criticize public men and measures." Such criticism, inevitably, will not always be reasoned or moderate; public figures as well as public officials will be subject to "vehement, caustic, and sometimes unpleasantly sharp attacks." *New York Times* v. *Sullivan* [1964]. . . .

Of course, this does not mean that any speech about a public figure is immune from sanction in the form of damages. . . . [W]e have consistently ruled that a public figure may hold a speaker liable for the damage to reputation caused by publication of a defamatory falsehood, but only if the statement was made "with knowledge that it was false or with reckless disregard of whether it was false or not." *New York Times*. False statements of fact are particularly valueless; they interfere with the truth-seeking function of the marketplace of ideas, and they cause damage to an individual's reputation that cannot easily be repaired by counterspeech, however persuasive or effective. . . . But even though falsehoods have little value in and of themselves, they are "nevertheless inevitable in free debate," *Gertz*, and a rule that would impose strict liability on a publisher for false factual assertions would have an undoubted "chilling" effect on speech relating to public figures that does have constitutional value. "Freedoms of expression require 'breathing space.'" *Philadelphia Newspapers, Inc.* v. *Hepps* [1986] (quoting *New York Times*). This breathing space is provided by a constitutional rule that allows public figures to recover for libel or defamation only when they can prove both that the statement was false and that the statement was made with the requisite level of culpability.

Respondent argues, however, that a different standard should apply in this case because here the State seeks to prevent not reputational damage, but the severe emotional distress suffered by the person who is the subject of an offensive publication. . . . In respondent's view, and in the view of the Court of Appeals, so long as the utterance was intended to inflict emotional distress, was outrageous, and did in fact inflict serious emotional distress, it is of no constitutional import whether the statement was a fact or an opinion, or whether it was true or false. It is the intent to cause injury that is the gravamen of the tort, and the State's interest in preventing emotional harm simply outweighs whatever interest a speaker may have in speech of this type.

Generally speaking the law does not regard the intent to inflict emotional distress as one which should receive much solicitude, and it is quite understandable that most if not all jurisdictions have chosen to make it civilly culpable where the conduct in question is sufficiently "outrageous." But in the world of debate about public affairs, many things done with motives that are less than admirable are protected by the First Amendment. In *Garrison* v. *Louisiana* [1964], we held that even when a speaker or writer is motivated by hatred or ill will his expression was protected by the First Amendment:

> Debate on public issues will not be uninhibited if the speaker must run the risk that it will be proved in court that he spoke out of hatred; even if he did speak out of hatred, utterances honestly believed contribute to the free interchange of ideas and the ascertainment of truth.

Thus while such a bad motive may be deemed controlling for purposes of tort liability in other areas of the law, we think the First Amendment prohibits such a result in the area of public debate about public figures.

Were we to hold otherwise, there can be little doubt that political cartoonists and satirists would be subjected to damages awards without any showing that their work falsely defamed its subject. *Webster's* defines a caricature as "the deliberately distorted picturing or imitating of a person, literary style, etc. by exaggerating features or mannerisms for satirical effect." . . . The appeal of the political cartoon or caricature is often based on exploitation of unfortunate physical traits or politically embarrassing events—an exploitation often calculated to injure the feelings of the subject of the portrayal. The art of the cartoonist is often not reasoned or evenhanded, but slashing and one-sided. . . .

Despite their sometimes caustic nature, from the early cartoon portraying George Washington as an ass down to the present day, graphic depictions and satirical cartoons have played a prominent role in public and political debate. Nast's castigation of the Tweed Ring, Walt McDougall's characterization of Presidential candidate James G. Blaine's banquet with the millionaires at Delmonico's as "The Royal Feast of Belshazzar," and numerous other efforts have undoubtedly had an effect on the course and outcome of contemporaneous debate. Lincoln's tall, gangling posture, Teddy Roosevelt's glasses and teeth, and Franklin D. Roosevelt's jutting jaw and cigarette holder have been memorialized by political cartoons with an effect that could not have been obtained by the photographer or the portrait artist. From the viewpoint of history it is clear that our political discourse would have been considerably poorer without them.

Respondent contends, however, that the caricature in question here was so "outrageous" as to distinguish it from more traditional political cartoons. There is no doubt that the caricature of respondent and his mother published in *Hustler* is at best a distant cousin of the political cartoons described above, and a rather poor relation at that. If it were possible by laying down a principled standard to separate the one from the other, public discourse would probably suffer little or no harm. But we doubt that there is any such standard, and we are quite sure that the pejorative description "outrageous" does not supply one. "Outrageousness" in the area of political and social discourse has an inherent subjectiveness about it which would allow a jury to impose liability on the basis of the jurors' tastes or views, or perhaps on the basis of their dislike of a particular expression. An "outrageousness" standard thus runs afoul of our longstanding refusal to allow damages to be awarded because the speech in question may have an adverse emotional impact on the audience. . . .

Admittedly, . . . First Amendment principles, like other principles, are subject to limitations. . . . In *Chaplinsky* v. *New Hampshire* [1942] we held that a State could lawfully punish an individual for the use of insulting "'fighting' words—those which by their very utterance inflict injury or tend to incite an immediate breach of the peace." These limitations are but recognition of the observation in *Dun & Bradstreet, Inc.* v. *Greenmoss Builders, Inc.* [1985] that this Court has "long recognized that not all speech is of equal First Amendment importance." But the sort of expression involved in this case does not seem to us to be governed by any exception to the general First Amendment principles stated above.

We conclude that public figures and public officials may not recover for the tort of intentional infliction of emotional distress by reason of publications such as the one here at issue without showing in addition that the publication contains a false statement of fact which was made with "actual malice," i.e., with knowledge that the statement was false or with reckless disregard as to whether or not it was true. This is not merely a "blind application" of the *New York Times* standard, . . . it reflects our considered judgment that such a standard is necessary to give adequate "breathing space" to the freedoms protected by the First Amendment.

Here it is clear that respondent Falwell is a "public figure" for purposes of First Amendment law. The jury found against respondent on his libel claim when it decided that the *Hustler* ad parody could not "reasonably be understood as describing actual facts about [respondent] or actual events in which [he] participated." . . . The Court of Appeals interpreted the jury's finding to be that the ad parody "was not reasonably believable," and in accordance with our custom we accept this finding. Respondent is thus relegated to his claim for damages awarded by the jury for the intentional infliction of emotional distress by "outrageous" conduct. But for reasons heretofore stated this claim cannot, consistently with the First Amendment, form a basis for the award of damages when the conduct in question is the publication of a caricature such as the ad parody involved here. The judgment of the Court of Appeals is accordingly

REVERSED.

HAZELWOOD SCHOOL DISTRICT V. KUHLMEIER
484 U.S. 260 (1988)

Ajournalism class at Hazelwood East High School in St. Louis County, Missouri, published a school newspaper called *Spectrum*. Reviewing the six pages scheduled for the May 13, 1983, issue, the school's principal objected to two stories, one describing student experiences with pregnancy and the other reporting the impact upon students when their parents divorce. Believing that there was not time to make changes in the stories before the publishing deadline, the principal decided to eliminate the two pages on which they were to appear. After publication of the truncated issue, three students who edited the paper sued, alleging a violation of First Amendment rights. The district court denied their claim, but the U.S. Court of Appeals for the Eighth Circuit reversed. The Supreme Court then sided with the school district.

Like *Bethel* v. *Fraser* (1986), *Kuhlmeier* limited the reach of *Tinker* v. *Des Moines* (1969), which held that students' silent wearing of black armbands to protest the Vietnam War was a form of protected speech. The *Kuhlmeier* Court read *Tinker* as governing only the expression of personal views and said that school-sponsored student speech was another matter entirely. This kind of speech, the Court held, is subject to editorial control by school authorities so long as "their actions are reasonably related to legitimate pedagogical concerns." Because school-sponsored activities could include "publications, theatrical productions, and other expressive activities that students, parents, and members of the public might reasonably perceive to bear the imprimatur of the school," the Court seemed to leave few contexts in which student speech could be personal in nature and thus protected by the more stringent standards of *Tinker*.

Opinion of the Court: **White**, Rehnquist, Stevens, O'Connor, Scalia. Dissenting opinion: **Brennan**, Marshall, Blackmun.

Hazelwood School District v. *Kuhlmeier* was decided on January 13, 1988.

OPINIONS

JUSTICE WHITE DELIVERED THE OPINION OF THE COURT . . .

Students in the public schools do not "shed their constitutional rights to freedom of speech or expression at the schoolhouse gate." *Tinker* v. *Des Moines* [1969]. They cannot be punished merely for expressing their personal views on the school premises—whether "in the cafeteria, or on the playing field, or on the campus during the authorized hours," *Tinker*—unless school authorities have reason to believe that such expression will "substantially interfere with the work of the school or impinge upon the rights of other students."

We have nonetheless recognized that the First Amendment rights of students in the public schools "are not automatically coextensive with the rights of adults in other settings," *Bethel School District No. 403* v. *Fraser* [1986], and must be "applied in light of the special characteristics of the school environment." *Tinker*. . . . A school need not tolerate student speech that is inconsistent with its "basic educational mission," *Fraser*, even though the government could not censor similar speech outside the school. Accordingly, we held in *Fraser* that a student could be disciplined for having delivered a speech that was "sexually explicit" but not legally obscene at an official school assembly, because the school was entitled to "disassociate itself" from the speech in a manner that would demonstrate to others that such vulgarity is "wholly inconsistent with the 'fundamental values' of public school education." We thus recognized that "[t]he determination of what manner of speech in the classroom or in school assembly is inappropriate properly rests with the school board," rather than with the federal courts. It is in this context that respondents' First Amendment claims must be considered.

We deal first with the question whether *Spectrum* may appropriately be characterized as a forum for public expression. The public schools do not possess all of the attributes of streets, parks, and other traditional public forums that "time out of mind, have been used for purposes of assembly, communicating thoughts between citizens, and discussing public questions." *Hague* v. *CIO* [1939]. . . . Hence, school facilities may be deemed to be public forums only if school authorities have "by policy or by practice" opened those facilities "for indiscriminate use by the general public," *Perry Education Assn.* v. *Perry Local Educators' Assn.* [1983], or by some segment of the public, such as student organizations. If the facilities have instead been reserved for other intended purposes, "communicative or otherwise," then no public forum has been created, and school officials may impose reasonable restrictions on the speech of students, teachers, and other members of the school community. . . .

The policy of school officials toward *Spectrum* was reflected in Hazelwood School Board Policy 348.51 and the Hazelwood East Curriculum Guide. Board Policy 348.51 provided that "[s]chool sponsored publications are developed within the adopted curriculum and its educational implications in regular classroom activities." The Hazelwood East Curriculum Guide described the Journalism II course as a "laboratory situation in which the students publish the school newspaper applying skills they have learned in Journalism I." The lessons that were to be learned from the Journalism II course, according to the Curriculum Guide, included development of journalistic skills under deadline pressure, "the legal, moral, and ethical restrictions imposed upon journalists within the school community," and "responsibility and acceptance of criticism for articles of opinion." Journalism II was taught by a faculty member during regular class hours. Students received grades and academic credit for their performance in the course.

School officials did not deviate in practice from their policy that production of *Spectrum* was to be part of the educational curriculum and a "regular classroom activit[y]." The District Court found that Robert Stergos, the journalism teacher during most of the 1982–1983 school year, "both had the authority to exercise and in fact exercised a great deal of control over *Spectrum*." For example, Stergos selected the editors of the newspaper, scheduled publication dates, decided the number of pages for each issue, assigned story ideas to class members, advised students on the development of their stories, reviewed the use of quotations, edited stories, selected and edited the letters to the editor, and dealt with the printing company. Many of these decisions were made without consultation with the Journalism II students. The District Court thus found it "clear that Mr. Stergos was the final authority with respect to almost every aspect of the production and publication of *Spectrum*, including its content." Moreover, after each *Spectrum* issue had been finally approved by Stergos or his successor, the issue still had to be reviewed by Principal Reynolds prior to publication. Respondents' assertion that they had believed that they could publish "practically anything" in *Spectrum* was therefore dismissed by the District Court as simply "not credible." These factual findings are amply supported by the record, and were not rejected as clearly erroneous by the Court of Appeals.

The evidence relied upon by the Court of Appeals in finding *Spectrum* to be a public forum . . . is equivocal at best. For example, Board Policy 348.51, which stated in part that "[s]chool sponsored student publications will not restrict free expression or diverse viewpoints within the rules of responsible journalism," also stated that such publications were "developed within the adopted curriculum and its educational implications." One might reasonably infer from the full text of Policy 348.51 that school officials retained ultimate control over what constituted "responsible journalism" in a school-sponsored newspaper. Although the Statement of Policy published in the September 14, 1982, issue of *Spectrum* declared that "*Spectrum*, as a student-press publication, accepts all rights implied by the First Amendment," this statement, understood in the context of the paper's role in the school's curriculum, suggests at most that the administration will not interfere with the students' exercise of those First Amendment rights that attend the publication of a school-sponsored newspaper. It does not reflect an intent to expand those rights by converting a curricular newspaper into a public forum. . . .

The question whether the First Amendment requires a school to tolerate particular student speech—the question that we addressed in *Tinker*—is different from the question whether the First Amendment requires a school affirmatively to promote particular student speech. The former question addresses educators' ability to silence a student's personal expression that happens to occur on the school premises. The latter question concerns educators' authority over school-sponsored publications, theatrical productions, and other expressive activities that students, parents, and members of the public might reasonably perceive to bear the imprimatur of the school. These activities may fairly be characterized as part of the school curriculum, whether or not they occur in a traditional classroom setting, so long as they are supervised by faculty members and designed to impart particular knowledge or skills to student participants and audiences.

Educators are entitled to exercise greater control over this second form of student expression to assure that participants learn whatever lessons the activity is designed to teach, that readers or listeners are not exposed to material that may be inappropriate for their level of maturity, and that the views of the individual speaker are not erroneously attributed to the school. Hence, a school may in its capacity as publisher of a school newspaper or producer of a school play "disassociate itself," *Fraser*, not only from speech that would "substantially interfere with [its] work . . . or impinge upon the rights of other students," *Tinker*, but also from speech that is, for example, ungrammatical, poorly written, inadequately researched, biased or prejudiced, vulgar or profane, or unsuitable for immature audiences. A school must be able to set high standards for the student speech that is disseminated under its auspices— standards that may be higher than those demanded by some newspaper publishers or theatrical producers in the "real" world—and may refuse to disseminate student speech that does not meet those standards. In addition, a school must be able to take into account the emotional maturity of the intended audience in determining whether to disseminate student speech on potentially sensitive topics, which might range from the existence of Santa Claus in an elementary school setting to the particulars of teenage sexual activity in a high school setting. A school must also retain the authority to refuse to sponsor student speech that might reasonably be perceived to advocate drug or alcohol use, irresponsible sex, or conduct otherwise inconsistent with "the shared values of a civilized social order," *Fraser*, or to associate the school with any position other than neutrality on matters of political controversy. . . .

Accordingly, we conclude that the standard articulated in *Tinker* for determining when a school may punish student expression need not also be the standard for determining when a school may refuse to lend its name and resources to the dissemination of student expression. Instead, we hold that educators do not offend the First Amendment by exercising editorial control over the style and content of student speech in school-sponsored expressive activities so long as their actions are reasonably related to legitimate pedagogical concerns. . . .

We also conclude that Principal Reynolds acted reasonably in requiring the deletion from the May 13 issue of *Spectrum* of the pregnancy article, the divorce article, and the remaining articles that were to appear on the same pages of the newspaper.

The initial paragraph of the pregnancy article declared that "[a]ll names have been changed to keep the identity of these girls a secret." The principal concluded that the students' anonymity was not adequately protected, however, given the other identifying information in the article and the small number of pregnant students at the school. Indeed, a teacher at the school credibly testified that she could positively identify at least one of the girls and possibly all three. It is likely that many students at Hazelwood East would have been at least as successful in identifying the girls. Reynolds therefore could reasonably have feared that the article violated whatever pledge of anonymity had been given to the pregnant students. In addition, he could reasonably have been concerned that the article was not sufficiently sensitive to the privacy interests of the students' boyfriends and parents, who were discussed in the article but who were given no opportunity to consent to its publication or to offer a response. The article did not contain graphic accounts of sexual activity. The girls did comment in the article, however, concerning their sexual histories and their use or nonuse of birth control. It was not unreasonable for the principal to have concluded that such frank talk was inappropriate in a school-sponsored publication distributed to 14-year-old freshmen and presumably taken home to be read by students' even younger brothers and sisters.

The student who was quoted by name in the version of the divorce article seen by Principal Reynolds made comments sharply critical of her father. The principal could reasonably have concluded that an individual publicly identified as an inattentive parent—indeed, as one who chose "playing cards with the guys" over home and family—was entitled to an opportunity to defend himself as a matter of journalistic fairness. These concerns were shared by both of *Spectrum*'s faculty advisers for the 1982–1983 school year, who testified that they would not have allowed the article to be printed without deletion of the student's name.

Principal Reynolds testified credibly at trial that, at the time that he reviewed the proofs of the May 13 issue during an extended telephone conversation with [Howard] Emerson [Stergos's replacement as faculty advisor to *Spectrum*], he believed that there was no time to make any changes in the articles, and that the newspaper had to be printed immediately or not at all. It is true that Reynolds did not verify whether the necessary modifications could still have been made in the articles, and that Emerson did not volunteer the information that printing could be delayed until the changes were made. We nonetheless agree with the District Court that the decision to excise the two pages containing the problematic articles was reasonable given the particular circumstances of this case. . . .

In sum, we cannot reject as unreasonable Principal Reynolds' conclusion that neither the pregnancy article nor the divorce article was suitable for publication in *Spectrum*. Reynolds could reasonably have concluded that the students who had written and edited these articles had not sufficiently mastered those portions of the Journalism II curriculum that pertained to the treatment of controversial issues and personal attacks, the need to protect the privacy of individuals whose most intimate concerns are to be revealed in the newspaper, and "the legal, moral, and ethical restrictions imposed upon journalists within [a] school community" that includes adolescent subjects and readers. Finally, we conclude that the principal's decision to delete two pages of *Spectrum*, rather than to delete only the offending articles or to require that they be modified, was reasonable under the circumstances as he understood them. Accordingly, no violation of First Amendment rights occurred.

The judgment of the Court of Appeals for the Eighth Circuit is therefore
REVERSED.

JUSTICE BRENNAN, DISSENTING . . .

Free student expression undoubtedly sometimes interferes with the effectiveness of the school's pedagogical functions. Some brands of student expression do so by directly preventing the school from pursuing its pedagogical mission: The young polemic who stands on a soapbox during calculus class to deliver an eloquent political diatribe interferes with the legitimate teaching of calculus. And the student who delivers a lewd endorsement of a student-government candidate might so extremely distract an impressionable high school audience as to interfere with the orderly operation of the school. See *Bethel School Dist. No. 403* v. *Fraser* [1986]. Other student speech, however, frustrates the school's legitimate pedagogical purposes merely by expressing a message that conflicts with the school's, without directly interfering with the school's expression of its message: A student who responds to a political science teacher's question with the retort, "socialism is good," subverts the school's inculcation of the message that capitalism is better. Even the maverick who sits in class passively sporting a symbol of protest against a government policy, cf. *Tinker* v. *Des Moines Independent Community School Dist.* [1969], or the gossip who sits in the student commons swapping stories of sexual escapade, could readily muddle a clear official message condoning the government policy or condemning teenage sex. Likewise, the student newspaper that, like *Spectrum*, conveys a moral position at odds with the school's official stance might subvert the administration's legitimate inculcation of its own perception of community values. . . .

This Court applied the *Tinker* test just a Term ago in *Fraser*, upholding an official decision to discipline a student for delivering a lewd speech in support of a student-government candidate. The Court today casts no doubt on *Tinker's* vitality. Instead it erects a taxonomy of school censorship, concluding that *Tinker* applies to one category and not another. On the one hand is censorship "to silence a student's personal expression that happens to occur on the school premises." On the other hand is censorship of expression that arises in the context of "school-sponsored . . . expressive activities that students, parents, and members of the public might reasonably perceive to bear the imprimatur of the school."

The Court does not, for it cannot, purport to discern from our precedents the distinction it creates. . . .

Nor has this Court ever intimated a distinction between personal and school-sponsored speech in any other context. . . .

The sole concomitant of school sponsorship that might conceivably justify the distinction that the Court draws between sponsored and nonsponsored student expression is the risk "that the views of the individual speaker [might be] erroneously attributed to the school." Of course, the risk of erroneous attribution inheres in any student expression, including "personal expression" that, like the armbands in *Tinker*, "happens to occur on the school premises." Nevertheless, the majority is certainly correct that indicia of school sponsorship increase the likelihood of such attribution, and that state educators may therefore have a legitimate interest in dissociating themselves from student speech.

But "'[e]ven though the governmental purpose be legitimate and substantial, that purpose cannot be pursued by means that broadly stifle fundamental personal liberties when the end can be more narrowly achieved.'" *Keyishian* v. *Board of Regents* [1967] (quoting *Shelton* v. *Tucker* [1960]). Dissociative means short of censorship are available to the school. It could, for example, require the student activity to publish a disclaimer, such as the "Statement of Policy" that *Spectrum* published each school year announcing that "[a]ll . . . editorials appearing in this newspaper reflect the opinions of the *Spectrum* staff, which are not necessarily shared by the administrators or faculty of Hazelwood East"; or it could simply issue its own response clarifying the official position on the matter and explaining why the student position is wrong. Yet, without so much as acknowledging the less oppressive alternatives, the Court approves of brutal censorship.

Since the censorship served no legitimate pedagogical purpose, it cannot by any stretch of the imagination have been designed to prevent "materia[l] disrup[tion of] classwork." *Tinker*. Nor did the censorship fall within the category that *Tinker* described as necessary to prevent student expression from "inva[ding] the rights of others." If that term is to have any content, it must be limited to rights that are protected by law. . . .

The Court opens its analysis in this case by purporting to reaffirm *Tinker's* time-tested proposition that public school students "do not 'shed their constitutional rights to freedom of speech or expression at the schoolhouse gate.'" That is an ironic introduction to an opinion that denudes high school students of much of the First Amendment protection that *Tinker* itself prescribed. . . . [T]he Court today "teach[es] youth to discount important principles of our government as mere platitudes." *West Virginia Board of Education* v. *Barnette* [1943]. The young men and women of Hazelwood East expected a civics lesson, but not the one the Court teaches them today.

I dissent.

TEXAS V. JOHNSON
491 U.S. 397 (1989)

In front of Dallas City Hall, at the end of a demonstration protesting Reagan administration policies, Gregory Lee Johnson doused an American flag with kerosene and set it on fire. Charged with violating a state law prohibiting the desecration of a venerated object, Johnson was convicted, sentenced to a year in prison, and fined $2,000. The Texas Court of Criminal Appeals overturned Johnson's conviction on First Amendment grounds, and then the U.S. Supreme Court, by a vote of 5 to 4, affirmed.

In this case involving "expressive conduct" (also called "non-verbal expression" or "symbolic speech"), the Court for the first time addressed the constitutionality of flag desecration. The issue had been raised before, in the late sixties and early seventies. But the Court had managed to decide those cases (without exception for the defendants) on narrow grounds, declining to resolve the constitutional issue.

Texas offered two justifications for its law: to prevent breaches of the peace resulting from flag-burning and to preserve the integrity of the flag as a symbol of national unity. The Court, with Justice Brennan writing, said that Johnson's flag-burning had not actually resulted in any immediate or later breach of the peace, and that the idea of protecting the flag as a symbol of national unity struck where it was constitutionally forbidden—at the communicative aspects of Johnson's conduct. Refusing to recognize what it called "a separate juridical category . . . for the American flag," the Court effectively affirmed a First Amendment right to burn the flag.

Johnson, arguably the Court's most important pronouncement ever on non-verbal expression—a type of speech it first recognized in *Stromberg* v. *California* (1931)—effectively nullified the flag-desecration statutes of forty-seven other states as well as the existing federal law. The case sharply divided the Court and produced unusual alignments, with Justices Marshall, Blackmun, Scalia, and Kennedy joining Justice Brennan in the majority, and Justices White, O'Connor, and Stevens joining Chief Justice Rehnquist in dissent. Not surprisingly, the decision stirred passions throughout the country. Congress responded by enacting a "content-neutral" law designed to protect the physical integrity of the flag. A year later, in *United States* v. *Eichman,* the Court, with the justices voting exactly as they had in *Johnson,* found that the "Flag Protection Act," as it was called, suffered "the same fundamental flaw" as the Texas statute.

Those disappointed with *Eichman* were left with only one option: a constitutional amendment making it possible to outlaw flag-burning. Repeated attempts to propose such an amendment, the latest in 1999, have fallen short of the necessary two-thirds vote in both houses of Congress.

Opinion of the Court: **Brennan**, Marshall, Blackmun, Scalia, Kennedy. Concurring opinion: **Kennedy**. Dissenting opinions: **Rehnquist**, White, O'Connor; **Stevens**.

Johnson v. *Texas* was decided on June 21, 1989.

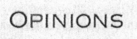

OPINIONS

JUSTICE BRENNAN DELIVERED THE OPINION OF THE COURT . . .

The Government generally has a freer hand in restricting expressive conduct than it has in restricting the written or spoken word. . . . It may not, however, proscribe particular conduct *because* it has expressive elements. . . . It is, in short, not simply the verbal or nonverbal nature of the expression, but the governmental interest at stake, that helps to determine whether a restriction on that expression is valid.

Thus, although we have recognized that where "'speech' and 'nonspeech' elements are combined in the same course of conduct, a sufficiently important governmental interest in regulating the nonspeech element can justify incidental limitations on First Amendment freedoms," *U.S.* v. *O'Brien* [1968], we have limited the applicability of *O'Brien*'s relatively lenient standard to those cases in which "the governmental interest is unrelated to the suppression of free expression." *O'Brien*. . . . In stating, moreover, that *O'Brien*'s test "in the last analysis is little, if any, different from the standard applied to time, place, or manner restrictions," . . . we have highlighted the requirement that the governmental interest in question be unconnected to expression in order to come under *O'Brien*'s less demanding rule.

In order to decide whether *O'Brien*'s test applies here, therefore, we must decide whether Texas has asserted an interest in support of Johnson's conviction that is unrelated to the suppression of expression. If we find that an interest asserted by the State is simply not implicated on the facts before us, we need not ask whether *O'Brien*'s test applies. . . . The State offers two separate interests to justify this conviction: preventing breaches of the peace, and preserving the flag as a symbol of nationhood and national unity. We hold that the first interest is not implicated on this record and that the second is related to the suppression of expression.

Texas claims that its interest in preventing breaches of the peace justifies Johnson's conviction for flag desecration. However, no disturbance of the peace actually occurred or threatened to occur because of Johnson's burning of the flag. Although the State stresses the disruptive behavior of the protestors during their march toward City Hall, it admits that "no actual breach of the peace occurred at the time of the flag-burning or in response to the flag-burning." The State's emphasis on the protestors' disorderly actions prior to arriving at City Hall is not only somewhat surprising given that no charges were brought on the basis of this conduct, but it also fails to show that a disturbance of the peace was a likely reaction to Johnson's conduct. The only evidence offered by the State at trial to show the reaction to Johnson's actions was the testimony of several persons who had been seriously offended by the flag-burning.

The State's position, therefore, amounts to a claim that an audience that takes serious offense at particular expression is necessarily likely to disturb the peace and that the expression may be prohibited on this basis. Our precedents do not countenance such a presumption. On the contrary, they recognize that a principal "function of free speech under our system of government is to invite dispute. It may indeed best serve its high purpose when it induces a condition of unrest, creates dissatisfaction with conditions as they are, or even stirs people to anger." *Terminiello* v. *Chicago* [1949]. . . .

Thus, we have not permitted the Government to assume that every expression of a provocative idea will incite a riot, but have instead required careful consideration of the actual circumstances surrounding such expression, asking whether the expression "is directed to inciting or producing imminent lawless action and is likely to incite or produce such action." *Brandenburg* v. *Ohio* [1969]. . . . To acccept Texas' arguments that it need only demonstrate "the potential for a breach of the peace," and that every flag-burning necessarily possesses that potential, would be to eviscerate our holding in *Brandenburg*. This we decline to do.

Nor does Johnson's expressive conduct fall within that small class of "fighting words" that are "likely to provoke the average person to retaliation, and thereby cause a breach of the peace." *Chaplinsky* v. *New Hampshire* [1942]. No reasonable onlooker would have regarded Johnson's generalized expression of dissatisfaction with the policies of the Federal Government as a direct personal insult or an invitation to exchange fisticuffs. . . .

We thus conclude that the State's interest in maintaining order is not implicated on these facts. The State need not worry that our holding will disable it from preserving the peace. We do not suggest that the First Amendment forbids a State to prevent "imminent lawless action." *Brandenburg*. And, in fact, Texas already has a statute specifically prohibiting breaches of the peace, which tends to confirm that Texas need not punish this flag desecration in order to keep the peace. . . .

The State also asserts an interest in preserving the flag as a symbol of nationhood and national unity. In *Spence* v. *Washington* [1974], we acknowledged that the Government's interest in preserving the flag's special symbolic value "is directly related to expression in the context of activity" such as affixing a peace symbol to a flag. We are equally persuaded that this interest is related to expression in the case of Johnson's burning of the flag. The State, apparently, is concerned that such conduct will lead people to believe either that the flag does not stand for nationhood and national unity, but instead reflects other, less positive concepts, or that the concepts reflected in the flag do not in fact exist, that is, we do not enjoy unity as a Nation. These concerns blossom only when a person's treatment of the flag communicates some message, and thus are related "to the suppression of free expression" within the meaning of *O'Brien*. We are thus outside of *O'Brien*'s test altogether.

It remains to consider whether the State's interest in preserving the flag as a symbol of nationhood and national unity justifies Johnson's conviction.

As in *Spence*, "[w]e are confronted with a case of prosecution for the expression of an idea through activity," and "[a]ccordingly, we must examine with particular care the interests advanced by [petitioner] to support its prosecution." Johnson was not, we add, prosecuted for the expression of just any idea; he was prosecuted for his expression of dissatisfaction with the policies of this country, expression situated at the core of our First Amendment values. . . .

Moreover, Johnson was prosecuted because he knew that his politically charged expression would cause "serious offense." If he had burned the flag as a means of disposing of it because it was dirty or torn, he would not have been convicted of flag desecration under this Texas law: federal law designates burning as the preferred means of disposing of a flag "when it is in such condition that it is no longer a fitting emblem for display," and Texas has no quarrel with this means of disposal. The Texas law is thus not aimed at protecting the physical integrity of the flag in all circumstances, but is designed instead to protect it only against impairments that would cause serious offense to others. . . .

Whether Johnson's treatment of the flag violated Texas law thus depended on the likely communicative impact of his expressive conduct. Our decision in *Boos* v. *Barry* [1988] tells us that this restriction on Johnson's expression is content-based. In *Boos*, we considered the constitutionality of a law prohibiting "the display of any sign within 500 feet of a foreign embassy if that sign tends to bring that foreign government into 'public odium' or 'public disrepute.'" Rejecting the argument that the law was content-neutral because it was justified by "our international law obligation to shield diplomats from speech that offends their dignity," we held that "[t]he emotive impact of speech on its audience is not a 'secondary effect'" unrelated to the content of the expression itself. . . .

According to the principles announced in *Boos*, Johnson's political expression was restricted because of the content of the message he conveyed. We must therefore subject the State's asserted interest in preserving the special symbolic character of the flag to "the most exacting scrutiny." *Boos.*

Texas argues that its interest in preserving the flag as a symbol of nationhood and national unity survives this close analysis. Quoting extensively from the writings of this Court chronicling the flag's historic and symbolic role in our society, the State emphasizes the "'special place'" reserved for the flag in our Nation. . . . The State's argument is not that it has an interest simply in maintaining the flag as a symbol of *something*, no matter what it symbolizes; indeed, if that were the State's position, it would be difficult to see how that interest is endangered by highly symbolic conduct such as Johnson's. Rather, the State's claim is that it has an interest in preserving the flag as a symbol of *nationhood* and *national unity*, a symbol with a determinate range of meanings. According to Texas, if one physically treats the flag in a way that would tend to cast doubt on either the idea that nationhood and national unity are the flag's referents or that national unity actually exists, the message conveyed thereby is a harmful one and therefore may be prohibited.

If there is a bedrock principle underlying the First Amendment, it is that the government may not prohibit the expression of an idea simply because society finds the idea itself offensive or disagreeable. . . .

We have not recognized an exception to this principle even where our flag has been involved. In *Street* v. *New York* [1969], we held that a State may not criminally punish a person for uttering words critical of the flag. . . . Nor may the government, we have held, compel conduct that would evince respect for the flag. . . .

In holding in *West Va. State Board of Education* v. *Barnette* [1943] that the Constitution did not leave this course open to the Government, Justice Jackson described one of our society's defining principles in words deserving of their frequent repetition: "If there is any fixed star in our constitutional constellation, it is that no official, high or petty, can prescribe what shall be orthodox in politics, nationalism, religion, or other matters of opinion or force citizens to confess by word or act their faith therein." In *Spence*, we held that the same interest asserted by Texas here was insufficient to support a criminal conviction under a flag-misuse statute for the taping of a peace sign to an American flag. "Given the protected character of [Spence's] expression and in light of the fact that no interest the State may have in preserving the physical integrity of a privately owned flag was significantly impaired on these facts," we held, "the conviction must be invalidated." . . .

In short, nothing in our precedents suggests that a State may foster its own view of the flag by prohibiting expressive conduct relating to it. To bring its argument outside our precedents, Texas attempts to convince us that even if its interest in preserving the flag's symbolic role does not allow it to prohibit words or some expressive conduct critical of the flag, it does permit it to forbid the outright destruction of the flag. The State's argument cannot depend here on the distinction between written or spoken words and nonverbal conduct. That distinction, we have shown, is of no moment where the nonverbal conduct is expressive, as it is here, and where the regulation of that conduct is related to expression, as it is here. . . . In addition, both *Barnette* and *Spence* involved expressive conduct, not only verbal communication, and both found that conduct protected.

Texas' focus on the precise nature of Johnson's expression, moreover, misses the point of our prior decisions: their enduring lesson, that the government may not prohibit expression simply because it disagrees with its message, is not dependent on the particular mode in which one chooses to express an idea. If we were to hold that a State may forbid flag-burning wherever it is likely to endanger the flag's symbolic role, but allow it wherever burning a flag promotes that role—as where, for example, a person ceremoniously burns a dirty flag—we would be saying that when it comes to impairing the flag's physical integrity, the flag itself may be used as a symbol—as a substitute for the written or spoken word or a "short cut from mind to mind"—only in one direction. We would be permitting a State to "prescribe what shall be orthodox" by saying that one may burn the flag to convey one's attitude toward it and its referents only if one does not endanger the flag's representation of nationhood and national unity.

We never before have held that the Government may ensure that a symbol be used to express only one view of that symbol of its referents. . . .

. . . To conclude that the Government may permit designated symbols to be used to communicate only a limited set of messages would be to enter territory having no discernible or defensible boundaries. Could the Government, on this theory, prohibit the burning of state flags? Of copies of the Presidential seal? Of the Constitution? In evaluating these choices under the First Amendment, how would we decide which symbols were sufficiently special to warrant this unique status? To do so, we would be forced to consult our own political preferences, and impose them on the citizenry, in the very way that the First Amendment forbids us to do. . . .

There is, moreover, no indication—either in the text of the Constitution or in our cases interpreting it—that a separate juridical category exists for the American flag alone. Indeed, we would not be surprised to learn that the persons who framed our Constitution and wrote the Amendment that we now construe were not known for their reverence for the Union Jack. The First Amendment does not guarantee that other concepts virtually sacred to our Nation as a whole—such as the principle that discrimination on the basis of race is odious and destructive—will go unquestioned in the marketplace of ideas. See *Brandenburg*. We decline, therefore, to create for the flag an exception to the joust of principles protected by the First Amendment. . . .

We are fortified in today's conclusion by our conviction that forbidding criminal punishment for conduct such as Johnson's will not endanger the special role played by our flag or the feelings it inspires. To paraphrase Justice Holmes, we submit that nobody can suppose that this one gesture of an unknown man will change our Nation's attitude towards its flag. See *Abrams* v. *United States* [1919] (Holmes, J., dissenting). . . .

We are tempted to say, in fact, that the flag's deservedly cherished place in our community will be strengthened, not weakened, by our holding today. Our decision is a reaffirmation of the principles of freedom and inclusiveness that the flag best reflects, and of the conviction that our toleration of criticism such as Johnson's is a sign and source of our strength. Indeed, one of the proudest images of our flag, the one immortalized in our own national anthem, is of the bombardment it survived at Fort McHenry. It is the Nation's resilience, not its rigidity, that Texas sees reflected in the flag—and it is that resilience that we reassert today.

The way to preserve the flag's special role is not to punish those who feel differently about these matters. It is to persuade them that they are wrong. . . . We can imagine no more appropriate response to burning a flag than waving one's own, no better way to counter a flag-burner's message than by saluting the flag that burns, no surer means of preserving the dignity even of the flag that burned than by—as one witness here did—according its remains a respectful burial. We do not consecrate the flag by punishing its desecration, for in doing so we dilute the freedom that this cherished emblem represents.

Johnson was convicted for engaging in expressive conduct. The State's interest in preventing breaches of the peace does not support his conviction because Johnson's conduct did not threaten to disturb the peace. Nor does the State's interest in preserving the flag as a symbol of nationhood and national unity justify his criminal conviction for engaging in political expression. The judgment of the Texas Court of Criminal Appeals is therefore

AFFIRMED.

JUSTICE KENNEDY, CONCURRING . . .

The hard fact is that sometimes we must make decisions we do not like. We make them because they are right, right in the sense that the law and the Constitution, as we see them, compel the result. And so great is our commitment to the process that, except in the rare case, we do not pause to express distaste for the result, perhaps for fear of undermining a valued principle that dictates the decision. This is one of those rare cases.

Our colleagues in dissent advance powerful arguments why respondent may be convicted for his expression, reminding us that among those who will be dismayed by our holding will be some who have had the singular honor of carrying the flag in battle. And I agree that the flag holds a lonely place of honor in an age when absolutes are distrusted and simple truths are burdened by unneeded apologetics.

With all respect to those views, I do not believe the Constitution gives us the right to rule as the dissenting members of the Court urge, however painful this judgment is to announce. Though symbols often are what we ourselves make of them, the flag is constant in expressing beliefs Americans share, beliefs in law and peace and that freedom which sustains the human spirit. The case here today forces recognition of the costs to which those beliefs commit us. It is poignant but fundamental that the flag protects those who hold it in contempt. . . .

CHIEF JUSTICE REHNQUIST, DISSENTING.

In holding this Texas statute unconstitutional, the Court ignores Justice Holmes' familiar aphorism that "a page of history is worth a volume of logic." *New York Trust Co.* v. *Eisner* [1921]. For more than 200 years, the American flag has occupied a unique position as the symbol of our Nation, a uniqueness that justifies a governmental prohibition against flag-burning in the way respondent Johnson did here. . . .

The flag symbolizes the Nation in peace as well as in war. It signifies our national presence on battleships, airplanes, military installations, and public buildings from the United States Capitol to the thousands of county courthouses and city halls throughout the country. . . .

No other American symbol has been as universally honored as the flag. In 1931, Congress declared "The Star-Spangled Banner" to be our national anthem. In 1949, Congress declared June 14th to be Flag Day. In 1987, John Philip Sousa's "The Stars and Stripes Forever" was designated as the national march. Congress has also established "The Pledge of Allegiance to the Flag" and the manner of its deliverance. The flag has appeared as the principal symbol on approximately thirty-three United States postal stamps and in the design of at least forty-three more, more times than any other symbol.

Both Congress and the States have enacted numerous laws regulating misuse of the American flag. Until 1967, Congress left the regulation of misuse of the flag up to the States. Now, however, Title 18 U.S.C. §700(a) provides that:

> Whoever knowingly casts contempt upon any flag of the United States by publicly mutilating, defacing, defiling, burning, or trampling upon it shall be fined not more than $1,000 or imprisoned for not more than one year, or both.

Congress has also prescribed . . . detailed rules for the design of the flag, the time and occasion of the flag's display, the position and manner of its display, respect for the flag, and conduct during hoisting, lowering, and passing of the flag. With the exception of Alaska and Wyoming, all of the States now have statutes prohibiting the burning of the flag. Most of the state statutes are patterned after the Uniform Flag Act of 1917, which . . . provides: "No person shall publicly mutilate, deface, defile, defy, trample upon, or by word or act cast contempt upon any such flag, standard, color, ensign or shield." . . .

The American flag, then, throughout more than 200 years of our history, has come to be the visible symbol embodying our Nation. It does not represent the views of any particular political party, and it does not represent any particular political philosophy. The flag is not simply another "idea" or "point of view" competing for recognition in the marketplace of ideas. Millions and millions of Americans regard it with an almost mystical reverence regardless of what sort of social, political, or philosophical beliefs they may have. I cannot agree that the First Amendment invalidates the Act of Congress, and the laws of forty-eight of the fifty States, which make criminal the public burning of the flag. . . .

But the Court insists that the Texas statute prohibiting the public burning of the American flag infringes on respondent Johnson's freedom of expression. . . .

. . . [T]he public burning of the American flag by Johnson was no essential part of any exposition of ideas, and at the same time it had a tendency to incite a breach of the peace. Johnson was free to make any verbal denunciation of the flag that he wished; indeed, he was free to burn the flag in private. He could publicly burn other symbols of the Government or effigies of political leaders. He did lead a march through the streets of Dallas, and conducted a rally in front of the Dallas City Hall. He engaged in a "die-in" to protest nuclear weapons. He shouted out various slogans during the march, including: "Reagan, Mondale, which will it be? Either one means World War III"; "Ronald Reagan, killer of the hour, perfect example of U.S. power"; and "red, white, and blue, we spit on you, you stand for plunder, you will go under." For none of these acts was he arrested or prosecuted; it was only when he proceeded to burn publicly an American flag stolen from its rightful owner that he violated the Texas statute. . . .

The result of the Texas statute is obviously to deny one in Johnson's frame of mind one of many means of "symbolic speech." Far from being a case of "one picture being worth a thousand words," flag-burning is the equivalent of an inarticulate grunt or roar that, it seems fair to say, is most likely to be indulged in not to express any particular idea, but to antagonize others. . . . The Texas statute deprived Johnson of only one rather inarticulate symbolic form of protest—a form of protest that was profoundly offensive to many—and left him with a full panoply of other symbols and every conceivable form of verbal expression to express his deep disapproval of national policy. Thus, in no way can it be said that Texas is punishing him because his hearers—or any other group of people—were profoundly opposed to the message that he sought to convey. Such opposition is no proper basis for restricting speech or expression under the First Amendment. It was Johnson's use of this particular symbol, and not the idea that he sought to convey by it or by his many other expressions, for which he was punished. . . .

The Court concludes its opinion with a regrettably patronizing civics lecture, presumably addressed to the Members of both Houses of Congress, the members of the forty-eight state legislatures that enacted prohibitions against flag-burning, and the troops fighting under that flag in Vietnam who objected to its being burned: "The way to preserve the flag's special role is not to punish those who feel differently about these matters. It is to persuade them that they are wrong." The Court's role as the final expositor of the Constitution is well established, but its role as a Platonic guardian admonishing those responsible to public opinion as if they were truant schoolchildren has no similar place in our system of government. The cry of "no taxation without representation" animated those who revolted against the English Crown to found our Nation—the idea that those who submitted to government should have some say as to what kind of laws would be passed. Surely one of the high purposes of a democratic society is to legislate against conduct that is regarded as evil and profoundly offensive to the majority of people—whether it be murder, embezzlement, pollution, or flag burning.

Our Constitution wisely places limits on powers of legislative majorities to act, but the declaration of such limits by this Court "is, at all times, a question of much delicacy, which ought seldom, if ever, to be decided in the affirmative, in a doubtful case." *Fletcher* v. *Peck* [1810]. Uncritical extension of constitutional protection to the burning of the flag risks the frustration of the very purpose for which organized governments are instituted. The Court decides that the American flag is just another symbol, about which not only must opinions pro and con be tolerated, but for which the most minimal public respect may not be enjoined. The government may conscript men into the Armed Forces where they must fight and perhaps die for the flag, but the government may not prohibit the public burning of the banner under which they fight. I would uphold the Texas statute as applied in this case.

RESPONSES

FROM THE *ATLANTA JOURNAL-CONSTITUTION,* JUNE 25, 1989, "CONSERVATIVE COURT, LIBERTARIAN STREAK"

Well, of course burning or otherwise desecrating the American flag "is wrong, dead wrong," as President Bush said in deploring the recent U.S. Supreme Court ruling. The court did not say otherwise, however. It did not welcome desecration. It only ruled that our Constitution's free-speech guarantee allows the surly, the sick, and the silly to trash the flag if they insist.

The justices could hardly have done otherwise. (And it is worrisome that four would have.) The principle has long been established that "speech" in the Bill of Rights does not mean only literal speech but other forms of personal expression as well—symbolic speech, as the term goes. To hold differently would be to crimp the guarantee into a narrow literal-mindedness that would erode its protections, especially in an age when televised and other images are a large part of the nation's political and social semaphore.

For most of us, the flag is a potent symbol of what we love about this country. And it is precisely because the flag is so potent that dissidents can't properly be denied its misuse to make a point. . . .

FROM THE *INDIANAPOLIS STAR,* JUNE 23, 1989

The court's ruling appears to nullify the laws of forty-eight states and a federal statute against flag desecration at peaceful protests. Only Wyoming and Alaska lack such laws. But it left open the possibility that flag-burning to incite a riot may be prosecutable as a crime.

That was wise. A great many Americans are strongly opposed to public burning of the flag, just as they would be to public burning of the Declaration of Independence and the Constitution. Even if such symbolic actions are, in the eyes of the law, words, to many they are fighting words, which can incite riots and other violence, and have done so often.

At present, the rights of protesters to destroy the symbols of American freedom are protected. Who will protect the rights of the millions who oppose destruction of the symbols of American freedom? Do they count for nothing in this supposedly enlightened age?

FROM THE SYNDICATED COLUMN BY GEORGE F. WILL, JULY 2, 1989

Speaking about the leftist whose arrest for flag-burning started [the flag controversy], Rep. Don Edwards (D-Calif.), a liberal, is distressed that "a nincompoop in Dallas, Texas, could do something that could trigger this reaction." Edwards does not understand. Five confused men in robes triggered this.

Their constitutional doctrine (by now it really is this, whether the justices know it or not) is that any behavior expressing an attitude that can be given a political coloration is protected "expression." A congressman wonders if fornication at high noon in Times

Square is protected. The answer is that fornication would blend into the background there, but would be protected if the participants said they were trying to shock the bourgeoisie into a higher consciousness.

After half a century of misconstruction, the First Amendment cannot be helped by a piddling-fiddling amendment about the flag. It needs serious thought about why the Amendment's framers, who used words more carefully than the Court does, used the word "speech" rather than "expression." The answer is that speech, meaning the use of words, is the sine qua non of reasoning and persuasion, and hence of democratic government. Democracy is, after all, the point of the Constitution, to which the Amendment is appended.

The fundamental problem is a social atmosphere saturated with a philosophy of extreme individualism. In many manifestations this philosophy is anti-democratic because it overrides the right of the community to speak and act. This philosophy has been absorbed by many judges, including some called conservatives, who have supported the assault on the rights of the community. . . .

There is no flag-burning problem sufficient to justify the radical step of amending the Constitution. . . .

No words on parchment will stymie litigious individualism. A change of constitutional words without a change of judicial and other minds will be unavailing. Go ahead, enact this amendment: "Nothing in this Constitution shall be construed to prevent states from protecting the flag from desecration." Then stand back. There will be an avalanche of litigation to determine if the use of the flag in advertisements, on clothing, with political slogans spray-painted on it, dragged in the dirt, or whatever, constitutes "desecration." . . .

MILKOVICH V. LORAIN JOURNAL CO.
497 U.S. 1 (1990)

In 1975 Michael Milkovich, an Ohio high school wrestling coach, sued a sports columnist for the *Lorain Journal* for suggesting that he had lied under oath in a judicial proceeding about a post-meet brawl in which several people were injured. The litigation in the Ohio courts, which spanned almost fifteen years, resulted in a summary judgment for the newspaper on the grounds that the sports column was "constitutionally protected opinion." On appeal, the U.S. Supreme Court reversed.

In *Milkovich* the Court was asked to distinguish between matters of opinion and assertions of fact and on that basis to recognize, as the majority opinion by Justice Rehnquist put it, "a wholesale defamation exemption for anything that might be labeled 'opinion.'" In declining this invitation, the Court said the issue is whether, regardless of how a statement might be characterized, it is "sufficiently factual to be susceptible of being proved true or false." Thus, an opinion that can reasonably be construed "as stating actual facts about an individual" may be subject to a defamation action. Plaintiffs bringing such cases, the Court emphasized, still had the burden of demonstrating culpability under standards developed in previous libel cases.

In a dissent joined by Justice Marshall, Justice Brennan also refused to create a special privilege for opinion. His disagreement with the Court instead concerned whether what the writer said about Milkovich really did imply any factual claims. Brennan said that there were none, that the column in question offered only "conjecture" about the coach's behavior, and that conjecture is constitutionally protected.

Opinion of the Court: **Rehnquist**, White, Blackmun, Stevens, O'Connor, Scalia, Kennedy. Dissenting opinion: **Brennan**, Marshall.

Milkovich v. *Lorain Journal Co.* was decided on June 21, 1990.

```
OPINIONS
```

CHIEF JUSTICE REHNQUIST DELIVERED THE OPINION OF THE COURT . . .

Respondents would have us recognize . . . still another First-Amendment-based protection for defamatory statements which are categorized as "opinion," as opposed to "fact." For this proposition, they rely principally on the following dictum from our opinion in *Gertz* v. *Robert Welch, Inc.* [1974]:

> Under the First Amendment, there is no such thing as a false idea. However pernicious an opinion may seem, we depend for its correction not on the conscience of judges and juries, but on the competition of other ideas. But there is no constitutional value in false statements of fact.

Judge Friendly appropriately observed that this passage "has become the opening salvo in all arguments for protection from defamation actions on the ground of opinion, even though the case did not remotely concern the question." *Cianci* v. *New Times Publishing Co.* [1980]. Read in context, though, the fair meaning of the passage is to equate the word "opinion" in the second sentence with the word "idea" in the first sentence. Under this view, the language was merely a reiteration of Justice Holmes' classic "marketplace of ideas" concept. . . .

Thus we do not think this passage from *Gertz* was intended to create a wholesale defamation exemption for anything that might be labeled "opinion." . . . Not only would such an interpretation be contrary to the tenor and context of the passage, but it would also ignore the fact that expressions of "opinion" may often imply an assertion of objective fact.

If a speaker says, "In my opinion John Jones is a liar," he implies a knowledge of facts which lead to the conclusion that Jones told an untruth. Even if the speaker states the facts upon which he bases his opinion, if those facts are either incorrect or incomplete, or if his assessment of them is erroneous, the statement may still imply a false assertion of fact. Simply couching such statements in terms of opinion does not dispel these implications; and the statement, "In my opinion Jones is a liar," can cause as much damage to reputation as the statement, "Jones is a liar." As Judge Friendly aptly stated: "[It] would be destructive of the law of libel if a writer could escape liability for accusations of [defamatory conduct] simply by using, explicitly or implicitly, the words 'I think.'" *Cianci*. . . .

Apart from their reliance on the *Gertz* dictum, respondents do not really contend that a statement such as, "In my opinion John Jones is a liar," should be protected by a separate privilege for "opinion" under the First Amendment. But they do contend that, in every defamation case, the First Amendment mandates an inquiry into whether a statement is "opinion" or "fact," and that only the latter statements may be actionable. They propose that a number of factors developed by the lower courts (in what we hold was a mistaken reliance on the *Gertz* dictum) be considered in deciding which is which. But we think the "'breathing space'" which "'[f]reedoms of expression require in order to survive,'" *Philadelphia Newspapers, Inc.* v. *Hepps* [1986] (quoting *New York Times Inc.* v. *Sullivan* [1969]) is adequately secured by existing constitutional doctrine without the creation of an artificial dichotomy between "opinion" and fact.

Foremost, we think *Hepps* stands for the proposition that a statement on matters of public concern must be provable as false before there can be liability under state defamation law, at least in situations, like the present, where a media defendant is involved. Thus, unlike the statement, "In my opinion Mayor Jones is a liar," the statement, "In my opinion Mayor Jones shows his abysmal ignorance by accepting the teachings of Marx and Lenin," would not be actionable. *Hepps* ensures that a statement of opinion relating to matters of public concern which does not contain a provably false factual connotation will receive full constitutional protection.

Next, the *Bresler–Letter Carriers–Falwell* line of cases [*Greenbelt Cooperative Publishing Assn., Inc.* v. *Bresler* (1970); *Letter Carriers* v. *Austin* (1974); *Hustler Magazine* v. *Falwell* (1988)] provide protection for statements that cannot "reasonably [be] interpreted as stating actual facts" about an individual. This provides assurance that public debate will not suffer for lack of "imaginative expression" or the "rhetorical hyperbole" which has traditionally added much to the discourse of our Nation.

The *New York Times–Butts* [*Curtis Publishing* v. *Butts* (1967)]–*Gertz* culpability requirements further ensure that debate on public issues remains "uninhibited, robust, and wide-open." *New York Times.* Thus, where a statement of "opinion" on a matter of public concern reasonably implies false and defamatory facts regarding public figures or officials, those individuals must show that such statements were made with knowledge of their false implications or with reckless disregard of their truth. Similarly, where such a statement involves a private figure on a matter of public concern, a plaintiff must show that the false connotations were made with some level of fault as required by *Gertz.* . . .

We are not persuaded that, in addition to these protections, an additional separate constitutional privilege for "opinion" is required to ensure the freedom of expression guaranteed by the First Amendment. The dispositive question in the present case then becomes whether or not a reasonable factfinder could conclude that the statements in the . . . [newspaper] column imply an assertion that petitioner Milkovich perjured himself in a judicial proceeding. We think this question must be answered in the affirmative. As the Ohio Supreme Court itself observed: "[T]he clear impact in some nine sentences and a caption is that [Milkovich] lied at the hearing after . . . having given his solemn oath to tell the truth." . . . This is not the sort of loose, figurative, or hyperbolic language which would negate the impression that the writer was seriously maintaining petitioner committed the crime of perjury. Nor does the general tenor of the article negate this impression.

We also think the connotation that petitioner committed perjury is sufficiently factual to be susceptible of being proved true or false. . . .

The numerous decisions . . . establishing First Amendment protection for defendants in defamation actions surely demonstrate the Court's recognition of the Amendment's vital guarantee of free and uninhibited discussion of public issues. But there is also another side to the equation; we have regularly acknowledged the "important social values which underlie the law of defamation," and recognize that "[s]ociety has a pervasive and strong interest in preventing and redressing attacks upon reputation." *Rosenblatt* v. *Baer* [1966]. . . .

We believe our decision in the present case holds the balance true. The judgment of the Ohio Court of Appeals is reversed, and the case remanded for further proceedings not inconsistent with this opinion.

JUSTICE BRENNAN, DISSENTING . . .

. . . I part company with the Court . . . because I find that the challenged statements cannot reasonably be interpreted as either stating or implying defamatory facts about petitioner. Under the rule articulated in the majority opinion, therefore, the statements are due "full constitutional protection." I respectfully dissent. . . .

No reasonable reader could understand Diadiun [writer of the column] to be impliedly asserting—as fact—that Milkovich had perjured himself. Nor could such a reader infer that Diadiun had further information about Milkovich's court testimony on which his belief was based. It is plain from the column that Diadiun did not attend the court hearing. Diadiun also clearly had no detailed second-hand information about what Milkovich had said in court. Instead, what suffices for "detail" and "color" are quotations from the OHSAA [Ohio High School Athletic Association] hearing—old news compared to the court decision which prompted the column—and a vague quotation from an OHSAA commissioner. Readers could see that Diadiun was focused on the court's reversal of the OHSAA's decision, and was angrily supposing what must have led to it.

Even the insinuation that Milkovich had repeated, in court, a more plausible version of the misrepresentations he had made at the OHSAA hearing is preceded by the cautionary term "apparently"—an unmistakable sign that Diadiun did not know what Milkovich had actually said in court. . . . Thus, it is evident from what Diadiun actually wrote that he had no unstated reasons for concluding that Milkovich perjured himself.

Furthermore, the tone and format of the piece notify readers to expect speculation and personal judgment. The tone is pointed, exaggerated, and heavily laden with emotional rhetoric and moral outrage. Diadiun never says, for instance, that Milkovich committed perjury. He says that "[a]nyone who attended the meet . . . knows in his heart" that Milkovich lied—obvious hyperbole, as Diadiun does not purport to have researched what everyone who attended the meet knows in his heart.

The format of the piece is a signed editorial column with a photograph of the columnist and the logo "TD Says." Even the headline on the page where the column is continued—"Diadiun says Maple told a lie,". . .—reminds readers that they are reading one man's commentary. Certain formats—editorials, reviews, political cartoons, letters to the editor—signal the reader to anticipate a departure from what is actually known by the author as fact. . . .

Although I agree with the majority that statements must be scrutinized for implicit factual assertions, the majority's scrutiny in this case does not "hol[d] the balance true" between protection of individual reputation and freedom of speech. The statements complained of neither state nor imply a false assertion of fact and, under the rule the Court reconfirms today, they should be found not libel "as a matter of constitutional law.". . . Readers of Diadiun's column are signaled repeatedly that the author does not actually know what Milkovich said at the court hearing and that the author is surmising, from factual premises made explicit in the column, that Milkovich must have lied in court.

Like the "imaginative expression" and the "rhetorical hyperbole" which the Court finds "has traditionally added much to the discourse of our Nation," conjecture is intrinsic to "the free flow of ideas and opinions on matters of public interest and concern" that is at "the heart of the First Amendment." *Falwell.* The public and press regularly examine the activities of those who affect our lives. . . . But often only some of the facts are known, and solely through insistent prodding—through conjecture as well as research—can important public questions be subjected to the "uninhibited, robust, and wide-open" debate to which this country is profoundly committed. *New York Times.*

Did NASA officials ignore sound warnings that the Challenger Space Shuttle would explode? Did Cuban-American leaders arrange for John Fitzgerald Kennedy's assassination? Was Kurt Waldheim a Nazi officer? Such questions are matters of public concern long before all the facts are unearthed, if they ever are. Conjecture is a means of fueling a national discourse on such questions and stimulating public pressure for answers from those who know more. . . .

What may be more disturbing to some about Diadiun's conjecture than, say, an editorial in 1960 speculating that Francis Gary Powers was in fact a spy, despite the Government's initial assurances that he was not, is the naïveté of Diadiun's conclusion. The basis of the court decision that is the subject of Diadiun's column was that Maple Heights had been denied its right to due process by the OHSAA. Diadiun, as it happens, not only knew this but included it in his column. But to anyone who knows what "due process" means, it does not follow that the court must have believed some lie about what happened at the wrestling meet, because what happened at the meet would not have been germane to the questions at issue. There may have been testimony about what happened, and that testimony may have been perjured, but, to anyone who understands the patois of the legal profession, there is no reason to assume—from the court's decision—that such testimony must have been given.

Diadiun, therefore, is guilty. He is guilty of jumping to conclusions, of benightedly assuming that court decisions are always based on the merits, and of looking foolish to lawyers. He is not, however, liable for defamation. Ignorance, without more, has never served to defeat freedom of speech. . . .

I appreciate this Court's concern with redressing injuries to an individual's reputation. But as long as it is clear to the reader that he is being offered conjecture and not solid information, the danger to reputation is one we have chosen to tolerate in pursuit of "'individual liberty [and] the common quest for truth and the vitality of society as a whole.'" *Falwell.* . . . Readers are as capable of independently evaluating the merits of such speculative conclusions as they are of evaluating the merits of pure opprobrium. Punishing such conjecture protects reputation only at the cost of expunging a genuinely useful mechanism for public debate. . . .

It is, therefore, imperative that we take the most particular care, where freedom of speech is at risk, not only in articulating the rules mandated by the First Amendment but also in applying them. "Whatever is added to the field of libel is taken from the field of free debate." *New York Times.* . . . Because I would affirm the Ohio Court of Appeals' grant of summary judgment to respondents, albeit on somewhat different reasoning, I respectfully dissent.

55

RUST V. SULLIVAN

500 U.S. 173 (1991)

In 1970 Congress passed a law providing federal funds for family-planning services. The statute—Title X of the Public Health Service Act—said that no appropriated funds could be used in programs that included abortion as a method of family planning. In 1988, Title X regulations were rewritten to provide better guidance on this point. The new regulations provided that a Title X project could not give advice on abortion as an instrument of family planning, nor could it, in referring women for other services, suggest an abortion provider, even upon specific request. Before the new regulations were enforced, Title X grantees in New York City challenged their validity on grounds including the First Amendment. They failed in district court, in the U.S. Court of Appeals for the Second Circuit, and in the Supreme Court, where their challenge was defeated 5 to 4.

As a First Amendment case, *Rust* concerned the doctrine of unconstitutional conditions, also known as the doctrine of conditional spending, under which the government may not impose unconstitutional conditions on the programs it creates and funds. In denying that the challenged regulations imposed unconstitutional free speech conditions on those working in Title X projects, the Court said that the government was simply "refusing to fund activities, including speech, which are specifically excluded from the scope of the project." The Court added that while doctors working in Title X programs could not engage in "abortion-related speech," they were not denied such speech because outside these programs they still could counsel on abortion.

Had the regulations at issue in *Rust* obligated the individuals who ran the projects, rather than the projects themselves, the outcome probably would have been different. The regulations were rescinded during the first term of the Clinton presidency.

Opinion of the Court: **Rehnquist**, White, Kennedy, Scalia, and Souter. Dissenting opinions: **Blackmun**, Marshall, O'Connor (in part), and Stevens (in part); **Stevens**; **O'Connor**.

Rust v. *Sullivan* was decided on May 23, 1991.

OPINIONS

CHIEF JUSTICE REHNQUIST DELIVERED THE OPINION OF THE COURT . . .

Petitioners contend that the regulations violate the First Amendment by impermissibly discriminating based on viewpoint because they prohibit "all discussion about abortion as a lawful option—including counseling, referral, and the provision of neutral and accurate information about ending a pregnancy—while compelling the clinic or counselor to provide information that promotes continuing a pregnancy to term." They assert that the regulations violate the "free speech rights of private health care organizations that receive Title X funds, of their staff, and of their patients" by impermissibly imposing "viewpoint-discriminatory conditions on government subsidies," and thus penaliz[e] speech funded with non–Title X monies. Because "Title X continues to fund speech ancillary to pregnancy testing in a manner that is not evenhanded with respect to views and information about abortion, it invidiously discriminates on the basis of viewpoint." Relying on *Regan* v. *Taxation With Representation of Wash.* [1983] and *Arkansas Writers Project, Inc.* v. *Ragland* [1987], petitioners also assert that, while the Government may place certain conditions on the receipt of federal subsidies, it may not "discriminate invidiously in its subsidies in such a way as to 'ai[m] at the suppression of dangerous ideas.'" *Regan* (quoting *Cammarano* v. *United States* [1959]). . . .

There is no question but that the statutory prohibition contained in [section] 1008 is constitutional. In *Maher* v. *Roe* [1977], we upheld a state welfare regulation under which Medicaid recipients received payments for services related to childbirth, but not for non-therapeutic abortions. The Court rejected the claim that this unequal subsidization worked a violation of the Constitution. We held that the government may "make a value judgment favoring childbirth over abortion, and . . . implement that judgment by the allocation of public funds." Here the Government is exercising the authority it possesses under *Maher* and *Harris* v. *McRae* [1980] to subsidize family planning services which will lead to conception and childbirth, and declining to "promote or encourage abortion." The Government can, without violating the Constitution, selectively fund a program to encourage certain activities it believes to be in the public interest, without at the same time funding an alternate program which seeks to deal with the problem in another way. In so doing, the Government has not discriminated on the basis of viewpoint; it has merely chosen to fund one activity to the exclusion of the other. "[A] legislature's decision not to subsidize the exercise of a fundamental right does not infringe the right." *Regan*. . . .

The challenged regulations implement the statutory prohibition by prohibiting counseling, referral, and the provision of information regarding abortion as a method of family planning. They are designed to ensure that the limits of the federal program are observed. The Title X program is designed not for prenatal care, but to encourage family planning. A doctor who wished to offer prenatal care to a project patient who became pregnant could properly be prohibited from doing so because such service is outside the scope of the federally funded program. The regulations prohibiting abortion counseling and referral are of the same ilk; "no funds appropriated for the project may be used in programs where abortion is a method of family planning," and a doctor employed by the project may be prohibited in the course of his project duties from counseling abortion or referring for abortion. This is not a case of the Government "suppressing a dangerous idea," but of a prohibition on a project grantee or its employees from engaging in activities outside of its scope.

To hold that the Government unconstitutionally discriminates on the basis of viewpoint when it chooses to fund a program dedicated to advance certain permissible goals because the program, in advancing those goals, necessarily discourages alternate goals would render numerous government programs constitutionally suspect. When Congress established a National Endowment for Democracy to encourage other countries to adopt democratic principles, . . . it was not constitutionally required to fund a program to encourage competing lines of political philosophy such as Communism and Fascism. Petitioners' assertions ultimately boil down to the position that, if the government chooses to subsidize one protected right, it must subsidize analogous counterpart rights. But the Court has soundly rejected that proposition. . . . Within far broader limits than petitioners are willing to concede, when the Government appropriates public funds to establish a program, it is entitled to define the limits of that program.

We believe that petitioners' reliance upon our decision in *Arkansas Writers Project* is misplaced. That case involved a state sales tax which discriminated between magazines on the basis of their content. Relying on this fact, and on the fact that the tax "targets a small group within the press," contrary to our decision in *Minneapolis Star and Tribune Co.* v. *Minnesota Comm'r of Revenue* [1983], the Court held the tax invalid. But we have here not the case of a general law singling out a disfavored group on the basis of speech content, but a case of the Government refusing to fund activities, including speech, which are specifically excluded from the scope of the project funded.

Petitioners rely heavily on their claim that the regulations would not, in the circumstance of a medical emergency, permit a Title X project to refer a woman whose pregnancy places her life in imminent peril to a provider of abortions or abortion-related services. This case, of course, involves only a facial challenge to the regulations, and we do not have before us any application by the Secretary to a specific fact situation. On their face, we do not read the regulations to bar abortion referral or counseling in such circumstances. Abortion counseling as a "method of family planning" is prohibited, and it does not seem that a medically necessitated abortion in such circumstances would be the equivalent of its use as a "method of family planning." Neither 1008 nor the specific restrictions of the regulations would apply. Moreover, the regulations themselves contemplate that a Title X project would be permitted to engage in otherwise prohibited abortion-related activity in such circumstances. . . .

Petitioners also contend that the restrictions on the subsidization of abortion-related speech contained in the regulations are impermissible because they condition the receipt of a benefit, in this case Title X funding, on the relinquishment of a constitutional right, the right to engage in abortion advocacy and counseling. Relying on *Perry* v. *Sindermann* [1972] and *FCC* v. *League of Women Voters of Cal.* [1984], petitioners argue that, "even though the government may deny [a] . . . benefit for any number of reasons, there are some reasons upon which the government may not rely. It may not deny a benefit to a person on a basis that infringes his constitutionally protected interests—especially, his interest in freedom of speech." *Perry.*

Petitioners' reliance on these cases is unavailing, however, because here the government is not denying a benefit to anyone, but is instead simply insisting that public funds be spent for the purposes for which they were authorized. The Secretary's regulations do not force the

Title X grantee to give up abortion-related speech; they merely require that the grantee keep such activities separate and distinct from Title X activities. Title X expressly distinguishes between a Title X grantee and a Title X project. . . . The Title X grantee can continue to perform abortions, provide abortion-related services, and engage in abortion advocacy; it simply is required to conduct those activities through programs that are separate and independent from the project that receives Title X funds.

In contrast, our "unconstitutional conditions" cases involve situations in which the government has placed a condition on the recipient of the subsidy, rather than on a particular program or service, thus effectively prohibiting the recipient from engaging in the protected conduct outside the scope of the federally funded program. In *FCC* v. *League of Women Voters of Cal.*, we invalidated a federal law providing that noncommercial television and radio stations that receive federal grants may not "engage in editorializing." Under that law, a recipient of federal funds was "barred absolutely from all editorializing," because it "is not able to segregate its activities according to the source of its funding," and thus "has no way of limiting the use of its federal funds to all noneditorializing activities." The effect of the law was that "a noncommercial educational station that receives only 1% of its overall income from [federal] grants is barred absolutely from all editorializing" and "barred from using even wholly private funds to finance its editorial activity." We expressly recognized, however, that were Congress to permit the recipient stations to "establish 'affiliate' organizations which could then use the station's facilities to editorialize with nonfederal funds, such a statutory mechanism would plainly be valid." Such a scheme would permit the station "to make known its views on matters of public importance through its nonfederally funded, editorializing affiliate without losing federal grants for its noneditorializing broadcast activities.["]

Similarly, in *Regan*, we held that Congress could, in the exercise of its spending power, reasonably refuse to subsidize the lobbying activities of tax-exempt charitable organizations by prohibiting such organizations from using tax-deductible contributions to support their lobbying efforts. In so holding, we explained that such organizations remained free "to receive deductible contributions to support . . . nonlobbying activit[ies]." Thus, a charitable organization could create . . . an affiliate to conduct its nonlobbying activities using tax-deductible contributions, and at the same time establish . . . a separate affiliate to pursue its lobbying efforts without such contributions. Given that alternative, the Court concluded that "Congress has not infringed any First Amendment rights or regulated any First Amendment activity[; it] has simply chosen not to pay for [appellee's] lobbying." . . . The condition that federal funds will be used only to further the purposes of a grant does not violate constitutional rights. . . .

By requiring that the Title X grantee engage in abortion-related activity separately from activity receiving federal funding, Congress has, consistent with our teachings in *League of Women Voters* and *Regan*, not denied it the right to engage in abortion-related activities. Congress has merely refused to fund such activities out of the public fisc, and the Secretary has simply required a certain degree of separation from the Title X project in order to ensure the integrity of the federally funded program.

The same principles apply to petitioners' claim that the regulations abridge the free speech rights of the grantee's staff. Individuals who are voluntarily employed for a Title X project must perform their duties in accordance with the regulation's restrictions on abortion counseling and referral. The employees remain free, however, to pursue abortion-related activities when they are not acting under the auspices of the Title X project. The regulations . . .

do not in any way restrict the activities of those persons acting as private individuals. The employees' freedom of expression is limited during the time that they actually work for the project; but this limitation is a consequence of their decision to accept employment in a project, the scope of which is permissibly restricted by the funding authority.

. . . It could be argued by analogy that traditional relationships such as that between doctor and patient should enjoy protection under the First Amendment from government regulation, even when subsidized by the Government. We need not resolve that question here, however, because the Title X program regulations do not significantly impinge upon the doctor-patient relationship. Nothing in them requires a doctor to represent as his own any opinion that he does not in fact hold. Nor is the doctor-patient relationship established by the Title X program sufficiently all-encompassing so as to justify an expectation on the part of the patient of comprehensive medical advice. The program does not provide post-conception medical care, and therefore a doctor's silence with regard to abortion cannot reasonably be thought to mislead a client into thinking that the doctor does not consider abortion an appropriate option for her. The doctor is always free to make clear that advice regarding abortion is simply beyond the scope of the program. In these circumstances, the general rule that the Government may choose not to subsidize speech applies with full force. . . .

The . . . regulations are a permissible construction of Title X, and do not violate either the First or Fifth Amendments to the Constitution. Accordingly, the judgment of the Court of Appeals is

AFFIRMED.

JUSTICE BLACKMUN, DISSENTING . . .

Until today, the Court never has upheld viewpoint-based suppression of speech simply because that suppression was a condition upon the acceptance of public funds. Whatever may be the Government's power to condition the receipt of its largess upon the relinquishment of constitutional rights, it surely does not extend to a condition that suppresses the recipient's cherished freedom of speech based solely upon the content or viewpoint of that speech. . . .

Nothing in the Court's opinion in *Regan* can be said to challenge this long-settled understanding. In *Regan*, the Court upheld a content-neutral provision of the Internal Revenue Code . . . that disallowed a particular tax-exempt status to organizations that "attempt[ed] to influence legislation," while affording such status to veterans' organizations irrespective of their lobbying activities. . . . [T]he Court explained: "The case would be different if Congress were to discriminate invidiously in its subsidies in such a way as to '"ai[m] at the suppression of dangerous ideas."' . . . We find no indication that the statute was intended to suppress any ideas or any demonstration that it has had that effect." [*Regan*, quoting *Cammarano* v. *United States* (1959), in turn quoting *Speiser* v. *Randall* (1958)]. . . .

It cannot seriously be disputed that the counseling and referral provisions at issue in the present cases constitute content-based regulation of speech. Title X grantees may provide counseling and referral regarding any of a wide range of family planning and other topics, save abortion. . . .

The Regulations are also clearly viewpoint-based. While suppressing speech favorable to abortion with one hand, the Secretary compels anti-abortion speech with the other. For example, the Department of Health and Human Services' own description of the Regulations makes plain that "Title X projects are required to facilitate access to prenatal care and social services, including adoption services, that might be needed by the pregnant client to promote her wellbeing and that of her child, while making it abundantly clear that the project is not permitted to promote abortion by facilitating access to abortion through the referral process." . . .

Moreover, the Regulations command that a project refer for prenatal care each woman diagnosed as pregnant, irrespective of the woman's expressed desire to continue or terminate her pregnancy. If a client asks directly about abortion, a Title X physician or counselor is required to say, in essence, that the project does not consider abortion to be an appropriate method of family planning. Both requirements are antithetical to the First Amendment. . . .

The Regulations pertaining to "advocacy" are even more explicitly viewpoint-based. These provide: "A Title X project may not encourage, promote or advocate abortion as a method of family planning." They explain: "This requirement prohibits actions to assist women to obtain abortions or increase the availability or accessibility of abortion for family planning purposes." The Regulations do not, however, proscribe or even regulate antiabortion advocacy. These are clearly restrictions aimed at the suppression of "dangerous ideas."

Remarkably, the majority concludes that "the Government has not discriminated on the basis of viewpoint; it has merely chosen to fund one activity to the exclusion of another." But the majority's claim that the Regulations merely limit a Title X project's speech to preventive or preconceptional services rings hollow in light of the broad range of non-preventive services that the Regulations authorize Title X projects to provide. By refusing to fund those family planning projects that advocate abortion because they advocate abortion, the Government plainly has targeted a particular viewpoint. . . . The majority's reliance on the fact that the Regulations pertain solely to funding decisions simply begs the question. Clearly, there are some bases upon which government may not rest its decision to fund or not to fund. For example, the members of the majority surely would agree that government may not base its decision to support an activity upon considerations of race. . . . As demonstrated above, our cases make clear that ideological viewpoint is a similarly repugnant ground upon which to base funding decisions.

The majority's reliance upon *Regan* in this connection is also misplaced. That case stands for the proposition that government has no obligation to subsidize a private party's efforts to petition the legislature regarding its views. Thus, if the challenged Regulations were confined to nonideological limitations upon the use of Title X funds for lobbying activities, there would exist no violation of the First Amendment. The advocacy Regulations at issue here, however, are not limited to lobbying, but extend to all speech having the effect of encouraging, promoting, or advocating abortion as a method of family planning. Thus, in addition to their impermissible focus upon the viewpoint of regulated speech, the provisions intrude upon a wide range of communicative conduct, including the very words spoken to a woman by her physician. . . .

The Court concludes that the challenged Regulations do not violate the First Amendment rights of Title X staff members, because any limitation of the employees' freedom of expression is simply a consequence of their decision to accept employment at a federally funded project. But it has never been sufficient to justify an otherwise unconstitutional condition upon public employment that the employee may escape the condition by relinquishing his or her job. . . .

The majority attempts to circumvent this principle by emphasizing that Title X physicians and counselors "remain free . . . to pursue abortion-related activities when they are not acting under the auspices of the Title X project." "The regulations," the majority explains, "do not in any way restrict the activities of those persons acting as private individuals." Under the majority's reasoning, the First Amendment could be read to tolerate any governmental restriction upon an employee's speech so long as that restriction is limited to the funded workplace. This is a dangerous proposition, and one the Court has rightly rejected in the past. . . .

The Government's articulated interest in distorting the doctor-patient dialogue—ensuring that federal funds are not spent for a purpose outside the scope of the program—falls far short of that necessary to justify the suppression of truthful information and professional medical opinion regarding constitutionally protected conduct. Moreover, the offending Regulation is not narrowly tailored to serve this interest. For example, the governmental interest at stake could be served by imposing rigorous bookkeeping standards to ensure financial separation or adopting content-neutral rules for the balanced dissemination of family planning and health information. . . . By failing to balance or even to consider the free speech interests claimed by Title X physicians against the Government's asserted interest in suppressing the speech, the Court falters in its duty to implement the protection that the First Amendment clearly provides for this important message.

Finally, it is of no small significance that the speech the Secretary [of Health and Human Services] would suppress is truthful information regarding constitutionally protected conduct of vital importance to the listener. One can imagine no legitimate governmental interest that might be served by suppressing such information. . . .

RESPONSES

FROM *AMERICA*, JUNE 8, 1991, "RUST V. SULLIVAN: A BETTER DEBATE"

. . . The cries of outrage from the "pro-choice" community after this decision . . . emphasize, of course, not the reality of abortion itself, but the abridgment of women's "choice" and doctors' "free speech." On Sunday morning, May 26, David Brinkley of ABC's "This Week With David Brinkley" was not untypical, but especially offensive, in questioning whether Judge David Souter (a particular disappointment to the libertarian establishment in this decision) was willing to abide by the Constitution. On Tuesday morning, May 28, the first business day after the holiday weekend, Planned Parenthood launched its counteroffensive with a full-page ad in the *New York Times* claiming, in inch-high type: "Americans Lost the First Amendment."

Most Catholics and, it is to be hoped, most Americans will take a different view, for they will recognize that the Supreme Court in *Rust* v. *Sullivan* has preserved distinctions crucial to a sensible debate.

1. Abortion cannot be equated with "family planning." The Supreme Court points out that the 1970 family planning legislation distinguished the two and intended to restrict Federal money to planning human life, not destroying it. This distinction is a legitimate one, says the Court, for the Federal Government may decide it has an interest in promoting childbirth but not in promoting abortion, even granting a woman's legal right to procure one.

2. The admission of a legal right (in this case, abortion) does not necessarily imply a duty on the part of the government to promote that right. Catholics understand the distinction well enough, for the parochial schools to which they have a right—schools that manifestly offer a service to the republic—receive virtually no government support. Proponents of abortion should be able to understand, therefore, how government might decline to support the "right" they wish to promote—a "right" that results in the "service" of 1.6 million abortions a year. As for the medical caregiver's free-speech rights to suggest or advise abortion, those are not violated, says the Court, because those rights can be exercised apart from facilities that use Federal money. . . .

FROM *THE PROGRESSIVE*, JULY 1991, "THE FIRST GOES TO RUST"

Physicians . . . have reason for concern. They, after all, are the people being gagged. The Court's decision allows the Government to wedge itself between doctors and their patients. By ordering doctors not to discuss the abortion option, it is ordering them to violate a long-standing code of ethics calling for medical advice to be *complete*. When a clinic doctor is treating a healthy woman with an unwanted pregnancy and fails to discuss abortion—a legal, safe, medical option in this situation—that is bad enough. But the Government made it clear in its oral argument before the Court that the rules also forbid the doctor to bring up abortion even when the life is endangered by her pregnancy.

Physicians who follow the Government's orders as the regulations now stand can be—and should be—seen as employing the same defense the Nazi doctors used to excuse their crimes in the death camps.

Massive resistance by doctors—refusal to obey—is the order of the day.

However, all of us—not just physicians—have reason for concern. Congress must take the blame for passing the vague law under which the Reagan Administration promulgated the gag rule, and it can partially atone by responding favorably to the movement now building to amend that law so physicians can get back to the ethical practice of medicine at Federally funded family-planning clinics. But the Supreme Court has done us a more permanent injustice: It has ruled that this sort of gag rule does not violate the Constitution's protection of freedom of speech.

If the Court can abolish the First Amendment in one case, it can abolish it in any case, at any time.

The anti-abortion lobby won this one; what comes next? Will the chemical lobby push through a law ordering agricultural extension agents not to talk about organic farming? Will the nuclear-power industry push through a law ordering scientists not to talk about solar energy? Will the National Rifle Association push through a law ordering police chiefs not to talk about gun control?

The danger to the First Amendment—done in its bicentennial year, no less—is unimaginable.

56

R.A.V. v. St. Paul
505 U.S. 377 (1992)

Robert A. Viktora, a white teenager, burned a cross on the lawn of a black family's house in St. Paul, Minnesota. Authorities charged the juvenile under a St. Paul ordinance prohibiting the display of symbols "including but not limited to a burning cross or Nazi Swastika, which . . . arouse anger, alarm, or resentment in others on the basis of race, color, creed, religion, or gender." Viktora moved to dismiss the count on grounds that the ordinance violated the First Amendment's free speech clause. The trial court granted the motion, but the Minnesota Supreme Court reversed. Viktora then appealed to the Supreme Court, which by a vote of 9 to 0 held the ordinance unconstitutional.

In *R.A.V.*, the Court for the first time addressed the constitutionality of "hate-crime" laws. All but four states had such laws, which are premised on the notion that crimes based on certain characteristics of a victim such as race, religion, or disability are particularly bad for society and may therefore be targeted for special punishment. A similar premise underlies speech-code regulations in force on many college and university campuses.

More significant than the result, which most court observers expected, was the majority's reasoning. In an effort to save a poorly drafted law, the Minnesota Supreme Court limited its reach to expressive conduct that amounts to "fighting words," i.e., "conduct that itself inflicts injury or tends to incite immediate violence." Citing the teaching of *Chaplinsky* v. *New Hampshire* (1942) that "fighting words" lack First Amendment protection, the Minnesota Supreme Court thus was able to hold that the ordinance reached only expression that under the Constitution could be proscribed. Justice Scalia, joined by Chief Justice Rehnquist and Justices Kennedy, Souter, and Thomas, accepted the Minnesota court's construction of the ordinance. But Scalia said the law was nonetheless unconstitutional. There are categories of speech—fighting words, obscenity, and defamation—that lack First Amendment protection, Scalia agreed, and government may regulate them. But in doing so government is not free, he said, to penalize some types of speech within an unprotected category but not others on account of their content. The problem in *R.A.V.*, Scalia continued, was that the St. Paul ordinance had done precisely that:

> Displays containing abusive invective, no matter how vicious or severe, are permissible [under the ordinance] unless they are addressed to one of the specified disfavored topics. Those who

wish to use "fighting words" in connection with other ideas—to express hostility, for example, on the basis of political affiliation, union membership, or homosexuality—are not covered. The First Amendment does not permit St. Paul to impose special prohibitions on those speakers who express views on disfavored subjects.

Justices White, Blackmun, Stevens, and O'Connor would have voided the law on a much narrower basis. These justices rejected the view of the statute adopted by the Minnesota Supreme Court—that it reached only fighting words that the First Amendment leaves unprotected. "The mere fact that expressive activity causes hurt feelings, offense, or resentment," wrote White in his separate opinion, which was joined by Blackmun, Stevens, and O'Connor, "does not render the expression unprotected." The ordinance thus reached unprotected as well as protected expression and was, wrote White, "fatally overbroad and invalid on its face."

Notwithstanding its agreement on the outcome, the *R.A.V.* Court was sharply divided. The four concurring justices were friendly to the idea behind the St. Paul ordinance, while the five justices forming the majority plainly were not. Disputing the majority's opinion on a number of points, the concurring opinions read more like dissents.

Opinion of the Court: **Scalia**, Rehnquist, Kennedy, Souter, Thomas. Concurring in the judgment: **White**, Blackmun, Stevens (in part), O'Connor; **Blackmun**; **Stevens**, White (in part), Blackmun (in part).

R.A.V. v. *St. Paul* was decided on June 22, 1992.

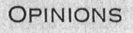

OPINIONS

JUSTICE SCALIA DELIVERED THE OPINION OF THE COURT . . .

In construing the St. Paul ordinance, we are bound by the construction given to it by the Minnesota court. . . . Accordingly, we accept the Minnesota Supreme Court's authoritative statement that the ordinance reaches only those expressions that constitute "fighting words" within the meaning of *Chaplinsky* v. *New Hampshire* [1992]. Petitioner and his amici urge us to modify the scope of the *Chaplinsky* formulation, thereby invalidating the ordinance as "substantially overbroad." . . . We find it unnecessary to consider this issue. Assuming, *arguendo*, that all of the expression reached by the ordinance is proscribable under the "fighting words" doctrine, we nonetheless conclude that the ordinance is facially unconstitutional in that it prohibits otherwise permitted speech solely on the basis of the subjects the speech addresses.

The First Amendment generally prevents government from proscribing speech . . . or even expressive conduct . . . because of disapproval of the ideas expressed. Content-based regulations are presumptively invalid. . . . From 1791 to the present, however, our society, like other free but civilized societies, has permitted restrictions upon the content of speech in a few limited areas, which are "of such slight social value as a step to truth that any benefit that may be derived from them is clearly outweighed by the social interest in order and morality." *Chaplinsky*. We have recognized that "the freedom of speech" referred to by the First Amendment does not include a freedom to disregard these traditional limitations. See, e.g., *Roth* v.

United States [1957] (obscenity); *Beauharnais* v. *Illinois* [1952] (defamation); *Chaplinsky* ("'fighting' words"). . . . Our decisions since the 1960s have narrowed the scope of the traditional categorical exceptions for defamation, see *New York Times Co.* v. *Sullivan* [1964]; *Gertz* v. *Robert Welch, Inc.* [1974]; see generally *Milkovich* v. *Lorain Journal Co.* [1990]; and for obscenity, see *Miller* v. *California* [1973], but a limited categorical approach has remained an important part of our First Amendment jurisprudence.

We have sometimes said that these categories of expression are "not within the area of constitutionally protected speech," *Roth; Beauharnais; Chaplinsky;* or that the "protection of the First Amendment does not extend" to them, *Bose Corp.* v. *Consumers Union of United States, Inc.* [1984]. . . . Such statements must be taken in context, however, and are no more literally true than is the occasionally repeated shorthand characterizing obscenity "as not being speech at all." . . . What they mean is that these areas of speech can, consistently with the First Amendment, be regulated because of their constitutionally proscribable content (obscenity, defamation, etc.)—not that they are categories of speech entirely invisible to the Constitution, so that they may be made the vehicles for content discrimination unrelated to their distinctively proscribable content. Thus, the government may proscribe libel; but it may not make the further content discrimination of proscribing only libel critical of the government. . . .

Our cases surely do not establish the proposition that the First Amendment imposes no obstacle whatsoever to regulation of particular instances of such proscribable expression, so that the government "may regulate [them] freely.". . . That would mean that a city council could enact an ordinance prohibiting only those legally obscene works that contain criticism of the city government or, indeed, that do not include endorsement of the city government. Such a simplistic, all-or-nothing-at-all approach to First Amendment protection is at odds with common sense and with our jurisprudence as well. It is not true that "fighting words" have at most a "de minimis" expressive content, or that their content is in all respects "worthless and undeserving of constitutional protection"; sometimes they are quite expressive indeed. We have not said that they constitute "no part of the expression of ideas," but only that they constitute "no essential part of any exposition of ideas." *Chaplinsky.* . . .

The proposition that a particular instance of speech can be proscribable on the basis of one feature (e.g., obscenity) but not on the basis of another (e.g., opposition to the city government) is commonplace and has found application in many contexts. We have long held, for example, that nonverbal expressive activity can be banned because of the action it entails, but not because of the ideas it expresses—so that burning a flag in violation of an ordinance against outdoor fires could be punishable, whereas burning a flag in violation of an ordinance against dishonoring the flag is not. . . . And just as the power to proscribe particular speech on the basis of a non-content element (e.g., noise) does not entail the power to proscribe the same speech on the basis of a content element, so also the power to proscribe it on the basis of one content element (e.g., obscenity) does not entail the power to proscribe it on the basis of other content elements.

In other words, the exclusion of "fighting words" from the scope of the First Amendment simply means that, for purposes of that Amendment, the unprotected features of the words are, despite their verbal character, essentially a "nonspeech" element of communication. Fighting words are thus analogous to a noisy sound truck . . . ; both can be used to convey an idea; but neither has, in and of itself, a claim upon the First Amendment. As with the sound truck, however, so also with fighting words: the government may not regulate use based on hostility—or favoritism—towards the underlying message expressed. . . .

The concurrences describe us as setting forth a new First Amendment principle that prohibition of constitutionally proscribable speech cannot be "underinclusiv[e]," (White, J., concurring in judgment)—a First Amendment "absolutism" whereby "[w]ithin a particular 'proscribable' category of expression, . . . a government must either proscribe all speech or no speech at all" (Stevens, J., concurring in judgment). That easy target is of the concurrences' own invention. In our view, the First Amendment imposes not an "underinclusiveness" limitation, but a "content discrimination" limitation, upon a State's prohibition of proscribable speech. There is no problem whatever, for example, with a State's prohibiting obscenity (and other forms of proscribable expression) only in certain media or markets, for although that prohibition would be "underinclusive," it would not discriminate on the basis of content. . . .

Even the prohibition against content discrimination that we assert the First Amendment requires is not absolute. It applies differently in the context of proscribable speech than in the area of fully protected speech. The rationale of the general prohibition, after all, is that content discrimination "raises the specter that the Government may effectively drive certain ideas or viewpoints from the marketplace," *Simon & Schuster, Inc.* v. *Members of N.Y. State Crime Victims Board* [1991]. . . . But content discrimination among various instances of a class of proscribable speech often does not pose this threat.

When the basis for the content discrimination consists entirely of the very reason the entire class of speech at issue is proscribable, no significant danger of idea or viewpoint discrimination exists. Such a reason, having been adjudged neutral enough to support exclusion of the entire class of speech from First Amendment protection, is also neutral enough to form the basis of distinction within the class. To illustrate: a State might choose to prohibit only that obscenity which is the most patently offensive in its prurience—i.e., that which involves the most lascivious displays of sexual activity. But it may not prohibit, for example, only that obscenity which includes offensive political messages. . . . And the Federal Government can criminalize only those threats of violence that are directed against the President . . . since the reasons why threats of violence are outside the First Amendment (protecting individuals from the fear of violence, from the disruption that fear engenders, and from the possibility that the threatened violence will occur) have special force when applied to the person of the President. . . . But the Federal Government may not criminalize only those threats against the President that mention his policy on aid to inner cities. . . .

Another valid basis for according differential treatment to even a content-defined subclass of proscribable speech is that the subclass happens to be associated with particular "secondary effects" of the speech, so that the regulation is "justified without reference to the content of the . . . speech." *Renton* v. *Playtime Theatres, Inc.* [1986]. . . .

Applying these principles to the St. Paul ordinance, we conclude that, even as narrowly construed by the Minnesota Supreme Court, the ordinance is facially unconstitutional. Although the phrase in the ordinance, "arouses anger, alarm, or resentment in others," has been limited by the Minnesota Supreme Court's construction to reach only those symbols or displays that amount to "fighting words," the remaining, unmodified terms make clear that the ordinance applies only to "fighting words" that insult, or provoke violence, "on the basis of race, color, creed, religion, or gender." Displays containing abusive invective, no matter how vicious or severe, are permissible unless they are addressed to one of the specified disfavored topics. Those who wish to use "fighting words" in connection with other ideas—to express hostility, for example, on the basis of political affiliation, union membership, or homosexuality—are not covered. The First Amendment does not permit St. Paul to impose special prohibitions on those speakers who express views on disfavored subjects. . . .

In its practical operation, moreover, the ordinance goes even beyond mere content discrimination to actual viewpoint discrimination. Displays containing some words—odious racial epithets, for example—would be prohibited to proponents of all views. But "fighting words" that do not themselves invoke race, color, creed, religion, or gender—aspersions upon a person's mother, for example—would seemingly be usable *ad libitum* in the placards of those arguing in favor of racial, color, etc., tolerance and equality, but could not be used by those speakers' opponents. One could hold up a sign saying, for example, that all "anti-Catholic bigots" are misbegotten; but not that all "papists" are, for that would insult and provoke violence "on the basis of religion." St. Paul has no such authority to license one side of a debate to fight freestyle, while requiring the other to follow Marquis of Queensberry rules.

What we have here, it must be emphasized, is not a prohibition of fighting words that are directed at certain persons or groups (which would be facially valid if it met the requirements of the Equal Protection Clause); but rather, a prohibition of fighting words that contain (as the Minnesota Supreme Court repeatedly emphasized) messages of "bias-motivated" hatred and, in particular, as applied to this case, messages "based on virulent notions of racial supremacy." One must wholeheartedly agree with the Minnesota Supreme Court that "[i]t is the responsibility, even the obligation, of diverse communities to confront such notions in whatever form they appear," but the manner of that confrontation cannot consist of selective limitations upon speech. St. Paul's brief asserts that a general "fighting words" law would not meet the city's needs, because only a content-specific measure can communicate to minority groups that the "group hatred" aspect of such speech "is not condoned by the majority." The point of the First Amendment is that majority preferences must be expressed in some fashion other than silencing speech on the basis of its content.

Despite the fact that the Minnesota Supreme Court and St. Paul acknowledge that the ordinance is directed at expression of group hatred, Justice Stevens suggests that this "fundamentally misreads" the ordinance. It is directed, he claims, not to speech of a particular content, but to particular "injur[ies]" that are "qualitatively different" from other injuries. This is wordplay. What makes the anger, fear, sense of dishonor, etc., produced by violation of this ordinance distinct from the anger, fear, sense of dishonor, etc., produced by other fighting words is nothing other than the fact that it is caused by a distinctive idea, conveyed by a distinctive message. The First Amendment cannot be evaded that easily. It is obvious that the symbols which will arouse "anger, alarm, or resentment in others on the basis of race, color, creed, religion, or gender" are those symbols that communicate a message of hostility based on one of these characteristics. . . .

The content-based discrimination reflected in the St. Paul ordinance comes within neither any of the specific exceptions to the First Amendment prohibition we discussed earlier nor a more general exception for content discrimination that does not threaten censorship of ideas. It assuredly does not fall within the exception for content discrimination based on the very reasons why the particular class of speech at issue (here, fighting words) is proscribable. . . .

. . . The dispositive question in this case . . . is whether content discrimination is reasonably necessary to achieve St. Paul's compelling interests; it plainly is not. An ordinance not limited to the favored topics, for example, would have precisely the same beneficial effect. In fact, the only interest distinctively served by the content limitation is that of displaying the city council's special hostility towards the particular biases thus singled out. That is precisely what the First Amendment forbids. The politicians of St. Paul are entitled to express that hostility—but not through the means of imposing unique limitations upon speakers who (however benightedly) disagree.

Let there be no mistake about our belief that burning a cross in someone's front yard is reprehensible. But St. Paul has sufficient means at its disposal to prevent such behavior without adding the First Amendment to the fire.

The judgment of the Minnesota Supreme Court is <u>reversed</u>, and the case is remanded for proceedings not inconsistent with this opinion.

JUSTICE WHITE, CONCURRING IN THE JUDGMENT.

I agree with the majority that the judgment of the Minnesota Supreme Court should be reversed. However, our agreement ends there.

This case could easily be decided within the contours of established First Amendment law by holding, as petitioner argues, that the St. Paul ordinance is fatally overbroad because it criminalizes not only unprotected expression but expression protected by the First Amendment. . . .

But in the present case, the majority casts aside long-established First Amendment doctrine without the benefit of briefing and adopts an untried theory. This is hardly a judicious way of proceeding, and the Court's reasoning in reaching its result is transparently wrong.

This Court's decisions have plainly stated that expression falling within certain limited categories so lacks the values the First Amendment was designed to protect that the Constitution affords no protection to that expression. . . .

Today, however, the Court announces that earlier Courts did not mean their repeated statements that certain categories of expression are "not within the area of constitutionally protected speech." . . . The present Court submits that such clear statements "must be taken in context," and are not "literally true."

To the contrary, those statements meant precisely what they said: the categorical approach is a firmly entrenched part of our First Amendment jurisprudence. Indeed, the Court in *Roth* reviewed the guarantees of freedom of expression in effect at the time of the ratification of the Constitution and concluded, "In light of this history, it is apparent that the unconditional phrasing of the First Amendment was not intended to protect every utterance."

In its decision today, the Court . . . holds that the First Amendment protects those narrow categories of expression long held to be undeserving of First Amendment protection—at least to the extent that lawmakers may not regulate some fighting words more strictly than others because of their content. The Court announces that such content-based distinctions violate the First Amendment because "[t]he government may not regulate use based on hostility—or favoritism—towards the underlying message expressed." Should the government want to criminalize certain fighting words, the Court now requires it to criminalize all fighting words.

To borrow a phrase: "Such a simplistic, all-or-nothing-at-all approach to First Amendment protection is at odds with common sense, and with our jurisprudence as well." [From the opinion of the Court.] It is inconsistent to hold that the government may proscribe an entire category of speech because the content of that speech is evil, . . . but that the government may not treat a subset of that category differently without violating the First Amendment; the content of the subset is, by definition, worthless and undeserving of constitutional protection.

The majority's observation that fighting words are "quite expressive indeed" is no answer. Fighting words are not a means of exchanging views, rallying supporters, or registering a protest; they are directed against individuals to provoke violence or to inflict injury. *Chaplinsky*. Therefore, a ban on all fighting words or on a subset of the fighting words category would restrict only the social evil of hate speech, without creating the danger of driving viewpoints from the marketplace. . . .

Any contribution of this holding to First Amendment jurisprudence is surely a negative one, since it necessarily signals that expressions of violence, such as the message of intimidation and racial hatred conveyed by burning a cross on someone's lawn, are of sufficient value to outweigh the social interest in order and morality that has traditionally placed such fighting words outside the First Amendment. Indeed, by characterizing fighting words as a form of "debate," the majority legitimates hate speech as a form of public discussion.

Furthermore, the Court obscures the line between speech that could be regulated freely on the basis of content (i.e., the narrow categories of expression falling outside the First Amendment) and that which could be regulated on the basis of content only upon a showing of a compelling state interest (i.e., all remaining expression). By placing fighting words, which the Court has long held to be valueless, on at least equal constitutional footing with political discourse and other forms of speech that we have deemed to have the greatest social value, the majority devalues the latter category. . . .

In a second break with precedent, the Court refuses to sustain the ordinance even though it would survive under the strict scrutiny applicable to other protected expression. Assuming, *arguendo*, that the St. Paul ordinance is a content-based regulation of protected expression, it nevertheless would pass First Amendment review under settled law. . . . St. Paul has urged that its ordinance, in the words of the majority, "helps to ensure the basic human rights of members of groups that have historically been subjected to discrimination. . . ." The Court expressly concedes that this interest is compelling, and is promoted by the ordinance. Nevertheless, the Court treats strict scrutiny analysis as irrelevant to the constitutionality of the legislation. . . .

Under the majority's view, a narrowly drawn, content-based ordinance could never pass constitutional muster if the object of that legislation could be accomplished by banning a wider category of speech. This appears to be a general renunciation of strict scrutiny review, a fundamental tool of First Amendment analysis. . . .

As with its rejection of the Court's categorical analysis, the majority offers no reasoned basis for discarding our firmly established strict scrutiny analysis at this time. The majority appears to believe that its doctrinal revisionism is necessary to prevent our elected lawmakers from prohibiting libel against members of one political party, but not another, and from enacting similarly preposterous laws. The majority is misguided.

Although the First Amendment does not apply to categories of unprotected speech, such as fighting words, the Equal Protection Clause requires that the regulation of unprotected speech be rationally related to a legitimate government interest. . . .

Turning to the St. Paul ordinance and assuming, *arguendo*, as the majority does, that the ordinance is not constitutionally overbroad . . . , there is no question that it would pass equal protection review. The ordinance proscribes a subset of "fighting words," those that injure "on the basis of race, color, creed, religion, or gender." This selective regulation reflects the city's judgment that harms based on race, color, creed, religion, or gender are more pressing public concerns than the harms caused by other fighting words. In light of our Nation's long and painful experience with discrimination, this determination is plainly reasonable. Indeed, as the majority concedes, the interest is compelling.

The Court has patched up its argument with an apparently nonexhaustive list of ad hoc exceptions, in what can be viewed either as an attempt to confine the effects of its decision to the facts of this case . . . or as an effort to anticipate some of the questions that will arise from its radical revision of First Amendment law. . . .

To avoid the result of its own analysis, the Court suggests that fighting words are simply a mode of communication, rather than a content-based category, and that the St. Paul ordinance has not singled out a particularly objectionable mode of communication. Again, the majority confuses the issue. A prohibition on fighting words is not a time, place, or manner restriction; it is a ban on a class of speech that conveys an overriding message of personal injury and imminent violence, *Chaplinsky*, a message that is at its ugliest when directed against groups that have long been the targets of discrimination. Accordingly, the ordinance falls within the first exception to the majority's theory.

As its second exception, the Court posits that certain content-based regulations will survive under the new regime if the regulated subclass "happens to be associated with particular 'secondary effects' of the speech . . . ," which the majority treats as encompassing instances in which "words can . . . violate laws directed not against speech, but against conduct. . . ." Again, there is a simple explanation for the Court's eagerness to craft an exception to its new First Amendment rule: under the general rule the Court applies in this case, Title VII hostile work environment claims would suddenly be unconstitutional.

Title VII of the Civil Rights Act of 1964 makes it unlawful to discriminate "because of [an] individual's race, color, religion, sex, or national origin," . . . and the regulations covering hostile workplace claims forbid "sexual harassment," which includes "[u]nwelcome sexual advances, requests for sexual favors, and other verbal or physical conduct of a sexual nature" that create "an intimidating, hostile, or offensive working environment." . . . The regulation does not prohibit workplace harassment generally; it focuses on what the majority would characterize as the "disfavored topi[c]" of sexual harassment. In this way, Title VII is similar to the St. Paul ordinance that the majority condemns because it "impose[s] special prohibitions on those speakers who express views on disfavored subjects." Under the broad principle the Court uses to decide the present case, hostile work environment claims based on sexual harassment should fail First Amendment review; because a general ban on harassment in the workplace would cover the problem of sexual harassment, any attempt to proscribe the subcategory of sexually harassing expression would violate the First Amendment.

Hence, the majority's second exception, which the Court indicates would insulate a Title VII hostile work environment claim from an underinclusiveness challenge because "sexually derogatory 'fighting words' . . . may produce a violation of Title VII's general prohibition against sexual discrimination in employment practices." But application of this exception to a hostile work environment claim does not hold up under close examination.

First, the hostile work environment regulation is not keyed to the presence or absence of an economic quid pro quo . . . but to the impact of the speech on the victimized worker. Consequently, the regulation would no more fall within a secondary effects exception than does the St. Paul ordinance. Second, the majority's focus on the statute's general prohibition on discrimination glosses over the language of the specific regulation governing hostile working environment, which reaches beyond any "incidental" effect on speech. *United States* v. *O'Brien* [1968]. If the relationship between the broader statute and specific regulation is sufficient to bring the Title VII regulation within *O'Brien*, then all St. Paul need do to bring its ordinance within this exception is to add some prefatory language concerning discrimination generally.

As to the third exception to the Court's theory for deciding this case, the majority concocts a catchall exclusion to protect against unforeseen problems, a concern that is heightened here given the lack of briefing on the majority's decisional theory. This final exception would apply in cases in which "there is no realistic possibility that official suppression of ideas is afoot." As I have demonstrated, this case does not concern the official suppression of ideas. The majority discards this notion out of hand.

As I see it, the Court's theory does not work, and will do nothing more than confuse the law. Its selection of this case to rewrite First Amendment law is particularly inexplicable, because the whole problem could have been avoided by deciding this case under settled First Amendment principles.

Although I disagree with the Court's analysis, I do agree with its conclusion: the St. Paul ordinance is unconstitutional. However, I would decide the case on overbreadth grounds. . . .

. . . Although the ordinance, as construed, reaches categories of speech that are constitutionally unprotected, it also criminalizes a substantial amount of expression that—however repugnant—is shielded by the First Amendment. . . .

In construing the St. Paul ordinance, the Minnesota Supreme Court drew upon the definition of fighting words that appears in *Chaplinsky*—words "which, by their very utterance, inflict injury or tend to incite an immediate breach of the peace." However, the Minnesota court was far from clear in identifying the "injur[ies]" inflicted by the expression that St. Paul sought to regulate. Indeed, the Minnesota court emphasized (tracking the language of the ordinance) that "the ordinance censors only those displays that one knows or should know will create anger, alarm, or resentment based on racial, ethnic, gender, or religious bias." I therefore understand the court to have ruled that St. Paul may constitutionally prohibit expression that, "by its very utterance," causes "anger, alarm, or resentment."

Our fighting words cases have made clear, however, that such generalized reactions are not sufficient to strip expression of its constitutional protection. The mere fact that expressive activity causes hurt feelings, offense, or resentment does not render the expression unprotected. . . .

Today, the Court has disregarded two established principles of First Amendment law without providing a coherent replacement theory. Its decision is an arid, doctrinaire interpretation, driven by the frequently irresistible impulse of judges to tinker with the First Amendment. The decision is mischievous at best, and will surely confuse the lower courts. I join the judgment, but not the folly of the opinion.

JUSTICE BLACKMUN, CONCURRING IN THE JUDGMENT.

I regret what the Court has done in this case. The majority opinion signals one of two possibilities: It will serve as precedent for future cases, or it will not. Either result is disheartening.

In the first instance, by deciding that a State cannot regulate speech that causes great harm unless it also regulates speech that does not (setting law and logic on their heads), the Court seems to abandon the categorical approach, and inevitably to relax the level of scrutiny applicable to content-based laws. As Justice White points out, this weakens the traditional protections of speech. If all expressive activity must be accorded the same protection, that protection will be scant. The simple reality is that the Court will never provide child pornography or cigarette advertising the level of protection customarily granted political speech. If we are forbidden from categorizing, as the Court has done here, we shall reduce protection across the board. It is sad that, in its effort to reach a satisfying result in this case, the Court is willing to weaken First Amendment protections.

In the second instance is the possibility that this case will not significantly alter First Amendment jurisprudence but, instead, will be regarded as an aberration—a case where the Court manipulated doctrine to strike down an ordinance whose premise it opposed, namely, that racial threats and verbal assaults are of greater harm than other fighting words. I fear that the Court has been distracted from its proper mission by the temptation to decide the issue over "politically correct speech" and "cultural diversity," neither of which is presented here. If this is the meaning of today's opinion, it is perhaps even more regrettable.

I see no First Amendment values that are compromised by a law that prohibits hoodlums from driving minorities out of their homes by burning crosses on their lawns, but I see great harm in preventing the people of Saint Paul from specifically punishing the race-based fighting words that so prejudice their community.

I concur in the judgment, however, because I agree with Justice White that this particular ordinance reaches beyond fighting words to speech protected by the First Amendment.

JUSTICE STEVENS, WITH WHOM JUSTICE WHITE AND JUSTICE BLACKMUN JOIN AS TO PART I, CONCURRING IN THE JUDGMENT.

[Note: All but the first two paragraphs of the following excerpts are from Part I.]

Conduct that creates special risks or causes special harms may be prohibited by special rules. Lighting a fire near an ammunition dump or a gasoline storage tank is especially dangerous; such behavior may be punished more severely than burning trash in a vacant lot. Threatening someone because of her race or religious beliefs may cause particularly severe trauma or touch off a riot, and threatening a high public official may cause substantial social disruption; such threats may be punished more severely than threats against someone based on, say, his support of a particular athletic team. There are legitimate, reasonable, and neutral justifications for such special rules.

This case involves the constitutionality of one such ordinance. Because the regulated conduct has some communicative content—a message of racial, religious, or gender hostility—the ordinance raises two quite different First Amendment questions. Is the ordinance "overbroad" because it prohibits too much speech? If not, is it "underbroad" because it does not prohibit enough speech? . . .

As an initial matter, the Court's revision of the categorical approach seems to me something of an adventure in a doctrinal wonderland, for the concept of "obscene antigovernment" speech is fantastical. The category of the obscene is very narrow; to be obscene, expression must be found by the trier of fact to "appea[l] to the prurient interest, . . . depic[t] or describ[e], in a patently offensive way, sexual conduct, [and], taken as a whole, lac[k] serious literary, artistic, political, or scientific value." *Miller* v. *California* [1973]. "Obscene antigovernment" speech, then, is a contradiction in terms: if expression is antigovernment, it does not "lac[k] serious . . . political . . . value," and cannot be obscene. . . .

I am, however, even more troubled by the second step of the Court's analysis—namely, its conclusion that the St. Paul ordinance is an unconstitutional content-based regulation of speech. Drawing on broadly worded dicta, the Court establishes a near-absolute ban on content-based regulations of expression, and holds that the First Amendment prohibits the regulation of fighting words by subject matter. Thus, while the Court rejects the "all-or-nothing-at-all" nature of the categorical approach, it promptly embraces an absolutism of its own: Within a particular "proscribable" category of expression, the Court holds, a government must either proscribe all speech or no speech at all. This aspect of the Court's ruling fundamentally misunderstands the role and constitutional status of content-based regulations on speech, conflicts with the very nature of First Amendment jurisprudence, and disrupts well-settled principles of First Amendment law.

Although the Court has, on occasion, declared that content-based regulations of speech are "never permitted," . . . our decisions demonstrate that content-based distinctions, far from being presumptively invalid, are an inevitable and indispensable aspect of a coherent understanding of the First Amendment. . . .

Our First Amendment decisions have created a rough hierarchy in the constitutional protection of speech. Core political speech occupies the highest, most protected position; commercial speech and nonobscene, sexually explicit speech are regarded as a sort of second-class expression; obscenity and fighting words receive the least protection of all. Assuming that the Court is correct that this last class of speech is not wholly "unprotected," it certainly does not follow that fighting words and obscenity receive the same sort of protection afforded core political speech. Yet, in ruling that proscribable speech cannot be regulated based on subject matter, the Court does just that. Perversely, this gives fighting words greater protection than is afforded commercial speech. If Congress can prohibit false advertising directed at airline passengers without also prohibiting false advertising directed at bus passengers, and if a city can prohibit political advertisements in its buses, while allowing other advertisements, it is ironic to hold that a city cannot regulate fighting words based on "race, color, creed, religion, or gender," while leaving unregulated fighting words based on "union membership . . . or homosexuality." The Court today turns First Amendment law on its head: Communication that was once entirely unprotected (and that still can be wholly proscribed) is now entitled to greater protection than commercial speech—and possibly greater protection than core political speech. . . .

In sum, the central premise of the Court's ruling—that "[c]ontent-based regulations are presumptively invalid"—has simplistic appeal, but lacks support in our First Amendment jurisprudence. To make matters worse, the Court today extends this overstated claim to reach categories of hitherto unprotected speech and, in doing so, wreaks havoc in an area of settled law. Finally, although the Court recognizes exceptions to its new principle, those exceptions undermine its very conclusion that the St. Paul ordinance is unconstitutional. Stated directly, the majority's position cannot withstand scrutiny.

RESPONSES

FROM *THE NATION*, JULY 13, 1992, "FIGHTING WORDS"

Friends of free speech can take cautious cheer from the Supreme Court's unanimous ruling on June 22 throwing out a St. Paul law prohibiting "hate symbols." Many states and local laws add special penalties to otherwise conventional crimes motivated by ethnic, religious, or sexual animus. But St. Paul's poorly drafted ordinance made a misdemeanor of expression alone—the mere appearance of such vicious and provocative symbols as swastikas and burning crosses. Had the law stood, it's not hard to imagine prosecutors in some future McCarthy era interpreting it to cover, say, a red flag or Malcolm's "X."

Still, *R.A.V.* v. *St. Paul* is hardly a definitive or even satisfactory ruling. Indeed, it seems fraught with danger, fostering the impression that hate crimes now enjoy the protection of the Constitution. Justice Scalia's majority opinion is nearly as poorly drafted as the original St. Paul ordinance itself. He seems at one moment to suggest that a wider law prohibiting *all* provocative symbols could have passed muster, and at another he implies that government has no power to give special consideration to hate speech or symbols of any sort. Both are frightening propositions. Acrimonious near-dissents by Justices Stevens, Blackmun, and White blasted Scalia's basic reasoning and scholarship. "An adventure in doctrinal wonderland," Stevens wrote of Scalia's opinion. Lobbyists for more effective bias-crime laws were left to ponder uncertainly Scalia's convoluted and murky reasoning.

More important than the St. Paul law itself are broader questions surrounding cultural expressions of racism, sexism and homophobia, etc. In defining free speech a quarter-century ago, the great civil liberties scholar Thomas Emerson drew a line between expression and action. Our dilemma today is that in an information age, expression seems perilously close to action. Racial, ethnic, and sexual invective and non-verbal images and symbols do hurt. They intimidate, and they ratify the confidence of those delivering the punches. To believe less is to deny the power of words and images to change society.

The challenge is to take that harm seriously without breathing life into the Frankenstein's monster of speech and image regulation by the government: to organize impassioned public censure, not empower the state censor. The danger in following the government-regulation route, even with the best intentions, is now starkly visible in Toronto, where enforcement of the Canadian Supreme Court decision embracing feminist legal scholar Catharine McKinnon's redefinition of pornography as a hate crime has begun. Ironically, the newly empowered censors' first target was a gay bookshop in Toronto, where police seized copies of a lesbian erotic magazine. The case demonstrates a central problem in regulating expression: Whether a swastika on the flagpole or degrading pornography in the corner store, free speech is inevitably defined by community standards, which can as easily promote oppression, like Toronto, as challenge it, like St. Paul.

It would be wrong for civil libertarians to react smugly to the *St. Paul* case. It demands that those who would defend social justice and civil liberties begin to articulate alternatives to codes of speech and censorship of images.

FROM *THE NEW REPUBLIC*, JULY 13 AND 20, 1992, "SPEECH THERAPY"

. . . This is an occasion for the friends of free expression to dance in the streets. By declaring unequivocally that even racist and sexist speech is protected by the First Amendment, . . . the Court has exposed the unconstitutionality of many state bias laws and virtually all campus hate speech codes. In a stroke, it has repelled the most serious threat to open debate that the current generation of students has experienced. But the consequences of Justice Scalia's bold reasoning may be more sweeping than even he intended. . . .

... Scalia held that even the traditional exceptions to the First Amendment—like fighting words, defamation, and obscenity—are "not entirely invisible to the Constitution," and the government may not use them to "handicap the expression of particular ideas." Minnesota could pass a general statute banning fighting words, but it could not single out only those fighting words that provoke violence on the basis of race or sex. Although the Court would have done better to abandon the "fighting words" doctrine altogether—it is absurd to assume that even face-to-face epithets are likely to provoke any reasonable person to reflexive violence—Scalia's alternative is an ingenious second best.

It is hard to imagine that any campus speech code in its current form should survive Justice Scalia's reasoning. (Private universities are obliged as a matter of principle, if not law, to abide by the decision.) First, any codes that target certain categories of speech—such as the Michigan and Stanford bans of speech that victimizes on the basis of race or handicap—are now impermissible. Second, any codes that focus, as Brown does, on the "feelings of impotence" or "anger" that speech arouses in others, rather than on its tendency to incite an immediate breach of the peace, can no longer masquerade as bans on "fighting words."

That leaves only one broad category of codes—those that rely on the EEOC's definition of sexual harassment, which includes speech that creates an "intimidating, hostile, or offensive work environment." We believe the "hostile environment" test is unconstitutional under traditional First Amendment principles; and as Justice White pointed out in his concurrence, it is clearly unconstitutional under Justice Scalia's new principles. Instead of a general ban on harassment that interferes with job performance, the "hostile environment" test singles out speakers who express views that the "reasonable woman" would find offensive. Scalia, disingenuously, dodged the question of whether he had inadvertently struck down part of Title VII.

Although the result of the *St. Paul* case could hardly be better, Scalia's novel theory of the First Amendment has some potentially pernicious implications. It is a good thing that, if taken seriously, Scalia's theory calls into question the "ethnic intimidation" laws many states have adopted, which carry special penalties for assaults on the basis of race, sex, and religion. But, taken to its logical conclusion, it may also cast doubt on some of the federal statutes passed after the Civil War specifically to protect blacks. ...

Nevertheless, the *St. Paul* decision deserves to be celebrated. The Rehnquist Court has not only reaffirmed but dramatically extended the principle that government may not silence speech on the basis of its content, and that no insults, no matter how sharply they sting, may be singled out for punishment.

FROM THE *DALLAS MORNING NEWS*, JUNE 24, 1992, "HATE CRIMES"

As unsettling as the high court's decision may seem, it needs to be put in perspective. Of all the "hate crime" ordinances and statutes passed in recent years, St. Paul's was perhaps the broadest. It punished "speech or thought crime." Even before this week's ruling, many legal experts considered that approach to be flawed.

Other cities and states, by contrast, address the problem by punishing action. Generally, they take existing crimes—such as assault, trespassing, and vandalism—and increase the penalties when the crimes were motivated by prejudice.

Texas legislators took a similar approach three years ago when they approved a statute that increased the punishment for certain types of vandalism.

Legal experts say it is unclear what message the Supreme Court was sending to state and local governments attempting to deal with the wave of hate crimes sweeping the country. But a logical response to the decision would be to assume that these other laws, which rely on stepped-up punishment, are as valid as ever.

Perhaps the best clue to the court's thinking can be found in Justice Scalia's summation: "Let there be no mistake about our belief that burning a cross in someone else's front yard is reprehensible. But St. Paul has sufficient means at its disposal to prevent such behavior without adding the First Amendment to the fire."

Hate, by itself, is not against the law, and our guarantee of free speech means we sometimes must listen to repugnant thoughts. But when prejudice flares up into illegal actions, we have a duty to deal with that conduct in the strongest terms possible.

57

HURLEY V. IRISH-AMERICAN GAY GROUP OF BOSTON
515 U.S. 557 (1995)

Since 1947 the South Boston Allied War Veterans Council had been authorized by the city of Boston to organize the annual St. Patrick's Day–Evacuation Parade, celebrating both St. Patrick's Day and the evacuation of royal troops and Loyalists from Boston in 1776. In 1992 a group of gay, lesbian, and bisexual descendants of Irish immigrants—with the acronym GLIB—applied to march in the parade. When the Council denied its request, GLIB obtained a court order requiring its inclusion in the parade. The following year GLIB again asked the Council for admission to the parade. Again the Council said no, whereupon the group sued in state court, alleging that the denial violated a state law prohibiting discrimination on the basis of sexual orientation in places of public accommodation. The trial court agreed with GLIB, and the Supreme Judicial Court of Massachusetts affirmed. The U.S. Supreme Court then voted unanimously to reverse.

In *Hurley* the Court was confronted with the novel question of whether private organizers of a parade could be forced to include a group expressing a message that the organizers did not wish to convey. Writing for the Court, Justice Souter found problematic not the Massachusetts public-accommodations law itself but its "peculiar" application, which "had the effect of declaring the sponsors' speech itself to be the public accommodation." Thus, wrote Souter, "any contingent of protected individuals with a message would have the right to participate in [the sponsors'] speech, so that the communication produced by the private organizers would be shaped by all those protected by the law who wished to join in with some expressive demonstration of their own." This use of state power, he concluded, would violate "the fundamental rule of protection under the First Amendment, that a speaker has the autonomy to choose the content of his own message."

Notably, the Court emphatically rejected the argument that might have been made in the case—"that the ultimate point of forbidding acts of discrimination toward certain classes is to produce a society free of the corresponding biases." Wrote Souter: "The very idea that a noncommercial speech restriction be used to produce thoughts and statements acceptable to some groups or, indeed, all people, grates on the First Amendment, for it amounts to nothing less than a proposal to limit speech in the service of orthodox expression. . . . While the law is free to promote all sorts of conduct in place of harmful behavior, it is not free to interfere with speech for no better reason than promoting an approved message or discouraging a disfavored one, however enlightened either purpose may strike the government."

Opinion of the Court: **Souter**, Rehnquist, Stevens, O'Connor, Scalia, Kennedy, Thomas, Ginsburg, Breyer.

Hurley v. *Irish-American Gay Group of Boston* was decided on June 19, 1995.

JUSTICE SOUTER DELIVERED THE OPINION OF THE COURT . . .

If there were no reason for a group of people to march from here to there except to reach a destination, they could make the trip without expressing any message beyond the fact of the march itself. Some people might call such a procession a parade, but it would not be much of one. . . . [W]e use the word "parade" to indicate marchers who are making some sort of collective point, not just to each other but to bystanders along the way. . . . Parades are thus a form of expression, not just motion, and the inherent expressiveness of marching to make a point explains our cases involving protest marches. . . .

The protected expression that inheres in a parade is not limited to its banners and songs, however, for the Constitution looks beyond written or spoken words as mediums of expression. Noting that "[s]ymbolism is a primitive but effective way of communicating ideas," *West Virginia Bd. of Ed.* v. *Barnette* [1943], our cases have recognized that the First Amendment shields such acts as saluting a flag (and refusing to do so), *Barnette*, wearing an arm band to protest a war, *Tinker* v. *Des Moines Independent Community School Dist.* [1969], displaying a red flag, *Stromberg* v. *California* [1931], and even "[m]arching, walking or parading" in uniforms displaying the swastika, *National Socialist Party of America* v. *Skokie* [1977]. As some of these examples show, a narrow, succinctly articulable message is not a condition of constitutional protection. . . .

Not many marches, then, are beyond the realm of expressive parades, and the South Boston celebration is not one of them. Spectators line the streets; people march in costumes and uniforms, carrying flags and banners with all sorts of messages (e.g., "England get out of Ireland," "Say no to drugs"); marching bands and pipers play, floats are pulled along, and the whole show is broadcast over Boston television. . . . To be sure, we agree with the state courts that in spite of excluding some applicants, the Council is rather lenient in admitting participants. But a private speaker does not forfeit constitutional protection simply by combining multifarious voices, or by failing to edit their themes to isolate an exact message as the exclusive subject matter of the speech. Nor, under our precedent, does First Amendment protection require a speaker to generate, as an original matter, each item featured in the communication. . . .

Respondents' participation as a unit in the parade was equally expressive. GLIB was formed for the very purpose of marching in it, as the trial court found, in order to celebrate its members' identity as openly gay, lesbian, and bisexual descendants of the Irish immigrants, to show that there are such individuals in the community, and to support the like men and women who sought to march in the New York parade. . . . GLIB understandably seeks to communicate its ideas as part of the existing parade, rather than staging one of its own.

The Massachusetts public accommodations law under which respondents brought suit has a venerable history. At common law, innkeepers, smiths, and others who "made profession of a public employment" were prohibited from refusing, without good reason, to serve a customer. . . .

After the Civil War, the Commonwealth of Massachusetts was the first State to codify this principle to ensure access to public accommodations regardless of race. . . . In prohibiting discrimination "in any licensed inn, in any public place of amusement, public conveyance or public meeting," the original statute already expanded upon the common law, which had not conferred any right of access to places of public amusement. . . . As with many public accommodations statutes across the Nation, the legislature continued to broaden the scope of legislation, to the point that the law today prohibits discrimination on the basis of "race, color, religious creed, national origin, sex, sexual orientation . . . , deafness, blindness, or any physical or mental disability or ancestry" in "the admission of any person to, or treatment in any place of public accommodation, resort, or amusement." . . . Provisions like these are well within the State's usual power to enact when a legislature has reason to believe that a given group is the target of discrimination, and they do not, as a general matter, violate the First or Fourteenth Amendments. See, e.g., *New York State Club Assn., Inc.* v. *City of New York* [1988]; *Roberts* v. *United States Jaycees* [1984]; *Heart of Atlanta Motel, Inc.* v. *United States* [1964]. Nor is this statute unusual in any obvious way, since it does not, on its face, target speech or discriminate on the basis of its content, the focal point of its prohibition being rather on the act of discriminating against individuals in the provision of publicly available goods, privileges, and services on the proscribed grounds.

In the case before us, however, the Massachusetts law has been applied in a peculiar way. Its enforcement does not address any dispute about the participation of openly gay, lesbian, or bisexual individuals in various units admitted to the parade. The petitioners disclaim any intent to exclude homosexuals as such, and no individual member of GLIB claims to have been excluded from parading as a member of any group that the Council has approved to march. Instead, the disagreement goes to the admission of GLIB as its own parade unit carrying its own banner. . . . Since every participating unit affects the message conveyed by the private organizers, the state courts' application of the statute produced an order essentially requiring petitioners to alter the expressive content of their parade. Although the state courts spoke of the parade as a place of public accommodation, . . . once the expressive character of both the parade and the marching GLIB contingent is understood, it becomes apparent that the state courts' application of the statute had the effect of declaring the sponsors' speech itself to be the public accommodation. Under this approach any contingent of protected individuals with a message would have the right to participate in petitioners' speech, so that the communication produced by the private organizers would be shaped by all those protected by the law who wished to join in with some expressive demonstration of their own. But this use of the State's power violates the fundamental rule of protection under the First Amendment, that a speaker has the autonomy to choose the content of his own message. . . .

Petitioners' claim to the benefit of this principle of autonomy to control one's own speech is as sound as the South Boston parade is expressive. Rather like a composer, the Council selects the expressive units of the parade from potential participants, and though the score may not produce a particularized message, each contingent's expression in the Council's eyes comports with what merits celebration on that day. Even if this view gives the Council credit for a more considered judgment than it actively made, the Council clearly decided to exclude a message it did not like from the communication it chose to make, and that is enough to invoke its right as a private speaker to shape its expression by speaking on one subject while remaining silent on another. The message it disfavored is not difficult to identify. Although GLIB's point (like the Council's) is not wholly articulate, a contingent marching behind the organization's banner would at least bear witness to the fact that some Irish are gay, lesbian, or bisexual, and the presence of the organized marchers would suggest their view that people of their sexual orientations have as much claim to unqualified social acceptance as heterosexuals and indeed as members of parade units organized around other identifying characteristics. The parade's organizers may not believe these facts about Irish sexuality to be so, or they may object to unqualified social acceptance of gays and lesbians or have some other reason for wishing to keep GLIB's message out of the parade. But whatever the reason, it boils down to the choice of a speaker not to propound a particular point of view, and that choice is presumed to lie beyond the government's power to control.

Respondents argue that any tension between this rule and the Massachusetts law falls short of unconstitutionality, citing the most recent of our cases on the general subject of compelled access for expressive purposes, *Turner Broadcasting, Inc.* v. *FCC* [1994]. There we reviewed regulations requiring cable operators to set aside channels for designated broadcast signals, and applied only intermediate scrutiny. . . . Respondents contend on this authority that admission of GLIB to the parade would not threaten the core principle of speaker's autonomy because the Council, like a cable operator, is merely "a conduit" for the speech of participants in the parade "rather than itself a speaker." But this metaphor is not apt here, because GLIB's participation would likely be perceived as having resulted from the Council's customary determination about a unit admitted to the parade, that its message was worthy of presentation and quite possibly of support as well. . . .

Parades and demonstrations . . . are not understood to be . . . neutrally presented or selectively viewed. Unlike the programming offered on various channels by a cable network, the parade does not consist of individual, unrelated segments that happen to be transmitted together for individual selection by members of the audience. Although each parade unit generally identifies itself, each is understood to contribute something to a common theme, and accordingly there is no customary practice whereby private sponsors disavow "any identity of viewpoint" between themselves and the selected participants. Practice follows practicability here, for such disclaimers would be quite curious in a moving parade. . . . Without deciding on the precise significance of the likelihood of misattribution, it nonetheless becomes clear that in the context of an expressive parade, as with a protest march, the parade's overall message is distilled from the individual presentations along the way, and each unit's expression is perceived by spectators as part of the whole.

An additional distinction between *Turner Broadcasting* and this case points to the fundamental weakness of any attempt to justify the state court order's limitation on the Council's autonomy as a speaker. A cable is not only a conduit for speech produced by others and selected by cable operators for transmission, but a franchised channel giving monopolistic opportunity to shut out some speakers. This power gives rise to the government's interest in limiting monopolistic autonomy in order to allow for the survival of broadcasters who might otherwise be silenced and consequently destroyed. The government's interest in *Turner Broadcasting* was not the alteration of speech, but the survival of speakers. In thus identifying an interest going beyond abridgment of speech itself, the defenders of the law at issue in *Turner Broadcasting* addressed the threshold requirement of any review under the Speech Clause, whatever the ultimate level of scrutiny, that a challenged restriction on speech serve a compelling, or at least important, governmental object. . . .

In this case, of course, there is no assertion comparable to the *Turner Broadcasting* claim that some speakers will be destroyed in the absence of the challenged law. True, the size and success of petitioners' parade makes it an enviable vehicle for the dissemination of GLIB's views, but that fact, without more, would fall far short of supporting a claim that petitioners enjoy an abiding monopoly of access to spectators. . . . Considering that GLIB presumably would have had a fair shot (under neutral criteria developed by the city) at obtaining a parade permit of its own, respondents have not shown that petitioners enjoy the capacity to "silence the voice of competing speakers," as cable operators do with respect to program providers who wish to reach subscribers. *Turner Broadcasting*. . . . Nor has any other legitimate interest been identified in support of applying the Massachusetts statute in this way to expressive activity like the parade.

The statute . . . is a piece of protective legislation that announces no purpose beyond the object both expressed and apparent in its provisions, which is to prevent any denial of access to (or discriminatory treatment in) public accommodations on proscribed grounds, including sexual orientation. On its face, the object of the law is to ensure by statute for gays and lesbians desiring to make use of public accommodations what the old common law promised to any member of the public wanting a meal at the inn, that accepting the usual terms of service, they will not be turned away merely on the proprietor's exercise of personal preference. When the law is applied to expressive activity in the way it was done here, its apparent object is simply to require speakers to modify the content of their expression to whatever extent beneficiaries of the law choose to alter it with messages of their own. But in the absence of some further, legitimate end, this object is merely to allow exactly what the general rule of speaker's autonomy forbids.

It might, of course, have been argued that a broader objective is apparent: that the ultimate point of forbidding acts of discrimination toward certain classes is to produce a society free of the corresponding biases. Requiring access to a speaker's message would thus be not an end in itself, but a means to produce speakers free of the biases, whose expressive conduct would be at least neutral toward the particular classes, obviating any future need for correction. But if this indeed is the point of applying the state law to expressive conduct, it is a decidedly fatal objective. . . . The very idea that a noncommercial speech restriction be used to produce thoughts and statements acceptable to some groups or, indeed, all people, grates on the First Amendment, for it amounts to nothing less than a proposal to limit speech in the service of orthodox expression. The Speech Clause has no more certain antithesis. . . . While the law is free to promote all sorts of conduct in place of harmful behavior, it is not free to interfere with speech for no better reason than promoting an approved message or discouraging a disfavored one, however enlightened either purpose may strike the government. . . .

Our holding today rests not on any particular view about the Council's message but on the Nation's commitment to protect freedom of speech. Disapproval of a private speaker's statement does not legitimize use of the Commonwealth's power to compel the speaker to alter the message by including one more acceptable to others. Accordingly, the judgment of the Supreme Judicial Court is reversed and the case remanded for proceedings not inconsistent with this opinion.

58

44 LIQUORMART, INC. V. RHODE ISLAND
517 U.S. 484 (1996)

A licensed retailer of alcoholic beverages called 44 Liquormart ran an advertisement in a Rhode Island newspaper identifying various brands of packaged liquor without stating any prices. The ad in fact noted that it was against Rhode Island law to advertise liquor prices. But it included the word "WOW" in large letters next to pictures of vodka and rum bottles, and it caught the eye of the Rhode Island Liquor Control Administrator, who concluded that the implied reference to bargain prices violated the statutory ban on price advertising. 44 Liquormart paid a $400 fine. Then, joined by Peoples Super Liquor Stores, the retailer filed a lawsuit in federal court challenging Rhode Island's price-advertising ban as a violation of the First Amendment. The district court agreed with the liquor stores. The U.S. Court of Appeals for the First Circuit sided with the state, but the Supreme Court voted unanimously to reverse.

Not until 1976, in *Virginia State Board of Pharmacy* v. *Virginia Citizens Consumer Council*, did the Court actually hold that commercial advertising enjoys First Amendment protection. The Court did not accord it the same degree of protection as noncommercial speech, however, and in 1980, in *Central Hudson Gas & Electric Corporation* v. *Public Service Commission of New York*, the Court announced a balancing test for reviewing restrictions on commercial speech: the regulation must directly advance a "substantial" state interest, and there must not be a more limited regulation that would serve equally well. Invoking this test, the Court in *Posadas de Puerto Rico Associates* v. *Tourism Co. of Puerto Rico* (1986) upheld Puerto Rico's prohibition of casino advertising.

In *44 Liquormart*, Rhode Island invoked the Court's reasoning in *Posadas* to justify its price advertising ban. But no member of the Court embraced the state's understanding of *Posadas*. Four justices—Stevens, Kennedy, Thomas, and Ginsburg—agreed that *Posadas*'s application of the *Central Hudson* test supported the state. But these justices concluded that *Posadas* "erroneously" employed that test by allowing suppression of speech when "a less speech-restrictive policy" was available. If *Posadas* was the meaning of *Central Hudson*, these justices were prepared to disavow it. The remaining justices thought that under *Central Hudson*, properly understood, the price-advertising ban was unconstitutional. Thomas, writing separately, was prepared to jettison the *Central Hudson* test.

44 Liquormart revealed a Court divided on the question of how restrictions on commercial speech should be analyzed. Even so, the Court was unwilling to adopt an analysis that would have saved Rhode Island's restriction. *44 Liquormart* thus was a case suggesting a more libertarian direction with regard to commercial speech. The Court continued in this direction three years later in *Greater New Orleans Broadcasting* v. *United States* (1999), when it voted unanimously to strike down the federal law prohibiting broadcast advertising of casino gambling.

The opinion by **Stevens** announced the judgment of the Court. Parts 1, 2, and 7 of his eight-part opinion were the opinion of the Court, as those parts were joined by Scalia, Kennedy, Souter, Thomas, and Ginsburg, and Part 8 was the opinion of the Court, as it was joined by Scalia, Kennedy, Souter, and Ginsburg. (Parts 3-6 were joined by fewer than four justices.) Concurring in part and concurring in the judgment: **Scalia**; **Thomas**. Concurring in the judgment: **O'Connor**, Rehnquist, Souter, Breyer.

44 Liquormart, Inc. v. *Rhode Island* was decided on May 13, 1996.

OPINIONS

JUSTICE STEVENS ANNOUNCED THE DECISION OF THE COURT AND DELIVERED THE OPINION OF THE COURT IN PARTS 1, 2, 7, AND 8 OF HIS OPINION. THE FOLLOWING EXCERPT IS FROM PART 3, JOINED BY JUSTICES KENNEDY, SOUTER, AND GINSBURG.

Advertising has been a part of our culture throughout our history. Even in colonial days, the public relied on "commercial speech" for vital information about the market. Early newspapers displayed advertisements for goods and services on their front pages, and town criers called out prices in public squares. . . . Indeed, commercial messages played such a central role in public life prior to the Founding that Benjamin Franklin authored his early defense of a free press in support of his decision to print, of all things, an advertisement for voyages to Barbados. . . .

In accord with the role that commercial messages have long played, the law has developed to ensure that advertising provides consumers with accurate information about the availability of goods and services. In the early years, the common law, and later, statutes, served the consumers' interest in the receipt of accurate information in the commercial market by prohibiting fraudulent and misleading advertising. It was not until the 1970s, however, that this Court held that the First Amendment protected the dissemination of truthful and nonmisleading commercial messages about lawful products and services. . . .

In *Bigelow* v. *Virginia* [1975], we held that it was error to assume that commercial speech was entitled to no First Amendment protection or that it was without value in the marketplace of ideas. The following Term in *Virginia Bd. of Pharmacy* v. *Virginia Citizens Consumer Council, Inc.* [1976], we expanded on our holding in *Bigelow* and held that the State's blanket ban on advertising the price of prescription drugs violated the First Amendment.

Virginia Pharmacy Bd. reflected the conclusion that the same interest that supports regulation of potentially misleading advertising, namely the public's interest in receiving accurate commercial information, also supports an interpretation of the First Amendment that provides constitutional protection for the dissemination of accurate and nonmisleading commercial messages. . . .

The opinion further explained that a State's paternalistic assumption that the public will use truthful, nonmisleading commercial information unwisely cannot justify a decision to suppress it. . . .

On the basis of these principles, our early cases uniformly struck down several broadly based bans on truthful, nonmisleading commercial speech, each of which served ends unrelated to consumer protection. . . .

At the same time, our early cases recognized that the State may regulate some types of commercial advertising more freely than other forms of protected speech. Specifically, we explained that the State may require commercial messages to "appear in such a form, or include such additional information, warnings, and disclaimers, as are necessary to prevent its being deceptive," *Virginia Pharmacy Bd.*, and that it may restrict some forms of aggressive sales practices that have the potential to exert "undue influence" over consumers. . . .

Virginia Pharmacy Bd. attributed the State's authority to impose these regulations in part to certain "commonsense differences" that exist between commercial messages and other types of protected expression. Our opinion noted that the greater "objectivity" of commercial speech justifies affording the State more freedom to distinguish false commercial advertisements from true ones, and that the greater "hardiness" of commercial speech, inspired as it is by the profit motive, likely diminishes the chilling effect that may attend its regulation.

Subsequent cases explained that the State's power to regulate commercial transactions justifies its concomitant power to regulate commercial speech that is "linked inextricably" to those transactions. *Friedman* v. *Rogers* [1979]. . . .

In *Central Hudson Gas & Elec. Corp.* v. *Public Serv. Comm'n of N.Y.* [1980], we took stock of our developing commercial speech jurisprudence. In that case, we considered a regulation "completely" banning all promotional advertising by electric utilities. Our decision acknowledged the special features of commercial speech but identified the serious First Amendment concerns that attend blanket advertising prohibitions that do not protect consumers from commercial harms.

Five Members of the Court recognized that the state interest in the conservation of energy was substantial, and that there was "an immediate connection between advertising and demand for electricity." Nevertheless, they concluded that the regulation was invalid because the Commission had failed to make a showing that a more limited speech regulation would not have adequately served the State's interest.

In reaching its conclusion, the majority explained that although the special nature of commercial speech may require less than strict review of its regulation, special concerns arise from "regulations that entirely suppress commercial speech in order to pursue a nonspeech-related policy." In those circumstances, "a ban on speech could screen from public view the underlying governmental policy." As a result, the Court concluded that "special care" should attend the review of such blanket bans, and it pointedly remarked that "in recent years this Court has not approved a blanket ban on commercial speech unless the speech itself was flawed in some way, either because it was deceptive or related to unlawful activity."

FROM PART 4 OF THE STEVENS OPINION, JOINED BY JUSTICES KENNEDY AND GINSBURG

As our review of the case law reveals, Rhode Island errs in concluding that all commercial speech regulations are subject to a similar form of constitutional review simply because they target a similar category of expression. The mere fact that messages propose commercial transactions does not in and of itself dictate the constitutional analysis that should apply to decisions to suppress them. . . .

When a State regulates commercial messages to protect consumers from misleading, deceptive, or aggressive sales practices, or requires the disclosure of beneficial consumer information, the purpose of its regulation is consistent with the reasons for according constitutional protection to commercial speech and therefore justifies less than strict review. However, when a State entirely prohibits the dissemination of truthful, nonmisleading commercial messages for reasons unrelated to the preservation of a fair bargaining process, there is far less reason to depart from the rigorous review that the First Amendment generally demands.

Sound reasons justify reviewing the latter type of commercial speech regulation more carefully. Most obviously, complete speech bans, unlike content-neutral restrictions on the time, place, or manner of expression . . . , are particularly dangerous because they all but foreclose alternative means of disseminating certain information. . . .

The special dangers that attend complete bans on truthful, nonmisleading commercial speech cannot be explained away by appeals to the "commonsense distinctions" that exist between commercial and noncommercial speech. *Virginia Pharmacy Bd.* Regulations that suppress the truth are no less troubling because they target objectively verifiable information, nor are they less effective because they aim at durable messages. As a result, neither the "greater objectivity" nor the "greater hardiness" of truthful, nonmisleading commercial speech justifies reviewing its complete suppression with added deference.

It is the State's interest in protecting consumers from "commercial harms" that provides "the typical reason why commercial speech can be subject to greater governmental regulation than noncommercial speech." *Cincinnati* v. *Discovery Network, Inc.* [1993]. Yet bans that target truthful, nonmisleading commercial messages rarely protect consumers from such harms. Instead, such bans often serve only to obscure an "underlying governmental policy" that could be implemented without regulating speech. *Central Hudson.* In this way, these commercial speech bans not only hinder consumer choice, but also impede debate over central issues of public policy. . . .

Precisely because bans against truthful, nonmisleading commercial speech rarely seek to protect consumers from either deception or overreaching, they usually rest solely on the offensive assumption that the public will respond "irrationally" to the truth. *Linmark Associates, Inc.* v. *Willingboro* [1977]. The First Amendment directs us to be especially skeptical of regulations that seek to keep people in the dark for what the government perceives to be their own good. That teaching applies equally to state attempts to deprive consumers of accurate information about their chosen products. . . .

FROM PART 5 OF THE STEVENS OPINION, JOINED BY JUSTICES KENNEDY, SOUTER, AND GINSBURG

In this case, there is no question that Rhode Island's price advertising ban constitutes a blanket prohibition against truthful, nonmisleading speech about a lawful product. There is also no question that the ban serves an end unrelated to consumer protection. Accordingly, we must review the price advertising ban with "special care," *Central Hudson,* mindful that speech prohibitions of this type rarely survive constitutional review.

The State argues that the price advertising prohibition should nevertheless be upheld because it directly advances the State's substantial interest in promoting temperance, and because it is no more extensive than necessary. . . . Although there is some confusion as to what Rhode Island means by temperance, we assume that the State asserts an interest in reducing alcohol consumption.

In evaluating the ban's effectiveness in advancing the State's interest, . . . we must determine whether the State has shown that the price advertising ban will significantly reduce alcohol consumption.

We can agree that common sense supports the conclusion that a prohibition against price advertising, like a collusive agreement among competitors to refrain from such advertising, will tend to mitigate competition and maintain prices at a higher level than would prevail in a completely free market. Despite the absence of proof on the point, we can even agree with the State's contention that it is reasonable to assume that demand, and hence consumption throughout the market, is somewhat lower whenever a higher, noncompetitive price level prevails. However, without any findings of fact, or indeed any evidentiary support whatsoever, we cannot agree with the assertion that the price advertising ban will significantly advance the State's interest in promoting temperance. . . .

The State also cannot satisfy the requirement that its restriction on speech be no more extensive than necessary. It is perfectly obvious that alternative forms of regulation that would not involve any restriction on speech would be more likely to achieve the State's goal of promoting temperance. As the State's own expert conceded, higher prices can be maintained either by direct regulation or by increased taxation. Per capita purchases could be limited as is the case with prescription drugs. Even educational campaigns focused on the problems of excessive, or even moderate, drinking might prove to be more effective.

As a result, even under the less than strict standard that generally applies in commercial speech cases, the State has failed to establish a "reasonable fit" between its abridgment of speech and its temperance goal. . . . It necessarily follows that the price advertising ban cannot survive the more stringent constitutional review that *Central Hudson* itself concluded was appropriate for the complete suppression of truthful, nonmisleading commercial speech.

FROM PART 6 OF THE STEVENS OPINION, JOINED BY JUSTICES KENNEDY, THOMAS, AND GINSBURG

The State responds by arguing that it merely exercised appropriate "legislative judgment" in determining that a price advertising ban would best promote temperance. Relying on the *Central Hudson* analysis set forth in *Posadas de Puerto Rico Associates* v. *Tourism Co. of P.R.* [1986], and *United States* v. *Edge Broadcasting Co.* [1993], Rhode Island first argues that, because expert opinions as to the effectiveness of the price advertising ban "go both ways," the Court of Appeals correctly concluded that the ban constituted a "reasonable choice" by the legislature. The State next contends that precedent requires us to give particular deference to that legislative choice because the State could, if it chose, ban the sale of alcoholic beverages outright. . . . Finally, the State argues that deference is appropriate because alcoholic beverages are so-called "vice" products. . . . We consider each of these contentions in turn.

The State's first argument fails to justify the speech prohibition at issue. . . . Rhode Island errs in concluding that *Edge* and *Posadas* establish the degree of deference that its decision to impose a price advertising ban warrants.

In *Edge*, we upheld a federal statute that permitted only those broadcasters located in States that had legalized lotteries to air lottery advertising. The statute was designed to regulate advertising about an activity that had been deemed illegal in the jurisdiction in which the broadcaster was located. Here, by contrast, the commercial speech ban targets information about entirely lawful behavior.

Posadas is more directly relevant. There, a five-Member majority held that, under the *Central Hudson* test, it was "up to the legislature" to choose to reduce gambling by suppressing in-state casino advertising rather than engaging in educational speech. Rhode Island argues that this logic demonstrates the constitutionality of its own decision to ban price advertising in lieu of raising taxes or employing some other less speech-restrictive means of promoting temperance.

The reasoning in *Posadas* does support the State's argument, but, on reflection, we are now persuaded that *Posadas* erroneously performed the First Amendment analysis. The casino advertising ban was designed to keep truthful, nonmisleading speech from members of the public for fear that they would be more likely to gamble if they received it. As a result, the advertising ban served to shield the State's antigambling policy from the public scrutiny that more direct, nonspeech regulation would draw. . . .

Given our longstanding hostility to commercial speech regulation of this type, *Posadas* clearly erred in concluding that it was "up to the legislature" to choose suppression over a less speech-restrictive policy. The *Posadas* majority's conclusion on that point cannot be reconciled with the unbroken line of prior cases striking down similarly broad regulations on truthful, nonmisleading advertising when non-speech-related alternatives were available. . . .

Because the 5-to-4 decision in *Posadas* marked such a sharp break from our prior precedent, and because it concerned a constitutional question about which this Court is the final arbiter, we decline to give force to its highly deferential approach. Instead, in keeping with our prior holdings, we conclude that a state legislature does not have the broad discretion to suppress truthful, nonmisleading information for paternalistic purposes that the *Posadas* majority was willing to tolerate. As we explained in *Virginia Pharmacy Bd.*, "[i]t is precisely this kind of choice, between the dangers of suppressing information, and the dangers of its misuse if it is freely available, that the First Amendment makes for us."

We also cannot accept the State's second contention, which is premised entirely on the "greater-includes-the-lesser" reasoning endorsed toward the end of the majority's opinion in *Posadas*. There, the majority stated that "the greater power to completely ban casino gambling necessarily includes the lesser power to ban advertising of casino gambling." It went on to state that "because the government could have enacted a wholesale prohibition of [casino gambling] it is permissible for the government to take the less intrusive step of allowing the conduct, but reducing the demand through restrictions on advertising." The majority concluded that it would "surely be a strange constitutional doctrine which would concede to the legislature the authority to totally ban a product or activity, but deny to the legislature the authority to forbid the stimulation of demand for the product or activity through advertising on behalf of those who would profit from such increased demand." On the basis of these statements, the State reasons that its undisputed authority to ban alcoholic beverages must include the power to restrict advertisements offering them for sale. . . .

Although we do not dispute the proposition that greater powers include lesser ones, we fail to see how that syllogism requires the conclusion that the State's power to regulate commercial activity is "greater" than its power to ban truthful, nonmisleading commercial speech. Contrary to the assumption made in *Posadas*, we think it quite clear that banning speech may sometimes prove far more intrusive than banning conduct. As a venerable proverb teaches, it may prove more injurious to prevent people from teaching others how to fish than to prevent fish from being sold. Similarly, a local ordinance banning bicycle lessons may curtail freedom far more than one that prohibits bicycle riding within city limits. In short, we reject the assumption that words are necessarily less vital to freedom than actions, or that logic somehow proves that the power to prohibit an activity is necessarily "greater" than the power to suppress speech about it.

As a matter of First Amendment doctrine, the *Posadas* syllogism is even less defensible. The text of the First Amendment makes clear that the Constitution presumes that attempts to regulate speech are more dangerous than attempts to regulate conduct. That presumption accords with the essential role that the free flow of information plays in a democratic society. As a result, the First Amendment directs that government may not suppress speech as easily as it may suppress conduct, and that speech restrictions cannot be treated as simply another means that the government may use to achieve its ends.

These basic First Amendment principles clearly apply to commercial speech; indeed, the *Posadas* majority impliedly conceded as much by applying the *Central Hudson* test. Thus, it is no answer that commercial speech concerns products and services that the government may freely regulate. Our decisions from *Virginia Pharmacy Bd.* on have made plain that a State's regulation of the sale of goods differs in kind from a State's regulation of accurate information about those goods. The distinction that our cases have consistently drawn between these two types of governmental action is fundamentally incompatible with the absolutist view that the State may ban commercial speech simply because it may constitutionally prohibit the underlying conduct.

That the State has chosen to license its liquor retailers does not change the analysis. Even though government is under no obligation to provide a person, or the public, a particular benefit, it does not follow that conferral of the benefit may be conditioned on the surrender of a constitutional right. . . .

Thus, just as it is perfectly clear that Rhode Island could not ban all obscene liquor ads except those that advocated temperance, we think it equally clear that its power to ban the sale of liquor entirely does not include a power to censor all advertisements that contain accurate and nonmisleading information about the price of the product. As the entire Court apparently now agrees, the statements in the *Posadas* opinion on which Rhode Island relies are no longer persuasive.

Finally, we find unpersuasive the State's contention that, under *Posadas* and *Edge*, the price advertising ban should be upheld because it targets commercial speech that pertains to a "vice" activity. The appellees premise their request for a so-called "vice" exception to our commercial speech doctrine on language in *Edge* which characterized gambling as a "vice." . . . The respondents misread our precedent. Our decision last Term striking down an alcohol-related advertising restriction effectively rejected the very contention respondents now make. See *Rubin* v. *Coors Brewing Co.* [1995].

Moreover, the scope of any "vice" exception to the protection afforded by the First Amendment would be difficult, if not impossible, to define. Almost any product that poses some threat to public health or public morals might reasonably be characterized by a state legislature as relating to "vice activity." Such characterization, however, is anomalous when applied to products such as alcoholic beverages, lottery tickets, or playing cards, that may be lawfully purchased on the open market. The recognition of such an exception would also have the unfortunate consequence of either allowing state legislatures to justify censorship by the simple expedient of placing the "vice" label on selected lawful activities, or requiring the federal courts to establish a federal common law of vice. . . . For these reasons, a "vice" label that is unaccompanied by a corresponding prohibition against the commercial behavior at issue fails to provide a principled justification for the regulation of commercial speech about that activity.

FROM PART 7 OF THE STEVENS OPINION, WHICH WAS THE COURT'S OPINION, JOINED AS IT WAS BY JUSTICES SCALIA, KENNEDY, SOUTER, THOMAS, AND GINSBURG

From 1919 until 1933, the Eighteenth Amendment to the Constitution totally prohibited "the manufacture, sale, or transportation of intoxicating liquors" in the United States and its territories. Section 1 of the Twenty-first Amendment repealed that prohibition, and 2 delegated to the several States the power to prohibit commerce in, or the use of, alcoholic beverages. . . .

As is clear, the text of the Twenty-first Amendment supports the view that, while it grants the States authority over commerce that might otherwise be reserved to the Federal Government, it places no limit whatsoever on other constitutional provisions. Nevertheless, Rhode Island argues, and the Court of Appeals agreed, that in this case the Twenty-first Amendment tilts the First Amendment analysis in the State's favor. . . .

In reaching its conclusion, the Court of Appeals relied on our decision in *California* v. *LaRue* [1972]. In *LaRue*, five Members of the Court relied on the Twenty-first Amendment to buttress the conclusion that the First Amendment did not invalidate California's prohibition of certain grossly sexual exhibitions in premises licensed to serve alcoholic beverages. Specifically, the opinion stated that the Twenty-first Amendment required that the prohibition be given an added presumption in favor of its validity. . . . We are now persuaded that the Court's analysis in *LaRue* would have led to precisely the same result if it had placed no reliance on the Twenty-first Amendment. . . .

Without questioning the holding in *LaRue*, we now disavow its reasoning insofar as it relied on the Twenty-first Amendment. As we explained in a case decided more than a decade after *LaRue*, although the Twenty-first Amendment limits the effect of the dormant Commerce Clause on a State's regulatory power over the delivery or use of intoxicating beverages within its borders, "the Amendment does not license the States to ignore their obligations under other provisions of the Constitution." *Capital Cities Cable, Inc.* v. *Crisp* [1984]. . . . [W]e now hold that the Twenty-first Amendment does not qualify the constitutional prohibition against laws abridging the freedom of speech embodied in the First Amendment. The Twenty-first Amendment, therefore, cannot save Rhode Island's ban on liquor price advertising.

FROM PART 8 OF THE STEVENS OPINION, WHICH WAS THE COURT'S OPINION, JOINED AS IT WAS BY JUSTICES SCALIA, KENNEDY, SOUTER, AND GINSBURG

Because Rhode Island has failed to carry its heavy burden of justifying its complete ban on price advertising, we conclude that R.I. Gen. Laws 3-8-7 and 3-8-8.1, as well as Regulation 32 of the Rhode Island Liquor Control Administration, abridge speech in violation of the First Amendment as made applicable to the States by the Due Process Clause of the Fourteenth Amendment. The judgment of the Court of Appeals is therefore

REVERSED.

JUSTICE SCALIA, CONCURRING IN PART AND CONCURRING IN THE JUDGMENT.

I share Justice Thomas's discomfort with the *Central Hudson* test, which seems to me to have nothing more than policy intuition to support it. I also share Justice Stevens' aversion towards paternalistic governmental policies that prevent men and women from hearing facts that might not be good for them. On the other hand, it would also be paternalism for us to prevent the people of the States from enacting laws that we consider paternalistic, unless we have good reason to believe that the Constitution itself forbids them. I will take my guidance as to what the Constitution forbids, with regard to a text as indeterminate as the First Amendment's preservation of "the freedom of speech," and where the core offense of suppressing particular political ideas is not at issue, from the long accepted practices of the American people. . . .

The briefs and arguments of the parties in the present case provide no illumination on that point; understandably so, since both sides accepted *Central Hudson*. The amicus brief on behalf of the American Advertising Federation *et al.* did examine various expressions of view at the time the First Amendment was adopted; they are consistent with First Amendment protection for commercial speech, but certainly not dispositive. I consider more relevant the state legislative practices prevalent at the time the First Amendment was adopted, since almost all of the States had free-speech constitutional guarantees of their own, whose meaning was not likely to have been different from the federal constitutional provision derived from them. Perhaps more relevant still are the state legislative practices at the time the Fourteenth Amendment was adopted, since it is most improbable that that adoption was meant to overturn any existing national consensus regarding free speech. Indeed, it is rare that any nationwide practice would develop contrary to a proper understanding of the First Amendment itself—for which reason I think also relevant any national consensus that had formed regarding state regulation of advertising after the Fourteenth Amendment, and before this Court's entry into the field. The parties and their amici provide no evidence on these points.

Since I do not believe we have before us the wherewithal to declare *Central Hudson* wrong—or at least the wherewithal to say what ought to replace it—I must resolve this case in accord with our existing jurisprudence, which all except Justice Thomas agree would prohibit the challenged regulation. I am not disposed to develop new law, or reinforce old, on this issue, and accordingly I merely concur in the judgment of the Court. I believe, however, that Justice Stevens' treatment of the application of the Twenty-First Amendment to this case is correct, and accordingly join Parts 1, 2, 7, and 8 of Justice Stevens' opinion.

JUSTICE THOMAS, CONCURRING IN PARTS 1, 2, 6, AND 7 AND CONCURRING IN THE JUDGMENT.

In cases such as this, in which the government's asserted interest is to keep legal users of a product or service ignorant in order to manipulate their choices in the marketplace, the balancing test adopted in *Central Hudson* should not be applied, in my view. Rather, such an "interest" is per se illegitimate and can no more justify regulation of "commercial" speech than it can justify regulation of "noncommercial" speech. . . .

In case after case following *Virginia Pharmacy Bd.*, the Court, and individual Members of the Court, have continued to stress the importance of free dissemination of information about commercial choices in a market economy; the antipaternalistic premises of the First

Amendment; the impropriety of manipulating consumer choices or public opinion through the suppression of accurate "commercial" information; the near impossibility of severing "commercial" speech from speech necessary to democratic decisionmaking; and the dangers of permitting the government to do covertly what it might not have been able to muster the political support to do openly.

In other decisions, however, the Court has appeared to accept the legitimacy of laws that suppress information in order to manipulate the choices of consumers—so long as the government could show that the manipulation was in fact successful. *Central Hudson* was the first decision to clearly embrace this position, although the Court applied a very strict overbreadth analysis to strike down the advertising ban at issue. In two other decisions, *Posadas* and *Edge*, the Court simply presumed that advertising of a product or service leads to increased consumption; since, as in *Central Hudson*, the Court saw nothing impermissible in the government's suppressing information in order to discourage consumption, it upheld the advertising restrictions in those cases.

The Court has at times appeared to assume that "commercial" speech could be censored in a variety of ways for any of a variety of reasons because, as was said without clear rationale in some post–*Virginia Pharmacy Bd.* cases, such speech was in a "subordinate position in the scale of First Amendment values." *Ohralik* v. *Ohio State Bar Assn.* [1978]. . . . I do not see a philosophical or historical basis for asserting that "commercial" speech is of "lower value" than "noncommercial" speech. Indeed, some historical materials suggest to the contrary. . . . Nor do I believe that the only explanations that the Court has ever advanced for treating "commercial" speech differently from other speech can justify restricting "commercial" speech in order to keep information from legal purchasers so as to thwart what would otherwise be their choices in the marketplace.

I do not join the principal opinion's application of the *Central Hudson* balancing test because I do not believe that such a test should be applied to a restriction of "commercial" speech, at least when, as here, the asserted interest is one that is to be achieved through keeping would-be recipients of the speech in the dark. Application of the advancement-of-state-interest prong of *Central Hudson* makes little sense to me in such circumstances. Faulting the State for failing to show that its price advertising ban decreases alcohol consumption "significantly," as Justice Stevens does, seems to imply that if the State had been more successful at keeping consumers ignorant and thereby decreasing their consumption, then the restriction might have been upheld. This contradicts *Virginia Pharmacy Bd.*'s rationale for protecting "commercial" speech in the first instance. . . .

Although the Court took a sudden turn away from *Virginia Pharmacy Bd.* in *Central Hudson*, it has never explained why manipulating the choices of consumers by keeping them ignorant is more legitimate when the ignorance is maintained through suppression of "commercial" speech than when the same ignorance is maintained through suppression of "noncommercial" speech. The courts, including this Court, have found the *Central Hudson* "test" to be, as a general matter, very difficult to apply with any uniformity. This may result in part from the inherently nondeterminative nature of a case-by-case balancing "test" unaccompanied by any categorical rules, and the consequent likelihood that individual judicial preferences will govern application of the test. Moreover, the second prong of *Central Hudson*, as applied to the facts of that case and to those here, apparently requires judges to delineate those situations in which citizens cannot be trusted with information, and invites judges to decide whether they themselves think that consumption of a product is harmful enough that it should be discouraged. In my view, the *Central Hudson* test asks the courts to weigh incommensurables—the value of knowledge versus the value of ignorance—and to apply contradictory premises—that informed adults are the best judges of their own interests, and that they are not. Rather than continuing to apply a test that makes no sense to me when the asserted state interest is of the type involved here, I would return to the reasoning and holding of *Virginia Pharmacy Bd.* Under that decision, these restrictions fall.

JUSTICE O'CONNOR, CONCURRING IN THE JUDGMENT.

. . . I agree with the Court that Rhode Island's price-advertising ban is invalid. I would resolve this case more narrowly, however, by applying our established *Central Hudson* test to determine whether this commercial-speech regulation survives First Amendment scrutiny.

Under that test, we . . . must decide whether the regulation "directly advances the governmental interest asserted, and whether it is not more extensive than is necessary to serve that interest." *Central Hudson.*

Given the means by which this regulation purportedly serves the State's interest, our conclusion is plain: Rhode Island's regulation fails First Amendment scrutiny. . . .

Rhode Island offers one, and only one, justification for its ban on price advertising. Rhode Island says that the ban is intended to keep alcohol prices high as a way to keep consumption low. By preventing sellers from informing customers of prices, the regulation prevents competition from driving prices down and requires consumers to spend more time to find the best price for alcohol. The higher cost of obtaining alcohol, Rhode Island argues, will lead to reduced consumption.

The fit between Rhode Island's method and this particular goal is not reasonable. If the target is simply higher prices generally to discourage consumption, the regulation imposes too great, and unnecessary, a prohibition on speech in order to achieve it. The State has other methods at its disposal—methods that would more directly accomplish this stated goal without intruding on sellers' ability to provide truthful, nonmisleading information to customers. Indeed, Rhode Island's own expert conceded that "'the objective of lowering consumption of alcohol by banning price advertising could be accomplished by establishing minimum prices and/or by increasing sales taxes on alcoholic beverages.'" A tax, for example, is not normally very difficult to administer and would have a far more certain and direct effect on prices, without any restriction on speech. The principal opinion suggests further alternatives, such as limiting per capita purchases or conducting an educational campaign about the dangers of alcohol consumption. The ready availability of such alternatives—at least some of which would far more effectively achieve Rhode Island's only professed goal, at comparatively small additional administrative cost—demonstrates that the fit between ends and means is not narrowly tailored. Too, this regulation prevents sellers of alcohol from communicating price information anywhere but at the point of purchase. No channels exist at all to permit them to publicize the price of their products.

Respondents point for support to *Posadas*, where, applying the *Central Hudson* test, we upheld the constitutionality of a Puerto Rico law that prohibited the advertising of casino gambling aimed at residents of Puerto Rico, but permitted such advertising aimed at tourists.

The Court there accepted as reasonable the legislature's belief that the regulation would be effective, and concluded that, because the restriction affected only advertising of casino gambling aimed at residents of Puerto Rico, not that aimed at tourists, the restriction was narrowly tailored to serve Puerto Rico's interest. The Court accepted without question Puerto Rico's account of the effectiveness and reasonableness of its speech restriction. Respondents ask us to make a similar presumption here to uphold the validity of Rhode Island's law.

It is true that *Posadas* accepted as reasonable, without further inquiry, Puerto Rico's assertions that the regulations furthered the government's interest and were no more extensive than necessary to serve that interest. Since *Posadas*, however, this Court has examined more searchingly the State's professed goal, and the speech restriction put into place to further it, before accepting a State's claim that the speech restriction satisfies First Amendment scrutiny. . . . [W]e [have] declined to accept at face value the proffered justification for the State's regulation, but examined carefully the relationship between the asserted goal and the speech restriction used to reach that goal. The closer look that we have required since *Posadas* comports better with the purpose of the analysis set out in *Central Hudson*, by requiring the State to show that the speech restriction directly advances its interest and is narrowly tailored. Under such a closer look, Rhode Island's price-advertising ban clearly fails to pass muster.

Because Rhode Island's regulation fails even the less stringent standard set out in *Central Hudson*, nothing here requires adoption of a new analysis for the evaluation of commercial speech regulation. . . .

Respondents argue that an additional factor, the Twenty-first Amendment, tips the First Amendment analysis in Rhode Island's favor. . . .

Nothing in the Amendment's text or history justifies its use to alter the application of the First Amendment. . . . The Twenty-first Amendment does not trump First Amendment rights or add a presumption of validity to a regulation that cannot otherwise satisfy First Amendment requirements. . . .

RESPONSES

FROM THE *NEW YORK TIMES*, MAY 15, 1996, "COMMERCIAL FREE SPEECH GETS FREER"

In one of this term's most significant First Amendment cases, the Supreme Court has struck down a Rhode Island ban on advertising liquor prices, thereby strengthening protections for "commercial speech" promoting lawful products. Although it did not address the issue, the Court's decision raises new questions about the constitutionality of the Clinton Administration's proposed restrictions on cigarette promotions.

There were four separate majority opinions—an indication that the Court is still groping for a firm policy on commercial speech. Nevertheless, all nine justices voted to overturn the ban. . . .

There was also a clear majority for the proposition that the Constitution's First Amendment protection of free speech takes precedence over the 21st, which repealed Prohibition and granted states broad authority to regulate alcohol. But the most important message of the case, broadcast in the four separate opinions staking out nuanced differences among the justices, is that the Court will judge harshly any absolute ban on commercial speech that is not precisely tailored to protect consumers against false or deceptive information.

The Court extended First Amendment protection to truthful advertising of lawful products twenty years ago. Recent rulings have broadened the scope of that protection, which still falls short of the safeguards awarded to political, artistic, and other noncommercial speech. . . .

Exactly what [this case] means for the proposed restrictions on cigarette advertising under consideration by the Food and Drug Administration is not clear. Rhode Island did not try to defend its advertising ban as a method of restricting young people's access to liquor. The focus of the FDA's cigarette plan is illegal sales to minors.

It seems unlikely that the Court will view favorably tobacco advertising that targets and manipulates children, who cannot legally buy cigarettes. But the justices may well object, as some did in the Rhode Island case, if they find that the Government could meet its goal of keeping cigarettes from children by methods that do not restrict information to adults—more prominent health warnings on packages, for example, or stricter penalties for selling cigarettes to minors, or a national education campaign.

FROM THE SYNDICATED COLUMN BY GEORGE F. WILL, MAY 16, 1996

. . . [O]n Monday the Supreme Court unanimously struck the forty-year-old fetters from Rhode Island's liquor dealers, holding that the ban on price advertising violates the First Amendment. This pleases conservatives who believe that granting less protection to commercial speech than to political or artistic speech is part of a dangerous derogation of economic liberty and property rights. But the decision should disturb conservatives who believe judges should strive to be deferential to legislative judgments, even some dotty ones. . . .

In a robust concurrence, Justice Thomas says that when government's asserted interest "is to keep legal users of a product or service ignorant in order to manipulate their choices in the marketplace," that interest no more justifies regulation of "commercial" speech than of any other kind.

Some conservatives have another view. It is that the First Amendment is part of a political document, the point of which is self-government. Hence the amendment, properly construed, gives special protection to political speech. It may well be sensible policy generally to refrain from restricting truthful communication about legal products, but the amendment does not require that policy. And it is paternalistic of the court to protect the people of Rhode Island from paternalistic laws they can petition their legislators to repeal.

RENO V. AMERICAN CIVIL LIBERTIES UNION
521 U. S. 844 (1997)

In 1996 Congress enacted comprehensive telecommunications legislation, one of whose titles was the Communications Decency Act. Two of the CDA's provisions sought to protect minors from harmful material on the Internet. One section criminalized the transmitting of "obscene or indecent" messages to anyone under 18; the other outlawed sending to anyone under 18 any message "that, in context, depicts or describes, in terms patently offensive as measured by contemporary community standards, sexual or excretory activities or organs." Soon after President Clinton signed the new telecommunications law, the American Civil Liberties Union and nineteen other organizations (later joined by twenty-seven more) brought a lawsuit in the Eastern District of Pennsylvania challenging the constitutionality of the CDA's anti-obscenity provisions. Finding the provisions in violation of the First Amendment, a three-judge panel entered an injunction forbidding their enforcement. The Supreme Court affirmed.

In the CDA case the Court for the first time indicated that the protections of the First Amendment extend to the Internet. "We agree," wrote Justice Stevens for the Court, ". . . that our cases provide no basis for qualifying the level of scrutiny that should be applied to this medium."

The Court found the CDA provisions constitutionally deficient on account of their imprecision. In particular, even as they denied minors access to potentially harmful speech, they also suppressed "a large amount of speech that adults have a constitutional right to receive and to address to one another."

Notably, the Court reaffirmed the test for obscenity it had articulated almost a quarter century earlier in *Miller* v. *California* (1973), saying that the test "controls to this day."

Opinion of the Court: **Stevens**, Scalia, Kennedy, Souter, Thomas, Ginsburg, Breyer. Concurring in the judgment in part and dissenting in part: **O'Connor**, Rehnquist.

Reno v. *American Civil Liberties Union* was decided on June 26, 1997.

OPINIONS

JUSTICE STEVENS DELIVERED THE OPINION OF THE COURT . . .

In arguing for reversal, the Government contends that the CDA is plainly constitutional under three of our prior decisions: (1) *Ginsberg* v. *New York* [1968]; (2) *FCC* v. *Pacifica Foundation* [1978]; and (3) *Renton* v. *Playtime Theatres, Inc.* [1986]. A close look at these cases, however, raises—rather than relieves—doubts concerning the constitutionality of the CDA.

In *Ginsberg*, we upheld the constitutionality of a New York statute that prohibited selling to minors under 17 years of age material that was considered obscene as to them even if not obscene as to adults. We rejected the defendant's broad submission that "the scope of the constitutional freedom of expression secured to a citizen to read or see material concerned with sex cannot be made to depend on whether the citizen is an adult or a minor." In rejecting that contention, we relied not only on the State's independent interest in the well being of its youth, but also on our consistent recognition of the principle that "the parents' claim to authority in their own household to direct the rearing of their children is basic in the structure of our society." In four important respects, the statute upheld in *Ginsberg* was narrower than the CDA. First, we noted in *Ginsberg* that "the prohibition against sales to minors does not bar parents who so desire from purchasing the magazines for their children." Under the CDA, by contrast, neither the parents' consent—nor even their participation—in the communication would avoid the application of the statute. Second, the New York statute applied only to commercial transactions, whereas the CDA contains no such limitation. Third, the New York statute cabined its definition of material that is harmful to minors with the requirement that it be "utterly without redeeming social importance for minors." The CDA fails to provide us with any definition of the term "indecent" as used in §223(a)(1) and, importantly, omits any requirement that the "patently offensive" material covered by §223(d) lack serious literary, artistic, political, or scientific value. Fourth, the New York statute defined a minor as a person under the age of 17, whereas the CDA, in applying to all those under 18 years, includes an additional year of those nearest majority.

In *Pacifica*, we upheld a declaratory order of the Federal Communications Commission, holding that the broadcast of a recording of a twelve-minute monologue entitled "Filthy Words" that had previously been delivered to a live audience "could have been the subject of administrative sanctions." The Commission had found that the repetitive use of certain words referring to excretory or sexual activities or organs "in an afternoon broadcast when children are in the audience was patently offensive" and concluded that the monologue was indecent "as broadcast." The respondent did not quarrel with the finding that the afternoon broadcast was patently offensive, but contended that it was not "indecent" within the meaning of the relevant statutes because it contained no prurient appeal. After rejecting respondent's statutory arguments, we confronted its two constitutional arguments: (1) that the Commission's construction of its authority to ban indecent speech was so broad that its order had to be set aside even if the broadcast at issue was unprotected; and (2) that since the recording was not obscene, the First Amendment forbade any abridgement of the right to broadcast it on the radio.

In the portion of the lead opinion not joined by Justices Powell and Blackmun, the plurality stated that the First Amendment does not prohibit all governmental regulation that depends on the content of speech. Accordingly, the availability of constitutional protection for a vulgar and offensive monologue that was not obscene depended on the context of the broadcast. Relying on the premise that "of all forms of communication" broadcasting had received the most limited First Amendment protection, the Court concluded that the ease with which children may obtain access to broadcasts, "coupled with the concerns recognized in *Ginsberg*," justified special treatment of indecent broadcasting.

As with the New York statute at issue in *Ginsberg*, there are significant differences between the order upheld in *Pacifica* and the CDA. First, the order in *Pacifica*, issued by an agency that had been regulating radio stations for decades, targeted a specific broadcast that represented a rather dramatic departure from traditional program content in order to designate when—rather than whether—it would be permissible to air such a program in that particular medium. The CDA's broad categorical prohibitions are not limited to particular times and are not dependent on any evaluation by an agency familiar with the unique characteristics of the Internet. Second, unlike the CDA, the Commission's declaratory order was not punitive; we expressly refused to decide whether the indecent broadcast "would justify a criminal prosecution." Finally, the Commission's order applied to a medium which as a matter of history had "received the most limited First Amendment protection," in large part because warnings could not adequately protect the listener from unexpected program content. The Internet, however, has no comparable history. . . .

In *Renton*, we upheld a zoning ordinance that kept adult movie theaters out of residential neighborhoods. The ordinance was aimed, not at the content of the films shown in the theaters, but rather at the "secondary effects"—such as crime and deteriorating property values—that these theaters fostered. . . . According to the Government, the CDA is constitutional because it constitutes a sort of "cyberzoning" on the Internet. But the CDA applies broadly to the entire universe of cyberspace. And the purpose of the CDA is to protect children from the primary effects of "indecent" and "patently offensive" speech, rather than any "secondary" effect of such speech. Thus, the CDA is a content based blanket restriction on speech, and, as such, cannot be "properly analyzed as a form of time, place, and manner regulation." *Renton.* . . .

These precedents, then, surely do not require us to uphold the CDA and are fully consistent with the application of the most stringent review of its provisions.

In *Southeastern Promotions, Ltd.* v. *Conrad* (1975), we observed that "[e]ach medium of expression . . . may present its own problems." Thus, some of our cases have recognized special justifications for regulation of the broadcast media that are not applicable to other speakers. . . . In these cases, the Court relied on the history of extensive government regulation of the broadcast medium . . . ; the scarcity of available frequencies at its inception . . . ; and its "invasive" nature. . . .

Those factors are not present in cyberspace. Neither before nor after the enactment of the CDA have the vast democratic fora of the Internet been subject to the type of government supervision and regulation that has attended the broadcast industry. Moreover, the Internet is not as "invasive" as radio or television. The District Court specifically found that "[c]ommunications over the Internet do not 'invade' an individual's home or appear on one's computer screen unbidden. Users seldom encounter content 'by accident.'" It also found that "[a]lmost all sexually explicit images are preceded by warnings as to the content," and cited testimony that "'odds are slim' that a user would come across a sexually explicit sight by accident.". . .

Finally, unlike the conditions that prevailed when Congress first authorized regulation of the broadcast spectrum, the Internet can hardly be considered a "scarce" expressive commodity. It provides relatively unlimited, low cost capacity for communication of all kinds. The Government estimates that "[a]s many as 40 million people use the Internet today, and that figure is expected to grow to 200 million by 1999." This dynamic, multifaceted category of communication includes not only traditional print and news services, but also audio, video, and still images, as well as interactive, real time dialogue. Through the use of chat rooms, any person with a phone line can become a town crier with a voice that resonates farther than it could from any soapbox. Through the use of Web pages, mail exploders, and newsgroups, the same individual can become a pamphleteer. As the District Court found, "the content on the Internet is as diverse as human thought." We agree with its conclusion that our cases provide no basis for qualifying the level of First Amendment scrutiny that should be applied to this medium.

. . . [T]he many ambiguities concerning the scope of [the CDA's] coverage render it problematic for purposes of the First Amendment. For instance, each of the two parts of the CDA uses a different linguistic form. The first uses the word "indecent," while the second speaks of material that "in context, depicts or describes, in terms patently offensive as measured by contemporary community standards, sexual or excretory activities or organs." Given the absence of a definition of either term, this difference in language will provoke uncertainty among speakers about how the two standards relate to each other and just what they mean. . . . This uncertainty undermines the likelihood that the CDA has been carefully tailored to the congressional goal of protecting minors from potentially harmful materials.

The vagueness of the CDA is a matter of special concern for two reasons. First, the CDA is a content based regulation of speech. The vagueness of such a regulation raises special First Amendment concerns because of its obvious chilling effect on free speech. . . . Second, the CDA is a criminal statute. In addition to the opprobrium and stigma of a criminal conviction, the CDA threatens violators with penalties including up to two years in prison for each act of violation. The severity of criminal sanctions may well cause speakers to remain silent rather than communicate even arguably unlawful words, ideas, and images. . . .

The Government argues that the statute is no more vague than the obscenity standard this Court established in *Miller* v. *California* [1973]. But that is not so. In *Miller*, this Court reviewed a criminal conviction against a commercial vendor who mailed brochures containing pictures of sexually explicit activities to individuals who had not requested such materials. Having struggled for some time to establish a definition of obscenity, we set forth in *Miller* the test for obscenity that controls to this day:

> (a) whether the average person, applying contemporary community standards would find that the work, taken as a whole, appeals to the prurient interest; (b) whether the work depicts or describes, in a patently offensive way, sexual conduct specifically defined by the applicable state law; and (c) whether the work, taken as a whole, lacks serious literary, artistic, political, or scientific value. . . .

Because the CDA's "patently offensive" standard (and, we assume *arguendo*, its synonymous "indecent" standard) is one part of the three prong *Miller* test, the Government reasons, it cannot be unconstitutionally vague.

The Government's assertion is incorrect as a matter of fact. The second prong of the *Miller* test—the purportedly analogous standard—contains a critical requirement that is omitted from the CDA: that the proscribed material be "specifically defined by the applicable state law." This requirement reduces the vagueness inherent in the open ended term "patently offensive" as used in the CDA. Moreover, the *Miller* definition is limited to "sexual conduct," whereas the CDA extends also to include (1) "excretory activities" as well as (2) "organs" of both a sexual and excretory nature. . . .

In contrast to *Miller* and our other previous cases, the CDA thus presents a greater threat of censoring speech that, in fact, falls outside the statute's scope. Given the vague contours of the coverage of the statute, it unquestionably silences some speakers whose messages would be entitled to constitutional protection. That danger provides further reason for insisting that the statute not be overly broad. The CDA's burden on protected speech cannot be justified if it could be avoided by a more carefully drafted statute.

We are persuaded that the CDA lacks the precision that the First Amendment requires when a statute regulates the content of speech. In order to deny minors access to potentially harmful speech, the CDA effectively suppresses a large amount of speech that adults have a constitutional right to receive and to address to one another. That burden on adult speech is unacceptable if less restrictive alternatives would be at least as effective in achieving the legitimate purpose that the statute was enacted to serve. . . .

It is true that we have repeatedly recognized the governmental interest in protecting children from harmful materials. But that interest does not justify an unnecessarily broad suppression of speech addressed to adults. As we have explained, the Government may not "reduc[e] the adult population . . . to . . . only what is fit for children." *Denver Area Ed. Telecommunications Consortium* v. *FCC* [1996]. . . .

In arguing that the CDA does not so diminish adult communication, the Government relies on the incorrect factual premise that prohibiting a transmission whenever it is known that one of its recipients is a minor would not interfere with adult to adult communication. . . .

Given the size of the potential audience for most messages, in the absence of a viable age verification process, the sender must be charged with knowing that one or more minors will likely view it. Knowledge that, for instance, one or more members of a 100 person chat group will be minor—and therefore that it would be a crime to send the group an indecent message—would surely burden communication among adults.

The District Court found that at the time of trial existing technology did not include any effective method for a sender to prevent minors from obtaining access to its communications on the Internet without also denying access to adults. The Court found no effective way to determine the age of a user who is accessing material through e-mail, mail exploders, newsgroups, or chat rooms. As a practical matter, the Court also found that it would be prohibitively expensive for noncommercial—as well as some commercial—speakers who have Web sites to verify that their users are adults. These limitations must inevitably curtail a significant amount of adult communication on the Internet. By contrast, the District Court found that "[d]espite its limitations, currently available user based software suggests that a reasonably effective method by which parents can prevent their children from accessing sexually explicit and other material which parents may believe is inappropriate for their children will soon be widely available."

The breadth of the CDA's coverage is wholly unprecedented. Unlike the regulations upheld in *Ginsberg* and *Pacifica*, the scope of the CDA is not limited to commercial speech or commercial entities. Its open ended prohibitions embrace all nonprofit entities and individuals posting indecent messages or displaying them on their own computers in the presence of minors. The general, undefined terms "indecent" and "patently offensive" cover large amounts of nonpornographic material with serious educational or other value. Moreover, the "community standards" criterion as applied to the Internet means that any communication available to a nationwide audience will be judged by the standards of the community most likely to be offended by the message. . . .

For the purposes of our decision, we need neither accept nor reject the Government's submission that the First Amendment does not forbid a blanket prohibition on all "indecent" and "patently offensive" messages communicated to a 17 year old—no matter how much value the message may contain and regardless of parental approval. It is at least clear that the strength of the Government's interest in protecting minors is not equally strong throughout the coverage of this broad statute. Under the CDA, a parent allowing her 17 year old to use the family computer to obtain information on the Internet that she, in her parental judgment, deems appropriate could face a lengthy prison term. . . . Similarly, a parent who sent his 17 year old college freshman information on birth control via e-mail could be incarcerated even though neither he, his child, nor anyone in their home community, found the material "indecent" or "patently offensive," if the college town's community thought otherwise.

The breadth of this content based restriction of speech imposes an especially heavy burden on the Government to explain why a less restrictive provision would not be as effective as the CDA. It has not done so. . . . Particularly in the light of the absence of any detailed findings by the Congress, or even hearings addressing the special problems of the CDA, we are persuaded that the CDA is not narrowly tailored if that requirement has any meaning at all. . . .

In this Court, though not in the District Court, the Government asserts that—in addition to its interest in protecting children—its "[e]qually significant" interest in fostering the growth of the Internet provides an independent basis for upholding the constitutionality of the CDA. The Government apparently assumes that the unregulated availability of "indecent" and "patently offensive" material on the Internet is driving countless citizens away from the medium because of the risk of exposing themselves or their children to harmful material.

We find this argument singularly unpersuasive. The dramatic expansion of this new marketplace of ideas contradicts the factual basis of this contention. The record demonstrates that the growth of the Internet has been and continues to be phenomenal. As a matter of constitutional tradition, in the absence of evidence to the contrary, we presume that governmental regulation of the content of speech is more likely to interfere with the free exchange of ideas than to encourage it. The interest in encouraging freedom of expression in a democratic society outweighs any theoretical but unproven benefit of censorship.

For the foregoing reasons, the judgment of the district court is
AFFIRMED.

JUSTICE O'CONNOR, CONCURRING IN THE JUDGMENT IN PART AND DISSENTING IN PART.

I write separately to explain why I view the Communications Decency Act of 1996 (CDA) as little more than an attempt by Congress to create "adult zones" on the Internet. Our precedent indicates that the creation of such zones can be constitutionally sound. Despite the soundness of its purpose, however, portions of the CDA are unconstitutional because they stray from the blueprint our prior cases have developed for constructing a "zoning law" that passes constitutional muster. . . .

Our cases make clear that a "zoning" law is valid only if adults are still able to obtain the regulated speech. If they cannot, the law does more than simply keep children away from speech they have no right to obtain—it interferes with the rights of adults to obtain constitutionally protected speech. . . . The First Amendment does not tolerate such interference. . . .

The Court in *Ginsberg* concluded that the New York law created a constitutionally adequate adult zone simply because, on its face, it denied access only to minors. The Court did not question—and therefore necessarily assumed—that an adult zone, once created, would succeed in preserving adults' access while denying minors' access to the regulated speech. Before today, there was no reason to question this assumption, for the Court has previously only considered laws that operated in the physical world, a world with two characteristics that make it possible to create "adult zones": geography and identity. . . .

The electronic world is fundamentally different. Because it is no more than the interconnection of electronic pathways, cyberspace allows speakers and listeners to mask their identities. . . .

Cyberspace differs from the physical world in another basic way: Cyberspace is malleable. Thus, it is possible to construct barriers in cyberspace and use them to screen for identity, making cyberspace more like the physical world and, consequently, more amenable to zoning laws. This transformation of cyberspace is already underway. . . .

Despite this progress, the transformation of cyberspace is not complete. Although gateway technology has been available on the World Wide Web for some time now, it is not available to all Web speakers, and is just now becoming technologically feasible for chat rooms and USENET newsgroups. Gateway technology is not ubiquitous in cyberspace, and because without it "there is no means of age verification," cyberspace still remains largely unzoned—and unzoneable. User based zoning is also in its infancy. . . .

Although the prospects for the eventual zoning of the Internet appear promising, I agree with the Court that we must evaluate the constitutionality of the CDA as it applies to the Internet as it exists today. Given the present state of cyberspace, I agree with the Court that the "display" provision cannot pass muster. Until gateway technology is available throughout cyberspace, and it is not in 1997, a speaker cannot be reasonably assured that the speech he displays will reach only adults because it is impossible to confine speech to an "adult zone." Thus, the only way for a speaker to avoid liability under the CDA is to refrain completely from using indecent speech. But this forced silence impinges on the First Amendment right of adults to make and obtain this speech. . . . As a result, the "display" provision cannot withstand scrutiny. . . .

The "indecency transmission" and "specific person" provisions present a closer issue, for they are not unconstitutional in all of their applications. As discussed above, the "indecency transmission" provision makes it a crime to transmit knowingly an indecent message to a person the sender knows is under 18 years of age. The "specific person" provision proscribes the same conduct, although it does not as explicitly require the sender to know that the intended recipient of his indecent message is a minor. Appellant urges the Court to construe the provision to impose such a knowledge requirement. . . .

So construed, both provisions are constitutional as applied to a conversation involving only an adult and one or more minors—e.g., when an adult speaker sends an e-mail knowing the addressee is a minor, or when an adult and minor converse by themselves or with other minors in a chat room. . . . Restricting what the adult may say to the minors in no way restricts the adult's ability to communicate with other adults. He is not prevented from speaking indecently to other adults in a chat room (because there are no other adults participating in the conversation) and he remains free to send indecent e-mails to other adults. The relevant universe contains only one adult, and the adult in that universe has the power to refrain from using indecent speech and consequently to keep all such speech within the room in an "adult" zone.

The analogy to *Ginsberg* breaks down, however, when more than one adult is a party to the conversation. If a minor enters a chat room otherwise occupied by adults, the CDA effectively requires the adults in the room to stop using indecent speech. If they did not, they could be prosecuted under the "indecency transmission" and "specific person" provisions for any indecent statements they make to the group, since they would be transmitting an indecent message to specific persons, one of whom is a minor. The CDA is therefore akin to a law that makes it a crime for a bookstore owner to sell pornographic magazines to anyone once a minor enters his store. Even assuming such a law might be constitutional in the physical world as a reasonable alternative to excluding minors completely from the store, the absence of any means of excluding minors from chat rooms in cyberspace restricts the rights of adults to engage in indecent speech in those rooms. The "indecency transmission" and "specific person" provisions share this defect.

But these two provisions do not infringe on adults' speech in all situations. And as discussed below, I do not find that the provisions are overbroad in the sense that they restrict minors' access to a substantial amount of speech that minors have the right to read and view. Accordingly, the CDA can be applied constitutionally in some situations. Normally, this fact would require the Court to reject a direct facial challenge. . . . Appellees' claim arises under the First Amendment, however, and they argue that the CDA is facially invalid because it is "substantially overbroad"—that is, it "sweeps too broadly . . . [and] penaliz[es] a substantial amount of speech that is constitutionally protected." *Forsyth County* v. *Nationalist Movement* [1992]. . . . I agree with the Court that the provisions are overbroad in that they cover any and all communications between adults and minors, regardless of how many adults might be part of the audience to the communication.

This conclusion does not end the matter, however. . . . There is no question that Congress intended to prohibit certain communications between one adult and one or more minors. . . . There is also no question that Congress would have enacted a narrower version of these provisions had it known a broader version would be declared unconstitutional. . . . I would therefore sustain the "indecency transmission" and "specific person" provisions to the extent they apply to the transmission of Internet communications where the party initiating the communication knows that all of the recipients are minors. . . .

The Court neither "accept[s] nor reject[s]" the argument that the CDA is facially overbroad because it substantially interferes with the First Amendment rights of minors. I would reject it. *Ginsberg* established that minors may constitutionally be denied access to material that is obscene as to minors. As *Ginsberg* explained, material is obscene as to minors if it (i) is "patently offensive to prevailing standards in the adult community as a whole with respect to what is suitable . . . for minors"; (ii) appeals to the prurient interest of minors; and (iii) is "utterly without redeeming social importance for minors." Because the CDA denies minors the right to obtain material that is "patently offensive"—even if it has some redeeming value for minors and even if it does not appeal to their prurient interests—Congress's rejection of the *Ginsberg* "harmful to minors" standard means that the CDA could ban some speech that is "indecent" (i.e., "patently offensive") but that is not obscene as to minors.

I do not deny this possibility, but to prevail in a facial challenge, it is not enough for a plaintiff to show "some" overbreadth. Our cases require a proof of "real" and "substantial" overbreadth, *Broadrick* v. *Oklahoma* [1973], and appellees have not carried their burden in this case. In my view, the universe of speech constitutionally protected as to minors but banned by the CDA—i.e., the universe of material that is "patently offensive," but which nonetheless has some redeeming value for minors or does not appeal to their prurient interest—is a very small one. Appellees cite no examples of speech falling within this universe and do not attempt to explain why that universe is substantial "in relation to the statute's plainly legitimate sweep." That the CDA might deny minors the right to obtain material that has some "value" is largely beside the point. While discussions about prison rape or nude art may have some redeeming education value for adults, they do not necessarily have any such value for minors, and under *Ginsberg*, minors only have a First Amendment right to obtain patently offensive material that has "redeeming social importance for minors." There is also no evidence in the record to support the contention that "many [e] mail transmissions from an adult to a minor are conversations between family members," and no support for the legal proposition that such speech is absolutely immune from regulation. Accordingly, in my view, the CDA does not burden a substantial amount of minors' constitutionally protected speech.

Thus, the constitutionality of the CDA as a zoning law hinges on the extent to which it substantially interferes with the First Amendment rights of adults. Because the rights of adults are infringed only by the "display" provision and by the "indecency transmission" and "specific person" provisions as applied to communications involving more than one adult, I would invalidate the CDA only to that extent. Insofar as the "indecency transmission" and "specific person" provisions prohibit the use of indecent speech in communications between an adult and one or more minors, however, they can and should be sustained. The Court reaches a contrary conclusion, and from that holding that I respectfully dissent.

RESPONSES

FROM THE *WASHINGTON POST*, JUNE 27, 1997, "YES, THE NET IS SPEECH"

Half an hour after the Supreme Court announced its ruling that key portions of the Communications Decency Act were unconstitutional, Internet users could tap in and read the full text of the court's opinion from nearly anywhere in the world. Such is the reach of the medium that now, thanks to the court's decision, has been freed to grow and develop as buoyantly in the future as it has up till now—freed, that is, from the so-called decency law, which if upheld would have constituted the most serious and potentially hobbling limitation that a U.S. court has sought to impose on the Internet in its short lifetime.

In voting 7 to 2 to overturn the hastily written decency provisions, which would have penalized the "knowing" transmission via the Internet of any "indecent" or "patently offensive" content to a minor, the court recognized and explicitly affirmed that the Internet is a medium of speech and, moreover, one that, unlike radio and like newspapers and magazines, is entitled to the highest level of First Amendment protection. It weighed in strongly with the view that the protection of children, though important, cannot be used as an excuse to muzzle this potential for vastly increased communication and interaction—in Justice John Paul Stevens's words, the ability to make "any person with a phone line . . . a town crier with a voice that resonates farther than it could from any soapbox."

The opinion upholds a unanimous Philadelphia appeals panel decision and, like it, lays much emphasis on the unprecedented nature of Internet communications: the lack of central control, the "low barriers to entry" resulting in millions of senders and receivers, and the absence from the Internet of characteristics that led lower courts to conclude it was acceptable to impose restrictions on TV and radio. Access to the Internet is neither "scarce," as broadcasting frequencies once were, nor "invasive," like a blaring radio, and less drastic means exist for filtering its raw elements. Sources of the Internet's strength, these qualities also make it impossible to apply the decency act's vague and imprecise standards without blocking adult access to vast amounts of speech that otherwise would be constitutionally protected. Such speech, Justice Stevens wrote, could include "a large amount of nonpornographic material with serious educational or other value . . . artistic images . . . and arguably the card catalog of the Carnegie Library." (A sole provision banning the transmission of obscenity, illegal anyway, was upheld.)

The Supreme Court sharply criticized the vagueness of the provisions as drawn, the failure to seek less restrictive means of protecting children, and the failure of Congress to hold any hearings on the measure before passing it. Even the dissent, by Justice O'Connor, concurred with the majority that most applications of the new law would be unconstitutional. It's unlikely that the Net, in its complexity, will remain totally free of regulation of any kind. After this debacle, though, perhaps future rounds will take at least some account of constitutional realities.

FROM THE *OREGONIAN* (PORTLAND, OREGON), JUNE 29, 1997, "CYBERSPACE CONTENT, BEDROCK BELIEF"

Parents are right to be concerned about their children stepping in smut as they foray into cyberspace.

But the Supreme Court is also right, in its first foray into cyberspace, to say Congress can't protect children by keeping smut from adults.

The court Thursday struck down a key part of a law that made it a crime to put "patently offensive" words or pictures on the Internet where children could find it. The Communications Decency Act was passed last year as part of the telecommunications bill. The high court agreed with librarians, civil libertarians, computer-makers, online services, journalists and booksellers that the act was too vague and too broad. It had the unnerving potential to make criminals of people posting legitimate material on the Internet dealing with health, art, science, and politics.

Parents, not the government, must take the final responsibility for what their children view on the Internet, just as at the library or the bookstore. Blocking-technology can help them. President Clinton's pledge to convene a group to find such technology and rating systems that "protect children in ways that are consistent with America's free speech values" should reassure them.

Further, this ruling doesn't threaten prohibitions against transmission of obscenity or child pornography over the Internet.

The government's argument in this case that people are avoiding the Internet as a result of smut is just silly. The Internet is growing like crazy, and this ruling will help ensure that free speech is protected as it does.

NATIONAL ENDOWMENT
FOR THE ARTS V. FINLEY
524 U.S. 569 (1998)

In June 1990 the National Endowment for the Arts denied grant applications submitted by performance artists Karen Finley, John Fleck, Holly Hughes, and Tom Miller. In a lawsuit filed in the Central District of California, the four complained that the NEA in rejecting their applications had violated their First Amendment rights. After Congress passed legislation—§954(d)(1)—requiring the NEA to ensure that "artistic excellence and artistic merit are the criteria by which [grant] applications are judged, taking into consideration general standards of decency and respect for the diverse beliefs and values of the American public," the plaintiffs added to their lawsuit a First Amendment challenge to the new statute. Siding with Finley, the district court struck down the law, and then the U.S. Court of Appeals for the Ninth Circuit affirmed. But the Supreme Court, by a vote of 8 to 1, reversed.

Finley arose from the public controversy swirling around the NEA as a result of two 1989 grants. Part of one grant funded the display of homoerotic photographs by Robert Mapplethorpe; the other grant supported the work of Andres Serrano, whose work included "Piss Christ," a photograph of a crucifix immersed in urine. Complaints about these grants led Congress to pass the "decency and respect" law.

Finley turned on the meaning of this law. The artists contended that the law discriminated against grant applicants whose art either failed to respect mainstream values or offended standards of decency. The government countered that the law was merely hortatory and did not impose discrimination on any applicant. Deferring to the government's understanding of the law, Justice O'Connor, writing for the majority, said, "We do not perceive a realistic danger that [the law] will compromise First Amendment values."

Finley generated two other opinions that disagreed as to what the result in the case should be but were in solid agreement that the "decency and respect" law constituted "viewpoint discrimination." The two opinions thus rejected the government's view of the law. "The law at issue in this case," wrote Justice Scalia (joined by Justice Thomas), concurring in the judgment, "is to be found in [its] text. . . . And that law unquestionably disfavors—discriminates against—indecency and disrespect for the diverse beliefs and values of the American people." In dissent, Justice Souter wrote: "One need do nothing more than read the text of the statute to conclude that Congress's purpose in imposing the decency and respect criteria was to prevent the funding of art that conveys an offensive message; the decency and respect provision on its face is quintessentially viewpoint based."

Opinion of the Court: **O'Connor**, Rehnquist, Stevens, Kennedy, Breyer, Ginsburg (in part). Concurring in the judgment: **Scalia**, Thomas. Dissenting opinion: **Souter**.

National Endowment for the Arts v. *Finley* was decided on June 25, 1998.

OPINIONS

JUSTICE O'CONNOR DELIVERED THE OPINION OF THE COURT . . .

Respondents raise a facial constitutional challenge to §954(d)(1). . . . To prevail, respondents must demonstrate a substantial risk that application of the provision will lead to the suppression of speech. . . .

Respondents argue that the provision is a paradigmatic example of viewpoint discrimination because it rejects any artistic speech that either fails to respect mainstream values or offends standards of decency. The premise of respondents' claim is that §954(d)(1) constrains the agency's ability to fund certain categories of artistic expression. The NEA, however, reads the provision as merely hortatory, and contends that it stops well short of an absolute restriction. Section 954(d)(1) adds "considerations" to the grant-making process; it does not preclude awards to projects that might be deemed "indecent" or "disrespectful," nor place conditions on grants, or even specify that those factors must be given any particular weight in reviewing an application. Indeed, the agency asserts that it has adequately implemented §954(d)(1) merely by ensuring the representation of various backgrounds and points of view on the advisory panels that analyze grant applications. . . . We do not decide whether the NEA's view—that the formulation of diverse advisory panels is sufficient to comply with Congress' command—is in fact a reasonable reading of the statute. It is clear, however, that the text of §954(d)(1) imposes no categorical requirement. The advisory language stands in sharp contrast to congressional efforts to prohibit the funding of certain classes of speech. . . .

Furthermore, like the plain language of §954(d), the political context surrounding the adoption of the "decency and respect" clause is inconsistent with respondents' assertion that the provision compels the NEA to deny funding on the basis of viewpoint discriminatory criteria. The legislation was a bipartisan proposal introduced as a counterweight to amendments aimed at eliminating the NEA's funding or substantially constraining its grant-making authority. . . .

That §954(d)(1) admonishes the NEA merely to take "decency and respect" into consideration, and that the legislation was aimed at reforming procedures rather than precluding speech, undercut respondents' argument that the provision inevitably will be utilized as a tool for invidious viewpoint discrimination. In cases where we have struck down legislation as facially unconstitutional, the dangers were both more evident and more substantial. In *R.A.V.* v. *St. Paul* [1992], for example, we invalidated on its face a municipal ordinance that defined as a criminal offense the placement of a symbol on public or private property "'which one knows or has reasonable grounds to know arouses anger, alarm, or resentment in others on the basis of race, color, creed, religion, or gender.'" That provision set forth a clear penalty, proscribed views on particular "disfavored subjects," and suppressed "distinctive idea[s], conveyed by a distinctive message."

In contrast, the "decency and respect" criteria do not silence speakers by expressly "threaten[ing] censorship of ideas." Thus, we do not perceive a realistic danger that §954(d)(1) will compromise First Amendment values. As respondents' own arguments demonstrate, the considerations that the provision introduces, by their nature, do not engender the kind of directed viewpoint discrimination that would prompt this Court to invalidate a statute on its face. Respondents assert, for example, that "[o]ne would be hard-pressed to find two people in the United States who could agree on what the 'diverse beliefs and values of the American public' are, much less on whether a particular work of art 'respects' them"; and they claim that " '[d]ecency' is likely to mean something very different to a septegenarian in Tuscaloosa and a teenager in Las Vegas." The NEA likewise views the considerations enumerated in §954(d)(1) as susceptible to multiple interpretations. . . . Accordingly, the provision does not introduce considerations that, in practice, would effectively preclude or punish the expression of particular views. Indeed, one could hardly anticipate how "decency" or "respect" would bear on grant applications in categories such as funding for symphony orchestras.

Respondents' claim that the provision is facially unconstitutional may be reduced to the argument that the criteria in §954(d)(1) are sufficiently subjective that the agency could utilize them to engage in viewpoint discrimination. Given the varied interpretations of the criteria and the vague exhortation to "take them into consideration," it seems unlikely that this provision will introduce any greater element of selectivity than the determination of "artistic excellence" itself. . . .

The NEA's enabling statute contemplates a number of indisputably constitutional applications for both the "decency" prong of §954(d)(1) and its reference to "respect for the diverse beliefs and values of the American public." Educational programs are central to the NEA's mission. . . . And it is well established that "decency" is a permissible factor where "educational suitability" motivates its consideration. *Board of Ed., Island Trees Union Free School Dist. No. 26* v. *Pico* [1982]; see also *Bethel School Dist. No. 403* v. *Fraser* [1986] ("Surely it is a highly appropriate function of public school education to prohibit the use of vulgar and offensive terms in public discourse").

Permissible applications of the mandate to consider "respect for the diverse beliefs and values of the American public" are also apparent. In setting forth the purposes of the NEA, Congress explained that "[i]t is vital to democracy to honor and preserve its multicultural artistic heritage." §951(10). The agency expressly takes diversity into account, giving special consideration to "projects and productions . . . that reach, or reflect the culture of, a minority, inner city, rural, or tribal community," §954(c)(4), as well as projects that generally emphasize "cultural diversity," §954(c)(1). Respondents do not contend that the criteria in §954(d)(1) are impermissibly applied when they may be justified, as the statute contemplates, with respect to a project's intended audience.

We recognize, of course, that reference to these permissible applications would not alone be sufficient to sustain the statute against respondents' First Amendment challenge. But neither are we persuaded that, in other applications, the language of §954(d)(1) itself will give rise to the suppression of protected expression. Any content-based considerations that may be taken into account in the grant-making process are a consequence of the nature of arts funding. The NEA has limited resources and it must deny the majority of the grant applications that it receives, including many that propose "artistically excellent" projects. The agency may decide to fund particular projects for a wide variety of reasons, "such as the technical proficiency of the artist, the creativity of the work, the anticipated public interest in or appreciation of the work, the work's contemporary relevance, its educational value, its suitability for or appeal to special audiences (such as children or the disabled), its service to a rural or isolated community, or even simply that the work could increase public knowledge of an art form." . . .

Respondent's reliance on our decision in *Rosenberger* v. *Rector and Visitors of Univ. of Va.* [1995] is therefore misplaced. In *Rosenberger*, a public university declined to authorize disbursements from its Student Activities Fund to finance the printing of a Christian student newspaper. We held that by subsidizing the Student Activities Fund, the University had created a limited public forum, from which it impermissibly excluded all publications with religious editorial viewpoints. Although the scarcity of NEA funding does not distinguish this case from *Rosenberger* . . . the competitive process according to which the grants are allocated does. In the context of arts funding, in contrast to many other subsidies, the Government does not indiscriminately "encourage a diversity of views from private speakers." The NEA's mandate is to make aesthetic judgments, and the inherently content-based "excellence" threshold for NEA support sets it apart from the subsidy at issue in *Rosenberger*—which was available to all student organizations that were "'related to the educational purpose of the University'"—and from comparably objective decisions on allocating public benefits, such as access to a school auditorium or a municipal theater. . . .

The lower courts also erred in invalidating §954(d)(1) as unconstitutionally vague. Under the First and Fifth Amendments, speakers are protected from arbitrary and discriminatory enforcement of vague standards. . . . The terms of the provision are undeniably opaque, and if they appeared in a criminal statute or regulatory scheme, they could raise substantial vagueness concerns. It is unlikely, however, that speakers will be compelled to steer too far clear of any "forbidden area" in the context of grants of this nature. . . . We recognize, as a practical matter, that artists may conform their speech to what they believe to be the decision-making criteria in order to acquire funding. . . . But when the Government is acting as patron rather than as sovereign, the consequences of imprecision are not constitutionally severe.

In the context of selective subsidies, it is not always feasible for Congress to legislate with clarity. Indeed, if this statute is unconstitutionally vague, then so too are all government programs awarding scholarships and grants on the basis of subjective criteria such as "excellence." . . . To accept respondents' vagueness argument would be to call into question the constitutionality of . . . valuable government programs. . . .

Section 954(d)(1) merely adds some imprecise considerations to an already subjective selection process. It does not, on its face, impermissibly infringe on First or Fifth Amendment rights. Accordingly, the judgment of the Court of Appeals is reversed and the case is remanded for further proceedings consistent with this opinion.

JUSTICE SCALIA, CONCURRING IN THE JUDGMENT.

"The operation was a success, but the patient died." What such a procedure is to medicine, the Court's opinion in this case is to law. It sustains the constitutionality of 20 U.S.C. §954(d)(1) by gutting it. The most avid congressional opponents of the provision could not have asked for more. I write separately because, unlike the Court, I think that §954(d)(1) must be evaluated as written, rather than as distorted by the agency it was meant to control. By its terms, it establishes content and viewpoint-based criteria upon which grant applications are to be evaluated. And that is perfectly constitutional. . . .

The phrase "taking into consideration general standards of decency and respect for the diverse beliefs and values of the American public" is what my grammar-school teacher would have condemned as a dangling modifier: There is no noun to which the participle is attached (unless one jumps out of paragraph (1) to press "Chairperson" into service). Even so, it is clear enough that the phrase is meant to apply to those who do the judging. The application reviewers must take into account "general standards of decency" and "respect for the diverse beliefs and values of the American public" when evaluating artistic excellence and merit. One can regard this as either suggesting that decency and respect are elements of what Congress regards as artistic excellence and merit, or as suggesting that decency and respect are factors to be taken into account in addition to artistic excellence and merit. But either way, it is entirely, 100% clear that decency and respect are to be taken into account in evaluating applications. . . .

This is so apparent that I am at a loss to understand what the Court has in mind (other than the gutting of the statute) when it speculates that the statute is merely "advisory." General standards of decency and respect for Americans' beliefs and values must (for the statute says that the Chairperson "shall ensure" this result) be taken into account (see, e.g., *American Heritage Dictionary* 402 (3d ed. 1992): "consider . . . [t]o take into account; bear in mind") in evaluating all applications. This does not mean that those factors must always be dispositive, but it does mean that they must always be considered. The method of compliance proposed by the National Endowment for the Arts (NEA)—selecting diverse review panels of artists and nonartists that reflect a wide range of geographic and cultural perspectives—is so obviously inadequate that it insults the intelligence. A diverse panel membership increases the odds that, if and when the panel takes the factors into account, it will reach an accurate assessment of what they demand. But it in no way increases the odds that the panel will take the factors into consideration—much less ensures that the panel will do so, which is the Chairperson's duty under the statute. Moreover, the NEA's fanciful reading of §954(d)(1) would make it wholly superfluous. Section 959(c) already requires the Chairperson to "issue regulations and establish procedures . . . to ensure that all panels are composed, to the extent practicable, of individuals reflecting . . . diverse artistic and cultural points of view."

The statute requires the decency and respect factors to be considered in evaluating all applications—not, for example, just those applications relating to educational programs, or intended for a particular audience. Just as it would violate the statute to apply the artistic excellence and merit requirements to only select categories of applications, it would violate the statute to apply the decency and respect factors less than universally. A reviewer may, of course, give varying weight to the factors depending on the context, and in some categories of cases (such as the Court's example of funding for symphony orchestras) the factors may rarely if ever affect the outcome; but §954(d)(1) requires the factors to be considered in every case.

I agree with the Court that §954(d)(1) "imposes no categorical requirement," in the sense that it does not require the denial of all applications that violate general standards of decency or exhibit disrespect for the diverse beliefs and values of Americans. . . . But the factors need not be conclusive to be discriminatory. To the extent a particular applicant exhibits disrespect for the diverse beliefs and values of the American public or fails to comport with general standards of decency, the likelihood that he will receive a grant diminishes. . . .

This unquestionably constitutes viewpoint discrimination.

That conclusion is not altered by the fact that the statute does not "compe[l]" the denial of funding, any more than a provision imposing a five-point handicap on all black applicants for civil-service jobs is saved from being race discrimination by the fact that it does not compel the rejection of black applicants. If viewpoint discrimination in this context is unconstitutional (a point I shall address anon), the law is invalid unless there are some situations in which the decency and respect factors do not constitute viewpoint discrimination. And there is none. The applicant who displays "decency" . . . and the applicant who displays "respect" . . . will always have an edge over an applicant who displays the opposite. And finally, the conclusion of viewpoint discrimination is not affected by the fact that what constitutes "decency" or "the diverse beliefs and values of the American people" is difficult to pin down—any more than a civil-service preference in favor of those who display "Republican-party values" would be rendered nondiscriminatory by the fact that there is plenty of room for argument as to what Republican-party values might be.

The "political context surrounding the adoption of the 'decency and respect' clause," which the Court discusses at some length, does not change its meaning or affect its constitutionality. . . .

. . . And it is wholly irrelevant that the statute was a "bipartisan proposal introduced as a counterweight" to an alternative proposal that would directly restrict funding on the basis of viewpoint. We do not judge statutes as if we are surveying the scene of an accident; each one is reviewed, not on the basis of how much worse it could have been, but on the basis of what it says. . . . It matters not whether this enactment was the product of the most partisan alignment in history or whether, upon its passage, the Members all linked arms and sang, "The more we get together, the happier we'll be." . . . The law at issue in this case is to be found in the text of §954(d)(1), which passed both Houses and was signed by the President. . . . And that law unquestionably disfavors—discriminates against—indecency and disrespect for the diverse beliefs and values of the American people. . . .

The Court devotes so much of its opinion to explaining why this statute means something other than what it says that it neglects to cite the constitutional text governing our analysis. The First Amendment reads: "Congress shall make no law . . . abridging the freedom of speech." . . . With the enactment of §954(d)(1), Congress did not abridge the speech of those who disdain the beliefs and values of the American public, nor did it abridge indecent speech. Those who wish to create indecent and disrespectful art are as unconstrained now as they were before the enactment of this statute. . . .

Section 954(d)(1) is no more discriminatory, and no less constitutional, than virtually every other piece of funding legislation enacted by Congress. "The Government can, without violating the Constitution, selectively fund a program to encourage certain activities it believes to be in the public interest, without at the same time funding an alternative program. . . ." *Rust v. Sullivan* [1991]. As we noted in *Rust*, when Congress chose to establish the National Endowment for Democracy it was not constitutionally required to fund programs encouraging competing philosophies of government—an example of funding discrimination that cuts much closer than this one to the core of political speech which is the primary concern of the First Amendment. It takes a particularly high degree of chutzpah for the NEA to contradict this proposition, since the agency itself discriminates—and is required by law to discriminate—in favor of artistic (as opposed to scientific, or political, or theological) expression. . . .

The nub of the difference between me and the Court is that I regard the distinction between "abridging" speech and funding it as a fundamental divide, on this side of which the

First Amendment is inapplicable. The Court, by contrast, seems to believe that the First Amendment, despite its words, has some ineffable effect upon funding, imposing constraints of an indeterminate nature which it announces (without troubling to enunciate any particular test) are not violated by the statute here—or, more accurately, are not violated by the quite different, emasculated statute that it imagines. "[T]he Government," it says, "may allocate competitive funding according to criteria that would be impermissible were direct regulation of speech or a criminal penalty at stake." The government, I think, may allocate both competitive and noncompetitive funding ad libitum, insofar as the First Amendment is concerned. Finally, what is true of the First Amendment is also true of the constitutional rule against vague legislation: it has no application to funding. Insofar as it bears upon First Amendment concerns, the vagueness doctrine addresses the problems that arise from government regulation of expressive conduct . . . , not government grant programs. In the former context, vagueness produces an abridgment of lawful speech; in the latter it produces, at worst, a waste of money. . . .

JUSTICE SOUTER, DISSENTING . . .

The decency and respect proviso mandates viewpoint-based decisions in the disbursement of government subsidies, and the Government has wholly failed to explain why the statute should be afforded an exemption from the fundamental rule of the First Amendment that viewpoint discrimination in the exercise of public authority over expressive activity is unconstitutional. The Court's conclusions that the proviso is not viewpoint based, that it is not a regulation, and that the NEA may permissibly engage in viewpoint-based discrimination, are all patently mistaken. Nor may the question raised be answered in the Government's favor on the assumption that some constitutional applications of the statute are enough to satisfy the demand of facial constitutionality, leaving claims of the proviso's obvious invalidity to be dealt with later in response to challenges of specific applications of the discriminatory standards. This assumption is irreconcilable with our long standing and sensible doctrine of facial overbreadth, applicable to claims brought under the First Amendment's speech clause. I respectfully dissent. . . .

It goes without saying that artistic expression lies within . . . First Amendment protection. . . . When called upon to vindicate this ideal, we characteristically begin by asking "whether the government has adopted a regulation of speech because of disagreement with the message it conveys. The government's purpose is the controlling consideration." *Ward* v. *Rock Against Racism* [1989]. The answer in this case is damning. One need do nothing more than read the text of the statute to conclude that Congress's purpose in imposing the decency and respect criteria was to prevent the funding of art that conveys an offensive message; the decency and respect provision on its face is quintessentially viewpoint based. . . .

A . . . basic strand in the Court's treatment of today's question, and the heart of Justice Scalia's, in effect assumes that whether or not the statute mandates viewpoint discrimination, there is no constitutional issue here because government art subsidies fall within a zone of activity free from First Amendment restraints. The Government calls attention to the roles of government-as-speaker and government-as-buyer, in which the government is of course entitled to engage in viewpoint discrimination: if the Food and Drug Administration launches an advertising campaign on the subject of smoking, it may condemn the habit without also having to show a cowboy taking a puff on the opposite page; and if the Secretary of Defense wishes to buy a portrait to decorate the Pentagon, he is free to prefer George Washington over George the Third.

The Government freely admits, however, that it neither speaks through the expression subsidized by the NEA, nor buys anything for itself with its NEA grants. On the contrary, believing that "[t]he arts . . . reflect the high place accorded by the American people to the nation's rich cultural heritage," §951(6), and that "[i]t is vital to a democracy . . . to provide financial assistance to its artists and the organizations that support their work," §951(10), the Government acts as a patron, financially underwriting the production of art by private artists and impresarios for independent consumption. Accordingly, the Government would have us liberate government-as-patron from First Amendment strictures not by placing it squarely within the categories of government-as-buyer or government-as-speaker, but by recognizing a new category by analogy to those accepted ones. The analogy is, however, a very poor fit, and this patronage falls embarrassingly on the wrong side of the line between government-as-buyer or -speaker and government-as-regulator-of-private-speech. . . .

. . . Since the decency and respect proviso of §945(d)(1) is substantially overbroad and carries with it a significant power to chill artistic production and display, it should be struck down on its face.

The Court does not strike down the proviso, however. Instead, it preserves the irony of a statutory mandate to deny recognition to virtually any expression capable of causing offense in any quarter as the most recent manifestation of a scheme enacted to "create and sustain . . . a climate encouraging freedom of thought, imagination, and inquiry."

Appendix

JUSTICES OF THE
UNITED STATES SUPREME COURT
1919–1999

Names of chief justices are printed in boldface type.

	Appointing President	Justice Replaced	Oath Taken	Term End
Joseph McKenna	McKinley	Stephen J. Field	Jan. 1898	Jan. 1925
Oliver Wendell Holmes	T. Roosevelt	Horace Gray	Dec. 1902	Jan. 1932
William R. Day	T. Roosevelt	George Shiras, Jr.	Mar. 1903	Nov. 1922
Horace H. Lurton	Taft	Rufus W. Peckham	Jan. 1910	July 1914
Charles Evans Hughes*	Taft	William H. Taft	Oct. 1910	June 1916
Edward D. White**	Taft	Melville W. Fuller	Dec. 1910	May 1921
Willis Van Devanter	Taft	William H. Moody	Jan. 1911	June 1937
Joseph R. Lamar	Taft	Edward D. White	Jan. 1911	Jan. 1916
Mahlon Pitney	Taft	John Marshall Harlan	Mar. 1912	Dec. 1922
James C. McReynolds	Wilson	Horace H. Lurton	Sept. 1914	Feb. 1941
Louis D. Brandeis	Wilson	Joseph R. Lamar	June 1916	Feb. 1939
John H. Clarke	Wilson	Charles Evans Hughes	Aug. 1916	Sept. 1922
William H. Taft	Harding	Edward D. White	July 1921	Feb. 1930
George Sutherland	Harding	John H. Clarke	Oct. 1922	Jan. 1938
Pierce Butler	Harding	William R. Day	Jan. 1923	Nov. 1939
Edward T. Sanford	Harding	Mahlon Pitney	Feb. 1923	Mar. 1930
Harlan F. Stone*	Coolidge	Joseph McKenna	Mar. 1925	July 1941
Charles Evans Hughes	Hoover	William H. Taft	Feb. 1930	July 1941
Owen J. Roberts	Hoover	Edward T. Sanford	June 1930	July 1945
Benjamin N. Cardozo	Hoover	Oliver Wendell Holmes	Mar. 1932	July 1938
Hugo L. Black	F. Roosevelt	Willis Van Devanter	Aug. 1937	Sept. 1971
Stanley F. Reed	F. Roosevelt	George Sutherland	Jan. 1938	Feb. 1957
Felix Frankfurter	F. Roosevelt	Benjamin N. Cardozo	Jan. 1939	Aug. 1962
William O. Douglas	F. Roosevelt	Louis D. Brandeis	April 1939	Nov. 1975
Frank Murphy	F. Roosevelt	Pierce Butler	Jan. 1940	July 1949

	Appointing President	Justice Replaced	Oath Taken	Term End
Harlan F. Stone	F. Roosevelt	Charles Evans Hughes	July 1941	April 1946
James F. Byrnes	F. Roosevelt	James C. McReynolds	July 1941	Oct. 1942
Robert H. Jackson	F. Roosevelt	Harlan F. Stone	July 1941	Oct. 1954
Wiley B. Rutledge	F. Roosevelt	James F. Byrnes	Feb. 1943	Sept. 1949
Harold H. Burton	Truman	Owen J. Roberts	Oct. 1945	Oct. 1958
Fred M. Vinson	Truman	Harlan F. Stone	June 1946	Sept. 1953
Tom C. Clark	Truman	Frank Murphy	Aug. 1949	June 1967
Sherman Minton	Truman	Wiley B. Rutledge	Oct. 1949	Oct. 1956
Earl Warren	Eisenhower	Fred M. Vinson	Oct. 1953	June 1969
John M. Harlan III	Eisenhower	Robert H. Jackson	Mar. 1955	Sept. 1971
William J. Brennan, Jr.	Eisenhower	Sherman Minton	Mar. 1957	July 1990
Charles E. Whittaker	Eisenhower	Stanley F. Reed	Mar. 1957	April 1962
Potter Stewart	Eisenhower	Harold H. Burton	May 1959	July 1981
Byron R. White	Kennedy	Charles E. Whittaker	April 1962	June 1993
Arthur J. Goldberg	Kennedy	Felix Frankfurter	Oct. 1962	July 1965
Abe Fortas	Johnson	Arthur J. Goldberg	Oct. 1965	May 1969
Thurgood Marshall	Johnson	Tom C. Clark	Oct. 1967	Oct. 1991
Warren E. Burger	Nixon	Earl Warren	June 1969	Sept. 1986
Harry A. Blackmun, Jr.	Nixon	Abe Fortas	June 1970	April 1994
Lewis F. Powell, Jr.	Nixon	Hugo L. Black	Jan. 1972	June 1987
William H. Rehnquist*	Nixon	John M. Harlan III	Jan. 1972	Sept. 1986
John Paul Stevens	Ford	William O. Douglas	Dec. 1975	
Sandra Day O'Connor	Reagan	Potter Stewart	Sept. 1981	
Antonin Scalia	Reagan	William H. Rehnquist	Sept. 1986	
William H. Rehnquist	Reagan	Warren E. Burger	Sept. 1986	
Anthony M. Kennedy	Reagan	Lewis F. Powell, Jr.	Feb. 1988	
David H. Souter	Bush	William J. Brennan, Jr.	Oct. 1990	
Clarence Thomas	Bush	Thurgood Marshall	Nov. 1991	
Ruth Bader Ginsburg	Clinton	Byron R. White	Aug. 1993	
Stephen Breyer	Clinton	Harry A. Blackmun, Jr.	Aug. 1994	

* Associate justice; later served as chief justice.
** Previously served as associate justice, 1894–1910.

BIBLIOGRAPHY

Abernathy, M. Glenn. *The Right of Assembly and Association.* 2d rev. ed. Columbia: University of South Carolina Press, 1981.

Abraham, Henry J. *Freedom and the Court: Civil Rights and Liberties in the United States.* 7th ed. Oxford: Oxford University Press, 1998.

Berns, Walter. *The First Amendment and the Future of American Democracy.* Washington: Regnery Gateway, 1985.

Bork, Robert H. "Neutral Principles and Some First Amendment Problems." 47 *Indiana Law Journal* (Fall 1991): 1–35.

Chafee, Zechariah, Jr. *Free Speech in the United States.* Repr. ed. New York: Atheneum, 1969.

———. "Freedom of Speech in War Time." 32 *Harvard Law Review* (1919): 932–73.

Constitution of the United States of America, The: Analysis and Interpretation. Washington: U.S. Government Printing Office, 1992.

Currie, David P. *The Constitution in the Supreme Court: The Second Century, 1888–1986.* Chicago: University of Chicago Press, 1990.

———. *The Constitution of the United States: A Primer for the People.* Chicago: University of Chicago Press, 1988.

Fried, Charles. "The New First Amendment Jurisprudence: A Threat to Liberty." 59 *University of Chicago Law Review* (Winter 1992): 225–53.

Hall, Kermit L., ed. *The Oxford Companion to the Supreme Court of the United States.* New York: Oxford University Press, 1992.

Hickok, Eugene W., Jr., ed. *The Bill of Rights: Original Meaning and Current Understanding.* Charlottesville: University Press of Virginia, 1991.

James Madison: Writings. New York: The Library of America, 1999.

Kelly, Alfred H., Harbison, Winfred A., and Belz, Herman. *The American Constitution: Its Origins and Development.* 7th ed. New York: Norton, 1991.

Lee, Rex. *A Lawyer Looks at the Constitution.* Provo, Utah: Brigham Young University Press, 1981.

Levy, Leonard. *Emergence of a Free Press.* Oxford: Oxford University Press, 1985.

———. *Legacy of Suppression: Freedom of Speech and Press in Early American History.* Cambridge: Belknap Press, 1960.

———. *Origins of the Bill of Rights.* New Haven: Yale University Press, 1999.

Lewis, Anthony. *Make No Law: The Sullivan Case and the First Amendment.* New York: Vintage Books, 1992.

Lowenthal, David. *No Liberty for License: The Forgotten Logic of the First Amendment.* Dallas: Spence Publishing, 1997.

Miller, John C. *Crisis in Freedom: The Alien and Sedition Acts.* Boston: Little, Brown, 1951.

"Near v. Minnesota: 50th Anniversary." Symposium in 66 *Minnesota Law Review* (1981): 1–208.

Rabban, David M. "The First Amendment in Its Forgotten Years." 90 *Yale Law Journal* (January 1981): 514–95.

Riesman, David. "Democracy and Defamation: Control of Group Libel." 42 *Columbia Law Review* (May 1942): 747.

Rosenberg, Norman. *Protecting the Best Men: An Interpretive History of the Law of Libel.* Reprint ed. Chapel Hill: University of North Carolina Press, 1990.

Rutland, Robert A. *Birth of the Bill of Rights, 1776–1791.* Chapel Hill: University of North Carolina Press, 1955.

Schauer, Frederick. *Free Speech: A Philosophical Inquiry.* New York: Cambridge University Press, 1982.

Smolla, Rodney. *Suing the Press: Libel and the Media.* Oxford: Oxford University Press, 1986.

Walker, Samuel. *In Defense of American Liberties: A History of the ACLU.* Carbondale: Southern Illinois University Press, 1999.

Index of Names and Topics

INDEX OF CASES

Note: Cases in **boldface** type are included in this book.

ABOUT THE EDITOR

Terry Eastland has written for numerous publications on a wide variety of political and legal issues. His books include *Energy in the Executive: The Case for the Strong Presidency; Ending Affirmative Action: The Case for Colorblind Justice;* and *Religious Liberty in the Supreme Court: The Cases That Define the Debate Over Church and State.*

Made in the USA
Monee, IL
28 August 2020